ETHNOSCAPES
Current Challenges in the Environmental Social Sciences

Series Editors: *David Canter and David Stea*

Ethnoscapes: Current Challenges in the Environmental Social Sciences
Volume 7

THE MEANING AND USE OF HOUSING

This book is dedicated to the attainment of a *decent home* for all people around the world, particularly for those at the margin of their societies.

The Meaning and Use of Housing

International perspectives, approaches and their applications

Edited by
ERNESTO G. ARIAS
The University of Colorado at Boulder

Avebury

Aldershot · Brookfield USA · Hong Kong · Singapore · Sydney

Published by
Averbury
Ashgate Publishing Limited
Gower House
Croft Road
Aldershot
Hants GU11 3HR
England

Ashgate Publishing Company
Old Post Road
Brookfield
Vermont 05036
USA

A CIP catalogue record for this book is available from the British Library and the US Library of Congress.

ISBN 1 85628 159 0

Printed in Great Britain by
Athenaeum Press Ltd, Newcastle upon Tyne.

Contents

v

viii

List of Figures

List of Tables

Acknowledgements

It is with honor, pleasure and great appreciation that I acknowledge the contributions and assistance from all the individuals, as well as the various institutional events and support responsible for the realization of this timely international reader.

I acknowledge first and foremost, the innovative research presented in the subsequent chapters. It is the work of a truly outstanding group of international scholars, serioulsy dedicated to improving the future of housing around our world. Their collaborations are responsible for the quality and timeliness of this book's contributions to the field of international housing studies. Collectively, their work is directly responsible for this book's procedural and substantive insightfulness, and clearly demonstrates the multidisciplinary nature and cultural richness of this important field of study.

Second, the input and dedication throughout the editing process of Graduate Research Assistant Mr. Mohan Penubarti; and the endless hours spent transcribing text and writing letters by Ms. Linda Stevens of the College's front office, have been invaluable in completing the project and attaining the final copy.

Thirds, the preparation of this book was made possible in great part by a fellowship from the Center for International Research and Education Programs, and by funding support from the College of Environmental Design at the University of Colorado-Boulder.

Last but not least, its conception is owed in part to the initiative and insightful leadership of the organizers of the "International Housing Symposium on the Meaning and Use of Home and Neighborhood," Fall of 1989; and its sponsors, the National Swedish Institute of Building Research and the International Association for the Study of People and Their Physical Surroundings (IAPPS). It was at this gathering in Sweden where the idea was conceived.

In closing, I acknowledge the responsibility for all editing oversights.

E.G. Arias

Series Editor's Preface

DAVID CANTER
University of Surrey

This is a remarkable book. It spans the globe, reviewing studies of every conceivable form of housing. In these studies, a wide range of social science, design, management and policy perspectives are harnessed to enrich our understanding of the central place in people's life, their homes. Yet throughout the diverse, geographically and metaphorically wide ranging topics of this volume, Ernesto Arias its editor, has managed to ensure that there is a clear central focus (no mean feat when the range of cultures and native languages of his authors are considered).

The intellectual core of this volume is as simple as it is novel. The creation of housing requires an understanding of its personal, social and cultural significance as well as its use. Furthermore, meaning and use interact with each other. The meaning of a house defines the range of its acceptable uses, and these meanings are themselves shaped by the activities that go on in and around them. The interplay between cognitive and emotional reaction to housing, on the one hand, and the actions that are supported by the socio–physical setting, on the other hand. This interplay is at the heart of any systematic analysis and design of acceptable housing.

The novelty of this perspective is apparent in every major city of the world. The rows upon rows of mass housing built only with a view to providing roofs and floor space for minimal domestic activity can be seen everywhere. These buildings focus on the use to which housing may be put without taking account of its meanings.

The empty housing, that can be found in many countries, in which there is still a sizeable population of homeless people, also shows that the mere presence of buildings for people to live in does not ensure the people will be living in them. In some third world countries these empty buildings are eventually filled by people for whom they were not intended, the problem that they were built to address remaining untouched. Vast resources are therefore wasted on engineering and architectural solutions that do not answer the human concerns that turn houses into a home.

Even within developed countries it is clear that movement between houses is not a simple consequence of functional demands on space use. The housing markets that are so central to western economies are driven by the desires of people to obtain a place to live that they regard as compatible with other aspects of their life style. As a consequence, wherever there is the slightest element of choice in housing there will be movement of people between places that have different meanings and significance to their residence. Rather than economic forces shaping and controlling our cities and suburbs, it is the meaning and use of houses that gives shape to key aspects of economic processes. Most housing managers and policy makers have assumed that fiscal processes are the dominant ones to manage and understand if a country's development is to be maintained. The contributions to the present volume, however, challenge the narrowness of that perspective and illustrate in many ways that the social, psychological and cultural processes that assign meanings to places are in fact the dominant themes which shape many aspects of our society.

These meanings of home grow out of a great mixture and history of transactions that people have with their place of residence. Thus, although, the visual aspects of houses carries some significance these are often masked by traditions and other social processes that add salience to the various physical forms. It is probably this complexity, above all else, that has taken the study of domestic meanings so long to develop. Any direct, one to one, relationship between particular aspects of physical form and particular meaning is extremely difficult to establish. A variety of methodologies that deal with the observable as well as the implicit need to be combined, taking into account current concerns as well as long term antecedents. Even then the processes of meaning that emerge will be open to different emphases amongst different sub-groups and people who are part of different cultures.

There is, thus, the central question of the present volume as to whether the use and meaning of housing has any common, or even universal, themes that are relevant across a large number of groups, or whether we should strive to identify the very particular constituents of the housing experience that characterise any given sub-group in a particular locality.

All the above considerations point to the essential requirement that if we are to develop our understanding of the meaning and use of housing and its application to management and policy issues, then our studies have to draw upon many disciplines, in many countries, using a variety of methodologies. David Stea and I coined the term "Ethnoscapes" precisely to describe that range of research and policy question which required cross–cultural and cross-disciplinary approaches for their resolution. The present volume epitomises the very best of work of this kind and shows how important it is to face up to such a significant current challenge in the environmental social sciences.

Homes, Housing, and the 21st Century: Prospects and Challenges

IRWIN ALTMAN
Distinguished Professor of Psychology
University of Utah

There is no question but that the topic of this volume—homes—is central to human well being in every part of the world. People are often born, marry, procreate, raise children, work, grow old, die, and function as part of economic, political and social systems in homes. Homes are anchors of human life—whether they be permanent or temporary, are located in one place or are transported from place to place, are owned or rented, or are in planned communities or squatter settlements. In some cases homes are closely associated with a culture's cosmology and world view, may be religiously sacred and holy, and may connect people to one another, to Gods and supernatural beings, to an ancestral past or to the future, and to the world and nature at large.

These qualities of homes are not universal, and there is enormous variation among cultures and over the course of history in the form, use, importance and role of dwellings in peoples' lives. Regardless of their variation across cultures, however, there is no escaping the fact that homes are among the most central physical settings of human life.

The physical, social and psychological importance of homes is brought to the forefront in instances of disruption, loss, upheaval, and trauma in peoples' lives. It is in such cases that we come to realize how central residences and dwellings are to human well-being, and to individual, family and cultural viability. And, disruption and upheaval has become part and parcel of everyday life in the 1980s and 1990s, and is likely to continue into the 21st century. Although many disruptions are portrayed as involving large scale events that affect the balance of power among nations and have major effects on macro-economic and political spheres, they ultimately reach down into the lives of ordinary people—a fact too often ignored, downplayed, or even rejected by power structures and power brokers. The fact is that national and international events intrude on and disrupt peoples' everyday religious, social and economic lives and physical settings—the most notable settings being their homes and immediate communities.

To place the issue in perspective I see a worldwide shift in the balance of centrifugal and centripetal forces that operate at almost every level of human functioning—from macro-political and social events to micro-interpersonal and individual events. As a dialectically oriented social and environmental psychologist I am struck by the pervasiveness of a centrifugal-centripetal dialectic in many aspects of everyday life. On the one hand people are affected by centripetal or unifying and communal processes that bind them to their neighbors, communities and cultures, some of which we described a number of years ago in respect to communal aspects of sitings, facades, interior decorations, and uses of homes (Altman and Gauvain, 1981; Gauvain, Altman & Fahim, 1983). At the same time there are a variety of centrifugal forces operating in human endeavors that propel people to seek individuality, uniqueness, and distinctiveness from one another. Thus we described how homes in many cultures are decorated and used to achieve distinctiveness and individuality and, at the same time, reflect the bonding of people with one another and with their culture.

At the risk of being presumptuous and applying this dialectic more broadly, the 1980s and 1990s have been times of worldwide centrifugal and centripetal forces. Centrifugal political and social changes of unprecedented magnitude in some parts of the world have resulted in fragmentation of everyday life. For example, a startling and dramatic centrifugal process has involved the breakup and collapse of communism in eastern Europe and the Soviet Union.

How amazing it has been to many observers to see communist ideology and its everyday economic political system fall apart in country after country in eastern Europe and in the republics of the Soviet Union. From this disunity and centrifugal flow old issues of religion, ethnicity and nationalism are emerging and are already bringing to the forefront and exacerbating deeply rooted and long standing political and social divisiveness among people. The disintegration of the communist political and social system has already led to social, economic, political and interpersonal conflicts and to death, maiming, homelessness, armed conflict and warfare, the destruction of homes and communities, forced displacement and relocation of populations, and the like. Surely, centrifugal forces are having major macro-political and economic effects. However, these centrifugal events are also reaching down in profound ways into the lives of ordinary people on a day to day basis—as they give up involuntarily their homes and work, are forced to relocate, take in relatives and friends, lose their possessions and social networks, and live in a state of upheaval.

Similar centrifugal processes have occurred in the Middle East, some of which have existed for years, and have been brought to the forefront by the recent Persian Gulf war. Thus long term Palestinian residents of Kuwait became victims of persecution by the Kuwaiti government, strife between Shiite and Sunni Muslims erupted anew, and long standing animosities between Kurds and the Iraqi government exploded, resulting in death, relocation, exoduses, and loss of homes and communities for hundreds of thousands of people. And, in Africa and Asia, unstable governments and traditional ethnic and national conflicts have come to the forefront in many countries—from South Africa to Cambodia. On a less disruptive scale, divisiveness continues to occur in Canada between French and English speaking constituencies. In the United States, a rising homeless population and a weakening economy have exacerbated tensions and stresses in many people's lives. And, there are simmering strains of ethnic upheaval in the United States that are likely to flare up in the 1990s and in the next century. The rising numbers and voices of minority populations—Hispanic/Latino-Americans, Afro-Americans, Native Americans and several groups of Asian-Americans will grow in many cities, states and regions. These minority groups are already demanding more access to the center of American society, and they have the potential for enormous political and social influence. Given the vested economic and political power structure of American society in a largely conservative, white, upper class strata, coupled with a weakening industrial and economic base and a sharply escalating unemployment rate, we can expect a volatility in American life in the 1990s and in the 21st century that will easily surpass the upheavals of the 1960s. Similar trends may occur in other nations with large immigrant or ethnic and national minority groups who face fragile economies and resultant social and political strains.

In a word, it does not take much skill or experience as a geopolitical expert to conclude that the 1990s will continue to see major centrifugal and divisive forces around the globe that involve breaking up of previously stable social-political systems, and consequent upheavals in nation after nation, society after society, and region after region. As discussed below, it is inevitable that these centrifugal events will disrupt and cause enormous difficulties in the lives of everyday people—much of which will be played out in their homes, neighborhoods, settlements and communities.

True to a dialectic perspective, however, there are also centripetal processes at work around the world, resulting in unifying, integrating and synthesizing trends in social, political, and economic spheres of life. Of special note is the development of the European economic community and its goal of collectively linking European nations for economic and political well-being. The traditional divisiveness among many European nations is, for the moment at least, giving way to attempts to bond centripetally in several areas of life. And, the dramatic and rapid events surrounding the reunification of East and West Germany makes salient the centripetal swing in Europe amidst the centrifugal events in eastern Europe and the Soviet Union. Furthermore, the unity of the United States with European, Middle Eastern, African and Asian nations during the recent Persian Gulf war, and the tentative lessening of overt animosities between Arab nations and Israel (and Israel's remarkable restraint in the face of missile attacks by Iraq on its cities) during and following the war speaks to the potential for even fragile centripetal unity in the Middle East. And, the Madrid Peace Conference of 1991 and successive negotiations on the Middle East, the seemingly new stance and new leadership among the Palestinian people, and the apparent flexibility by some Arab nations and Israel raises the prospect of centripetal trends in an otherwise traditionally unstable region of the world.

Analogous centripetal trends are occurring elsewhere. For example, long standing and hostile relationships between North and South Korea appear to be softening, a unified Cambodian government has been formed, the United States and Vietnam are exploring new relationships, and so on. So, we are seeing instances of both centripetal and centrifugal trends among societies and nations.

Congruent with a dialectic perspective, the interplay of centrifugal and centripetal forces in geopolitical and social domains is neither stable nor wholly predictable. And, in a philosophical sense, neither centrifugal nor centripetal trends are "good or bad", although in human terms the costs and outcomes can be enormous. Thus the centrifugal events around the world that I described have had a devastating effect on the lives of hundreds of thousands of human beings—in the form of relocations and displacements, losses of homes and occupations, death and disease, and degradation of everyday life in the face of disruptions of macro-social, economic and political systems.

At the same time, centripetal trends can also produce social problems of enormous magnitude. For example, the unification of Germany has resulted in a massive migration of Germans from east to west, economic reverberations in a previously stable West Germany, and social and political disruptions. Such problems are likely to continue until the prosperous and democratic West Germany and the economically marginal and communist

East Germany are woven together. Similarly, powerful centripetal trends in the USSR beginning with the Communist revolution eventually produced a stagnating economy, a monolithic social structure, and restrictions on personal freedom and opportunity that unduly stifled creativity and initiative, and yielded a homogeneous and restricted lifestyle for everyday citizens. So, both centrifugal and centripetal forces of the type now occurring globally have the capacity to produce upheaval in peoples' lives.

What lies before us, therefore, in the 1990s and 21st century are dramatic shifts in worldwide centrifugal and centripetal social, political, and economic forces. These forces have already and are likely to continue to create major upheavals in the lives of everyday people whether they be residents of high technology and industrial societies or members of traditional societies; rural, suburban or urban residents; established national systems or emerging nations; Buddhists, Muslims, Christians or Jews; lower, middle or upper socioeconomic groups; adults or children; males or females; agricultural, factory or office workers, merchants or consumers; homeowners, home renters, or that fast growing worldwide species of human being the "homeless."

And, ultimately, centrifugal and centripetal trends place a burden on ordinary people, as their homes and home life, and communities and work are uprooted. For example, with ethnic and nationalist conflict emerging in the former Soviet Union and eastern Europe, people may lose their homes, communities, and work, and may be forced to migrate and reestablish themselves in new communities, and live in temporary camps or residences that are incompatible with their cultural values and lifestyles. Thus hundreds of thousands of people around the world have lived in squatter settlements, relocation centers or internment camps for many years. And, in the United States, homeless shelters and other settings have become temporary or even semi-permanent homes for many people.

In summary, contemporary and future centrifugal and centripetal worldwide trends ultimately affect the physical, psychological and social survival of ordinary people in terms of families and friends, homes and residences, proximate neighbors and community, and their everyday work and means of livelihood. Policy planners and government leaders may develop all sorts of macro-geopolitical and economic plans to address these problems, but solutions must ultimately address and enhance the everyday lives of people in homes, workplaces and communities.

The reality and power of these worldwide centrifugal and centripetal forces on the daily life of ordinary people make the contributions in this volume crucial. At the same time, it is important to recognize that policy makers, researchers and environmental designers of homes and communities face a formidable task. Voluminous research and design expertise about homes and communities in different cultures is needed, but it takes years to gain culturally relevant skills. And, research and design are hampered by political and social factors that often place homes, housing and communities low in governmental priorities in the face of political pressures to support military, industrial and political interests—which then claim to enhance the lives of ordinary people in the guise of one or another form of "trickle down" theory. But in spite of such pragmatics and barriers the work of research and environmental design must go on, and it is going on, as testified to by the contributions in the present volume.

The fundamental question before us concerns the research and design agenda to be addressed in the 1990s and 21st century in the face of these powerful centrifugal and centripetal forces. How does the present volume fare in meeting these challenges, and how do the chapters in the volume point the way toward the future? Let me address these issues in the context of my views about research and design needs in the coming years.

First and foremost, we will live, research and design in a world of pluralism and multiculturalism in which there will be an extraordinary interplay of racial, ethnic and national groups. Centrifugal and centripetal forces described earlier will often involve disparate cultures intermingling by virtue of migrations, shifts in demographics, birth rates etc. This intermingling will occur day by day as cultures live, work and play with or near one another on a daily basis. At the same time, some racial, ethnic and national groups in different parts of the world will establish separate enclaves as they search for unique group identities that may have been suppressed previously by governmental policies and social pressures. With either separatism or intermingling, research and design must be sensitive to cultural values about housing and lifestyle. For example, unlike the traditional monolithic and homogeneous housing of the 1950s-1970s in the United States, Great Britain, the USSR and elsewhere, or relocation communities in Africa built in connection with dam and riverine development, many of which largely ignored cultural needs and values of different populations, we must now be unusually sensitive to the rising tide of ethnic and national identities in both culturally intermingled and separatist living. A complex and difficult set of research and design issues indeed!

How to achieve this goal? One way illustrated in several chapters in the present volume is to highlight aspects of homes and residences in a range of technologically advanced, emerging, and traditional cultures. In addition, the contributions in the volume illustrate how it is crucial, as never before, for research and design on housing and home environments to include the perspectives of many disciplines in the social sciences and environmental design fields. Historians, anthropologists, geographers, regional experts, psychologists, and sociologists and others must be sensitive to one another's work and, where possible, join forces to understand a particular issue. At the same time, social scientists and architects, landscape architects, interior designers, urban and regional planners and other design professionals must collaborate, else all we do is learn but not act, or act without learning. Surely the pragmatics of all these disciplines working together is idealistic and not wholly achievable. But, at a minimum, we can learn about work in other disciplines in volumes such as the present one, and through exemplary collaborative projects. Difficult, yes, but absolutely necessary!

Second, family structures are changing in many parts of the world. Mobility, migration, technology, alternative lifestyles, womens' movements, and employment patterns have contributed to changes in family functioning in many cultures. Divorce and separation is prevalent in the western world, resulting in many single parent families and heads of households (usually women); the massive entry of women into the work force is increasing worldwide; the introduction of technology has changed gender and other role relationships in many cultures. Moreover, the rising homelessness rate in many countries has affected family life and ties to communities. These shifts in family functioning partially derive from and are occurring in the context of the worldwide centrifugal and centripetal forces noted earlier, and obviously have implications for homes and housing. Researchers and designers must focus their attention and skills on the unique and emerging needs of people in these changing family and life circumstances. Chapters in the present volume deal with one or another aspect of these issues in terms of shared housing, collective housing, relocation, homelessness, and the like. Extraordinary research and design efforts need to be mounted to extend the work reported in this volume. We must work to cope constructively with the inviolable fact that family life and social life are changing dramatically, and that innovative and alternative residential forms need to keep pace with these social and cultural changes.

Third, the realities of large scale centrifugal and centripetal forces accentuate the fact that we are dealing with complex hierarchical and nested socio-physical systems. Individuals are nested in families and other groups, groups are nested in neighborhoods and small communities, who in turn are nested in larger social systems and cultures. The relationships and tensions between these different social systems contribute to the reality and complexity of the 1990s and of the 21st century, and bear directly on homes and residences. Although we must learn about and design separately the interiors of individual dwellings, the individual structures themselves, and communities, neighborhoods and villages which incorporate dwellings, it is also essential that we attend to the culturally relevant nested relationships between homes and streets, homes and communities, homes and neighboring homes, and the like. We have readily come to appreciate the idea of home/settlement systems at micro- and macro- levels, which can range from a residence and its yard or street, to a residence and the community in which it is embedded. Here again, the dramatic centripetal and centrifugal forces of the 1990s and beyond provide special challenges, as lifestyles, demographics and cross cultural changes within and between groups yield new configurations of people and places. Several chapters in the present volume highlight the hierarchy of places within which homes and residences are located, and the relationships and intrinsic bonds of these different levels. Another challenge for researchers and designers to pursue in the coming years.

Fourth, the breadth, scope and range of issues facing environmental designers and researchers in respect to homes and communities demand openness to alternative philosophical, theoretical and methodological strategies. The social sciences of the 20th century have largely adopted a philosophy of science built around one or another form of positivistic philosophy, including the value of dimensional analysis, antecedent-consequent causation, observer objectivity, separation of subject and object, and other philosophical principles involving "proper" rules of evidence. This philosophy of science has necessarily guided the form and shape of theories for decades, and has also had an important influence on research methodology and means for accruing and evaluating information and knowledge. Without launching a full discussion here, it is sufficient to note that a number of scholars and practitioners in several disciplines have begun to explore complementary and alternative philosophies of science (Altman and Rogoff, 1987; Stokols and Altman, 1987). I believe that it is imperative to continue enhancing our philosophical, theoretical and methodological strategies because of the enormous complexity of the problems of design and research that must be addressed. Frankly, I am raising the possibility that traditional philosophies and strategies may not be wholly applicable to contemporary and future issues associated with homes and communities. One type of alternative approach goes by any of several labels— contextualism, transactionalism, systems analysis. Its focus is on treating events and phenomena as holistic units composed of inseparable aspects, understanding unique historical and social events, treating observers as part of phenomena, adopting a formal cause criterion of understanding (identifying and describing patterns of relationships rather than strictly antecedent-consequent concepts of causation). These approaches call for an enhanced range of research methodologies, including case studies of single events, qualitative analyses, holistic phenomenological perspectives, and the like.

Philosophy of science, theory and methodology in respect to research and design of homes and residences is complicated and not easily resolved. But these seemingly abstract matters warrant attention as we attempt to understand and address research and design of homes and communities in the 1990s and 21st century. And, the first several chapters in the present volume address aspects of these weighty matters in ways that command attention and set the stage for future discussions.

The present volume addresses the major issues that need to be addressed in the coming years, and sets forth an agenda for future deliberations. The centrifugal and centripetal forces operative around the world are complex, momentous, often unpredictable, and not easily or quickly understood. And, while many commentators and policy makers address these forces at macro-geopolitical levels, the fact is that centrifugal and centripetal dynamics ultimately affect the lives of ordinary people as they go about their everyday activities in homes, neighborhoods and communities, and as they explore and struggle with new lifestyles, family structures, and relationships in their own culture and with other cultures.

It is surely difficult to comprehend and act constructively to resolve the complex problems of the times, but we have no alternative but to begin and carry on the process. It is only by doing so that there is any hope for creating environments for and with people to improve and enhance their lives in the face of the complexities and realities of the times. The present volume points the way and provides us with encouragement, advice and stimulation to follow on with new research and new environmental designs for homes, residences and dwellings.

References

Altman, I. & Gauvain, M. (1981) "A cross-cultural and dialectic analysis of homes." In L. S. Liben, A.H. Patterson, & N. Newcombe (Eds.) *Spatial representation and behavior across the life span.* (pp. 283- 320). New York: Academic Press.

Altman, I. and Rogoff, B. (1987). "World views in psychology: Trait, interactional, organismic, and transactional perspectives." In D. Stokols & I. Altman (Eds.) *Handbook of Environmental Psychology.* Volume 1. (pp. 1- 40). New York: Wiley.

Gauvain, M., Altman, I. & Fahim, H. (1983) "Homes and social change: A cross-cultural analysis." In N. R. Feimer & E. S. Geller (Eds.) *Environmental psychology: Directions & perspectives.* (pp. 80-218). New York: Praeger.

Stokols, D. & Altman, I. (Eds.) (1987) *Handbook of environmental psychology.* Volumes 1 and 2. New York: Wiley.

Introduction

Ernesto G. Arias *et al*
University of Colorado

Use gives meaning to housing, and at the same time meaning guides how housing is used. How housing is used and what it means to those who reside in it ... and to those who do not have a house to reside, are probably the two most important topics to housing policy, planning or design in any cultural context around the world. Given the increasing concern in housing policy on these intrinsically related topics, this book introduces various concepts and methodological approaches to study present and future issues fundamental to the use and meaning of residential settings in various countries and cultural contexts. These conceptual and methodological approaches, together with the interdisciplinary and international perspectives presented, will afford readers the basis to make necessary and important comparisons across issues, disciplines, and countries, without relying on traditional comparative international analyses of the topic.

The book evolved from the very successful "International Housing Symposium on the Meaning and Use of Home and Neighborhood," sponsored by the National Swedish Institute of Building Research and the International Association for the Study of People and Their Physical Surroundings (IAPPS) in the Fall of 1989. The symposium demonstrated the present interest in the topic by a diverse and interdisciplinary group of participating planners, architects and social and behavioral scientists from all continents represented by over twenty countries. The chapters of the proposed book are a selection of the research presented at the conference, supplemented by especially invited contributions from other researchers whose work is internationally recognized as being on the cutting-edge of housing research (see Contributors).

Trends and implications

New approaches utilized to study different important aspects directly related to the use and meaning of housing are presented in the various contributions. These approaches have been developed to respond to an increasing concern for the environmental qualities of residential settings. Their importance will increase further, as more and more people in the future will remain at home and in neighborhoods to carry out non-residential activities. This increase in populations and uses of residential settings is an outcome of the variety of changes currently observed around the world. For example, first, as Franck points out in her introduction to the section on "Overlooked Populations," the changing household composition, occupations and life style patterns are changing traditional needs and uses of residential settings. This poses the major question of how existing home interiors, new housing design standards and unconventional housing arrangements meet and will meet the evolving needs of present and future housing uses by traditional and special populations in different countries.

Second, stricter public budget limitations imposed on the delivery of social welfare assistance have generated an increasing dependency on informal social network and support systems found in residential environments. This dependency may become more apparent as we witness the unfolding of economic and socio-political transitions taking place today in the delivery of housing in many areas around the world, as very clearly pointed out by Altman's "Foreword" and by van Vliet in his conclusion chapter and elsewhere (van Vliet 1987). Therefore, as Anthony indicates, new approaches to research the meaning and use of unconventional housing arrangements become imperative in future housing studies.

Finally, we are also witnessing different utilizations of the home interior from such trends as the increasing use of the housing environment for a workplace. This is clearly illustrated by Lawrence's introduction and the chapters of Bernard, Barbey and Giuliani et al, in this book. Likewise, these different utilizations have been also portrayed in Third World self-help housing and squatter settlements studies (Ward 1982, Turner,1976, among others). Similar patterns are being experienced in the more developed countries due to technological innovations such as the computer and the increasing access to electronic communication systems. These trends will continue to have increasing and direct implications for the study of the meaning and use of the home and the changing neighborhood.

Need

All these trends highlight the importance of environmental qualities of housing—the home and neighborhood's physical attributes; its users (the traditional family, special and overlooked populations, or the newly evolving unconventional households); and its dynamics of change. Thus, as a new century approaches, the importance of the meaning and use of the residential environment around the world will become even more pronounced. Therefore, a re-evaluation of housing policy, planning, design and management research which involves new perspectives, theories and methods such as those introduced by this book is timely and necessary.

The study of home environments has held for many years major national and international prominence in policy, planning, design and management of housing (van Vliet 1987, Lawrence 1987, Francescato *et al.* 1979). Recently, it has moved to the central arena of environmental and behavioral studies (Altman and Werner 1985). However, the use and meaning of housing as the organizing theme of a collection of international research on housing did not surface until the 1989 "International Housing Symposium on the Meaning and Use of Home and Neighborhood," at Gavle, Sweden.

Even though there has been much world interest on this topic, as illustrated by the conference, such work has remained hidden as a set of scattered individual pieces under the larger rubric of person-environment studies. In general, as Despres points, while some of this work is from various disciplines, most of this literature has defined the meaning and use of housing for traditional households and has in most cases overlooked new evolving ones (Despres 1989). A further limitation of this body of literature in general is that it does not present methodological approaches and applications on this topic in any systematic manner which allows the reader to make intelligent comparisons between different housing contexts, cultures or disciplinary perspectives.

More specifically, while there are clearly sound contributions in the existing literature, they represent a further need for this book to build upon their work, and to address some of their limitations. For example, Michelson's *Behavioral Research Methods in Environmental Design*, 1975, has been overtaken by new developments, while Michelson, Becthel and Marans' more recent *Methods for Environmental and Behavioral Research*, 1988, does not address the meaning and use of housing or neighborhoods; conversely Rapoport's seminal work *House Form and Culture*, 1969, while addressing residential settings, does not cover research methods. Two contributions which indeed reflect the growing excitement and potential of interdisciplinary research in the psychological experience of dwelling and the meaning of built form are Altman and Werner's *Home Environments*,

1985, and Rapoport's *The Meaning of the Built Environment*, 1982. While both contributions provide a comprehensive basis on meaning and use, they also have limitations, some of which are addressed by this book, such as the lack of an explicit focus on methods and their applications, and a very limited international perspective on the meaning and use of housing.

Purpose and philosophy

The Meaning and Use of Housing: International Methodological Approaches and Their Applications is intended to be a contribution to the study of housing for the social and behavioral sciences, as well as various related professions in various countries and cultures. The reader presents a collection of work organized for the first time around this topic, and represents a needed re-evaluation of housing policy, planning, design and management research involving new perspectives, concepts, and methods to address emerging concerns in the field. The need for new approaches to the study of use and meaning of housing, such as those presented in this book, arises from an increasing concern for the environmental qualities of residential settings around the world.

Methodologically, the contributions collectively present the philosophy that the central concern in the study of this topic is not the competition between qualitative versus quantitative approaches but rather the appropriateness of each to the housing situation and cultural context being studied. Conceptually, it holds the perspective that not all strategies aimed at a concern about use or meaning are equally effective in the attainment of a housing objective, but rather, that the nature of any strategy is contingent on the specific situation and its cultural context. Therefore, it is the situational variables describing a particular application that are important for the reader in understanding the relationships between concepts, methods, and "real" situations of concern to policy, planning, design and management for each country. Additionally, the book strives to make a unique contribution to housing studies by clearly linking theory, research and practice.

Organization

The contributions in this book are organized in seven parts and two concluding chapters. Each part represents domains of concern to policy, planning, design or management in the study of "meaning" and "use" of housing around the world. A set of incisive essays introducing the various parts provide this volume with critical perspectives on each of the selected concerns of its topic. Part I, as introduced by Studer, presents the general theoretical basis to understand use and meaning as concepts, as well as the methodological approaches and issues to study the various implications of these concepts in and of housing. The essays by Lawrence and Arias introduce Parts II and III, which respectively cover meaning and use relative to the home's "interior" and its "design." Then, the chapters in Part IV introduced by Yen, address the neighborhood's dynamics, and it's spatial and non-physical aspects at the more aggregate levels of concern to housing policy and planning. Chockor, from a comprehensive African perspective, introduces the studies on the use and meaning of housing for the traditional family in different countries included in Part V; while Anthony's essay in Part VI introduces issues and perspectives about the research on unconventional housing arrangements, such as cooperative and collective housing being re-examined with great interest in order to address the new housing needs of newly evolving unconventional households. Finally, Franck's provocative essay introduces the chapters in Part VII concerned with the use and meaning of overlooked populations such as the elderly, women, children, and the homeless. The chapters by Studer and van Vliet represent the concluding part which looks into major procedural and substantive implications and directions of future work.

Each chapter has been structured to systematically address the topic by presenting some conceptual and methodological base; their applications to some real housing concerns for a given culture or country; and a discussion of the findings and their implications to theoretical and practical aspects of policy, planning, design or management of housing. Such systematic organization represents a way to clearly articulate and provide a better cross-disciplinary and cross-cultural understanding of the topic for the comparative purposes of the reader.

Summary[1]

The main purpose of this summary is to give the reader a road map and a quick overall insight of the various parts and chapters. It is hoped that the overview will help place specific needs and interests of the reader against the broader perspective of the whole book, e.g., one or few chapters; similar methodological approaches utilized to address different concerns in different cultures or countries; different approaches to address the same concern; or simply an expedient way for the reader to find out if her needs or interests

---

[1] Excerpts from the contributions have been used to construct the subsequent chapter summaries.

related to policy, planning, design or management are addressed by chapters in the book.

Meaning and use: A basis of understanding

The two chapters of this part introduce the substance of "meaning and use," as well as the methodological concerns in studying their implications to housing policy, planning and design. The chapter "Meaning and Use" by Francescato, seeks to sketch a conceptual framework by discussing the terms of the title of this book. A systemic perspective is proposed to examine issues related to the multiplicity of meanings arising from the diversity of goals held by the various "stakeholders" in the system. Implications of the levels of housing scale such as room, dwelling, neighborhood and community are explored. Definitions of the term "use" are discussed and the process of semantization by which objects of use are attributed meaning is presented. The effect of time and change on the meaning and use of housing is examined from a transactional perspective. Implications of this conceptual overview include a number of needs: to go beyond the economic, technological and political biases that have informed a large proportion of housing research; to confront the frequent incompatibility of goals among the various participants in the housing sector; to identify the various levels of scale at which housing occurs; and to develop dynamic and adaptive strategies of study, policy making and interventions better suited to reflect aspects of time and change. The focus on use and meaning as an inseparable bundle is seen as a way to firmly anchor the study of housing to its human and social significance.

"Methodological Issues and Approaches: A Critical Analysis," by Lang, tells how all housing policies and designs are based on images of reality and good life. These images, Lang maintains, are based on some approach, casual or systematic, qualitative or quantitative. The nature of housing research and the assessment of its quality and implications has been marred by confusion over the nature of methodology, paradigms, models and methods. There has been a special need to distinguish between positive theory, which is descriptive and explanatory, and normative theories, or design ideologies. There have been two major research and design approaches to the creation of housing policies and housing architecture during the twentieth century: Rationalism and Empiricism. The limitations of the positive theoretical basis for much Rationalist thinking has lead to the growth in Empirical housing studies. The goal of Empirical research has been to build a sound knowledge base on which creative policies and habitable, cognitively rewarding, and enjoyable housing environments and housing units within specific cultural frames can be formulated. The research design task was to develop methods of working analogous to the scientific method in order to remove the biases inherent in Rationalist thinking. Pure Empiricist research methods have also been challenged by recent approaches to research such as phenomenology and hermeneutics. Examples of these approaches may be found in the contributions by Barbey on interior design and Chawala's work on the meaning of home from a child's perspective. Each approach has contributed much to our understanding of the housing environment. However, Lang reminds us that each has its limitations, and that all research findings are biased by the method used. The potential contribution and limitations of each approach must be understood and the results integrated into a positive theoretical basis which is open to challenge and development.

In this manner, as Studer points out, Francescato and Lang's chapters form a substantive and procedural basis of understanding from which to view the methodological approaches and perspectives presented in subsequent chapters. A basis which is also necessary to review relevant implications which these perspectives, approaches and applications to study meaning and use may have in furthering the theory and praxis "in" and "of" the planning, design and management of housing.

The meaning and use of home: Its interior

The introduction by Lawrence and the three chapters of Part II argue that probably the most utilized, and therefore the most meaningful physical domain of a home is its interior. Yet, as Giuliani et al point out in their chapter, there is little research available providing an understanding about the way different groups of people actually organize and use their interior domestic space. These chapters aim at presenting an explanatory background of the home's interior relative to its physical characteristics and behavioral attributes of users.

"The Interior Use of Home: Behavior Principles Across and Within European Cultures," by Bernard *et al*, demonstrates how a comparative method provides one of the most fruitful basis for a global speculation about a specific behavior. The gradual integration of observations on various societies or in different countries helps to show the specificity of the observed behavior as it emerges from the various complex interactions between physical, social and cultural factors. This chapter builds conceptually Altman's research orientation of the establishment of universal principles of behavior across cultures, and the attempt to understand a culture on its own terms in relation to its unique beliefs attitudes and values without imposing external values on that culture ("A cross cultural and dialectic analysis of Homes," 1981). The chapter shows how, using data collected with an identical protocol, the data processing selected makes it possible to display clearly the specificity of practices observed in France, Italy, England, or Sweden, as well as the way in which these practices structure different social worlds. Bernard elaborates on the two research goals. First, the comparative analysis aims at identifying the structurally more important characteristics differentiating the behaviors related to the use of the home space. These characteristics are not the features describing the initial corpus, but they are complex organizations of these features. The aim is not to describe a representative behavior of all the French, Italian, or Swedes but to detect in each of these countries the variables or groups of variables identified by the analysis from which to establish the social groups differentiation in each country. Second, once the patterns of variables characterizing a group of people are identified, to know who are those people and to look if people grouped according to attitudes and values can be characterized by common sociological variables, it is then possible to compare these new associations between countries. It then presents the different steps of the methodological approach: data collection, sampling, features coding, and choice of data analysis (Correspondence Analysis, Hierarchical Classification). The positive aspects of each of these techniques are critically reviewed in the context of comparative analysis. The chapter then presents the results, statistically displaying the existence in each culture of significant and consistent patterns among the variables considered. Finally, it examines the results, revealing the existence in each country of characteristic and differentiated patterns of interior residential arrangements regarding both, the existing elements and the relationships amongst them. The comparison also stresses equally the existence of identical relations between some social groups and some spatial layouts.

In "Spatial Archetypes and the Experience of Time: Identifying the Dimensions of Home," Barbey concentrates on the relationship between the home, its use, meaning and time as a transactional process between physical and affective factors. Additionally, as time passes, buildings undergo certain physical transformations. Their meanings and uses change. Therefore, the historical value of personal representations of domestic space can provide a way to understand and accommodate meaningful relationships between residents and their home. To this end, the chapter argues for a methodology that originates from a dual 'structuralistic' perspective which includes both, a typomorphological and a behavioral analysis. Home is thus considered as a combination of fixed spatial archetypes, such as individual rooms or suites, and the corresponding experience of time spent at home. The chapter identifies spatial archetypes which are characteristic of a standard dwelling unit as related to some typical experiences of home which are illustrated by literary sources and residential biographies. Therefore, utilizing this research approach, the results demonstrate that space identity is dependant upon the individual's ability to convert a physical space into a meaningful mental world based on cultural norms and values, yet, also reflecting personal aspirations and goals. Additionally, results indicate that people behave according to previous experiences of space and social norms governing status symbols. Moreover, the values involved in the identification process with the home are subject to social and cultural variations. Thus, through the application and results, the chapter is able to support the dual perspective approach as an instructive method to enrich our understanding of the meanings associated with the use of home; and to demonstrate how the identification of the common dimensions between the spatial form of domestic space and the lived experience of home can be helpful in establishing valuable qualitative criteria aimed at designing specific parts of the dwelling unit.

Giuliani *et al* in "The Spatial Organization of the Domestic Interior: The Italian Home," utilize a multivariate analysis to illustrate how current research on house form and meaning highlights a growing discordance between users' requirements and housing standards in western societies. Among the major causes of this discordance particular emphasis is placed on the dwelling designers' and planners' neglecting of individual differences in dwelling habits. Individual differences seem currently to be magnified by socio-demographic changes in household composition and by changes in systems of transmission of cultural models among different social worlds. However, little empirical evidence is yet available about the way in which different groups of people actually organize and use their domestic space. This is probably because of the difficulty in describing the great variety of situations present in the real world, as determined by the interaction between household structure, spatial characteristics of homes, and personal values as well as preferences. The chapter argues that multivariate analysis can be an useful tool in order to unify and summarize in one comprehensive framework the several interactions underlying the observed data. As an example of this statistical technique, Correspondence Analysis and Cluster Analysis are applied in a survey exploring the way different households spatially realize daily living activities in Rome, Italy. The theoretical assumption underlying this study is that the main dimension in the ordering of domestic space is the socialization–privacy dimension, and that changes in meaning and use of the dwelling will affect primarily this dimension. The results presented reveal that the application of multivariate analyses allow to identify similarities and differences among households in patterns of spatial organization of two basic dwelling activities—eating and sleeping. The implications of these results in planning housing standards are discussed.

In this manner, these three chapters will acquaint the reader with the importance of the home's physical interior due to its functional and symbolic roles in satisfying many of the housing needs of dwellers in different cultural contexts. In addition, they clearly illustrate the significance of the different methodological approaches introduced to studying the meaning and use of the home's interior in various European countries.

The meaning and use of home: Its design

Although the interior is very important in studying housing, as is illustrated previously, the contributions in Part III argue that its meaning and use are also derived from other significant interior and exterior aspects which are directly influenced by residential design, e.g. continuity, security, self-identity, or personal and social status. These aspects become apparent only when we turn our attention to understand design as process and outcome.

In "Connotative Meanings of House Styles," Nasar looks into symbolic inferences by the public from various styles of home. The chapter looks at similarities and differences in those meanings across socio-cultural groups and regions, and whether architects share or know public meanings. A diverse sample of adults in Columbus, Ohio and Los Angeles rated six styles of home in terms of desirability, and the friendliness and status of assumed residents. Sixty five Columbus architects answered the same questions and tried to guess how the Columbus public responded. Utilizing conventional non-parametric analyses, the study analyzed the rank-order data to obtain results from the survey. The results revealed clear differences in preference and meaning associated with different stylistic content. Further, they revealed shared meanings, with stability across geographically, culturally and environmentally distinct cities. The public in Columbus and Los Angeles had the same pattern of connotative response to the house styles. The chapter the shows how both groups rated Farm and Tudor as the "most desirable," Mediterranean and Saltbox as "least desirable," Farm as "most friendly," Colonial as "unfriendly," Colonial and Tudor as "highest in status," and Saltbox and Mediterranean as "lowest in status." Further, this chapter explains how some differences in meaning emerged across various "tastes" or socio-cultural groups, and how the architects responded differently from and misgauged the public responses.

"User Group Preferences and Their Intensity: The Impacts of Residential Design" by Arias, argues that housing has been the object of serious research and public concern for almost a century in the U.S.A.; yet, housing preferences, probably the most fundamental building block of housing analysis, are still poorly comprehended. Even though, as decisions made by the consumer, preferences are centrally responsible for the initial development of "meaning," way before "use" plays a role. The chapter presents the development of an effective methodological approach to study consumer preferences and their intensities in residential design, utilizing existing knowledge about concepts and approaches from other disciplines. It introduces this integrative framework to study a general but central question to design: "how are consumer housing preferences altered by outcomes of the design process?" In addressing it, the focus is on the intensity of preferences as an important knowledge gap, given that such knowledge is essential to the provision of sensitive and affordable housing. The chapter conceptualizes the designer and consumer decision processes and contexts, and then introduces the integrative framework to study preferences. The final part describes an illustrative experiment and the application of some aspects of the framework to address the question above. The chapter ends with a discussion of the findings on the intensity of consumer preferences, and the implications and limitations of this methodological approach in the study of the meaning and use of housing.

Finally, Luckey's "The Meaning of the Corredor in Costa Rica: An Integrated Methodology for Design" presents how the fit of meaning and use with form evolves over time in housing as new designs are introduced to an area of this Latin American country. As housing undergoes these transitions many questions need to be understood in order to provide efficiently housing sensitive to the needs of its residents, e.g., how do different generations think about and use the same design elements in the new housing? Or, does the new design introduced take into consideration those critical aspects of traditional form which have evolved incremental over time as a result of a "trial and error" process to attain the best "fit" between residential form and behavior? The chapter presents an integrated methodology to study the evolution of meaning and use in Costa Rica's Golfito area. An evolution which has been brought about by the introduction of new housing designs for the workers of foreign banana companies. More specifically, the chapter focuses on a particular design element of the "company house" relative to those of the "traditional house" such as the "corredor" in this unique southern coastal region of Costa Rica.

Thus, the chapters in Part III introduce the design of a home as both, process and outcome, and how the concepts and methodological approaches introduced in their respective research can be utilized to inform not only design, but other problem-solving activities such as planning or management, in order to attain effective and sensitive residential settings for different user groups.

The meaning and use of neighborhood: Spatial attributes and social dynamics

The chapters of Part IV, collectively argue that the meaning and use of housing change as scales of residential aggregations increase from home to neighborhood, and as the element of time is introduced. Its chapters examine how over time spatial attributes and social change affect the residents' perceived meaning and uses of the neighborhood.

"The Meaning and Use of Public Space" by Blaw utilizing a deductive reasoning approach, argues that housing, while it should meet people's need for privacy, should also provide facilities for community. The chapter considers public spaces mainly as meeting places, and argues that by definition they are expected to fulfill this social function. This argument presupposes the possibility to effect people's behavior with the help of spatial arrangements. Referring to this research, the chapter concludes that even in such prestructured situations as "neighboring," people need an argument to contact each other. Thus, the reason why public spaces should meet certain requirements. Therefore, the chapter presents the support to its arguments that: to function as meeting places, public spaces should facilitate the possibility for users to see each other and for varying groups to behave in various ways; public spaces should be perceived as safe and have sufficient physical attributes to attract people; and that users of public spaces should be able to recognize public spaces as such and should know how to behave in public life. Finally, Blaw in this chapter explores the likelihood for public spaces as a consequence of actual social changes in neighborhoods. The chapter concludes that notwithstanding the technological developments which seem to make public spaces redundant, other developments, both economic and demographic require the planner's attention to carefully design them.

Bogus, in "Neighborhood Gentrification: Dynamics of Meaning and Use in São Paulo, Brazil," studies through an integrative methodological approach the questions related to residential location and spatial mobility of the population in the urban environment. It also looks into their implications for the meaning and use of neighborhood which have become more and more important to urban studies, mainly in Third World countries such as Brazil. The chapter discusses the theoretical and methodological aspects of those questions. Taking in account the demographic, socio-economic variables, and especially those variables reflecting real state increasing values, the objective is to explain the set of changes which occurred in a specific peripheral area of the city of São Paulo. Those changes were due to a governmental re-urbanization program that resulted in a gentrification process with serious consequences to the resident families altering their life and housing conditions. According to the perspective of this study, the analysis of the changes in the use of home and neighborhood also passes through the study of the family which takes over the character of a methodological tool. The option for the case study and the longitudinal study justifies itself by the fact that these modalities of analysis permit one to reconstruct the social processes present in the city as a whole. Bogus elaborates on how the integrative use of case study analysis, life history and the study of personal and familiar trajectories is of great importance for understanding the dynamics of neighborhood changes which took place in that area. Particularly those changes in the meaning at both, the home and neighborhood scales.

Finally, "The Space of Citizenship: Visually Perceived Non-Spatial Dimensions of Housing" by Carvalho, draws a cross-national profile of some low-income housing estates in Brazil and in Britain. It focuses on the interrelatedness between spatial patterns in housing, the residents' attitudes towards them (and corresponding morphological process of change) and the role of the State in the decision process that produced or allowed those patterns to be created (organizational participatory arrangements). It begins by proposing a conceptual and methodological framework of analyses based on visually perceived indicators of residents' and State's interpretation of their roles in that interrelationship. Some participatory mechanisms of upgrading (and managing) residential environment are described in their different disguises (State-led decentralization, tenants' Cooperatives, Action groups) and their impact analyzed (by means of applying those indicators) in relation to the gradual transformation of certain standard shapes of selected housing estates. The relative weight of the State and of citizenship (as acknowledged individual rights towards proposing and deciding over the dwelling) on the housing space are examined by comparing the two different contexts. One is the Brazilian authoritarian structure of power and corresponding centralized process of production and characteristic design. The other context is the British democratically structured housing system and peculiar style of design (production) and management (consumption) of space. The chapter closes summarizing the relevant aspects identified in this research about the roles played by the dweller (in transforming the housing estate), the space patterns of the housing estate, and by the State.

In this manner, this part addresses concerns which are more directly relevant to urban policy and planning decisions in different countries. For example, how neighborhood's physical and locational characteristics act as the intermediaries in the transitions and conflicts between public and private domains; how the dynamics of social change are reflected in the filtering or gentrification of neighborhoods; or how the State perceives its role in the visually perceived indicators of residents. Thus, it introduces the reader to possible approaches and perspectives to derive policy interventions aimed at central housing concerns related to use and meaning such as residential location, mobility, and satisfaction.

The meaning and use of housing: The traditional family

The concern of the chapters in Part V is that housing, in a behavioral sense, plays major functional and symbolic roles which sustain the social concept of the traditional nuclear family. The contributions of this part introduce the reader to a conceptual understanding of the family as a behavioral, social, and economic unit; and of expected or evolving changes in its attributes such as composition (e.g. larger to smaller families, or extended to nuclear) or socio-economic behavior as a unit (e.g. production and consumption, or life style changes).

Michelson in "The Behavioral Dynamics of Social Engineering: Lessons for Family Housing," examines the dynamics of such effects on social behavior which professionals who create housing expect will occur as a consequence of their design work. The chapter goes beyond the presence of such effects to explain under what circumstances they may appear. The analysis is based on three kinds of data gathered simultaneously in eight housing areas in Sweden during the winter and spring of 1988. Half of these areas are experimental, in that their designers attempted to foster enhanced social contact, inter-generational contact, lessened household work, and easier child care through specific physical designs and forms of social organization, separately and together. The other half are matched control areas. Survey data, time-use data, and systematic observational data are drawn upon to assess the extent that one or more of the goals specified are found in more pronounced form in experimental as opposed to control areas. Further analysis concerns which experimental treatments enhance effects, as well as the strength of interaction effects. These data show that while the experiments are largely successful in terms of the effects expected, these effects are a function of an antecedent condition—the self-selection of residents to particular housing situations. The effects of environment are not deterministic. Nonetheless, self-selection is carried out with specific reference to the experimental conditions. Thus, attempts at "social engineering" are hardly irrelevant if based on a sound understanding of the relationship between human behavior and its immediate environmental contexts. But they require human recognition and motivation to achieve their goals.

"Housing Characteristics, Family Relations, and Family Lifestyle: An Empirical Study of Estonian Families" by Niit, relies on the theoretical framework that each socio-physical system (e.g., a family in the apartment) should be described as a unity of place, activity and relations. The chapter demonstrates that we cannot understand none of these descriptors without considering them in relation to the others. It describes a study of 200 families in new housing estates in Tallinn and Tartu, Estonia . In each family, members completed a similar survey which included a privacy preference scale, Rotter's Locus of Control Scale, Moos' Family Environment Scale, and several other questions about family relations and activity patterns of the family members. Additionally, the location of furniture and material artifacts in the apartment, as well as usual locations of about 20 activities for each family member were recorded. Using Smallest Space Analysis, six clear facets of privacy preferences are distinguished. These are: solitude, openness, intimacy, reserve, avoidance of interaction, and anonymity. On the basis of the privacy preferences of different family members, the privacy indices were constructed for the whole family and their relationships with the other parameters of the socio-physical system were analyzed. The chapter describes the relationships between residential density (as a characteristic of place), family relations (measured with Moos' Family Environmental Scale), and the 11 activity indices (e.g., cultural interests, or domestic activities) constructed from frequencies of 35 activities (e.g., going to the cinema, or watching TV). Thus, the study is able to distinguish several family lifestyles from the activity patterns, as well as discussing the relationship between several housing characteristics (e.g., floor of residence or residential density) with these lifestyles (e.g., active or passive), and emphasizing the implications for apartment and neighborhood design and planning.

The last chapter, "Inheritability and Attachment: The Detached House in Japan" by Narumi, explains how in Japanese traditional society the "Ie," which literally means "house," played a central role with its other meaning of social unit. Culturally, the "Ie" means a system of successive family genealogy. A meaning which continues to be strongly associated with detached housing in agricultural areas. It has also been carried over to contemporary industrial Japan, where many families do not expect a social welfare system to take care of its members during their "old age." Instead, in these families it is expected that the sons or daughters will do so. Given this meaning and tradition, the desire of many Japanese families is to own a detached house. This is true not only in rural areas of the country, but in the large cities where land area is minimal. Judging from the fact that there is this strong desire to own a detached house, Narumi points out that it is important to consider what should the future housing in Japan learn and adopt from the detached house. To this end, the chapter considers two points. First, it looks into the observation that even for a detached house, it is rare that it is succeeded by a single "Ie," this is particularly true in large cities. It considers how privately owned detached houses are inherited as assets and how people think this inheritance should be. The second observation studied is that a detached house can be easily improved by its physical reorganization through remodeling or additions. Through the analysis of this consideration the chapter clarifies the role of the physical house in conveying culture from one generation to the next in Japanese families.

Thus, these chapters of Part V introduce the reader to central topics in the study of the traditional family; as well as to methodological approaches, implications and relationships of some of the approaches and findings to various semantic concepts and theoretical interpretations of the meaning and use of housing to the family, e.g. home as permanence and continuity, or inheritability and the economic, social and psychological functions and interpretations of home in different cultural contexts.

The Meaning and use of housing: Unconventional arrangements

The chapters of Part VI present the student of housing with an introductory discussion about housing for shared cooperative and collective living arrangements; as well as discussing housing types which represent different and unconventional arrangements, such as the trailer home. They also acquaint the reader with new methodological approaches to re-examine these arrangements and their affordances in meeting the new housing needs of unconventional households, and those resulting from the changing compositions of the traditional ones.

The first chapter, "A Hybrid Strategy in a Study of Shared Housing" by Despres, argues that home cannot be interpreted only as a personal construct, since it is also a social practice and a physical entity; and, that meanings expressed by respondents represent only a fragment of this reality. Further, it argues that researchers must learn to read two levels of discourse when people talk about their home: the "intermediate discourse" (accessible through verbal data) and the "meta-discourse" (uncovered only through the contradictions and pre-conceived notions of home). To this end, the chapter introduces a general methodological strategy which puts two research traditions in a dialectical relationship, so as to generate original data. The research design combines quantitative instruments from cognitive psychology with qualitative research procedures from other disciplines such as human geography and phenomenological sociology, in order to explore the meaning and experience of home for unrelated households in shared housing arrangements. The data was gathered through the application of face-to-face interviews with a cross-sectional sample of 70 homesharers. Due to the limited empirical data available on shared housing, the research was "hypothesis generating" rather than "hypothesis testing." Three cognitive tasks — rating task, paired comparison task and sorting task— were used to provide quantitative indicators of sample trends, and as a means to generate open-ended comments. Additionally, qualitative techniques such as multidimensional scaling (MDS), structural text analysis, and structural built form analysis allowed to unfold levels of discourse which respondents cannot always articulate, and were used to investigate factors which shape the meaning of share housing. Thus, the study utilizing this hybrid design is able to find out from respondents (1) what categories of meaning are valued most in relationship to their ideal home and to their current shared home; and (2) what dimensions of home are most critical in shared housing, that is, the ones that present the most discrepancies between their idea of what a home should be and their current experience; and (3) what sets of factors can explain the gaps between ideal and current shared housing.

Vestbro's "Methodological Problems in the Study of Collective Housing" focuses on various dilemmas arising from the application of an integrative methodology consisting of some eleven methods to study the meaning and use of collective housing in Sweden. In this chapter, Vestbro selects nine significant aspects of collective housing for the analysis: the role of collective housing in Swedish housing policy, the goals for collective housing, participation in planning and administration, recruitment of suitable inhabitants, a profile of inhabitants in collective housing, integration of age and social groups, municipal service in collective housing, house types and spatial organization, and the function of communal meals and dining hall. The methods utilized in the study range from archival research (Analysis of research documents, official documents, newspaper articles, and organizational reports), interviews (Key person interviews, Group interviewing, Semi-structured user interviews, and Enquiries), observation and participant observation, and the analysis of architectural plans. The chapter also explores the opportunities and constraints, i.e. the level of contribution, of each of the methods applied to address the various the major aspects of collective housing in studying its use and meaning. For example, the chapter reveals the great methodological importance of utilizing observation and analysis of plans to study housing prototypes and spatial organization, while showing the limited contribution of organizational report analysis to study the use and meaning of the very same housing prototypes and spatial organization of collective housing in Sweden.

In "The House Trailer: Assimilation and Accommodation of an Innovation," Wallis discusses how the introduction of material innovations in societies involves dual processes of assimilation and accommodation. Through assimilation the physical characteristics of an innovation, as well as its meaning and pattern of use, are altered in order to make the innovation more acceptable. At the same time, the growing use of an innovation involves accommodation through which the perception of other objects and practices related to the same activities as the innovation are themselves transformed acknowledging acceptance of the innovation. Evidence of the operation of these dual processes is found in the physical transformation of the object and in formal changes in its meaning. This chapter presents the methodological use of the case study for a single innovation in housing—the house trailer. House trailers first came into popular use in the U.S. in the mid-1920's. Within thirty years they had evolved into the modern mobile home which now provides up to a quarter of all new housing produced annually in this country. The first part of this article presents a methodology for the use of court cases dealing with various aspects of house trailers. Court cases provide an excellent archival record of changing attitudes toward and the evolving meaning of the house trailer and mobile home. The second part of this case uses court opinions to reconstruct the chronological evolution of the house trailer into the mobile home. Four specific periods of development are identified. The analysis deals with issue such as whether a trailer or mobile home can legally be considered a house and, if so, what features it must contain in order to be considered permanent housing. The third part of this analysis looks at current attitudes and practices regarding the use of house trailers and mobile homes and demonstrates how practices in various states and communities reflect different phases in the development and acceptance of trailers and mobile homes. The final section deals with the broader methodological and public policy aspects of this type of analysis for understanding resistance to socially useful innovations. More broadly, it suggests a methodology for determining the relative level of integration of innovations and for analyzing the structure of resistance to their use.

In addition to the methodological approaches introduced, the inherent importance of Part VI rests in the fact that in many areas of the world, stricter public budget limitations imposed on the delivery of social welfare assistance have generated an increasing dependency on informal and formal unconventional housing arrangements for social support. In addition, just as there are increasing trends in the proportion of evolving non-traditional households and other special populations of users, there is an evolving variety of unconventional housing arrangements and types for them as presented by these chapters.

Overlooked populations

The aim of the chapters of Part VII is twofold. First, it is to introduce the reader to perspectives and approaches to study aspects of meaning and use of housing for overlooked populations in various cultures. And second, it is to make her aware that while the family continues to be a major household type, changing household composition around the world is resulting in an increasing number of new household types which need to be addressed in the policy, planning, design and management of housing.

In "The Homeless and "Doubled-Up" Households," Huttman discusses how a growing number of persons, both singles and families, lack a permanent abode of their own in the U.S.A. The National Coalition for the Homeless has estimated the number as high as two million. Besides those on the street or temporarily housed in shelters, motels or welfare hotels, there are those living in cars or recreational vehicles (RVs) and those doubling up with relatives or friends. To these individuals, whether single, unemployed, mentally ill or alcoholic, or, instead, families, couples or solo parents, poor, victims of violence and/or substance abusers, the "meaning of home" is in terms of very basic elements, though these may have added dimensions for homeless families other than those demanded by singles. The chapter demonstrates how for all, the main hope is to have one's own unit, that is a permanent home, however substandard. The street provides little adequate shelter; certainly living under a bridge or freeway entrance, or in a doorway, is not adequate accommodation. Nor is the large city shelters with their dormitories, often barrack-like, with row on row of cots, and communal baths and toilets, and with their regulations and demand for daily exit, and reapplication each night. All these features make them a non-permanent type of accommodation. The special family shelters or welfare hotels, including those for battered women, are only slightly better, with users asked to leave during the day, and limited in their stay, although unlike the city shelters for singles the stay is usually guaranteed for a month or even two. Doubling-up is again sharing a unit. Further, this contribution examines the "meaning of home" for the homeless as a unit that has the basic amenities that most Americans assume exists in every home. For the single homeless simply having a room of their own, even if the toilet is down the hall, is a desirable state, though a room with bath and toilet are preferred. For families, it is more than a room, but having a unit not only with one's own bathroom, but, in addition, one's own kitchen where the mother can cook for her family. Neither the shelter, the car, nor the doubling-up situation usually allow this, and certainly street living does not. In addition, the chapter analyzes why the "meaning of home" can also be in terms of having privacy and safety—for singles, one's own room where you can lock the door and keep your possessions, and or families, an apartment rather than a communal accommodation, even if one has a separate room. In the past transient hotels offered singles such even though they were substandard as did slum apartment units; now they are mostly gone. For both singles and families meaning of home can be where one lives independently without regulations or a set routine or agency personnel telling you what to do, or disciplining your children for you.

Louise Chawla's "Home is Where You Start From: Childhood Memory in Adult Interpretations of Home" presents how childhood homes and neighborhoods get turned into something less and something more through the alchemy of memory. Both housing researchers and the people whom they study necessarily adopt cultural frameworks of interpretation in defining the meaning of home. To this end, the chapter examines some major cultural interpretations of the significance of remembered childhood homes. It reviews this process in the life spans of four distinctive but diverse men and women, with a focus upon the connections to childhood memory that they have established at the approach of old age. Its method is phenomenological, as it seeks to attend to their descriptions of the quality of memory as openly as possible. It is also hermeneutic, because rather than stressing shared qualities of human experience, it explores how self-understanding is an interpretive act in which memories acquire meaning and value within an individual's particular time and place in history. Case studies are presented based on the poetry of four successful contemporary American poets: Audre Lorde, one of the most anthologized and reprinted African-American women poets; Marie Ponsot, hailed as one of the most important young Catholic poets of the post-World War II period; David Ignatow, who since young has continued Wm. Carlos Williams' tradition of uncompromising urban poetry in more than a dozen books; and William Bronk, who won the National Book Award in 1982 for poems that now span more than forty years. Through the medium of the case studies of these four men and women, who are articulate and self-conscious about the traditions that they draw upon, the chapter looks at how childhood memories persist in adult constructions of the meaning of home. In each case, choices of meaning are adaptive rather than passive: subjects select and shape cultural possibilities in keeping with parental relations and social and political status. Their resulting concept of home synthesizes adult conclusions with childhood origins. The results indicate that to understand childhood sources of the meaning of home, it is necessary to integrate remembered physical qualities of the home and neighborhood, family relations, sociopolitical status, and adult world view.

Danermark and Ekstrom in "The Elderly and Housing Relocation in Sweden; A Comparative Methodology," argue that the realistic contrafactual reasoning and intra/inter-individual comparative approach, developed by British scholars, solves many of the problems concerning causality. During recent decades there has developed widespread research into the significance of the social and physical situation of the elderly and their physical and mental health. Most of this research is more or less explicitly of a causal nature. Second, the chapter presents and discusses various imaginative research designs that are relevant to the study of causal relations in this field. Common are the various quasi-experimental extensive designs that are based on quantitative methods of data collection and on statistical analysis. Given the growth of the elderly population in all countries, it is becoming increasingly important to gather information about their situation with the aid of relatively simple and inexpensive methods of data collection. Concurrently, there is skepticism regarding the possibility of conducting investigations of elderly populations by way of survey instruments such as interviews, and especially questionnaires. Therefore it is safe to assume an inverse relationship between the methodological problems and the quality of the information. This chapter stresses the importance of acquiring greater knowledge as to what methodological considerations should be taken into account when looking at the elderly's housing situation. To this aim, it focuses on prescriptive methodological approaches to the study of the meaning and use of elderly housing. It introduces an intensive process-oriented design, focusing on the development of events in case studies of individuals. The purpose is to clarify concrete mechanisms, connections and relations between various circumstances, events, acts, meanings and states. Instead of seeking statistically significant correlations, causal relations are clarified through "contra-factual reasoning" and through "intra" and "inter-individual" comparisons. The authors argue that these research designs are complementary, and that there is need of process-oriented case studies which are more theoretically aware. In this manner the chapter investigates the social and health consequences of the relocation of elderly movers in Orebro and introduces a research design which integrates a register study, field survey with interviews, and a postal questionnaire. An evaluation of the applied design is presented and the methodological findings are discussed in terms of issues such as data quality, non-responsiveness, or evasive bias. Different sources of error are discussed, as well as the advantages and disadvantages, possibilities and drawbacks, of different survey methods.

Egyptian Norms, Women's Lives: A New Form and Content for Housing by El-Rafey and Sutton, introduce an ethnographic study that provides insight into how Egyptian women's cultural reality affects daily routines and compromises their capacity to achieve a sense of "at homeness" in contemporary housing. The chapter presents a study based on middle-income women with differing degrees of adherence to traditional values who lived in two multifamily complexes in Cairo. The research approach develops composite portraits on typical afternoons in the lives of four of them. These composites are drawn as one way to illustrate the spatial problems that women encounter depending on their cultural and religious values. To address women's inequality, embodied in inadequate housing designs, the chapter argues that although physical space is a reflection of the cultural values which shape it, simply redesigning the residential environment will do little to improve the lives of Egyptian women; unless, some consideration is given to changing the structural inequities that allow housing projects, such as those reviewed, to be built. The chapter concludes by outlining an interdependent conceptual approach to the physical and social transformation of domestic space in Egypt. This conceptual model considers the configuration of physical space and a dialogic social process for addressing the personal and societal values that give meaning to space. The parameters for physical change include a reconsideration of the activities that occur among specific groups of people in different types of space - all focused on increasing a sense of at-homeness among middle-income Egyptian women. The proposed dialogic social process in the framework is seen as taking place in several arenas which range from informal to institutional and involve diverse participation of stakeholders in Egyptian society. One arena of discourse is in the Ministry of Housing. There, formal or informal networks might form to advocate for changes in housing policy and design. Another is the institution of the university, were applied and theoretical approaches to addressing women's housing needs might be developed. A third is in primary and secondary schools where curricular and extracurricular activities might be designed to stimulate an awareness of the effect of the environment on the quality of life. A fourth arena is in the community where women can begin to define for themselves their sociospatial needs. Each arena can provide "safe places" to forge the shared values, strategies, and outcomes that are needed to fundamentally change the way domestic space in Egypt is designed and used. In this manner, the chapter provides an approach to implement a needed strategy to place the individual accommodations that women are making in their homes into a collective medium. An approach which suggests that both components - physical space and social process - be elaborated through research and practice.

Again, in this manner, the chapters in this part familiarize the reader with shifts in the growing trends of overlooked populations, their descriptive attributes and housing needs. Thus, making him and her aware that the outcomes of these shifts are an increasing concern for the environmental qualities of residential settings, and a need for new approaches to study the meaning and use of housing for these overlooked populations.

Conclusion: Future Implications and Directions

The aim of this concluding set of chapters is to primarily to remind us about some procedural and substantive concerns. They strive to provide the reader with a basis for understanding the implications and possible directions of future work addressing research and policy concerns about the meaning and use of housing. In a parallel manner as Part I, the chapters of this concluding part also address praxis and substance.

"Getting from What Is to What it Should Be: Procedural Issues" by Studer, points out that what has complicated the procedural agenda in housing praxis is recognition of the problems associated with instrumental rationalism and the related challenge of post- positivist perspectives of the housing enterprise. The chapter argues that procedural issues in housing research and housing praxis are differentiated, primarily by a focus on procedural issues in praxis. In order to illuminate these issues, questions encountered in housing decision processes must be critically reviewed, since one of the major challenges in praxis involves linkages between knowledge and problems about sociophysical systems. Therefore, the chapter offers four metastrategies for generating knowledge required in housing praxis: research *on* decision processes, research *for* decision processes, research *in* decision processes, and generative decision processes. The chapter suggests that all these should be considered in future work as components of a general program to address the multifaceted substantive and procedural issues and concerns. Implicitly suggested is the development of some sort of technology (analogous to established physical technologies) linking basic and applied sociophysical knowledge to situation-specific housing problems.

The final chapter by Van Vliet, "A House is not an Elephant: Centering the Marginal," while acknowledging other worthy domains for research on the meaning and use of housing, purposely focuses attention on distributional questions, and issues related to poverty in the face of affluence. The chapter further argues that differences in the meaning and use of housing are usually not random, but, instead, follow systematic patterns. It focuses attention on differences arising out of inequities that are created and reinforced by systems of housing provision. These differences are largest in nations where housing is foremost treated as a commodity, to be produced and traded for profit. In these countries, households that are too poor to translate their housing needs into an effective market demand become residualized. Such marginality characterizes the daily life of a majority of the population of the less industrialized world. Relationships of economic dependency on the industrialized world set an important constraining context for ameliorative policies. The chapter in it's conclusion reminds us that as we strive to perfect some of the tools contained in the chapters of this book, we must not forget about the contexts within which they become useful. Just as we must be committed to rigor in the application of methods, so also must we be committed to rigor in the selection of the ends to which they are applied. We must ensure that our applications are impartial to these ends. We must also ensure that our selection of these ends is partial to the values that we seek to uphold. In this regard it is as important to avoid the pretense of neutrality as the folly of dogma. Thus, the central implication raised by the chapter for future developments in housing policy, planning, design and management, proposes that the processes that marginalize poor households ought to be a central concern of researchers and professionals when addressing their design, planning, or policy interventions.

Conclusion

Throught this volume's organization and summary above, our purpose is to insure that it does not impose a linear structure to the reader, but rather one which allows a flexibility for the reader to imposed her/his own structure based procedural or substantive needs and interests. It is also hoped that the combination of this general and individual chapter organizations, methodological and conceptual philosophies, and its interdisciplinary and international perspectives on the topic, *The Meaning and Use of Housing: International Perspectives, Approaches and Their Applications* will assist the reader in making important housing comparisons across issues, concerns, disciplines and countries. In this manner, it represents a comprehensive re-evaluation of the study of use and meaning "in" and "of" residential environments; and provides interested researchers and practitioners from various disciplines and fields around the world with different perspectives, innovative methodological approaches and their respective cultural applications to various important aspects of the topic.

References

Altman, I. and Werner, eds., *Home Environments*, Plenum Press, 1985.

Altman, I. & Gauvain, M., "A cross cultural and dialectic analysis of Homes," in L.S. Liben, A.H. Patterson, & N. Newcombe (Eds.) *Spatial Representation and Behavior Across the Life Span.* New York: Academic Press, pp.283-320, 1981.

Becthel, Robert and Robert Marans, *Methods for Environmental and Behavioral Research*, 1988.

Despres, Carole, "The Meaning of Home: Literature Review and Directions for Future Research and Theoretical Development," paper presented at the International Symposium on the Meaning and Use of Home and Neighborhood, Sweden, 1989.

Francescato, G., S. Weidemann and J.R. Anderson, "Residential Satisfaction: Its Uses and Limitations in Housing Research," in van Vliet, W., *et al* (eds) *Housing and Neighborhoods: Theoretical and Empirical Contributions from North America and Europe.* 1987.

Francescato, G., S. Weidemann and J.R. Anderson, *Resident Satisfaction in HUD-Assisted Housing: Design and Management Factors.* Washington, D.C.: USGPO, 1979.

Lawrence, R. *Housing, Dwellings and Homes: Design Theory, Research and Practice.* New York: Jhon Wiley and Sons, 1987.

Michelson, Wm., ed., *Behavioral Research Methods in Environmental Design,* Dowden. Troudsburg, PA.: Dowden, Hutchinson and Ross, Inc., 1975.

Michelson, Wm., R. Becthel and R. Marans, *Methods for Environmental and Behavioral Research.* 1988.

Rapoport, Amos, *House Form and Culture.* Englewood cliffs, N.J.: Prentice-Hall, Foundations of Cultural Geography Series, 1969.

Rapoport, Amos, *The Meaning of the Built Environment.* Beverly Hills: Sage Publications, 1982.

Turner, John F.C. T, *Housing by People.* Pantheon Books, Mansell Publishing Limited, 1976.

Ward, Peter M., *Self Help Housing: A Critique.* Mansell Publishing Limited, 1982.

van Vliet, Willem, ed., *Housing Markets and Policies under Fiscal Austerity.* Greenwood Press, 1987.

Part I
Meaning and Use:
A Basis of Understanding

Meaning and Use: A Basis of Understanding

RAYMOND G. STUDER
University of Colorado

As evidenced by the title and contents of this volume, those involved in the field of housing seek to realize housing environments which are, above all, meaningful and useful to their inhabitants. Focusing on this superordinate goal leads directly to consideration of implicit sub-goals (e.g., "shelter", "affordability"), and a hierarchy of related empirical and nominative issues. With regard to meaning and use, as well as other dimensions of housing, we are collectively engaged in the search for useable knowledge, including the procedures for generating and using this knowledge. In the two chapters which follow, various substantive and procedural issues attendant to this search are explicated as a guide to the enterprise. The purpose of this introduction is to illuminate aspects which are addressed in more detail in these two chapters.

Although functionally interdependent, "meaning" and "use" connote conceptually distinct phenomena. In psychological discourse, meaning has been characterized as that which one intends to or is conveyed or communicated; that which a symbolic act or object refers to or (denotively or connotively) signifies in the conventional or socially agreed-upon sense. Meaning is also seen as an attribute of an object or idea that makes it of emotional value or concern, arousing in a person or persons certain associations, cognitions or affects. Such elements stand for and communicate particular ideas or values of those agents who present them in order to confirm an intention (English and English, 1958). In philosophic discourse, meaning is seen as "a highly ambiguous term with at least four pivotal senses, involving: a) intention or purpose, b) designation or reference, c) definition or translation, d) causal antecedents or consequences." (Runes, 1959).

Use suggests overt behavior, the employment of objects or ideas to facilitate an action. Indeed it would be convenient to look at use as manifesting *effective* behavior, and meaning as manifesting *affective behavior*. However, in the following chapter Francescato points out that use involves both effective and affective (e.g., "perceptual, affective, symbolic") responses. In any event, elements in the environment can be seen to provide behavioral instructions to its users. Many such elements, of course, operate in both modalities. That is, they provide instructions for use on the one hand, and signify, symbolize or stand for something on the other. The entrance to a dwelling, for example, provides an understood point of ingress and egress, instructional (discriminative) stimuli connoting the appropriate behaviors, a meaningful symbol for a socially salient event or ritual, and presentation of an idea, value or intent on the part of those who produced it. In this sense, elements which embody meaning and direct appropriate use are amalgamated in housing environments.

It is difficult to imagine an environment that could be either highly meaningful and completely useless, or quite useful but meaningless. Given this reality, is meaning implicit in use, or is use implicit in meaning? That is, since meaning and use are intertwined, can one be defined in terms of, or indexed by, the other? In which case, what is the unit of analysis, and what is measured and how? Ascertaining information regarding meaning or use clearly involves quite different questions, i.e., "what does this mean to you" or "how do (or would) you *use* this?" Regarding use, one would expect an answer like: "to *do*, or possibly not do, something" (e.g., "enter here", "relax", "socialize", "stay out"); in the case of meaning, one would expect an answer like: "to *communicate* something" (e.g., "repose", "wealth", "isolation"). Sorting out the conceptual and methodological issues in assessing meaning and use is the implicit theme underlying the following chapters.

However conceptualized and measured, *whose* meaning and use is at issue? That is, the conceptual and procedural problems implicit in assessing and accommodating meaning and use requirements generally are compounded when one considers the complex array of stakeholders or clients involved in housing decisions, e.g., users, landlords, developers, analysts, designers. It is understood that meaning and use propensities vary with particular population and setting types. But even within these, any decision-making context involves the assessment of different, generally conflicting goals, perceptions, values and propensities (vis-a-vis meaning and use) both within and across various types of stakeholders. The conceptual and methodological issue here is: how can the multiplicity of requirements, (e.g., goals, meanings, uses) be accurately assessed, generalized and/or weighted across heterogeneous aggregates of users or potential users and other stakeholders? The complex methodological problems attendant to sorting out the empirical and nominative claims and requirements of heterogeneous populations are well known. It is also well known that conventional (positivist) procedures have not been found fully effective in addressing this problem.

An individual's, a family's, or a group's most salient and intimate experience vis-a-vis meaning and use is no doubt manifest within the boundary of the dwelling place. However, this is clearly only part of the experiential continuum. A reasonable premise is that the most successful housing configurations are those that exhibit continuity—are interdependent—with larger sociophysical aggregates, e.g., neighborhood, community. How then are the concepts and requirements of meaning and use to be extended and accommodated along the scale continuum? This continuum of requirements needs to be considered in the context of what Altman correctly identifies in the Foreword as the centripetal and centrifugal dialectic operating in any scale of human enterprise.

Getting a handle on multiple, conflicting meaning and use objectives and criteria at various scales is made more difficult with the realization that human systems are continuously changing. Among emerging changes affecting housing are, e.g., new home-work relationships, new lifestyles and family compositions, and entirely new ways of integrating various types of activities generally. In any event, rates of change generally relate to various scales from individuals (including life span changes) to larger aggregates. Regardless of the scale of concern, the reality is that sociophysical requirements generally change before they can be met; that is, the human dynamic can never be fully accommodated by environments we create to support human purposes. Supply will inevitably lag demand in the built environment, because it is essentially a static system organized to support dynamic human processes. In short, assessing and accommodating meaning and use requirements in housing at a particular point in time, while problematic, becomes even more so when one considers the accelerating changes in human systems at various scales and levels of aggregation.

A rather fundamental and long-standing question raised in considering the dynamics of people-environment systems is this: is the built environment a product, or an engine of social change? Social scientists would no doubt support the former, while environmental designers would probably insist that it is the latter; perhaps it is both. Nevertheless, planning, design and management are goal-directed processes, committed to moving human settings or systems from where they are to where they should be. This brings us to consideration of the nature of process, and methodological issues and strategies implicit in assessing and accommodating, among other things, meaning and use requirements in housing.

As the processes of organizing and realizing built environments evolved from unselfconscious to selfconscious (Alexander 1964, Studer 1987), various specialists emerged. This specialization accelerated during the scientific and technological revolution. Essentially, the processes shifted from those in which inhabitants configure their own built environments, to those in which these are organized and produced by others with specialized competencies. In time this led to systematic efforts to better understand human requirements and procedures for accommodating these.

A general interest in the scientification of praxis, particularly following the second world war, led to programs of research to better understand people-environment relations and decision-making methods to improve human system and setting performance. Predicated on the modernist precept of functionalism, documentation of human requirements of built environments (via the methods of positive science) became the major focus. Such programs were driven by the implicit assumption that the knowledge generated would lead directly to its utilization to effect more viable, well-fitting habitats.

The test of knowledge usability is its direct relevance to praxis—to decision processes and issues encountered in situation-specific contexts. As it developed, a great deal of the people-environment research agenda has been predicated on the demands of social science rather than those of physical planning, design and management. The designer who would use the knowledge accumulated is typically faced with a vast catalogue of primarily descriptive studies, many of them excellent. What has become apparent, however, is that the prospect that any one or a combination of these findings will match a particular problem setting is quite remote. Veracity and generalizability are, of course, not the only issues; the more fundamental one is the conceptual linkage between knowledge of people-environment relations and decision-making processes and design synthesis. In short, the vision of a science of people-environment relations yielding predictive models directly applicable to design decisions has obviously not been fulfilled. But even if we overlook nomological knowledge of environment-behavior systems, we would still be left with the reality that factual and valuative claims are inevitably amalgamated in decision processes.

A by-product of the scientification of praxis is *instrumental rationalism*, a form of reasoning which focuses on the identification, assessment and selection of the most effective means, the value of which are taken for granted. Attempts to effect "scientific" decision processes focusing on the "objective facts" of the situation eventually stimulated the so-called rationality debate. This debate has given rise to consideration of alternative axiological platforms, and methods of generating useful knowledge (see e.g., Dunn 1980, Forester 1989). If a people-focused design paradigm is to be sustained, many in the field have come to recognize that alternative platforms and strategies need to be considered. As documented by various chapters in this volume, in dealing with practical human problems such as housing, we continue to struggle with the conceptual and procedural issues and tensions attendant to an emerging post-positivist axiology. Central to the intellectual struggle in which we are engaged are the methodological issues addressed in the chapter by Lang.

Systematic consideration of meaning and use in housing thus leads us into difficult terrain, a great deal of it uncharted. Among the issues involved are those of appropriately conceptualizing these classes of variables, understanding their interrelationship, and developing reliable and valid ways of measuring them for purposes of realizing more viable housing environments. We must develop an understanding and procedures to accommodate or resolve conflicting claims and requirements of heterogeneous users and other stakeholders. We must also develop conceptual and procedural means of dealing with the scale continuum with respect to meaning and use. We must also come to grips with the problems attendant to accelerating change in human contexts, goals and propensities. In the following chapter, Francescato develops a more detailed analysis of these and other substantive issues.

In responding to meaning and use requirements in housing, as in other areas of praxis, substantive and procedural issues are closely interwoven. Procedural issues in housing are formidable, and in a state of considerable flux. In approaching methodological aspects of housing as a form of praxis, three types of knowledge generation must be considered: 1) general knowledge of people-housing environment relations, 2) instrumental (situation-specific) knowledge of these relations, and 3) related planning, design and management procedures. These three classes of knowledge generation are interrelated and all three are driven by competing axiological commitments. The planning, design and management of housing presently operates in a milieu which embodies an array of dialectical perspectives. Among these are modernist vs. post-modernist precepts, rationalist vs. empiricalist epistemologies, research vs. praxis, positivist vs. post-positivist platforms, and quantitative vs. qualitative methods. Recognition of these dialectical perspectives provides an appropriate context for Lang's chapter on methodological issues and approaches.

References

Alexander, C. 1964, *Notes on the Synthesis of Form*, Cambridge, MA: Harvard University Press.

Dunn, W., 1980, Introduction, Symposium on Social Values and Public Policy, *Policy Studies Journal*, Vol. 9, No. 4, 519-534.

English, H. and A. English, 1969, *A Comprehensive Dictionary of Psychological and Psychoanalytical Terms*, New York: David McKay Company, Inc.

Forester, J., 1989, *Planning in the Face of Power*, Berkeley: University of California Press.

Runes, D. D., 1959, *Dictionary of Philosophy*, Ames: Littlefield, Adams and Co.

Studer, R., 1987, *Prospects for Realizing Congruent Housing*, in W. van Vliet-, H. Choldin, W. Michelson and D. Popenoe (Eds.), New York: Greenwood Press, 29-41.

Studer, R., 1990, The Scientification of Design: Alternative Platforms, *Triglyph*, No. 10, 16-21.

Chapter 1

Meaning and Use: A Conceptual Basis

GUIDO FRANCESCATO
University of Maryland

This chapter seeks to sketch a conceptual framework by discussing the terms of the book title. A systemic perspective is proposed to examine issues related to the multiplicity of meanings arising from the diversity of goals held by the various "customers" of the system. Implications of the levels of housing scale such as room, dwelling, neighborhood and community are explored. Definitions of the term use are discussed and the process of semantization by which objects of use are attributed meaning is presented. The effect of time and change on the meaning and use of housing is examined from a transactional perspective.

Implications of this conceptual overview include a number of needs: to go beyond the economic, technological and political biases that have informed a large proportion of housing research; to confront the frequent incompatibility of goals among the various participants in the housing sector; to identify the various levels of scale at which housing occurs; and to develop dynamic and adaptive strategies of study, policy making and interventions better suited to reflect aspects of time and change. The focus on use and meaning as an inseparable bundle is seen as a way to firmly anchor the study of housing to its human and social significance.

Introduction

The prudent navigator does not leave port without first obtaining the clearest possible understanding of the nature of the voyage. The ship's destination, the features of the seas, coastlines and harbors, the likely weather patterns to be encountered, the rules and practices of seamanship and those pertaining to entering and leaving foreign ports are all important aspects of a general picture of the trip. They fashion a conceptual basis, which guides the navigator's subsequent actions such as the determination of a specific route and speed.

The reader who approaches this book may likewise find it useful to start from a general understanding of the nature and characteristics of its subject. This chapter seeks to offer some reflections that may be useful in navigating through the contributions of other authors and approaching the concepts of meaning and use in housing. The metaphor of the sea voyage seems particularly appropriate, because the topic involves discussions of both route and destination. Housing processes, strategies, programs and plans define routes, possible courses of action; residential environments and their inhabitants identify destinations, the targets of these efforts.

Alas, the waters to be traversed in our voyage are charted in a manner perhaps more reminiscent of the enigmatic maps available to Magellan and Columbus than of those guiding contemporary shipping. As Jon Lang points out in the next chapter, much uncertainty remains and is perhaps inherent in the subject. Still, navigation with a somewhat uncertain chart is preferable to piloting with no chart at all. This chapter is written with this assumption in mind.

Meaning or meanings?

The term "meaning" in the title of the book signals the intention to approach housing from a communication angle. In human terms, the goal of communication is not merely the transmission of information, but also the interpretation of information, the elucidation of its meaning. In turn, interpretation implies a hermeneutic viewpoint, an acceptance of diversity of meanings. Different interpreters will find different meanings in the same information, depending on their experiences, intent, interests, goals and a number of other factors. So if we wish to define the meaning of housing we first must ask: meaning for whom?

A systemic perspective may help to answer this question. General systems theory offers a way of looking at phenomena as sets of parts, elements, or factors that interact in pursuit of certain goals. The goals are those of the customers of the system, that is of those who stand to benefit from its operations (Churchman, 1968).

Housing is a system with multiple customers. This simple observation introduces a number of problems, among them that of defining who is the primary customer or customer group. We plan, design and build houses for people to live in, which would suggest that the residents are the principal raison d'être of any housing activity. But residents, however privileged their place in the constellation of housing customers may (or should) be, are still only one of a number of customer groups. Policy makers, planners, architects, engineers and technicians of all kinds, developers, bankers, housing managers, and others are also members of the universe of customers.

Policy makers seek to satisfy their political and economic ideologies; planners, architects and technicians do the same for their professional ones; developers and bankers pursue profits; and so on. Such goals as the stimulation of the economy, the appeasement of labor unions, the elimination of racial discrimination, the growth of corporate profit, the pursuit of stylistic concerns, the efficiency of transportation networks, and many other more or less worthy objectives are among those which housing may be required to meet.

Rapoport (1980) pointed out that housing has been approached as a product, as a commodity, as a process, as a place (including such concepts as the expression of identity, self-worth and status of the inhabitants), as territory, as private domain, as a "behavior setting" (a unit of analysis in ecological psychology), or as the response to a set of purely functional requirements (as a locus of activities). He noted that the definition of housing, that is the matter of its meaning, has been neglected "possibly because, since we all live in housing, we feel that we know what dwellings are". But the real reason for the neglect is probably the very multiplicity of meanings that can be attributed to housing, including those he identified.

If housing is a complex system which seeks to fulfill the goals of a variety of customers, it is legitimate to ask whether such goals are congruent or not. It is perhaps surprising that, in the discussion of housing issues—and especially at the policy level, where for obvious reasons this is particularly crucial—the question is often ignored. Inevitably, there is a degree of inconsistency among multiple goals. Some goals are incompatible, mutually contradictory: pursuing one may make it effectively impossible to also attain the other.

For example, Meehan (1979) analyzed the reasons for the dramatic problems experienced by the St. Louis Housing Authority, which resulted in the demolition of the notorious Pruitt-Igoe public housing project, among other undesirable consequences. He traced some of the causes of this failure to the lack of compatibility among stated and unstated goals of the original public housing legislation and between those goals and others that had been overlaid onto it over time. The contradictions were simply ignored by the policy makers. But they existed, and in the end it became clear that they had been ignored at great peril for the success of the enterprise.

It is beyond the scope of this chapter to outline specific strategies for reconciling and harmonizing conflicts among contradictory housing goals. But it is important to call attention to the issue. At the very least, these conflicts must be explicitly recognized; policies, plans, designs and intervention strategies must take their effect into account. Even more important, if a multiple-goal system is to attain its goals with reasonable efficiency and a minimum of unwanted side-effects it must be under the control of a "management subsystem" (Churchman, 1968). What does this mean in the context of resolving conflicting housing goals? What further problems does this introduce?

The management subsystem, in order to perform its task, must have a criterion with which to guide conflict resolution. The management subsystem's task is essentially that of monitoring the performance of the overall system, that of evaluating the system's output over time. But to evaluate is to assess performance against a criterion. Which, then, is an appropriate criterion in the case of housing?

This question is related to the identification of the system's customer. If one accepts the notion that the residents are the ultimate customers of any housing system, the primary criterion of satisfying the inhabitants should govern any attempts at managing the system. In case of conflict, other goals must be subordinated to achieving housing that satisfies the residents' expectations. "Housing" may or may not hold the same meaning for bankers and inhabitants, but if these two groups attribute two different and conflicting meanings to it, then it is the meaning held by the bankers that should be adjusted (or, at the limit, discarded), not that held by the inhabitants.

But rarely are these customer groups homogeneous either in characteristics of their constituent populations or of these populations' goals. The inhabitants themselves, in particular, obviously constitute as varied and heterogeneous a population as one could conceive. Residents do not share the same goals just because they all happen to live in houses. On the contrary, various inhabitants subgroups are likely to pursue goals that are incompatible to various degrees. A current example is the introduction of mentally or physically impaired homeless persons and households in subsidized housing that until recently had been restricted to occupancy by the elderly. Perhaps unavoidably, the old and new residents attached widely different goals to their homes. Conflict occurred where harmony had existed for many years.

In contemporary societies, whether in the industrialized or in the less industrialized world, policies and decisions tend to be made by those who hold economic, political and technological power, not by the general public. To the extent that democratic political structures permit it, the public does have an indirect influence on housing policies and decisions. In some countries this influence may, for selected sectors of the population, approach participatory levels. Still, by-and-large, conflicts between the goals of the residents and those of other population groups are likely to remain (This becomes a particularly acute problem in the case of disadvantaged social groups and is a primary reason for the appropriate but disproportionate attention to housing for low and moderate income households that one finds in the literature). For instance, until recently a large proportion of the research presented at meetings of certain scientific and professional societies approached housing quality from a technological point of view (Francescato, 1989). Often, the application of this technical approach to real housing has resulted in environments considered unsatisfactory by their users. For more than two decades now, a growing number of social and behavioral studies have shown the insufficiency of purely technical approaches to quality. Fortunately, the beginnings of a change in this attitude can now be discerned throughout the research community.

Adopting an appropriate primary criterion does not mean that other criteria, reflecting the goals of other customers of the housing system, can or should be ignored. Indeed, overlooking the interests of politicians, "experts", developers, planners, designers and others that have a role in the housing process is both unrealistic and likely to yield undesirable outcomes. Rather, there should be some agreement on an explicit hierarchy of criteria, so that a degree of control can be kept over the interrelationships and conflicts of interests that are bound to exist. To what extent this is possible is of course arguable. But this is an argument that can only be settled in the political arena, not in the realm of empirical research.

In sum, housing is bound to have a variety of meanings, depending on the goals it meets for different groups of people. It is important to recognize that these goals exist and are often incompatible. It is equally important to devise monitoring and control structures, management subsystems that address the diversity and possible incongruence of goals.

Meaning and scale

Definitions of housing are also affected by the scale of reference, that is, by the scale domain one has in mind: is it that of the home, building, complex, neighborhood, community, city or even the entire region?

Norberg-Schulz (1985) suggested that, in its broadest meaning, to "dwell" is to "be at home" in an environment. (In this sense, even the natural environment may be thought of as housing). In material quantitative terms, he noted, a dwelling is "a roof over our head and a certain number of square meters at our disposal". But, in qualitative terms, the home acquires social meaning by virtue of the continuum of which it is but a part. He identified four separate but interdependent domains in this continuum: the "settlement", the "urban space", the "institution" and the "house."

Rapoport (1980) pointed out the influence of culture on the relationship between meaning of housing and levels of scale. Activities which in one culture take place within the home may, in another, occur elsewhere. As an example, he cited Hartman's (1963) study of Boston's West End, in which stoops, streets and shops were found to be among the settings for activities that in most American households would ordinarily happen inside the house.

The scale of analysis has an effect on the meaning attributed to housing. One can approach housing at the level of room and dwelling unit, where certain concepts, such as intimacy, privacy, domesticity, and commodity (Rybczynsnki, 1986) or symbolism and self reference (Cooper, 1974) may well become prominent. But it is equally legitimate to discuss housing at the scale of the neighborhood and community, and at this level issues such as education, jobs or racial division (Louis Harris and Associates, 1978; Wood, 1979; Lake, 1980) would acquire primacy.

There is some disagreement on the structural relationships among levels of scale. Canter and Rees (1982) contrasted two different views: one in which scale domains are viewed as "nested", the other in which each level is seen as separate from the other and having a specific focus of concern. In the first, they argued, experiences and perceptions in the larger scale domains, such as the city or the neighborhood, are considered to be mediated by those in the smaller domains, such as the home. In the second, each level is conceived as independent from all others, and the mode of interaction between people and their housing, say, at the neighborhood level is viewed as "similar yet distinct" with respect to the levels of the development and the individual dwelling.

Regardless of the precise nature of their structural relationship, scale levels clearly impinge on housing meaning, as Ernesto Arias notes in the introduction and is reinforced by the chapters on spatial attributes and social dynamics of neighborhoods. Therefore, when discussing housing, it is necessary to identify whether one is looking at issues related to the home itself or whether the residential environment as a whole is being considered. Any comprehensive study of housing issues should take into account the larger continuum.

Indeed, a case can be made that in the field of housing there has been a general failure to focus on the intimate relationship between housing as dwelling and housing as community. This may be a reflection of public trends exemplified by the perceived general preference for single family housing that is commonly found in countries as diverse as the United States and Mexico. The result is a tendency to conceive housing as a mono-use condition. Although such elements as schools are commonly viewed as a part of the housing community, other activities are banished, both conceptually and—with the help of zoning—in practice.

Is this compartmentalization of "home", away from work, away from cultural activities, mostly even away from the daily necessities of shopping, an inevitable consequence of contemporary economics and production techniques? Does it represent an appropriate residential environment for the emerging post-industrial societies where it is more and more prevalent?

These are not just academic questions, involving theoretical models. They frame fundamental housing issues because they involve the actual shape of our residential communities. They affect not only the meaning we attribute to housing, how we think about it and therefore how we structure our collective responses and interventions, but also very practical problems for which there seems to be at present little hope of solution: for example, those connected with the time consuming, energy-intensive, often nerve racking daily commute of millions of urban dwellers obliged to travel large distances between home and workplace.

In short, it seems clear that the various scale levels through which housing is linked to the daily lives of its inhabitants require much attention, not simply as the external context in which housing is obviously embedded, but as an integral aspect of the residential environment.

Meaning and use

As mentioned earlier, to discuss meaning is to adopt a communication perspective. But to couple "meaning" with "use" is to signal that communication is not the only process worth considering in housing. Further, and more important, it is to recognize that communication relies on use, that meaning stems from use. And, of course, use—that is "to house", not "to communicate"—is the original reason for building houses in the first place.

A specific home may mean a number of different things to an individual, it may be associated with events and experiences that have personal significance. In this sense, each of us uses the home in individual ways. But there is also a social meaning, that is, meaning shared by a group, meaning that is bound up with social use.

A number of well-known studies have examined some dimensions of personal meaning. For example, Bachelard (1969) applied concepts from Jungian psychology to an exploration of the relationship between one's childhood home and meanings attributed to a variety of spaces in adulthood; Cooper (1974) looked at the home as a symbol of self; and Korasec-Serfaty (1979) distinguished between what she called "social and psychological determinants" of housing and focused on the latter in a study of personal meaning evoked by attics and cellars (1984). More recent interest in the concept of attachment to place by a number of researchers may bring about further study in this area. Yet, perhaps because housing research initially emerged from concerns about unmet social goals, it is meaning connected with social use that has received most of the attention of the research community.

"Use" itself needs to be defined. The term has often been taken to mean engaging in "activities". In planning and architecture it tends to be synonymous with "function". But these interpretations may connote a somewhat restrictive meaning, as they imply action or overt behavior. In the context of this book, it seems more appropriate to think of use as any interaction of people with their residential environment, including perceptual, affective and symbolic processes that may not necessarily be related to actions.

Semiotics offers a useful point of departure to examine both this view of use and the relationship between meaning and use. Barthes (1964, 1967) described at length the process by which, "from the moment society begins" any use of an object becomes an act of communication. This may first involve the individual user, acting only to identify the just discovered usefulness so that it can be remembered should the need arise for further use. Later, however, it may become necessary to communicate the discovered usefulness to other members of society, and to make this possible a certain meaning is assigned to a specific use by means of a "sign". In this sense, housing may be viewed as a sign, or more correctly as a system of signs—a "text" (Eco, 1967; 1976)—signifying the potential use to which it may be put.

In purely functional terms, meaning that is thus attached to an object of use involves a simple (or "primary") activity. The house becomes a text signifying perhaps the possibility of obtaining shelter from the weather and from danger (denotative meaning). But Barthes points out that with many objects of use the process goes much further. It involves higher and higher (connotative) levels of semantization. Thus housing may acquire not just the meaning of protecting one from weather and roaming beasts, but also additional meanings supported on the original one. Shelter from weather and danger may then become extended to other vicissitudes of existence, to the general notion of "refuge". What has happened is that a connotative level of meaning has been built upon the denotational level. The chapters by Jack Nasar, on house styles and by Wim Blauw on public spaces, among others, discuss some aspects of this relationship.

Although housing may be "intended" originally as shelter, social semantization begins to overlay additional intentions which, through further use related to new aims, in turn generate even more varied and broader meanings, and so on. Consider the discovery that the home may come to symbolize relative household status in the community. From this humble beginning, already present in preliterate cultures such as the Bororo tribes of the Brazilian jungle (Lévi-Strauss, 1970), new meanings may spring over time, together with housing types intended to convey them. For example, in the reign of Louis XIV, a strict codification emerged as to the physical characteristics and the lawful denomination of housing for certain classes of French society, ranging from the "palais" to the "hotel", the "maison" and the "maison particulaire" (Amendola, 1989).

This semantization is not restricted to physical objects, but involves housing processes as well, such as programs of governmental assistance. For instance, it is well known that the meaning associated with public housing in the United States, as alluded to in the relevant legislation, evolved over time. In the beginning, the "users" of this housing were referred to as working families of limited means, the "deserving poor". Consequently public housing was thought of as a relatively temporary waystation on the way to self-sufficiency, as a stepping stone towards achieving the "American dream". But with the changing socio- economic conditions of the American population, the users became the "truly needy", that is mostly the unemployed, single-parent households and others on welfare. In our day, public housing programs have come to be regarded as the last-resort, ghettoized institutionalization of emarginated populations, frequently minority groups perceived as unable or unwilling to participate in productive activities.

Through the process of semantization, use defines domains of experience and meaning. But environmental experiences vary across cultures, social groups, people's life cycle, and even among individuals belonging to the same group. Indeed, as alluded to earlier, differentiating the residents as the main customer group of the housing system from other customer groups, should not be taken to suggest that the residents themselves are in any way a homogeneous population. The meaning of housing and the patterns of use need not be the same for each subgroup of this population, nor the appropriate form of housing. Public housing tenants, for example, have frequently expressed dismay about what they perceive as a tendency of agencies, architects and managers to regard them as a homogeneous group having the same needs and aspirations (Francescato, et al., 1979).

Yet most contemporary housing tends towards sameness and homogeneity. For instance, Ahrentzen (1989) has pointed out that in the United Sates a large proportion of the population consists of non traditional households. The traditional married couple family, she noted, accounts for only 21 percent of the households created since 1980. But the housing being built does not seem to recognize this phenomenon: it is largely the typical three-bedroom house for a family of father, mother and children. Groth (1989) noted that between one and two million Americans live in single room occupancy (SRO) hotels.[1] Still, planning and design practice have virtually ignored this population and this housing type until very recently.

The focus on meaning and use also concerns the interrelationships of national and regional culture with housing. Even in the industrialized world, in which tendencies toward uniformity are reinforced by economic structures and mass communication, there are noticeable regional differences in both the characteristics of the housing stock and people's expectations about housing. Concurrently, there are discernible differences in policies, programs, and even in research approaches and emphases. The chapters by Vittoria Giuliani on the interior of Italian homes and by Kunihiro Narumi on attachment to home in Japan are examples of this.

Cultural and social diversity has begun to be recognized — at least on American campuses and among social observers — as a source not only of potential conflict, but also of richness and renewal. Diversity affects both meaning and use. It is necessary to understand the web of relationships tying meaning, use, and socio- cultural variety if we wish to obtain a credible conceptual picture of housing.

Meaning, use and time

As mentioned earlier, time is an essential dimension in the process of housing semantization. Moreover, meaning and use are linked by cultural codes, not unlike signifier and signified in communication systems; indeed, like signifier and signified, meaning and use should be viewed as two facets of the same entity. In human communication, cultural codes change over time. But perhaps more important, cultural codes cannot be understood without reference to the continuous process of their transformation. Just as evolution is inherent in verbal language phenomena, so that to study language

---

[1] Groth also states that single room occupancies (SROs) house more people than the entire U.S. Public Housing program (1989). However, this is not a plausible claim, since approximately 1.3 million public housing units are occupied by more than one person. It is interesting to note, though, that Adams' (1987) major overview of current housing issues in the United Sates, for one, does not even mention SROs. Whatever the number is, SROs are a housing issue of increasing concern as homelessness grows in the U.S.

means essentially to study its transformations (Chomsky, 1968), change is an intrinsic quality of the meaning-and-use construct.

Because of this, it may be useful to examine the meaning-and-use of housing through the lens of a paradigm that views time and change as integral aspects of phenomena. Altman and Rogoff (1987) describe the focus of this emerging paradigm, which they call the "transactional perspective" in environmental psychology, as the study of the "changing relationships" among aspects of the environment-behavior "event," a formulation that seems particularly apt in housing.

The central point of the transactional approach is that time is not merely a component, but rather an inherent aspect of human-environmental phenomena. For this reason, change is viewed as intrinsic in such phenomena, as an inseparable participant in the interaction among elements of a system rather than as a result of that interaction.

This view suggests that, as the role of housing evolves, it does so with social, economic and cultural changes. Housing may respond to change or inspire it, or both at the same time. Use mutates, new or different meanings arise which, in turn, suggest new uses, and so on. Understanding housing issues requires an attitude that recognizes this process. Studying the patterns of changing configurations of meaning and use should shed light on the dynamic relationships of the housing system, including the changing relationships among those earlier identified as its various customers.

Housing change may entail general processes, as those discussed in this book by Karen Franck in regard to "overlooked" populations and by Elizabeth Huttman about the homeless, or localized changes, as those examined by Lucia Maria Bogus in her chapter on gentrification in Sao Paulo, Brazil.

Change also plays an important role in different uses of housing during the life cycle of the occupants, hence on the meaning attributed to housing at various ages. Lawton (1975), Howell (1976) and Danermark and Ekstrom (in this book), among others, have investigated the special conditions pertaining to housing for the elderly, a type whose singularity in terms of life cycle consists in being occupied exclusively by a relatively homogeneous age group.

Transactional perspectives present the field with a severe challenge. Because they view environment-behavior phenomena as holistic events, traditional research strategies and methods based on analytical approaches can no longer be employed. Researchers need to develop new attitudes and methodologies focused more on rendering the process of change more intelligible, hence more effectively managed, than on predicting outcomes of interventions. This may seem a paradox, since prediction has been central to scientific endeavors until recently. However, the emergence of chaos theories in mathematics and physics suggests that understanding the behavior of non-predictable systems is extremely useful in practice, precisely because of the difficulty or impossibility of predicting the outcomes of such systems (Lorenz, 1979).

But time and change-centered perspectives also pose another problem. Developing and implementing housing policies, strategies and plans tends to require long periods, to stretch over years, when not decades. The post-World War II efforts of the United States, Europe, Japan and the Soviet Union did not run their course until the present. Indeed, the outcomes of these endeavors are themselves the subject of current attempts to deal with unforseen and undesired consequences of interventions (e.g., van Kempen, 1986). In other words, in our time social, economic and political changes often occur at a quicker pace than the implementation of housing policies. Here again, study and decision-making structures need to evolve methods of monitoring change and of responding more quickly and more effectively to changing conditions. These, however, are not easily attained objectives.

The challenge, then, is to develop housing systems and approaches to housing that reflect the dynamics of contemporary society. Transactions between people and the residential environment are forever evolving. An appropriate conceptual picture of housing should reflect this recognition, should embody the dimensions of time and change as co-equal aspects of the housing system. It remains to be seen, of course, whether extant political and decision making structures, including professional and institutional ones, are able to conform to such dynamics, to respond to the challenge of change within ever shortening time–windows.

Conclusion

A great proportion of the scholarship and attention devoted to housing issues, especially in the United States, has reflected economic, technological and political biases of institutions such as professional groups, governments, normative organizations and funding agencies. Within the ethos of the "market economy", this emphasis possesses a superficial appeal: it seems to address concrete problems and tangible strategies for their solution, it appears to deal with the harsh realities of a world increasingly concerned with material objects, material standards of quality and material wealth.

But, although there is an important role for this type of approach, the result is quite often the dehumanization of an issue which is, above all, a personal and social one. Is it then surprising that so many efforts in a variety of vastly different national, political and economic conditions have resulted in utter failure?

Among those who participate in housing processes, no group can be exempted from having contributed to this unfortunate outcome. Policy makers have frequently emphasized the quantitative facets of housing, be it in attempting to cause vast numbers of housing units to be built or in trying to remedy economic problems of a structural or conjunctional nature. Engineers and other technical personnel have tended to focus on standards of physical performance and on technological efficiencies. Architects and planners have too often privileged so-called functional aspects or normative aesthetic theories over the expectations and preferences of the users. Researchers have paid inordinate attention to criteria of scientific methodology and to factors that lend themselves to be included in statistical analyses. The concepts of use and meaning of housing that are the subject of this chapter seek to counterbalance these tendencies.

Focusing on the inseparable bundle of meaning and use firmly anchors the study of housing to its human and social significance. Confronting the purpose of housing with the often incompatible objectives of its multiple customers defines the difficulties intrinsic in what remains, at bottom, a social and political enterprise. Identifying the various scale domains at which housing occurs, and on which it sustains its own processes, both sharpens and broadens the significance attributed to meaning and use. Including time and change as inseparable constituents of housing transactions challenges the scholar, the politician and the practitioner to develop and employ more dynamic and adaptive strategies and methods for approaching and solving housing issues.

As Jon Lang points out in the next chapter, all housing policies and interventions are based on some understanding of the nature of housing transactions, that is of the relationships between people and their residential environments. The inquiry presented in this chapter is intended as a contribution to such an understanding.

References

Adams, J.S. (1987) *Housing America in the 1980s.* New York: Russel Sage Foundation.

Altman, I and Rogoff, B. (1987) "World views in psychology: Trait, organismic transactional perspective" in I. Altman and D. Stokols (eds.) *Handbook of environmental psychology.* Vol. 1. New York: Wiley.

Amendola, G. (1989) "Postmodern architects' people" in R. Ellis and D. Cuff (eds.) *Architects' people.* New York: Oxford University Press.

Bachelard, G. (1969) *The poetics of space.* Boston: Beacon Press.

Barthes, R. (1964) *Elements de semiologie.* Paris: Editions du Seuil. English transl.: A. Layers and C. Smith (1967) *Elements of semiology.* New York: Hill and Wang.

Canter, D. and Rees, K. (1982) "A multivariate model of housing satisfaction" *International Review of Applied Psychology,* 31, 185.

Chomsky, N. (1968) *Language and mind.* New York: Harcourt, Brace & World.

Churchman, C.W. (1968) *The systems approach.* New York: Dell Publishing Co.

Cooper, C. (1974) "The house as symbol of self" in J. Lang, C. Burnette, W. Moleski, and D. Vachon (eds.) *Designing for human behavior.* Straudsburg, PA: Dowden, Hutchinson and Ross.

Eco, U. (1967) *La struttura assente.* Milan: Bompiani.

Eco, U. (1976) *A theory of semiotics.* Bloomington: Indiana University Press.

Francescato, G.; Weidemann, S.; Anderson, J.R. and Chenoweth,R. (1979) *Residents' satisfaction in HUD-assisted housing: Design and management factors.* Department of Housing and Urban Development.

Francescato, G. (1989) "Planning and design aspects in the quality of multifamily-housing: The U.S. and European experience" in *Quality for Building Users Throughout the World,* Theme 1, vol. 1. Paris: International Council for Building Studies and Documentation.

Groth, P. (1989) "Non-people: A case study of public architects and impaired social vision" in R. Ellis and D. Cuff (eds.) *Architects' peoples.* New York: Oxford University Press.

Korosec-Serfaty, P. (1979) " Une maison a soi." *Determinants psychologiques et sociaux de l'habitat individuelle* (vol 3.). Strasbourg: Direction Regional du Ministere du Cadre de Vie.

Korosec-Serfaty, P. (1984) "The home from attic to cellar." *Journal of Environmental Psychology,* 4(4), 303-321.

Hartman, C.W. (1963) "Social values and housing orientations", *Journal of Social Issues,* 19(2), 113-131.

Howell, S. (1976) "Recent advances in studies of the physical environment of the elderly." Presented at the Program in Environmental Psychology, City University of New York Graduate Center.

Lake, R. (1980) "Racial transition and black homeownership in American suburbs" in G. Sternlieb and J.W. Hughes (eds.) *America's housing: Prospects and problems.* New Brunswich, NJ: Rutgers University Center for Urban Policy Research.

Lawrence, R.J. (1981) "The appropriation of domestic space: A cross-cultural perspective" in A.E. Osterberg, C.P. Tiernan and R.A. Findlay (eds.) *Design research interactions.* EDRA 12. Washington, DC: Environmental Design Research Association.

Lawton, M.P. (1975) *Planning and managing housing for the elderly.* New York: Wiley.

Lévi-Strauss, C. (1970) *Tristes tropiques.* New York: Atheneum.

Lorenz, E.N. (1979) "On the prevalence of aperiodicity in simple systems" in Mgremela and J. Mardsen (eds.) *Global Analysis.* New York: Springer-Verlag.

Louis Harris and Associates (1978) *The 1978 HUD survey on the quality of urban life.* Washington, DC: U.S. Department of Housing and Urban Development.

Meehan, E.J. (1979) *The quality of federal policymaking: Programmed failure in public housing.* Columbia, MO: The University of Missouri Press.

Norberg-Schulz C. (1985) *The concept of dwelling: On the way toward figurative architecture.* New York: Electa/Rizzoli.

Rapoport, A. (1980) "Towards a cross-culturally valid definition of housing". Presented at the 11th Environmental Design Research Association Conference.

Rybczynski, W. (1986) *Home: A short history of an idea.* New York: Viking Penguin, Inc.

van Kempen, E. (1986) "High-rise estates and the concentration of poverty" in *The Netherland Journal of Housing and Environmental Research,* 1(1), 5-26.

Wood, J.E. (1979) "Race and Housing" in G.S. Fish (ed.) *The story of housing.* New York: Macmillan.

Chapter 2

Methodological Issues and Approaches: A Critical Analysis

JON T. LANG
University of New South Wales

All housing policies and designs are based on images of "reality" and "a good life." These images are based on some research approach, casual or systematic, qualitative or quantitative. The nature of housing research and the assessment of its quality and implications has been marred by confusion over the nature of methodology, paradigms, models and methods. There has been which is descriptive and explanatory, and normative theories, or design ideologies. There have been two major research and design approaches to the creation of housing policies and housing architecture during the twentieth century: Rationalism and Empiricism. The limitations of the positive theoretical basis for much Rationalist thinking has lead to the growth in Empirical housing studies. The goal of Empirical research has been to build a sound knowledge base on which creative policies and habitable, cognitively rewarding, and enjoyable housing environments and housing units within specific cultural frames can be formulated. Each approach has contributed much to our understanding of the housing environment; each has its limitations. All research findings are biased by the method used. The potential contribution and limitations of each approach must be understood and the results integrated into a positive theoretical basis which is open to challenge and development.

Introduction

All housing policies and housing designs are based on some understanding
of the nature of people, the nature of the built environment, and the relationship between them. They are also based on some assumptions about
how the decision making process is, and should be, carried out. The knowledge a decision maker has about housing, its uses and meanings, is biased
by the techniques they use for examining it. In addition, what people
pay attention to depends on their motivations, purposes and their existing
knowledge. So it is with the researcher too.

Knowledge is developed in a number of ways. Much depends on our
personal experiences. Such experiences are encoded in images of the environment, anecdotes, rules of thumb, and principles of social and design
quality. Over the last thirty years, however, systematic research has enhanced our understanding of people and the meaning and use of housing
forms within different terrestrial, socio-economic, and cultural contexts. It
has also enhanced our understanding of research methods. At the same
time, there has been considerable debate over what the appropriate research paradigms are and how the methods used bias the results obtained.
In particular, questions have been raised over the relative merits of quantitative and qualitative approaches to design. Approaches to research and
design are, however, neither right nor wrong in themselves. Their utility
depends on what they can and cannot accomplish.

The objective of this chapter is to put into perspective the research
processes which have been used to build theory and formulate policies and
designs. It is neither to present accolades nor to denigrate particular approaches to research, but rather to present our current understanding of
their utilities. The first step in doing so is to point out the ambiguities
in some key terms used in this chapter and elsewhere in discussions of
research processes (see also Lang, 1987). With those meanings in mind,
the two intellectual traditions in housing research and design—Rationalism
and Empiricism—can be discussed. Most recent housing research has been
within the Empiricist mold but scientific and quasi-scientific methods have
limitations that phenomenological, hermeneutic and historiometric studies
are trying to remedy.

The argument presented in this chapter is that these approaches, while
competitive in many respects, can best be regarded as complementary. Yet
however thorough the housing theories and research findings at the disposal
of policy makers and architects are, policy and environmental design will
be carried out under uncertainty. Research can reduce that uncertainty by
enhancing our knowledge of housing uses and meanings in cultural contexts;
it cannot eliminate it.

Methodology, paradigms, models, and methods

Methodology is, strictly speaking, the study of methods but the word is very loosely used in the social sciences as a synonym for the set of steps and research methods used in doing a research study—the research design. Methods are techniques, or procedures, for carrying out specific tasks. Within research methodology there are a number of research paradigms. Paradigms are general approaches to carrying out an activity. During this century there have been two major approaches which still coexist today in housing design which imply a research tradition. They are the Rationalist and Empiricist approaches. In recent times it has been the Empiricist approach to research which led the way but it has been constantly challenged by researchers who feel it is too limited an approach.

All human actions are based on models of reality. We can seldom, if ever, pay attention to all the variables which might affect our actions. Models are abstractions of reality. They come in various forms: verbal, mathematical, iconic. A good model is said to be one which is simple but powerful. By simple is meant that it consist of the fewest variables possible to explain the phenomena under consideration; by powerful is meant that the model actually describes, explains, and above all for policy makers, predicts well. The term "model" and the term "theory" are often used synonymously. Theory is more appropriately a schema tying together a system of ideas or statements, whereas a model is really a philosophical position that imposes a structure on reality.

Substantive and procedural models

There are two sets of models of importance to the policy maker, architect, and research alike. The first set has to do with the nature of the world and, the second, with the methods of studying and designing it. The models in the first set, for want of a better term, have been called "substantive models" and, the second set, "procedural." The goal of theory building research is to fill out these sets. The meaning and use of housing are substantive concerns.

Recent research and clinical psychological experience has considerably enhanced our substantive understanding of housing. It has produced more powerful models than housing designers previously had at their disposal. These models are of people (Maslow, 1987), culture and housing (Rapoport, 1969, 1977; Lowe and Chambers, 1989), the person-environment relationship (Lang, 1987), housing, generally (Cooper and Sarkissian, 1986), and housing for specific groups of people (e.g. Regnier and Pynoos, 1987; Franck and Ahrentzen 1990; Chawla, 1991). Similarly there has been a substantial increase in the understanding of research processes (Bechtel, Marans, and Michelson, 1987) and the nature of the family of decision making processes of which public policy formation and architectural design are examples (Lang 1987).

Positive and normative theories and models

Positive theories and models are those that describe and explain phenomena — substantive or procedural. Their goal is to be value free, but any goal is a value laden statement in itself. Positive models of designing, policy formation and research are simply statements of how they are done to achieve different purposes. The development of positive models and theories is the goal of the physical and social sciences. Normative theories and models, in contrast, state what a good world and its attributes are, or they may be procedural models of how specific processes should be carried out. Research paradigms tend to be normative statements. Housing designs are the behavioral correlate of a normative position. Both build on positive models.

Housing use and meaning research

There are two basic types of research on the meaning and use of housing: theory building research and problem solving research. Many of the methods used are the same but the goal is different. Theory building research is aimed at making generalizations about the patterns of housing form and what they afford different people within different cultures. Problem solving research is focused on the peculiar instance, the situation at hand. Research is an integral part of the design process (Zeisel, 1981; Farbstein and Kantrowitz, 1991). The goal of such research is neither to develop theory nor general models, but rather to solve a particular set of problems. Theory guides problem solving research and theory building may be its by-product, but it is not the research goal. The goal is to provide the information base for the design of a public policy, a neighborhood plan, a building or a housing unit. The study of the results of the outcomes of public policy decisions to inform future policies and designs is known, borrowing from Kurt Lewin, as "action research" (Wisner, Stea, and Kruks, 1991). Theory and models guide problem solving research and its quality depends much on the quality of the models that are available to the practitioner. Without such theory and models, practitioners have to rely on their own experiences rather than the cumulative experience of the housing field.

Theory building research on the meaning and use of housing has primarily been based on the assumption that housing policy and design has had the goal of fulfilling human needs. A number of such models of human needs co-exist, but the most widely used to organize thinking about design goals is that of Abraham Maslow (1987). Maslow proposed a hierarchy of basic needs from the need for survival to the need for self-actualization and allied with them cognitive and aesthetic needs. Many of the needs are fulfilled through the carrying out of activities, but needs for affiliation and self-esteem and both cognitive and aesthetic needs have a high symbolic aesthetic component to them.

Theory building research focuses on developing abstract models of the housing environment and what different patterns of housing afford people in terms of uses and meanings within particular cultures. In doing so it borrows and forms models of culture appropriate for asking questions about the potential uses and meanings of housing forms at both a policy and architectural level (Rapoport 1969, Low and Chambers 1989). This research has focused on developing models of household activities and work activities in relationship to each other, family organizations and how they are evolving, social and gender roles in society and within the household, attitudes to and the roles of children within families, attitudes towards nature and gardening, and towards the meanings of different forms of housing and housing unit design.

Research issues

The goal of scientific research is to disinterestedly make generalizations and build theories about the world and how it functions. This goal has not been easy to achieve as research is almost inevitably biased by motivations other than disinterested observation. In doing research we have come to recognize that we are part of a system as well as observers of it. We are learning to recognize the biases any approach to examining the world brings with it. Arguments will persist about how best to pursue research ends and the degree of objectivity that is possible using various research strategies and designs. While there is a perception that use research can be done quasi scientifically, the research strategies for the study of meaning have been more difficult to design. Yet there is a considerable body of knowledge about the nature of meaning that has come out of empirical research (Lang 1987, Nasar 1988, Krampen 1991). The fear is that deeper meanings such as those embedded in myths are being missed.

There have been two basic theory building research strategies—building knowledge from the bottom up and from the top down. Bottom up approaches involve coming to an understanding of individual variables and assembling the understanding piece by piece into global models. Top down approaches involve developing global models of the world and then testing their components piece by piece to see whether they are accurate representations of reality. There have been many arguments about how best to proceed. It may well be impossible to build theory from a strictly bottom up approach—some image of the whole is necessary to guide research. Similarly, in policy design and in architectural design it may well be impossible to move forward without some image of a solution in mind at the outset. These images include schemata of the uses that should be afforded by the housing environment and also aesthetic images in which the symbolism communicates a set of meanings.

The fundamental question in assessing the quality of any research is: "How valid are the results?" There are two issues of concern: the internal validity of the study and the external validity—the degree to which the study applies in non-research situations. Many studies of meaning, for instance, ask categories of people to respond, using semantic differential tests, to slides or photographs of buildings. Statistical techniques are used for relating attributes of the scene in the slides to attributes of people and attributes of their responses. The external validity of such tests is open to challenge, although indications are that slides of scenes are a good surrogate for scenes themselves. One of the major problems to be overcome in many housing studies is the control of potentially intervening variables. This control is particularly necessary in evaluation studies and the studies of meaning. For instance, in housing quality assessment, the state of mind of the subject of a study may well bias the responses given (Gutman and Westergaard, 1974; Preiser, Rabinowitz, and White, 1988).

The appropriateness of specific research methods has to be seen not only in terms of the questions being addressed and what the techniques used may yield but also within the cultural frame in which the research is being done. This necessity holds particularly in problem solving research where, for instance, access to interviewing of important users (e.g. women or children) is only possible under specific circumstances by specific people, or where specific research approaches are seen as invasions of privacy, or some topics are taboo. Not only do research approaches have to be topic specific but culture specific. The problems facing researchers today is that most research approaches have been developed in Europe and North America. Their utility in other cultures may vary considerably from their utility within the cultures in which they were developed.

Rationalism and empiricism in housing design

There have been two major intellectual traditions in housing design during the twentieth century. They have been contrasted in various ways: Platonic versus Aristotelian, Continental versus Anglo-American, Progressive Utopian versus Regressive Utopian are examples. The clearest distinction is between Rationalism and Empiricism as research and design paradigms. Rationalism is the research approach that stresses logical reasoning rather than information derived from the senses as the foundation of certainty in knowledge. Empiricism stresses the role of observation and experimentation as the basis for drawing conclusion about the world. The two approaches to developing housing policies, plans and designs are readily discernible in housing schemes around the world.

Rationalist approaches to housing design and research

The Rationalists from René Descartes (1596-1650) onwards have argued for a unity of thinking and for a fundamental belief in the facts of existence, without the necessity of confirmation (Sharp, 1973). Rationality and Rationalism in policy formation and in architectural design are not necessarily allied terms. Rationalism has become a synonym for functionalism in architecture and the definition of what constitutes functional housing is seen to be rational. Yet, the definition of "function" has been found to be a narrow one based on a narrow model of the human being (Stringer, 1980; Lang, 1987; Ellis and Cuff, 1989). It has excluded questions of meaning in housing and the consideration of the educative nature of the environment. The concern in design was with efficiently providing for air, sun, and access to parks. It was concerned with the efficiency in carrying out rational, or sensible, household activities (see Wingler 1960 on the work of Hannes Meyer, for instance). The question of meanings was left to be dealt with implicitly within the architect's aesthetic ideology. The prevailing Rationalist aesthetic philosophies were derived from research on what artists, particularly the Cubist and Purists, were doing.

Rationalist approaches to design were widely used by the major architects of the Bauhaus (Wingler 1960) and of individuals associated with the International Style of the Continental schools of architectural thought as exemplified by the work of Le Corbusier (Le Corbusier, 1960; Sharp, 1978; Broadbent, 1990). It remains the main approach to research within the mainstream of the profession of architecture. Rationalist policies and designs have stood for radical change in the way people should live and as a result have produced neighborhood and housing schemes radically different from the past. Applications of these design types exist across the world

(Marmot, 1982). The housing design in Brasilia, and to a lesser extent, Chandigarh are products of Rationalist thought as are many housing projects in the United States with Pruitt Igoe being the most notorious (see Montgomery, 1966). Such housing designs stand in contrast to Empiricism with Empiricism's concern with understanding the present.

Empirical approaches to housing design and research

There has been considerable criticism of Rationalist approaches to housing design (e.g. Blake, 1977; Lang, 1987). Designs based on the designers' logical reasoning of how people should behave, what social organizations should exist, and the tastes that people should possess have been poorly related to how people wish to live and the meanings that they wish the environment to hold for them. Empiricists, in contrast, base design decisions on experience and observation. The term, "Empirical", has come to mean, rightly or wrongly, the use of scientific or quasi scientific approaches to research. Much that has passed for empirical research in design, however, has been the casual observations of housing reformers and architects of what they believe, in their own terms, to be good and bad environments. As a result much housing policy and design has been an advocacy for picturesque environments based on past models of neighborhoods and houses which have worked well or, more likely, were imagined to have worked well (Broadbent 1990). The results have been closer to the aspirations of the people to be housed but subject to what the designers thought were appropriate and inappropriate uses of the environment and the appropriate and inappropriate meanings it should communicate. These attitudes are associated with a number of design movements during this century from the Garden City movement at its beginning (e.g., Howard, 1902) to the Neo-traditional movement in urban design which is currently a strong one (L. Krier 1987; Duany, 1989). During the past thirty years Empiricist research has moved towards a more rigorous approach akin to the scientific method.

The scientific method

The scientific experiment is often held up as the exemplar of unbiased empirical research. Experiments involve the study of the impact of deliberately changing an independent variable on a dependent variables. To be labeled "scientific" such research has to follow specific rules. Three basic rules for observation and description of phenomena are that the variables be operationally defined so all can understand what is meant by them, that observations be controlled so that the relationship between an independent variable and a dependent variable can be understood, and that observations be repeated so that conclusions are not drawn from a few instances. In addition, it is assumed that unless the results can be generalized to a class of phenomena they are uninteresting. The rules for explanation are that the results are consistent and that they confirm previous results. If they do not confirm previous results, then a new explanation is needed which will stand until a better one can be found or devised. Theories are tentative. They stand until more thorough explanations are found.

How scientific can the research be that is used as the basis of housing policy and housing design? The goal of the scientific method is to reduce personal biases in the observation of phenomena to the extent that it is possible. This is a laudable goal. Yet how interesting is the understanding of isolated variables? In housing policy design a whole set of interacting variables have to be considered. Major efforts have been made to respond to this question and observation.

Recent empirical research and its challenging approaches

Typological and Empirical research approaches have been the two major empirical approaches attempting to be, at least, both quasi scientific and simultaneously dealing with bundles of variables. Typology is the study of types. In housing, the focus has been on use types, structural (technological) types, and formal (geometric) types (see Sherwood, 1978; R. Krier 1979). Ecological approaches have focused on the effort to more holistically describe and explain behavior in the built environment in a multi-dimensional manner.

Typological research has been closely related to the way policy planners and architects work. In the typological approach to design, the design of a policy or a building is an adaptation of a particular type to a particular circumstance. The basic assumption is that patterns of the environment meet certain human needs that are difficult to articulate, but are implicit in types. This assumption applies to both the uses and meaning of housing environments and housing units. Much recent research in housing design has focused on the necessity and development of new types in response to changes in the demography of the family (e.g., Franck and Ahrentzen, 1990).

Ecological approaches to research attempt to bring together two diverse approaches to theory building and research—the ecological theory of perception and meaning as developed by James J. Gibson and his colleagues, and the study of behavior settings as developed by Roger Barker and his colleagues (Kaminski, 1989). The basic assumption is that research has to be carried out in the everyday environment not in the laboratory. In design this approach argues that policies and designs should be based on an under-standing of human needs, the behaviors and environmental meanings that are important in fulfilling them, and the trends in environmental uses and meanings that are occurring. It assumes an Aristotelian approach to cre-ating the future. Much empirical research however remains piecemeal and atheoretical and has focused descriptively on the use of the environment and environmental preferences.

Phenomenology

There is a fear that quasi scientific Empiricist approaches to research can only focus on piecemeal analyses and bottom up approaches to building the-ory. The perception is that the limitations of the such research are inherent in its philosophy rather than in present research methods and research de-signs being used. The phenomenological approach to environmental and housing research is a descriptive approach based on careful observation and interpretation of what is observed by thoughtful observers (De Rivera, 1984). "The phenonmenologist hopes that through sincerity, perseverance, and care, he or she will see the phenomenon more fully and deeply" (Sea-mon, 1987). The accuracy of the description is established through the comparison of one phenomenologist's insights with another's. Some impor-tant works on the built environment have been based on phenomenological observation (e.g., the work on the sense of place by Tuan, 1977 and Nor-berg Schulz, 1980). The degree to which one can generalize from the views of erudite observers to broader populations is still open to question. Phe-nomenology is nevertheless an important advance over casual observation and promises much in developing insights into both uses and meanings of housing which can then be more rigorously tested. Phenomenology can present a top down approach to housing research and theory building al-though theory building is shunned by many phenomenologists (Seamon 1987).

Rationalism revisited: hermeneutics

A recent development in architectural research, particularly in the study of meaning has been to turn to hermeneutics. Hermeneutics is a posi-tive theory of understanding and interpretation (Ricouer, 1975; Gadamer 1975). It is an intuitive form of reasoning created originally to interpret religious texts and later applied to complex ethical and legal ones. The assumption is that the built environment can be treated as a text to be read. Hermeneutics uses rhetoric and metaphor to develop understanding. It is an approach that eschews evidence from the world itself. It assumes that because Empiricism has not addressed many issues of meaning in design, it cannot. Hermeneutics has had little to say, as yet, about the use of the housing environment. Whether or not it can be adapted to deal with activities and the affordances of specific housing forms is open to question.

Empirical research methods

Despite the challenge from phenomenology and hermeneutics most current housing research follows some form of mainstream Empiricism. Within it there are but two groups of methods for obtaining information—direct observation and mediated observation—but there have been many permutations of specific research techniques. In the design of housing research, direct observation has been applied primarily to the study of how housing areas are used and mediated observation to both the use of exterior and interior environments and the study of the meanings of house forms and types.

Direct observation

Direct observation is that carried out by the researcher; mediated observation relies on getting information though the observations of other people— by asking them. The scientific experiment is the most rigorous observation technique. Such research has focused more on the study of meanings in the environment than on the uses it provides. In such studies patterns of the environment are the independent variable and perceptions of meaning the dependent (Krampen 1991). The use of experiment has also been used to determine anthropometric and ergonomic factors in housing design (Grandjean 1973) including designing for the disabled. It is an obtrusive technique—people involved know they are being studied even though they do not know exactly what the subject of the study is. Unobtrusive direct observational approaches to research vary considerably in their degree of rigorousness. Casual observations of people as part of their own everyday lives is the least rigorous approach but has yielded many potential hypotheses to be tested. Research approaches which have been applied to housing design are the natural experiment in which the experimental situation (e.g., housing types) is manipulated but the population being studied is not. They are simply the people who are there or turn up. Simple observation is also widely used. In simple observation neither the environment nor the population is manipulated but rigorous time sampling and recording is used. It is not an easy method to apply and can be time consuming. It has yielded considerable information on how the exterior housing environment is being used but it is difficult to study the use of interior environments unobtrusively in this way, although the use of television cameras and/or time lapse photography on topics such as culture and room usage have been carried out this way. Such research has also been used in studying uses of the public environment and has resulted in the development of now widely used design principles (e.g. Whyte, 1980).

A number of unobtrusive observational techniques are now available to the housing researcher (Zeisel, 1981; Bechtel, Marans, and Michelson, 1987). These include such procedures as behavior setting analysis and behavioral mapping. Participant observation in which the observer becomes part of the system of behavior being observed has been used to get first hand information, but the observer has to be capable of being unobtrusive and the validity of the results may well be distorted by the presence of the observer changing the system. The observation of how the environment is eroded through usage and how elements have been added to it by users themselves is another technique which has informed housing design (Zeisel, 1981).

Mediated observation

Mediated observation involves looking at the environment through some-body else's eyes. The major way of doing this is through asking people what they know and feel about the environment. Studies of this type have taken various forms: experimental studies of asking people to respond to scenes before them, to scenes in slides, or simply interviewing them, either face to face about their attitudes or asking them to fill out surveys (Krampen 1991). Completing questionnaires is the basis of most mediated observational approaches.

Interviews and surveys using questionnaires are widely used in research for both the study of use and meaning as the basis for housing design for a number of reasons. Some of these reasons are logistical and others are conceptual. The logistical reasons are firstly, that it is possible to obtain much information in a relatively short period of time using questionnaires and, secondly, that many situations are not open to observation. The conceptual reason is that it is difficult to devise other approaches for obtaining information about people's hopes and aspirations for the future. While it is possible to observe behavioral tendencies, it is considerably easier to ask people about their attitudes. The accuracy of the response depends largely on how the research is designed. People's beliefs about themselves do not necessarily correspond with how they behave or would behave given the opportunity (Michelson, 1976).

There are a number of other mediated observation techniques such as the content and historiometric analyses of architectural criticism, films, novels, and diaries (Krippendorf, 1980; Simonton, 1984). These techniques involve defining the variables of concern operationally and the use of statistical techniques to define samples, to identify the correlations between variables, and to hypothesize about the causal relationships among them.

Research design

Designing research studies is a highly creative activity. Ultimately the quality of the results of any research, its external validity, depends on the quality of the questions posed, the quality of models used to guide it, and the set of operations that form the research method. The basic questions that one has to address apply to all types of research. How are the variables of concern to be defined? From the array of techniques available which ones get at the question being asked best? How is the sample of population of concern selected? How are extraneous factors controlled?

One of the major issues in doing research for housing is identifying the population of concern. In designing custom houses this task is easy, because the individuals of concern are known and the relationships among them are relatively clear. The sponsor and the user are the same. In new mass housing, it is not as easy. The specific users are unknown. One has to identify a surrogate population to study or rely on existing knowledge. In contrast, in existing housing the population is in place and their views can be ascertained directly.

Much research is biased by the way the population and samples of situations to be studied and people of concern are identified. Often the process of selecting both is a haphazard one—the situations and people who are available to be studied are studied rather than those that need to be studied. It is essential that policy makers and designers using research results know how the samples are selected. Without this knowledge it is difficult for them to understand the degree of confidence they should place in the information yielded. While a random sample is often the ideal, in much housing research the concern is for a structured sample in which the various sub-populations of the concern are represented.

In experimental research, the way in which the subjects of the study are allocated to the experimental conditions and the degree to which they are naive subjects effects the results obtained. In using an interview approach to design a whole set of concerns arise regarding the nature of questions to be asked and the order in which they are asked. In addition, the nature of interviewing, the structure of questionnaires, and who does the interviewing are likely to bias results.

A variety of statistical techniques are used to test the reliability of data obtained, degrees of correlation, and covariance. The manner in which data are recorded and conclusions are drawn vary considerably from study to study. They need to be clearly designed and specified. The more complex the statistical methods used, the greater the importance of doing this because each technique has a series of assumptions built into it.

An appraisal

There is an array of approaches for looking at different aspects of housing policy and the designs that result (see, for instance: Michelson, 1975; Zeisel 1981; Bechtel, Marans, and Michelson, 1987; Wisner, Stea, and Kruks, 1991, Farbstein and Kantrowitz, 1991). The relative merits of each approach is open to considerable debate. As a result there are different ways of studying the same phenomenon. In studying meaning there are semiotic and environmental psychological approaches (Krampen 1991). In the study of use there are rigorous simple observation techniques and phenomenological approaches (Franck 1987). Within architecture there is considerable debate over the relative merits of typological and empirical approaches to the study of housing meanings and uses as the basis for design. These debates cannot be resolved here, but some observations can be made.

Rationalism as the basis for housing policy formation and housing design has proven to have severe limitations. It was based on a set of fallacious assumptions (Blake 1977). Yet all design requires some Rationalist thought for it deals with the future and making the future. Rationalists thinking does, however, have to be coupled with a sound empirical understanding of people and environment if it is to be rational. The mainstream of housing research into the future will undoubtedly be an Empirical one.

Phenomenology and participant observation by trained researchers, unlike casual observation, yields important insights into general understandings of meanings and uses. Casual observation is highly biased by the observer's life style and values and so provides design information useful only in a very limited sphere, but it can yield important hypotheses for more rigorous study, including psychological experimentation. The study of meaning will almost inevitably continue to follow a variety of routes— clinical psychological, semiotic and environmental psychological approaches will persist. The first two approaches like phenomenology are more likely to produce hypotheses worth testing than enabling strong conclusions to be drawn and theories to be built.

Much planning and design is carried out under extreme time constraints. Inevitably researchers in these circumstances will have to use techniques which provide information rapidly which means that they will resort to face to face interviews and/or the use of questionnaires and surveys. Such approaches are also essential in ascertaining people's dreams about the future. The design and conducting of interviews and surveys is as much an art as a science. Casual methods can lead to highly misleading results. Much has been learnt about the how best to conduct research of this type over the past twenty years so that many pitfalls can be avoided.

No research approach is foolproof. Multiple approaches to the same research questions have already yielded fruitful information and enhance the quality of debate about the descriptions and explanations of phenomena. Researchers invest considerable intellectual and psychological energy in the techniques they use and/or develop, yet they have to remain open to what other research approaches can achieve and their approaches cannot. It is not easy to be open minded in this way!

Conclusion: designing under uncertainty

In making policies and designing houses, housing complexes, and neighborhoods there is inevitably a clash among different design objectives—to have much space and to have high accessibility, to have high quality living environments for all and limited resources, to have a pleasant living environment today and meet tomorrow's needs, and, above all, between fulfilling human needs in the short run, and the broader needs of ensuring a habitable planet in the long run.

Housing research has a short history. Our knowledge about how different housing policies and designs work in different cultural contexts has made considerable advances since World War II. Much remains to be understood so decisions will continue to be made under uncertainty. The consequences will no doubt be studied and researchers will learn from them. New research approaches and sharper methods will be developed, old controversies will become irrelevant and new ones will emerge. Difficulties that we face today in designing studies will be overcome but new difficulties will emerge as new concerns arise.

Theory based on systematic research however thoroughly it has been developed can only tell a policy maker or architect about the past and the present. It can enable the policy maker to make better predictions about the future, but policies, plans, housing developments, and houses are designed. At times of slow social and technological change the predictions are likely to be accurate but at times of more rapid change the degree of uncertainty under which one formulates a design increases. The future is created by our actions.

References

Alexander, Christopher, Sara Ishikawa and Murray Silverstein. *A Pattern Language: Towns, Buildings, Construction.* New York: Oxford University Press, 1977.

Bechtel, Robert, Robert Marans, and William Michelson, eds.. *Methods in Environmental and Behavioral Research.* New York: Van Nostrand Reinhold. 1987.

Blake, Peter. *Form Follows Fiasco: Why Modern Architecture Hasn't Worked.* New York: Atlantic/ Little Brown, 1977.

Broadbent, Geoffrey. *Emerging Concepts in Urban Space Design.* London: Van Nostrand Reinhold International, 1990.

Chawla, Louise. "Homes for Children in a Changing Society." In Ervin H. Zube and Gary T. Moore, eds., *Advances in Environment, Behavior, and Design*, Volume 3. New York: Plenum, 1991: 187-228.

Cooper Marcus, Clare and Wendy Sarkissian. *Housing as if people Mattered.* Berkeley and Los Angeles: University of California Press. 1986.

De Rivera, J.. "Emotional Experience and Qualitative Methodology." *American Behavioral Scientist* 27, 1984: 677-688.

Duany, Andres. "Traditional Towns." *Architectural Design Profile* 81, 1981: 61-64.

Ellis, Russell and Dana Cuff, eds. *Architects' People.* New York: Oxford University Press, 1989.

Farbstein, Jay and Min Kantrowitz. "Design Research in the Swamp." In Ervin H. Zube and Gary T. Moore, eds., *Advances in Environment, Behavior, and Design*, Volume 3. New York: Plenum, 1991: 297-326.

Franck, Karen A. "Phenomenology, Positivism, and Empiricism as Strategies in Environment-Behavior Research." In Ervin H. Zube and Gary T. Moore, eds., *Advances in Environment, Behavior, and Design*, Volume 1. New York: Plenum, 1987: 59-67.

Franck, Karen A. and Sherry Ahrentzen, eds.. *New Households, New Housing.* New York: Van Nostrand Reinhold, 1990.

Gadamer, Hans-Georg. *Philosophical Hermeneutics.* Berkeley and Los Angeles: University of California Press. 1976.

Grandjean, Etienne. *The Ergonomics of the Home.* New York: Halsted.

Gutman, Robert and Barbara Westergaard. "Building Evaluation, User Satisfaction and Design." In Jon Lang, Charles Burnette, Walter Moleski, and David Vachon, eds.. *Designing for Human Behavior: Architecture and the Behavioral Sciences.* Stroudsburg, PA: Dowden, Hutchinson and Ross, 1974: 320-329.

Howard, Ebenezer. *Garden Cities of Tomorrow.* London: Sonnenschein, 1902.

Kaminski, Gerhard. "The Relevance of Ecologically Oriented Conceptualizations to Theory Building in Environment and Behavior Research." In Ervin H. Zube and Gary T. Moore ed., *Advances in Environment, Behavior, and Design,* Volume 2. New York: Plenum, 1989: 33-36.

Krampen, Martin. "Environmental Meaning." In Ervin H. Zube and Gary T. Moore, eds., *Advances in Environment, Behavior, and Design.* New York: Plenum, 1991: 231-271.

Krier, Leon. "Master Plan for Poundberry Development in Dorchester." *Architectural Design Profile* 79, 1987: 46-55.

Krier, Rob. *Urban Spaces.* New York: Rizzoli, 1979.

Krippendorf, Klaus. *Content Analysis: An Introduction to its Methodology.* London: Cage, 1980.

Lang, Jon. *Creating Architectural Theory: The Role of the behavioral Sciences in Environmental Design.* New York: Van Nostrand Reinhold. 1987.

Le Corbusier. *My Work.* Translated from the French by James Palmer. London: Architectural Press, 1960.

Low, Setha and Erve Chambers, eds.. *Housing. Culture and Design—A Comparative Perspective.* Philadelphia, PA: University of Pennsylvania Press. 1989.

Marmot, Alexi. "The Legacy of Le Corbusier and High Rise Housing." *Built Environment* 7, no. 2, 1982: 82-95.

Maslow, Abraham. *Motivation and Personality.* New York: Harper and Row (third edition revised by Robert Frager, James Fadiman, Cynthia McReynolds and Ruth Cox). 1987.

Michelson, William. *Behavioral Research Methods in Environmental Design.* Stroudsburg, PA: Dowden, Hutchinson and Ross, 1975.

Michelson, William. *Man and his Urban Environment: A Sociological Approach.* Reading, MA: Addison Wesley. 1976.

Montgomery, Roger. "Comment on 'Fear and House as Haven in the Lower Class,"' *Journal of the American Institute of Planners*, 32, no. 1: 31-37.

Nasar, Jack, ed.. *Environmental Aesthetics: Theory, Research, and Applications.* New York, NY: Cambridge University Press.

Norberg Schulz, Christian. *Genius Loci: Towards a Phenomenology of Architecture.* New York: Rizzoli, 1980.

Rapoport, Amos. *House Form and Culture*, Englewood Cliffs, NJ: Prentice Hall, 1969.

Rapoport, Amos. *Human Aspects of Urban Form.* New York: Pergamon. 1977.

Regnier, Victor and Jon Pynoos. *Housing the Aged: Design Directives and Policy Considerations.* New York: Elsevier 1987.

Ricouer, Paul. *The Rule of Metaphor: Multidisciplinary Studies in The Creation of Meaning in Language.* Translated from the French by Robert Czerny. Buffalo and Toronto: University of Toronto Press, 1975.

Seamon, David. "Phenomenology and Environment-Behavior Research." In Ervin H. Zube and Gary T. Moore ed., *Advances in Environment, Behavior, and Design*, Volume 1. New York: Plenum, 1987: 3-27.

Sharp, Dennis. "Introduction," in Dennis Sharp, ed., *The Rationalists: Theory and Design in the Modern Movement.* London: Architectural Press, 1978: 1-5.

Sherwood, Roger. *Modern Housing Prototypes.* Cambridge, MA: Harvard University Press. 1978.

Simonton, D. K., *Genius, Creativity and Leadership: Historiometric Inquiries.* Cambridge, MA: Harvard University Press.

Stringer, Peter. "Models of Man in Casterbridge and Milton Keynes." In Byron Mikellides, ed.. *Architecture for People.* New York: Holt, Rinehart and Winston,

1980: 176-186.

Tuan, Yu-Fu. *Space and Place: The Perspective of Experience.* Minneapolis, MN: University of Minnesota Press, 1977.

Whyte. William H. *The Social Life of Small Urban Spaces.* New York: The Conservation Foundation, 1980.

Wingler, Hans. *The Bauhaus.* Translated from the German by Wolfgang Jabs and Basil Gilbert. Edited by Joseph Stein. Cambridge, MA: MIT Press.

Wisner, Ben, David Stea, and Sonia Kruks. "Participatory and Action Research Methods." In Ervin H.Zube and Gary T. Moore, eds. *Advances in Environment, Behavior, and Design.* New York: Plenum, 1991: 271-296.

Zeisel, John. *Inquiry by Design: Tools for Environment-Behavior Research.* Monterey, CA: Brook/Cole 1981.

Part II
The Meaning and Use of Home:
Its Interior

The Meaning and Use of Home: It's Interior

RODERICK J. LAWRENCE
University of Geneva

Home evokes a wide range of divergent images and concepts which reflect its multidimensional nature. The meanings and uses of home, like that of housing, are not only complex and elusive, but they vary from person to person, between social groups in the same society, across cultures and during the course of time (Cf. Altman and Werner, 1985; Duncan, 1981; Kent, 1990; Kron, 1983; Lawrence, 1987; Low and Chambers, 1990). In recent decades many theoretical perspectives, concepts and research methods have been used to study home and housing.

A housing unit is a human artefact which defines and delimits space for the members of a household. It provides shelter and protection for domestic activities. Yet, the fact that houses in the same society have quite different shapes and sizes, and are built with a range of construction materials, suggests that, beyond pragmatic parameters, other factors are of at least equal importance in determining their design. For example, one purpose of the design of each dwelling unit is to distinguish between public and private domains. These spatial relations express the administrative, cultural, judicial and sociopolitical rights of the residents, visitors, neighbors and strangers. From the perspectives of law, economics and politics, the tenure status of housing, with its implications for personal control is the critical variable that defines "what makes a house a home". However, this emphasis on tenure status ignores the large portion of the population—even in affluent countries like Switzerland—who choose to rent. Thus, like a simple spatial interpretation of homes, this one too, is limited.

The three chapters in this section show that a home is more than just "a territorial core" (Porteous, 1976) and not just "an ordering principle in space" (Dovey, 1978). Home is a complex entity that defines and is defined by cultural, socio-demographic, psychological, political and economic factors. In this respect, it is noteworthy that only one of the nine dimensions identified by Hayward (1975) to define home referred solely to physical variables, suggesting that human relations are equally if not more important. Similarly, Saegert (1985, p. 187) notes that home is a more elusive notion that house: "Not only is it a place, but it has psychological resonance and social meaning. It is part of the experience of dwelling - something we do, a way of weaving up a life in particular geographical spaces". Moreover, Saegert (1985, pp. 187-188) states:

> The notion of dwelling highlights the contrast between house and home. First it does not assume that the physical housing unit defines the experience of home. It connotes a more active and mobile relationship of individuals to the physical, social and psychological spaces around them. It points to a spiritual and symbolic connection between the self and the physical world... (and)... emphasizes the necessity for continuing active making of a place for ourselves in time and place.
>
> Simultaneously, it points to the way in which our personal and social identities are shaped through the process of dwelling.

Although, the meaning and use of home have commonly been investigated in relation to housing units, it should be borne in mind that larger settings, such as an institution, a neighborhood, a geographical region, or a country, can also mean home to many people (Sopher, 1979). This section explicitly focuses on the intimate relationship between the meaning and use of the interior of housing units. Although each chapter is primarily concerned with the interpretation and use of the internal organization of domestic space, and the ordering of household life, the demarcation made by anyone between the exterior and the interior, and between public, collective and private spaces in residential areas is not absolute, nor static, as cross-cultural and historical studies have shown (Daunton, 1983; Kent, 1990; Lawrence, 1986). Consequently, the geographical and societal context of housing and home should not be overlooked. In this respect, although no single chapter in this book presents an exhaustive, contextual analysis of the meaning and use of housing and home, this set of contributions can and should be considered in a complementary way.

Bearing this qualification in mind, the three contributions in this section show that the design, meaning and use of home interiors are intimately related to sets of cultural, socio-demographic and psychological dimensions, and that the reciprocal relations between these dimensions should be studied synchronically and also with a temporal perspective. This kind of approach can relate the long-term architectural and social history of housing units in specific localities to those short-term processes concerning the construction, decoration and use of homes by households and individuals (Lawrence, 1985; 1986). Hence, the complementary nature of housing and home can be interpreted in relation to these processes, as the chapters in this section show by using different yet complementary research methods.

In the first chapter of this section, Yvonne Bernard presents the results of a comparative, cross-cultural study which examined the means residents in France, Italy and Sweden adopted to express their social identities within the domestic realm. This study focused on those material constituents, or sets of constituents, in the living room which enable its arrangement and decoration not only to be differentiated between countries, but also between social groups within each country.

In this respect, the study reexamined the confirmed hypothesis that the decoration of the living room is an indicator of the social identity of the inhabitants. Yet, this chapter presents a more in depth analysis of home interior decoration than many previous studies: on the one hand there is a more detailed study of the material constituents; on the other hand, the discriminating characteristics of the respondents have been studied in relation to their age (5 classes) as well as their socio-professional status (7 classes).

The main constituents that play a discriminating role in the decoration and organization of home interiors in France, Italy and Sweden are the treatment of walls, floors and fenestration openings, as well as the nature and layout of furnishing, including plants. Whereas there are common constituents in each of the three countries concerning the treatment of walls, floors and fenestration openings, this study also identifies the discriminating characteristics between these countries. These characteristics include the nature and layout of furniture which is attributed a more important role in Italy than in France and Sweden; the spatial organization of interiors including the attributed function of plants is more important in France than in Italy or Sweden; and the aesthetic function attributed to colors, shapes and materials used in home decoration is more important in Sweden than in the other two countries.

This chapter also presents certain discriminating characteristics common to specific groups of respondents in the three countries. For example, in comparison with the aesthetic function, the upper classes in each country attribute a relatively higher value to the distinctive function of the decoration of home interiors. In contrast, the middle classes with ascending mobility in each country convey their social status by being taste-makers, whereas those of the youngest generation of respondents who occupy the same professional position as their fathers commonly repeat the conventional decorative treatment of their parental homes.

In the second chapter, Gilles Barbey argues for a systematic analysis of how daily domestic life is intimately related to the spatial organization, the nomenclature and the furnishing of rooms; as well as how these may remain constant or change during the course of time. In order to develop this explicit, interdisciplinary, historical analysis this chapter discusses how and why homemaking can be considered as an illustration of place-making: Place and place-making are interpreted in relation to place identity. In this respect, Barbey develops and illustrates a spatial, socio-psychological and historical approach which complements the comparative, synchronic method presented in the previous chapter.

When the complementary perspectives presented by Bernard and Barbey are applied, it is possible to identify those meanings and uses of home interiors that have changed or remained constant, in spite of many societal developments, such as innovations in house planning, and changes to life-styles and household structure. Consequently, important questions for researchers, planners and designers are evoked: for example, will the continuing increase in residential mobility engender any modifications to the design, meaning and use of home interiors? In order to answer this question, Barbey shows that it is necessary to identify the intrinsic spatial configurations and psychological processes of home-making. These qualities are generic and preempt only aesthetic, functional, or economic interpretations of housing. Rather, these qualities suggest that archetypal spaces and socio-psychological processes form a matrix of the meanings and uses attributed to home interiors. In this respect, it is precisely the kind of approach advocated in this chapter which enables us to identify and comprehend the persistence of a prescribed setting in the home for eating formal meals, which Bernard and others have found in numerous countries irrespective of "objective" space standards (Lawrence, 1987). Moreover, it is also instructive to examine the duplication of settings for eating formal and informal meals that has been identified in several countries and which Giuliani found in Rome.

In the third chapter, Maria Vittoria Giuliani presents the rationale for and the results of a study of how households in Rome qualify and use their home interiors. Like the preceding chapter, this one also argues for an historical understanding of housing and home. However, Giuliani focuses on the historical relationship between the size of dwelling units and household composition. Although this relationship is a neglected subject of contemporary housing studies it has important historical roots that should not be ignored (Daunton, 1983; Lawrence, 1986). Studies of the serial of housing legislation and policy show that there was an intentional relationship between household composition and the recommended size of housing units. In particular these contributions confirm that the number, age and gender of children in a household have been a determining factor for the calculation of the recommended number of rooms per dwelling since the mid-19th century in several countries.

In contrast to historical studies of households and their home interiors, Giuliani's study reexamines this subject from the point-of-view of a sample of inhabitants living in Rome today. This study found that the number, age and gender of children play a crucial role in the furnishing and use of rooms: there were no cases in this study in which brothers and sisters over 12 years of age shared the same bedroom.

This study is also interesting because it identifies the strategies and practices adopted by those residents that are confronted with an "objective" lack of interior space. There is a consistent hierarchical principles which the study identified as:

1) the separation of the parents' bedroom from the children's bedroom (which often clashes with a preference to distinguish between spaces attributed for diurnal and nocturnal activities);

2) diurnal activities are usually attributed a higher priority than nocturnal activities (e.g. the function of a bedroom is added to that of a living room, whereas the reverse is extremely rare);

3) spaces for daytime activities are often differentiated between each other by functional classes as well as individual and shared uses. As there is an increase in leisure activities inside the home, the polyvalent use of rooms for leisure activities commonly occurs when there is a need for additional space for sleeping.

4) there is a consistent practice of duplicating settings for eating formal and informal meals whenever the "objective" floor area or number of rooms enables this to occur.

These results underline the pertinence of studying the strategies and practices that people use within their homes to accommodate their domestic affairs. Although the home is usually interpreted as a holistic unit (at least when considered from a material, judicial or tenureship point of view),the three chapters presented here indicate the relevance of studying the spaces or zones that are defined both conceptually and physically by the residents. Furthermore, these chapters illustrate that the classification and demarcation of activities and spaces define and are mutually defined by cultural, socio-demographic and psychological dimensions.

In sum, this section confirms that home interiors are complex subjects of study. In order to comprehend this complexity it is necessary to identify and study the interrelations between all the dimensions that define and are mutually defined by the design, meaning and use of housing and home interiors. In this respect, these chapters argue for and apply research methods which ought to be considered in terms of an integrative, conceptual framework as well as a temporal perspective.

Hence, beyond the content of each chapter in this section, the most important lesson to be given by this set of contributions is the need to elaborate this conceptual framework. In order to achieve this goal a redefinition and reorientation of much contemporary research is required, and each contribution in this section provides important cues.

Agenda for future research

First, it is necessary to reject any hierarchical model, used often in housing studies, which is claimed to order "variables" in terms of their weight or force. In this respect, and to cite but one example, it is noteworthy that Rapoport's (1969) claim that cultural variables have primacy over all others in the determination of house form is still frequently accepted a priori by scholars. This hierarchical interpretation is not only partial, as Lawrence (1987) has shown. It has also been argued that extremely broad conceptual tools, such as "culture" need to be replaced by intensive analyses that define not only the dimensions operative in specific contexts but also the reciprocal relations between them.

Second, it is also necessary to reject any atomistic-mechanistic model, used in some housing studies to identify and study cause-effect interactions between two "variables" isolated from the context in which they occur. One example of this kind of interpretation is the study of residential mobility, housing choice and the satisfaction of residents in terms of "pushes and pulls". This kind of study has been challenged by Michelson (1977) who has presented an alternative perspective.

In contrast to the two models just mentioned it is necessary to develop and apply an integrative, conceptual framework which accounts for the multiple dimensions of housing as well as the reciprocal relations between them, and the contextual conditions in which they occur.

The aim of formulating an integrative, conceptual framework is primarily to aid researchers and practitioners to address the complexity of housing and home as subjects of enquiry. This framework enables scholars to account for the design, meaning and use of dwellings using an integrative rather than a selective perspective. With this conceptual model, researchers and practitioners can situate their study, forcibly partial rather than all-inclusive, in terms of a holistic framework. Nonetheless, an important prerequisite for considering any case as a whole is the definition and comprehension of the constituents, and the reciprocal relations between them. Although this is not the appropriate place to elaborate this kind of framework, one model that can help achieve this goal, was initially formulated in 1986, and applied to the study of vernacular houses (Lawrence 1990). This framework is meant to aid scholars to identify those dimensions of housing and home which are pertinent in a precise context, at a specific point in time, as well as the reciprocal relations between them. The model should be reapplied in order to implement a temporal perspective. This framework comprises three main sets of dimensions: geographical, physical and material; societal including cultural dimensions; and individual human factors. All of these dimensions have been illustrated by studies of housing and home but few scholars have considered them simultaneously, either at one point in time, or over an extended period. Therefore, this analytical model is presented as a conceptual framework for future research that seeks an integrative perspective.

References

Altman, I. and C. Werner (eds) (1985) *Home Environments: Human Behavior and Environment.* Volume 8. New York: Plenum Press.

Daunton, M. (1983) *House and Home in the Victorian City: Working-Class Housing, 1850-1914.* London: Edward Arnold.

Dovey, K. (1978) "Home: an ordering principle in space." *Landscape* vol. 22, no. 2, pp. 24-30.

Duncan, J. (ed) (1981) *Housing and Identity: Cross-cultural Perspectives.* London: Croom Helm.

Hayward, G. (1975) "Home as an environmental and psychological concept." *Landscape* vol. 20, no. 1, pp. 2-9.

Kent, S. (ed) (1990) *Domestic Architecture and the Use of Space.* Cambridge: Cambridge University Press.

Kron, J. (1983) *Home-Psych: the Social Psychology of Home Decoration.* New York: Clarkson N. Potter.

Lawrence, R. (1985) "A more humane history of homes: research method and application." In I. Altman and C. Werner (eds) *Home Environments: Human Behavior and Environment*. Volume 8. New York: Plenum Press, pp. 113-132.

Lawrence, R. (1986) *Le Seuil franchi: logement populaire et vie quotidienne en Suisse romande, 1860-1960* (Stepping across the threshold: popular housing and daily life in the french-speaking region of Switzerland, 1860-1960). Geneva, Georg Editeur.

Lawrence, R. (1987) *Housing, Dwellings and Homes: Design Theory, Research and Practice*. Chichester: John Wiley.

Lawrence, R. (1990) "Learning from colonial houses and lifestyles." In M. Turan (ed.) *Vernacular Architecture: Paradigms of Environmental Response*. Aldershot: Gower, pp. 219-257.

Low, S. and E. Chambers (eds.) (1989) *Housing, Culture and Design*. Philadelphia: University of Pennsylvania Press.

Michelson, W. (1977) *Environmental Choice, Human Behavior and Residential Satisfaction*. New York: Oxford University Press.

Porteous, D. (1976) "Home: the territorial core." *Geographical Review*. vol. 66, no. 4, pp. 383-390.

Rapoport, A. (1969) *House Form and Culture*. Englewood Cliffs: Prentice Hall.

Saegert, S. (1985) "The role of housing in the experience of dwelling." In I. Altman and C. Werner (eds) *Home Environments: Human Behavior and Environment*. Volume 8, New York: Plenum Press, pp. 287-309.

Sopher, D. (1979) "The landscape of home: myth, experience, social meaning." In D. W. Meinig (ed) *The Interpretation of Ordinary Landscapes*. New York: Oxford University Press, pp. 128-149.

Chapter 3

The Interior Use of Home: Behavior Principles Across and Within European Cultures

YVONNE BERNARD
Université René Descartes, Paris

MIRILIA BONNES
Université di Roma "La Sapienza", Roma

M. VITTORIA GIULIANI
Instituto di Psicologia, Consiglio Nazionale delle Ricerche, Roma

This chapter builds conceptually on Altman's research orientation of the establishment of universal principles of behavior across cultures, and the attempt to understand a culture on its own terms in relation to its unique beliefs, attitudes, and values without imposing external values on that culture. A comparative study of France, Italy, and Sweden reveals the existence in each country of characteristic and differentiated patterns of interior arrangements regarding the existing elements and the relationships amongst them. The study stresses the existence of identical relations between some social groups and some spatial layouts.

81

Introduction

For years, sociologists have been interested in the arrangement of domestic space as a factor revealing the social identity of its dwellers. Chapin (1935) and Sewell (1940) used analysis patterns of furniture to predict the socio-economic status of the inhabitants. Based on a number of factors, Laumann and House (1970) established four distinct types of interior decoration associated with social classes characterized by both income and social lifestyle. In this study, the authors clearly showed that the dimension which contrasted the traditional and the modern equally contrast the Anglo-Saxon "WASPS" against socially mobile classes who are eager to validate their recently acquired social status by displaying a certain disdain for tradition and taste for mass consumer products in fashion. The effect of social status on the housing arrangement was also showed in an original manner by Duncan and Duncan (1976) who proposed the permeability of social networks as an explanatory variable. When an individual belongs to an imperme-able social network in which his socio- economic status is known to all, it is not necessary to assert it through the interior decoration of his home. In permeable social networks where individuals are, on the contrary, likely to enter in contact with new members, the arrangement and the decoration of his dwelling become a privileged display of the social status to which he belongs or to which he wishes to belong. The research which we have conducted in France (Bernard, 1978) confirmed the existence of patterns of arrangements of domestic space closely linked to the social class to which the individual belongs.

The acknowledgement of the relationship between social identity and dwelling arrangements therefore seems obvious. However, we may speculate as to whether the means used by the inhabitants to interpret this identity are still the same or if on the contrary, each country in accordance to its culture and its social system, which is more or less hierarchic, produces its own differentiating criteria.

The objective of the comparative research that we will present here is meant to examine this question. The three countries which were compared were France, Italy, and Sweden, three European countries which are similar and different at the same time, enabling us to use this comparative method.

The data on which we worked were pictures of living rooms. This room was chosen, as Goffman (1959) emphasized, because it is the privileged area of a "stage setting", where the dweller proposes to show an image of himself and what he wishes others to have of him; a dual message whose elements are closely linked. A personal image exists foremost through the eyes of the others.

Precursors of the comparative analysis

While we may find references to climate and seasons which have an effect on cultural differences in the works of Hippocrates, Plato and Aristotle and other ancient writers, we may generally admit that the first attempt in comparative statistical analysis of cultural facts was made at the end of the nineteenth century. In a lecture, the English anthropologist Tylor in 1888 attempted to establish the existence of scientific facts by showing that the development of institutions may be studied on the basis of data classification in order to distinguish the real association between facts, associations which should be expected to be based on the law of sheer chance. Using the term of adhesion, the predecessor of the term correlation, the author had taken the precaution of specifying that "adhesion" between two facts may not be used to conclude that a causal relationship between these two facts indeed exists. Used mostly by the adherents of evolutionist anthropology, the comparative method, all the while arousing criticisms, was developed and used successively by diffusionists, functionalists, and finally by structuralists. The huge comparative investigations done in the United States made it possible to improve this method. This was how Murdock, an American anthropologist in charge of the Yale Cross Cultural Survey which dealt with the comparison of 250 types of societies, introduced in 1948 the important idea that the comparison should be founded "not on cases which were dealt outside their cultural context but rather on functional associations of observed features, each one dealing with cultural differences."

Meanwhile, in France, comparative sociology was developing, using the method of concomitant variables formulated by Stuart Mill and developed by Durkheim. Applied in particular to the analysis of many societies, similar in their general nature but different where certain behavior is concerned, the objective of the analysis was to prove to what point the similarities and differences on a given point are accompanied by a similarity and differences on others. The synthesis of the results should enable the isolation of the constant relations between facts; constant relations on which, according to Durkheim, every scientific explanation should be founded.

Modern multi-dimensional methods, and especially those which we have used within the framework of the research that we are presenting herein, directly resulted from principles proposed in the nineteenth century. The application of these principles, particularly the treatment of numerous and complex data, were considerably alleviated with the advent of computers.

Objectives of the comparative research on domestic space

The comparative research on domestic space whose results are herein presented pursues a double objective:

1) Starting from a set of living room photos, each one described by a number of features, the analysis should identify structurally important characteristics which differentiate behavior with regard to the arrangement of domestic space. These characteristics are not features which describe the initial setting; they represent complex functions of the said set of features. It is important to understand that our goal was not to describe the behavior of the French, the Italians, or the Swedish concerning dwelling, a method which would imply a representative sampling of the population of each country, but rather to detect how behaviors in each country are different. It is not the goal of the comparison of these countries to see how, with regard to each variable, the subjects behave differently, but to observe if the same variables or group of variables associated by the analysis structure the differentiations in each country.

2) After we detect those variable patterns which express the behavior of a group of subjects, the second objective is to identify the subjects and to see if the individuals who were grouped according to their attitudes and their choices in relation to dwelling could be characterized by sociological variables which are also common. Although this method does not require an wide sampling of subjects, it is however imperative, and in particular with the perspective of an international comparison, to constitute samples which would offer a similar representation of the large categories of socio-cultural variables likely to discriminate the subjects and to explain their way of living and their use of domestic space. It is essential to emphasize here the difficulties encountered when we matched samples from different countries. If age and educational background are variables that are easy to define, the classifications of socio-professional categories which are generally used, should be carefully analyzed and precisely defined.

Methodological steps

In order to reach the first proposed objective, i.e., to discover the underlying structure with regard to the set of behaviors concerning the appropriation of domestic space, the method consisted of three stages: 1) find a coding system to define the field of observation; 2) select a method of treatment of data which may be applied to this field in order to show the explanatory factors; and 3) interpret these factors to understand the underlying logic which explains their appearance.

The coding system

The observation unit is an area: the living room. The observed areas were understandably different from each other. Knowing that the shape of the room facilitated or made it impossible to make certain arrangements, we consider that the coding system should express all potentials for behavior with regard to space appropriation. This is defined by a set of features. It is understandably not possible to consider a comprehensive description of the totality of the features. The coding consisted of selecting the features supposed to enable a better differentiation of behavior; the features which may be termed as diagnostic. The choice of diagnostic features depends on the aims of the research, the size, and the type of the sample used for observation. Thus, during a study done in France on the influence of cultural patterns, a relatively fine description of the style of furniture made it possible to clearly show the relatively subtle differences between the choices of subjects having the same educational background but with a different social origin. However, it proved costly and useless to conserve these descriptive traits in the codes which were retained for purposes of international comparative research. On the one hand, they were not relevant in describing the assembly of furniture elements which were observed, yet on the other, when inserted in a descriptive space of a larger context, they lost their classifying power. However, within the framework of a global analysis, certain features inherent in the French became diagnostic with regard to the Italian samples.

After an initial exploratory stage of qualitative study of the photographic material collected for the purpose of identifying certain main patterns of apparent differences between the various interiors examined, a descriptive system was devised to deal respectively with: (1) the type of element present; and (2) the type of relationships existing between the elements present.

Elements present in the room

A coding system was devised which consists of a list of objects that, although not exhaustive, is aimed at giving priority to certain objects with respect to others—as well as to certain characteristics rather than others. Thus, the elements have been identified on the basis of their significance with regard to the room's functional specialization, and described according to general categories making specific reference to the patterns which the object fulfils: (a) its specific function (e.g. for sofas and arm-chairs, the description was made mainly in the direction of such characteristics as hardness/softness, existence of arms or high backs, etc..., in view of its comfort and socializing potential); and (b) its possible decorative function with reference to perceptually relevant aspects, i.e. those connected for instance with the brightness of color, variety of materials, respectively. The intention was to relate the choice of these elements by the occupants back to implicit underlying value systems expressed in terms of the following value dimensions: old/new, valuable/worthless, conventional/non-conventional, etc...

Types of relationship

The type of relationship existing between the element present was identified on the basis of their capacity for affecting: (a) the global space structure; (b) the spatial organization and arrangement; and (c) the decoration.

Structuring of global space

Although there is no denying the existence of architectural constraints, the occupant is free to modify the perception of global structure of his space if he so wishes. This modification occurs in two basic ways: expansion or contraction. These may be further subdivided into three types of possible actions: raising or lowering the perception of height, widening or narrowing, and filling or emptying. Whether it consists of a simple color pattern or a more significant modification of volume, this part of the coding refers mainly to relationships of nearness, contrast or continuity between the constituent elements of the space, i.e. floor, walls, ceiling, doors and windows.

Spatial organization and arrangement

The spatial layout of the elements and the geometric pattern of the composition form the subject of a detailed analysis. The existence of zones, their degree of conspicuousness and the predominance of one zone over another were all initially noted. Each zone is then studied from the standpoint of the relationship between its constituting elements—i.e., furniture arrangement, existence of focal points, centralization, and symmetry or non-symmetry. These relationships are mainly geometric in nature and are organized according to a coordinate system.

Decoration of the space

Although the majority of characteristics or relationships already described can be considered as decoration, i.e., aimed at obtaining an aesthetic impression from the space, we have included under this heading the variables denoted by Berlyne (1971) as collative variables. These variables account for the individual's varying tendency to live in a rich, complex, and ambiguous environment.

Ambiguity: An evaluation of the flexibility or rigidity of the environment is one of the first important elements of information. This evaluation must basically be founded on the clarity or ambiguity of the overall perceivable structure of the room. The impression that there has been an accidental formal juxtaposition of the elements is opposed by that of solidly established conventional relationships. This evaluation, along with that of apparent order or disorder may appear subjective. The agreement of several coders is necessary to ensure the validity of incongruous or misused objects which also represent factors of ambiguity.

Complexity: Complexity primarily depends on the quantity of elements and their diversity. Visual diversity will be analysed through homogeneity or heterogeneity of colors, shapes, materials, and lighting; cultural diversity through the diversity of styles, the types and the origin of the objects of decoration. Complexity will also be studied through the system of relationships. Points of visual focus and the attempt to create dissonance must also be noted, as well as redundancy—series of objects or trinkets, accumulation of cushions or green plants, the presence of covers or napkins, repetitive spatial arrangements, reinforcement of signs referring to a given style, etc. Special attention must be paid to wall decoration and to picture hanging patterns. The arrangement of objects and trinkets on the various surfaces will also be observed. Centrality, symmetry and non-symmetry will in this case be interpreted as indications of complexity.

Treatment of data

The data to be dealt with consisted of a logical description table. Each set of rooms, is described by a set of features characterized in terms of presence or absence. For example, for each feature compared to another, as in the case of walls painted in white and the floor carpeted in green, three situations are possible: 1) the two features are present in the same room, like white paint and green carpet; 2) none of these two features is present, like walls covered by a flower-designed wall paper and the carpet being red; and 3) one feature is present and the other is not—the walls are white and the carpet is red. Description tables summarize the totality of association of details between the features described. In the same way, we can relate the subjects and the describing features, thus establishing the closeness of two subjects. Two subjects will be very close to each other if the description of their living rooms show similar choices or, on the contrary, set them apart if they do not have any choice in common.

Choice of method

The choice of a method is linked to the nature of the objective being pursued. If emphasis is placed on the synthesis, as in the case of the description of the features which characterize the arrangement of the living room, a geometrical method is chosen wherein data is represented in the shape of a cloud of points in the vectorial space of finite dimension. If emphasis is placed on the basis of classification, meaning on the necessity of entering each element in each category, as in the case of the subjects, we will have to use the algebraic method wherein data are represented in the form of partitions of class hierarchy. We therefore, used two methods successively: 1) a factor representation of the features described; and 2) a classification of subjects.

Geometrical representation

The main methods of geometrical representation are MDS (Multidimensional Scaling) and Factor Analysis. With MDS, starting from a table of distances between objects, we choose an algorithm to make a representation, as precise as possible, by means of points whose position shows the initial distances. Indeed, the distance between the points reflects the similarity, the dissimilarity or the nearness between objects. If two objects are alike, the distance between points which represent them is rendered null. The farther they are from each other, the more the distance is emphasized. Among these methods, the INDSCAL method could not be chosen since it cannot define inter-individual differences. The steps taken consisted of searching for common factors in groups of Italian, French and Swedish subjects and to search for the weight of these factors in each group. In an attempt to put in evidence specific factors, the choice of the INDSCAL method proved to be the less ideal.

Like the MDS, the factor analysis was to search for a spatial presentation of data, but in the form of independent factors, without any correlation between them. The factors which were taken one after the other explain, on the basis of their respective weights, the inertia of the cloud of points. The factors obtained were derived from a linear combination made by the features described and in so doing, enabled the structuring of the information contained in the initial table. The different methods of factor analysis differ in the choice of distance and the manner with which the cloud of points is constructed. The method that we have chosen is the Correspondence Analysis method, proposed by Benzecri (1976) and described in English by Lebart *et al.* (1984). It applies to a case wherein two sets are placed in a statistical correspondence. The independence corresponds to the $H0$ hypothesis. If this is rejected, the analysis will enable us to see how data differ from $H0$ and in which direction it sets itself from independence. The analyses of correspondences are distinct from other factor analysis methods due largely to the fact that the zero hypothesis corresponds to a table wherein lines and columns are not equal to each other, but have the same profile, meaning that they are proportional to each other. The differences in weight between the rows and the columns are thus eliminated and cannot hide the structure. Several relatively rare but nevertheless associated features constitute the form of a behavior pattern.

Hierarchical classification

The analysis of correspondences enabled us to clearly show the underlying structure of the features observed and to detect from which explanatory factors the synthesis was formed. The second step consisted of identifying the subjects which were grouped on the basis of behavior patterns outside the preceding analysis. The problem then arises in a different manner. In describing the structure of the arrangement of the living room we only retained the features which explained the emergence of the structure—i.e. those having a strong contribution to the axes. For the subjects, we had to identify the position of each of them, therefore giving then a place in a group whose composition is defined by the factorial axes previously extracted. This way, we may say, for instance that individual 'x' belongs to group 21, which differs from group 22 on the second axis. This result may be obtained by applying a method of hierarchical classification. The hierarchy obtained showed the similarities and dissimilarities observed in the behavior of the subjects. Two subjects who live in identical apartments are thus superimposed. The principle of construction is simple: right from the beginning, two subjects are placed on the point where distance is least. Then, we draw a distance table between the remaining subjects and the group formed through the incorporation of the first two subjects. We pursue the construction closer and closer until the two groups of subjects reach a union of all of the subjects. This means that the two incorporated groups which are lowest in the hierarchy will be relatively close while two incorporated groups high up in the hierarchy are very dissimilar.

Presentation of results

Factorial structure of descriptive features

We must remember that the first goal pursued was to detect through factorial analysis of correspondences the existence of elements which would allow us to understand what features or set of features in each of the countries compared differentiate the manner in which the living room is arranged and decorated. The first phase of interpretation consists of distinguishing the significant factors from those which are not. The set of factors take into consideration the entirety of inertia of the cloud of points but the percentage of inertia explained by each one of them enables us to attribute relative importance. The percentage is given by eigenvalues which explain the dispersion of features on the considered factor and take into consideration the explained variance. The factors are then interpreted in relation to the order of descending eigenvalues until the given value whose relative importance is considered to be too little to justify the interpretation of the factor. Then, we look into which elements have contributed to the elaboration of the factor and this is again in relation to the relative importance of their contribution. Therefore, it is by analysing the characteristics of the groups of elements which determine a factor that we attain the first objective, meaning that it is by putting emphasis on these features which enables us to differentiate and oppose the subjects.

The projection on the axis allows for the visualization of the proximities and facilitates interpretation. Unfortunately, an article is not the right medium wherein these projections can be presented efficiently. The number of elements represented on the projection makes it impossible for us to decipher it. We, therefore, chose to present the results in the form of a synthetic table (Table 3.1) which, through the different categories of code description, shows the type of features in each country that play a determining role in the formation of the various axes. The elements which contribute to the formation of the first two axes are the elements which play an important role in the differentiation (Bonnes *et al.*, 1987).

We noticed immediately that certain features play a discriminating role in the three countries. The treatment of the walls, i.e., the choices between sobriety (white painting or neutral colors) and decoration or wall paper with flower or stripe designs show a clear opposition between subjects in each country. The treatment of the ground and the openings also appear on axis 1 and 2 in the three countries. However, if we then examine what other

Table 3.1: Results of factorial analysis in each country

	FRANCE	ITALY	SWEDEN
ceiling, type of paper, paint, color	[1][2]3 4	[1] 3 4	[1][2]3 4
floor, type of floor, carpeting	[2] 4	[1]	[1][2]3 4
ouvertures, draping of windows with or without curtains	[1][2]	[2]3	[2]3 4

Set 1 : Structuring of global space

		FRANCE	ITALY	SWEDEN
general arrangement of the living-room		[2]3 4	[1][2] 5	3 4
complet set or disparaging set		[2]	[1]	[1]
lighting		4	[1]	3 4
green plants		[1] 4	[1] 4	[2]3 4
arrangement furnitures and objects	centrality	[1][2]3	4	3 4
	symmetry	[1][2]3	4	3 4
flexibility rigidity		[1][2]	[2]3	4
order disorder		[1]	3 4	3

Set 2 : Organisation and arrangement

		FRANCE	ITALY	SWEDEN
density of space utilization	floor	3 5	[1] 4 5	
	walls	3 5	[1] 3 4	
decorative density		3 4	[1] 3 4	[1] 4
kind of furniture		[2]	[1][2]3 4	[1][2]3 4
kind of lighting		[1][2]	[1][2]3 4	
type of mural decoration		[1][2]3 4	[2]3	[1][2]3 4
book arrangement		[1]	[2]	[1][2]
variety of lighting				[2]
variety and heterogenity	materials	[2]		[1]
	shapes			[1]
variety and heterogenity	color	4		3
	style	[1]		[1][2]
wall decoration	type	[2] 4	4	[1]
	arrangement	[1] 3	[2] 5	3
variety of knick-knacks		[1]		[1][2]
decoration of the lg. room	dining table	[2]3 4	[1] 4	[2]
	center table	[2] 4	[2] 4	[2]

Set 3 : Livening the space decoration

features contribute to the characterization of the first axis, slight differences appear. In Italy, the composition and the nature of the furniture seem to play a particularly important role. A meticulous analysis will show us what characterizes the difference between groups of subjects is that the variation in size and quality of dwelling is greater in Italy than in France or Sweden. That is, if we are interested, for instance, in the furniture, having or not having a living room corner, even if it is only composed of two armchairs, can be a discriminating factor where Italy is concerned. These features appear in France on the second factor and in Sweden, where workers have big-sized apartments, they appear only on the 3rd and 4th factors.

In France alone the first factor is explained mostly by variables in the organization of space. If the manner in which green plants are arranged, grouped or isolated, seems to be the differentiating criterion in the three countries, the manner in which the furniture is arranged–the paintings and the objects–reflect in France a distinct opposition between those who put emphasis on a central arrangement, symmetry, order–in short on rigidity– and those who, on the contrary, seem to live in a more flexible universe; less orderly, e.g., chairs are not always around the table. What is striking is that in other countries, these features don't appear on the 3rd or 4th factor.

The manner in which low or high tables are decorated is a criterion which appears on the the second factor in the three countries. If we exclude this, variables which characterize decoration especially those which express a variety and heterogeneity of materials, shapes and colors, play a relatively negligible role in France and are practically non-existent in the Italian factors. However, in Sweden, whatever the social category, dwellings are quite large and the importance of economic factors are less obvious, and differentiations are shown more distinctly in relation to aesthetic choices which characterize the decoration. The style of furniture, the variety of shapes and colors of materials and the type of mural decoration are the features which explain the first factor.

Classification of subjects

After discussions between researchers in the first two countries, France and Italy, it was decided to retain two variables as basic conferring variables: age and socio-professional status. Age was divided into 5 categories: from 20 to 30, from 31 to 40, from 41 to 50, from 51 to 60, and over 60.

The nature of the research led us to adopt a socio- professional typology different from those usually used and we excluded farmers in as much as our research concerned urban sites. However, we have selected two groups of subjects, who in our opinion represent special characteristics both in

Table 3.2: Hierarchical classification of subjects

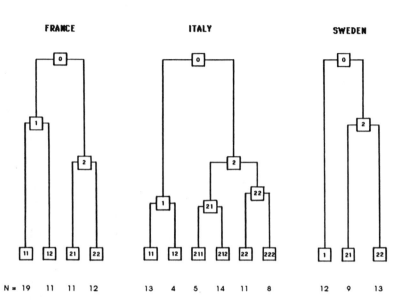

their lifestyle and their relation to domestic space: the first one is that of architects and artists, the second is that of intellectuals. Grouped together under this heading are journalists, writers, and teachers of higher education. Other categories retained have been established taking into consideration profession as well as income and educational attainment. Each subject classified under this category comes under a socio-professional name: 1) workers, 2) handcraftsmen, 3) employees, lower-level executives, 4) senior executives, 5) self-employed, company directors 6) artists, architects, and 7) intellectuals.

The way we grouped subjects is pictured in the shape of a tree, the reading of which is done from top to bottom. The higher the knots connecting groups, the greater the distance between these groups. Interpretation is achieved both by the place of groups on the factorial plan and by frequency analysis of the appearance of features for each group differentiated in the classification (Table 3.2: Hierarchical Classification of Subjects in the Three Countries).

France

In France, the partition observed at the highest knot stems from the variables which characterize the first axis, and which oppose two lifestyles characterized mostly by variables in furnishing and animation. The set of features gathered on the negative pole of axis 1 evoke a modern and relaxed atmosphere, characterized by flexibility in the furnishing as well as by a kind of apparent untidiness. To this, on the positive pole, is opposed a more rigid style of furnishing and a carefully maintained order. This opposition could have been due to a difference in generations. That is not so. If one bisects the tree so as to retain only groups of subjects sufficiently numerous to justify a collective interpretation, one finds an equivalent distribution of the various age categories in each of the four groups.

On the other hand, the partition conveys a real sociological differentiation between subjects. Group 2 includes all the artists and architects of the sample, a few of the intellectuals, 3 senior executives, all under 40 years of age. Group 1 includes all others, the blue collar workers, all the lower executives and employees, and most senior executives. All have in common an affinity for order, centrality, symmetry and, more generally, the formal features of the traditional "bourgeois" class patterns to which they belong or which they refer to as a model.

In group 2, walls are in most cases white, apertures are emphasized, interior closing apparatus are not used and, above all, the density of decoration is low, on walls as well as on the floor. One can feel a search for aesthetic values, sometimes conveyed by an alteration of floors and volumes. The furniture is heterogeneous, often mixing antique and contemporary pieces. The elementary rules of symmetry have been respected, except in the hanging of pictures or the positioning of objects. Group 2 often appears to be torn between two models: the bourgeois model to which, as we can observe, most of them are connected, by the education they received based on their origins, and the avant-garde aesthetic model to which they are drawn by professional or personal affinities.

Group 1 is divided into two branches at a high level. The two subgroups are highly differentiated in the social characteristics of their subjects. One finds in group 11, 8 senior executives, 6 lower executives or employees, 4 intellectuals and only 1 blue collar worker. The living-room is large, walls are white or of a neutral color. The floor, whether parqueted or wall-to-wall carpeted, is often covered with rugs. Windows are often framed with drapes. Generally speaking, whether on the walls or on the floor, the volume of furnishing is highly dense. One notes the presence of large pieces of furniture. In the majority of cases, the living room area includes at least one couch and numerous armchairs around a rectangular or round coffee table on which precious objects and potted plants are usually displayed. The furniture is almost always antique. Furniture pieces, as well as objects and pictures, are usually set in a symmetrical manner in the center of walls or surfaces. The mural decoration is rich and varied.

Situated on the same main branch as group 11, group 12 shares with it a number of common features. Totally different in sociological composition—we find in it practically all the blue collar workers (6 out of 7) of the sample—this group shares with group 11 an affinity for order, though with a more characterized rigidity. It is only in this category that we find a specific kind of wall paper, characterized by its geometrical pattern. Windows are usually dressed with plain curtains. The furniture is contemporary or stylized. Here as well, the floors are crowded with furniture, but the walls are not covered with pictures. The living room of these subjects is usually small and in half the cases there is no conversation corner. The dining room—it is the only group where we found this trait—is furnished with a complete set: a table, matching chairs, and a sideboard. The furniture is grouped in the center of the room and one finds here again the symmetry which characterized the previous group. There is little variety in the choice of colors and decorative objects. These are usually small and of little artistic value (animals, souvenirs). One often notes the presence of a bunch of cut flowers on the dining room table, the center of which is almost always covered with a doily.

Italy

In Italy, as in France, the highest knot of the tree separates subjects on axis 1. On the left, we find group 1 (17 subjects), on the right all the other subjects. Axis 1 being entirely determined by its negative pole, this partition conveys the very strong characterization of group 1 in relation to the others. If we identify the subjects which form this group 1, we find that this characterization is also of a sociological nature. Here we find 8 blue collar workers, and 9 craftsmen or employees, all of modest extraction, without diplomas and with a low or average income. The television set is often the focal point of the living room area. There is almost never a coffee table but there is a contemporary leather or velvet couch with one or two matching armchairs. The dining area often occupies an important place. Next to the table around which chairs are carefully arranged there is a sideboard or bookshelves with bar and sideboard, a typical piece of furniture on which china and a few books are displayed. The wish to adorn the dining room table with a doily or a vase of flowers appears as a characteristic of this group, the decorative paucity of whose environment is usually obvious. On the granito floor—a type of covering typical of inexpensive housing in Italy—

there are no carpets. There are no drapes on windows and–a relatively exceptional feature in the three countries surveyed–there are no potted plants. Apart from a few color-prints, the wall decoration is practically nil. Generally speaking, investment in decoration is low, though this may not be necessarily due to lack of financial means.

In opposition to the group which has just been described are all the other subjects, divided in turn into two subgroups, which can be regrouped for the purpose of a first interpretation. Group 21 is opposed to group 22 in their respective position on axis 2. Axis 2 opposes tradition to modernity, a feature conveyed not only through the style of the furniture but also through the management of space and the way of life it seems to imply.

In group 21, the living room area is almost always a drawing room. 11 subjects out of 19 have a separate dining room or a living-dining room of vast proportion which allows for large and comfortable conversation corners. More than half these subjects own at least two couches with many extra armchairs. In the center of this set one almost always finds a large coffee table made of stone or glass on which are displayed silver objects, ash trays, cigarette boxes, as well as other objects, all conveying the hosts' wish to receive their guests with care. The general atmosphere is convivial. The floors are covered with antique rugs. Lighting is provided by numerous lamps placed on the floor or on the furniture. Although books are usually kept in another room, office or library, we found in this type of apartment the drawing room displaying a wall entirely covered with books. All the subjects in group 21 were either senior executives or of equivalent status. They were all, by birth, from the upper or middle class, a fact which explains that they are, in most cases, the owners of homes situated in the center of Rome or in residential districts. Their income is usually high. In that group, it is to be noted that the older subjects maximize in their behavior the features which characterize their reference group.

The connecting factor among the subjects of group 22 is the absence of a traditional arrangement. The rooms we surveyed were mostly living-dining areas without clearly established zones. The dining area is usually reduced to a table and a few chairs, with no sideboard. The living area is usually less organized than in the previous group. If one usually finds there a couch and a few armchairs, these do not necessarily match and are often placed in a divergent manner. A fairly rare disposition which can be explained, among other reasons, by the quasi-general absence of a coffee table as the focal point.

In this group there is an evident desire for an aesthetic treatment of the global space. Walls are white. There are usually no curtains or drapes. Pieces of furniture, of antique or design style, are harmoniously blended and placed in a manner which suggests a deliberate and thought-out wish for flexibility. Mural decoration, which includes numerous posters and prints, is rich and diversified. The hanging of pictures reveals complexity and a wish to do away with centrality or symmetry. It is only in this group that are found rugs of ethnic origin and objects from far away cultures. Newspapers, objects of every day life, strewn about on the dining room table may give the impression of a certain untidiness, but they mostly convey the free and easy way in which the room is used. When analyzing the sociological composition of group 21, one finds all 5 architects of the sample, 2 artists, 4 intellectuals, 2 senior executives but also 4 employees. These subjects are, as we have already stated, fairly young, but they mostly come from upper or middle classes. Of average income, they live in average size, even relatively small, apartments, but these are usually situated in or near the center of Rome.

Sweden[1]

Results concerning Sweden have, on a comparative basis, to be carefully analyzed. First, the number of subjects surveyed is smaller than in France or Italy, and second Lund is a much smaller city than Rome or Paris. The balance between the different age categories and their socio-economic background has nevertheless been respected, with a smaller number of subjects in each category.

The variables which discriminate groups are markedly different from those in the two other countries, perhaps due to a less marked interference of socio-economic factors—e.g., it is a fact that, whatever the income or the social background of their inhabitants, all the houses and apartments we surveyed were large. In opposition to what was true in France or Italy, a quick survey of photographs did not permit the immediate perception of a differentiation. However, we did observe a comparable differentiation between subjects, although partitions did not stem from the same group of variables. Structuration of global space as well as visual animation played there a very important part.

As in Italy, on the first axis, one group is markedly opposed to all of the other subjects. Group 1 includes 12 subjects, essentially workers or employees of various ages. Two thirds of the rooms surveyed were living-dining rooms, the other third living rooms only. As we noticed in group 12 in France, one finds in this group a relatively typical wall paper pattern with flowers or stripes. Nevertheless, walls are never plain. Windows are dressed with half curtains, usually of lace, a type of traditional window

---

[1] Swedish data were collected by Sven Sandstrom and Janice Gillquist. We thank them for their participation in this research.

dressing only found in our Swedish sample, and only in this group. As in Italy, what we called bookshelves with bar and sideboard seems to be a standard piece of furniture. Bound books, china and knick-knacks are displayed on it. Couches, almost always of a flower design, are placed at an angle when there are two, which was the case in more than half the rooms surveyed. This disposition, although sometimes present elsewhere, seems to characterize the furnishing in group 1.

However, the most important variables are those which concern certain aspects of decoration, mainly mural decoration, abundant and very specific. Paintings, usually framed, large and very realistic, show landscapes, boats or children's portraits. There are also snapshots of family members and many knick-knacks and objects made of glass or china. There are potted plants in all Swedish homes but there are significant differences in the way they are displayed. In group 1, plants are separated and often placed on the floor or on furniture. The second axis also contributes to distinguish group 1 by the manner in which the dining room table is decorated. As in France and Italy, placing a doily on which are set a flower vase or a fruit bowl in the center of the dining room table constitutes a discriminating factor.

Opposed to group 1, the entirety of the other subjects is again divided into two subgroups. Group 21 presents the strongest sociological character- istics as it includes 5 out of the 6 architects in our sample, no intellectuals, no blue collar workers, but 2 lower managers and 2 senior executives. Age distribution here is again balanced. Subjects in group 21 earn an average or high income and most are university graduates. Their characterizing fea- ture is modernity, conveyed by their choice of furniture and even more by wall decoration. Only in this group did we find posters and contemporary prints on walls generally painted white. The furniture, consisting mainly of small pieces, seems relatively flexible.

Group 22, which includes the rest of the sample, is relatively heteroge- neous. We find there 6 senior executives as well as 2 workers, 3 intellectuals, 1 lower manager and 1 architect. The subjects in this group are relatively older. This group is markedly opposed to group 1 by its decoration of space. Walls are painted white and one observes a great variety of shapes, mate- rials and lighting. Variety, heterogeneity and complexity are the variables which most determine the first axis of the factorial analysis. The furniture is characterized by a blending of antique and contemporary styles. Couches are no longer of a flower design but plain. Windows also are dressed in a different way from that observed in the first group. Curtainless windows are framed by white or very lightly shaded drapes.

Discussion

Comparative analyses are usually based on classic methods such as interviews and questionnaires. These methods raise translation and interpretation problems. The gathering of photographic documents enabled us to be more objective. Based on visual facts, whose variety and complexity seem to defy analysis, we attempted to discover the logic in behavior without forming any hypothesis other than the existence of differentiated behaviors. Factorial treatment showed the different axes around which these differentiations were regulated, thus providing a solid base for comparative interpretation.

Furthermore, the hierarchic classification of subjects on the different factorial levels enabled us to come to a number of conclusions. If one compares the different classifications of subjects defined in each country, one observes a number of points in common which argue in favor of social determinism in aesthetic choices in furnishing and decorating the habitat. Although, as we have seen, discrimination between groups was established only on the basis of common practices. Individuals belonging to these groups often present the same socio-cultural profile as well as, though markedly less so, the same income level. Age, except in Italy, does not seem to play a decisive part. However, one observes very evidently in Italy, that the older subjects tend to maximize the features of their group pattern.

One also observes that groups aggregated at a very low level, that is groups presenting the most homogeneous practices, are also groups where the sociological identity of the subjects is the most marked, both by their occupation and by their social origin. From that stand point, senior executives and sons of senior executives are in the same situation as workers and sons of workers. These are relatively impermeable social groups, as Duncan (1976) showed in his study. The social status of their individuals is known by all and does not have to be constantly re-stated and at the mercy of fashion changes. Laumann (1970) as well had observed this trait while referring to Anglo-Saxons, who, when they occupy the same social position as their fathers, retain the same traditional atmosphere.

Among the well-to-do members of the upper class, the distinctive function of decoration is more important than the aesthetic function. Decoration conveys the belonging to a group and in this situation one observes an erasing of individual initiatives to the benefit of a statement of collective superiority.

Among middle class members in ascending mobility, individuals must convey their status, sometimes as Weblen (1899/1953) demonstrated by referring to patterns of classes immediately above theirs, sometimes, when they feel that they will not be readily accepted by members of traditional upper classes, by turning towards new and fashionable styles which will enable them to state their affinities and identity while symbolically rejecting traditional patterns.

These social groups, whose sociological composition is fairly unstable, are the followers of a group, found in all three countries, which Lynnes called the taste-makers, and which is a fairly homogeneous group. In France, in Italy, and in Sweden, we find a group generally opposed to the totality of the others, which includes architects, artists and professionals in art, some intellectuals, among them writers and journalists and a few members of a profession.

The signs which differentiate those groups are difficult to apprehend for they are characterized by attitudes rather than by solutions. Flexibility of use, variety and complexity in selecting materials, objects, works of art, and in displaying them promote originality in individual initiatives. Whereas in previous groups decoration, relatively static, did not discriminate between people, but between social classes, here belonging to the group is brought about through the originality of personal expression and through traditional claims of creation.

Lastly we note that, in spite of the variable incidence of economic factors, Swedish workers usually have an area which is two or three times larger than their French or Italian counterparts–yet, one finds constants in all three countries. A high density of furniture and aesthetic choices characterize the workers group in relation to the others. In all three countries we find a specific though different type of wall paper with a geometrical, flowered or striped patterns. A type of furnishing element, the one we called bookshelves with bar and sideboard whose function is to display objects, knick-knacks and eventually books, plays an important part in the aesthetic of daily life. We find this care, too, in the decoration of the dining room table with, in all three countries, its doily, potted plant or vase for cut flowers.

References

Benzecri, J.P. *La pratique de l'analyse des données.* Paris: Dunod. 1980-1982.

Bernard, Y. and M. Jambu. "Espace habité et modeles culturels," *Ethnologie Francaise*, Vol. 8, 1978, p.7-20.

Bonnes M., V. Giuliani, F. Amoni, and Y. Bernard. "Cross cultural rules for the optimization of the living-room," *Environment and Behavior*, Vol. 3, 1987, p. 204-227.

Chapin, F.S. *Contemporary American institution: A sociological analysis.* New York: Harper and Brothers, 1935.

Duncan, J.S. and N.J. Duncan. "Housing as presentation of self and the structure of social networks," in Moore, G.T. and R.G. Golledge, Editors, *Environmental Knowing.* Stroudsburg, PA: Dowden, Hutchinson & Ross, 1976.

Goffman, E. *The presentation of self in everyday life* New York: Doubleday, 1959.

Laumann, E.O. and J.S. House. "Living room styles and social attributes: The patterning of material artifacts in a modern urban community." in Laumann, E.O., P.M. Siegel, R.W. Hodge, Editors. *The logic of social hierarchies.* Chicago: Markham, 1970.

Lebart, L., A. Morineau, and K. Warwick. *Multivaried descriptive statistical analysis.* New York: John Wiley, 1984.

Murdock. *The social structure.* 1948.

Sewell, W.H. "The construction and standardization of a scale for the measurement of the socio-economic status of Oklahoma farm families," *Technical Bulletin,* Vol. 9, 1940. Stillwater, Oklahoma: Oklahoma Agricultural and Mechanical College.

Tylor, E.B. "On a method of investigating the development of institutions applied to laws of marriage and descent," *Journal of the Royal Anthropological Institute of Great Britain and Ireland,* 1888, p. 245-269.

Weblen, T. *The theory of the leisure class.* New York: American Library, 1953 (original work published 1899).

Chapter 4

Spatial Archetypes and the Experience of Time: Identifying the Dimensions of Home

GILLES BARBEY
École Polytechnique Fédérale de Lausanne, Switzerland

This chapter explores some implicit dimensions related to the meaning of home considered as a combined residence and work place. A dual socio-psychological and historical research perspective is outlined. The concepts of place and placemaking enable homemaking to be reinterpreted in relation to place identity, whereby home is conceptualized both as a social symbol and an extension of the self. The actual conversion process of an anonymous hotel room into a meaningful and personalized world provides an overview of the complex meanings attached to home; Simultaneously, domestic space is infused with the nostalgia of an eternal time, as illustrated by the great human myths, which emphasize the importance of a stable home. Based on such an interdisciplinary perspective, it seems possible to demonstrate that a global reconsideration of the meanings related to the home can lead to an alternative approach to architectural design, that considers both the affective ties between the inhabitants and the spatial configuration of their home interiors.

Introduction

The aim of this chapter is to study some of the dimensions associated with the meaning of home considered in its narrow acceptation of combined residence and work place. This interpretation contrasts with other more universal domestic meanings such as those reviewed in the *Landscape of Home* (Sopher, 1979). In spite of an ongoing change in life styles, the basic meanings of home seem to remain constant. During recent years, research on domesticity has been extended to the various disciplines of the social sciences, with an increasingly multidisciplinary outlook. Although it is difficult to achieve an overview of studies of homes, this chapter suggests that a historical perspective has frequently been missing from recent research. Nonetheless it is suggested that this perspective provides important cues for understanding the meanings and uses of domestic space.

Consequently, this chapter will concentrate on the relationship between the home, its use, meaning and time as a transactional process between physical and affective factors. Since homes can be considered a "warehouse of human experience," it seems important to explore those personal and affective ties which each individual has with his dwelling during his lifetime, in order to understand how specific space acquire differential values for members of the same family. As time passes, buildings undergo certain physical transformations. Their meanings and uses change. Therefore, the historical value of personal representations of domestic space can provide the way to understand and accommodate a meaningful relationship between residents and their home.

Orientations and methods

During the last three decades, the growth of interest in urban and housing history has produced a large volume of studies that have examined broad, societal parameters, or themes, such as housing policies, economics, and legislation. In this respect, research by architects, economic, social and urban historians has examined dwelling units built for different socio-economic classes in a wide range of locations and societies, some limited to specific towns and others to specific periods of time. Concurrently, there has also been a growing volume of studies by social scientists about the history of households and families as Lawrence (1985) has discussed. Nonetheless, many contemporary housing studies give scant consideration to the lifestyle and values of the residents. Apart from many functionalist studies of the use of dwelling interiors, there has rarely been any systematic consideration of how domestic daily life is related to the spatial organization, the nomenclature and the furnishing of rooms; or how these change during the course of time. In general, the interrelations between societal and personal ideas, processes and values, and the design and use of dwelling units, have commonly been overlooked. In order to overcome this limitation, Barbey and Lawrence (1985) suggest that a dual historical perspective relates housing history to residential bibliographies.

Placemaking and homemaking

During a recent international conference entitled 'Place and Placemaking,' Dovey (1985, p. 94) argued that 'place' is not primarily physical but rather experiential. Tuan (1975) describes 'place' implies both people and meaning. Quality or 'sense' of place then depends on the quality of the experience and the depth of meaning. Dovey differentiates the 'spirit of place' from the 'sense of place' and 'home.' Sime (1985, p. 295) defines the concept of 'place affiliation' and its components: identity, attachment and actualization. The meanings of place are infused with the dialectics of home and journey, person and setting, individual and community (Dovey, 1985, p. 99).

'Homemaking' can be considered as an illustration of placemaking. 'Place identity' is a physical environmental referent to the more well known term of 'self identity.' For each person the definition of self or what is referred to as 'the self', 'self image' and 'self identity,' necessarily includes dimensions of place and space which collectively constitute what we have called place identity (Proshansky, 1976, p. 38). Furthermore, the home provides opportunities for personal and social activities and longterm processes. How these enable self impression and expression is one profound centre of significance that contributes to a sense of place identity (Sixsmith, 1986, 291). Although Graumann (1988, p.60) defines home as "the place where I live, I dwell, I make my home," it is also a place for the recollection of memories associated with different places experienced in the past. Home is an exceptional place characterized by a moderate pace of time. This implies that the life world dimension is an integral part of the understanding of home.

Home as a symbol of self

Paraphrasing Cooper's (1972) illuminating essay, we can assume that home is the expression and symbol of the self. It corresponds to the vision that people have of the ideal life and makes use of symbols which serve a culture by making concrete its ideas and feelings (Rapoport, 1969, p. 47). For example, living room decoration and furnishings tend to reflect the conscious and unconscious attempts of the residents to express their social identity.

It is suggested that people decorate their home according to their level of cultural awareness and values; less educated people are likely to value traditional furniture more than the upwardly mobile, who favour a more informal style of interior decoration (Laumann and House, 1969).

All the above observations about the use of space should incorporate the temporal dimension. It is important to visualize the linkage between space and time using the perspective of Gaston Bachelard, who argues that space is like "encapsulated and compressed time" (Bachelard, 1957/1969).

Text analysis

It is useful to relate individual domestic behavior to more universal myths and symbols. Analysis of texts is one method to decipher these relationships in relation to domestic space and objects, as Lawrence (1985) has shown. Many writers describe their study room as a 'microcosm' which combines different features reminiscent of the diversity of the World. When asked to describe their personal relationship to their home and workplace, some authors refer to the metaphor of a prison cell, implying that it is characterized by an everlasting provision of time. At the same time, the constrained living in a prison is equivalent to a challenge to escape from its seclusion. It is noteworthy that individual reactions to familiar places can be ambiguous or contradictory. For example, in the correspondence exchanged with Nanny Wunderly Volkart from Zurich, the Austrian poet Rainer Maria Rilke describes and sketches the hotel room where he spent three months of his life during the winter 1919-1920 at Locarno, Switzerland (Rilke, 1977, pp. 23166). Rilke was renting two rooms at the Pension Villa Muralto. These were composed of a large study and a tiny bedroom, and were separated by a corridor. In the study, the furniture is displayed in the periphery of the room, against the walls as shown in his sketch of the room.

It is organized in such manner that it corresponds to specific activities and periods of the day. There is a breakfast corner and a place to sit down and read. There is a table for writing, which is located in the middle of the room. Perhaps the most significant feature is a chest of drawers, which serves as a kind of altar. It is covered with a table cloth, a vase containing roses and a picture hung on the wall. These material artefacts have far-reaching spiritual connotations and constitute a link between the poet and some of his closest friends. Rilke occasionally remembers the happy evenings shared chatting with Nanny as he watches the picture of the 'Stubli' (a small and cosy room).

The description of this room reflects the mental transformation of a random hotel room into an intimate place, where the personality of the

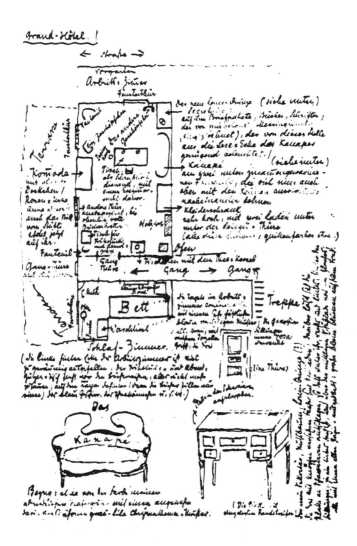

Figure 4.1: Rilke's *Stübli* at Villa Muralto

writer is safe guarded. His lifeworld is the sphere of writing where the table is the focus. There must be an ample provision of time at hand and no sign of disturbance whatsoever. The feeling of freedom is also the liberty to move back and forth through the space. Rilke states that it took some effort to achieve a satisfactory layout of furniture which required various trials before it was finalized. During this process, it was important to appropriate the various zones of the study, which became material extensions of the self. Armchairs and tables were almost considered as living creatures which lead a life of their own, and were supposed to play a role in the life of the poet. There cognition of the 'personality' characterizing the surrounding artefacts is like an attempt to achieve a comforting though undisturbing company. The same applies to the room as a whole, which is reputed to have experienced happy times, as candles were lit, with a feeling of peace filling the space. These sensations tend to provide a feeling of homeliness and security like the ambiance of the paintings and sketches of the Swedish artist Carl Larsson.

Such literary descriptions of home seem to express an inner development of the self. The total equation of self and home epitomizes the home as a way of being in the world. The structure, layout, style, decoration and furnishings of the home make it a place unlike any other, where self expression is possible (Sixsmith, 1986, p. 290). The setting is perceived as a whole and it is impossible to examine the quality of the space independently of that associated with the artefacts. The analysis of domestic meanings extracted from Rilke's correspondence emphasizes the personal dimension of home experience. This experience may be somewhat egocentric and restrictive, since the room is not open to social interaction. One could suggest that the setting is to some extent a place of potential mystery and secrecy, not accessible to anyone, and yet a place of legitimate privacy (Korosec Serfaty and Montagna, 1989).

The relevance of domestic myths

In his famous essay on the myth of the eternal return, Eliade (1949, p. 41) reminds us that nothing can last unless it is lively and inhabited by a soul. When faced with the futilities of destiny, people have no other choice but to attribute a meaning to what they are forced to accept. Eliade explains that in primitive societies the abolition of time may only occur through the imitation of certain behavioral archetypes and the repetition of paradigmatic gestures. Anything that does not conform to a given model does not hold any relevant meaning. Thus, every newly built house is like an 'absolute beginning' and reflects a time which does not belong to history. Man is forced to negate time while recreating the cosmogony. The myth of the eternal return is meant to contradict the cyclical conception of time and restore its reversibility. Home is by essence characterized by the capacity to be a familiar place, a place of eternal return.

Another important domestic myth endeavours to treat home as the centre of the world. Eliade studies the symbolism of ascension located in the centre of the house and manifested by a central pole or a staircase which constitutes a cosmic axis (Eliade, 1952, p. 59). The house is compared to the universe and seen to be located at the centre of the world. The ascension is the symbol of the path leading to the absolute truth. It enables the communication between the different levels of the human being. It is therefore always of prime importance to recreate a centre, a microcosm and an imago mundi, which help providing the illusion of permanence. In Greek mythology, Hestia, the goddess of the hearth, occupies a fixed position in the house, whereas Hermes symbolizes motion and transition (Vernant, 1974, p. 124). The mythological coupe "Hestia + Hermes" is a representation of the home space: the interior being feminine and the exterior masculine. The myth is an important key to the meaning of home as it incorporates an interpretation of time which provides man with the illusion that he is eternal. Buddhist mythology endeavours to prove that transcending space is equivalent to transcending the flow of time. Budha is not only capable of abolishing time, but he can also move upstream and reverse the course of history. Nowadays, the influence of domestic myths may be remote and unconscious to modern man, who no longer considers his dwelling as part of a mythical process. Yet, he is forced to conform to the domestic morale which forces him to settle down and lead a regular life.

The ideology of sedentarity

'Grieving for a lost home' describes the reaction of many people to forced relocation as one of grief, painful loss, continued longing, a sense of help-lessness and difficulty in adapting to the new situation (Fried, 1963). Other authors such as Gans (1962) or Coing (1966) explain the tragic experience of relocation following the process of urban renewal, whereby a whole net-work of social and affective ties is destroyed. It is evident that residential expropriation is disruptive of existential processes and values.

At another level, nomadism and vagabondism are considered as a social plague. Bohemians and Gypsies are suspected to be unreliable and dan-gerous people as they do not conform to what appears as a fixed pattern of life and residence. Until recently in history, the traveller and the alien were mistrusted, as witnessed by numerous stories depicting the rejection of strangers and wanderers wherever they went.

In the popular literature of domestic chronicles, mobility and alienship are condemned universally. The example of a stable and sober homebound life is valued as a religious morale. Sedentarity proves to be the only accepted mode of residence, except in special cases when social groups such as shepherds must earn a living based transhumance. Nowadays, a parallel growth in residential mobility and homelessness is becoming universal, so that it may well affect the meaning of home for a vast part of the world population.

Changing patterns of domestic life

The analysis of housing types shows that these fall into two opposite categories. Firstly, the institutional housing, where inhabitants are transient boarders as illustrated by monasteries, hospitals, army camps, boarding schools and various kinds of 'social housing' where everyday life is subjected to a house rule and a daily program of scheduled activities. In such environments, sometimes built for the labouring classes in many European cities during the 19th century, space and time are controlled and regulated so that residents behave according to certain accepted patterns of life. The imposed discipline is reflected in the spatial layout of houses which consist traditionally of several rows of identical cells lined up on a central corridor leading to common rooms.

Second, and in contrast, residential housing which originated in royal courts and in aristocratic mansions, corresponds to a more leisurable use of space at home. Individuals are not expected to live according to identical patterns and therefore enjoy more domestic freedom. In this context sociability characterizes a range of spaces whose dimensions and uses reflect a more liberal lifeworld.

It is interesting to note that the industrial revolutions have simultaneously reinforced and suppressed these domestic distinctions. Although a significant part of Third World populations are housed in miserable conditions with up to 10 people or more per room the difference between the institutional and residential categories of housing is presently being diminished owing to architectural ideology and economic parameters.

Changing uses of space and facilities

Concurrently, Medam (1977, p. 70) describes the fast changing patterns of life and the corresponding impoverishment of the relations between members of the same family in their home. The author notes that the former togetherness of the family around the kitchen table was an important factor of socialization, which is no longer available in contemporary dwellings, where life is far more individualised and influenced by the media. During this process, the home becomes less meaningful and rewarding on the affective level.

Demographic studies in many countries show that the traditional household is being increasingly replaced by other categories of residents such as single parent families or youth communities, and that home is consequently subjected to other values and use patterns. As housing units progressively became more specific and autonomous after the industrial revolution for example, rooms were distinguished solely according to their use; likewise it is now obvious that homes are undergoing a new redistribution of roles and functions. The home and work place which were separated during the last century or so tend to be combined again, as residents are increasingly involved with professional work at home. When confined between the four walls of his apartment during the major part of the day, the resident becomes more conscious of the affective ties between him and his home or work place. He finds himself in the same situation as an author, like Rilke, who 'dwells' in the world of writing and values his home as a place for creativity. He is therefore likely to identify more strongly with such a living and working place than with a dwelling unit which would merely be occupied like a dormitory. One hypothesis worthy of study is that the meaning of home could well be related to the amount of time spent there: the greater the confinement at home, the more relevant its meaning, as proved by the room as a cell with its constrained framework, which is occupied almost continuously day and night. Furthermore, what could be termed the 'intentionality of home usage' is dependant upon the variety of meanings associated with the home and the individual capacity of spatial appropriation.

Synthesis and discussion

The aim of this study is to gain a better understanding of the identification processes of the individual to his familiar home. If part of the feeling of being at home is dependant upon the adequacy of the dwelling unit in terms of space and equipment, the other part of it is related to the human ability to sublimate the image of everyday life in a place invested with such intensive care and attachment. Thus, the home place becomes something more than a mere dwelling place, somehow equivalent to a private kingdom.

Recent studies confirm that 'home' is a label applied voluntarily and selectively to one or more environments to which a person feels some attachment (Hayward, 1975, p. 3; Lawrence, 1987, pp. 34). In recent work in philosophy and the social sciences, there has been a growing interest in the themes of dwelling and home. To dwell is to be at home with one's own place, to live in a world where one feels comfortable and at ease. Dwelling is the final conceptualization of the key aim in all of Heidegger's work: to resurrect an ontological scheme that relocates person in world (Seamon, 1983, p. 6). Furthermore, lived space refers to space as it is actually experienced and has a close relationship to life world and a phenomenology of the body. Each person has a 'natural place' to which he belongs, and only this place can properly be called the zero point of his reference system. Normally, this natural place is the home (Seamon, 1982, p. 129).

This observation may still be relevant today, but at the same time it is infused with contemporary meanings which derive from space controlling techniques, commonly identified as "integrated home services" (Amphoux, 1988, p. 4). These include, for example, systems of communication designed for comfort, information, or security. Their extensive use will undoubtedly influence the spatial conception of homes and notably the demarcation and accessibility of domestic, private space to household members and outsiders. However, these observations should by no means signify that the organization of space in the home is becoming proportionally less important.

Whereas most architects tend to apply existing prototypical layouts to the design of residential buildings, this paper argues that it is necessary to reconsider the linkage between existential values and the physical properties of home interiors. Beginning with an analysis of specific spatial archetypes such as the cell or the suite, which incorporate a social dimension and correspond to a fixed spatial order. For example, it is evident that the monastery cell was conceived as a place for individual confinement, solitary work and meditation. If Le Corbusier kept reusing this spatial type in many buildings, it is because he valued the significance of creative work in everyday life and he projected his own point of view into his design, as witnessed by the tiny office at the Rue deSevres, or the Cabanon at Cap Martin.

A history of *building types* was proposed by Nikolaus Pevsner who analyses the successive or parallel changes occurring in the distribution of space in various types of buildings. His survey is quite useful but incomplete, as it does not take into account housing and dwelling types. A group of Italian authors is accredited with the tentative interpretation of urban morphology and building typologies in terms of their mutual inferences (Aymonino, 1975). However, the above mentioned studies do not really attempt to relate behavioural observations to the organization of domestic space.

Some basic research work was achieved by the French and English historians of domesticity (Alliaume *et al.*, 1977; Daunton, 1983) who related dwelling patterns to housing types. More recently, architectural historians with a broad understanding of environmental sociology and psychology surveyed the treatises of architecture of the 17-18th centuries and their in-fluences on the conception of domestic space (Bauhain, 1989; Eleb-Vidal, 1989).

Apart from some initial work by Mayer Spivak on *archetypal space*, there is little systematic reflection on the relations between the various categories of domestic space associated with them (Spivak, 1973). While we are rejecting architectural determinism, we can still demonstrate that the combination of domestic spaces consists in a limited number of components, that can be identified as *spatial archetypes* (Barbey, 1990).

The variation of spatial archetypes is so important that their combina-tion is illimited to the extent that they can accommodate almost any type of living. Spatial archetypes are illustrated by features such as galleries, suites, rooms, etc. The Utopian phalanx was nothing else than an original combination of individual dwelling units combined with access galleries to be shared by the residents on various opportunities, thereby creating more communality. The same attempt at providing more convivial lifestyles than usual can be observed in the work of the Russian constructivists, who in-vented the labourer's club and the common house (don kommuna) in the 1930's (Guinzbourg, 1924). These examples demonstrate that more socially or communally oriented dwelling patterns do not result automatically from innovative floor plans but can be considerably facilitated (or inhibited) by (in)appropriate design.

It is important to acknowledge certain intrinsic qualities associated with specific spatial configurations, as experienced in everyday life. An example of the experiential values associated with the home can be identified in the descriptions of writers who were interviewed about the affective relationship to their workplace (David, 1982). They report that their home and work place correspond and adapt to their personality: on the courtyard side of the apartment, the darker rooms seem to echo the most secret part of the self, whereas the sunny side of the house matches the open and social facet of their ego. The constant association of the physical features of domestic space such as orientation or lighting to the psychological attitudes of residents proves to be relevant information for the design of new housing types and the renovation of old buildings.

Conclusion

This chapter has argued that a multi-disciplinary approach to the study of home is important in order to enrich our understanding of the meanings and uses of domestic space. The behavioral dimensions presented here can be related to a historical or temporal perspective. Hence, architectural history would combine a macro level of analysis (with respect to the evolution of building types, construction methods and services) and also a micro level perspective concerned with the residential biographies of the inhabitants. In sum, it is instructive to explore the intimate and affective ties between the individual and his or her home. It is also important to bear in mind the relations between social behavior and spatial configurations. It has been shown that space identity is dependant upon the individual ability to convert a physical space into a meaningful mental world based on cultural and societal norms, customs and values yet also reflecting personal aspirations and goals.

Above all, the spatio-temporal perspective of home presented here indicates that people behave according to previous experiences of space and social norms governing status symbols. Moreover the values involved in the identification process with the home are subject to cultural and social variation. The subjective meanings attached to the concept of home require that their exploration is pursued in great depth in order to be fully comprehended. A dual sociopsychological and historical perspective is therefore an instructive method to enrich our understanding of the meanings associated with home.

References

Aillaume, J.M. *et al.* (1977) *Politiques de l'habitat, 1800-1850.* Paris: Corda.

Amphoux P. (1988) *L'intelligence de l'habitat* (The intelligence of habitat). Paris: Paper presented at the Symposium 'Domotics=Integrated Home Services' (January).

Aymonino, C. (1975) *Il significato della città.* Bari, Ed. Laterza.

Bachelard G. (1969) *The Poetics of Space.* Boston: Beacon Press.

Barbey, G. and Lawrence, R. (1985) "Mediation between behavioral and historical studies of people and the built environment." Workshop at CUNY during EDRA 16, 1985.

Barbey, G. (1990) *L'évasion domestique. Essâi sur les relations d'affectivité au logis.* Lansanne. PPUR.

Bauhain, C. (1989) "Les familles bourgeoises françaises au XIX-siède," in N. Haumont et M. Segaud. *Familles, modes de vie et habitat.* paris: L'Harmattan.

Coing H. (1966) *Rénovation urbaine et changement social.* L'ilot no 4 (Paris 13e) (Urban renewal and social change: The Sector No. 4 in Paris). Paris: Editions Ouvrieres.

Cooper C. (1972) *The House as Symbol of Self.* Berkeley: Institute for Urban and Regional Development, University of California (May).

David F. (1982) *Intérieurs d'écrivains* (Home interiors of writers). Paris: Le dernier terrain vague.

Dovey K. (1985) "An Ecology of Place and Placemaking: Structures, Processes, Knots of Meaning." In K Dovey *et al.* (Eds.), *Place and Placemaking.* Melbourne: Proceedings of the PAPER 85 Conference: 93110.

Eleb-Vidal, M. (1989) *Architectures de la rie prirèe.* Bruxelles: AAM.

Eliade M. (1949) *Le mythe de L'éternel retour.* Archtypes et répétition (The myth of the eternal return). Paris: NRF, Gallimard.

Eliade M. (1952) *Images et symboles. Essai sur le symbolisme magico-religieux* (Images et symbols: An essay on magical and religious symbolism). Paris: Gallimard.

Fried M. (1963) "Grieving For a Lost Home." In L Duhl (Ed.), *The Urban Condition.* Basic Books.

Gans H. (1962) *The Urban Villagers: Group and Class in the Life of Italian Americans.* New York: Free Press.

Graumann C. (1988) "Toward a Phenomenology of Being at Home. Looking Back to The Future." Delft, NL: Proceedings of the 10th IAPS Conference: 5665.

Guinzbourg, M. (1924) *Le Style et L'épogue.* Liège, Ed. Mardaga.

Hayward G. (1975) *Home As an Environmental and Psychological Concept.* Landscape. 20:1.

Korosec Serfaty P and Montagna C. (1989) "Demeure et altérité: mise à distance et proximité de l'autre," (The Home: Secret and proximity of the other). *Architecture and Behavior* 5:165177.

Lauman Ed and House J. (1969) "Living Room Styles and Social Attributes: The Patterning of Material Artefacts in a Modern Urban Community." San Francisco, CA: Paper read at the 64th Annual meeting, A.S.A. (August).

Lawrence R. (1987) *Housing, Dwellings and Homes: Design Theory, Research and Practice.* Chichester, New York, Brisbane, Toronto, Singapore: John Wiley & Sons.

Medam A. (1977) "Loger en famille" (Family dwelling). Paris: Cahiers de psychologie de l'art et de la culture: De la construction de l'espace à l'espace de la création. ENSBA (Automne): 6175.

Pevsner, N. (1976) *A history of building types.* London, Thames and Hudson Ltd.

Proshansky H. (1976) "The Appropriation and Misappropriation of Space." Appropriation of Space. Strasbourg: Proceedings of the 3rd IAPS Conference: 3145.

Rapoport A. (1969) *House Form and Culture.* Englewood Cliffs, New Jersey: Prentice Hall.

Rilke R. M. (1977) *Briefe an Nanny WunderlyVolkart* (Letters to Nanny Wunderly Volkart).
Frankfurt: Insel.
Seamon D. (1982) "The Phenomenological Contribution to Environmental Psychology." *Journal of Environmental Psychology,* 2:119140.

Seamon D. (1983) "Heidegger's Notion of Dwelling and One Concrete Interpretation as Indicated by Hassam Fathy's Architecture For The Poor." *Geosciences and Man,* 13.

Sime J. (1985) "Creating Places or Designing Spaces: The Nature of Place Affiliation." In K Dovey *et al.* (Eds.), *Place and Placemaking.* Melbourne: Proceedings of the PAPER 85 Conference: 275292.

Sixsmith J. (1986) "The Meaning of Home: An Exploratory Study of Environmental Experience." *Journal of Environmental Psychology,* 6:281298.

Sopher D.E. (1979) "The Landscape of Home: Myth, Experience, Social Meaning." In D.W. Meining (Ed.), *The Interpretation of Ordinary Landscapes.* New York: Oxford University Press.

Spivak, M. (1973) "Archetypal Space," in *Architectural Forum,* 140, No. 3, 1973, pp. 44-49.

Tuan Y. (1975) "An Experiential Perspective." *The Geographical Review,* 65 (2):151165.

Vernant J.P. (1974) *Mythe et pensée chez les Grecs* (Myth and thought in the ancient Greek culture). Paris: Maspero: (I) 125.

Chapter 5

The Spatial Organization of the Domestic Interior: The Italian Home

M. VITTORIA GIULIANI
Instituto di Psicologia, Consiglio Nazionale delle Ricerche, Roma

GIUSEPPE BOVE
Université di Roma "La Sapienza", Roma

GIUSEPPINA RULLO
Instituto di Psicologia, Consiglio Nazionale delle Ricerche, Roma

The variety of ways of organization and use of the interior of the home has not been investigated much through empirical research. This chapter aims to utilize multivariate analysis based on the theoretical assumption that the main dimension in the ordering of domestic space is the socializing-privacy dimension; and further, that the differences in meaning and use of the dwelling are reflected in this dimension. The results reveal some general 'rules' in the organization of the homes under investigation. A social space is realized even where the dwelling size is small so that the nighttime privacy is not guaranteed for each member of the household. However, when the dwelling size allows for at least one social room, the nighttime privacy for children is guaranteed. The need for a room for the child (or children) is usually the first requirement where there is not. In addition, a general rule is concerned with the presence of two places for eating. The most formal one is used in more 'ritual' occasions, such as taking meals on a holiday or when there are guests.

Introduction

In 1850, Orson S. Fowler, the American phrenologist, sex educator and amateur architect, was putting the finishing touches on a house built on the banks of the Hudson River which was intended to represent the model for a new way of residential life. Octagonal in shape, the house consisted of three storeys and some sixty rooms, "but not one too many", as Fowler himself claimed. The underlying building principles and the technical instructions for the construction are set out in a manual, the main aim of which was "to bring comfortable dwellings within the reach of the poorer classes" (Fowler, 1973, p. 3). One of the main requisites Fowler considered necessary for a comfortable home was a sufficient number of rooms. He uses convincing arguments to explain why every member of the family should have a separate room exclusively to him/herself, and enumerates the advantages of having many places for entertaining friends, a play-room for the children, a gymnastics room for females, a dancing room, and a number of special purposes rooms, such as a sewing room, milk room, pantry, or lumber room.

The organizing principle used by Fowler is obviously that of maximum differentiation of space (Altman and Chemers, 1980). Despite Fowler's recommendations, the size of urban dwellings in the industrialized countries makes it impossible to attain this principle for most of the population, and much less for the poorer among them.

The assignment of one room for each function also clashes with an increasingly strongly felt need, i.e., that of the individual's discretion in using the space. This need involves a territorial organization of the domestic space which tends to extend the individual's spaces to the detriment of the shared spaces (Sebba and Churchman, 1983). In coming to terms with space limitations, the inhabitants are thus obliged to make a number of decisions which will be dependent on the relative importance attributed to the satisfaction of the various needs. The hierarchical ordering of the needs, and therefore also the space-organizing strategies, vary among different cultures (Altman and Gauvain, 1982; Lawrence, 1987) as well as within the same culture, as a function of numerous individual and social factors (Bonnes *et al.*, 1987; Giuliani, 1987).

In Western societies in particular individual differences seem currently to be magnified by socio-demographic changes in household composition (Bonvalet, 1989). A growing number of theoretical and empirical studies argue for the central role of household structure in affecting the meaning and use of the home. However, little empirical evidence is available about the impact of the household structure on the actual organization and use of the domestic space (Rosenblatt and Budd, 1975; Tognoli and Horwitz, 1982; Giuliani and Rullo, 1988; Giuliani, Rullo, and Bacaro, 1989). A major cause of this may be the difficulty experienced in describing the great variety of situations present in the real world, as determined by the interactions between household structure, spatial characteristics of homes, personal values and preferences.

In Italy, average dwelling size has increased over the past thirty years from 3.3 rooms per dwelling in 1951 to 4.2 in 1981 (Ricci, 1986). During the same period average family size dropped from 4.0 to 3.0 (Golini, 1986). In spite of this, the impression is that the home is growing smaller. What Fowler considered to be enjoyable luxuries are increasingly considered as vital needs by the modern urban family, e.g. the needs for social life, entertainment, security, which require a larger space than that currently available (Ragone, 1988).

The present chapter presents a survey about the way different households spatially perform their living activities in an Italian city is analysed. By applying multivariate statistical analysis techniques, some light is shed on the relations between the organization and use of the domestic space, the household type and the spatial characteristics of the dwelling.

Methodology

The subjects

The survey was carried out on 532 households from different districts of Rome[1]. In order to characterize these cases, the main features of the household structure and of the dwellings will be described here. One quarter of the 532 households investigated have two members, followed by three-member (23%) and four-member (22%) households. The remaining 30% are divided up equally between the two extreme values, i.e., one-member and five, or more, member households, respectively. The vast majority of the households consists of nuclear families. In 15% of the households, one or more relatives cohabited with the family. Household types are shown in Tables 5.1 and 5.2.

The dwellings are apartments in medium-rise buildings, except in a very small number of cases. As regards the size of the dwelling, the main indicator used in the analysis, was the number of separate rooms, excluding bathrooms, kitchens and balconies (see Tables 5.3 and 5.4).

---

[1] This set of cases is a part of a stratified random sample of 1484 households. Such a sample was drawn from the population by the CENSIS, charged from the City Council of Rome to carry out a survey of the housing situation in Rome. All the families registered in the City Council of Rome in December 1988 served as the population for the CENSIS survey (Centro studi investimenti sociali, 1989).

V. *Giuliani, G. Bove,* and *G. Rullo*

Table 5.1: Household types

Household type	Tot.(%)
childless couple	18.0
couple with children	52.0
single parent family	9.5
single	15.0
non-family households	5.5
Tot.	100.0

Table 5.2: Number of children per household type (%)

	1 child	2 children or more
couple with chidren	43	57
single parent family	48	52
non-family households	21	3

Table 5.3: Number of rooms in dwellings

N. of rooms	(%)
1	2.5
2	27.0
3	48.5
4	17.0
5 or more	5.0
Tot.	100.0

Table 5.4: Dwelling size (sq.m.) per number of rooms

Rooms	Dwelling size (%)				
	$> 40\ m^2$	$41\text{-}60\ m^2$	$61\text{-}80\ m^2$	$81\text{-}100\ m^2$	$< 100\ m^2$
1	77.0	23.0	0.0	0.0	0.0
2	9.0	57.0	30.0	4.0	0.0
3	0.0	5.5	52.0	37.0	5.5
4	0.0	0.0	5.0	44.0	51.0
5 or more	0.0	0.0	0.0	11.0	89.0

Table 5.5: Inside density

number of people	number of rooms				
	1	2	3	4	5+
one	S	S	L	L	L
two	D	S	S	L	L
three	C	D	S	S	L
four	C	C	D	S	S
five	C	C	C	S	S
more	C	C	C	D	S

Note:

L = Low density (16.0%)

S = Standard (50.0%)

D = High Density (18.5%)

C = Critical high density (15.5%)

The different levels of inside density in each case were also considered. Such a density was estimated on the basis of the ratio of people per rooms suggested by CENSIS, as shown in Table 5.5.

The questionnaire

The closed-end questionnaire focused on three main types of information on the basis in which various possible types of dwelling behavior could be described. The first type refers to the socio-demographic characteristics of the inhabitants, such as the type of household, the number and age of the members, their professional status and educational background. The second type refers to characteristics of the dwelling, i.e. the overall size, the number of rooms and the available facilities, as well as the location of the neighborhood and the type of building. The third type is specifically related to the way in which the home is organized around four main aspects. The first aspect refers to the functional allocation of the various rooms with the emphasis on the structure of and the rules for using the shared spaces. The second is concerned with the habits related to the place where meals are eaten. The eating activity was selected because of its major role in social interaction in Italian culture, both in family interaction and in social exchange with friends or guests. The third aspect is focused on the different patterns of privacy in the home. The feature of the sleeping space of household members was selected because of the primary importance of bedrooms as individual areas. In particular, the availability of private space for the various members of the household and any sharing of the nighttime space were examined. Finally, preference was elicited concerning the designation of a hypothetical extra room, in order to ascertain the unsatisfied needs in each household.

Analysis of data

Different methods were used to analyze the information obtained from the survey. Beyond traditional statistical analysis, multivariate statistical procedures were applied to the data to unify and condense it into a single comprehensive framework the several relationships underlying the observed data.

The data collected, in fact, can be represented by a very large multiway contingency table crossclassifying many categorical variables (i.e. the items considered in the questionnaire). The common approach reducing the multiway table to several two-way tables on which to apply the chi-square test of independence reveals all its limits in this context. First, given that many attributes are involved, the possible two-way tables would proliferate unmercifully. Furthermore many important hypotheses cannot be expressed using two-way tables alone because they ignore higher-order associations, i.e. interactions between 3 or more variables. Thus, it is more appropriate to apply multivariate statistical methods.

A two-phase strategy was adopted. First, an exploratory analysis was carried out using Correspondence Analysis and Cluster Analysis[2] in order to detect both the main patterns describing different dwelling habits (factor dimensions) and the main features of the household typologies. Secondly, Loglinear modelling methods were applied to subsets of variables pointed out by the previous analyses (Bishop, Fienberg and Holland, 1975). This allowed us to perform confirmatory analyses by expressing the relationships between the different variables in each subset.

Results

The way the home is functionally organized and used will be dealt with in two sections. In the first one, a global description of single variables and of their association will be presented. In the second section, different patterns of organization of the domestic space will be identified.

---

[2] The multivariate analyses were carried out using SPAD.N routines (Lebart, Morineau and Lambert, 1987).

Main features in the structuring of the domestic space

The first aspect of interest is the organization of the daytime quarters. In most cases (73%) the daytime living space consists of a single room, mostly in the form of a dual-purpose living-dining room. In 23% of cases there are two or more daytime rooms, and in 4% there was no daytime living space. In 9% of the homes there is a private room (usually a study or a workshop). In all these cases where a daytime private room exists, at least one shared room is present too.

By considering these results together, we can argue that, in general, the need for at least one shared room is very important, while the organization of the space set aside for daytime private use is secondary to that of having at least one shared space. In order to retain this result and use it in the multivariate analysis, a new variable was created by reorganizing the earlier information, based on the ratio between the number of daytime private and shared rooms.

Moreover, two new variables were created on the basis of the structure as well as the function of the shared space (or spaces). In the vast majority of cases (82%) this shared space is organized to allow the family to live in it or to entertain guests. In only 3% of cases is the single shared room considered to be reserved for guests, and in 4% of homes there is both a "formal" room and a room open to the family.

A second feature of interest is the way in which meals are taken. As far as intra-family socializing is concerned, it is significant that practically all (86%) the families take their meals together, i.e. both lunch and dinner, on weekdays and on holidays. The frequency of extra-family socializing tends to be more variable. The vast majority entertain both close friends and guests (81%) to eat, while in several cases only close friends are involved (7%), and in other cases outsiders are always considered as guests (5%).

Another important aspect of interaction during meals is the place where the activity takes place in relation to its temporal aspects (Werner, Altman and Oxley, 1985). Are meals taken always in the same place or is the place changed for reasons of space, comfort or to give a better impression? Changing from an informal place (e.g. kitchen or breakfast room) to a more formal place (e.g. dining or living room) appears to be a further indication of the kind of socializing that occurs in the home.

In one third of the cases, a change of room occurs when outsiders are being entertained, whether or not they are close friends or guests, while in several cases the change occurs only when there are guests (10%). However, it is interesting to note that in several cases (16%) there is a change of place in the case of dinner on a holiday, which is probably felt to be a more ritual occasion than dinner on other days. There is generally a strong tendency to differentiate the place where meals are taken, organizing a more daily and informal place and another more formal one for use on more ritual occasions (Lamure, 1976). On the other hand, in cases where no change occurs, the reason does not seem to be due to the lack of space alone. For instance, in the majority of cases (62%) in which the kitchen is used, there is also another place where meals could be taken.

As far as privacy patterns are concerned, the indicators were the sharing of nighttime space and the availability of a bedroom for the various members of the family.

In addition to the case of couples sharing the bedroom, the sharing of a bedroom by children is the most common situation in families with two or more children (64%). The sharing of nighttime space is often retained to ensure the existence of a social room. Age and sex of children play a very important role in the sharing of their nighttime space. In one quarter of the households, the social room is also used as a bedroom. The percentage of households in which at least one of the members does not have an actual bedroom of their own rises to 43% in families with two or more children. In fact, there are no cases where sisters and brothers aged over twelve share the same bedroom.

Let us conclude this overview with a brief account of preferred ways of using an extra room. It is significant that a comparatively large number of interviewees declared that they did not need any more space (38%). In the higher age group, this percentage rises to 67%. A comparatively large number of individuals (31% of the total) would instead use any extra room as a bedroom for the children. This percentage rises to 70% in families with two or more children. It is interesting to note the low percentage (6%) of choices regarding using the additional space for social purposes compared with the wishes expressed for a more individual space, such as a study or hobby room (13%).

In order to obtain a global description of the set of associations among variables, Correspondence Analysis was performed on a set of 41 variables which had previously been divided up into active variables (17) and supplementary variables (24). While the first set of variables is considered to define different patterns of use and organization of the interior space, the second one allows for a pre-identification of the structural features of the households and dwellings significantly related to these patterns. In this application, the study focused on the first five axes which reproduced 31% of the total information (inertia).

The first two factorial axes were interpreted using the absolute contributions together with two-dimensional graphical representations. The first axis represents a new complex dimension relating the need of space (i.e. preference for an extra room) with both the inside density and the sharing of the nighttime space. The second axis emphasizes the close relationship between the number of rooms and both the number of social rooms and the ratio "social/private" rooms.

Furthermore it emerges from the analysis that the features of dwelling size and inside density interact in determining what people would like as an extra room while only the former seems to have any effect on the availability of social spaces in the home. This result has been confirmed by an additional analysis in which households with only one room were excluded from the set of cases.

Aspects of the information concerning the preference for an extra room and the sharing of the nighttime space by children (termed 'children's privacy') can be further investigated by using a Loglinear modelling approach. In particular it is interesting to investigate if there is any association between the previous variables and the structural features of the household (e.g. educational background, professional status, age, etc.).

In the first analysis a non saturated loglinear model was considered, in order to study the association between the children's privacy (CP), the dwelling size (DS) and educational background (EB). The backward elimination procedure available in the SPSSX program was used and the final model (G=4.29, p=0.36) obtained is:

$$EB \longrightarrow DS \longrightarrow CP$$

An indirect association between EB and CP is thus evident, indicating that sharing of bedrooms is more a function of dwelling size than of educational background. When the phenomenon of sharing is considered separately for both high and low levels, a higher frequency of sharing between different sex children characterizes the high educational level. By contrast, no significant associations were detected in the models considering the professional status.

The second analysis was performed in order to study the association between the preference for an extra room (PER), the educational background (EB), the ratio social/private rooms (RSP), and the age of the head of the family (AGE). This time the backward elimination procedure detects the final model (G=57.4, p=0.42):

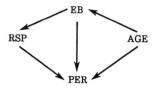

in which all three variables are important in determining the choice of the type of extra room. If the household type (HT) is considered instead of the age, the model (G=45.21, p=0.79) assumes the following form:

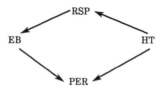

Patterns of organization and households

A detailed characterization of the different patterns of organization of the domestic space was obtained by applying a hierarchical method of cluster analysis in the factorial space of the first five axes. In this way, a 9-group partition was found at a level of 86% for the inter/total inertia ratio. The main features characterizing the groups are summarized in Table 5.6. A more detailed description is presented in the following pages.

The first group (GR 1) is the largest. It consists of 159 households and accounts for 29.89% of the sample. It represents the mean situation since the barycenter of the group is actually located near the origin of the two first axes. The typical layout of the home is represented by a social room (100%) and two (52%) or one (37%) bedrooms. The daytime room is generally a dual-purpose living room, while the daytime private rooms are completely absent. This is the group with the widest scatter of preferences. In fact all possible options are represented in it. In this group the essential needs have probably been satisfied and therefore it is the individual needs related to the life style which emerge more clearly. Very few always have their meals in the kitchen, 30% always eat in the living room, while the majority move from the kitchen to the living room on "ritual" occasions, which include holidays and when outsiders are present. There is practically no sharing of bedrooms except by the couple, also because of the very low percentage of cohabitations or of large family size. The most common type is that of the three-member household (45%), followed by the two-member household (36%). Fifty-two percent of cases consist of couples or a single parent with an only child, and only in 17% of cases are there two or more children. However, in 20% of the cases nighttime privacy is ensured by using a daytime room as bedroom, and this shortage of space is indicated by the choice of using any additional room as a child's bedroom. This type of household model does not seem to be linked to any particular socio-demographic variables. In particular, the age of the head of the family corresponds exactly to the age distribution of the sample.

The second group (GR 2: N=84=15.76%) also occupies a central position as far as the projection on to the factorial axes is concerned. The most typical layout closely resembles that of the preceding group, although the home is smaller in size. Two-room apartments predominate (52%), followed by three-room ones (40%). All homes have a rather small daytime social room. This group differs from the preceding one both in the way the space is used and in its family typology. For instance, it is significant that a rather large percentage of the families always have their meals in the kitchen (37%). It should be noted however that a rather high proportion of the households declare that they never have outsiders to dinner (14%). There are no cases of sharing the nighttime space, except by the couple. The household consists mainly of a single person (58%) or at most two (24%). The typical family could be defined as "residual," with a high percentage of widows. Nearly half the heads of the family (45%) are over 65 years of age. The majority (68%) would have no use for an extra room, although it is interesting to note the importance attached by this group to guest rooms, which is rarely found in other cases. In 11% of the households such a room already exists, while a further 8% would like to have one.

The next two groups (GR3 and GR4) have in common a ratio between social rooms and daytime private rooms which, compared with the other groups, tends to favor private rooms. This is particularly true in the case of GR3. In both cases there is plenty of space available to the occupants. It is interesting to examine the differences between the two groups.

The most common type found in GR3 (N=26=4.89%) is composed of a dual-purpose living room (77%), a study (96%) and one (61%) or two (35%) bedrooms. The daytime social space appears to be used less often; only a very small percentage have all their meals in the living room (19%) and a significant percentage consider this room to be reserved for guests (15%). Despite the abundant space available, nearly 40% would have a use for an extra room, preferably as an exercise or a hobby room. As regards the childrens' privacy, the low percentage of those sharing rooms is probably linked to the comparative absence of children. In those cases in which an extra room would be made into a bedroom for the children there is no sharing and the social room is used also as a bedroom. As regards family type, the group is characterized by the presence of singles under the age of 60 (27%), and by a large number of childless couples (31%). The head of the family tends to be highly qualified (35% have a degree) and to have a correspondingly high professional status.

Like GR3, GR4 (N=17=3.20%) is characterized by the presence of a study (100%) but differs from the latter in that it has two social rooms, one of which is reserved for guests in 35% of the cases. The house itself is quite large, with a terrace, double living room and two or more bathrooms.

Table 5.6: Summary of cluster analysis results

GROUPS	SS. N	SS. %	people	HOUSEHOLD STRUCTURE hous.types	HOUSEHOLD STRUCTURE age	education	DENSITY	home as a whole
1	159	30%	2 or 3	-couples + 1 child -single par. + 1 child	various	-----	-----	2 or 3 rooms: 1 social + 1 or 2 bedrooms
2	84	16%	1 or 2	-couples -widows	elderly	low	-----	idem (but smaller)
3	26	5%	1 or 2	-singles: -couples:	-young or adults -various	high	low	3 or 4 rooms: 1 social + 1 study + 1 or 2 bedrooms
4	17	3%	3 or more	-couples + 1 or more children	adult (middle age)	middle- -high	the lowest	4 or more rooms: 2 social + 1 study + 1 or 2 bedrooms
5	10	2%	4 or more	-couples + 2 or more children	adult	various	-----	2 social + 2 or more bedrooms
6	68	13%	1 or 2 (or more)	-couples -singles	elderly	middle- -high	-----	2 social + 1 or more bedrooms
7	87	16%	4 or more	-couples + 1 or more children -& cohabit.	adult (young age)	middle	standard- -high	1 social + 2 or more bedrooms
8	61	11%	4 or more	-couples + 2 or + ch. -single par. -& cohabit.	adult (middle age)	low	high	2 or 3 rooms: 1 social + 1 or more bedrooms
9	20	4%	1, 2, or more	-singles: -couples + 1 child: -single par.	elderly young	-----	standard- (or high)	-1 single room (50% of cases) -2 or 3 bedrooms

Table 5.6: Continued: Summary of cluster analysis results

| ORGANIZATION OF HOME | | EATING PLACES | | NIGHT PRIVACY | | DESIDERATA |
social rooms	study/work	within-family	with-guests	sharing-bedroom	beds-not-in-bedroom	
1: bifocal	no	-kitch.normally living in holydays -living	living	no, only couple	- no - one child in social room (20% of cases)	- all types - room for children
1	no	kitchen	-living -some people never receive	idem	- - - - -	- 'I don't know' - room for guests
1: bifocal	yes	kitchen	living	- no, only couple - children share (a few)	- - - - -	- hobby room
2: one is reserved for guests	yes, in all cases	dining	living	- no, only couple - young children share (a few)	- - - - -	- 'I don't know'
2: bifocal (1 reserved for guests)	no	dining	living	yes, also children share	- - - - -	- various - room x children (a few cases)
2	no	kitchen	living	no, only couple	- - - - -	- - - - -
1: bifocal	no	kitch.normally living in holydays	- - - - -	yes, also children share	- no - a few in a daytime room	- room x children - study
1	no	-family room -kitchen	family room	yes, 2 or more children share	yes, children in social or other rooms	- room x children
there isn't	no	kitchen	-kitchen -some people never receive	- no - a few children share	- no - a few cases	- social room or a kitchen-living r. - room x children - 'I don't know'

This group has the highest room/occupant ratio and is the one with the highest percentage of occupants (71%) that would not know what to do with an extra room. Furthermore, the entertaining of outsiders to dinner does not change the way the rooms are used as the family itself prefers to have their meals in the dining room. As in GR3 it is rare for the bedroom to be shared by members of the family other than the couple itself, although there are some cases, particularly when there are small children. The most common type of household is that of a couple with one or more children, somewhat on in years and with a medium-high socio-cultural status.

A clear-cut preference for the social use of daytime space is made by the next two groups, GR5 and GR6. Both groups have at least two social rooms and no private daytime room.

In GR5 (N=10=1.88%) priority seems to be given to the social use of space not only over private daytime space but also over private nighttime space. All the families in this group have at least two children. In all cases at least one pair of children shares the bedroom and in only two cases would an extra room be used as a child's bedroom. As in GR4 even the family itself has its meals in the dining room, at least in the evening and on holidays. One of the two social rooms is reserved for guests more frequently than in GR4. More frequently than in the other groups the dining and living room functions are kept spatially distinct. In this group the typical family is rather large, with a head of the family aged less than 60. It has no clear-cut socio-cultural characterization, except for the spouse's high educational level.

GR6 (N=68=12.78%) differs from GR5 in the less formal distinction made between the social rooms, although only 14% customarily have their meals in the dining room and nearly half eat there only when outsiders are being entertained. The household mainly consists of elderly childless couples with a medium-high socio-cultural status.

The next two groups (GR7 and GR8) reflect a situation that is the exact opposite of the latter, particularly as far as inside density is concerned.

GR8 (N=61=11.47%) is characterized (85% of cases) by using daily areas (e.g. family room, but also entrance halls or corridors) also as children's bedrooms and by having two or more children, even of different sexes, share the nighttime space (95%). It is therefore not surprising that an extra room would be used as a children's bedroom (90%). The actual home is rather small (59% with two rooms and 33% three rooms). Meals are often taken in the family room even when no guests are being entertained (34%). The household consists of a couple with children or a single-parent family (16%). In 30% of the cases some form of cohabitation is practiced, in particular with married children. Significant features are the age of the head of the family (46 to 55), and a low educational level, corresponding to a relatively unqualified professional status. This group has the smallest percentage of home owners (29%).

GR7 (N=87=16.35%) differs from the previous group in that the existence of shared bedrooms is accompanied by the use as bedrooms of other domestic spaces only in 9% of cases. The home tends to be larger than in the previous group and the social room is mostly a dual-purpose living room (68%) which the family moves to for meals on holidays. Private daytime rooms are completely absent. Nevertheless the need is felt for them, although to a lesser degree than for a bedroom for the children. The most frequent family type is that of a couple with children. The younger age groups are more strongly represented than in the previous group and in 17% of the cases at least one parent cohabits. The majority of heads of the family and their spouses have at least some higher education, and 30% of them are employed as office workers or teachers.

The distinctive feature of the last group, GR9 (N=20=3.76%) is the complete absence of a daytime social space, separated from the kitchen. In most cases this is the result of the small size of the home, which in 50% of the cases consists of a single room. It probably corresponds, however, in some cases to a decision to give priority to private space, in particular during the night, over social space. In fact, this group includes also homes with two or three rooms and, conversely, not all one-room dwellings are included in it. The need felt for social space is indicated by the decision to use any extra rooms as a living-dining room or in order to extend the kitchen (35% of the cases). Obviously, meals are taken in the kitchen even when guests are present (95%). Moreover, it is not surprising that this is the group with the highest percentage (15%) of those who never invite guests to dinner. The typical family consists of singles (40%), mostly elderly, although there are a few instances of young couples with one child or single-parent families.

Conclusions

The results presented above give food for thought at different levels. From a purely descriptive point of view, the situation concerning dwellings in Rome, as it emerges from the evidence at hand, appears to be characterized by considerable hardship due to the objective lack of space.

The expression of preferences concerning the way a hypothetical extra room would be used, together with the large percentage of the interviewees who declared they did not need an extra room, reveal that the widespread conviction that planning cannot be based on user requests because the latter are excessive and unrealistic is untrue.

Preference analysis interpreted in terms of behaviour with regard to the organization of individual and community space allows several hypotheses to be proposed concerning the hierarchical ordering of spatial requirements.

The first need seems to be to separate the nighttime space of children from that of their parents. This need often clashes with another need, i.e. that of differentiating daytime space from nighttime space. The same room may have to be used both as a daytime social space and an individual nighttime space. The conflict is usually resolved by giving priority to the social function of the space, i.e. the function as bedroom is added to that of living room, while the reverse is extremely rare. Greater differentiations are made as the amount of available space increases. This is true for both daytime space and the ratio between daytime space and nighttime space.

Daytime space may be organized by function (e.g. by separating the dining room area from that of conversation), according to the social designation (by separating a family room from a room for entertaining outsiders), or else according to the individual, as opposed to community, use of the space (by devoting at least part of the nighttime space to a study).

When the daytime space is given priority over the nighttime space the nighttime space is then shared among the other members of the family other than the married couple. Conversely, the tendency to guarantee nighttime privacy to all members of the family leads to a compression of the daytime space, which thus becomes polyfunctional.

From a methodological point of view, the results seem to confirm the adequacy of the system of analysis chosen. By using multivariate analyses it was possible both to describe the relations between the two main variables affecting the organization of the domestic space, i.e. inside density and composition of the household, and to identify a relationship between the organizational models used and family type. However, the Loglinear analyses show that no single sociodemographic variable can be considered as the explanatory variable.

Several patterns of dwelling model development seem to emerge clearly, for instance, the persistent tendency to duplicate the place where meals are taken and a greater need for private spaces inside the dwelling, which are sometimes play related (exercise or hobby room).

References

Altman, I. and Chemers, M.M. *Culture and Environment.* Monterey, CA: Brooks-Cole, 1980.

Bishop, Y.M.M., Fienberg, S.E., and Holland, P.W. *Discrete Multivariate Analysis: Theory and Practice.* Cambridge, Mass.: MIT Press, 1975.

Bonnes, M., Giuliani, M.V., Amoni, F., and Bernard, Y. "Cross-cultural rules for the optimization of the living room," *Environment and Behavior*, Vol. 19, 1987, p. 204-227.

Bonvalet, C. "Evolution des structures familiales et consequences sur l'habitat en France," in N. Haumont et M. Segaud, Editors, *Familles, modes de vie et habitat*, p. 31-53. Paris: Editions L'Harmattan, 1989.

Centro Studi Investimenti Sociali. *La condizione abitativa a Roma.* Roma: CENSIS, 1989.

Fowler, O.S. *The Octagon House: A Home for All.* New York: Dover Publications, 1973.

Giuliani, M.V. "Naming the Rooms: Implications of a Change in the Home Model," *Environment and Behavior*, Vol. 19, 1987, p. 180-203.

Giuliani, M.V. and Rullo, G. "Territorial Organization of Domestic space in Different Types of Households," in H. van Haogdalem, N.L. Prak, T.J.M. van der Voordt, and H.B.R. van Wegen, Editors, *Looking Back to the Future*, p. 353-362. Delft: Delft University Press, 1988.

Giuliani, M.V., Rullo, G., and Bacaro, C. "Structures Familiales et Modeles Territoriaux," in N. Haumont et M. Segaud, Editors, *Familles, modes de vie et habitat*, p. 262-273. Paris: Editions L'Harmattan, 1989.

Golini, A. "La famiglia in Italia: tendenze recenti, immagine, esigenze di ricerca," *Annali di Statistica*, 115, serie ix, Vol. 6, 1986, p. 15-38.

Lamure, C. *Adaptation du logement a la vie familiale.* Paris: Eyrolles Editeur, 1980.

Lawrence, R.J. *Housing, Dwellings, and Homes: Design Theory, Research and Practice.* Chicester: John Wiley & Sons, 1987.

Lebart L., Morineau A., and Lambert T. *SPAD.N: Systeme Portable pour l'Analyse des Donnees*, Version 1.0. Sevres: CISIA, 1987.

Ragone, G. "Case piccole e grandi citta," *Rassegna*, X, 35/3, p. 65-69.

Ricci, R. "Condizioni abitative delle famiglie e politica della casa in Italia," *Annali di Statistica*, 115, serie IX, Vol.6, 1986, p. 283-297.

Rosenblatt, P.C. and Budd, L.G. "Territoriality and Privacy in Married and Unmarried Cohabiting Couples," *Journal of Social Psychology*, Vol. 97, 1975, p. 67-76.

Sebba, R. and Churchman, A. "Territories and Territoriality in the Home," *Environment and Behavior*, Vol. 15, 1983, p. 191-210.

Tognoli, J. and Horwitz, J. "From Childhood Home to Adult Home: Environmental transformations," in P. Bart, A. Chen, and G. Francescato, Editors, *Knowledge for Design*, p. 321-328. Washington, D.C.: Environmental Design Research Association, 1982.

Werner, C.M. "Home Interiors: A Time and Place for Interpersonal Relationships," *Environment and Behavior*, Vol. 19, 1987, p. 169-79.

Part III
The Meaning and Use of Home:
Its Design

The Meaning and Use of Home: Its Design

ERNESTO G. ARIAS
University of Colorado

The purpose of this brief introduction is primarily to provide a definitional context for reading the three chapters of this part and thinking about design with respect to housing. The research presented in this part by Nasar, Arias and Luckey represents a well rounded set of methodological approaches to study implications of design on the meaning and use of housing from their respective concerns — aesthetics, consumer preferences, and functional elements of residential design. Thus, these chapters conceptually view residential design as process and outcome.

Design — What is it?

Comprehensively, design may be viewed as an *activity* and as the consequences or *outcome* from that activity. Therefore, residential design includes settings, processes, and outcomes. Defined in this general manner, residential design includes not only the physical, but also the social, economic, and political dimensions of housing (addressed by other contributions in other parts of this book). However, this introduction focuses on design from a physical perspective, while understanding that its relevancy, both as outcome or process, rests on the other non-physical dimensions which influence and are influenced by design.

As an activity, in the most general sense, all of us design whenever we have a purpose in mind and devise a way to attain it. Yet, there are some definitional differences when we start to view the activity with more rigor,

as it relates to housing. Then its central aim becomes clearly one of intervention toward the resolution of a housing problem. Thus, it is a form of
problem solving process based on *reflection in action* (Schon 1983) and *creativity* (Lang 1987). Design as an outcome can be seen, in turn, as both a
set of design choices, as well as a residential setting. The reason behind this
duality is simply that when we view design's aim as an intervention, outcomes are only decisions (before implementation) which affect and become
part of the setting (once implemented) at a subsequent time in a housing
analysis.

Utilizing this conceptual definition, then various concerns related to the
meaning and use of housing in this part can be put in perspective, e.g.,
Nasar's concerns with aesthetics, Luckey's work on residential elements, or
Arias' interest in decision making and preferences. In addition, the implications and importance of design sensitive to other traditional, procedural
and substantive areas of research in housing may be better understood, e.g.,
the work on housing quality, satisfaction, participation, or decision-making.

The nature of problems in design

The most difficult part of the residential design process as a problem solving
process is defining the problem! A design problem, conceptually speaking,
may be defined as the fundamental difference that exists between "what is"
versus "what should" or "ought to be." While there are fundamentally two
types of problems, tame (have solutions) and wicked (only have resolutions);
as mentioned, those addressed by residential design are ill behaved. These
latter problems conceptually have three fundamental characteristics:

- They are as Simon points out, ill structured (1973), i.e., their context
  changes even as resolution takes place;

- They lack valuative clarity (right/wrong) i.e., they have multiple criteria and are viewed from perspectives which include multiple objectives given the variety and constant flux of the stakeholders in
  housing;

- They have no stopping point, i.e., unlike the tame problem in which
  it is known when the right solution is attained, time deadlines or cost
  and resource limitations are the only references which let us know
  when to stop;

From a more practical point of view, keeping in mind the conceptual
points above, the definition should also include the following attributes
which characterize the "real-world" housing problem:

- *Cause-effect* – this relationship is particularly important in development and evaluations of design alternatives.

- *Intensity* – it is extremely relevant to an understanding of the quantitative and qualitative urgency of a problem.

- *Distributions* – housing problems are dispersed socially across populations and spatially over residential districts or dwelling units with given attributes.

- *Perceptions* – whose problem is it anyway? This innocent question is the center of much of the equity argument in the re-distribution of resources to address housing inefficiencies.

Design as a problem solving activity

As a problem solving activity, the aim of design is to move toward a more favorable future housing state from the problematic present setting; its focus is on intervention in the physical part of the residential environment, but with a knowledge of the implications to the non-physical concerns of housing. The focus in residential design is more likely to be concentrated on the scale of the dwelling or neighborhood. This process takes place within a context of: *uncertainty* due to on-going change; *uniqueness* given that in housing, because of its nature, there is no single right answer; and *conflict* because of different stakeholders who constantly change or change in attitudes, values, and other characteristics (e.g., age, income, education, etc.) are brought into the process since they are either affected by (resident satisfaction) or effect (participatory design) design interventions. Therefore, in this context there are no design solutions, only resolutions since by nature its problems are "wicked" or "ill behaved" ones (Rittel and Weber 1973).

There is a reliance on four characteristics when design is viewed from the definitional context briefly elaborated above. In this context, design as a problem solving activity relies fundamentally on decision making, reflection in action, thinking flexibility, and creativity. Briefly, the reasons behind the necessity for this reliance are:

- *Decision making* — reliance on this characteristic stems from the fact that decision making is fundamental in any problem solving activity. When thinking about design relative to housing, two central requirements of decision making must be interdisciplinarity, given the nature of housing, and implementation. If we accept that the aim of design as a decision-making process is to attain problem resolutions then implementation is a most critical requirement, since it represents the reallocation of resources and a change of behavior.

- *Reflection in action* — by nature, design as an activity aimed at interventions has to be guided by a permanent "feedback" with the problem environment. Reliance on this characteristic is also fundamental if indeed there is to be a movement from "what is" to "what it should be" for any given housing problem.

- *Thinking flexibility* — there has to be reliance on the designer[3] to continuously move backwards and forwards between descriptive, valuative and prescriptive reasoning in order to push the process toward design resolutions. Such movement is evoked by arguments (with herself/himself and others) or by relations with the housing problem. Both, the reflection in action and thinking flexibility are fundamental characteristics of design as a problem solving process given the dynamic nature of housing problems.

- *Creativity* — it is both functional and aesthetic, and its realization is through integration of concepts and forms in new ways which can only be attained when there is an ability to look at the world differently (upside-down) at appropriate times of the process. Thus, reliance on this characteristic is also fundamental to design as a problem solving activity in housing as is demonstrated by the respective concerns of the three chapters in this part. Also, reliance on this characteristic is necessary particularly when decisions have to be made against a background of major constraints and limitations as is the case of many housing situations, e.g., some of the situations described by Altman in his Foreword, or those faced by populations at the margin as van Vliet points out in his chapter.

Design as outcome

As an outcome, it must be understood that once the design choices, decisions, and alternatives are implemented they become part of a housing setting. A setting which is characterized by a set of relationships between design attributes of housing units and attributes of households. Obviously, these relationships are not static over time. On the contrary, they undergo

---

[3]when looking at design as a problem solving activity, designers are all those stakeholders who actively participate in a physical housing intervention for themselves or others.

constant change as a function of changes in characteristics of both the individual and the dwelling unit, e.g., changes in household composition as result of marriages, divorces, births and deaths; and dwelling-unit changes resulting from physical deterioration, renovations, or hazards.

These dwelling unit and household dynamics create incongruities in a housing setting between the housing that people have and the housing they need (Michelson 1977). The degree of excellence to which the setting is capable of attaining the objectives of its primary user group — the residents — in order to bring a closer "fit" between what they have and what they need may be viewed as *quality*. This degree of excellence is a function of both: observable and measurable physical and non-physical attributes of housing, and subjective perceptions as to how well those attributes attain the objectives of residents.

Therefore, design as outcome is a central concern in housing research given its basic relation to the general concept of housing quality. Its importance relative to quality stems from the direct and indirect implications design has on the objective and subjective indicators of quality. Objective indicators are those derived from people's housing environments, and are therefore used in research as descriptors of the physical and social state of a residential setting, i.e., housing attributes which are observable and measurable. Subjective indicators on the other hand, are those derived from people's perceptions of the "fit" between the existing objective attributes of residential environments (social and physical) and their needs, values and attitudes.

In this sense, Luckey and Nasar's chapters view design as an outcome, but focus on physical attributes as objective and subjective indicators respectively. While Luckey focuses on the "corredor" as a residential element which has resulted over time in Costa Rican housing design; the research presented in Nasar's chapter is concerned with aesthetics in terms of resident assessments of the physical outcome. My chapter on consumer preferences and their intensities could be viewed as looking at design as both process and outcome. While it is principally concerned with design as a process fundamentally based on the participants making decisions (designers and residents as the consumer), it is also concerned with preferences made on individual residential elements which are themselves examples of design as outcome. Thus, the work presented in "Connotative Meanings of Housing Styles" and "The Meaning of the Corredor in Costa Rica" are examples of research focusing on design as outcome to inform design as process; while the chapter, "User Groups Preferences and Their Intensity," is an example of research focusing on design as process to inform decision-making and evaluation in housing.

References

Lang, J. (1987), *Creating Architectural Theory: The Role of the Behavioral Sciences in Environmental Design*. New York: Van Nonstrand Reinhold.

Michelson, Wm. (1977), *Environmental Choice, Human Behavior, and Housing Satisfaction*. New York: Oxford Press.

Rittel H.W.J. and M. Weber (1973), "Dilemmas in a General Theory of Planning," in *Policy Sciences*, 4:155-169.

Schon, D.A. (1983), *The Reflective Practicioner: How Professionals Think in Action*. New York: Basic Books Inc.

Simon, H.A. (1973), "The structure of Ill-structured Problems,"in *Artificial Intelligence*, 4: 181-210.

Chapter 6

Connotative Meanings of House Styles

JACK L. NASAR
Ohio State University

This chapter reports studies of the connotative meanings the public infer from various styles of home. It looks at similarities and differences in those meanings across socio-cultural groups and regions, and whether architects share or accurately gauge public meanings. A diverse sample of 118 adults in Columbus, Ohio and 102 adults in Los Angeles rated six styles of home in terms of desirability, and the friendliness and status of assumed residents. 65 architects in Columbus answered the same questions and tried to guess how the Columbus public responded. The public in Columbus and L.A. had the same pattern of connotative response to the houses. Both groups rated Farm and Tudor as most desirable, Mediterranean and Saltbox as least desirable, Farm as most friendly, Colonial as unfriendly, Colonial and Tudor as highest in status, and Saltbox and Mediterranean as lowest in status. Some differences in meaning emerged across various "taste" or socio-cultural groups, and the architects responded differently from and misgauged the public responses.

[0]The author thanks Brian Zaff, Leigh Ann Dunnworth, Jack Duran and Al Rezoski (for their help with the Columbus public data), Marianne Merrick Ziegler (for her data gathering in L.A.) and Tae Sun An, Maria Elene Kambitsi, and Sang Zoon Kwon (for their help with the architect interviews). An earlier version of this paper was presented at the 1988 Environmental Design Research Association Conference in Pomona, California. It was first published in *Environment and Behavior* 21, 3, May 1989, p. 235-257.

Introduction

Low income Colombians living in pre-fabricated housing paint the unit exterior to improve its appearance, before addressing severe problems with insulation or security (Nasar, & deNivia, 1987). Home-buyers are known to select the house they want on the basis of "curb-side" appeal. Part of the failure of Pruitt Igoe has been attributed to its milieu (Newman, 1972). This anecdotal evidence suggests that aesthetics of the house is of central importance. Empirical research confirms this view. For example, studies have found that aesthetics accounted for the highest proportion of variance in resident judgments of the quality of their residential environment and has a major influence on residents feelings of satisfaction with their community (Carp, Zawadasky and Shokrun, 1976; Lansing, Marans, and Zehner, 1970). Public policy initiatives (NEPA, 1969; CZMA, 1972) and decisions by state and federal courts in the U.S. have also recognized the importance of aesthetics (Pearlman, 1988).

Of course, architects have long considered aesthetics a central concern. Research shows that they still focus their attention on the aesthetic merits of certain formal arrangements and styles (Groat, 1982; Hershberger & Cass, 1974). With the rejection of the international style, some architects began promoting Post-Modern architecture, claiming it communicates desired meanings to the public (Jencks, 1977). For example, Scott Brown (1980) talked of the pluralistic values that the architect must satisfy. Venturi (Venturi, Scott Brown & Izenour, 1972) wrote that the public needs "explicit...symbolism," and he described post-modern architecture as carrying the symbolism, "people's architecture as they want it." Although the intent may be admirable, the architecture of these architects may well fail to convey the favorable meanings to the public. Through inclination (McCaulley, 1981), education and experience (Michelson, 1968), architects have developed different values from the public. Thus, they have been consistently found to differ from the public in their evaluations of buildings (Canter, 1969; Hershberger & Cass, 1974; Leff & Deutsch, 1973; Nasar & Kang, 1989 a; Purcell, 1986).

The differences go beyond differences in intensity to differences in direction. Gans (1978) has argued that architects like "high" styles and reject the "popular" styles preferred by the public. When Groat (1982; Groat & Canter, 1979) compared architect and accountant responses to Post-Modern buildings, she found that the two groups used different criteria for evaluating the buildings. The accountants, unlike the architects, did not distinguish between the two styles. The buildings most liked by the accountants were among the least satisfactory to the architects.

Another study which used a more diverse comparison group than accountants found that the educated public judged "popular" styles as the more meaningful, coherent, clear and pleasant, while architects judged "High" styles as the more meaningful, coherent, clear and pleasant (Devlin & Nasar, 1989). A replication in Australia found that the differences occur early. First-year architecture majors preferred the "high" styles and other first-year students preferred the "popular" styles (Purcell & Nasar, 1991). Groat's (1982, p. 20) conclusion still applies: "While certain architects ...may be sensitive to the presence of differing codes among architects and laypeople, they may as yet be ineffective in using that sensitivity for the purpose of conveying intended meanings through architecture." Designs could better meet the aspirations of the public, if the design decisions were informed by information on the symbolic meanings which styles convey to the public.

This is particularly important in situations where the design is approved and paid for by a client, who differs from the eventual occupants. Such clients include corporations, the government, schools and universities. Even in private housing, constraints of cost and availability may limit the ability of buyers or renters to find housing fitting their symbolic aspirations.

What do I mean by symbolic meaning in buildings? Humans experience architecture through mediating variables—properties that relate to the building but are not the building itself. These properties reflect the individual's mental image of the building (Moore, 1989) and associations with that representation and building. These associations can take several forms. Judgments about what a building is (a church, office, or house) or what a style is (modern, post-modern, tudor) represent denotative aspects of meaning. Beyond that, inferences about the evaluative and affective qualities of a building, its use and inhabitants represent connotative aspects of meaning. For example, two houses, which differ only in exterior style—one "Tudor" and one "Farm" style—might be grouped as having the same denotative meaning—single family houses, but they might convey different connotative meanings. Passersby might infer differences in the costs of the houses, and personality, values, and other characteristics of the residents.

In agreement with Lang (1987, p. 204), I define the term symbolic meanings as a result of "a cognitive process whereby an object acquires a connotation beyond its instrumental use." In the case of architecture, then people may infer emotional and other qualities from style or schema. Where the connotative meanings are pleasurable, we can talk about a symbolic aesthetic experience. Of particular importance is what Rapoport (1982) calls pragmatic meaning, the meaning of a style to users. But what is style?

In theory, an individual's experience of an object depends on the interaction between the object's features and the individual's representation in memory of past experience related to that building type (Mandler, 1984). It has been argued that these representations in memory have a hierarchical organization (Rosch, 1977) which moves from a general or superordinate level such as "animal," to a basic level such as "dog," to a subordinate level such as basset hound. Research has confirmed that knowledge structures in relation to the physical environment have a hierarchical organization with each category having associated properties (see Kaplan and Kaplan, 1989 for a discussion of environmental categories). With regard to architecture, buildings would represent a superordinate level, building uses (such as single-family home, suburban office) a basic level, and style within a use a lower level.

Style is dynamic. When a designer first puts together a particular set of physical properties and relationships, that set of properties and relationships, called a formal structure, stands alone (Norberg-Schulz, 1965). As individuals encounter other examples with similar formal structures (or descriptions of the formal structure), they begin to categorize them internally (assign denotative meanings): The instances become examples of a "style." The probability and strength of the style depends on the frequency that the individuals encounter the family of formal structures. With more and more related examples, the probability that individuals construe a style category should increase. A style, then, results from an interaction between an internal prototypical "formal organization" in relation to a system of forms (Norberg-Schulz, 1965). Research confirms this perspective. Groups have been found to set up style categories, and instances in these categories have been found to have unique formal properties (Espe, 1981; Devlin & Nasar, 1988; Groat, 1982; Verderber & Moore, 1977). Recognition of style organizes and simplifies our encounters with our complex surroundings.

Brunswik (1956) offers a useful framework for understanding symbolic meaning in relation to style. He says that we use probabilistic strategies in drawing inferences from environmental cues. Through experience, we evaluate the accuracy of the inferences, and we change. Through repeated and long-term experience with buildings and styles, individuals might learn to associate different meanings with particular building types or styles. The research has confirmed such differences across building types (cf. Kaplan and Kaplan, 1989). Stylistic differences have not been examined. Similar to other models of meaning, such as Rapoport's (1977) cultural filters model and the semiotics model (Lang, 1987), this model differentiates the actual environment from the experienced environment; and it argues that environmental meaning (a product of environmental cues and individual factors such as personal/cultural filters or social contract) results from an individual's experience and interaction with the environment.

This framework suggests that socio-cultural groups with different environmental experience might differ in the symbolic inferences they draw from styles. Their differences in experience would result in different inferences. At the same time, however, these groups may also develop certain shared meanings from common experiences in our culture. The research on architectural meaning provides some tentative support for both shared and idiosyncratic meanings in relation to housing styles.

With regard to differences, Newman (1972) argued that architects and housing professionals misjudge the housing milieu desired by lower income residents. Others have shown that people of different education, income and social class view certain aspects of housing differently (Michelson, 1976; 1987; Royse, 1969; Wethman, 1968). These findings receive further support in historical studies (cf. Cherulnik and Wilderman, 1982), which show the socio-economic segregation of American cities and reveal appearance as a major element used to create neighborhoods appropriate to the status of the intended resident. This pattern of segregated development would give different socio-economic groups different experiences and thus associations with housing appearance.

With regard to commonalties, Venturi and Rauch (1977) speculated that the Colonial style homes meet public aspirations. Research on housing in a New York exurb and Columbus, Ohio confirms the dominance of the Colonial style (Duncan, 1974; Fusch and Ford, 1986). Interviews with residents of six planned communities also found Colonial as preferred to Modern (Lansing, Marans and Zehner, 1970). The findings for Colonial may be biased by selectivity in respondents or in what developers, who have different stylistic preferences from the public (Tuttle, 1983), provide.

Still, other evidence suggests the presence of commonalties. Purcell (1986) showed that the public preferred small discrepancies from a known style. Cherulnlik and Wilderman (1986) found that students discriminated in a consistent fashion between lower-middle and upper-middle class nineteenth-century homes. While these studies did not test responses to style per se, other studies did attempt to manipulate and test responses to style. Kinzy (Langdon, 1982) obtained responses from Buffalo suburbanites to black-and-white elevations of eight popular home-styles. He found that the suburbanites preferred Tudor and Farm to Contemporary and Modern. Ranch, Mediterranean, Early American and Colonial fell in the middle. Tuttle (1983) obtained responses from Wisconsin suburbanites to black-and-white perspective drawings of 24 styles. He found that the suburbanites responded most favorably to Colonial, followed closely by Tudor, Queen Anne, Farm, and Saltbox. Both studies found vernacular styles favored to modern styles, and favorable reactions to Tudor and Farm styles.

While these studies represent important first efforts, they had some

problems. Responses to Kinzy's (Langdon, 1982) use of unrealistic mechan-
ically drawn elevations might not have reflected response to real buildings.
Furthermore, non-stylistic variations in the test homes (their size, number
of stories, presence and size of garage, amount of windows) may have biased
his results. Tuttle's (1983) findings may also have been biased by variation
in non-stylistic factors (such as drawing quality, letters labelling each style,
vegetation and size) across the styles.

This present research sought to reduce such problems. By reconsid-
ering stylistic meaning with different methods, stimuli and respondents it
examined the stability of shared public preferences for Tudor and Farm
styles. This research also extended the work in several ways. First, it
went beyond preference to consider other important symbolic meanings—
perceived status and friendliness. While preference is important (Russell
and Ward, 1981), the public also makes inferences about personal identity,
social status and friendliness from building styles (Cooper, 1976; Duncan,
1973; Rapoport, 1982). Duncan (1973) and Royse (1969) identified the importance of social status inferences drawn from environmental cues. Tuttle
(1983) identified the importance of messages of warmth, friendliness and
invitingness.

Second, it sampled a more diverse and representative group of people
than the suburbanites in the Kinzy (Langdon, 1982) and Tuttle (1983)
studies. This allowed a test of whether the styles conveyed similar meanings
to a diverse group of observers. In light of the extensive empirical evidence
of commonalties in aesthetic values (cf. Nasar, 1988), I expected to find
some shared meanings.

The sample also allowed tests of differences in meaning across the groups
by age, education, occupation, gender and environmental experience. Because of likely differences in their local experience, various socio-demographic
groups were expected to have some idiosyncratic patterns of meanings.

Third, it obtained responses from individuals in two cities—Los Angeles
and Columbus, Ohio to allow a comparison of responses across cities. These
cities differ in many ways including their size, climate, building materials,
housing costs and ethnicity. Size of city has been found to influence one's
experience of the environment (Wohlwill and Kohn, 1973). Differences in
local architecture (the product of such things as climate, materials and culture) may also create different expectations and inferences from the styles.
This may account for some of the differences in the findings of Tuttle (1983)
and Kinzy (Langdon, 1982) in Wisconsin and New York respectively. With
the differences in climate, available building materials, costs and culture of
Los Angeles and Columbus, the likelihood that these cities would develop
similar housing seems remote. One study that compared house-styles in
Columbus with those in San Diego, a neighbor of Los Angeles found dif-

ferences. The predominant house-styles in Columbus, Ohio was Colonial, while the predominant house-style in San Diego was Contemporary Garage Dominant L (Fusch and Ford, 1986). Thus, I expected the comparison of house-style meanings in the two cities to reveal differences as a result of unique local experiences.

Fourth, this study reconsidered architect responses to the styles. Architects were asked for their preferences and meanings. I expected the consistent findings of differences between architects and non architects to be confirmed (Devlin & Nasar, 1989; Groat, 1982; Groat & Canter, 1979; Hershberger & Cass, 1974; Leff & Deutsch, 1973; Purcell, 1986). But, the research also tested a more relevant question: Do architects accurately gauge public preferences and inferences from styles? Remember the Post-Modernists, claim to be conveying desirable messages to the public through design, while researchers have claimed that the architects' image of user values is inaccurate (Michelson, 1968; Newman, 1972). Given the differences in educational experience, motivation, and personality style between architects and the public (Hershberger & Cass, 1974; McCaulley, 1981; Purcell, 1986), I expected to find that the architects misjudged the public meanings. The research also considered how well architects gauged the responses of their architectural peers. Here, professional norms and similarities in education were expected to produce accurate guesses.

In sum, this research had the following hypotheses with regard to symbolic meanings of styles in single-family homes:

1. Home styles would convey meanings to the public, and in particular, the previously found preference for Tudor and Farm styles would show stability.

2. There are regional (experiential) differences in stylistic meanings.

3. There are differences in symbolic meanings across socio-demographic groups.

4. Architects see different meanings from the public.

5. architects misjudge public meanings.

6. Architects accurately accurately gauge inferences made by their local peers.

Method

Respondents

Three groups participated in this research: 102 adults in Los Angeles; 118 adults in Columbus, Ohio; and 65 architects in Columbus, Ohio. Interviewers contacted the architects at 12 randomly selected architectural firms in Columbus, Ohio. For the other respondents in Columbus and Los Angeles, students and I selected several census tracts, each with populations of distinct socio-demographic characteristics (such that one tract had more blue collar families, another had more elderly empty-nesters, another had more well-educated professionals and so on). Then, within each census tract we chose one supermarket as an interview location. At these sites, at various times of day and days of the week male and female interviewers approached every other passerby of the opposite sex of the previous interview.

The samples of the public in each city included a diversity of people, but the samples had similar distributions to one another in gender (45 % male, 55 % female), education (16-18 % high school graduate, 27-31 % some college, 23-29 % college graduate, and 24-32 % more education), and occupation (15-17 % blue collar, 22-25 % technician/aid, 27-30 % sales/administrator, 22-25 % professional, and 6-7 % student). The Los Angeles sample had a higher proportion of respondents age 18-34 (62 %) than did the Columbus sample (48 %), and a lower percentage of people age 35-49 (18 %) than in Columbus (18 %). Otherwise the distributions for ages 50-64 (18-19 %) and for 64+ (3 %) were similar.

The Columbus architects had a higher proportions of males (83 %), well-educated (35 % college graduate, 65 % more), professionals (100 %) than did the sample of the Columbus public. This difference, however, reflects differences in the demographic characteristics of the profession and the public. The sample of architects also included a variety of practice experience. 41 percent had been in practice for 0 - 7 years, 19 percent for 8-15 years, and 30 percent for more than 15 years.

Procedure

Six styles of homes were selected from among the hundreds of artists renderings for a plan service (Home Planners, Inc., 1986) to represent Farm, Tudor, Mediterranean, Saltbox, Colonial and Contemporary styles. The homes were all two-story detached houses. Beyond that, they were selected such that they were similar in view, size, height and number of windows. Through manipulations of photocopies, other features, such as vegetation and shading of the picture, were controlled such that the homes were alike except for the stylistic differences. Figure 6.1 shows the six styles. As black and white pictures, these styles were mounted unlabeled on 4" x 6" cards for the study.

Interviewers told participants that we were studying housing evaluation. They shuffled and gave each participant the six cards displaying the house styles, informed them that there were no right or wrong answers and told them we were only interested in their honest opinions. Interviewers neither showed nor told respondents the labels for any style.

Interviewers asked questions designed to tap three aspects of meaning: evaluation, friendliness, and status. To strengthen external validity, the questions were designed to put the respondent into a realistic decision-making scenario. For preference, participants were told to imagine winning the "Dream House Lottery" and having to choose the home to receive for free. They were asked to place the homes in order from the most desirable to the least desirable.

For perceived friendliness, they were told to imagine having a flat-tire on a street with the six houses. They were asked to rank order the homes in terms of which they would feel most comfortable approaching for help.

For perceived status, they were told to assume that the residents worked together, and participants were asked to rank order the homes in terms of which resident would take charge and lead the group.

Before each question, interviewers reminded participants that the size, cost, layout and location of the homes were equal. The interviewers re-shuffled the cards before each question, and they varied the order of questions at random for each respondent. After the home-style questions were answered, interviewers asked respondents to fill out a form requesting socio-demographic information.

The architects were asked the same questions, but in addition, they were asked to guess the public responses to the questions and to guess how other local architects would respond. Architects were also asked if they believed there to be differences in preference across different socio-economic classes.

Results

The individual responses to each home were coded according to rank from 1 (most favorable) through 6 (least favorable) on each scale separately. Where there were ties, each style was assigned the score of the mean of the tied ranks. For example, if two homes were classified as second most friendly, they were coded as 2.5, and the next highest rank was coded as 4. Non-parametric analyses were used to analyze these rank-order data.

Farm

Colonial

Salt Box

Figure 6.1: The six house styles tested

Note: Clockwise from the top left the styles are Farm, Contemporary, Mediterranean, Tudor, Salt Box, and Colonial. ©Home Planners, Inc. (1986).

Contemporary

Mediterranean

Tudor

Figure continued from opposite page.

Shared Meaning

Do different styles convey different symbolic meanings? As shown in Tables 6.1, 6.2 and 6.3, the results indicate that they do. Table 6.1 presents the statistics and rank order of the styles for each respondent group in terms of desirability. Tables 6.2 and 6.3 show similar information for perceived friendliness and status respectively.

Consider the public ratings of desirability (columns 1 and 2 in Table 6.1). For both the L.A. and Columbus public, the results indicate significant differences in desirability across the styles. Respondents in each city ranked the Tudor and Farm as the most desirable. These styles accounted for 46 percent and 51 percent of the first place ranking in Columbus and Los Angeles respectively. Mediterranean and Saltbox ranked as significantly less desirable than any other style. Saltbox alone accounted for 42 and 35 percent of the last place rankings.

The results for public ratings of friendliness (Table 6.2) and status (Table 6.3) also reveal significant differences across the styles. Laypersons in each city ranked the Farm style as the one most comfortable to approach for help. It accounted for 44 percent of the first place rankings in each city. They ranked Colonial and Contemporary as least friendly. These styles accounted for 57 percent and 47 percent of the last place scores in Los Angeles and Columbus respectively. With regard to status, respondents ranked Colonial as the most likely to house a leader. It accounted for 66 percent and 42 percent of the first place rankings in Los Angeles and Columbus respectively. They ranked Saltbox as significantly less likely than any other style style to house leaders. It accounted for 38 percent and 43 percent of last place rankings in each city. Inspection of the architect responses on each scale also indicates significant differences across the styles in desirability, friendliness, and leadership.

Thus, the results indicate the variations in home-style do produce differences in symbolic meanings inferred from those styles. Now, we turn to the second question: Do respondents from different cities differ in the meanings they associate with the styles?

The results indicate that the L.A. and Columbus lay respondents did not differ. Instead, they exhibited strikingly similar pattern of response to the styles. Compare the rankings of the styles between these two groups. For desirability and status (Tables 6.1 and 6.3), the rankings had only one minor difference: Tudor and Farm tied for most desirable in Columbus, and ranked first and second in Los Angeles. For friendliness, Los Angeles respondents rated Saltbox lower and Contemporary higher than did Columbus residents.

Previous studies had found favorable responses to Tudor and Farm style homes. This present findings confirmed the stability of that preference.

Overall, the public in each city responded most favorably to Tudor and Farm, and least favorably to Mediterranean and Saltbox. Responses to Colonial varied. It ranked highest in status, neutral in desirability, and lowest in friendliness.

In sum, respondents in each city showed consistent patterns of response to the styles, responding most favorably to Farm and Tudor and less favorably to Mediterranean and Saltbox. In spite of these commonalties, we can not assume that groups within each city respond alike. In the next section, we will consider socio-demographic differences in response.

Socio-demographic differences

Recall that socio-demographic groups were expected to exhibit differences in their responses to the styles. The sample of respondents in each city was split into groups by education, occupation, age, sex, locations of childhood home and length of residence, and the responses of each group were compared. The results reveal differences in response across the various groups.

First consider the results for the Columbus public. Most differences emerged in relation to the Colonial and Contemporary styles. In agreement with Newman (1972) and Venturi and Rauch (1977), the desirability of Colonial increased as education level decreased and as occupational class decreased from Blue Collar to Technician/aid to Professional ($\chi^2 = 11.22$, 3df, $p < 0.01$; $\chi^2 = 10.72$, 3df, $p < 0.05$). Colonial was judged as friendlier by respondents between 35 and 49 than by either younger or older groups $\chi^2 = 6.30$, 3df, $p < 0.0$). In contrast to Colonial, the desirability and perceived status of Contemporary increased with education level ($\chi^2 = 12.30$,3df, $p < 0.01$; $\chi^2 = 8.72$, 3df, $p < 0.05$) and occupational class, from Blue Collar to Technician/aide to Professional ($\chi^2 = 8.42$, 3df, $p < 0.01$), but decreased with increases in age ($\chi^2 = 8.56$, 3df, $p < 0.05$). Respondents who grew up in a suburb ranked Contemporary as more desirable than did respondents who grew up in rural or urban settings ($\chi^2 = 12.14$, 3df, $p < 0.01$)

Females judged Farm as more desirable than did males ($Z = 2.40$, 1df, $p < 0.05$), and respondents older than 50 judged Farm as slightly more desirable and friendly than did their younger counterparts ($\chi^2 = 5.23$, 3df, $p = 0.07$; $\chi^2 = 6.60$, 3df, $p < 0.05$). The longer respondents lived in Columbus, the more likely they were to attribute high status to residents of the Farm-style home ($\chi^2 = 6.57$, 3df, $p < 0.05$).

Technicians/aids ranked the Mediterranean as less desirable than did either Professional/Administrators or Blue collar workers ($\chi^2 = 15.01$, 3df, $p < 0.01$). The oldest group of respondents ranked the Mediterranean residents as slightly more friendly and the Tudor residents as slightly less friendly than did other age groups ($\chi^2 = 5.14$, 3df, $p = 0.07$; $\chi^2 = 5.41$,

Table 6.1: Rankings of styles for desirability

L.A. Public (n = 102)			Columbus Public (n = 118)			Columbus Architects (n = 65) Guess of public			Own judgments		
Tudor	2.08	a#	Tudor	2.42	a	Colonial	1.94	a	Contemporary	1.77	a
Farm	2.52	b	Farm	2.41	a	Tudor	2.72	b	Farm	2.74	b
Contemporary	2.54	b	Contemporary	2.74	b	Contemporary	2.82	b	Colonial	2.80	b
Colonial	2.70	b	Colonial	2.88	bc	Farm	2.94	b	Tudor	3.08	b
Medit.	3.84	c	Medit.	3.67	c	Saltbox	3.80	c	Saltbox	3.75	c
Saltbox	4.34	d	Saltbox	3.92	c	Medit.	3.83	c	Medit.	3.89	c
Kruskal Wallis χ^2 (5df) = 34.44**			82.77**			57.16**			66.27**		

** $p < 0.01$

(Means; 1 = most desirable, 6 = least desirable)

For any group, means with the same letter are not significantly different.

Table 6.2: Rankings of styles for perceived resident friendliness

L.A. Public (n = 102)			Columbus Public (n = 118)			Columbus Architects (n = 65)					
						Guess of public			Own judgments		
Farm	1.66	a#	Farm	1.95	a	Farm	2.03	a	Saltbox	2.42	a
Tudor	2.79	b	Saltbox	2.86	b	Saltbox	2.55	ab	Farm	2.54	ab
Contemporary	3.13	bc	Tudor	3.05	bc	Medit.	2.65	b	Medit.	2.97	abc
Saltbox	3.24	bc	Medit.	3.37	c	Contemporary	3.18	c	Contemporary	3.09	bc
Medit.	3.37	c	Colonial	3.38	c	Tudor	3.32	c	Tudor	3.20	c
Coonial	3.89	d	Contemporary	3.41	c	Colonial	4.40	d	Colonial	3.83	d
Kruskal Wallis χ^2 (5df) = 23.72**			63.60**			35.16**			28.74**		

** $p < 0.01$
(Means; 1 = most desirable, 6 = least desirable)
For any group, means with the same letter are not significantly different.

Table 6.3: Rankings of styles for perceived resident status

L.A. Public (n = 102)			Columbus Public (n = 118)			Columbus Architects (n = 65)				
						Guess of public			Own judgments	
Colonial	1.13	a#	Colonial	1.59	a	Colonial	1.28	a	Saltbox	1.51	a
Tudor	1.81	b	Tudor	1.97	b	Contemporary	2.06	b	Farm	1.88	a
Contemporary	3.22	c	Contemporary	2.14	b	Tudor	2.20	b	Medit.	2.42	b
Farm	3.29	c	Farm	3.80	c	Farm	4.00	c	Contemporary	3.69	c
Medit.	3.98	d	Medit.	4.06	c	Medit.	4.18	c	Tudor	4.09	cd
Saltbox	4.61	e	Saltbox	4.47	d	Saltbox	4.29	c	Colonial	4.45	d
Kruskal Wallis χ^2 (5df) = 115.93**			311.01**			190.83**			169.2**	

** $p < 0.01$

(Means; 1 = most desirable, 6 = least desirable)

\# For any group, means with the same letter are not significantly different.

3df, p = 0.06). The desirability of Saltbox increased with the age of the respondent (χ^2 = 8.22, 3df, p < 0.05).

In Los Angeles, fewer socio-demographic differences emerged. There were no significant differences in response by education, occupational class, or years of residence. However, younger respondents rated Farm as higher status and Meditteranean as lower status than did older respondents (χ^2 = 6.74, 2df, p < 0.05; χ^2 = 5.16, 2df, p < 0.05). Comparisons by gender revealed one difference: As in Columbus, females judged Farm as friendlier than did males (Wilcoxon Z = 2.73, 1 df, p < 0.01). Comparisons by childhood home revealed that respondents who had lived in suburbia as a child judged Tudor as more desirable than did those who had lived in urban or rural locations (χ^2 = 7.00, 2df, p < 0.05).

In sum, the results indicate some differences in response across various socio-demographic groups to select styles. However, the results do not show strong and consistent patterns of differences across the various groups. Now, let us turn to a specific socio-cultural group, the architects.

Architect comparisons

Recall that there were three questions with regard to the architects: Would their responses differ from those of the public? Would they misjudge the responses of the public? Would they accurately gauge the response of their local peers? The answer to each question is yes.

The architects differed from the public in the meanings they inferred from the styles. In tables 6.1 through 6.3, compare the Columbus architect (column 4) and public rankings (column 2) of the styles. These rankings differ on two of the three scales. Statistical comparisons of responses to each style revealed that the Columbus architects in comparison to the Columbus public ranked Contemporary as more desirable, Tudor as less desirable, (Z= 2.62, p < 0.01; Z=3.52, p < 0.01), Farm and Colonial as less friendly (Z=2.36, p < 0.05; Z=1.88, p=0.06), and Saltbox as more friendly (Z=1.88, p = 0.06).

The architects also misjudged public preferences. When asked if there were socio-economic differences in response, the architects unanimously agreed that such differences did exist. Yet, as can be seen in columns 2 and 3 of the tables, the architects systematically misjudged the public responses, underestimating the desirability of Farm and the friendliness of Colonial to the public (Z = 2.08, p < 0.05; Z = 3.19, p < 0.01), and overestimating the friendliness of Mediterranean and the desirability and status of Colonial to the public and (Z = 3.19, p < 0.01; Z = 3.77, p < 0.01; z = 2.36, p < 0.01).

Finally, the results indicate that the architects accurately judged their peer responses. They only misjudged two items, underrating the friendliness of Tudor and Saltbox to their peers (Z = 2.15, 1 df, p < 0.05; Z = 2.25, 1 df, p < 0.05).

Thus, the results confirm that the architects have different preferences from the public and, more importantly, they misjudge public preferences and meanings. They have a good idea of the stylistic meanings to their architectural peers, however.

Discussion

It was particularly striking that people gave immediate answers to the questions about meaning. Such rapid judgments not only about the desirability of a style but also about the qualities of the likely residents suggest that people have robust mental images or knowledge structures with regard to house-style, and that style may have immediate and strong impacts on building meaning. Whether the inferences are accurate or not, they may well influence behavior, not only affecting purchase or rental decisions, but also affecting the degree to which people visit and spend time in areas of a certain stylistic character. Research suggests that inferences about residents from home exteriors are accurate (Cherulnik & Wilderman, 1986; Sadalla, Vershure and Burroughs, 1987): The cues chosen by the resident to reflect their personality communicate that message to others.

The results revealed clear differences in preference and meaning associated with different stylistic content. They also revealed shared meanings, with stability across two geographically, culturally and environmentally distinct cities. Speculation about the desirability of Colonial (Venturi and Rauch, 1977) received partial support. In both cities, Colonial ranked in the middle in desirability and low friendliness, but ranked highest on perceived resident status. Its ratings improved for respondents with less education, occupational status, older ages, and urban or rural residents.

Other styles scored better. In particular, the results support the stability of popular preferences for Tudor and Farm styles (Langdon, 1982; Tuttle, 1983). In both cities, Farm and Tudor emerged as the most desirable. Presumed residents of the Farm style were ranked as friendly and middle in status, while Tudor residents were judged as high in status and moderately friendly.

These findings may not generalize to other kinds of buildings. For example, response to Tudor style may vary depending on whether it occurred in single family housing, row housing or a garden apartment. For urban design, it is the streetscape of one style or multiple styles that takes on importance; and clearly further research is needed to examine the impact of various streetscapes on human preferences and inferences. Building type or use has an important influence on public reactions to buildings (Groat and Canter, 1979) such that evaluative criteria vary with building type (Michelson, 1976). People may respond differently to a Tudor style in an office, home or gas station. Some confirmation for this can be found in a study of stylistic meanings in suburban offices (Nasar, & Kang, 1989 b) which found more favorable response to an abstract style than had occurred in the housing studies. The findings that inferences relate to style points to the need for further study of stylistic meanings in other building types. One important implication of these findings, then, is that in designing buildings such as dorms and public housing, where the client and occupant differ, the stylistic aspirations of the occupants should be gauged.

I did not test the six styles to see if they represented styles salient in the perception of respondents or a realistic cross-section of styles that people would encounter and recognize in their surroundings. For purposes of applications, the styles tested should be salient in respondents' perceptions. In fact, a study completed after the present research (Kang, 1990) suggests that most of the styles are salient in public perceptions of styles, but that a more complete set of perceptually relevant styles would have included other styles. Kang (1990) first selected forty-five prototypes (representing 15 stylistic categories derived from a historical analysis, examination of developer housing, and interviews with builders). He displayed these homes in color photographs (controlled through the use of computer image capture technology, so that they were alike in all ways except style, and they still looked like color photographs of real houses). Analysis of Q-sorting of these styles by thirty undergraduates in Columbus, Ohio produced 10 distinct salient clusters. Five of his clusters—Farm, Greek Revival, Spanish, Georgian/Tudor, Garrison Colonial—fit five styles in the present study— Farm, Colonial, Meditteranean, Tudor, and Saltbox. Additional clusters included French, International (which may be similar to Contemporary), Post-modern, Queen Anne, Italianate, and Federal. Thus, within a subset of salient styles, the present results may have applicability.

However, the styles were not tested to see if they represented good examples of each style to the public. If they vary in perceived typicality, this might confound the results. Typicality has been found to influence preference (Purcell, 1987). Comparing the styles to the best examples derived in Kang's (1990) study, it seems likely, that the styles (with one exception, which I will discuss later) are good examples. Beyond that, the homes have been marketed and published by a national plan service and purchased under the labels. A post hoc survey of four graduate students confirmed that all but the Mediterranean were good examples of each style. The problem with Mediterranean was confirmed in Los Angeles where some respondents did not recognize it as such. Furthermore, when compared to the Spanish group in Kang's (1990) study, the Meditteranean style lacks some distinctive features of the style, such as the arches. However, the results for the other styles may well have applicability.

Unexpectedly, one scale produced remarkably consistent responses: the perceived status of residents. All groups and responses ranked Colonial first, Tudor second, Contemporary third, Farm fourth, Mediterranean fifth and Salbox last. The convergent results for status suggests that our schemas for status in housing are robust, resistant to change. This speculation receives support from Cherulnik and Wilderman's (1986) finding that contemporary observers accurately judged the status of residents in homes from over 80 years ago! The findings for status also suggest that where status is a design goal, the decisions by the architect may convey the expected message.

While respondents were not queried for reasons, the pattern of results and the character of the styles suggest some tentative explanations for the meanings. Consider the findings for status. The large columns on the Colonial, the stained-wood ornament on the Tudor and the brick on both may have been cues to status, but styles may also call up associations with Great Britain and the royalty, and in the case of Colonial with Southern plantations, Monticello or the White House. While local forms may affect these association, I suspect that an examination of the content of mass-media advertising and entertainment would find Colonial and Tudor elements used more often than others in association with high status objects. The styles that ranked low in status—Meditteranean and Saltbox–are simpler. The materials and absence of ornament may have led respondents to see them as cheaper and lower status.

With regard to friendliness, the favorable ratings for Farm style as a place to go for help may have been cued by the protected porch. All the homes have protected entries, but Farm's porch affords the most protection. Farm may also have benefitted from associations with an easier-going life in rural/farm locations.

The public's judgments of desirability may depend on perceptions of friendliness and status. Consider the most desirable styles: Tudor and Farm. The first ranked high on status and neutral on friendliness, and the second ranked high in friendliness but neutral in status. Colonial, which ranked first in status but last in friendliness, ranked in the middle in desirability. These findings considered in light of Purcell's (1986) schema discrepancy model suggest that slight variations on the Tudor or Farm style might yield highly favorable meanings to the public.

The results also confirmed differences in response by various sociodemographic groups. Of course, some of the socio-demographic factors are interrelated. In Columbus, for example, education and occupational group are related ($\chi^2 = 115.10$, 20df, p < 0.01); males have higher level occupations than females ($\chi^2 = 11.92$, 5 df, p < 0.05); and people growing up in a suburb have more education than others ($\chi^2 = 16.39$, 8df, p < 0.05). Nevertheless, the differences support the view that meanings are affected by experience. The Contemporary style, the architect's favorite, was valued more by well-educated young, professionals like themselves than by others.

Beyond that and in agreement with Michelson (1968), the architects misjudged public values. The structure of the errors is informative. Architects guessed that the public would most like Colonial, a style which according to the architects, the public would see as unfriendly but high in status. Note that the architects rated their own first choice—Contemporary—in a similar way, unfriendly but high in status. Did their misjudgments of public preferences result from a misjudgment of the relative importance of status vs. warmth to the public? Could this result in part from their clients, who in seeking architectural advise, are also seeking a status design? These questions takes on added importance in light of the architects accurate guesses of status judgments by the public and are questions worth pursuing in further research.

Sales figures for the homes in this research shed further light on the architect errors. The 1986 Ohio sales orders for homes matched the Columbus public rankings on status and the architects' guesses at public preferences: Colonial (25), followed by Tudor (16), Contemporary (12), Farm (6), Mediterranean and Saltbox (0,0). The sales rankings in California—Contemporary (28), followed by Colonial (15), Farm (7), Tudor (6), Mediterranean (2) and Saltbox (0)—and in the nation—Colonial (312), followed by Contemporary (299), Farm (193), Tudor (30), Saltbox (26) and Mediterranean (12)—differ from those in Ohio, but the California sales, like those in Ohio, echo the status rankings.

This could be taken as evidence that the architects know the public preferences, but such a view neglects variations in the plans, the unique population buying the plans and the unique purposes (vacation home) for which some of these homes are built. Still, the figures may hold a clue to the architects' misjudgments. The profile of the average buyer—39 year old, male, married with one to two children and an income of 60 thousand dollars a year–may fit the profile of many clients of architectural services. If so, the architects may have learned and accurately guessed stylistic preferences of clients but inaccurately assumed those preferences to apply to the public.

This research raises a number of questions. Did the drawings accurately depict the schema for each style? How well do the findings generalize to other examples of the styles? To on-site response? Will the similarities found for Los Angeles and Columbus emerge for other cities in the U.S.?

At what age do we form stylistic inferences? (I received a letter from someone who tested the styles on their five year old daughter who gave the same rankings as the adult respondents.) How do these inferences change during the life-span? How would individuals respond to neighborhoods or blocks of each style, or to mixtures of styles? What meanings do people infer from styles in other building types, particularly prominent or public buildings such as offices, libraries or civic centers?

Given the architects' misjudgments of public responses, however, the value of further inquiry into stylistic meaning is evident. In general, it can help delineate the ways in which architectural style can be used to create meaningful and desirable public places. For specific projects, rather than relying on the inaccurate judgment of an architect, clients can use consumer-research to select and create designs conveying the image they desire.

References

Brunswik, E. (1956) *Perception and the representative design of psychological experiments.* Berkeley: University of California Press.

Canter, C. (1969) "An intergroup comparison of connotative dimensions in architecture." *Environment and Behavior*, 1, 37-48.

Carp, F. M., Zawadski, R.T. & Shokron, H. (1976) "Dimensions of urban environmental quality." *Environment and Behavior*, 8, 239-264.

Cherulnik, P.,D. and Wilderman, S.K. (1986) "Symbols of status in urban neighborhoods: Contemporary perceptions of nineteenth-century Boston." *Environment and Behavior*, 18, 604-622.

Coastal Zone Management Act. (1972) 1451 (CZMA 302). Congressional hearings, and 1452 (CZMA 303) "Congressional declaration of policy." Public Law 89-454 Title II, 302 and 303 as added Public Law 92-583.

Cooper, C. (1976) "The house as a symbol of self." In J.Lang, C. Burnette, W. Moleski, and D. Vachon (eds.) *Designing for Human behavior: Architecture and the behavioral sciences.* Stroudsburg, PA: Dowden, Hutchinson & Ross, Inc.

Devlin, K. & Nasar, J. L. (1989) "Beauty and the beast: Some preliminary comparisons of "Popular" vs."High" residential architecture and public vs. architect judgments of same." *Journal of Environmental Psychology*, 9, 333-344.

Duncan, J. Jr. (1973) "Landscape taste as a symbol of group identity: A Westchester County Village." *The Geographical Review*, 63, 334-355.

Espe, H. (1981) "Differences in perception of national socialist and classicist architecture." *Journal of Environmental Psychology*, 1, 33-42.

Fusch, R. & Ford, L. (1986) "Architecture and the geography of the American City." *The Geographical Review*, 79, 324-340.

Gans, H. (1978) "Towards a human architecture: A sociologist view of the profession." *Journal of Architectural Education*, 2, 26-31.

Groat, L. (1982) "Meaning in Post-Modern architecture: An examination using the multiple sorting task." *Journal of Environmental Psychology*, 2, 3-22.

Groat, L. & Canter, D. (1979) "Does Post-Modernism communicate." *Progressive Architecture*, 12, 84-87.

Hershberger, R.G. & CASS, R. (1974) "Predicting user responses to buildings." In D.H. Carson (ed.) *Man-Environment Interactions*, EDRA 5, pp. 117-143.

Home Planners, Inc. (1986) "Two Story Homes." Farmington Hills, Mich.

Jencks, C. (1977) *The Language of Post-Modern Architecture*. New York, Rizzoli.

Kang, J. (1990) *Symbolic inferences and typicality in five taste cultures*. Unpublished dissertation, Columbus, Ohio: The Ohio State University.

Kaplan, R. & Kaplan, S. (1989) *The Experience of Nature: A Psychological Perspective*. New York: Cambridge University Press.

Lang, J. (1987) *Creating Architectural Theory: The Role of the Behavioral Sciences in Environmental Design*, New York, NY: Van Nostrand Reinhold Co.

Langdon, P. (1982, April 22) "Suburbanites Rating House Styles," *New York Times*, p. C12.

Lansing, J.B., Marans, R.W. & Zehner, R.B. (1970) *Planned Residential Environments*. Ann Arbor, MI: The Survey Research Center, University of Michigan.

Leff, H. & Deutsch, P. (1973) "Construing the physical environment: Differences between environmental professionals and lay persons." In W. Preiser (ed.) *Environmental Design Research*: Vol. 1 Selected Papers EDRA 4, pp. 284-297. Stroudsburg: Dowden, Hutchinson & Ross.

Mandler, J.M. (1984) *Stories, Scripts and Scenes: Aspects of Schema Theory.* Hillsdale, N.J.: Erlbaum Associates.

Mccaulley, M.H. (1981) *Jung's Theory of Psychological Types and the Myers-Briggs Type Indicator.* Gainesville, Fla: Center for Applications of Psychological Types.

Michelson, W. (1968) "Most people don't want what architects want." *Transaction*, 5, 8, 37-43.

Michelson, W. (1976) *Man and his Urban Environment.* Reading, MA.: Addison-Wesley.

Michelson, W. (1987) "Groups, Aggregates, and the Environment." In E.H. Zube, & G. T. Moore (Eds.) *Advances in Environment, Behavior, and Design*, Vol. 1, pp. 161-185. New York: Plenum.

Nasar, J.L. (1988) *Environmental Aesthetics: Theory, Research and Applications.* New York: Cambridge University Press.

Nasar, J.L. & de Nivia (1987) "A post-occupancy evaluation for the design of a light pre-fabricated housing system for low income groups in Colombia." *Journal of Architectural and Planning Research*, 4, 199-211.

Nasar, J.L. & Kang, J. (1989 a). "A post-jury evaluation: The Ohio State University design competition for a center for the visual arts." *Environment and Behavior*, 21, 464-484.

Nasar, J.L. & Kang, J. (1989 b). "Symbolic meanings of building style in small suburban offices." In G. Hardie, R. Moore, & H. Sanoff (Eds.) *Changing Paradigms*: EDRA 20, pp 165-172. Oklahoma City: E.D.R.A.

National Environmental Policy Act (1969). Public Law 91-190. Eighty-third Stat., 852-856.

Norberg–Shulz, C. (1965) *Intentions in Architecture.* Cambridge, MA: The M.I.T. Press.

Pearlman, K. T. (1988) "Aesthetic regulation and the courts." In J.L. Nasar (Ed.) *Environmental Aesthetics: Theory, Research and Applications* (pp. 476-492). New York: Cambridge University Press.

Purcell, A.T. (1986) "Environmental perception and affect: A schema discrepancy model." *Environment and Behavior*, 18, 3-30.

Purcell, A. T. & Nasar, J. L. (1990). "Australian architect and non-architect students experiences of American houses." Paper presented at the Conference of the International Association of Empirical Aesthetics, Budapest, Hungary, August 22-25.

Rapoport, A. (1977) *Human aspects of urban form: Towards a man environment approach to urban form and design.* Oxford, Pregamon Press.

Rapoport, A. (1982) *The meaning of the built environment: A nonverbal communication approach.* Beverly Hills: Sage.

Royse, D.C. (1969) *Social inferences via environmental cues.* Doctoral Dissertation, MIT, Cambridge, Mass.

Russell, J. & Ward, L. (1981) "The psychological representation of molar physical environments." *Journal of Experimental Psychology: General,* 110, 121-152.

Sadalla, E.K., Verschure B. & Burroughs, J. (1987) "Identity symbolism in housing." *Environment & Behavior,* 19, 599-587.

Scott Brown, D. (1980) "Architects' task in a pluralistic society." *Harvard Architectural Review.*

Tuttle, D.P. (1983) *Surban fantasies.* Master's Thesis, University of Wisconsin, Milwaukee.

Venturi, R. & Rauch, D. (1977) *Signs of Life: Symbols in the American City.* Washington, DC: Aperture.

Venturi, R., Scott Brown, D. & Izenour, S. (1972) *Learning from Las Vegas.* Cambridge, Mass.: MIT Press.

Verderber, S. & Moore, G. T. (1979) "Building imagery: A comparative study of environmental cognition." *Man-Environment Systems,* 7, 332-341.

Vining, J. & Orland, B. (1989) "The video advantage: A comparison of two environmental representation techniques." *Journal of Environmental Management,* 29, 275-283.

Wethman, C. (1968). *The social meaning of the physical environment.* Unpublished Doctoral Dissertation, University of Southern California.

Wohlwill, J.F. & Kohn, I. (1973) "The environment as experienced by the migrant: An adaptation-level view." *Representative research in social psychology,* 4, 35-164.

Chapter 7

User Group Preferences and Their Intensity: The Impacts of Residential Design

ERNESTO G. ARIAS
University of Colorado

Housing preferences are still poorly comprehended in residential design. Yet they directly affect, and are directly affected by the meaning and use of housing. The objective of this chapter is to provide a better understanding of the role of housing preferences in design. Specifically, its aim is to see if consumer housing preferences are altered by the outcomes of a design process, and how this information could be of use in a more efficient and sensitive delivery of housing for different user groups, e.g., elderly, single headed households, or children. To this end, the relationship between preferences, use and meaning is considered; the intensity of preferences is reviewed as an important knowledge gap; the context of design and consumer decisions is examined; a methodological framework to study preferences is introduced; and a pilot study focusing on the intesity of preferences is presented, utilizing in part this framework.

Introduction

The most visible evidence of a household's relative well-being, as well as the second largest component of personal consumption, is housing. The use and meaning of housing has been the object of serious research and public concerns in the U.S. for almost a century. During this time, most aspects have been studied theoretically as well as empirically from various perspectives. Virtually every academic discipline, from psychology and anthropology to law and architecture, has been concerned with questions and issues on housing. Yet consumer housing preferences, the most fundamental building block of housing analysis, are still poorly comprehended in architectural theory and practice (MacLennan and Williams 1979, Drake 1984, Rapoport 1985).

The objective of this chapter is to explore what effects decisions made in the process of residential design may have on the housing preferences made by consumers through visual inspection of the physical unit as the outcome of design. It focuses on the intensity of the preference as a way to explore these effects. The chapter includes an introduction and three subsequent parts. The introduction presents a brief look at the relationships between preferences, meaning and use. It then reviews knowledge gaps about preferences in the literature. The second part represents a conceptual basis for the general study of housing preferences in residential design. To this aim it first reviews the contexts in which consumers and designers make decisions and then introduces a conceptual framework to study the intensity and other knowledge gaps of housing preferences for design and planning applications. The third part describes an illustrative experiment on the intensity of preferences which was carried out at the College of Environmental Design of the University of Colorado, Boulder. This pilot research represents a partial aplication of the framework. It explores how consumer housing preferences may be affected by outcomes of the design process. Therefore, it provides a basis to address questions such as: how much, if any, do the outcomes of phases of the design process have on the rank order and intensity of residential preferences of a user group (e.g., students, women, elderly)? What importance elements versus total unit designs play in residential preferences of these groups in housing markets? Or, how can residential satisfaction and economy be optimized in the development and delivery of housing for different user groups? The final part concludes with a discussion of implications and limitations of this methodological approach to residential design as it pertains to some of these questions.

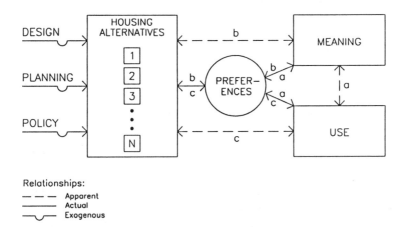

Figure 7.1: Role of preferences in housing's meaning and use

Preferences, meaning and use

The importance in trying to understand preferences while studying use and meaning is simply that the relationships between meaning, use and residential alternatives are defined via housing preferences (Figure 7.1). The aim of this part is to provide a brief conceptual understanding of preferences of housing alternatives, and the meaning and use of those alternatives. Before moving into these relationships, let us briefly define what is meant by these terms. A preference is a choice of a housing alternative over others in a universe of residential alternatives available to an individual or household. A complete definition of a preference must include rank order, intensity, and the reason(s) behind the preference. Finally, housing preferences are either "ideal," i.e., those not bound by limitations of the individual or household, nor by real constraints of the market place; or "revealed," i.e., those expressed by the consumer through an actual housing choice bound by the individual or household's real constrains.

Utilizing Herbert Gans' (1968) terms, the use of any housing alternative may be "effective" or "potential." For example, the effective use of a housing unit may be for traditional residential activities household members actually carry out, such as sleeping, entertaining, eating, etc., yet there may be potential uses of it such as the possibility of using it as a combined workplace-home setting. Both, effective and potential uses depend on the capabilities and predispositions of individuals or households. Meaning, on the other hand, is the significance a housing alternative has to its users. This significance stems from two different perspectives, those of the user's housed in it, e.g., meanings of home, safety, investment; and the significance of a residential alternative to others not living in it, e.g., status, success, or incentive.

Housing alternatives may be described by physical and non-physical attributes. Some of them are direct outcomes of the design process such as the floor plan of a unit (e.g., number of rooms and functional arrangement) or costs (e.g., construction costs). Others however, are not necessarily outcomes of design, for example, location and type of ownership. These attributes are a direct function of market forces and result from other on-going economic, demographic or political processes. Although not directly related to design these processes must be kept in mind since they play very important roles in preference formation.

Finally, the centrality of preferences (P) in relating use (U) and meanings (M) to housing alternatives can be discerned if we examine four basic unidirectional relations between them: "P$\longrightarrow$U," "P$\longrightarrow$M," "U$\longrightarrow$P," and "M$\longrightarrow$P." For example, the preference of a housing alternative's location not only affects the duration of its use by household members (e.g., they can spend more time at home if the house is close to the workplace or schools), but also its image to the user and others alike (e.g., perceptions of ourselves or of others elicited from living on "the other side of the railroad tracks"). In addition, use over time influences what a household prefers, e.g., preferences of room sizes, functional arrangements of floor plans, and even location of a unit are affected through previous residential experiences. As any housing alternative is used, its meaning is inevitably affected, both, in an absolute sense to the user and the unit; as well as in a relative sense to other users and other units. As these absolute or relative meanings of housing are gained over time, such as security to users or status to neighbors, they in turn affect the household's future preferences by seeking or avoiding housing alternatives with characteristics which evoke these positive or negative meanings.

Intensity and other knowledge gaps about preferences

Much has been learned from the observation of what families buy or rent (Rossi 1980). In the U.S., preferences are assessed indirectly through the analysis of government statistics about households and housing units, such as those gathered by the Bureau of the Census (HUD Annual Housing Survey 1986), the Federal Housing Administration, and more recently the base information on residential behavior of low income households for a variety of design characteristics and settings gathered for the experimental housing allowance program (Lawton 1978, Barnet 1976). Through analysis of market behavior some research has shown that certain groups prefer certain architectural styles or housing types, e.g. the preference of Jewish families for modern architecture over early American styles (Rapkin & Grigsby 1960). Another type of information has been gathered from studies which address ideal preference directly by the home building industry and realtors. For example, visitors to model homes are frequently asked to fill out questionnaires telling what they like or dislike about various parts of the model homes (Research Services Inc. 1985). Other revealing studies of particular aspects of residential environments which families like and dislike have been conducted to explain why households move (Rossi and Shlay 1982, Rossi 1980, McAuley & Nutty 1982), attributes of the neighborhood (Onibokun 1974, Glaster & Hesser 1981, Lawton 1978), attitudes towards single family and multiple family housing types (Michelson 1966), high and low-rise living preferences (Michelson 1977, 1979; Williamson 1981), and interior arrangements (Sanoff 1973).

Given the previous research briefly described above, there appears to be general aspects related to housing preferences which are still relatively unexplored. However, of central concern to this chapter is the knowledge gaps related to the intensity of preferences for various design characteristics of housing. The accuracy of measuring preferences is a problem with most of these findings. Since participants were expressing an ideal preference, the issue of preference intensity was not addressed. In addition detailed knowledge of current preferences may not be especially helpful in formulating designs which seek to change preferences by offering something new and different via design, since related aspects which are visually assessed by consumers and directly influence their preferences have not been fully considered.

Intensity for our purposes may be defined as degrees of preference between rank orders of alternatives; in other words, how much more one characteristic of housing is preferred over others from a universe of alternatives. Due to the nature of housing as a "bundle of goods," these characteristics are numerous and range broadly from physical (design) to non-physical (economic or social), simple (house) to complex (housing systems), and include various levels of spatial and temporal aggregations.

Intensity is closely related to the variation in preferences among similar groups (Longley and Wrigley, 1984). Its importance stems from the fact that if the intensity of a preference is not known, the degree to which various sub-markets are linked in terms of similar design aspects, also cannot be known. Our lack of knowledge in this regard seems especially critical when one considers the fact that some of the most closely linked sub-markets contain quite dissimilar housing unit designs (Grigsby 1963). Various authors have devised approaches for getting at the strength of preferences through the use of economic behavioral data to estimate demand elasticities. These approaches have been deficient due to incorrect assumptions that preference functions can be revealed by economic behavioral data (Ellickson, Fishman & Morrison 1977). Some research has tried to measure the strength of the preferences in a similar manner as presented here (Whitbread 1979; Gustafson, Harsman & Snickars 1977), however they have principally concentrated on planning aspects, only used very few variables to describe design characteristics, and, except for Whitbread (1979), have not included visual descriptors to their methodologies.

A very important methodological issue in planning and design related to the intensity of preferences is the additivity of the intensity in multiattribute decisions, such as the purchase of a home. In the process of design, the designer decomposes the objective of this process, in this case the design of a housing unit, into integral components, e.g., a bath, bedroom, or kitchen; and these in turn are desegregated into sets of attributes, e.g., materials or size. In a creative leap, not very well understood (Lang 1987), decisions are made by the designer combining these components into arrangements to attain "the design," which results in the functional and aesthetic characteristics of a housing unit the consumer sees, e.g., a floor plan or an exterior elevation. Looking into the additivity of intensities of individual attributes may prove to be insightful in understanding better the relation between designer decisions and user group preferences in turn-key style housing of industrialized countries. It may also prove insightful in the analysis of housing which evolves over time, as is the case of housing of the very poor in the less industrialized world.

A clear understanding of reasons behind preferences is another knowledge gap related to intensity (Hinshaw & Allot 1973). It is very difficult to determine from market information the value that consumers place on each design characteristic or the reason(s) behind the preference. This difficulty stems from the fact that a multitude of individual design characteristics comprising a housing unit are combined and marketed as the "bundle of goods" previously mentioned. A bundle of goods which cannot be purchased nor assembled one at a time, cafeteria style. Following some pioneering work in the 60's (Lancaster 1966), housing analysts have pursued the notion of conjoint measurement (Findikak & Danjai 1982, Curry et al. 1978), and also the "hedonic indices" much used in the automobile industry and other marketing research (Butler 1982). These indices place market values on selected housing characteristics.

However, these approaches have never been applied specifically to design. The number of characteristics considered in both types of studies is still very limited, and there has been a scant attempt to relate these characteristics to consumer needs and desires mentioned above (Brueckner 1983). As a consequence, important planning and design knowledge such as knowing the extent to which the large suburban yard is sought-after because it offers status, privacy, or recreation is unknown. Previous research points out that when families seek a place to live, they try to satisfy not only basic shelter needs (Rainwater 1973a, 1973b) but also, to varying degrees, their desire for a host of functional and symbolic attributes that a dwelling provides, such as the needs for comfort, safety, security, privacy, status, peer group acceptance, ease of operation, proximity to natural environment, or interior and exterior aesthetics (e.g., see Cooper-Marcus 1977, Diaso et al. 1971, Merton 1966). Different design characteristics of a unit (number of bedrooms, style and type of housing unit, or site layout), and neighborhood (densities, street layout, or open space distribution), contribute in differing degrees and ways to housing satisfaction. We can begin to understand more about reasons and interests of these characteristics through theories of housing needs (Drake 1984, Marans 1975, Cooper 1975, Grigsby 1975), or psychological theories of human motivation and the "hierarchy of needs" (Maslow, 1970).

A final gap of importance to design and very much related to the intensity of preferences which has been missing to a great extent in previous research is an understanding of the visual attributes of the unit and the neighborhood. Very broadly, the desires home and neighborhood satisfy can be classified as aesthetic and functional, representing the integral, substantive components of architecture. Imbedded in each are the physiological, psychological, and sociological desires of residents as described in earlier work (Francescato *et al.* 1979, Becker 1977, Duncan & Duncan 1976, Cooper 1975).

A conceptual basis of understanding preferences

A great deal of useful knowledge of concepts, methodologies, and findings from previous research related to housing preferences is already available to designers and planners. A central premise in developing a framework is to integrate existing knowledge from various fields which is useful to study design decisions and their implications on consumer choices. The methodological integration of concepts and apporaches provides the framework a capacity to analyze how consumer judgments are made through the visual inspection of alternative housing designs, e.g., preferences for interior and exterior functional and aesthetic qualities of a housing unit. Such understanding is necessary to guide the creation as well as use of residential environments in order to address some of the knowledge gaps discussed, and to be be more responsive to the needs and aspirations of different user populations in housing, e.g., the elderly, children, women headed households, or the handicapped. Prior to introducing such a framework, the contexts within which consumers and designers make decisions are examined.

Consumer decisions and the design process

Consumers make judgments about the aesthetic and functional design qualities of a dwelling unit on the basis of visual inspection. However, this is done only after satisfycing housing decisions relative to other issues such as affordability, employment, neighborhood schools and safety, or street-side appearance. These issues are associated with more aggregate spatial levels beyond the unit and its site, e.g., city, neighborhoods, and the block (Figure 7.2). While some preference work has been done at these levels of aggregation (Rossi and Shlay 1982, Anselin and Arias 1981, Glaster and Hesser 1981, Rossi 1980), only very few efforts have related preferences made by the consumer through visual inspection of the functional and aesthetic attributes of the unit's design or site plan. Further, these few studies have barely begun to address the gaps mentioned (e.g., Peterson 1976, Rabinowitz & Coughlin 1971, Louviere 1979, Whitbread 1979). Once decisions based on the more macro issues are made (employment, income, and schools), consumers then focus on direct outcomes of the design process, e.g., the housing unit's functional and aesthetic attributes.

The residential design process can be seen as taking place in two major phases: a programmatic structural understanding followed by a functional creative integration (Figure 7.3). The designer decomposes the concept of a residential unit into basic components during the first phase, e.g., the interior plan, the exterior facades, and the site. Each component is then understood as a group of program elements such as the kitchen, bathroom or bedrooms. The designer further views each of these elements relative to layout, size or other design aspects which he or she then considers in term of design alternatives, e.g., an "island kitchen" versus a "galley" layout. This hierarchically analytic thinking provides the designer with a comprehensive understanding of the integral elements of the dwelling unit. In the second phase, through a reflection in action process, the designer combines the various selected design alternatives for each element to arrive at the "plan" of the unit. This same "functional synthesis" also produces design solutions

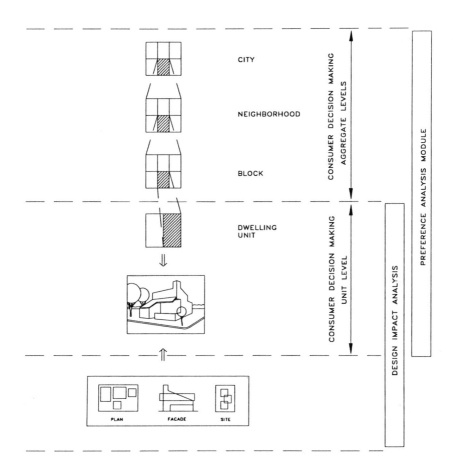

Figure 7.2: Context of consumer residential decisions

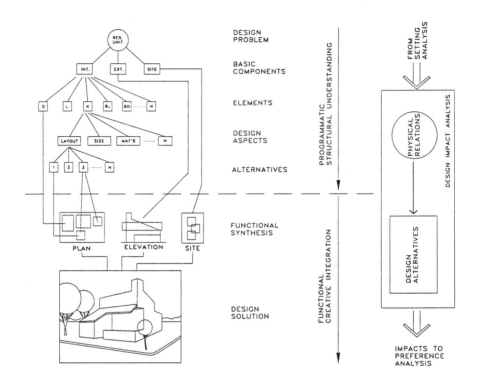

Figure 7.3: Context of residential design decisions

for each of the other components, thus resulting in the plan, elevations, and site layout of a residential unit's design solution (Figure 7.3).

The methodological framework to be introduced next provides a conceptual basis for understanding intensity and other knowledge gaps relating them to the context of design decisions. The programmatic structural understanding and the functional creative integration phases discussed are included in the "residential setting analysis" and "design impact analysis" modules. The context of consumer decisions is represented in both, the design impact analysis and the preference analysis modules of the subsequent framework (Figures 7.2, 7.3 and 7.4).

The framework

The proposed framework provides a methodological context to study intensity and additivity of preferences for individual design aspects. It integrates gaming and simulations approaches with consumer trade-offs of design aspects, with the use of visual aids to represent these aspects. The integration of the concept of trade-offs (Veldhuisen, Thijsen & Timmermans 1984) affords the framework a capability to place the study in a real-world situation where decisions have to be made between competing "alternatives" in order to achieve the best possible array of choices (Hecht, Paxson & Juhasz 1980). This approach is in dramatic contrast to approaches which simply sample from outcomes people may find desirable.

The framework consists of three main modules, the 'residential setting analysis', 'design impact analysis', and the 'preference analysis' (Figure 7.4). Each module in turn includes sub-modules to express relations (circles) and/or outcomes of relations (blocks). The sub-modules themselves are seen as being capable to include descriptions of variables, relations, and methodologies in the most flexible manner. Therefore, the framework can include other substantive topics of housing in addition to residential design.

The residential setting analysis has two submodules which describe the household (HH) and the physical dwelling unit (DU) for any proper application of market segmentation. The "HH" sub-module includes non-physical variables (socio-economic, behavioral) to describe the attributes of a household in terms of demographic descriptors and life-style profiles. The "DU" sub-module, on the other hand, includes physical variables to define design attributes of a dwelling unit, e.g., descriptors of the interior layout, exterior facade, and site aspects of the residential unit.

The design impact analysis module includes the "physical relations" between the various components and elements of the "DU." These relations are those manipulated by the designer to attain various residential design alternatives generated through the application of an analytic hierarchical process to arrive at a structural model of residential design (Alexander 1964)(Figure 7.3). The various relations between design attributes produce residential design "alternatives" of elements, e.g., design variations of a bathroom, kitchen, or bedroom; and major components of a unit, e.g., interior plan layouts, facades, or site plan layouts. Each alternative represents outcomes from the design process to which the consumer reacts and makes decisions through visual inspection of a housing unit (Figure 7.2). These decisions represent the "impacts" in the subsequent preference analysis module of the framework.

The third and most important module is the preference analysis module.

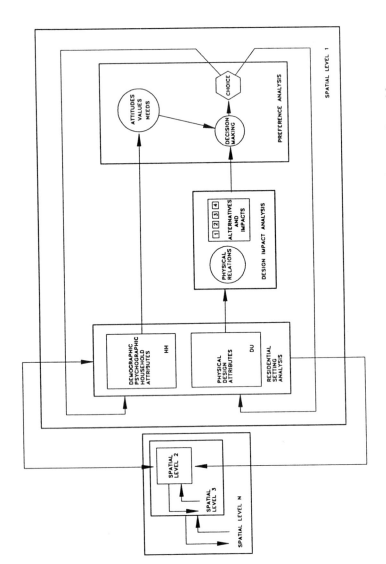

Figure 7.4: A conceptual framework for the study of preferences in residential design

It consists of three sub-modules, each dealing with a specific part of the decision making process. The first includes the "attitudes, values and needs" of the consumer, or household (HH), in which the data on the "HH," from the residential setting analysis, are combined to yield the relevant household welfare functions necessary to evaluate design alternatives. The output of this submodule, together with the physical design alternatives and impacts form the inputs of the "decision making" submodule. This module is also applicable to study decision making by the designer as discussed, specifically, those decisions made in the functional creative integration phase of the design process (Figure 7.3).

The "decision making" submodule analyzes the consumer's housing choice from an available universe of alternatives. Its operationalization may be attained through an integrated set of methodologies. These include first, a "decision-analytic process," similar to that used in growth management of cities to select between locational alternatives of development actions (Anselin and Arias 1983). The structure of such a process can be applied to a hierarchical structural definition of residential design from the previous module to obtain performance ranking of design attributes (Saaty 1977). A second methodology is the "trade-offs" methodology (Hetcht and Juhasz 1982). It is useful in identifying preferences and their intensities from different design attributes, or from design components as clusters of attributes, e.g. different kitchen prototypical layouts, or unit floor plan alternatives.

Other relevant methodological perspectives can also be integrated to operationalize this submodule. For example, the "reflective-dialectical" methodology (Studer 1982) could be integrated to identify changes in preferences of the same design attribute(s) through participation in discussions, e.g., change in rank order and/or intensity of preference for the same kitchen layout after discussion and learning. Another might be "market segmentation" which can be used to join specific residential design attributes and household characteristics for the different housing sub-markets. To attain the segmentation of a new housing market into sub-markets, the methodology uses the preferable design attributes of the residential unit obtained from the above methodologies, and associates them with the life style characteristics of a household using a psychographics approach. These life styles may be described by groups of demographic variables from the "attitudes/values/needs" submodule. What must be kept in mind while integrating various approaches to operationalize this submodule is that its outcomes are the different consumer choices of residential design attributes in the form of "revealed preferences."

"Choice" is the final submodule of the preference analysis module. It contains the "revealed preferences" for the different types and characteristics of households produced in the "decision" submodule. In subsequent time periods of a simulation, these choices become inputs of the residential setting analysis. Thus, utilizing the framework for simulations over periods of time, these choices represent the changing expectations, future preferences and new objectives of the household in a housing market (e.g. the single family housing market), or sub-markets (e.g. single family attached housing sub-market). Also, specific effects from the implementations of residential designs can be traced and compared to original designs which could lead to new design decisions. Via the residential setting analysis module of the framework, consumer choices as inputs, not only affect the unit level (spatial level 1), but also affect (and are affected by) residential aspects at other spatial levels of concern to policy, planning, or management, e.g., neighborhood, city, or metropolitan region — spatial levels 2, 3,... n.

This integrative framework represents a methodological approach to residential design which may be utilized by future research in order to provide a better understanding of existing knowledge gaps about housing preferences, such as:

1. housing preference variations among similar socio-economic groups of households,

2. intensity of preference for various design attributes of the unit and the additivity of these intensities to assess the impacts of design in creating the functional and aesthetic arrangements of residential components and their corresponding design attributes,

3. reasons behind preferences of specific design attributes of residential prototypes, or

4. design attributes of the unit which directly affect housing preferences.

The application of this methodological framework can provide other research studies with a more complete understanding of the decision process the consumer goes through before a housing choice is made. Better understanding of this process is central to residential design, since as a rule, it is practiced in a housing context which is in a constant state of flux— households either move into or out of housing units, existing households in the same unit change over time, and the physical unit attributes change due to either deterioration, obsolescence, or adaptation through renovations over time.

The framework, as will be illustrated in the final part of the chapter, can be applied to study the intensity of preference for each residential design element (e.g. three alternative bathroom layouts), or complete interior and exterior arrays (e.g. a 2 bedroom-2 bath apartment layout).

The framework also has the capacity to address both, preference variations between different user groups (e.g., preference variations for similar or different housing design elements or arrays between the elderly and children), and variations between populations with similar socio- economic or demographic characteristics (e.g., variations within the hispanic poor, or elderly). The application of the framework also forces the development of systematic and comprehensive methods of questioning respondents about visual representations of design attributes in models. This area of study can lead to an improvement in the use of visual messages by designers, as well as to a greater responsiveness of housing producers to latent consumer demand (Seaton *et al.* 1972).

A pilot research application: preferences in student housing

The research study presented in this section addresses in part the issue of intensity in housing preferences. We can learn through additivity of intensity between the rank ordered preferences whether the meaning and use of a housing unit change when viewed as a set of discrete design components (e.g. bedroom or kitchen) versus as an integrated whole. There is housing literature which supports the notion that the consumer does not always like what the architect likes (Michelson 1968, Rainwater 1973, Proshansky 1974, Lang 1987); nevertheless, a generally accepted hypothesis in architectural practice has been that design decisions "can" and "do" affect consumer decisions in a positive sense. This inconsistency between research and practice brings us to the question raised at the onset of the chapter: Are consumer housing preferences altered by outcomes of the design process, and if so, how? This final part of the chapter will address this query by exploring the following questions:

1. Can we understand the preference of a dwelling unit as a whole through an understanding of the consumer preferences for the individual elements of the unit only?

2. Is the design of the elements of a unit, e.g. bathroom, kitchen, bedroom, etc., more important than the design of the functional unit layout to consumer housing preferences?

3. How much influence, if any, do the outcomes of the integrative phase of a design process have on consumer preferences and their intensity? That is, do better layouts change the order rank of the preference or only their intensity?

The exploration of these questions will be through the review of the pilot research carried out at the College of Environmental Design which focused on the intensity of preferences for hypothetical student housing. This part presents briefly how the experiment was carried out, and discusses the findings to address these questions. Finally, some of the implications and conclusions drawn from the framework and the findings of the experiment are discussed.

The experiment

This pilot research is principally organized around the "Design Impact Analysis" and the "Preference Analysis" modules of the framework. The "Residential Setting Analysis" module only guided decisions with respect to the selection of the physical design attributes of area and elements of an average student apartment, and the economic attribute of average rent in Boulder, Colorado. In terms of household attributes, the experiment was carried out with thirty six undergraduate students from the College. While the psychographic or demographic attributes describing this particular user group were not considered, the framework makes it possible to do so.

The decisions about the development and design manipulations of the 3-D scale models used in the simulations were guided by the Design Impact Analysis. These design manipulations parallel the "programmatic structural understanding" and the "creative functional integration" phases of the residential design process discussed (Figure 7.3). Scale models at 1/2" = 1'-0" were developed for three alternative layouts of the various elements (master and second bedrooms, full and half baths, kitchen, living room, and dining room), and to create floor plan alternatives of complete units. Their use allowed visualization in order to elicit rent preferences from the students for design attributes of the housing unit. The "Preference Analysis" was the other module of the framework used to guide the actual simulations carried out in the two phases of the experiment (Figures 7.5 and 7.6). Play money for rent was given to each respondent in the amount of $600.00. This amount was determined by the Campus Housing Office of the University of Colorado. Utilizing the trade-off methodology, students revealed their preference intensities for the discreet elements comprising the average unit, the relative intensities for different design layouts of each element, and for different functional layouts of the "whole unit."

The DU as a Set of Discreet Elements. The first phase of the experiment includes two steps aimed at understanding preferences for the elements of a dwelling unit (DU) (Figure 7.5). This phase presented the unit very similarly to the way a designer might see the unit for a programmatic structural understanding (Figure 7.2). In the first step of this phase, the

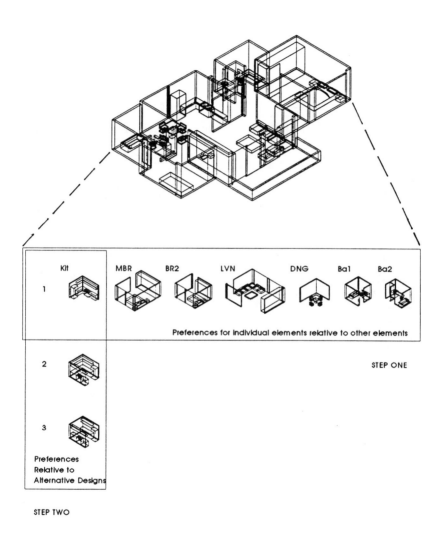

Figure 7.5: First Phase: Preferences relative to unit elements and to design alternatives of elements

Ernesto G. Arias

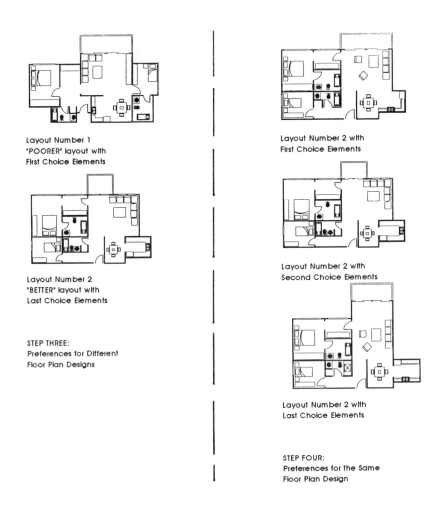

Figure 7.6: Second Phase: Preferences between whole unit layouts

Table 7.1: Intensity of preferences of elements relative to other elements

Elements of DU	Rank	Mean	Range	Range Limits
Kitchen	3	102.00	100.00	60.00 - 160.00
Msrt Bdrm	2	130.00	130.00	80.00 - 240.00
Bdrm 2	5	75.00	125.00	05.00 - 130.00
Living	1	140.00	165.00	35.00 - 200.00
Dining	6	44.00	100.00	00.00 - 100.00
Bath 1	4	80.00	110.00	40.00 - 150.00
Bath 2	7	29.00	90.00	00.00 - 090.00
Sum of Means	600.00			

Note: $n = 36$, missing obs. $= 0$.

respondents were presented with an apartment in terms of a set of discreet elements. They were then asked to reveal their preferences by distributing their rent across the elements, and the corresponding amounts of play money were placed in front of each element. This step provided the base information on the rank order and intensity of preference for the individual elements relative to the other elements comprising a unit, when the unit is viewed as a functionally desegregated set of elements (Table 7.1).

The second step presented the students with two additional layouts of each element, making a universe of three design alternatives for each element from which to choose. They were then asked to rank them in order of preference, with their first, second and third choices in three rows— front, middle and real rows respectively. Utilizing a trade-offs approach, each of the elements from the front row were removed one at a time. The students were asked each time how much money would they take back in order to be "satisfied" with their second preferred layout for the particular element being removed from the universe of choices. The same procedure was carried out between second and third preferences for each element. This step provided information on the rank order of each of the layouts of each element, and the intensities of the preferences between first and second choices, second and third choices, and consequently first and third choices (Table 7.2).

The DU as a Functional Whole. The second phase includes steps 3 and 4 of the experiment. Its aim was to test preferences of consumers for design of the "whole" unit, again utilizing visualization to complement rent costs in the simulations. In this case, models showing the functional relationships (location and circulation) between the elements were designed using the various individual elements (Figure 7.6). The data from the first phase was

Table 7.2: Inference of preference between alternative layouts of each element

Elements of DU	1st & 2nd Choices		2nd & 3rd Choices		1st & 3rd Choices	
	Mean	Range Limits	Mean	Range Limits	Mean	Range Limits
Mstr. Bdrm.	13.0	.0 - 40.0	19.0	.0 - 50.0	32.0	5.0 - 70.0
Bdrm 2	9.0	.0 - 40.0	16.0	.0 - 50.0	25.0	5.0 - 80.0
Kitchen	12.0	.0 - 40.0	17.0	.0 - 60.0	29.0	0.0 - 70.0
Living	16.0	.0 - 60.0	24.0	.0 - 95.0	40.0	0.0 - 105.0
Dining	7.0	.0 - 40.0	9.0	.0 - 60.0	16.0	0.0 - 95.0
Bath 1	8.0	.0 - 30.0	10.0	.0 - 30.0	18.0	0.0 - 60.0
Bath 2	5.0	.0 - 20.0	5.0	.0 - 20.0	10.0	0.0 - 30.0
Sum of Means	70.0		100.0		170.0	

then reviewed through a frequency analysis to identify the preferences of the various design alternatives of each element in terms of their rank order and intensities. Based on this information, whole unit layouts of apartments to be used in these final two steps of the experiment were then constructed. These layouts represent the outcomes of a creative functional integration of individual elements in the design process (Figure 7.3).

In the third step, the respondents were asked to evaluate two different unit layouts which were composed utilizing the best and least preferred sets of elements. One of the layouts was hypothesized by designers as the "better" plan, but constructed with the least preferred elements. The second layout was composed using the first preference elements, but was evaluated by designers as the "poorer" plan because of privacy and functional reasons (layout 1 and 2 in the third step of Figure 7.6). The respondents were given $1,200.00 in play money and were asked to bid up to $600.00 for each of these two layouts, thus providing rank order and intensity between the two layouts.

In the last step of the experiment, three units were constructed using the "better plan" (layout No. 2), with the first, second, and third choice elements respectively (Step 4 in Figure 7.6). The students then bided up to $600.00 for each of the units in a similar fashion as in the previous step. In this manner, the second phase provides information on housing preferences when the consumer views a the residential unit as a functional and aesthetic "whole." The experiment illustrates a research application of the framework which provides an approach to study the effects residential design (decisions and outcomes from the programmatic and creative integration activities) has on the consumer preferences in housing. The findings from such applications can provide insights to the various questions above.

Some of the findings

Thirty six students from the College of Environmental Design participated in this research. Two thirds of the students actually paid over $400.00 per month for their housing. The majority of respondents characterized their present housing as low-rise multi-family apartments with two or one bedrooms and one bath. Cost was considered by over half of the students (58%) as the most important concern in making their housing choice, followed by the location of the unit, with design and appearance their least concern. Additionally, in the selection of their present housing arrangements, the interior layout was the design aspect considered by the great majority (83%) as most important in influencing their housing preference, while the building facade, and site layout and landscaping were viewed as second and least influential, respectively.

The preference of a unit as a whole could be assessed through an understanding of the consumer preferences for individual elements. It must be made clear that the findings are not statistically significant, nor do they represent a true sample of the student population. They are presented for illustrative purposes. In comparing the findings from the two phases of the experiment, it is clear that while intensities did change, the rank order of the preferences did not. For example, rank orders remained the same when the consumer viewed the unit either as a set of discreet elements or as a functional whole. This finding can be seen when comparing the sums of the mean for the 1st, 2nd, and 3rd choice elements attained in the first phase (Table 7.2) with the means for the preferences of the three layouts in step 4 of the second phase (Table 7.3).

The outcomes of the activities in the creative functional integration of design do impact the intensity of preferences. However, as mentioned, in the case of the students these activities did not affect the rank order of the preferences. It was found through analysis of the statistical means, that the intensities between least and most preferred elements decreased, i.e. these elements improved when incorporated in the "better" layout of the whole unit, but their rank order remained the same as in the first phase of the experiment (Tables 7.2 and 7.3). The sum of the statistical mean for the intensities between 1st and 3rd choices of the individual elements (Table 7.1) was reduced by $49.00 when compared to the intensity between the two layouts composed of the same elements, and by $46.00 when compared between 2nd and 3rd choices. These findings are consistent for both steps of the second phase.

Table 7.3: Intensity of preferences between unit layouts

	1st & 2nd Choices		2nd & 3rd Choices		1st & 3rd Choices	
Layouts of DU	Mean	Range Limits	Mean	Range Limits	Mean	Range Limits
Step 3: 1 / 2	N/A	N/A	N/A	N/A	144.00	5.00 - 600.00
Step 4: 1 / 2 / 3	67.00	5.00 - 200.00	54.00	5.00 - 200.00	121.00	0.00 - 200.00

Note: $n = 36$, missing obs. $= 0$.

These findings also illustrate the capability of this approach to tell us how a particular user group views the various design elements of their housing as a set of separate functional spaces. For example, the students preferred the living room over other functional spaces such as the master bedroom or kitchen (Table 7.1). We can also see that an intensity of $10 separates the living room from the master bedroom, while the intensity between master bedroom and kitchen is almost tripled. Likewise, we can begin to understand that students do not place much emphasis on a second bathroom. This knowledge for the various resident groups is valuable to see how a user group views the discreet elements of its housing. Such understanding allows us to know where the design emphasis should placed for different user groups (e.g., elderly, singles, or overlooked groups like the single parent, female headed household) in order to optimize satisfaction and economy through the design of their respective housing.

Additionally, it was found that the first priority of concern for the students was cost rather than design. Relative to design of the unit itself, the interior layout (plan) was viewed as most important in selecting their present housing arrangements over facades and site layouts. That is, function was considered over aethetics by the students. From these initial findings, it is interesting to note that design plays a background role when viewed relative to other socio-economic concerns associated with other spatial levels of aggregation. Also, it was expected that issues such as unit design or aesthetics would be at the forefront of the concerns of these architectural students. This finding starts to point to the hypothesis that occupation as an attribute of the user may not play a major role in housing preferences.

The results from this pilot application of the framework to the concept of preference intensity, start to provide an understanding for questions of importance in the consumption of housing which have been raised throughout the chapter: How can satisfaction and economy in residential design be optimized in development and delivery of housing for particular users groups? For example, we can see that for the students a design emphasis on the enhancement of living, bedroom or kitchen areas at the expense of dining space or a second bath may optimize the satisfaction and economy of their housing (Table 7.1). The same information can be revealed for the various alternative designs of each element (Table 7.2).

A better understanding of the effects of design on intensity and additivity on consumer preferences for various design variables will be extremely useful to both architectural practice and the housing industry. Expected results from applications of the framework such as the one above will contribute to a better understanding of the user-client relationship in residential design — a relationship which in design theory and in practice has brought criticism over time from several disciplines (Michelson 1968, Proshansky 1974, Cooper-Marcus 1977, Lang 1978, Drake 1984, among others).

Implications significance of applications of the framework

There are implications and limitations of the choice of visual aids in the research methodology relative to finding a reasonable balance between verisimilitude, cost, experimental rigor, and number of design variables. Ideally, the choice for future work is to use large scale models in which interior design attributes and functional relationships (elements, sizes, unit plan layouts, etc.), exterior unit facade (massing, styling, and materials, etc.), and site attributes (unit location-orientation, access, landscaping, etc.) can be independently manipulated to simulate different housing settings. The study relaxed some rigor to gain verisimilitude and comprehension by manipulating the variables in the 3D scale models. In addition, the pilot study looked at a limited number of variables which were aggregated according to prototypical market conditions of student housing in Boulder, Colorado. The assumption was that the market place has created significant aggregates of variables that could be traded off in groups, e.g. prototypes of design components such as the massing or fenestration of the building facades. We did find through the pilot study that the use of models does allow for a realistic manipulation of variables into prototypical groups for particular aspects of a housing unit. The very reduction in the number of variables increases verisimilitude since the consumer is unable to comprehend very large sets of design variables (Miller, 1956; Dowall & Juhasz, 1977, 1978; Timmermans, 1984). For example the students found it manageable to determine and evaluate three design alternatives of a bathroom layout. However, it became apparent that it can be extremely difficult for a respondent to trade off between all possible relevant design dimensions of a bathroom, e.g., types of fixtures, materials, color of materials, circulation, lighting, among others.

The significance of the proposed framework lies in the expected results which relate to architectural design theory and practice; in its procedural contribution to the understanding of intensity, additivity, and reasons in housing choice; in an integrative methodology to explore new ways to achieve market segmentation in order to study variations associated with different socio-economic groups; in the implications for fields which attempt to understand and regulate housing markets; and in its substantive contribution to research methodology. In a general sense, the applications of future studies could generate a model of housing preferences which, for the first time, may offer features of preferences which are testable and based on genuine empirical data collection.

More specifically, this pilot application began to demonstrate that techniques such as using three dimensional visual aids with high verisimilitude to real life conditions in the simulations, can elicit housing preference statements over a greater range of variables and with greater accuracy than previous work. In addition to having the ability to focus on the dwelling unit level in terms of design variables of the interior layout, the building exterior and the site of a prototypical residential unit within a specific market area; other housing characteristics can also be grouped into categories at aggregate levels for which planning decisions instead of design decisions have the major implications. At these levels we can assess the implications of such planning variables on housing preferences such as location in terms of accessibility to employment, or neighborhood environment (Weiss et al. 1973, Weichhart 1983). This information is critical for the improvement of existing urban growth management models (Anselin and Arias 1983, Arias 1986), or for the construction of planning models to predict the effects of various national housing trends and public policies of markets in metropolitan areas (Anselin and Arias 1981).

References

Alexander, C. *Notes on the Synthesis of Form.* Cambridge, Mass: Harvard University Press, 1964.

Anselin, L.E., and E.G. Arias. "A Microsimulation Approach to Intra-urban Residential Movement: A Conceptual Approach," in Voght and Mickle, Editors, *Modeling and Simulation*, Vol. 12, 1981, p. 999-1003.

Anselin, L.E., and E.G. Arias. "A Multicriteria Framework as a Decision Support System for Urban Growth Management Applications: Central City Redevelopment," *European Journal of Operations Research*, Vol. 13, 1983, p. 300-309.

Arias, E.G. "Development of Simulations and Games to Understand Decisions in Planning Physical Urban Environments." A Teaching and Learning Grant, The Undergraduate Enrichment Program, University of Colorado, Boulder, Principal Investigator, 1985-1986.

Barnet, C.L. "Using Hedonic Indexes to Measure Supply Response to Housing Allowances." WN-8686-HUD, The Rand Corporation, 1976.

Bearchall, C.A. Jr. "Psychographic Profiles of Selected Groups of a New and Used Home Buying Families." Bureau of Business Services and Research, School of Business Administration and Economics, California State University, 1973.

Becker, F.D. *Housing messages*. Stroudsburg, Pa.: Dowden, Hutchinson and Ross, 1977.

Brueckner, J.K. "The Economics of Urban Yard Space: An 'Implicit-market' Model for Housing Attributes," *Journal of Urban Economics* Vol. 13, 1983, p. 216-234.

Burnett, J. A. *Social History of Housing 1815-1970*. Newton Abbot, England: David and Charles, 1978.

Butler, R. "The Specification of Hedonic Indexes for Urban Housing," *Land Economics*, Vol. 58(1), 1982, p. 96-108.

Cooper, C. "The House as a Symbol of Self," in J. Lang, C. Burnette, W. Moleski, and D. Vachon, Editors, *Designing for Human Behavior*. Stroudsburg, Pa.: Dowden, Hutchinson, and Ross, 1974.

Cooper, C. *Easter Hill Village: Some Social Implications of Design*. N.Y.: Macmillan, 1975.

Cooper-Marcus, C. "User Needs Research in Housing," in S. Davis, Editor, *The Form of Housing*. N.Y.: Van Nostrand Reinhold Co., 1977.

Curry, D.J., Levin, I.P., and Gray, M.J. *A Comparison of Additive Conjoint Measurement and Functional Measurement in a Study of Apartment Preferences.*

Iowa City, IO.: The Institute of Urban and Regional Research Technical Report No. 98, 1978.

Diaso, R.D., *et al.* "Perception of the housing environment," Urban and Environmental Health Planning Papers, University of Pittsburgh, 1971.

Dowall, D. and J. B. Juhasz. "A new methodology for citizen participation in land use planning," in B. McDowell, Editors, *Innovation and action in regional planning.* Urbana: University of Illinois Press, 1977, 226-236.

Drake, J. "Architects and user requirements in public-sector housing: Towards an adequate understanding of user requirements in housing," *Environment and planning B: Planning and design*, Vol. 11, 1984, p. 417-433.

Duncan, J.S. and N.G. Duncan. "Housing as presentation of self and the structure of social networks," in G. Moore and R. Golledge, Editors, *Environmental knowing.* Stroudsburg, Pa.: Dowden, Hutchinson and Ross, 1976, p. 32-45.

Duncan, J.S. "The house as a symbol of social structure: Notes on the language of objects among collectivistic groups," in I. Altman and C. M. Werner, Editors, *Home environments*, Vol. 8. New York: Plenum Press, 1985, p. 133-152.

Ellickson, B., B. Fishman, and P.A. Morrison. "Economic analysis of urban housing: A new approach," R-2024-NSF, The Rand Corporation, CA., July 1977.

Findikak, I., and Dajani, J.S. "Conjoint-analysis of residential preferences," *Journal of the Urban Planning and Development Division of the American Society of Civil Engineering*, Vol. 108(1), 1982, p. 15-29.

Francescato, *et al. Resident's satisfaction in HUD-assisted housing: Design and management factors.* Washington, D.C.: USGPO, 1979.

Gans, Herbert, *People and Plans.* New York, Basic Books, 1968.

Glaster, G.C. and G. W. Hesser, "Residential Satisfaction: Compositional and contextual correlates," *Environment and Behavior*, Vol. 13(5), November 1981, p. 735-758.

Good, W.S. and O. Suchsland. "Consumer lifestyles and their relationship to market behavior regarding household furniture," *Michigan State University Research Bulletin*, No. 28, 1970, East Lansing, MI.

Grigsby, W. G. "Housing needs and objectives: A conceptual view," in W. G. Grigsby and M. Rosenburg East, Editors, Urban Housing Policy. N.Y.: APS Publications, Inc., 1975, p. 31-58.

Grigsby, W. G. *Housing Markets and Public Policy.* Philadelphia, PA.: University of Pennsylvania, 1963.

Gustafson, J.R., J.R. Harsman, and F. Snickars. "Housing demand models and consumer preferences," Papers of the Regional Science Association, Vol. 38, 1977.

Hecht, P. and J.B. Juhasz. "Employing trade-off techniques for impact assessment and environmental education," in C.P. Osterberg, C.P. *et al.*, Editors, *Design Research Interactions.* Washington, D.C.: EDRA, 1982.

Hecht, P. R., L. Paxson, and J. B. Juhasz. "Optimizing, compromising, and trading-off," in R. Stough, A. Wandersman and S. Sanders, Editors, *Optimizing environments: Research, practice and policy.* Washington, D. C.: Environmental Design Research Association, 1980, p. 60-64.

Hinshaw, M.L. and Allot, K.J. " Environmental preferences of future housing consumers," in J. Pynoos *et al.*, Editors, *Housing Urban America.* Chicago: Aldine Publishing Co., 1973, p. 191-202.

HUD, *The annual housing survey.* Washington, D.C.: USPG, 1986. Jacobson, E. and J. Kossoff. "Self-percept and consumer attitudes toward small cars," *Journal of Applied Psychology*, Vol. 47, August 1963, p. 242-245.

Kassarjian, H.H. "Social characteristics and differential preferences for mass communication," *Journal of Marketing Research*, Vol. 2, May 1965, p. 146-153.

Lancaster, K.J. "A new approach to consumer theory," *Journal of Political Economy*, Vol. 74(2), 1966, p. 132-157.

Lang, J.T. *Creating Architectural Theory.* 1987.

Lang, J.T., "The built environment and social behavior: Architectural determinism re-examined," *VIA*, Vol. 4, 1978.

Lawton, M.P. "The housing problems of community-resident elderly," In HUD-PDR *The occasional papers in housing and community affairs*, Vol. 1. Washington, D.C.: USGPO, 1978 (HUD-PDR-497), p. 39-74.

Longley, P.A., and Wrigley, N. "Scaling residential preferences—a methodological note," Tijdschrif voor Economische en Sociale Geografie, Vol. 75(4), 1984, p. 292-299.

Louviere, J.J. Modeling individual residential preferences: A totally disaggregate approach. Iowa City, IO: The Institute of Urban and Regional Research Technical

Report 100, 1979 (26 pages).

MacLennan, D. "Information, space and the measurement of housing preference and demand," *Scottish Journal of Political Economy*, Vol. 24, June 1977.

MacLennan, D. and N.J. Williams. "Spatial choice—Searching for a theoretical framework," Working Paper, University of Glasgow, March 1979.

Marans, R.W. *Basic human needs and the housing environment*. Ann Arbor, MI.: Institute for Social Research University of Michigan, 1975.

Maslow, A. *Motivation and personality* (2nd ed.). N.Y.: Harper and Row, 1970.

McAuley, W.J., and Nutty, C.L. "Residential preferences and moving behavior— A family life-cycle analysis," *Journal of Marriage and the Family*, Vol. 44(2), 1982, p. 301-309.

Merton, R. "The social psychology of housing," in W. Wheaton, G. Milgram and M.E. Meyerson, Editors, *Urban housing*. New York: The Free Press, 1966.

Michelson, W. "An empirical analysis of urban environment preference," *Journal of the American Institute of Planners*, Vol. 32, 1966, p. 355-360.

Michelson, W. "Most people don't want what architects want," *Trans-action*, July-August 1968, p. 37-43.

Michelson, W. Environmental choice, human behavior, and housing satisfaction. New York: Oxford University Press, 1977.

Michelson, W. *Man and his urban environment: A sociological approach*. Reading: Addison- Wesley, 1979.

Munsenger, G.M., *et al.* "Joint home purchasing decisions by husbands and wives," *Journal of Consumer Research*, Vol. 1, March 1975, p. 60-66.

Onibokun, A. "Evaluating consumer's satisfaction with housing: an application of a systems approach," *Journal of the American Institute of Planners*, 1974, Vol. 40, p. 189-200.

Peterson, G.L. "A model of preference: Qualitative analysis of the perception of the visual appearance of residential neighborhoods," *Journal of Regional Science*, 1976, Vol. 7, p. 19-31.

Proshansky, H. M. "Environmental psychology and the design professions," in J. Lang, C. Burnette, W. Moleski and D. Vachon, Editors, *Designing for human behavior: Architecture and the behavioral sciences.* Stroudsburg, PA.: Dowden, Hutchinson and Ross, Inc. 1974, p. 72-97.

Quigley, J.M. "What have we learned about urban housing markets," in Mieszkowski, P. and Straszheim M., *Current Issues in Urban Economics.* Baltimore: The John's Hopkins University Press, 1979, p. 391-429.

Rabinowitz, C.B. and R.E. Coughlin. "Some experiments in quantitative measurement of landscape quality," *Regional Science Research Institute Discussion Paper Series,* Vol. 43, 1971.

Rainwater, L. "Fear and the house-as-heaven in the lower class," in Pynoos, J. *et al., Housing urban America.* Chicago: Aldine Publishing Co., 1973a, p. 181-190.

Rainwater, L. "The Lessons of Pruitt-Igoe," in Pynoos, J., *et al., Housing urban America.* Chicago: Aldine Publishing Co., 1973b, p. 548-555.

Rapkin, C. and W.G. Grigsby. *The demand for housing in racially mixed areas.* Berkeley: University of California Press, 1960.

Rapoport, A. "Preference, habit selection and urban housing," *Journal of Social Issues,* 1980, Vol. 36(3), p. 118-134.

Rapoport, A. "Thinking about home environments: A conceptual framework," in I. Altman and C. M. Werner, Editors, *Home environments 8,* New York: Plenum Press, 1985, p. 255-286.

Research Services. *The Denver Housing Study Interview Questionnaire.* Denver, Co.: Research Services Inc., September 1985 (31 pages).

Reynolds, F.D. "Psychographics: A conceptual orientation," Athens, GA: Research Monograph No. 6, College of Business Administration, U of GA., 1973.

Reynolds, F. D. "An analysis of catalog buying behavior," in *Journal of Marketing,* 1974, Vol. 38, p. 47-51.

Rossi, P.H. *Why families move,* 2nd edition. Beverly Hills, CA: Sage Publications, 1980.

Rossi, P.H. and Shlay, A.B. "Residential mobility and public policy issues: "Why families move" revisited," *Journal of Social Issues,* 1982. Vol. 38(3), p. 21-34.

Saaty, T. "Scaling method of priorities in hierarchical structures," *Journal of Mathematical Psychology,* 1977, Vol. 15, p. 234-281.

Samuelson, P.A. "Consumption theory in terms of revealed preference," *Economics*, 1948, Vol. 15, p. 243-253.

Sanoff, H. *Integrating user needs in environmental design*. Springfield, Va.: National Technical Information Service, National Institute of Mental Health, 1973.

Seaton, R. W., *et al.* "Validity and reliability of ratings of simulated buildings," *Environmental design: Research and practice*, EDRA 3/AR8, Los Angeles, 1972.

Smith, T.E. "A representational approach to the joint determination of housing market segmentation and housing preferences," RSRI Discussion Paper Series, 1980.

Smith, T.E. "Housing market search behavior and expected utility theory: Measuring preferences for housing," *Environment and planning A*, 1982, Vol. 14, p. 681-698.

Stigler, G.J., and Becker, G.S. "De gustibus non est disputandum," *The american economic review*, 1977, Vol. 67, p. 76-90.

Studer, R.G. *Normative Guidance for the Planning, Design and Management of Environment-Behavior Systems*, Ph.D. dissertation. Pittsburg: University of Pittsburgh, 1982.

Timmermans, H. J. P. "Decomposional multiattribute preference models in spatial analysis," *Progress in Human Geography*, 1984, Vol. 8, p. 189-221.

Veldhuisen, K. J., A. P. Thijssen and H.J.P. Timmermans. "Conjoint Measurement Applied to the Judgement and Design of Dwellings," *Open House*, 1984, vol. 9, p. 17-33.

Veldhuisen, K. J. and H.J.P. Timmermans. "Specificiation of Residential Utility Functions," *Environment and Planning* 1984, Vol. 16, p. 1573-1583.

Weichhart, P. "Assessment of the Natural Environment: a Determinant of Residential Preferences," in *Urban Ecology*, 1983, Vol. 7, p. 325-343.

Weiss, S., Burley, R., Kaiser, E., Donnelly, T., and Zehner, R. *New Community Development: A National Study for Environmental Preferences and the Quality of Life*. Chapel Hill, N. C.: Institute for Research in Social Science, 1973.

Wells, W.D. "Psychographics: A Critical Review," *Journal of Marketing Research*, Vol. 12, May 1975, p. 196-213.

Whitbread, M. *Attitudes to Residential Environments*. Research Series, 28, Center for Environmental Studies, May 1979.

Whitbread, M. "Two Trade-off Experiments to Evaluate the Quality of Residential Environments," *Urban Studies*, Vol. 15, June 1978, p. 149-166.

Williams, J.A., Jr. "The Multifamily Housing Solution and Housing Type Preferences," *Social Sciences Quarterly*, Vol. 52, 1979, p. 543-559.

Williamson, Robert C. "Adjustment to the High Rise: Variables in a German Sample," *Environment and Behavior*, Vol. 13, 1981, p. 289-310.

Chapter 8

The Meaning of the "Corredor" in Costa Rica: An Integrated Methodology for Design

DONNA LUCKEY
University of Kansas, Lawrence

The meaning and significance of the corredor *as a design element of housing in Costa Rica is examined from a methodology based on the integration of several approaches. These include content analysis of graphic material, as well as a historic review, current document review, and a survey instrument. The combination of several techniques into one anaysis allows different levels of understanding and approaches to meaning of the built environment. In this case, the design element under consideration is the* corredor.

[0]Research in Costa Rica has been supported by the University of Kansas General Research Fund, the Hall Center for the Humanities, and the Fulbright Central American Republics Research Program. The author also wishes to acknowledge assistance provided by K.C. Tsui, Cheryl Pratt, Susan L. Pinto, Marcos Chavez, and the women of the Alianca de Mujeres in Golfito, Costa Rica. Special thanks go to Maria Eugenia Bozzoli de Wille, Charley Stansifer, and Darrell Hill.

Introduction

The material presented in this chapter is part of a study of housing form and quality, focused on the South Pacific, or Brunca, Region of Costa Rica. The goal of the ongoing research is to provide design knowledge which can be used to make more informed decisions concerning housing design elements and their relationships to cultural and social aspects of the built environment in this part of Costa Rica. The intent of this chapter is to explore the relationship between an integrated methodology and these design decisions. This will be demonstrated by focusing on a single housing element, the *corredor*, found not only in Costa Rica but in many other Latin American countries and areas once under the Spanish colonial influence. By keeping the present review focused, the integrated methodology as developed can be considered in terms of its contribution to knowledge necessary for design decisions. Parts of the larger study, which began in 1987, have been presented elsewhere and will be published in various forms in the future.

Trejos Dittel indicates that the house of Costa Rica is "constantly changing, yet it keeps a certain physical form, a possible result of tradition" (1945, p. 2). Visible throughout the different regions of Costa Rica, the *corredor* has emerged as one of the common housing elements. This chapter thus explores the meaning and use of this design element, which reflects continuous changes while maintaining certain physical requirements. The specific methodologies integrated into the overall study are presented, followed by the background and historic perspective. A discussion of the results which relate to the design element of *corredor* follows, while another section comments on the design significance and possible misuse of this housing element. The results of the integrated methodology, its use in approaching wicked problems (Rittel and Webber, 1972), and its usefulness to designers are also discussed. Conclusions regarding both the *corredor* and the integrated methodology are presented.

Methodology

Background for integrated methodology

Designers of the built environment face many difficulties, especially when working within different cultures and unique political and economic settings. The wickedness of design problems is even more evident under these circumstances. That is, among the several possible characteristics contributing to wicked problems (WPs), there are no clearly defined solutions, no correct solutions, and no indication from where knowledge necessary to resolve the problem may come. In response to the nature of these design problems, Rittel has outlined several principles of design (which he labelled "second generation" design principles (1972, p. 400). Among these is found the symmetry of ignorance, which reiterates the fact that the designer knows no better than anyone else where the necessary information may lie which will help resolve any given WP.

Through a variety of methodological approaches, including a historic review, the relationship of meaning and evolving tradition is explored. This is in keeping with the proposal made by Rapoport, who states that "... environmental design research must be cross cultural and historical ... and must go beyond material aspects of environments ..." if understanding is to occur (1980, p. 8). The methodological approaches necessary to respond to the various characteristics of wicked problems can also clarify meaning in design. Altman, Rapoport, and others have indicated a wide range of methodologies may be necessary to address the various elements of design (1980; 1988; Low and Chambers, eds., 1989). In addition, various perspectives from which to view the built environment have been outlined by Ittleson et al.; these perspectives include: history, sociology, psychology, geography, and anthropology, as well as views from architectural design (1974).

In the social sciences, much work has been done to address the concerns outlined above. For example, Lawrence points out that "In recent years it has become increasingly common for social anthropologists, other social scientists, and architects, to examine extant buildings in terms of a range of cultural and social dimensions" (1989, p. 90). Within the perspective of phenomenology, many different qualitative methods have been developed with which it is possible to better understand the motives and beliefs behind people's actions (Taylor and Bogdan, 1984). This can be expressed through the concept of symbolic interactionism, as seen in Figure 8.1. Qualitative methods are generally defined as those which provide a holistic view, allow flexibility in research and direct observations, and which produce descriptive data, or, as Taylor and Bogdan put it, "written or spoken words or observable behavior" (1984, p. 12). It is assumed here that for purposes of designing, descriptive data must also include visual, or graphic material.

The methodology of the larger study for the Brunca Region of Costa Rica utilizes this full range of descriptive data, along with other forms. That research is designed to integrate various existing models of analysis in such a way as to provide a more holistic structure, or overview, of the design knowledge in question. Briefly, the existing models used are: (1) the development of a building typology for recording house styles, construction materials, etc.(such as those discussed by Rossi, 1966; Moneo,

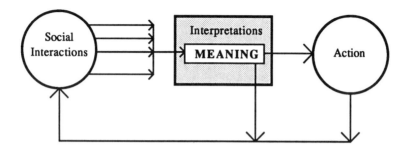

Figure 8.1: A model of meaning through symbolic interactionism

Note: After Taylor and Bogdan, 1984.

1979; Aguilar, 1980; Norberg-Schultz, 1985; and Brunskill, 1987); (2) a Geographic Information System (GIS) to record climatic topographic and other resource data in a graphic form (this also allows information such as transportation systems, cultural spheres of influence, and actual patterns and distributions of house forms or/and material usage to be mapped) (e.g., Walsh, 1985 and Huxhold, 1991, among others); and (3) qualitative and quantitative data from questionnaires, census material, and so on (see Figure 8.2).

Another model to consider, then, is how design information becomes available to the designer as knowledge from which to base decisions. The general model, which Rittel has adapted from Ashby, Figure 8.3a, shows this relationship in terms of Context Variables (CVs), Design Variables (DVs), and Performance Variables (PVs) (1974; based on Ashby, 1970). Design Variables are those under the control of the designer, who actually makes decisions on those issues, while Context Variables inform the designer from the wide range of issues out of the control of the designer. To look more specifically at the current model of integrated methods, Figure 8.3b presents the CVs as filters, through which information or data passes, and the different filters yield values for these variables, the "input" for designers to use when making design descisions (that is, for informing the decisions made, as DVs).

For the purposes of this study, specific graphic descriptive data are also available from visual surveys of house plans, exteriors and interiors as recorded in photographs, and plan diagrams from interviews. These various

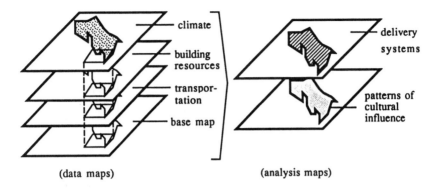

(data maps)   (analysis maps)

Figure 8.2: Adaptation of a GIS to this research

forms of descriptive data can then be integrated with other sources of design knowledge. Historic and archival material in both written and graphic form, census data on housing quality, building materials, and usage, as well as the analysis of questionnaires administered in this region of Costa Rica, all provide data sources for the study of the *corredor* as a design element. This would suggest that design information would result from the full variety of forms represented in the integrated methodology. Figures 8.4a and 8.4b represent the various characteristics of WPs, as well as those of qualitative methods, which are applicable to this study of environments in order to inform designers.

Specific methods

The specific research methods utilized to understand the meaning of the *corredor* in Costa Rican housing are fourfold: (1) a historic review of documents, both written and graphic; (2) collecting visual material and data (maps, floor plans, photographs and slides, diagrams, etc.); (3) reviewing and analyzing existing data bases (previous questionnaires, census material,etc.); and (4) developing and administering a questionnaire. The multiple approach is in keeping with much of the work done in environment behavior studies, as mentioned above (also see: Michelson, 1975; Low and Chambers, 1989, etc). Each of the four basic methods utilized here is discussed in more detail below.

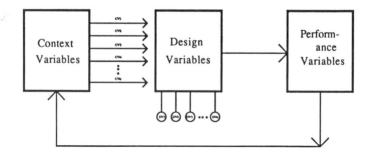

Figure 8.3A: A model of the design process, where context variables are outside of the control of the designer which, along with the design variables determine the outcome, as seen in the values of the performance variables (from Rittel, 1974; after Ashby, 1970).

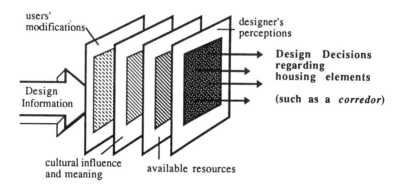

Figure 8.3: A model of the design process

Figure 8.3B: Resultant design elements from context variables acting as filters for design variables.

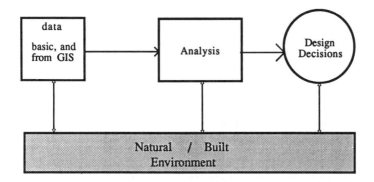

Figure 8.4A: A model of the distribution of design knowledge.

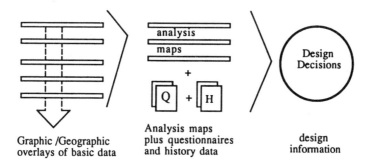

Figure 8.4: How research informs the designer

Figure 8.4B: How design information results from the integration of different types of analysis and basic data.

Historic review and analysis

A literature and document search was undertaken (in English and Spanish) to provide the basis of a historical analysis. Literature from the fields of archaeology, anthropology, history, and architecture was considered. Visual documents include field notes and their interpretation, diagrams developed from historic letters and documents, as well as existing etchings and photographs from the 16th century forward. Archival documents and descriptions in Costa Rica were included as well.

Graphic and visual data collection

In the summer of 1987 an initial photographic survey was done of housing in Golfito and the surrounding Brunca Region. A collection of maps and architectural or engineering documents was begun at that time. Two brief trips in 1989 allowed photographic documentation of some of the changes occurring in Golfito, providing material on housing and community infrastructure from that period also. During the 1990-1991 academic year, additional photographs were taken, some in conjunction with the survey instrument discussed below. Maps and other drawings were also obtained during that year, supplementing the existing graphic data base. Thus current graphic documentation includes not only specific diagrams and photographs of houses where interviews took place, but also material from historic and current references,architectural drawings and diagrams, and maps.

Other visual data were collected through direct observation of exterior changes made to company-built houses in Golfito. Utilizing the same coding procedure developed for the analysis of the questionnaires, all of the five barrios in Golfito containing "Arquitectura Bananera" were reviewed, and changes recorded. These data provide verification of responses made to questions during the interviews done in these barrios. It also contributes to a longitudinal visual data base of housing in Golfito. Earlier data are from the 1987 and 1989 visits; for Barrios Las Alamedas and Parrochial, an appraisal done in 1982 extends the historic record. Photographs, floor plans, elevation drawings and economic analyses exist for all company properties in these two barrios at that time.

Existing data bases

Various previous studies for the region have been reviewed. These include questionnaires done in Golfito, in the indigenous communities and reserves in the area, and in the Brunca Region in general. Two of the Golfito questionnaires contributed to the design of the survey instrument administered in longitudinal data longitudinal data 1991, discussed below. This was done to develop a longitudinal data base, with earlier questions about the community of Golfito dating from 1984. Costa Rican census material has also been reviewed, as it provides a third longitudinal study. Specific data about housing styles, uses, appliances, and building materials are found in census documents from 1963, 1973, and 1983. While the design element *corredor* is not specifically mentioned in the housing census material, other aspects are significant for the broader study.

Questionnaire

The final method used to collect data was an extensive questionnaire survey. It was designed to elicit information regarding the social and cultural aspects of housing in Golfito and the surrounding region. It contained five sections: (A) Demographic data; (B) Opinions about Golfito/your community; (C) The house and its location; (D) Diagram and use of the house;and (E) The city/community. The demographic data and opinions, sections A and B, are follow up for the earlier studies mentioned above (M.E. Bozzoli, 1985, for example). The current analysis of the use and evolution of the *corredor* draws directly from sections A, C, D,and the floor plan diagrams.

The survey instrument was intended for use as an interview questionnaire, since the rate of return for mailed questionnaires without interviews in this situation is essentially 0%. A pilot study and two rounds of revisions improved the clarity of the questions. After the test cases were reviewed, a stratified sample of Golfito was established based on the 14 existing barrios. Interviewers obtained cluster samples of an assigned size for each sub- area. The survey instrument was then modified to reflect regional communities in general, and was administered in selected neighboring towns. This secured data for purposes of comparison with Golfito. Figure 8.5 shows the communities selected and the sample stratification in Golfito, while Tables 8.1 and 8.2 provide the sample size for each stratum in the overall data sample.

The questionnaire was intentionally designed to contain mostly open-ended questions. In this manner, both qualitative and quantitative analyses are possible. This approach also allows more diversity and freedom in responses. However, it places a larger burden on the coding of the answers and the analysis of the questionnaire variables. In response to this demand, the vast majority of the coding was done by Costa Ricans familiar with Golfito. The quantitative analysis of variables is thus limited to nominal and ordinal scale data, mostly nominal. However the ability to examine the direct and diverse responses within an overall context analysis is critical to the project and the integration of methods. The qualitative thus reinforces the visual analysis done, while the quantitative allows support for correlations which may occur.

Figure 8.5: The Brunca region and sample locations

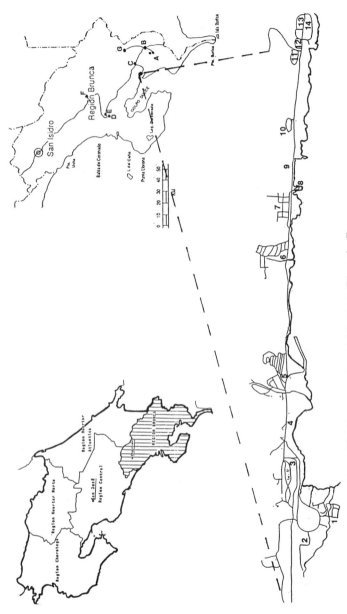

Note: The Brunca region within Costa Rica, the Brunca region communities, and the barrios in Golfito as sampled. The lists in Tables 8.1 and 8.2 correspond to these maps.

Table 8.1: Stratified sample selection in Golfito

Barrio (North to South)	Type of housing	Sample size: desired	actual
1. Llano Bonito	company	5	5
2. (San Juan)	INVU	5	5
3. Las Alamedos	company	10	10 (+2)
4. Parrochial	company	5	5
5. Bella Vista	company	20	20 (+3)
6. Kilometro Uno	company	20	22(+2)
7. Pueblo Civil	(self-built)	20	19 (+1)
8. San Andreas	INVU	5	5 (+4)
9. Kilometro Dos	self-built	5	5 (+3)
10. San Martin	INVU	5	5
11. Kilometro Tres[1]	INVU (1)	5	5
12.	INVU (2)	5	5
13. 7 INVU (3)	5	10	
14. Kilometro Tres	(Casas de la Playa)	40	31 (+2)
15. Afuera de Golfito	(self-built)	10	10 (+1)
	TOTALS:	165	180

(See Figure 8.5 for parallel indications of the locations of these samples)

1. It should be noted that the sample for Barrio Kilometro Tres, including three INVU projects for that area, was intentionally high in response to requests by INVU and the community for better information regarding this barrio. Specific questions were added to the survey instrument to address these concerns, to be asked only of residents in that area.

Table 8.2: Sample for communities in the region

Name South to North	Type of housing	Sample size desired	Sample size actual
A. COTO 47, 49	company[1]	10	10
B. Ciudad Neilly	self-built	10	10
Ciudad Neilly	INVU	10	9
C. Rio Claro	self-built	5	5(+1)
D. Palmar Sur	company	10	9(+1)
E. Palmar Norte	self-built	5	5
F. Buenos Aires	self-built	10	11
	INVU	5	1(+1)
	company[2]	5	
G. San Vito[3]	(self-built)	15(10+5)	0
	TOTALS:	85	62

(See Figure 8.5 for the locations of these communities in the region)

1. United Fruit Company
2. Pindeco (Del Monte Pineapple)
3. No returns yet. Questionnaires distributed for possible comparison for cultural viewpoint since this is an Italian colony.

The approach utilized in the present study is intentionally hybrid, for the following reasons:

1. A system of checks and balances is built in to verify or corroborate data in various forms.

2. Verbal explanations of spatial experiences are often limited; for cross-cultural studies this becomes even more critical.

3. Historic information, like contemporary studies, provides interpretations which may need revision or adaptation.

4. Longitudinal data are desired when trying to understand changes in meaning and tradition.

5. The discipline of design has no single tradition of inquiry; thus, a variety of research methods is usually helpful. These often include both quantitative and qualitative methods.

Background and historic setting

The adaptation and prevalence of the *corredor* throughout Costa Rica can be argued to be seen in part as its reflection of the traditional, indigenous houses which were variations on the rancho. These can be traced from settlement patterns of the three main Pre-Colombian groups. The Chorotega of the Nicoya Peninsula had villages with central plazas, surrounded by rectangular structures, while the Huetara and Boruca, or Brunca, tribes developed patterns with large communal, circular houses (Chapman, 1974; León, 1943). Each group utilized available natural resources to produce thatched houses, the various shapes of which can be considered predecessors of the rancho seen today – post and beam construction, open or partially blocked walls, with grass or palm thatched roofs (Figure 8.6). Thus while none of the Pre-Colombian structures are known to have a *corredor* per se, the open rancho structure, responsive to climatic forces, is an important aspect of historic and current shelter in the entire Mesoamerican region.

The results of three centuries of Spanish rule in Costa Rica are noticeably different than the colonial experience in other Central American countries. While the hacienda, the plantation, and the adobe house were all present in Costa Rica, the architectural forms, from religious and institutional buildings to housing, were much more modest. Trejos Dittel points out that the earliest building materials of the colonists in Costa Rica were wood and "bahareque" (much like wattle and daub construction) (1945); wood shows up in early hybrid systems with the rancho form (Figure 8.7).

Figure 8.6: 16th century etching of indigenous *rancho*

Note: 16th century etching of indigenous *rancho* (by Benzoni, Gerolamo; first published in "Dell' Historie del Mondo Nuovo," as seen in *Enciclopedia de Costa Rica: su historia, tierra y gentes*, Rojas R., Joerge L., general coordinator, for Océano, 1987 (p. 71).

He further verifies Len's position that, especially in the Nicoya area, the rough wooden plank house and rancho combination seen today is a direct descendant of the early use of wood introduced during the Spanish era (1943). Especially in the Guanacaste area, where the Chorotega's rancho was often open on the sides, the evolving house form began to include an open yet covered area, as an antecedent to today's *corredor*.

The settlement and development pattern of the hacienda is also important in the evolution of the *corredor*. Melndez and Len describe the granado hacienda of Guanacaste as a form well adapted to the activities of the cattlemen in the dry tropical climate; the large main ranch house, or casona, was surrounded by a series of corrals, followed by outlying pastures (1977; 1943). Trejos Dittel indicates that most of the casonas were ringed by a galeria, with wooden rails. The galeria faced the front as well as interior patios. The collection of wooden structures "might take the form of traditional Spanish buildings" serving a variety of purposes (1945; p. 18). Layers of corrals were used for branding cattle, but they also served as protection during a fight or attack. In addition they housed critical social functions: after a day of hard work the corrals became stage areas for bullfights, dances and other fiesta activities. The galerias were integral parts of these fiestas as well.

Figure 8.7: Illustration of a typical hacienda

Note: Illustration of a typical hacienda, as seen in *Enciclopedia de Costa Rica: su historia, tierra y gentes*, Rojas R., Joerge L., general coordinator, for Océano, 1987 (p. 141).

Fonseca notes that to own a hacienda provided social and economic prestige; the owner frequently lived in town or the capital, and visited the hacienda infrequently (1983). This confirms Len's description, which excluded the owner from the occupants; rather, ranch hands and cattlemen lived there and stored tools in the structure (1943). Stephens provides several descriptions of the haciendas encountered in his travels through the region in the 1840s (1929). One hacienda he visited was a two-story structure, with stairs on the outside and the lower floor serving as the bodega (storage area). The house was "well sited, with a tosco balcony on all four sides,..." (in Guaria, 1929; p. 78). In the owner's absence the major domo slept in a hammock outside; the kitchen was a separate structure nearby. Another hacienda Stephens visited had corrals on three sides. There was a small area of the large 200,000 acre holding set aside to cultivate vegetables grown for the workers, while the entire properties were large in order to assure sustained use by rotating crops and pasture lands. The hacienda therefore evolved from a unique combination of characteristics: geography, climate and vegetation, as well as limited technological resources, a low labor supply, and little need or availability of capital. The hacienda form was quite resistant to change, which is why it is still seen in Guanacaste. The gallery, or *corredor*, is highly visible in the house form today.

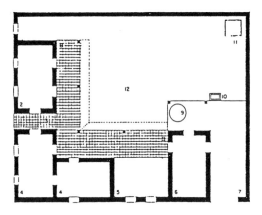

Figure 8.8: Evolution of the *corredor*

Note: The *coredor* as evolved from full gallery which would surround an indoor courtyard.
From Paris, after Léon (1943).

Adobe houses became possible only as Costa Rican colonists became a
bit more prosperous. Further, their presence was generally limited to the
Meseta Central (the Central Valley), where the majority of the Spanish
colonists lived; the temperate climate required more completely enclosed
houses than in the tropical coastal lowlands. The *corredor* itself is perhaps more clearly understood in the context of the traditional adobe house
imported from Spain. According to Guaria, most of the Spanish colonists
who settled in Costa Rica came from Andalucia and Castilla (Ricardo Fer-
nandez, 1925 edition; p. 44). The house type brought with these Spanish
settlers was one with an internal patio, surrounded by a gallery, or "cloister
- like arcade" is confirmed by Paris (1989) (See Figure 8.8). More formal houses in Costa Rica today, as in other Central and Latin American
countries, still reflect this form, with an internal patio and its surrounding
corredor (Paris, 1989 and others).

One of the reasons adobe survived so long in Costa Rica as a building
material, and thus as a house form, is its direct relationship to bahareque,
one of the Pre-Colombian technologies (Meléndez; 1977; Madrigal, et al.).
The hybrid bahareque/adobe construction has proven to be highly resistant
to seismic forces, as clarified by Stephens:

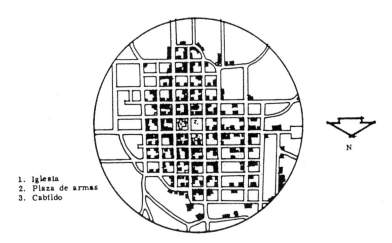

1. Iglesia
2. Plaza de armas
3. Cabildo

Figure 8.9: The town of Escazú

Note: Early layout of the town of Escasú; note corner location of older adobe houses; a
typical plan for these is given in Figure 8.8 (From León, 1943).

> The Costa Rican houses are the best in all of Central Amer-
> ica for resisting tremors. They are low and long and when the
> adobe blocks are smooth they are placed with posts between
> one another, so that when the sun dries them, it converts the
> wall into a solid mass which moves with the surface of the earth.
> (1929; p.92).

The adobe house thus evolved to become one of the symbols of Costa
Rica, as highly visible throughout the Meseta Central during the 19th and
early 20th centuries as the Spanish grid and central plaza settlement pattern
from the 1573 law (Costa Rica; no date). Urban adobe houses were built
around the plaza and on the grid corners. This pattern is still visible in
Barva de Heredia, where the entire plaza area and surrounding buildings
are preserved for historic reasons.

Madrigal and Léon also illustrate the grid system, exemplified by Escazú
with adobe houses on the corners (Figure 8.9). The 19th century home for
the President in San Jose was built in this tradition: two story, adobe block,
tile roof, and upper level balcony (in Guaria, 1929). Similarly, many houses
in Cartago, the earlier capitol of Costa Rica, utilized covered walkways, or
modified *corredors*.

Another form of vernacular housing in Costa Rica is that attributed to the Black population in Limon and along the Atlantic Coast. The Antilles Blacks settled these areas in three main waves: first as plantation workers for the Spanish, then as the tortugueros arriving to live independently along the coast, and finally as workers brought over at the end of the 19th century, to build the railroad and banana plantations (Palmer, 1986). These Blacks brought with them many cultural traditions, one of which was the house form seen in that area today. A different settlement pattern also evolved, with a single manzana, or city block, serving as the homestead site. The house would be located vaguely in the center of the block, with rambling outbuildings, no fences, and gardens or yard space all around. Usually simple wood structures, the houses were raised on posts for climatic and health reasons, with a gallery running across the front, or around the entire house (Paris, 1988; Ponce, 1982). This suggests another version, or variation to, the *corredor* as it developed in Costa Rica.

In contrast, there are houses built in Costa Rica designed without any form of *corredor*. The United Fruit Company developed banana plantations and supporting infrastructure throughout the last century in Costa Rica. The port town of Golfito, built 50 years ago as headquarters for exporting bananas from the South Pacific Region, contains many excellent examples of houses built by the Company. Identified by Flores as Arquitectura Bananera, a full typology of house forms was designed and built, in Golfito clearly identifying the socio-economic structure of the company itself (1985). Five of the 14 barrios in Golfito contain these structures. Most of these house forms, while well adapted to the tropical climate, do not provide *corredors*. Due to the Company's decision to move out of Golfito after eliminating its banana production in the area, many changes are taking place in that setting. These changes and houses are the focus of the larger study, of which the current chapter is only a small part.

Results

Results of the various methods occur in different forms. Initial results of the questionnaire will be presented here, with corroboration and supporting data from other aspects of the investigation given throughout the discussion that follows. The existence of the *corredor* as an element in the house design will be presented, then its use will be discussed.

From a content analysis of the answers to the question, "Que es para Usted una casa antigua de Costa Rica?" A very clear trend is evident. Table 8.3 breaks down the answers to this question, while Table 8.4 gives the responses to "Que es para Usted una casa typica de esta comunidad?" Interpretation of the responses that included "adobe, mud, or bahareque"

Table 8.3: Responses to the question: "What is a traditional Costa Rican house?"[1]

Descriptors	Responses	
	in Golfito	in other Communities
poor/bad	3	1
good/beautiful	16	16
rustic/old	9	0
wooden	7	12
a rancho[2]	16	17
colonial	5	0
adobe[3]	70	22
with a patio	2	0
with a *corredor*	9	1
TOTALS:	137	66

1. "Qué es para Usted una casa antigua de Costa Rica?"
2. A *rancho* is a thatched, pole and beam, usually open-sided structure.
3. Following the Costa Rican census categories, "adobe" also includes the terms: "bahareque", "barro", "tejas", and "labrillo".

assumes the house form with corresponding patio and or *corredor*. Responses that included "Arquitectura Bananera, casa de la playa, or rancho", would not be interpreted to have patio or *corredor*, as these houses represent different types. This interpretation indicates that 70 (51%) of 137 respondents in Golfito consider adobe the traditional house form, while outside of Golfito 22 (29%) of 63 gave this response. When the terms *corredor* and patio are included, the total responses are 86 (63%) and 23 (30%) respectively.

This interpretation is confirmed and clarified when the floor plan diagrams from the questionnaires are analyzed. While not specifically asking the interviewers to address the element of *corredor* there was an expressed intent to get information regarding outside spaces, beyond walls of the sheltered portion of the dwelling. From respondents outside of Golfito, 40 (64.5%) of 62 diagrams had spaces labeled as *corredor*; of these 40, 10 (25%) had an area labelled patio. Of the 22 with no area identified as a *corredor*, 10 (45.5%) were Company houses, (Arquitectura Bananera, Pindeco's INVU housing), and another 4 (18%) were from the Ciudad Neilly INVU project. Within Golfito, 76 (46.3%) of the 164 diagrams reviewed indicated a *corredor* or a patio. Of these 76, 43 (56.6%)were Arquitectura Bananera, which means a *corredor* had been added in the last 5 years.

In April of 1991 a complete count of visible exterior changes was made

Table 8.4: Responses to the question: "What is a typical house in Golfito/this community?"

Descriptors	Responses	
	in Golfito	in other Communities
Company[1]	48	6
a rancho[2]	30	13
wood	14	13
Casa de la Playa[3]	4	(na)
other	5	0
adobe	0	6
cement	0	5
TOTALS:	101	43

1. Arquitectura Bananera, or houses built by the United Fruit Company
2. Same as note 2, Table 8.3.
3. These are the stilt houses, especially in Kilometro Tres, or "Hong Kong", in Golfito.

for the barrios of Arquitectura Bananera in Golfito. The houses in Las Alamedas and Parrochial are not conducive to the addition of a *corredor* due to their two storey construction above a piso baso. In the Barrios of Bella Vista and Kilometro Uno, many of the houses are multiple units. However this has not prevented conversions: often the *corredor* is built in front of only one half of the structure. The survey for these two barrios indicates that 62 of 258 units in Bella Vista, or 24% have an added *corredor*, while in Kilometro Uno 52 of 228, or 22.8% houses, have these additions. Overall these represent lower figures than the sample taken.

Discussion

In a country like Costa Rica, where cultural traditions are not a strength either of the people or of the built environment, then many issues need to be considered. This supports the approach of addressing meaning in the environment from a full range of perspectives. Based on the suggestions of Ittlement et al., several social sciences are necessary along with architectural design to understand urban and community settings (1974). It can equally be argued that these same realms of study are necessary for informing decisions in architectural design itself. For example, the use of and meaning assigned to an element like the *corredor* can be analysed in the psychological terms of perception, cognition, and behavior. However the contributions of political, religious or economic institutions as they structure the Costa

Rican society are also important.

Further, it is useful to examine the application of an integrated methodology, such as the one presented here. This is necessary not only to evaluate
the structure of this specific, proposed model, but also to consider the use
of a model of this type with respect to its contributions to knowledge useful to designers. The process of design has no clear end point, as Rittel
and Webber acknowledge in the discussion of WPs (1972). Rather, design
problems are resolved, over and over again, with varying degrees of success.
This is one argument for including historic analysis in the investigation of
housing elements. This is done not only to discovere precedents, in the
more formal design typological sense, but also to recognize the degrees of
success various design resolutions have provided for cultural patterns or
behavior.

Discussion of *corredor* as a housing element

From the historic review, it is seen that in the traditional Spanish house
and its variations, the *corredor* provided access to several rooms. This
was, first, a remnant of the full gallery function found originally in this
house type, and, second, a response to the simplified house form which
evolved in Costa Rica. For example, when the Andalusian Spanish adobe
house was imported in form and material to the new world, it was modified
within the different geographic settings, as well as in response to other
variables. In Costa Rica, with the colonists more involved in an agrarian
subsistence economy, a larger house, more formal and with an internal
courtyard fully surrounded by a gallery, was often well beyond their means
(Fonseca, 1983; Ground, 1978). The form was modified, as can be seen
in the "corner" urban adobe houses presented by León and others (1943).
(Seen in figure 8.9.) This modification gives a faade similar to the original
courtyard plan house, but protects in fact a more modest structure. The
rear may only have a patio, with a *corredor* between that and the inside.
Or, with economic means increased, the patio may have developed into
the full courtyard again, with its accompanying gallery. The *corredor* has
served as a passage, or hallway space, to allow entry to several internal
rooms. This format with multiple access is visible in both urban and rural
houses, inside and outside of Costa Rica. In more formal houses, an actual
vestibule might develop, moving the entry transition function inside.

In urban areas of Costa Rica two story houses often developed. In
these, the second floor always had a covered gallery, or *corredor*-like space.
In Puntarenas, the historic port city on the Pacific Coast, the two story
house form was traditional, with an upstairs gallery and its railing (Len,
1943; Paris, 1988). Living quarters in Puntarenas were upstairs in response

to the need for commercial uses at ground level. Similar to the houses in Limn and on the Atlantic Coast, the living quarters were also raised in response to the climate, to better capture sea breezes and to avoid insects and pests. In Limn the use of the veranda was perhaps more diverse than elsewhere, however; descriptions indicate clothes cleaning and drying, child care, musical gatherings, and social games and relaxation all took place in this area (Ponce, 1982; Palmer, 1986).

The main difference between the raised balcony, veranda, or gallery, and the *corredor* is that climate has dictated raised living spaces for the former set of spaces. This vertical change also assures better privacy, and separation from street or water level activities. The climate and social functions of this zone fit the *corredor* as well. The buffer space assures shading of the wall surface, reducing solar gain to the interior (Olgyay, 1963). As protection from rain, heat and sun, while providing usable outdoor space, the *corredor* serves a variety of activities. Historically the *corredor* was an area to dry grain, or coffee beans (Ground, 1978). Now it is used for sleeping, relaxing, food preparation or eating, and receiving visitors (ITC, 1964). Further, as a semi- private space, occupants or the *corredor* can maintain privacy without intrusion as they address passers-by in the street.

Historically, in the countryside the Spanish colonists' first houses were wooden cabin structures, usually with an attached rancho. Then, after time and if more economic stability occurred, a full hacienda or adobe casona could be built. The form and use of the attached rancho naturally merged with the *corredor* of the later house forms; houses in all stages of this transition are still visible, not only in Costa Rica, but in neighboring Nicaragua and Panama, as well as in countries further south, such as Venezuela (Gasparini, 1962).

In Costa Rica the hybrid form of the *corredor*, reflecting an evolution occurring in indigenous homes is quite visible. In Matamb, near Nicoya, the reservation dwellers in the early part of this century had only one entry to their home, off the interior patio and *corredor*. Now with a second entry on the street side, the house is still protected by the *corredor*. In this hybrid form it can be argued that the *corredor* exists in all parts of Costa Rica. While internal colonization of the Pacific South Region occurred mostly during the middle of the 20th century (Bozzoli, 1989), the indigenous populations of the Brunca Region show the hybrid rancho wooden house, with a shed rancho often acting as a *corredor*, similar to the houses in Nicoya. More recent settlements in this region contain a house form borrowed from the Central Valley, which is itself only remotely modelled after an adobe house. Thus the direct tie is removed even farther from the traditional adobe house. However with the climatic and social requirements of the transition space provided by a *corredor*, it becomes one of the first additions made by new occupants of institutionally built housing.

The *corredor* shows up in other countries as well; a brief review of the usage is presented here. In neighboring Nicaragua and Panama, the multiple entry adobe house is more visible than in Costa Rica today. This may be due to the high rate of burglary in Costa Rica, as well as to changing availability of building materials (concrete block, prefabricated items, etc.). In Paraguay the *corredor* has many entries to internal rooms, but it is more clearly identified as a hybrid from indigenous uses, and less clearly as an evolved form based on a gallery surrounding a patio (Marin; 1991). In Puerto Rico, however, a *corredor* refers to a hallway transition space, which mayor may not be completely enclosed (Jopling, 1988).

The historic precedent of a full gallery surrounding the Spanish interior courtyard has evolved into many different forms. The *corredor* found in Costa Rica and elsewhere is only one of many ways this design element is expressed. From a study of house forms in the Central Valley undertaken as a group thesis project at UCR, the architecture students treated the transition space as one of many defining variables (see Figure 8.10; Chavez, et al., 1987). The various terms used to describe this outdoor - indoor transition space can also be briefly reviewed. Krier discusses variations of public space, which include verandas, porches, and entry halls (1980). He also indicates that arcades, more often seen on non-residential structures, have an ambiguity: it is not clear whether they belong to the street or to the actual building. These intermediary spaces also exist with balconies, galleries, and *corredors*. It is important to recall that various disciplines have their own terminology, and that historians, anthropologists, and architects might all give the same space a different name. However by focusing on common usage, meaning can be more readily determined. The changes and uses of the *corredor* space, as indicated by the results from the questionnaire, are important factors in clarifying meaning. These are now discussed.

Going beyond the historic analysis, the graphic materials (photographs, existing plans and construction documents) reinforce the design aspects and the prevelance of the *corredor* in Costa Rica. Direct observation along with the visual documents confirms the usage and functions generally attributed to the *corredor*. Where there is a clear change in social structure and consequently access to housing, as occurred in Golfito, then visual observations of changes and modifications made to the Arquitectura Bananera may be more convincing than verbal responses to the survey instrument. This may be attributed to several different possibilities. The first is that, to a Costa Rican, a *corredor* is so necessary, and common, that it may hardly be discussed. The data from the questionnaires, for example, did not show the *corredor* to be one of the three most important spaces in the housing. However, it is necessary to remember that the questionnaire was

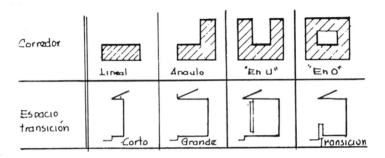

Figure 8.10: A classification system of the *corredor*

Note: Classification system from a formal typology which utilizes both the form of the corredor and the condifuration of the transition space as identifying design elements. (From Chavez *et al.*, 1988).

not explicitly designed to elicit data on *corredors* alone; rather as part of a larger survey objective. sted in the original structure. For example, of the Company houses in Golfito, the houses built in Barrios Las Alamedas and Parrochial had elevated living quarters. The piso baso, a lattice-enclosed ground level space, thus took the place of a *corredor* and no specific *corredor* was provided. Among the other plan types built by the Company in Golfito, none initially had any outdoor *corredor* space. Therefore, when reviewing the diagrams drawn for Golfito, the location or barrio must be taken into account, one of the requirements dictating the stratified sample. Of the 164 houses in Golfito with no *corredor*, 76 of these were Arquitectura Bananera. In addition, there is an ill-defined poorly enforced preservation code in Barrios Las Alamedas or Parrochial (Matarrita, 1990). This suggests that structures in these two barrios remain intact with no significant modifications.

When looking at the recorded changes made to houses in Golfito, a few socio-economic factors, not to mention political ones, are visible. The first trend reflects a pattern of adapted changes to structures within a given barrio. What happens is that an initial change is made by one resident; it next appears up and down that street, then elsewhere in that barrio. This phenomenon is directly tied to the fact that different plan types and densities are used in the different barrios, originally intended as a direct indication of socio-economic status. Thus what works well for one house in that barrio presumably would work well for all of the other houses of that type present in that barrio. The trend may also simply reflect a desire to "keep up with the Joneses ".

The second trend is a reflection of the relationship of a given house, or series of houses, to the main street of Golfito. There is a clear pattern which shows more exterior changes made to houses closer to this street, which functions in many ways as a central plaza might in other towns.

That is, visibility and social functions seem to be as critical to one's location relative to the main street. Whether or not the occupants of the houses closest to the street have more money available to make improvements has not been clearly determined. However within the sample obtained, responses indicate that many residents of the two barrios involved, Bella Vista and Kilometro Uno, purchased the house they occupied at the time the Company left. Again, the presence of a social structure in terms of original housing assignments cannot be determined with the material available at this time. Suffice it to say that pressures may exist to change the Company built house, adding, for example, a *corredor*. It is interesting to note that a similar trend is evident in the housing projects built by INVU/IMAS in the area. This trend is reflected in both Ciudad Neilly and the new IMAS project in Golfito; houses closer to the main thoroughfare show improvements sooner.

However, the addition of a *corredor* for political, or status, reasons has led to a new design dilemma. While the significance of this housing element in Costa Rica has been confirmed by this research, the meaning of the *corredor* has perhaps been elevated to a level of importance beyond its pragmatic requirements. The actual transition space from the street to the house may now be more abrupt, depending on the yard space around the added *corredor*. And, the climatic performance of the structure may be compromised. While the protection from sun and rain still exists, cooling breezes may no longer reach interior spaces. In tropical climates, this ventilation is often considered the critical cooling factor (Luckey, 1989); when it is reduced, interior activities must move outside. Whether or not these activities would have initially occurred in the *corredor* or not is difficult to determine.

Design implications

Within an integrated research approach, as with any inquiry in search of design information, it is appropriate to recognize and allow limitations. While it is important to develop an improved and ongoing understanding of meaning within the built environment, there is no complete substitute for a designer's experience and personal involvement in a design project. The intent of research undertaken for architects and designers is generally to allow them to apply new knowledge. Within the natural constraints of wicked problems, this can only be attempted, and resolved; it is never finally solved (Rittel, 1972). Regarding the hybrid methodology, then, its application is necessary to maintain a variety of viewpoints. To perceive cultural meaning, historic and current usage must be examined to understand traditions and change (Rapoport, 1989). Other disciplines must be considered, to ascertain the applicability of both methods and knowledge gained from them (Ittleson, et al., 1974). An overall willingness to adjust to,or work within, evolving research methods is important for design approaches (Taylor and Bogdan, 1984). Further, it is interesting to note the parallel form the various models presented take. That is, with performance variables providing feedback to the context, the model in Figure 8.4b parallels the symbolic interactionism model, or diagram, for "meaning". Similarly, the use of the typological structure within the framework of a GIS is reiterated in the specific CV filters, or screens, of this model.

As various parts of this study, or of housing design decisions, are considered, certain fields of knowledge will be included, or not, as appropriate. For example, when reviewing the use of building materials for different zones of Costa Rica, the availability of resources, transportation systems, and engineering knowlegde may play a more significant role than they do now, when considering the meaning and the use of the design element known as the *"corredor"*. Thus the intent of an integrated methodology is not simply to allow both quantitative and qualitative, or statistical and descriptive data, to be examined together. It is also intended to be flexible enough to adjust to the different factors or variables contributing to the specific design issues under consideration. Hopefully, also, as new knowledge is found, it can be included and integrated in the overall methodolgy as well, without requiring a completely new model.

In terms of information gained, there is much to be learned here for designers. First, caution is indicated: relying solely on symbolic meaning of spaces is insufficient. Usage contributes to meaning, and both evolve and change as part of tradition, or ongoing cultural evolution. In addition, preconceived notions,whether in the form of design vocabulary or that of other professionals, may be seriously misleading. The full range of architectural terms for an indoor - outdoor transition from public to private realms are unknown to the users of *corredors* in Costa Rica. However the space described by this simple, almost generic term is no less significant to their homes. Thus, especially in a country which is rediscovering or re-establishing its cultural identity, as is Costa Rica, what is tradition and important may be revealed more clearly by understanding the ordinary. The importance of the consistency, or tenacity, of the *corredor*, in spite of its spatial variations, for existing and future housing stock cannot be denied.

Finally, with the integrated approach, it may be possible to continue to supplement the data bases produced through research. Here, for example, the larger study for the Brunca Region is providing longitudinaly data for research projects begun in 1984. Also, the flexibility required in qualitative approaches, as Taylor and Rogdan indicated, which is visible in this integrated methodology, allows new sources of and analysis for design knowledge as it develops and evolved (1984).

Conclusions

There are several different conclusions which can be reached at this point. Initially, in terms of housing in Costa Rica, it is clear that a *corredor*, at a minimum, is a critical design element. It may also be appropriate to have a patio, or courtyard, or other form of outdoor space, as explained below. Not only has the need for the *corredor* been demonstrated through its visible presence within different historic periods and cultural influences, but also through its current usage and prevelance. This is seen in the addition of a *corredor* to housing solutions built under various institutional structures, such as the United Fruit Company in Golfito, or the Costa Rican government in INVU projects. Further, housing solutions presently under construction or projects being designed are now including a *corredor*, albeit usually a very modest one. Examples in the Brunca region are houses in the IMAS/INVU project in Golfito, designed in part by the community housing committee, as well as self-help housing underway as part of the Integrated Rural Development Project of the European Communities.

While the actual form of the *corredor* may vary, its presence was consistent. Thus the verandah in Limn may be seen to serve similar roles with parallel meanings to the *corredor* elsewhere in Costa Rica. In many houses, especially more formal ones, a patio or an internal courtyard is also present. All of these elements are presented here as relatives of the *corredor*, although this conclusion is somewhat more tentative and needs further study for different countries and cultural realms. While this point still needs additional verification, the fact that a transition space occurs for purposes of moving from light to shade, from public to private, and to contain specific functional and perhaps ritual uses is well documented. What remains to be confirmed is how the full range of formal variations moves from public arcade, to public or private galleries around a courtyard, to verandahs, balconies, porches, and finally to the *corredor*, whether as a hall space or an entry from the outside to several interior spaces.

Another level of conclusion may be reached regarding how the design process is informed.

There are many different realms which contribute context and design knowledge. Just considering this one design element, factors identified are those which contribute to the meaning of *corredor* through the interpretive filters seen in Figure 8.4b: (1) the users' built modifications to and observable behaviors within the housing solutions; (2) the available resources (human, transport, materials); (3) the historic and cultural influences; and (4) the designer's perceptions. While each of these realms enhances the context and contributes to the understanding of *corredor*, design decisions must still be made. What has been demonstrated, however, is that informed decisions, such as those made during the design process for the IMAS/INVU project in Golfito, can more directly serve both functional and meaning, or symbolic needs, through design choices. Thus, design decisions regarding the *corredor* in Costa Rica are informed by history, culture, meaning and use.

All of these factors become clearer, or are better demonstrated, through the use of the proposed integrated methodology. As with most design related data, visual and graphic content and analyses were useful, and they reinforced the basic conclusions found in the survey data. Direct observations and recordings, not only of behavior but also of the built forms themselves, were also useful. Placed in the context of historic analysis and review, again using both verbal and graphic data, along with documentation which provides statistical distributions of house forms, cultural understanding evolves more readily.

In the end designers must beware looking for an easy approach. The desire to make the process of designing more transparent, to find information which improves accountability, is strong. In cross cultural or other less complex situations the temptation exists to find a solution, or knowledge for a design answer, from other professions. This may be from research studies which can direct design decisions. Visible evidence from direct observation should not be discounted, whether or not it has been formally documented or analyzed. Further, history cannot be denied, as precedent for architectural form as well as usage and meaning; nor is it a design panacea. By developing a combined set of methods which provide the necessary design knowledge in a unique, current situation, then meaning may be better understood and applied in the resolution of WPs, in the design process.

References

Aguilar A., Eduardo, *Estudio de la Vivienda Rural en Guatemala*, Editorial Universidad Guatemala, 1980

Altezor F., Carlos, *Arquitectura Urbana en Costa Rica: Exploracin histrica 1900–1950*, Cartago, Costa Rica, Editorial Tecnologica de Costa Rica, 1986

Altman, Irwin, "Human Behavior and Environment: Advances in Theory and Research", in Vol. 4, *Environment and Culture*, Amos Rapoport and Joachim F. Wohlwill, eds., New York, Plenum Press, 1980

Altman, Irwin and Martin Chemers, *Culture and Environment*, Monterey, CA, Brooks/Cole Publishing Company, 1980

Ashby, William R., *The Process of Model Building in the Behavioral Sciences*, Columbus, The Ohio State University Press, 1970

Bechtel, Robert B., Chapter 9 in Low, above, "Behavior in the House: A Cross-Cultural Comparison Using Behavior–Setting Methodology", PP. 164-187

Bozzoli de Wille, Maria–Eugenia, "El desarollo de la Region Brunca: Tendencias y Perspectivas", Ceincias Sociales, Esp. 2: 1985 (pp. 23-32)

Brunskill, R. W., *Illustrated Handbook of Vernacular Architecture*, 3rd edition, London, Faber and Faber, 1987

Censos de Población de los años 1963, 1973, y 1984 de la Dirección General de Estadística y Censos de Costa Rica

Chapman, Anne M., "Los Nicarao y Los Chorotega segun Las Fuentes Historicas", in: Publicaciones de la Unversidad de Costa Rica, Serie Historica y Geografía #4, 1974, Ciudad Universitaria Rodrigo Facio, Costa Rica

Chavez C., Erick, et al., "Un Analysis Tipologico Habitacional Comparative en el Valle Central", thesis for University of Costa Rica, 1987

Costa Rica, *Colección de Leyes y Decretos, San José*, Costa Rica, Imprenta Nacional

de Oviedo, Fernández and Gonzalo Valdés, Historia General y Natural de las Indias, Madrid, Ediciones Atlas, Biblioteca de Autores Espaoles, Vol. IV, 1959

Fernández, León, Colleccion de documentos para la Historia de Costa Rica, Vol. 3, San José, Costa Rica, Imprenta Nacional, 2nd edition (date?)

Flores C., Luis Guillermo, Arquitecto, Golfiteo, personal coversations, San Pedro, Costa Rica, 1985 & 1987.

Fonseca C., Elizabeth, Costa Rica Colonial: La Tierra y El Hombre, Ciudad Universitaria Rodrigo Facio, Costa Rica, Editorial Universidad Centroamericana, 1983

Gasparini, Graziano, La Casa Colonial Venezolana, Caracas, Venezuela, Universidad Central de Venezuela, 1962

Ground, Richard L., "Styles of Development in Costa Rica: The rise of coffee and the transfer of the subsistence economy", findings of Phase I - Report, unpublished manuscript, 1978

Guardia, Ricardo Fernndez, Costa Rica en el Siglo XIX, Ciudad Universitaria Rodrigo Facio, Costa Rica, Editorial Universitaria Centroamericana (EDUCA), 1929

Guardia, Ricardo Fernndez, Historica de Costa Rica, San Jos, Costa Rica, Lehmann Libreria, 1925 edition and 1967, 43rd edition

Gutiérrez R., Manuel E., Arquitecto, *La casa de adobes costarricense*, Ciudad Universitaria Rodrigo 'Facio, Costa Rica, Publicacción de UCR, 1972

Huxhold, William E., *An Introduction to Urban Geographic Information Systems*, New York/Oxford, Oxford University Press, 1991

Instituto de Tierras y Colonización (ITC), "Estudie de Comunidades de indigenas zonas: Boruca–Térraba, China–Kicha", San José, Costa Rica, bound manuscript; 1964

Ittleson, William H., et al., *An Introduction to Environmental Psychology*, New York, Holt, Reinhart and Winston, 1974

Jopling, Carol F., *Puerto Rican Houses in Sociohistorical Perspective*, University of Tennessee Press, 1988

Krier, Rob, *Elements of Architecture*, London, A. D. Publishers, Ltd. (1980)

Lawrence, Roderick J., Chapter 6 in Low, below, "Translating Anthropological Concepts into Architectural Practice", (pp. 89 - 113)

León, Jorge, Nueva Geografía de Costa Rica, San José, Costa Rica, Soley y Valverde, 1943 edition

Low, Setha M., and Erve Chambers, eds., *Housing, Culture and Design: A Comparative Perspective*, Philidelphia, University of Pennsylvania Press, 1989

Luckey, Donna, "Hot wet climate, building in", *Encyclopedia of Architecture: Design, Engineering and Construction*, Vol. 2, ed. Wilkes, John; New York, John Wiley; 1988 (pp. 827 - 838)

Madrigal M., Manuel, Arquitecto, *La Vivenda del Costarricense hasta mediados del siglo XIX*, San José, Costa Rica, Imprenta Nacional, 1988

Marín, Gustavo, Paraguan national, personal communications in Lawrence Kansas, 1991

Matarrita A., Carlos, Arquitecto, et al., "Diagnostico del sistema ecologico de la ciudad de Golfito", bound manuscript, Coceyma, S. A., San José, Costa Rica, November 1990

Meléndez C., Carlos, *Tierra y Poblamiento en la Colonia*, San José, Costa Rica, Editorial Costa Rica, 1977

Michelson, William, ed., *Behavioral Research Methods in Environmental Design*, Stroudsburg, PA, Dowden, Hutchinson & Ross, Inc., 1975

Moneo, Rafael, "On Typology", in Oppositions #13, Cambridge, Mass., the MIT Press, 1979

Norberg-Schultz, Christian, *Meaning in Western Architecture*, revised edition, New York, Rizzoli, 1980

Norberg-Schultz, Christian, *The Concept of Dwelling: On the way to Figurative Architecture*, New York, Rizzoli, 1985

Norberg-Schultz, Christian, *Meaning and Place*, New York, Rizzoli, 1988

Olgyay, Victor, *Design with Climate*, Princeton, N.J., Princeton University Press, 1963

Palmer, Paula, *"Wa'apin Man": La historia de la costa talamanqueña de Costa Rica, según sus protagonistas*, San José, Costa Rica, Instituto del Libro, 1986

Palmes, J. C., *Sir Bannister Fletcher's: A History of Architecture*, revised edition, London, Athlone Press, 1975

Paris, Richard Woodbridge, "La Historia de Arquitectura de Costa Rica", thesis for Universidad Iberoamericana, Mexico; 1988

Patton, Carl V., ed., *Spontaneous Shelter: International Perspectives and Prospects*, Philadelphia, Temple University Press, 1988

Ponce, Juan Bernal, Arquitecto, "La Vivienda del Negro Limonense", in Habitar, (Revista del Colegio de Arquitectos de Costa Rica) #9, July 1982 (pp. 31-33)

Rapoport, Amos, *The Meaning of the Built Environment*, 2nd Edition, 1989

Rapoport, Amos, Chapter 3, in Patton, above: "Spontaneous Settlements as Vernacular Architecture" (pp. 51–77)

Rapoport, Amos, Chapter 11, in Altman, Irwin, and Werner, Vol. 8: *Home Environments*, "Thinking about home environments: A conceptual framework" (pp. 255–286)

Rittel, Horst W. J. and Melvin W. Webber, "Dilemmas in a General Theory of Planning", *Policy Sciences*, Vol. 4, 1973 (pp. 155-167)

Rittel, Horst W. J., "Structure and Usefulness of Planning Information Systems", *Bedrifts Økonomen*, No. 8., October 1972 (pp. 398-401)

Rittel, Horst W. J., class notes, University of California, Berkeley, 1974

Rossi, Aldo, *The Architecture of the City*, Cambridge, Massachusetts, MIT Press, 1982

Stephens, John Lloyd, "Incidentes de viaje en Centro America, Chiapas y Yucatan", in Guardia, above, pp. 47 - 102

Taylor, Steven J., and Robert Bogdan, *Introduction to Qualitative Research Methods: A search for Meaning*, 2nd edition, New York, John Wiley, 1984

Trejos Dittel, Eduardo, "Evolucion y Problemas de la Vivienda en Costa Rica" – Thesis, University of Costa Rica, 1945

Walsh, S. J., "Geographic Information Systems for Natural Resource Management", *Journal of Soil and Water Conservation*, 40(2) , 1985 (pp. 202-205)

Part IV
The Meaning and Use of Neighborhood:
Spatial Attributes and Social Dynamics

The Meaning and Use of Neighborhood: Spatial Attributes and Social Dynamics

MARIA M. YEN
University of California, Berkeley

Neighborhoods are more than groups of homes joined by contiguous lots, streetscapes and public spaces. Neighborhoods, and more specifically the community organizations and residents who dwell within them, provide planners, policy-makers and designers opportunities for partnerships in addressing problems related to housing and the context within which housing occurs. Whether the issue is the physical desperation of slum dwellings in some urban areas of Asia, Africa or Latin America or the social desperation permeating some urban neighborhoods in the countries of Europe or North America, it is valuable to take a broader view both spatially and temporally by examining housing and community challenges in their neighborhood contexts.

At least part of the total package of solutions to the dilemmas facing the world's neighborhoods must come from the wisdom of community members themselves. A community's parents and elders, sick of violence, work tirelessly to provide their young people with opportunities to enjoy their childhoods, hoping to guide them safely into the twenty-first century. Tenants join together to fight for decent housing. Squatter settlement residents pool their resources into a fund for neighbors afflicted by the loss of a wage earner. The most creative, cost-effective and appropriate solutions come from those who deal daily with neighborhood challenges. While the three authors of this section approach their explorations of the meaning and use of neighborhood from various cultural contexts using different assumptions and methods, their calls for action reveal their commitment to a participatory planning approach.

Public sections of European neighborhoods are contemplated by P. Wim Blauw in "The Meaning and Use of Public Space." The author encourages planners and architects to remain committed to the design of public spaces for both urban and suburban communities. To better design these arenas for social contacts, he urges practitioners to go deeply into public life, observe the needs of neighborhood residents for socializing, and design accordingly. Blauw recognizes the changes occurring at the neighborhood level due to technological advances in information dissemination. He calls for a simultaneous change in the design of public spaces to reflect a new emphasis by neighborhood residents on recreational needs, especially in suburbia.

Lucia Maria Machado Bogus provides insights into the gentrification process of an urban fringe neighborhood in her chapter, "Neighborhood Gentrification: The Dynamics of Meaning and Use in São Paulo, Brazil." Using an integrative case study methodology, the author traces changes in familial and individual residency over time. She discovers a pattern familiar to cities throughout the world—as neighborhoods become the focus of government renewal programs, the original residents are driven out by rising housing costs. The author's call to action concerns a critical examination of government re-urbanization programmes in developing countries, an examination also fitting for urban policies in other countries.

The final author of this section uses both physical and social variables to examine public housing estates in Great Britain and Brazil. The quality of the physical design of public housing along with the involvement of its residents in policy making combine to form successful, liveable neighborhoods. In "The Space of Citizenship: Visually Perceived Non-Spatial Dimensions of Housing," Thereza C. Carvalho uses observations and informal interviews during four cross-cultural case studies to determine which modes of public involvement work best when the goal is an environment suitable to the needs of consumers. She calls for an incorporation of residents' decisions into the planning of public estates and argues for a decentralization of state power into the hands of those directly affected by housing policies. Carvalho highlights the need for governments to recognize, support and encourage public housing dwellers' efforts to transform institutional settings into true neighborhoods.

As academics and practitioners, the need to study and work at the scale of the neighborhood is as crucial as the need to comprehend the meaning and use of housing. More than just conglomerations of houses and families, neighborhoods carry many meanings and uses which are especially noticeable when communities are compared cross-culturally. In some nations, neighborhoods are natural extensions of home, with the public and private lives meshing and becoming almost one. Houses are designed with open, fluidly connected courtyards while streets and public spaces provide a theater of activity leaving little space left for privacy. In areas of other nations, neighborhoods consist of sprawling homes separated by tree-lined streets through which dwellers drive cars into and out of two-car garages without having to leave the sanctuary of the auto or the home. Guards may even prevent undesirables from entering these neighborhoods, thereby further insulating an individual from the possible discomfort of unplanned human contact. Clues to a society's vision of family, community and social responsibility are apparent from an examination of the spatial attributes of its neighborhoods.

Neighborhoods provide glimpses into aspects of a culture's norms and therefore into the appropriate designs and plans for a culture's citizens. Additionally, neighborhoods are pulse-points for the health of a nation's economy and the priorities of its political system. Serving as units of control and information dissemination, neighborhoods in China have reflected a government more concerned with orderly development than individual freedoms. However, Chinese neighborhoods also serve as clearinghouses for the delivery of essential services such as health care, reflecting a political commitment lacking in many other nations. Neighborhoods can also serve as quiet springboards for revolutionary activities—seedbeds of social change. Churches, community organizations and residents have formed powerful coalitions to change existing political systems, as they did during the Civil Rights Movement in the United States of America during the 1960s.

The economic health of a nation is likewise reflected in the mood and appearance of its neighborhoods. Economic policies which appear sound when drawn on paper napkins (the basis for one administration's economic approach in the United States of America) may be revealed as flawed by walking the streets of central cities. Uneven economic development, common in nations throughout the world, is most vividly apparent by a visit to posh neighborhoods of affluence after spending time in crowded neighborhoods of poverty.

Recognizing the clues to a nation's cultural, political and economic realities is only part of the usefulness of studying neighborhoods. Most relevant to planners, designers and policy makers is that neighborhoods provide a base from which to seek solutions to challenges facing urban areas today. While policies may be implemented at scales larger than the neighborhood, these policies will be more effective if they are conceived with the participation of residents on the front lines of urban decay. Yet some do argue for caution in allowing neighborhood dwellers to have too great an impact on city planning and design decisions. Residents may recognize the symptoms of community illness and may reject certain cures for the illness, however "...their ability to diagnose problems and the range of preventive and remedial interventions they can conceive is limited (Grigsby, Baratz, Galster and Maclennan, 1987)."

Indeed, a call for action among those passionate about housing, communities and social change should not blind us to the role of master planning, future envisioning and thoughtful academic contemplation in diagnosing and treating neighborhood ills. However, these tried-and-true approaches cannot be the only panaceas for the challenges facing neighborhoods today and those which will grow to crisis levels in the future. While larger, systemic issues need to be addressed, some planners and designers have found the solutions proposed by the people living in the neighborhoods to be remarkable in their effectiveness. Though the residents of neighborhoods are clearly far from impartial observers, this same partisanship toward their communities gives them wisdom a planner, architect or policy maker should regard as a resource worth working with, just as professional urban practitioners provide their own set of resources to communities. A participatory planning approach can help in the implementation of the visions put forward in this section on the "Meaning and Use of Neighborhood: Spatial Attributes and Social Dynamics."

References

Grigsby, Baratz, Galster and Maclennan. "Formulating Neighborhood Stabilization and Revitalization Strategies," Chapter 9, *Progress in Planning*, Vol. 28, Part 1, p. 73, 1987.

Chapter 9

The Meaning and Use of Public Space

P. WIM BLAUW
Erasmus Universiteit Rotterdam

Public spaces by definition are open to the public, although in practice there are often different limits to accessibility (only for certain categories of people, only accessible on certain conditions, visual thresholds, and difficult to reach). Another characteristic is that public spaces are expected to stimulate public life and are considered as meeting places. This characterization presupposes, that 1) it is possible to affect social contacts with the help of spatial arrangements, and 2) there is a sufficient number of potential users who, under certain conditions, will use public spaces.

This chapter argues that social homogeneity proves to be the most determining factor for social contacts (with neighbors). However, the built environment, urban versus suburban, has an autonomous effect on social contacts given certain social conditions.

The chapter points out that with regard to public spaces, the following physical conditions are considered to be particularly relevant: it should facilitate the public to watch each other unobtrusively, it should be safe, should have architectural quality, and should be appropriate to a variety of behavior. Further, with regard to social conditions, the chapter finds it necessary that: people can recognize a public space as such, the public has some familiarity with the place, the public can watch and join a variety of behavior (although the types of behavior should not be too conflicting), and that the people should know how to behave in public.

Introduction

There proves to be a growing interest in public spaces of cities. The architectural quality of public squares and public buildings are recognized as attractive not only for accidental pedestrians, but are also considered to be of economic interest as a factor for both business companies and their high qualified employees to settle down in such cities. Given the interest in public spaces one could wonder: what is characteristic of public spaces and under which conditions do they function as they are meant to do? According to the authorities' reports public spaces are meant to be meeting places (for example a Dutch national report of the Ministry of Housing, Physical Planning and Environmental Control, 1988). This characterization presupposes, that: 1) it is possible to effect social contacts with the help of spatial arrangements; and 2) there is a sufficient number of potential users, who under certain conditions will use public spaces.

This chapter deals with both assumptions through a deductive process based on a descriptive and argumentative rationale. First, after having described the characteristics of public spaces some models will be discussed, which might help to explain a possible relationship between the urban environment and people's behavior, in particular with regard to their social contacts. Secondly, the general conditions for use of public spaces, both physical and social, will be explored. Finally, the possible consequences of actual social changes for the phenomenon of public spaces will be discussed.

Public spaces

Public spaces by definition are open to the public: *accessibility* for everyone, regardless one's background, is required (Blauw 1989a). In that sense streets and squares are public spaces. However in case of designing public spaces, architects and town-planners have more in view than just accessibility. When designing a theatre, or a shopping centre, there is also the definite wish to bring about, with spatial arrangements *public life* (Blauw 1989b). For example, when designing a theatre the director would like that the theatre evokes certain behavior of visitors such as chatting in the lobby during the break, about the quality of the play or, if wanted, about the clothes of the people present. Likewise it could be desirable, that a new shopping-centre would not only afford buying certain goods, but also affords sauntering and looking at each other from a bench. That is the quality of the built environment we have in mind in this chapter, when talking about public spaces.

Accessibility

Accessibility of public spaces is not always maximal. With regard to accessibility, there may be different limits:

1) The accessibility of what is meant to be a public space is often intended for certain categories of people. The parking place is only accessible to visitors of the nearby office building and the club only to members. A certain category of people can be excluded: sometimes openly, sometimes covered, for example when unwanted people are refused the admission of a discotheque, with the argument that "it would be too crowded inside". On the other hand, someone can be admitted, because there are no legitimate reasons for not letting him or her in, but from the behavior of the people present, one has to conclude that one is an unwanted visitor.

2) Public spaces can also be accessible on certain conditions: the casino is only accessible to men wearing a tie. Moreover, it applies to this and many other places, like stadiums, that one is only admitted after paying a certain price of admission. On the other hand the city park is without any limit accessible to everybody; one should only pay attention to the rules mentioned at the entrance. Like the rule that one must have left the park before dark. In other words, the access is limited to certain periods of time.

3) Sometimes there is a visual threshold: a park can be accessible to everybody, but it could be completely hidden, so that only the insiders know how to find it. Or the bus station could only be reached by a long and dark tunnel, so that one prefers travelling by car.

4) Public spaces should be within reach of facilities: if, for example, a shopping center, situated in the middle of nowhere, is not to be reached by public transport, the accessibility is highly limited to the less (auto)mobile part of the population.

Public life

Public spaces are expected to stimulate public life. The sociologist Hans-Paul Bahrdt, who uses the concept of public life (offentlichkeit) in this sense, considers the market as the pre-eminent example of this type of social contact (Bahrdt 1969). Imagine a goods-market, as it is being held on several squares in cities. At that market buyers and sellers can easily contact each other. The buyer can ask how much the exposed merchandise costs and the seller can bring to the passer-by's attention the sales, that one cannot let slip. Nevertheless the passer-by can continue his way, after having judged the recommended product, with or without the excuse "I'll look a bit further." According to Bahrdt, the "incomplete integration of a social context" is characteristic for public life. One does not know each other's background. If any contact is made at all, this is in regard to certain matters, in this example buying or not-buying of goods. Opposite to this incomplete integration, is a social context, which can be characterized as closed. In such a context nobody is unfamiliar with the background of the other. In an ideal typical closed-village community everybody knows each other, not only by name, but including each other's life-history. It is typical for such a community, that the backdoor is open and that the people of the neighborhood can walk in freely. In that situation there is no public and no private life. In big cities, on the contrary, people can more easily retire in the private sphere and, because they use these possibilities more often, this will strengthen their need for public life. Conversely, in public life (for example in the crowd on the street or in a meeting at work), a need will be aroused to retire oneself into the private home, the 'back region' (Goffman 1959, 109-140), where people can be sure that they will not be disturbed by unwanted persons.

Gehl (1987) characterized these social contacts in public life as "low intensity" contacts. However, under the condition of mutual interest these contacts might change into high intensity contacts. Thus, public life offers a type of social contact, which is appreciated as such, but, and this is another attraction of public life, it also offers opportunities to start more intimate contacts.

Urban environment and social contacts

As remarked in the introduction to this chapter, designing public places, which are meant to be meeting places presupposes that the built environment effects people's behavior. Theoretically, we have to consider the possibility that the built environment does not have any effect on people's behavior. If people behave in the same way in different spatial situations, this might be a right proposition (Fischer and Jackson's simple null model) (Fischer and Jackson 1976). However, people's behavior does vary with the built environment. For example, neighboring proves to be more frequent in the suburban than in the urban environment, both in the U.S. and in the Netherlands (Fischer and Jackson 1976; Blauw 1986 and 1987). The next question is: if this difference can be observed, which variables can explain the difference?

Planners might be inclined to stress the physical characteristics of the environment. Against this 'physical determinism' Gans (1972a) stresses the importance of individual characteristics as explaining variables, notably class and life-cycle stage. Fischer and Jackson use some other models, which simultaneously take into account both the effect of the built and social environment. With regard to the built environment they pay attention to the metropolitan character of central cities, the availability of a variety of facilities. As a second factor regarding the built environment they indicate the distance (to the city-center), and consequently the costs to reach the facilities. Both factors prove to support the deliberately chosen contacts (with friends and acquaintances). The suburban environments on the contrary proves to be more appropriate to neighboring.

Social homogeneity, the degree in which people feel that they are alike to their neighbors, proves to be decisive. A multivariate analysis shows that, nevertheless, the built environment has an autonomous effect on neighboring (Blauw 1986 and 1987). However, this applies to the population of working men without children and not to women with young children and without a job. It can be supposed that women have their young children as an argument for making contact with their neighbors (by taking care of each others children or at least by exchanging their experiences with their children). For them this mutual interest is a sufficient condition for neighboring contact: regardless the built environment, they make contact with each other. Men lack such an obvious common interest. For them the built environment does facilitate the making of social contact with their neighbors.

To conclude, even for neighboring, a situation in which it is relatively easy to meet, there is a need for a purpose before making contact. In other words, we assume that people are not inclined to commit themselves unless they have a reason. They do not like to stand before their house with no other purpose than to ask for contact. Thus, the built environment, whether urban or suburban, should contain places, where people can meet non-committedly. The analysis so far does not take into account the fact that, whether the built environment will be used or not, is dependent on the users' interpretation of the environment. When describing the conditions the possibility of different interpretations of a certain place has to be considered. Subsequently, both the conditions with regard to the physical characteristics of public spaces and those with regard to the potential users will be traced.

Physical conditions

Having described the characteristics of public spaces we now want to explore the conditions for the functioning of public spaces. Both public space and the potential users have to meet certain conditions, here indicated as physical and social conditions. The following physical conditions seem to be essential:

To see and to been seen

In the public sphere, the chance for people to decide freely whether or not to make contact with others presupposes that people must be able to see each other and to be seen by others. Outdoor terraces, but also indoor terraces behind glass walls (like in Paris), make this two-way watching of others possible.

Safety

It is important that people feel safe in a public space. If not, people will concentrate their attention to potential insecurities and will not be accessible to others. The increased crime rate on streets paralyzes public life, while in turn, the deserted streets jeopardize the neighborhood. The reason being that if the streets are quieter, then more people will be reluctant to go out. Social control could work preventively with regard to crime. However, anonymity reduces the chances to deter criminal behavior in public spaces. In this situation it will also be unlikely that the violator of the law will mind others. Nevertheless, it might be expected, that, mutual visibility, even though it is not a sufficient condition, contributes to the increased safety of a public space.

Architectural qualities

When people like to stay in a certain space, this condition also contributes to public life. To this end, the space must have certain architectural qualities concerning matters like 'human scale' and 'nice atmosphere', although hard to define. The Dutch define a nice atmosphere with the not translatable word "gezelligheid". A reason why the Dutch author Rudy Kousbroek in an essay judged cafés by their G-factor. Anyhow, adequate spatial dimensions and use of colours can attribute to this quality of public spaces.

Variety of behavior

Another challenge for designers is to see to it that planned public spaces have facilities for a variety of behavior. In other words, public spaces should be multi-functional (Bahrdt 1974, 35-37). A square in the city center is only a good square if there are, for example, benches to sit and watch, appropriate space for dancers or musicians to show their performances, or the fountain is not only refreshing, but also invites the play of children.

Social conditions

By interchanging the terms 'public' and 'public spaces', as Bahrdt does, the suggestion could arise, that in a certain kind of space a certain kind of behavior is evoked automatically. However, it is not that simple. Designers, on the ground of their experience and intuition, can do their very best to create a space which could function as a public space. Yet, it cannot be guaranteed that the space will be used as intended. For that reason it is necessary that: people can recognize a public space, there exists familiarity with the space, attracts a variety of people, and affords public behavior.

People can recognize a public space

Even if an architect succeeds in designing a certain space in accordance with his vision about a public space, it is still questionable whether that space will be used that way. As Gans (1972a) said: a potential environment is not the same as an effective environment. For example, a hall, on which the entrances of several apartments opened out to and which was meant to be a public space, was not used as such. It turned out that the selected dwellers moved into the apartments because of their size, not to socialize in the hall.

Whether and how a space will be effectively used depends on the social and cultural background of the potential users. Imagine a native of the jungle, dropped at 5th Avenue or the Champs Élysées. For this person the red traffic-light will have no meaning, a lamppost will be used as a tree and the sight of a knife will not be interpreted as a request for one's wallet, but as a challenge to a hand-to-hand fight. Another example, in old neighborhoods the public road was often seen as an extension of the house: one put a chair on the pavement and at the same time one kept an eye on the children who were playing in the street. Nowadays the 'public' road in the residential districts above all has traffic as its major function.

This difference of interpretation of space will not only be manifest between different social classes, but also between people of different ethnic origins. For example, there are indications, that, for the Mediterranean fellow-citizens the street-market is not only important as a place where one can buy vegetables, but for them it is relatively more important as a place to meet each other (DenDraak 1989). Hall (1969) points out that in Southern-Europe restaurants are more often used as public places than in West-Europe or North America. In Italy, Spain and France the tables in the restaurants are situated in such a way that they stimulate as much as possible the contact between the guests at different tables. Everyone can see what one's neighbor eats and, if one likes, can easily start a conversation. In countries like Germany or the United States tables are situated along the walls and separated by partitions so that one can create a private sphere within the public space.

Familiarity with the public space

Whether someone in a public space will interact with other people, also depends on one's familiarity with the situation. Is the situation part of someone's "Umwelt" (Bahrdt 1974), an environment, in which someone can give the right meaning to the physical characteristics of the situation and to the behavior of others? If not, the chance is small, that an individual will enter that public space, let alone, interact with other people. When an outsider tries to contact other people in the setting, it might lead to awkward painful situations for the persons involved. The reactions of the people present in a public place can convince a harmless visitor that the place is not as public as has been thought. Imagine the reactions of a lady, who enters the pub filled with loud men, or the reactions of a group of Hells' Angels, when a gentleman enters their common home, wearing a bowler and having an umbrella in hand.

A variety of people

By definition public spaces should be accessible to all people. However, this does not mean that all public spaces are frequented by all types of people. Yet, it can be argued that public spaces should attract a variety of people. A variety of people with a variety of cultural backgrounds is conducive to a greater richness of behavior, which makes a public space more worthwhile to spend time.

So if these conditions are met, it could be possible that at a square in the city a mime player draws the attention of shopping housewives, the businessman reads the *Financial Times* on his bench, the ice-cream man sells his products to school-children, and somewhere else in the square followers of Hare Krishna try to convince other people to join their religious movement. However, this description might be somewhat utopian. In fact, the confrontation of different types of users with different life styles is problematic (e.g., cultural high brow versus street corner society).

Public behavior

Behavior on the 'front stage' (Goffman 1959) requires the ability to play and change roles easily. To play a role one needs to behave in a more or less prescribed way and use the right attributes. In such a situation one has to be aware of other people's expectations, which are however difficult to find out as the others are by definition strangers. What can be done is to conform to norms which are rather universal.

For example, before entering a public meeting, the newcomer will first check if he or she is prepared: the hair be combed quickly, the woman may redden her lips or the man checks his tie. Then the situation is examined: one lingers at the door, sees who is present and wonders in which direction to move into the setting (Lofland 1973). When a desired position has been located, dependent on the fact whether the preferences can be shown openly, one moves more or less gradually into the direction of the desired position. The meeting can be more or less private (a staff meeting), but it can also be accessible to people who do not, or hardly know each other. In that case, special requirements are needed for making contact. When one does not know the background of others, people are judged by external appearances, which can be observed (face-information) (Karp 1977). The first impression is decisive. And as people cannot fully prepare on such meetings with strangers, it is even more difficult to hide oneself from them than from those with whom one is familiar (Alberoni 1987, 123-126). The importance of the first impression also explains why in an urban environment people behave more showily. It facilitates making contact with similar people. Bahrdt (1969) speaks about the necessity of drawing attention ("Darstellung") and of making oneself recognizable ("Representation"). Informal clothes (sweater, jeans and sport-shoes) evokes informal behavior of others, like being on familiar terms or a friendly pat on the back. In the red-light district, blond-put-up-hair, a décolleté, a short and tight skirt, stiletto heels and covetous eyes in a woman will be interpreted by men as signs of an invitation to paid-sex.

A future for public spaces?

In the sixties and seventies expectations to plan and manipulate society ran high. The expectation that architects and town planners could effect peoples' behavior with the help of spatial arrangements followed naturally from these implicit expectations.

Eventually, as a reaction to these expectations which proved not to be realizeable, some architects became utterly cynical about their possibilities to contribute to society by designing the built environment, and in particular public spaces. According to the British architect Martin Pawley: "Public space does not have a function anymore. It has become a dangerous, corrupt space without economic value". In other words, it is not possible to design public spaces and there is no need for them either. "There is no reason to speak about public spaces and public spirit any more. That is the last thing to do. We have to allow that telecommunication takes over the physical movement" (translated from De Tijd, 22-12-1989). Before him some other intellectuals have raised their voices to say that public life and public spaces are threatened or even "dead" (Sennett 1974). In western societies, it is said, people are inclined to withdraw themselves from public life into their separate autonomous spaces (Alexander 1966) looking for some "Gluck-im-Winkel" (Bahrdt 1969).

As has already been suggested, technological developments have led to a change in the functions of public spaces (see also Oosterman 1989). The square before the townhall is no longer the place where the news is announced: instead people listen to their radio or watch television. In order to speak to others it is not necessary to meet them face-to-face, instead people can use a telephone. It seems like an anachronism to speak about public spaces in the computer era. Only if we suppose that meeting other people face-to-face has some surplus value, public spaces will still make sense.

On the long term, economic development has allowed increasing incomes and consequently increasing expenses of transportation. With regard to social contacts, people have become less dependent on their own place and have more freedom to choose where and with whom to contact socially. Thus, city centers with their wide range of facilities can be frequented more often.

However, just now, in Western societies households have statistically at least one car to their disposal, therefore the need for restricting car traffic has become so urgent that in the near future people might become again more committed to their neighborhood. This will particularly apply to those who cannot pay the increasing costs of transportation or who are not able to travel easily, like children or the elderly.

The third factor to be mentioned here is the demographic one. It is too obvious to say, but public spaces need public. The terraces have to be filled up with people having some leisure time, as well as some money to spend. In this sense public places are supported by a growing number of singles and double-income households, who live in or close to the city centers.

This same factor can explain the lack of comparable public spaces in the suburbs. The family-oriented population is bounded to their own home: (to keep to the familiar image) commuting fathers coming home late after a tiring work day and mothers caring for small children do not easily go out for a drink in a pub. However, the given description is becoming a stereotype. First, it can be hypothesized that the suburbanites did not loose their need for public life. The typical suburban facilities like swimming pools, tennis courts and primary schools can be considered as 'functional equivalents' to the sidewalk terraces and bars in the city centers, although the public in the suburbs is socially more homogeneous than in the city centers.

Secondly, the composition of the population might change as a consequence of future demographic processes. Young parents are becoming the middle aged people with adolescent children and the latter will be retiring and jobless. That will enlarge their need for some public life and for some adequate public spaces to meet. As a group of adolescents, their children have earlier asked for more lively places in the suburbs than are presently available (DenDraak 1989). For some suburbanites the lack of public life might even lead to an escape in the direction of the central cities, however, for the majority this is not a serious option.

The social and cultural developments effect public life and consequently the character of public spaces. Private and public life do not have a meaning independent of time and place. As Habermas (1962) showed, private life, particularly in European societies, has been and still is threatened by an increasing interference of the state in the lives of its citizens.

Privacy in the preceding century has been an ideological justification of the bourgeois to protect themselves from the 'dangerous class' of poor people (Brunt 1989). The continuing process of individualization of Western societies has brought about a tremendous spatial impact (Burgers 1989). Literally, public places have lost space on behalf of private space. Today, the public and private spheres are becoming more and more interwoven: public life is brought into the privacy of homes, and conversely, the private secrets of politicians and artists are becoming public property.

To conclude, as face-to-face contacts are no longer prerequisite for social contacts mass media have become functional equivalents for the communication from the state to its citizens. Still public places proved to be important for the political manifestations to radical changes in society as has been demonstrated recently in the East European countries. Besides this political function, three other functions remain important (Billiard 1988, 111). First, although not discussed here, public places are the connecting spaces between streets. Second, public places can be symbols for a city's identity, for the power of the political rulers or for the solidarity of its citizens. Third, public spaces, as has been discussed extensively, facilitate meeting other people face-to-face.

Thus, for architects and planners it is still worthwhile to go deeply into public life in order to design public spaces, which facilitate the kind of social contacts people desire.

References

Alberoni, Francesco (1987), *Pubblico & Privato*, Milan: Garzanti.

Alexander, Christopher (1966), "The City as a Mechanism for Sustaining Human Contact." Berkeley, Cal.: Institute of Urban and Regional Development, University of California.

Bahrdt, Hans-Paul (1969), *Die moderne Grossstadt. Soziologische Überlegungen zum Städtebau.* Hamburg: Wegner Verlag.

Bahrdt, Hans-Paul (1974), *Umwelterfahrung. Soziologische Betrachtungen über den Beitrag des Subjekts zur Konstitution von Umwelt.* München: Nymphenburger.

Billiard, Isabelle (ed.) (1988), *Espaces Publics.* Paris: La Documentation Francaise.

Blauw, P. Wim (1986), *Suburbanisatie en sociale contacten.* Amsterdam: Erasmus Universiteit.

Blauw, P. Wim (1987), "Neighbouring in an urban and suburban context". *Netherlands Journal of Housing and Environmental Research*, vol. 2, nr. 3, 233-246.

Blauw, P. Wim (1989a), "Ruimte voor openbaarheid: een introductie," in: P. Wim Blauw (ed.), *Ruimte voor Openbaarheid.* The Hague: VUGA, p. 9-17.

Blauw, P. Wim (1989b), "Het gebruik van de openbare ruimte", in: P. Wim Blauw (ed.), *Ruimte voor Openbaarheid.* The Hague: VUGA, p. 62-73.

Brunt, Lodewijk (1989), "Oost west, thuis best". Openbaarheid en persoonlijk leven, in: P. Wim Blauw (ed.), *Ruimte voor Openbaarheid.* The Hague: VUGA, p. 19-33.

Burgers, Jack (1989), "Publieke voorwaarden voor private woonmilieus," in: P. Wim Blauw (ed.), *Ruimte voor Openbaarheid.* The Hague: VUGA, p. 34-48.

DenDraak, Jan (1989), "Openbaarheid in stedelijke en suburbane gebieden", in: P. Wim Blauw (ed.), *Ruimte voor Openbaarheid*. 's-Gravenhage: VUGA, p. 74-90.

Fischer, Claude S. and R.M. Jackson (1976), "Suburbs, Networks and Attitudes", in: Barry Schwarz (ed.), *The Changing Face of the Suburbs*. Chicago-London: Chicago University Press, p. 279-307.

Gans, H. J. (1972a) "The Potential Environment and the Effective Environment", in: *People and Plans*. Harmondsworth: Penguin Books, p. 4-13.

Gans, Herbert J. (1972b), "Planning and Social Life: Friendship and Neighbour Relations in Suburban Communities". In: *People and Plans*. Harmondsworth: Penguin Books, p. 123-139.

Gehl, J. (1987), *Life between Buildings. Using Public Space*. New York: Van Nostrand Reinhold.

Goffman, E. (1959), *The Presentation of Self in Every Day Life*. Harmondsworth: Penguin Books.

Habermas, Jürgen (1962), *Strukturwandel der Öffentlichkeit*. Neuwied-Berlin: Luchterhand.

Hall, E. T. (1969), *The Hidden Dimension*. New York: Anchor Books/Doubleday.

Karp, D.E., G.P. Stone and W.C. Yoels (1977), *Being Urban. A Socio Psychological View of City Life*. Lexington, Mass./Toronto: Heath.

Lofland, Lyn (1985) (original 1973), *A World of Strangers. Order and Action in Urban Public Space*. Prospect Heights, Ill.: Waveland Press.

Ministerie van Volkshuisvesting, *Ruimtelijke Ordening en Milieubeheer* (1988), Vierde Nota over de Ruimtelijke Ordening. The Hague: Staatsuitgeverij.

Oosterman, Jan (1989), "Stadspleinen: hoogtepunten van stedelijk leven?", in: P. Wim Blauw (ed.), *Ruimte voor Openbaarheid*. The Hague: VUGA, p. 93-105.

Sennett, R. (1974), *The Fall of Public Man. On the Social Psychology of Capitalism*. Boston: Faber & Faber.

Chapter 10

Neighborhood Gentrification: Dynamics of Meaning and Use in São Paulo, Brazil

LUCIA MARIA M. BOGUS
Pontifícia Universidade Católica de São Paulo

The questions related to the residential location and spatial mobility of the population in the urban environment and their implications for the meaning and use of neighborhood have become more and more important to urban studies, mainly in Third World countries such as Brazil. The chapter's purpose is to discuss the theoretical and methodological aspects of those questions.

Taking into account the demographic, socio-economic, and especially those variables related to the real estate increasing values, the objective is to explain the set of changes which occurred in a specific peripheral area of São Paulo. The chapter elaborates on how the integrative use of case study analysis, life history, and the study of personal and familiar trajectories is of great importance for understanding the dynamics of neighborhood changes which took place in that area, particularly concerning changes observed in the meaning at both the home and neighborhood scales.

Introduction

When the course of the process of population substitution in a specific area is studied, many and varied consequences are observed. This chapter attempts to analyze the characteristics and effects of that process, as it took place in a neighborhood in the periphery of the city of São Paulo, Brazil, as consequence of an urban renewal project there. The urban renewal had an immediate effect on the local real estate market, the socioeconomic profile of the resident population, the housing conditions, and on the relationships among the neighbors. This chapter also attempts to show that the use itself of the home and the neighborhood area underwent substantial changes during the transformation process of the neighborhood as a whole.

There are many works which discuss the different meanings of the term "gentrification", as well the different forms which this process can assume. (See, for example, Teeland: 1988; Beauregard: 1986; London: 1980: Marcuse: 1986). In this case, gentrification is understood as the replacement of a low-income population residing in an area by another population with different characteristics in terms of higher income, job occupation, and educational level. This substitution of residents was a consequence of a series of improvements made by the State government in the neighborhood under study—Vila do Encontro—through an urban renewal project which accompanied the construction of a nearby subway station.

In this case, the process was set in motion by State action—indirectly, through the construction of the subway as part of the extension of urban transportation services and directly, through the urban renewal project in the area: infrastructure services and facilities for public use, such as daycare centers, schools, and hospitals. The effect on the real estate market was quickly seen in higher prices for houses and lots. This work will point out some characteristics of the area studied, within the context of the city of São Paulo, in addition to methodological considerations regarding the research, the main changes in terms of neighborhood relationships (including statements by the resident population), the use of space in the home and neighborhood and how these questions are related to the process of real estate speculation and the housing market. Finally, this chapter will attempt to understand the gentrification process, intra-urban migration, and socioeconomic-spatial segregation of the population, as components of an urbanization process taking place in Brazilian cities, of which São Paulo is the biggest and best example.

Urban renewal and change: profile of an area undergoing transformation

The area studied, whose process of transformation has been under study since 1978, is located in southern part of the city of São Paulo. It began being the target starting when the subway station for the north-south line began to be built there. The transformations became more accentuated when the State carried out a series of urban renewal projects there as part of a policy of densification in the area, important in order to obtain a quick return on the capital invested in that mode of urban transports, causing an immediate increase in rents and the consequent expulsion of the renters, as well as a rapid process of "verticalization" with the construction of many multi-storied apartment buildings (for additional information see Bogus: 1988). It is important to point out that the population originally residing in the area, at the time of the beginning of the changes, was basically made up of migrants from the rural areas of Northeast Brazil, with an average family income about two minimum salaries[1], employed in the poorly-paid service sector, and with very little schooling and little job qualification. People went to live there, starting in the 1950's, because the price of property and rents were lower. The irregular topography of the land and the type of subdivision of the lots, also irregular, with narrow, deep lots[2] favored the construction of slum dwellings and the appearance of nuclei of shacks ("favelas" or shanty-towns) whenever there were two or more neighboring lots still unoccupied.

The highest part of the area, near the main avenue leading to other parts of the city, saw the better quality houses being built there from the very beginning, when the purchasing power of the population was a little bit higher, but still not greater than a family income of 6 minimum salaries. The social relationships existing at that time in the area were basically those of solidarity, since with the relatively homogeneous socioeconomic situation, the residents had similar difficulties and problems, giving them common interests. The long-time residents still remember the time when the neighbors would get together and socialize. "Before they built the area for the subway roundabout, the streets up here all had the names of birds. I was born and raised here. Everybody knew each other." When the long-time residents moved, expelled by the expropriations, demolitions, and

---

[1] The minimum salary today in Brazil is about US$ 60, using the official dollar exchange rate.

[2] It is common to find in Vila do Encontro, even today, lots which are 5 meters wide and 50 or 60 meters deep. On these lots there are still some slum dwellings which, after a superficial remodelling, (some were merely painted), were re-rented at much higher prices.

mainly by the process of higher property values and taxes, new residents began to arrive, to live in the apartment buildings, the new houses, and to enjoy in some way the advantages that an urbanized area offers. As one of the new residents said: "Buying an apartment here in Vila do Encontro was a good deal. This area is already valuable and it is going to become much more valuable. These 'shacks' and 'dens' are going to disappear. It's going to be a great area." (Elizabeth, 24 years old, recent resident.)

The profile of the new inhabitant is totally different from the original ones: the purchasing power is greater, with an average family income of 5 - 10 minimum salaries, with much higher educational and job qualification level. Generally, they are young couples who came to live in the apartment buildings, seeking an area with good services, where they could live and where the prices were lower and more accessible than in the traditional middle-class areas in São Paulo. In an attempt to hold out against the increased property values, some strategies were sought by the old residents to enable them to remain in the area and enjoy the benefits which the area is beginning to offer. Calling our attention among these strategies is the joining together of two families to live in the same dwelling and divide the rent and dwelling expenses (light, water, taxes).

Methodological framework

Social standing cannot be experienced individually by men; it only occurs through a social group which, historically, has been the one responsible for the organization of survival strategies, whether at the rural or urban environment. In this sense, the family, historically placed, assumes the feature of a methodological tool, standing itself while mediation between the individual and the social life experience takes place. The family - as a "domestic group" or the "group of persons linked by kinship ties, affinities or economic bounds living under the same roof"[3]—came to be our "unit of analysis," since it constitutes the privileged group for carrying out the analyses of the series of alterations observed in a given area of the city, where the gentrification process occurs, and which can only be made through a demographic, socioeconomic and political approach. The unit of consumption, or the "subgroup of elements of the domestic group sharing the one and same family budget,"[4] was the criterion adopted for detecting the presence, in the same domestic group, of one or more families.

Starting from this supposition, the analysis of the family was adopted

---

[3] This criterion was originally adopted by the "Pesquisa Nacional sobre Reprodução Humana". CEBRAP, São Paulo, 1974.

[4] Idem, ibidem.

as a criterion for approaching the subject under study. Particularly in what the dwelling is concerned to, the family takes over great importance in facing up to the arising problems and in searching for ways to solve them. The family group appears as a mediator in the concrete experience of the production-consumption process (including the house's, the quarter's, and the city's) by the individuals who compound it, since it is there that strategies for reproducing their existential conditions are generated.

The average income of the families originally resident in Vila do Encontro is rather low, making it unfeasible to stay in the area after the increase in real estate values which followed the public policies of re-urbanization. This situation was harder on the persons who rented houses. In these cases, the association of two families—with no kinship ties between themselves— sharing a single and same house and summing up budget items which each family alone could not face by itself, was the formula discovered by them for staying in the area, giving rise to a new kind of family group—the "compound family"—which divides between themselves the physical spaces of the house in order to afford to stay and consume the series of benefits the quarter offers. Although less frequently, the existence of compound families has already been detected in other areas of the metropolitan region of São Paulo through studies carried out by the Dieese (Inter-Union Department of Statistics and Socioeconomical Studies), in the early 80's.[5] This Dieese's study shows that the "compound families" constitutes around 5% of the total families residing in the metropolitan region and that the greater percentage of them are found in income groups receiving up to 2 minimum salaries (34,6%) and from 2 to 5 minimum salaries (42,1% of the total number of the compound families analyzed).

Another important point is that related to the stage of the vital cycle in which such families are generally found: they are young couples, with young children, if not the woman alone, who are unable to solve by themselves the surviving questions; therefore having to associate themselves with another family in order to have someone stay at home to take care of the children, making possible new arrangements for dividing house tasks and, mainly, to deal with the question of dwelling, which is today the most expensive item in the labour class' reproduction cost, in São Paulo. Some studies (Bruschini: 1990) have approached the association between levels of family income and types of family, pointing out that the poorer families tend to aggregate new elements to the group as a way of increasing the family income and sharing the expenses. In the case of Vila do Encontro, where the percentage of families with young children is high (32% of the population is concentrated in the age group from zero to 10) and where the raising in the lot land

---

[5] See, Dieese - "Padrão de vida, emprego e desemprego na Grande São Paulo".

Table 10.1: Evolution of land prices in Vila do Encontro

Year	Price per m^2 in Vila do Encontro 1972 = 100	Price per m^2 in the Municipality of São Paulo (*) 1972 = 100
1972	100.00	411.27
1973	301.39	—
1974	369.34	459.22
1975	653.11	—
1976	476.05	508.23
1977	349.91	—
1978	286.54	420.59
1979	276.53	424.79
1980	167.61	388.92
1981	203.71	452.28
1982	493.88	—
1983	634.16	246.97
1984	543.29	207.55
1985	406.25	193.27

- Evolution of prices per m^2 for land located in Vila do Encontro and in the municipality of São Paulo, during the period 1972-1985.

- (*) Prices per square meter for land in the municipality of São Paulo had as base the year 1975. For comparison purposes these data were transferred to 1972 using the Consumer Price Index from FIPE. São Paulo, 1985.

- *Source*: For Vila do Encontro, data from EMBRAESP, São Paulo. For the Municipality of São Paulo, data from EMBRAESP apud MARCONDES, M. J. A.,— Formacao do Preco do Solo Urbano no Municipio de São Paulo, Masters' dissertation, PROPUR, UFRJ, Rio de Janeiro, 1986.

prices (Table 10.1) has caused an abrupt increase in the dwelling rents, the joining of families presented itself as the most convenient measure for 15% of the families under study, who stayed in the area.

Obviously, the option for the re-composition of the domestic group implies a loss in privacy, which the former individual dwelling offered. Notwithstanding, the acceptance of a worsening in the life conditions "inside home" is made out of the possibility of enjoying a better quality of urban life, of living in the best equipped and easily accessed quarter, of reducing the time spent in going from home to work, of not being "pushed" farther away to the distant peripheries where the workman family does not live in, "it hides itself in," as a popular saying puts it so well.

According to our point of view, the study of the changes in the use of the home and neighborhood necessarily passes through the study of the family, here understood as the "locus of reproduction of the labor force", which takes over the character of a methodological tool, placing itself while mediation. The option for the case study and the longitudinal study justifies itself by the fact that these modalities of analysis—from the study of an area of the city—permit one to reconstruct the social processes and those of the economical assessments present in the city as a whole. It is our understanding that although the processes of building-up and alteration of urban peripheries have common explanatory mechanisms, there exists specificities in the processes which occur in different areas of the city, whose aspects vary in accordance with the socioeconomical characteristics of the affected populations. This makes a case of each case, making generalizations unpractical. Although there exist studies on the effects of public policies on the processes of increasing real estate prices, few approach the mechanisms used by the families to face such processes in the attempt to remain in the area under intervention. It has been demonstrated that the use of many modalities of analysis, in an integrate and complementary way, is of great usefulness and importance for capturing the characteristics the gentrification process takes over in a given area, besides permitting the analysis of the impact of the changes on the area, as well as on the resident population, along a period studied.

The substitution of population, the proliferation of apartment buildings, the demolition of old houses and slum-dwellings to give room for new dwellings of better standard, the movement of "resistance" on the part of families which found out in co-habitation a way to, at least, postpone the pushing-way process—all of these—were phenomena apprehended through the constant visits to the area and through the successive surveys carried out along the period studied. This collecting of facts included three surveys—in 1970, 1982 and, 1985—(Bogus: 1988), besides a number of interviews with residents, real estate agents, governmental agents and, representatives of local institutions (churches, schools, health posts, day-care centers). The option for these methodological procedures and techniques of data collecting had a decisive importance for the comprehension of the processes observed.

Both, the "longitudinal study" and the analysis of the migratory courses carried out through life histories, have also enabled one to capture the magnitude of the intra-urban migratory movements which were caused almost always by the difficulties in accessing the dwelling, configuring the existence of truly urban nomads, mainly among the low-income population (Patarra & Bogus: 1981).

Old and new residents in an area of contrasts: social bonds in disaggregation

The series of changes observed in Vila do Encontro, attracting population of other areas of the city and pushing gradually away the poorer residents, has prevented the mechanisms of segregation, commonly present in other areas of the city, to occur there in the same way, up to the present. There still live, side-to-side, the poor residents of slums and hut dwellings and the young middle-class couples who came to live in the area attracted by the prices of houses. The conflict of interests between the old and the new resident is, then, inevitable! It is showed up in the way the occupation of the area occurred, where the existing standards of segregation were de-structured in order to give space to a different standard in dwellings and social level.

The relationships of cooperation and mutual assistance continue to exist in the ties of solidarity among the old families who are trying to stay in the area, showing up in various forms: more than one family living together in the same house, loans of money, help in caring for children while the mother is at work. But, in general, it is the relationships of conflict between two different social segments living in Vila do Encontro today which predominate, reproducing a broader process which occurs in São Paulo as a whole, where the poorer people are "pushed" into the worst areas of the city, without services or infrastructure, making up a true situation of urban nomads.[6] The old residents who are still there live, for the most part, in the worst sections of the area—the bottom of the valley which is still not urbanized, in nuclei of shacks and old slum dwellings still standing—in a process of internal segregation within the neighborhood itself.

In spite of the conflict of interests with regard to occupation of the area, the women who live in the slum dwellings and shacks provide domestic services to the newly-arrived families. According to one of the new residents, contracting the work of someone who lives nearby is advantageous for both parties: "For me, it is advantageous because she arrives on time everyday, and if she doesn't arrive, I can go to her house and see what is happening. For her it is also good, because she doesn't have to spend any money on transportation, she's at work and at the same time she's at home." (Anesia, 34 years old, recent resident in the apartment building).

---

[6] In order to give a better idea of the volume of demand for housing, transportation, and other basic social services, it should be remembered that the city of São Paulo received nearly 1,700,000 immigrants during the decade of the 70's, from various parts of the country, who came to São Paulo, the largest city in the country, in search of better living conditions and job opportunities (for the most part, they have little schooling, very few job qualifications).

In truth, the biggest advantage exists for the employer, since the proximity of the employee's housing works as an element of control. At first sight, there appears to be a shared interest between the poor families/long time residents and the more recently arrived families, who employ the female labor force in the area for domestic work. Nevertheless, this sharing of interests is precarious, since the new residents, and primarily the owners of the real estate, are interested in "a better neighborhood", "in the disappearance of the shacks and slum dwellings", so that the area continues to increase in value. This situation expresses, in reality, not a sharing but a conflict of interests, between different social groups which the urbanization process has joined in the same portion of urban space, at a specific moment in the expansion of the city. The former relationships of a neighborhood governed by friendships and tranquility were replaced by suspicion (of the rich with regard to this neighbor, a poor person, who might want to rob him), and of fear by some that their houses will be demolished and not knowing if there will be enough money next month to pay the higher rent. The originality of existing community ties were overcome by the relationships predominant in the capitalist class society, where individualism is the dominant characteristic and where the interests of capital superimpose themselves above all others.

Final considerations

Being a case study, this paper does not permit generalizations. However, it can be affirmed with a high margin of safety, that whenever a certain area is the object of a governmental urban renewal plan, in similar circumstances to those of Vila do Encontro, the same results will be repeated: real estate speculation, expelling of the long-time residents (especially those with lower incomes), new construction to house the new residents, all of this producing alterations in the social relationships between neighbors with implications even with regard to the use of the internal space of the dwelling, which is sometimes shared by two families who previously lived in separate houses.

In this sense, the gentrification process is intimately linked to intra-urban and intra-metropolitan migratory movements and can even be cited as one of the key elements in the causal chain of the movements. Through a process of horizontal expansion of the city and of its neighboring municipalities, the urban perimeter incorporates areas which are subtracted from the rural environment through clandestine subdivisions[7]. They lack

---

[7] The clandestine subdivisions are those made with no observance of urban legislation. Since they have not been approved by the City government, they do not receive any public services, thus presenting very precarious conditions.

municipal public services, such as water, light, sewers, and transportation, as well as other collective services essential to community living (schools, day-care centers, hospitals, etc.). It is these precarious areas which house the lower-income social groups which are expelled from the more central areas being improved.

On the other hand, the gentrification process (as it occurred in Vila do Encontro) is also a consequence of the expulsion process of social groups who were previously resident in more central and valuable areas of the city, who, in turn, were replaced by another group of higher income. It is possible to see clearly, the existence of an income gradient in the occupation of city space. The neighborhoods which are more central and better equipped tend to concentrate the high-income social groups in nice houses and tall, modern apartment buildings. As we move away from the center towards the periphery, the height and the number of buildings decreases, the standard of the dwellings becomes simpler and the trees disappear from the streets. At the same time, the number of shacks, and the slum dwellings all increase. Should this process of horizontal expansion of the city continue, consequence of the continual need for new dwellings, many other areas like Vila do Encontro will be gentrified, as they become the target of public policies of urbanization or urban renewal.

Thus, the gentrification process and the social relationships resulting from it, the intra-urban migrations and the public policies aimed at the use and occupation of urban space (the State acts as a mediator, whose "trusted scale" always ends up leaning in favor of the same side) are aspects of an uncontrolled urbanization process, in which changes in the use of the home and the neighborhood are part of the daily lives of a large segment of the populations at the margin.

References

Beauregard, Robert. "The chaos and the complexity of gentrification." pp. 35-55 in Smith, N. and Williams, P. (Eds), *Gentrification of the city*, Boston: Allen, 1986.

Bogus, Lucia M. M. *(Re) urbanizacao: por que e para quem?* Doctoral thesis presented to the Department of Architecture and Urban Studies of the University of São Paulo, 1988.

Bruschini, C. "Estrutura familiar e trabalho na Grande São Paulo. Cadernos de Pesquisa," *Fundacao Carlos Chagas*, n. 72, Fev. 1990, pp.39-57.

London, Bruce. "Gentrification as urban reinvasion: some preliminary definitions and theoretical considerations." In Laska, S. and Spain, W. (Eds) *Back to the city. Issues in neighborhood renovation.* Oxford: Pergamon Press, 1980, pp. 79-95.

Marcuse, Peter. "Abandonment, gentrification and displacement: the linkages in New York city." In Smith, N. and Williams, P. *Gentrification of the city.* Boston: Allen and Unwin, 1986, pp. 153-178.

Patarra, Neide e Bogus, L.M.M. *Percursos migratorios e ocupacao do espaco urbano: um estudo de caso ANAIS 2o.* ENCONTRO ABEP São Paulo, 1981, pp.239-247.

Teeland, L. *Components of gentrification in Sweden.* Department of Sociology, University of Gothenburg, Sweden. Mimeo, 1988.

Chapter 11

The Space of Citizenship: Visually Perceived Non-Spatial Dimensions of Housing

THEREZA C. CARVALHO
Oxford Polytechnic

This chapter draws a cross-national profile of some low-income housing estates in Brazil and in Britain. It focuses on the inter-relatedness between spatial patterns in housing, the residents' attitudes towards them (and corresponding morphological process of change) and the role of the State in the decision process that produced or allowed those patterns to be created (organizational participatory arrangements). The relative weight of the State and of citizenship (as acknowledged by individual rights towards proposing and deciding over the dwelling) on the housing space are examined by comparing the two different contexts. One is the Brazilian authoritarian structure of power and corresponding centralized process of production and characteristic design. The other context is the British democratically structured housing system and peculiar style of design (production) and management (consumption) of space. The chapter closes summarizing the relevant aspects identified in this research of the roles played by the dweller (in transforming the housing estate), by the space patterns of the housing estate and by the State.

Introduction

The accelerating physical deterioration of state-subsidized social housing stock is a common feature in the landscape of more than one country. Another common feature is the visually perceived 'no change' aspect that often characterizes such residential environments (unlike the neighborhoods around them which change gradually with the gradual changes in residents lifestyles). Visually perceived physical and spatial changes in housing estates often only occur through state intervention. Residents' changing lifestyles and consequent changing demands on their residential environment are stifled and frustrated or they are clandestine and condemned. State intervention in housing has often been evaluated on the basis of homogeneous order or decay with which the appearance of the housing estates has been associated.

These two visually perceived 'problem' features, decay and no-change, appear to derive from both physical and political-organizational aspects of the housing issue. The physical aspect concerns design and structural concepts and procedures that have only been adopted in public sector housing. Because of this uniqueness two problem-generating circumstances have frequently arisen. On the one hand some unique forms of housing have quickly become unpopular as they do not fit into the vernacular architectural context of their neighborhood. They have been consequently stigmatized as visual signs of their residents' dependency on the welfare state. On the other hand, time has shown that some of those forms of housing and building procedures have severe conceptual flaws and structural faults, while others, apparently, need only relevant 'cosmetic' and symbolic changes to be accepted.

The political aspect concerns the investment programs and fund-cutting measures that have alternately characterized government's involvement with housing provision in both its production and maintenance-consumption stages. The organizational aspect of government's involvement, in terms of operational systems devised to administrate its policies locally also matters. Their achievement seems to be in proportion to the degree of local autonomy. This autonomy varies in at least two main respects, first, in terms of decision power allowed to local authorities by central government, and second, in terms of how much support and participation from citizen-residents the local government has encouraged, supported or tolerated.

In Britain one of the means devised to counteract the physical degradation of the public housing stock was by encouraging the decentralization of local government housing services. Localized management mechanisms were supposed to be the means of counteracting it. Visually perceived decay in council houses was seen as a sign of failure of local government administration. In Brazil municipalization ideals have been pursued, together with privatization of former state provided or subsidized services, as the means to respond to the new demands placed on the Government. These new demands have derived from the continued use of the existing two million stock of low-income subsidized dwellings, produced for sale, while demand for new housing has also increased, exponentially.

Decentralization in Britain appeared in different guises. The principle of the state sharing responsibility for service provision with the client (who then becomes, to a certain extent, a self-provider) seemed implicit. The concept of participatory management mechanisms has been 'backed up' by both fund-cutting measures and privatization of the best council dwelling units apparently as a set of complementary strategies to reduce maintenance costs. Three objectives seemed clear: 1) to counteract the visually perceived decay; 2) to change the established political basis of provision and; 3) to reinstate a 'new order' in the relationship between the state and its citizen-residents.

The new order significantly changed the responsibilities and rights of each side. It appears to have been based, in many cases, on self-help, team-work and individual initiative and on greater involvement of the private sector in the provision of formerly public services. What has it achieved? For whom? These are the points this chapter addresses.

The second section of this chapter, Methodological Procedures and Measures of Success, presents the analytical framework, and its three working hypotheses, which are based on research previously carried out in Brazil, then revised, adjusted and tested in the case-studies conducted in Britain.

Sections 3, 4 and 5 examine the performance of housing projects under the light of the findings of the investigation. The evaluation criteria adopted relates the physical-spatial attributes of selected projects to four visually perceived non-spatial factors that influence the perception and the manipulation of the project by the residents. The following factors were regarded as determinant: state system of provision; the housing estate morphology and residents' expectations. The way each one of those factors affect the performance of a housing project, how they affect each other, and the visually perceived restructuring role they play in different contexts, are addressed in the sixth section. The last section, the Conclusions, brings together the findings and the results of the comparative analysis and presents the issues for further research.

Objectives

The objective of this chapter is therefore to present the application of the findings of the investigation of the impact of different State related resident-based strategies on the promotion of the necessary revitalization and overall improvement of living conditions in certain public sector housing. This investigation was originally conducted as partial fulfillment of the requirements of the Council for National Academic Awards for the Degree of Doctor in Philosophy at Oxford Polytechnic.

Three interrelated aspects were examined: some housing estates and their designs; residents' patterns of space consumption materialized through changes in its fabric; cases where participatory mechanisms of revitalization have been tried with residents' participation; and the relative weight of the State in the resulting participatory investment and design decision-making process. The indicator adopted here for achievement is recognition by residents and the local state of the potential of certain housing estates for revitalization. This recognition was examined by observing gradual transformations (spatial revitalizations) of the residential environment and through unstructured interviews with residents (and in some cases staff) to assess their participation in the process of recognized change. Those three aspects and indicator of achievement are considered here as interrelated, affecting each other in different ways contingent on the peculiarities of the local context.

Methodological procedures and measures of success

The proposed analytical framework, after the initial testing and subsequent revisions took place, include citizens' estate-based participation, and the means jointly devised by residents and the local state to obtain legitimacy and acknowledgement for their individual or collective contributions in the making or re-making of their housing environment, both in terms of design and investment decisions.[1] It comprises three working hypotheses. The first working hypothesis is that some housing forms and estate layouts allow for transformations while others do not. Differentiating factors would include the tightness of the physical link between dwellings, the nature of the adjacent spaces, and of the link with the public open spaces around them. The second working hypothesis is that some mechanisms of management-decentralization and other similar forms acknowledge and support residents' initiatives while others do not. Here differentiating factors would be the

---

[1] The widening of the empirical net is theoretically supported by Duncan and Goodwin (1988), Castells (1983), Dickens et al. (1985), Perlman (in Susskind et al., ed., 1983), Ravetz (1988) and Moudon (1986). The contribution of these authors to the argument of this thesis is demonstrated in sections 4 and 5 of this chapter.

role of the state, the rigidity of the hierarchy, power structure and staff attitudes in terms of self-preservation and social change. The third working hypothesis is that where design and management mechanisms, favorable to both physical change and to residents' taking the initiative to direct those changes to their best interests, have come together the potential for growth (and development) of the residential environment was strongly enhanced.

The level of achievement in such management mechanisms were expected to vary significantly, however, depending on the ability of residents and the state to renegotiate the balance in that 'self help based new order', in terms of rights to use space regardless of tenure. Exercise of these new rights was expected to be visually perceivable.

Participatory mechanisms based on such assumptions were examined as possible routes (policy) for strengthening citizens' participation in the administration of the unevenness of development expressed in their own housing environment, through residents and local institutions joint efforts (management), interacting between them and with specific morphological configurations of selected housing estates (product).

The selected case-studies

The three case-studies in Britain, and the one in Brazil, have been used as steps in the process of investigating the evolving relationship between the state, the citizens-residents and housing estates. The comparison between different contexts served two different purposes: first, as a means of identifying differentiating links between apparently common structures and their localities; second, to avoid the risk of taking the experiment for the model; third, to also avoid the risk of being parochial and ethnocentric.

Each one of the interrelated aspects (the revised working hypotheses for this research) which address the relations between the state, the space(of the estate) and residents, through policy administration and management strategies were selected and refined as significant, partly by the case-studies' experience. Broadwater Farm in the London Borough of Haringey, illustrates, in particular, the role of the state and its relation with residents. Byker, in the City of Newcastle-upon-Tyne, on the other hand highlights the relationship between the state and the space of the housing estate while Easterhouse in the outskirts of Glasgow seems to bring the three aspects together. Each housing estate also characterizes a particular trend in housing design, building procedure and urban policy in Britain. Easterhouse has the standard four-storey-walk-up shape and scale of the quantitatively geared strategies of housing provision of the '50s while Broadwater Farm bears the also characteristic overwhelming shape and scale, and concrete fabric, of the system built architectural follies of the mid seventies. Byker illustrates the more ambitious agenda of the late seventies when progressive planning encouraged participatory processes in design.

The case-study in Brazil, Cidade Alta in Rio de Janeiro, based on previous research, has a similar four storey-walk-up standard shape of the quantitatively geared housing strategies characteristic of the '60s in Brazil and was selected for the exceptional performance of residents (and design) in terms of exploring the potential for change of the space of the estate[2].

Choice of indicator

The investigation on participatory mechanisms for revitalization strategies was based on the interrelatedness of the three working hypothesis previously presented. Visually perceived transformations in housing estates, their shape and scale would indicate whether improvement or rehabilitation have been "centrally" decided, or locally, whether there were one group of organized residents or more, and, which is even more important, how the resulting achievement in social and economic terms were effectively expressed in the changed design image. Jacobs' "clues" to looking at cities (1985) helped to provide the necessary thread to knit together the patterns of space transformation in the consumption stage of a housing estate, the organizational and political dimensions of participatory mechanisms emphasized by Churchman (1988), the social factor in terms of levels of mobilization, the personal factor in terms of creative potential of individual residents (Cooper-Marcus,1986; Perlman,1983) and the space and design potential for change (Moudon,1986; Carvalho,1985). Unlike Zeizel (1981,p.105) who argues for the observation of physical traces of changes in a housing environment as signs of conceptual design flaws, to be corrected, they are regarded in this chapter as indicators that help to answer

---

[2] The Brazilian case-study was on the basis of personal research done in the Metropolitan area of Rio de Janeiro comprising both unstructured interviews and observational studies on the various sites. This investigation was carried out through sample surveys in twenty one housing estates. The sample was selected according to three different size and scale brackets: average small (with less than 500 dwellings per estate), average medium (from 500 to 1000 dwellings per estate) and average large (more then 1001 dwellings per estate). The research identified four different aspects, besides the physical-spatial one, of the housing projects analyses, which permeate through the visually perceived image of a given scheme and with this maintains a likewise visually perceived relation of physical proportion ,or scale, and for this reason are here called dimensions. They are: a the psycho-social or the perceived image dimension; b) the socio-cultural or community making/place-making dimension; c) the economic- productive dimension; and (d) the spatial related adminiorganisational dimension. The performance of a given housing project was evaluated by relating its physical-spatial attributes to each one of the referred dimensions. The explanatory variable consisted in the needs and values of the group of residents as they were expressed through their visually perceived initiatives to fulfill them.

questions related to the past of the housing estate in its production stage, its evolution in terms of management, State and residents relationship, and respective achievements, up to the present 'state of the art'.

The interrelationship between these 'patterns', 'dimensions' and 'factors' would account for the acknowledged success of participatory processes and their physical outcomes, and for the latter's responsiveness to users' changing needs for self-expression and social acknowledgement.

Not all designed spaces respond equally to gradual changes and additions. The physical forms of the housing estates were analyses according to perceived potential for change. This required looking at the spatial patterns of certain specific design aspects (spatially closer to the residents' visual control). The improvement of the interface between the dwelling, unit or block, and the area around/adjacent to it (the semi-private/semi-public boundary) was considered to be an appropriate aspect for sample study, covering, as it does, a full range of issues from policy to practice.

The gradual transformation of this adjacent space would highlight the effectiveness of participatory based systems of housing provision and management, in terms of both technical and political performance. In technical terms this was for at least two reasons. The first was the generally accepted expectation that localized service management necessarily leads to improved residents satisfaction. The second was that within the housing estate the perceived image of the dwelling (its external fabric and design features) and of its adjacent spaces would be one of the key issues that would directly affect residents' satisfaction with their homes (it is the one that 'obligatory' changes with tenure). In political terms the selected aspect would also indicate both the nature of the residents' involvement in the decision-making process and the role of the State in it. The relationship between the residents and the State would be expressed in the acknowledgement and legitimization of the residents' capacity to decide over that matter

Key areas for investigation

The key areas for investigation required to provide evidence for the analytical framework and working assumptions are embodied in the following seven factors. The first one is the situational context including morphological characteristics of the housing and predominant administrative system. The second and third factors to be considered are government perspective and the way residents' participation, acknowledged or not, affect the physical setting. Fourth and fifth in this list are, respectively, the factors of characterizing power relationship between central and local decision makers and between the latter and the residents and the way it affects the morphological, the administrative and the social aspects of the estate. Finally, the potential for change of the physical setting had also to be examined vis-a-vis the assumed interrelationship between the management strategies and residents' initiatives, with or without government involvement. The background goals of the evaluator were regarded as the seventh and constant factor. Unstructured interviews, and spatial observations, were conducted focusing on the three major issues.

Application and findings related to the state system of provision

Some significant aspects of the relationship between the state and its citizens were observed to be materialized in the social and spatial inequalities that often characterize social housing, (a feature which is highlighted when compared to the 'high street' model, both in Brazil and Britain). In Brazil, social and spatial inequalities are associated with the publicized image of the country: very poor slum areas and middle-class high-rise sea-shore dwellings. In Britain these 'inequalities' have been observed throughout this research, both within selected housing estates such as in Easterhouse, and between these and the neighborhood, as in the case of Broadwater Farm. The acknowledged quality of design in Byker has apparently preserved that estate from the visual stigma associated with social and spatial inequalities.

Community initiatives regarded as successful and resulting in environmental improvement have more often than not occurred outside the government's sphere of influence. They have often been labelled 'informal', as they by-passed bureaucratic controls in order to fulfill their aims. This 'by-pass' disguises a reduction of prevailing space or building standards and of bureaucratic requirements carried out by the 'informal' producer-consumer. The acknowledged success of some of these initiatives has been sometimes attributed in Brazil to this 'informality'. It conciliates poverty with the established standards, in a compromise that is negotiated on site and therefore locally adequate. Such initiatives are, however, often deprived of legitimacy by the label 'informal', which both stigmatizes and condemns them to clandestine status.

Government involvement has sometimes hindered the process of development it was supposed to support. This is because its main concern has often been both in Brazil and in Britain, basically regulatory, implying bureaucratic controls that are often 'alien' to the interests of the local community. The degree of 'alieness' increases significantly when the government's main mechanisms of control are geared to the financial feasibility criterion. In Brazil, where housing programs are based on home ownership, this criterion has accounted for some distortion, as the benefitted community has not been identical to the targeted one. Family income has therefore in these circumstances often been determinant of government's support. In Britain more recently the same criterion (the cost-value ratio) has been applied with similar consequences in terms of increasing social and spatial inequalities. Different levels of internal social mobilization among different groups of a given community, shortage of resources, and the consequent competition for the little available, have also aggravated the problem when that distortion has occurred.

In the British context (Glasgow, Easterhouse) power relationships between different levels of State and the residents played an important role in carrying out changes. Corresponding organizational arrangements formalized those efforts both in terms of space and shape and in terms of localized management mechanisms. The changes that started ephemeral "and gradually developed into some level of formalization, whether spacial or organization, have sometimes appeared more successful in terms of achievement in the eyes of the residents".

In both countries, recent developments points to ambitious national programs based on home ownership and private-sector involvement to generate inflated house prices. This has produced, in Brazil, increasing cuts in government's financial support for new developments and reduced government's ability to keep up the same rhythm of production. The decrease in government subsidies to low-income housing has pushed up the rents in the private sector and, pushed more and more people into house buying, at prices they could not really afford. The prevalence of this private sector approach has helped to maintain and increase profit margins at the expense of rising homelessness and significantly accelerated deterioration of the existing housing stock.

The last ten years of change in British housing policies has made this analysis valid, to a certain extent, for both Britain and Brazil. Housing policies based on home ownership and private-sector involvement have generated rising inflation in house prices. Tax relief on mortgages and the right-to-buy strategy helped to channel public funds into the private sector. Further cuts in public sector housing provision have also helped to push more people into buying their houses at almost any cost, initially. In 1985 this resulted in 11,000 repossessions by building societies in 1985 (Ospina,1987,p.14), "and even more registered and unregistered homelessness". The same applies to local authority stock sold under the right to buy which the owner-occupiers cannot afford to maintain. To diminish the consequences of this and to maintain the existing public-sector housing stock, large resources would be required, which central government is not prepared to pay. Instead the structural change in the government's expected and accepted social role has led to a redefinition of responsibilities for both provision and maintenance. Provision of new houses seems to be almost completely left with the private sector. For maintenance and management some alternatives were devised. One was to force local authorities to dispose of their stock, to either sitting tenants or private developers, so as to reduce the level of public spending on maintenance. Another strategy was to encourage or organize residents participation in sharing responsibility for maintenance through some form of localized management arrangement (trust, agency, association or residents' cooperatives).

Application and findings related to morphology

The case-studies selected contributed to confirm directly or by default and each one in its different way, the visual sign of good social and spatial performance of social housing considered in this research to be the transformation of the estates into real neighborhoods. The good spatial and social performance was associated with perceived morphological, organizational (administrative) and economic characteristics closer to the traditional ('real') high-street model, with mixed functions and varied facades and accesses. The envisaged product was the gradual transformation of the blocks within existing housing estates in order to accommodate local residents' changing and mixed demands. This would be achieved through residents' initiatives and joint decisions which would be constantly and visually negotiated with the state, as well as those deriving from external pressures from the city around.

The two space-patterns, the parsimonious, bleak and conspicuous housing estate on one end and the richly explored and experienced traditional street on the other, form the extremes of a continuum that varies in complexity of function and activities performed and in space and place experienced. The same activities related to education, health, social contacts, production, administration, leisure, communication and transportation are present in both extremes and at each situation in between although with significantly different qualitative aspects. The same individual resources in terms of residents' creativity, expectations, initiative and ambitions of improvement are also present. The complexity varies, together with the degree of individual choice allowed, contingent on a series of local and external issues comprising among others political will and material space and social resources available. Access to opportunities for improvement are also consequently and correspondingly influenced.

Along that continuum there is a hierarchy of 'links' between design and management of the urban space (the residential area), between the dweller and the state. Those links vary in the degree of freedom that they allow the dwellers in terms of negotiating their space and their status with the state. The first link in that continuum corresponds in terms of building typologies to either individual or terraced houses in the high street. In that circumstance the residents have a direct and individualized link with the space outside their dwellings and with the services provided by the state. Their individual identities as residents (citizens) is confirmed by that address. They can negotiate it with the State, change or abide by the law or by the collective street image, individually or as part of the local community of non-dependent on state support.

The second degree of freedom in the continuum is the block in the high street where the residents have to abide by restrictions imposed by the routine of living in a condominium. They have therefore a corresponding weaker link with the space outside their dwellings depending on the ratio between total number of dwellings per block. The adjacent space to the dwelling becomes public or semi-public or semi-private, and consequently affects the access routes and services provided by the state. Going down that continuum, the private development close of blocks of flats is the next weaker link in terms of spatial relationship between the dwellers and the state. However economic and political clout of the residents can change weakness into strength. Services originally provided by the State can be in this circumstance privatized sometimes to the advantage of the residents depending on their political and economic purchasing capacity.

The next weaker link is the council estate of individual or row houses. Although these building typologies would resemble the stronger links enunciated in this continuum they present one significant distinct feature. An intermediate management level deals with the residents as a collective dependent group. The governing administration of that residential space has therefore distinct rules from the high street model. That distinction does not necessarily show on the sidewalk so perhaps there will not be any stigma attached to the area and the residents. Once introduced the changed rules and corresponding intermediate level of collective administration of the area freedom to change decreases step by step along that continuum unless the deal with the state is re-negotiated through residents' organized endeavors, such as some of the ones observed in Easterhouse.

The other high-street building typologies repeat themselves, in a different political and spatial status, as housing estates with decreasing acknowledgement (increasing stigma) of residents' capacity (and right) to negotiate their individual space and status with the state. The bottom line in that regression is the multi-storey council estate of slabs and tower blocks and reticular lay-out with 'locked in' routes of access such as observed in Broadwater Farm. The rigid 'locked in' fly-over pedestrian routes reduce even further the degree of freedom available in the project for individual users to manipulate the space. Localization of certain housing functions can in some cases aggravate the state-dweller relationship by reducing even further the degrees of freedom allowed them. This reduction in freedom can derive from self-preservation attitudes of the government bodies involved or lack of government commitment to social development (social change).

Those differences along that state-cum-space continuum can be therefore correspondingly reduced or enhanced also contingent on local and external factors. A set of three factors has been observed. One factor is the role that the state plays in controlling and maintaining those spatial differences [and their social implications which are called for the sake of this research social and spatial inequalities]. Democratically based policies and practices regarding the housing issue, both in the provision and more particularly in the management and consumption sides of the issue, are fundamental to create favorable conditions for those gradual changes to take place. State's control regulations over use of space influences strongly the development of differentiated (through individual and group initiatives) patterns of space-consumption.

Another influential local factor is space as designed and defined by tradition or by local enterprising initiatives. Some spaces allow for expansion and for change of use while other spaces do not. This potential for change can be favored or obstructed by certain design features such as the nature of the grid of accesses to the estate and to its various parts, as well as the design and location within the existing fabric of certain activities and service-points. Ill-defined tenure over certain spaces, whose assigned functions are often also equally ill-perceived, can, in the same way, obstruct the envisaged gradual transformations. Both Byker and Broadwater Farm illustrates this point, respectively, in its positive and negative aspects.

The third factor that can influence these spatial transformations significantly is the residents' creative potential and confidence to carry on changes. Both the potential and the confidence can be undermined or boosted by social opinion and self-image, by a paternalistic style of management and by the impermeability of certain physical features. The issue has actually appeared in this research when comparing England and Scotland with respect to residents' informal initiatives towards improving their income through some sort of home-based production or service. National characteristics and pride in their different self-images were called upon to answer for the observed differences.

Application and findings related to residents' expectations

Social and spatial articulation was found to derive from three basic factors. The first was cultural, stemming from within the community of residents, how they see themselves and their relationship with the world around. Their image of themselves and of the world affects spatial orientation, motivation and the decisions of all the agents involved in the creation and gradual re-creation of the residential setting, such as in Lochend Homesteading Group as opposed to Easthall Dampness Group in Easterhouse. The second factor was the social structure of the local community of residents, which is composed of elements that perform certain roles in the society outside of their domain. Their links with the process of production and with existing formal organizations can be manipulated both personally and collectively to create the necessary conditions for change to take place (Easthall in Easterhouse). The third factor was the physical structure, comprising elements spatially distributed, which is organized into distinct sub-spatial distributions, each one with a different meaning for the resident users.

A direct relationship was identified, within certain specific public housing schemes, between the perception of success by its users and the degree of freedom offered both by the design and by its management. This freedom is the extent to which the estate has provided the residents with the necessary conditions to enable them to reshape the common spaces and interfaces within their immediate environment. The main contribution of this evaluation consisted in attributing a positive aspect to the design of schemes whose common areas and interfaces allowed for changes, and were therefore effectively altered by their residents, as opposed to those that did not.

The investigation conducted has also provided evidence, from different cultural origins, to question certain myths. The myth of the negative connotations of policies geared to physical improvements disregards the importance of the perceived image of a place for its community to achieve its envisaged social acknowledgement. Budgets and political priorities express commitment to certain groups and not to others and thus determines social legitimacy of some at the expense of others. Running after a lorry for shopping at monopolistic prices in Easterhouse illustrate the level of deprivation in environmental, social and in economic terms to which the local residents are subjected.

The myth of the tenant not bothering about external areas in the estate has also revealed itself in a different light with some of the Scottish experi-

ence described at this thesis. Both the cooperative and the dampness group
in Easterhouse seemed very concerned with perceived image and external
appearance of their dwellings, of their blocks and of their neighborhood.
The representatives of the Easthall Dampness Group were actually eager
to propose changes to that scale and to participate, if allowed, in the discussion of other city-wide spatial-economic revitalization strategies. The myth
seems to derive from five interrelated aspects often found in low-income
housing estates. First is the legal basis for tenure which would account for
the 'I don't care for what I don't own' assumed attitude. The second is the
administrative basis for that myth: who is responsible for the maintenance
and management of the various spaces in the estate? Thirdly is the design
basis for it. Where no or little visually perceived distinction is made between private, semi-private, semi-public and public spaces, issues such as
tenure and maintenance may suffer. As boundaries between those spaces
become muddled signs of 'tenants' not bothering' such as graffiti, rubbish
and vandalism may clutter the already unclear paths.

The fourth aspect is the social basis for that myth, again related to the
previous ones. The negative feeling towards certain communities, due to
their no longer acknowledged right to a state provided house accounts for
the stigma of dependency associated with their estate, its shape, location.
Finally, the ethnical (cultural) basis for that myth where ethnic minorities
with different values in relation to inhabiting are not accepted. Together
those five aspects can build up a barrage of prejudice which support that
myth against contrary visual evidence included (through value-based perception you see what you want) as the riot in Broadwater Farm illustrates
(5th, Oct. 1985). The stereotypes of 'model aspirations' in terms of building typologies have followed the same line of questioning. Even the loathed
flats have done well enough once adequately dressed up (Ravetz, 1988).

The myth of self-sufficiency of the minimalist-based neighborhood unit
concept of housing design, still surviving, needs a final coup de grace. Neither the size of certain functional buildings nor their functional segregation
have, up to now, proved to be appropriate to the scale of activities that
take place on state-subsidized housing estates for the low-income groups.[3]

---

[3] The shops and communal equipment such as schools and commercial facilities in the
housing estate of Zaira Duna, for instance, are placed at the end of the plot, for the
'exclusive use of the estate residents'. These residents, most of which belong to the same
low-income bracket, have little resources to make for the shop leaser's expected profits.
What very often happens is the subsequent closure of these facilities. No attention is
paid, in most cases, to the interface between the estate and its adjacent area. The
housing scheme turns its back and its dust-bins to the neighborhood. The shopping
facilities of the housing estate of D. Jaime Camara on the other hand illustrates the
spatial relationship geared to the high street model. They were successfully located in
front of the existing square, singular feature in the local urban pattern of the area, on

This resembles more closely the economic and related social practices of the smaller rural villages, not in its productive side but in its consumption/retail aspect. The area of the shopping facilities appropriately bears a physical relationship to the amount and nature of the average consumer's shopping and to its frequency. This often means, for instance, buying two eggs instead of the super-market minimum standard of six. This also means that not much space was required to stock merchandise.

The myth of cost-efficiency adopted as paradigm for service provision and as criterion for performance evaluation disguises political priorities and ideological principles often alien to the residents' best interests. The aspect of offering residents choice', again on an income segregating basis linking choice to purchasing capacity, works as poor compensation for the cost-effective reduction carried out in the housing provision service. Choice has been in that respect manipulated into a status of item of luxury, a reward for achievers. But is it?

Comparing and contextualizing: citizenship, home, and neighborhood

Citizenship has to do with the political significance of choice; the prevalence of residents' criteria in the use of the space has to do with the economic significance of choice; self-image and self-confidence has to do with the social significance of choice; variety and identity of a place has to do with the cultural significance of choice. All those significants and their signifying concern illustrate the spatial and physical significance of choice. They are interrelated and have to do with choice on an equal basis, i.e. with no segregating condition.[4] Cost-effectiveness as sole criterion for decision in rendering housing as a public service segregates the service and the public. Segregation has again political, economic, social, cultural and spatial sig-

---

the interface between the housing estate and the adjacent neighborhood, instead of in the usual geometric centre.

[4] Another aspect that enforces the residents awareness of their lack of choice consists in the building regulations, plus the development control regulations that support the insurance companies regulations, without which you cannot obtain a mortgage in Brazil. That all together legally marginalize the great majority of the poorer's initiatives towards building their own house and environment. Ignorance and the still high level of illiteracy favor the maintenance of the described context as the information about those policies and their respective implied regulations, when they are made available to the public, is often spelled out in terms which are not accessible to the vast majority of the population. That has also been identified by Prak (1 977,p.88): Users consider the built environment first of all as an instrument or a tool comparable to telephone, typewriter, pencils or cars; an instrument that is a help or a hindrance in their activities. That interpretation proved to be he more effective the poorer were the community.

nificance. All leading to residualization and deterioration of the stock and of the residents' living conditions one way or another.

This research has provided some arguments to support the underlying assumption that to incorporate residents' participatory initiatives in the decision-making process of creating and re-creating the environment through some form of decentralized structure of state support is a positive step forward in improving social housing. The externalization of 'new' socio-cultural-economically meaningful articulations within a dwelling and in the area adjacent to the dwelling, has a ripple effect in the area. It can generate new forms,functions and expectations that are potentially usable for socio-physical articulation.

This incorporation into the process determines acknowledging and legitimizing the residents' right and capacity to influence decisions as well as legitimizing their creative individual efforts. That step however can neither be taken from a distance, as another 'fountain pen-stroke', nor take for granted residents' support to the 'pen-holder's interpretation of their perspective. It requires local and visual negotiation and consequently a clearly defined and mutually agreed 'interface' between the state and the local community of residents interested in carrying out individual or group spatial changes. That interface implies a democratization process in terms of access to relevant information and to decision levels to keep the space (environment) gradually evolving and alive through constantly re-negotiating it.

A significant aspect of that interface lies in the very nature of the dwelling as a living space, in its relationship with the residents, the city and the state, which contains and is contained within the political system of state power and control. It is in the space adjacent to the dwelling, to the block and to the estate, in the interface with their immediate environment, where the social, the economic, the cultural and the political aspects come together inter-linked with the housing issue in its most intimate aspects and are ultimately and constantly being negotiated by the residents both collectively and individually.

The evidence provided by this investigation indicates that the more the balance struck, between spatial and non-spatial aspects of a given project, proved to be compatible with the residents' potential for improving their living conditions, the more improvements the area would show as a consequence. The opposite was also found to be implicitly valid. It follows that alterations in the design of the dwellings: layout or external physical shape, are interpreted as positive indicators of success of the built environment thus produced and of good performance of state-subsidized housing programs.

In the Brazilian context the social/spatial articulation or potential for growth of a housing environment, when and where it was observed, was found to derive from the presence of certain physical attributes such as: a) spatial repertoire with a significant degree of permeability to changes of functions and forms; b) topological structure of the grid with clearly perceived routes and significant density of use; c) clear and visually perceived spatial definition of statutory responsibilities over public and semi-public spaces; d) accessibility with a significant degree of choice; e) variety in terms of forms, functions and scale of activity.

These factors favor but do not guarantee effective manipulation of the space by residents, as the prevalent organizational decision-making aspect will also have great influence. The main contribution of that evaluation to the development of the further stages of this investigation consisted of attributing a positive aspect to the design of schemes whose common areas and interfaces allowed for changes, and were therefore effectively altered by their residents, as opposed to those that did not.

The residents tended to regard their houses as tools for improving their living conditions. This has shown to be their major criterion of assessment of 'good' or 'bad' environments. That interpretation proved to be more effective the poorer the community. Their objective approach to the matter of dwelling, when allowed to be freely and physically expressed in the recreation of the immediate housing environment built up variety in functional and spatial terms. The energy and time spent in the negotiation of this process of recreation builds up the community. In some housing estates the residents soon put to use the perceived margin allowed, or left over, for recreation. The more common process of appropriation observed in Rio, additions were made to the existing buildings, filling in the 'gaps' perceived in the design, as well as, opening or closing projected passage-ways. Accessibility was quickly identified by the residents as a major asset, fundamental to the flourishing of any commercial or productive activity . Yet, in at least one case, Cidade Alta housing estate, these margins were assessed by the professionals involved in the project evaluation as a waste and consequently as a mistake requiring correction in further developments. The margins were professionally condemned because they did not contribute to the overall perceived image of the project', or to the financial return for the private and public sector partnerships involved in the operation.

Byker housing estate in Newcastle, illustrates the conflict in the view of tenants' attitudes towards much praised design features of the estate that they want removed, as these tend to catalyze the gregarious tendencies of adolescents to the annoyance of the older residents. Architects would thus often be blamed for reinventing society and/or local socially established practices to suit their own ideals around which they would shape the environment. Problems of mismatch are thus inevitable and the consequent reappropriation of the built result by the residents, according to the local dominant values, takes place if physical conditions and State rules over space consumption are favorable.

There were however some obstructions to those changes both in spacial and in organizational terms. In spatial terms the stronger the design image as a whole of a given project, the stronger, in expressive terms, the coherence of its overall perceived image. Although it may sound like a positive quality in architectural terms, that perceived unity can in some circumstances negatively affect the perception, and consequently the articulation of changes, of each one of its parts. This was observed in the housing estate of Broadwater Farm, London. The overall image of the project overrides the perception of its components, which are bound together, in a rigid way, in order to build up the strength of the design image. This affects negatively the potential for new 'articulations' of the different parts that the residents' use may require. No alterations can be introduced in that design that will favor the making of the human environment. There were no visual boundaries along the access routes. Orientation was made very difficult and motivation almost impossible in consequence. In organizational terms, the paternalistic approach to housing provision and residents and consequent peculiar style of management found in the housing estate of Byker curtails the potential for growth which the physical structure presents making invisible residents' changing needs and initiatives.

By the same token, the housing designs that allow for greater changes to be made through use are the ones with a weaker overall perceived design image. Standard buildings loosely put together, with physical margins in the immediate surrounding areas of the dwelling units, offer more potential for 'new' articulations, changes of space/functions/meanings, to be introduced. This type of building and lay-out was found both in Britain, such as Easterhouse, and in Brazil, such as Cidade Alta. Spatial changes have been observed in both although the role of the State in allowing, facilitating or ignoring such changes has differed significantly.

Conclusions

Vital places are those where people have the freedom to make day-to-day changes to their environment. Collectively these small transformations can lead to the slow aging of a place of a kind often associated with very much appreciated old European towns which show and favor a significant degree of prosperity, adding to the integrity of the place. They can also be interpreted as visually perceived signs of the potential and local (and 'informal') knowledge available in a given locality.

Considering prosperity to be an overall ambition of society new uses, functions and activities, are being proposed by the minute. Some are expressed, squeezed into the gaps, potentially rich leftovers of the existing socio-spatial structure. The role of resolving conflicts through suppression, often attributed to design in rehabilitation works, appears to be only applicable in very specific circumstances, and for a limited period of time, where health hazards are involved and even then a discussion of hazards versus benefits could be appropriate.

There is a conflict 'in the making' as residents strive to add their local, personal, 'informal' knowledge to the existing socio-spatial structure of the area, requiring new settings through new uses, additions, transformations, or expansion. The objective of design, therefore, could be to propose areas for conflict, i.e. demarcating spaces whose potentially rich topological structure can support transformations. To provide such an initial 'footprint' in terms of basic unit of space, individual or block- type plots, gridirons of access, and building typologies could allow for incremental changes to take and make place.

Small alterations, however, may show only what residents are able to do within their prevailing constraints, not what they might have liked to do had circumstances been different in spatial, material and institutional terms. Though it does contribute to human dignity, and is not something to be despised, sharing in decisions is no panacea, no general cure for the evils of injustice and arbitrary power (Barrington Moore, quoted in Cox (1976), p.171).

'Ad hoc' approaches to problem-solving, and their frequent polarization effect, tend to reproduce similar patterns of spatial and social inequalities even though often changing the object area. Uneven development is, in these circumstances, apparently maintained, interpreted as necessary, in economic and in functional terms, to preserve the level of profit in the areas 'turned equal' through some form of generalized improvement or unhindered decay. Resident-citizens participated, in the described contexts, formally or informally, either individually or collectively, for the sake of their own development, to overcome these policies' limitations. Negative political evaluations, uneven development and social and spatial inequalities, appear to maintain a causal-effect-causal relationship with the 'ad hoc approach' to problem-defining-cum-problem-solving in housing, which administrative routines can help to maintain.

The objective of participatory mechanisms of economic and spatial revitalization in relation to purpose designed housing estates could therefore be to negotiate or mediate changes, in economic and spatial terms, on an individual or collective basis, with residents and with formal or informal organizations interested and/or involved in, and compromising with, emerging and remnant ones.

The role of the State in this context would be to adopt the strategy of allowing and supporting these gradual transformations to take place. It has been said that only "concerted and powerful forces can disrupt the original footprint" of a place (Moudon, 1986). Slum clearance and large-scale housing programs in general seem to draw their energy to materialize from that source of "concerted and powerful forces". The impact of these forces can be damaging enough at the moment of production of a housing project and does not need to be prolonged through design concepts that disguises spaces with ill-defined tenure, and management systems that impose conditions on consumption.

The relationship between design and management within specific structures of power and their corresponding housing systems has been traditionally associated with rent or mortgage payment control and maintenance of communal areas. The spatial analysis of selected housing estates in this research has provided the visually perceived evidence that the traditional approach to that relationship between management and design may not always serve the residents' nor the State's best interests.

The importance of incorporating residents' creative potential for development in the planning and decision-making process increases with poverty. It becomes paramount in Brazil. Paulo Freire restated the value of local knowledge, individual perception, personal experience, as an adult literacy training method in Brazil. Through raising consciousness of the worth of one's own culture, on the perception of choice, and on the dignity and rights of human beings as actors in their environment, Freire educated a process of critical thinking and analysis emerging from people's own experience'. Perlman (1983) has regarded this process as immensely interesting to incorporate into the planning approach. Carvalho (1957), in a different time and space context, supported and implemented the same thesis as development strategy in the poorer areas of Brazilian innerland. This research provided the evidence that Freire's contribution remains valid in the specific contexts analyses.

Issues for further research

The basic question of this investigation was twofold. First, was how to integrate the state and the participation of the residents into the process of creation and re-creation of the housing environment through some form of participatory mechanism of management. Second, when and where this 'integration' has occurred how responsive to changes have been selected design concepts materialized in the space of the estates chosen. The research carried out to answer this question raised a series of related issues which express the complexity of this matter.

First on the agenda is the issue of legitimation by the State and society of the efforts already carried out by the individual, or group, towards the making or improving of their housing and/or built environment. This task requires further studies of the relationship between the built environment, its nature, shape and scale, and the small-scale scattered appropriating initiatives, where they happened. It also includes identifying, divulging and encouraging the mechanisms and the necessary inputs that support, or that simply do not obstruct, those initiatives in economic, socio-political, financial and organizational terms.

Second in this series of related study requirements is the institutional aspect of the process of design. A new approach to design that takes into consideration the space related issues described above is necessary. This new approach would affect the roles both architect and town planner play in the making of the built environment.

An investigation into this field would also imply, as a third related issue, significant changes in the nature of the relationship between the local state and the local developers and (or) consumer producers. New guidelines and development control regulations should be issued to allow for, if not to promote directly, a margin for gradual improvement of the built environment. These would comprise physical, spatial and technological factors, and their socio-economic basis, related to design and construction of houses in general. The mechanism of functional zoning should also be revised in its alleged objective of regulating land-use as it often ends up being an instrument of income-based spatial segregation that benefits specific groups.

Another aspect related to the integration of the community based knowledge to the formal process of housing provision which deserves attention is the issue of the role of the State in relation to community based or grassroots movements concerned with the improvements of their environment. Many different proposals have been made concerning the nature of the necessary government support to these movements. They comprise, among other things, the administrative restructuring of the local State through decentralization of certain functions, as in Britain, the creation of a new government body to deal exclusively with those communities, as in France, or the slackening of regulations and control over the group or individual initiatives towards the improvement of their leaving and environment, as in Italy. This aspect brings back the issue of legitimizing these initiatives and the alternative to do so through granting or acknowledging statutory identity to those which would be community based.

The fifth issue regards the implicit economic base and aim of the residents' initiatives towards the improvement of their housing environments. The research conducted in Brazil provided relevant evidence that there is a relationship between the nature, shape and scale of the built environment produced through the housing programs and the scattered small scale individual initiative of residents towards improving their income and living conditions (Carvalho, 1980). To incorporate the participation of the residents into the process of housing improvement, as an acknowledged part of the overall process of urban development, will require taking into consideration the whole spectrum of economic activities that compose it, whether 'formal' or 'ephemeral'. This brings back the issue of legitimization of individual initiatives by the state and the society in general and the political social, economic, cultural, spatial, physical implications of this support.

References

Associacao Brasileira de Normas Tecnicas (1985) Partial reports of the Committee on Urbanistic Norms, Brazilian Assoc, of Technical Norms, ABNT, Rio de Janeiro.

Carvalho,M.P.; *Desenvolvimento agr'kola e industrial para pequeno. medio e grande produtores: umaabordagem integrada.* Pos-graduate diss., Instituto Superior de Estudos Brasileiros; Rio de Janeiro; 1957.

Carvalho,T.C.; *Contribuiao ao estudo da ordenacao espacial de conjuntos habitacionais de baixa renda*: Msc. diss., COPPE - Coordenacao de Programas em P6s-graduaao de Engenharia, Federal University of Rio deJaneiro; 1980.

"As Dimensoes da Habitaao"; Projeto: 77 July 95-105;1985.

Churchman, A and Neaman,S.; "Resident Participation in Neighborhood Programs: some Issues to be Resolved"; in *Looking Back to the Future (vol.2): Proceedings of the 10th IAPS Conference in Delft 5-8 July 1988.* ed. H.Van Hoogdalem and others, 325-334; Delft; Delft University Press; 1988.

Cooper-Marcus,C. and Sarkissian,W.; *Housing as if People Mattered*: Berkeley; University of California; 1986.

Cox,W.H.; *Cities-the Public Dimension*: Harmondsworth; Penguim; 1976.

Delson, R.M. (1979) *New Towns for Colonial Brazil* Dept. of Geography, Syracuse University, Michigan.

Escola Nacional de Habitacao e Poupania (1984) Partial Report: National Training Programme for the Implementation of Self-Help Housing programs, unpublished, Rio de Janeiro.

Friedman, Zube and Zimring (1978) *Environmental Design Evaluation*. Plenum Press, New York.

Hillier, R. & Hanson, J. (1984) *The Social Logic of Space*, Cambridge University Press, New York.

Instituto de Pesquisas Tecnologicas (1975) *Nivel de Satisfaao em Conjuntos Habitacionais da Grande Sao Paulo*, (Level of Satisfaction in Housing Estates of Great Sao Paulo), 2 vol., Research Institute of Technology, IPT, Sao Paulo.

Instituto Brasileiro de Administracao Municipal(1980) *Quando a Rua vira Casa*, (When Streets become Houses), Centre for Urban Research, Brazilian Institute of Municipal Administration, Rio de Janeiro.

Jacobs, A.; *Looking at Cities*: Cambridge, Mass.; Harvard University; 1985.

Lerup, L. (1977) *Building the Unfinished*. vol.53, Library of Social Research, Sage Publications, London.

Moudon, A.V.; *Built for Change*: Cambridge, Mass.;MIT press;1986.

Ospina,J.; *Housing Ourselves*; London; Hillary Shipman; 1987.

Perlman, J.ln Susskind, L. and Elliot,M. ed.; *Paternalism Conflict and Coproduction*; New York; Plenum Press:1983

Prak, N. (1985) *The Visual Perception of the Built Environment*. Delft University Press, Delft.

Reis FQ, N. G. (1980) *Estrutura Urbana e Politica Habitacional*. paper presented in the Simposium of Building Costs Reduction, Bahia, unpublished.

Part V
The Meaning and Use of Housing:
The Traditional Family

The Meaning and Use of Housing: The Traditional Family

BOYOWA ANTHONY CHOKOR
University of Benin, Nigeria

Housing studies and the meaning of housing to various groups including the family is continuing to attract considerable research attention on an international and cross-cultural scale. The house is a protective shell of the family but perhaps much more fundamentally, a unit of socio-physical space where the family identity is most effectively represented, symbolized and preserved. Thus for all man's range of spatial movements, journeys, economic activities and as well as social exchanges and interaction, the house is both a point of return and refuge or centre of existence/reference for the family of household group (see also Seamon 1979). Without being overly deterministic, as the household or family composition, ties, values and activities change over time so do the value, meaning and use of housing alter. Conversely, from the ways particular housing forms are designed so also are family ties, lifestyles, activities and relations affected or destroyed. This perhaps is the central theme which chapters in this section set out to explore. A major assumption is that the success of design as well as policies on housing for human habitation must be assessed in context of the degree of congruence between structural form and family values, needs and activities. This current underlies the requirement for greater critical research into the social meanings of housing at the family scale.

Context

Over the world, the concept of the family and household as traditionally defined, has undergone some considerable change and modification. In technology advanced, industrialized and socially transformed urban societies of the twentieth century, the composition and identity of the family is far more complex and it includes the one-parent family, working or professional mother's household, teenage family groups, etc., with varying housing requirements and special needs. In the tropical African setting, in spite of some emerging nuclear families, the use of the house even goes beyond the extended family to embrace community/neighbourhood members and peers, househelps and occasional strangers and visitors. However, for all the changes, Western and East European societies are still largely characterized by the traditional nuclear family, while in a number of non-Western societies and nations of the Third World, extended family ties criss-cross neighbourhoods both in the city and in the countryside with varying housing heritage and values reflective of the bonds of family association.

The varying and changing nature of housing and the family is perhaps what informs the methodological and philosophical perspectives of chapters in this part as well as some other works in this volume. Given the dynamic and increasingly complex character of housing and the family, and the difficulty of capturing the essence of housing meaning and values in relation to the family or individual, cross-national coverage is not only evident but also the adoption of a wide-ranging quantitative and qualitative methodologies in exploring the full range of interior, exterior and neighbourhood housing attributes and values should be viewed as most appropriate. Sadly and very significantly, however, Africa with a rich heritage of traditional and modern housing designs, complex extended family ties as well as a known history of design for different cultural groups that incorporated the social activities and beliefs of the people into housing organization is represented only by this introduction and the chapter on Egyptian housing. This must be viewed as a significant omission. The value of any approach to housing research, however, lies in the ability to demonstrate sensitivity to the physical, cultural, social and economic contexts of housing and to capture the essence of the relationship between the individual, group and physical form. Both behavioural/observational analysis and experiential/interpretive approaches are relevant to the task of housing quality and needs assessment. This is a major mark of this book. Indeed as shown in an African context, both qualitative and quantitative research complement one another in so far as man-environment study is concerned and could be blended to achieve better results in the analysis of the interrelationships between people, places and physical settings (Chokor 1991; see also Lang 1991).

One obvious gap across most of the chapters in this volume, however, is the overemphasis on the functionalists role of housing and on the geometrical, behavioural properties of design especially in relation to human activities. In context of the family in particular, housing research theory and methodology, I believe, still has a lot to gain from experiences in Africa. One fact other than physical qualities and structural properties of buildings that imbued the African family house with extra value, meaning and social significance was its association with personal roots, existence and group lineage identity. The family house and home territory is often seen as a geographical node which links the individual to an ancestry on arrival and departure from the world (Chokor 1988, p. 61). Such family houses are viewed as 'real home' in some sense similar to the Japanese case addressed by Narumi's chapter in this section. The home is a zone of family inheritance, a ring of shared meanings, established precepts and blood relationships with a recognized founding or reigning ancestral head, family tree, family records and continuity. The traditional social structure based on lineage, genealogy and feeling of continuity is important to human identity and existence, promoting considerable attachment to the ancestral family house. The modern professional town planner trained in Western traditions who proposes neighbourhood or housing revitalization and 'slum' redevelopment schemes without taking such cultural symbols into consideration runs the risk of stiff and articulate opposition and eventually failure (See Chokor 1989a, Marris 1961).

Undoubted unity and social harmony cut across physical housing form and people in the Third World, which carries the meaning of buildings greatly beyond the ordinary physical functional setting. As Rapoport (1981, p. 59) points out in one context, the seemingly unplanned, disorderly physical environment is highly organized in terms of social groups and relationships. Thus in the traditional African family compound, changing family pattern, economic status, social cultural beliefs and religious values and expectations are often reflected in the houses, and designs are employed to define access to and use of space amongst groups, including children, elders, chiefs, wives, outsiders and visitors (Chokor 1989b; Urquhart 1971; Fadipe 1970, Schwerdtfeger 1982; Moughton 1964). In Yoruba cities of Southwestern Nigeria, compound activities and control were highly regulated by the 'Baale' or compound head who had wide ranging disciplinary powers, as only few offenses were placed by custom outside his jurisdiction (Fadipe 1970 p. 108). Similarly, amongst the Binis in Edo State, Nigeria, who live in low income, low quality housing districts in the core of Benin City, pre-existing family patterns, varied cultural practices, ethnocentric traits and beliefs, such as home identification, common family house ownership, communal/family festivals, dances, family rites, age group membership, worship of a common deity, common ancestral shrines and family head's role in settling disputes are some of the key variables creating a great sense of belonging and attachment to place and family housing, while at the same time posing some constraints to the renewal of run down districts. The Binis may not mind less of a second home to demolition for the sake of renewal but to them it is abominable or even close to a taboo to wipe out the ancestral family house that depicted one's roots. Such ancestral houses are not only historically valuable and interesting but bring history to life (Ishegbe 1991 pp. 64-65). Many chiefs desired to be buried within the confine of the family house as a mark of final departure and which is one reason why public housing is unpopular and family or individual ownership of housing a symbol of manhood and achievement.

Unfortunately, in face of modernization and global change, Africa increasingly lacks a sufficient design and planning philosophy that is sensitive to the social and cultural context of housing (see Chokor 1989b; Sule 1982; Gyuse 1980). And as Marris (1977) points out, in several developing countries, with central indigence housing communities and culture, the demand of capital, market forces, land values and modern economic pressures tend to continue to have a major control over their own needs and to preserve and protect group communal goals, values and ideals.

Methodologically, what all this means is that more humane perspectives must be developed to access the physical, functional, behavioural and cultural value of housing internationally in order to achieve a more integrated view of housing quality and meanings. In the face of rapid economic change globally (which it is hoped, the timely 1992 IAPS Conference on socio-physical metamorphosis in Greece will address), housing protection policies and conservation schemes are still vital to the task of enhancing the quality of life and the identity of people in an increasingly homogeneous and uniform world. The interest of the traditional family, traditional lifestyle and housing design in different cultures and societies must be protected. Further, what does seem apparent is that while acknowledging the role of scaling and quantitative analysis in housing studies, there is a growing need to explore more personal and community case histories in order to appraise more deeply how cultural beliefs and practices feed into housing meaning and thus identify the direction of change over time. Historical studies grounded on hermeneutic frameworks could be helpful in this regard.

Empirical evaluation

Three chapters are included in this section of the volume and the efforts are quite bold. The primary objective of designers and architects of buildings is to satisfy the needs of clients but sometimes these needs are ill-defined, ambiguous conflicting, obscure and difficult to anticipate for the full range prospective users. Inadequacies in design are readily blamed on the architect and it is perhaps this factor which moved the famous architect Le Corbusier, while reflecting on his own works to say that it is always life that is right and the architect who is wrong (Bouden 1972, p. 2). However, one mark of a good design is flexibility and adaptability which make it possible for the client to 'personalize' an abstract space and for the house to be adapted to its occupants instead of the occupants having to adapt to the house (Bouden 1972, p. 116). The first two contributions by Michelson and Niit in this context, explore the gulf between what is intended by the designer and what inhabitants of housing estates desired and experienced in a sense similar to Bouden's assessment of Le Corbusier's Pessac housing project in France in the 1920s; where in spite of the conflict between design and people, the occupants were still able to make a range of conversions of the original design to suit personal interests and desires. However, by some contrast, both chapters also attempted to define housing and explore the propriety of design in terms of systems of activities, especially in context of the role and importance of different housing features (Rapoport 1980a pp. 313-4) or how congruent various environments are with activity system, life styles and so on (Rapoport 1980b p. 130).

Michelson's work on the behavioural dynamics of social engineering is based on a study of eight housing areas in Sweden, where housing designers attempted to foster enhanced social contact, inter-generational contact, lessened household work, and easier child care through specific physical design and forms of social organization, is a practical attempt to explore the relationship between theory and practice design concept and reality. Specifically, the chapter examines if planners and designers actually succeed in fulfilling certain behavioural expectations and activity patterns in their physical design and whether the social values and roles intended to be projected are met in design settings; or whether in fact what designs are originally intended for, ultimately encourage other behavioural modifications or self-selection. As he puts it, do designs become the antecedents for actions and behaviour of the family?

As he finds out, physical designs while attempting to engineer certain social behaviours, are not after all always deterministic; while the experiments are largely successful in terms of the outcomes expected, these effects are a function of an antecedent condition—the self-selection of residents to particular housing situations'. This signifies the role of personal adjustment and adaptability in housing habitation and in bridging some of the gaps between professional designs objectives and the ideals of ordinary people.

Are planners and designers in today's world really going to be able to anticipate fully the future behaviour and values of prospective occupants of houses, especially viewed against the background of the dynamism of family social life, economic activities and the societal values thrust on the person in everyday life of a fast changing world. I venture to suggest that a greater degree of alienation from design is expected to emerge globally. One option out of the coming crisis is to create more flexible designs as already pointed out for family groups, leaving greater room for users to feel in the 'gaps' as demands and expectations change. Finally, while Michelson's methodology is largely experimental and observational, the combined use of the survey approach is commendable but perhaps future studies more than focusing on experimental and control groups should also explore the life and times of ordinary people in different housing settings in an historical context, through narratives, stories, riddles, group discussions and the value judgements made by affected groups in housing districts as suggested elsewhere in this volume.

If people are limited in choice and behaviour in established privately developed neighbourhoods, public housing estates impose an even greater constrain on the family. Niit's paper is another bold empirical attempt to examine the dilemma of those constrained to live in publicly, massively built houses as in several Eastern European nations. The study examined 200 families in new housing estates in Tallinn and Tartu in the newly independent Republic of Estonia. The major focus was on the scaled value of housing in terms of privacy, family social relations and activity patterns, taking the family in an apartment as a socio-physical system. The internal organization of household materials were also explored. Small Space Analysis, a multi dimensional procedure was used, to identify six clear facets of privacy preferences, namely, solitude, openness, intimacy, reserve, avoidance of interaction and anonymity. Furthermore, an analysis of certain parameters that describe aspects of the socio-physical system, for example, privacy, residential density and family relations was made in context of some 35 activities (e.g. watching TV). Also, different categories of family lifestyle were identified from the activity patterns.

Obviously, an exploration of activity patterns and family lifestyles hold much importance for both public and private apartment development and neighbourhood design as indeed argued by the author. One goal of design is to strike a balance as well as harmony between housing form/characteristics and human activities and lifestyles. Methodologically, given the varied indices that can describe human activities, values, preferences and physical settings, the use of small space analysis which is capable of structuring the major facets or dimensions of attributes is certainly to be supported. However, as in most multimensional scaling analysis, the criteria for differentiation are sometimes difficult to identify and describe. Perhaps, as argued by Chokor (1991), such methods provide a key basis for structuring the major lines along which more subjective, qualitative interviews with affected community members could be pursued.

Housing has in recent years and as earlier analyzed in the African context taken on the colour of something infused with social values, lifestyles, personal histories and human identity. The third contribution by Narumi on inheritability and attachment to the detached house in Japanese traditional society comes closest to that of the African traditional Yeruba compound where family histories and identity are woven into the ordinary physical shell to give it the meaning and socio-cultural significance beyond the ordinary visual setting. And therein lies the importance of the focus on cross-cultural and cross-national housing studies and comparisons of which this book is an embodiment.

Narumi's chapter demonstrates clearly that family housing could be a symbol of genealogy and continuity. The concern over one's security and care in old age in traditional Japanese society (rather than rely on state supported social welfare system), brings in the role of the family unit as an integral part of human identity and survival and of which attachment to the family house especially the detached house becomes an important component. Thus the people's identity and social life expectations are inseparable from the physical house. Historical links and inheritance and attachment to the 'Ie' or family compound as in Africa, becomes part of that identity.

Detachment and detached housing are mere symbols of the individual family uniqueness and individuality. Will capitalism and global upturn into a free market economy accommodate and preserve such group family values? Can the family identity as symbolized in housing survive in the face of formal, impersonal competition for space? How do we guarantee the identity and survival of the less privileged who may not be able to afford the cost of preserving their self-identity? These are crucial questions which policy and research must address, as there is often the conflict between peoples' desire to retain traditional valued ways of life and the forces of modernization and socio-economic transformation which pay less and less attention to the individual and self-identity. Perhaps, personal as well as group inputs into remodeling and change should increasingly be accorded a role as Narumi seems to suggest. House and the family are important because of the role of the physical house in conveying culture from one generation to the next.

Future research and policy

As these and some other contributions show, the changing composition of families and households, the varied uses to which the house is put and the emergence of home-based work schedules as well as the computerization of household activities and home management pose tremendous challenges for housing design standard and criteria. The figure below shows a simple representation of the possible relationship between the house, the family, housing meaning, design and policy. It reveals the fact that the house as currently designed for the family unit supports a range of activities and behaviour which may have economic, socio-cultural, life goals and other dimensions. The experiences generated in turn transform into housing meanings; preferences and fulfillments as well as images of self-identity and a sense place. The underlying thing is that such meanings and values where sufficiently distilled and articulated, could provide an important context for future housing design, and policies on housing improvement.

A house should be viewed as a place; and place is a center of action, activity and intention; a focus where we experience the meaningful events of our existence (see Relph 1976, p. 42). Today, with growing modernization, capitalistic values and instincts, especially in traditional non-Western societies, certain social and cultural qualities have been disinvested of places and housing, and people suffer some moral, spiritual and social loss; dislocation and disorientation. Economic rationalization of housing and land use and functionalistic concerns in urban design seem to take precedence in environmental and physical planning matters. While I agree with Harris (1967) that science and humanism have inherent limitations in planning, Fromm (1972) long ago asserted that the demands of an industrial society and the central purposes of planning which serve the aim of production, technology and corporate organization and the failure to understand human nature are perhaps some of the forces working against the desirable goal of planning to enhance human well-being and thus the emergence of the culture of violence as well as the boredom, anxiety and isolation that is recurrent in society.

Philosophically and methodologically, the chapters previewed in this section do not address fully the social consequences of the growing gulf between housing design and needs in context of the family. However, one is generally pleased about the concern for the future design and planning implications of their works. Part of the issue of social alienation in housing design may be addressed focusing more on humanistic, historically and socially sensitive housing research.

Relationships between form, family, and meaning/policy

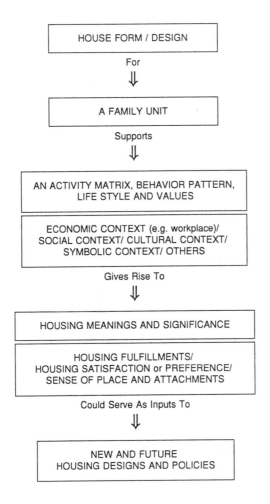

Note: A model of the relationships between house form, the family, and housing meaning and policy.

Today we no longer have planners and designers with 'prophetic' qualities and powers of divination but still most are trained to embrace future considerations. While indeed they are not to be regarded as prophets, successful design and planning also implies the capacity to anticipate the range of future uses of housing within the cultural context. We are told that founders of ancient cities consulted astrologers and geomancers and downplayed economic considerations (Tuan 1974, p. 171). Biblical priests and builders sought the approval and divine hands of God. In traditional Yoruba cities, in order to ward off evil spirits and guarantee psychological well-being for occupants, rituals and rites were important and preceded the founding of family compounds and 'quarters'. These symbols add to the meaning and social significance of housing for the family. The failure of modern housing to sustain community and fulfil family life expectations and create greater sense of belonging or more profound association may be traced in part to the loss of cultural symbols and continuity in our environment. I share the view of Canter et al (1988) that the recognition of the significance of group processes extend to the view that design is fundamentally a social process, that the furthering of continuity activity in design is of great significance.

References

Bordon, P. (1972) *Lived-in Architecture.* London, Lund Humphries.

Canter, D., Krampen, M. and Stea, D. (1988) *Environmental Perspectives.* Aldershot, Avebury.

Chokor, B. A. (1988) "Cultural Aspects of Place Consciousness and Environmental Identity" in *Environmental Perspectives,* Eds. D. Canter, M. Krampen and D. Stea. Aldershot, Avebury pp. 54-71.

Chokor, B.A. (1989a) "Motorway Development and the Conservation of Traditional Third World Cities," *Cities* 6, pp. 317-324.

Chokor, B.A. (1989b) "Changing housing form and organization in Urban Nigeria: Lessons for Community Planning," *African Urban Quarterly* (in press).

Chokor, B.A. (1991) "Triadic Comparison judgements and place significance," *Area* 23, 136-149.

Fadipe, M. (1970) *The Sociology of the Yoruba Ibadan.* Ibadan University Press.

Fromm, E. (1972) "Humanistic Planning," *Journal of the American Institute of Town Planners* 33, pp. 324-355.

Gyuse, T.T. (1980) "Culture and the Built Environment," reprinted in *Housing in Nigeria,* Ed. P. Onibokun, Ibadan, NISER, pp. 407-414.

Harris, B.C. (1967) "The Limits of Science and Humanism in Planning," *Journal of the American Institute of Town Planners* 33, pp. 324-335.

Ishegbe, V.O. (1991) *Housing Quality and Socio-economic and Cultural Constraints to Urban Renewal: A Study of Benin City Core Sector*, M.Sc. Project, School of Postgraduate Studies, University of Benin, Benin City.

Lang, J. T. (1991) "Methodological issues and approaches: a critical analysis," in *The Meaning and Use of Housing*, Ed. E.G. Arias, Aldershot, Averbury.

Marris, P. (1961) *Family and Social Change in an African Society: A Study of Rehousing in Lagos.* London, Routledge and Kegan Paul.

Marris P. (1977) "The Meaning of Slums and Patterns of Change," *International Journal of Urban and Regional Research* 1, 419-441.

Moughton, J.C. (1964) "The traditional settlements of the Hausa people," *Town Planning Review* 35, pp. 21-34.

Rapoport, A. (1980a) "Towards a cross-cultural valid definition of housing," in *Optimizing Environments* (EDRA 11) Eds. R.R. Stough and A. Wandersman, Washington, EDRA, pp. 310-316.

Rapoport, A. (1980b) "Environmental preference, Habitat Selection and Urban Housing," *Journal of Social Issues* 36, pp. 118-134.

Rapoport, A. (1981) "Culture and the Urban Order," in *Cities in Cultural Context*, Ed: J. Agnew, London, Croom Helm pp. 50-75.

Relph, E. (1976) *Place and Placelessness.* London, Pion.

Schwerdtfeger, F. (1982) *Traditional Housing in African Cities.* New York, Wiley.

Seamon, D. (1979) *A Geography of the Life-World.* London, Croom Helm.

Sule, R. (1982) *Urban Planning and Housing in Nigeria.* NY, Vantage Press.

Tuan, Yi-Fu (1974) *Topophilia: A Study of Environmental Perception Attitudes and Values.* Englewood Cliffs, Prentice Hall.

Urquhart, A.W. (1977) *Planned Urban Landscapes of Northern Nigeria.* Zaria, Ahmadu Bello University Press.

Chapter 12

The Behavioral Dynamics of Social Engineering: Lessons for Family Housing

WILLIAM MICHELSON
University of Toronto

Utilizing survey, time-use, and systematic observational data, this chapter demonstrates that while the effects of environment are not deterministic, attempts at "social engineering" are hardly irrelevant if based on a sound understanding of the relationship between human behavior and its immediate environmental contexts. But they require human recognition and motivation to achieve their goals. The study is based on eight housing areas in Sweden, equally divided into experimental and matched control areas.

[0] Presented at the XII World Congress of Sociology, Working Group on Housing and the Built Environment, Madrid, Spain, July 11, 1990. The data on which this chapter is based were collected in collaboration with Professor Birgit Krantz, Institute for Building Functions Analysis, University of Lund, Sweden, under a grant from the Swedish State Council for Building Research. It was facilitated by grants from the Humanities and Social Sciences Research Committee of the University of Toronto Research Board. I am grateful for valuable help and support from Birgit Krantz, Elizabeth Dalholm, Cecilia Henning, Karin Palm Linden, Britt Pedersen, Bill O'Grady, and Eva Oeresjoe.

Introduction

Social engineering has an ominous ring to it. It suggests that someone is attempting to determine someone else's behavior through systematic methods. The reality can be anywhere from despotic to benevolent, depending on the degree that those so engineered are aware of and share the objectives of the engineer and participate in the process. The more explicit and benevolent the situation, the more likely it is to consider the dynamics as supporting desired behavior and the less likely it is to be deterministic.

Architects, planners, and others involved in the creation of housing are increasingly urged by design researchers and social scientists to pay sensitive attention to the behavioral needs and desires of both conventional families and residential groups whose requirements are becoming only now recognized (e.g. women, single parents, nonrelated adults, teenagers living away from the nuclear family). (c.f. Cooper & Sarkissian, 1986; Huttman & Van Vliet, 1988; Franck & Ahrentzen, 1989) Researchers have also stressed the need to document the outcomes of such design experiments as are implemented, so as to assess the fruitfulness and hence future applicability of designs with behavioral objectives (Michelson, 1976; Zeisel, 1981; Bechtel *et al*, 1987).

This chapter is an attempt to go one step further, to explore not only what the outcomes of some behaviorally-oriented design experiments are, but the dynamics underlying the effects found. It is grounded in results from a study of several Swedish attempts to improve the qualitative side of housing through innovations with behavioral objectives.

Housing experimentation in Sweden

Sweden is known for the high standards of its housing and site planning. But, like other nations, its priorities have changed according to objective conditions. It has progressed since World War II through emphases on how to expand metropolitan residential structure and on sheer numbers of housing units. Now that Swedish cities no longer face desperate housing shortages and their infrastructures are rationally organized, attention in housing has turned to qualitative improvement.

One major shortcoming noted as an aftermath of the mass housing construction era was the relative absence of interaction among neighbors in the residential context. People were felt isolated in their home environments. Although privacy is much valued in Sweden, this was thought too extreme from a social perspective. Therefore attention was paid to ways of increasing social contact within residential areas.

A specific case thought worthy in its own right is intergenerational contact. With increasing scale of metropolitan development, in addition to geographic mobility, the generations have less contact with each other. Hence, a second objective in residential design is to find ways of increasing the possibility that young and old will rub shoulders, to the benefit of each.

Furthermore, in a period when most adult women have paid employment, ways to decrease household work and to facilitate child care are considered worthy of pursuit. Residential environments with such behavioral objectives are therefore encouraged.

Experimentation in housing created to achieve these kinds of behavioral outcomes has been fostered by various levels of authority in Sweden and its cities. There is no single path to the millennium. A variety of physical design and social organization innovations have been tried, some more frequently than others. On the physical side, these include shared spaces and rooms for specific activities in multiple family buildings (Figures 12.1a and ??b). Outside spaces are also formed with increasing attention to behavioral ends beyond free play, aesthetics, and fresh air. In several locations, experimentation has been made with the use of glass roofs over what would normally be a street between several blocks of row houses and over the courtyards of apartment quadrangles; these provide light, shelter from the elements, and considerable amenity, instead of outside space in a northern climate.

The most explicit experiment in social organization in recent years has been "collective" housing. Cooperative housing has become a relatively conventional form of tenure, popular as a way of accumulating capital in a multiple dwelling, protected against arbitrary landlords by membership and participation in a nonprofit owner/developer association. But collective houses go beyond the cooperative because the residents themselves have responsibility for carrying out many managerial tasks personally and in teams. Residents also decide on the nature of common facilities, and they organize use of these facilities. One common practice is the preparation of dinners on weeknights, with food purchase and preparation by rotating teams. There is a common kitchen and dining room (Figure 12.1a.

The most typical objective in such experimentation is the fostering of social contact among neighbors. A housing exposition was held in the City of Upplands-Vaesby in 1985, featuring a variety of housing areas by different developers, all representing attempts to enhance social contact. The collective houses generally combine a form of social organization, intended not only to lower costs but to bring residents together, with one or more of the design innovations facilitating common activities, intergenerational integration, and child care (Figure 12.2). Collective dinners and a trade-off of marginal apartment space for group-maintained common space are

Shared spaces in housing complexes help bring neighbors together. But the extent of social contact a is function of what contributions the spaces make in terms of social programming and environmental amenity/protection for the various segments of the residential population. Figure 12.1a: The dining room in the collective house, Praesthaard-shagen, in Stockholm, where rotating teams make dinner available every weeknight.

Figure 12.1: Shared spaces

In Figure 12.1b: Children play in ill-defined but protected shared space under the glass roof in Gaardsaakra, Esloev.

Figure 12.2: Shared spaces: Child care in play areas

A mother supervises small children in a simple play area located in an outside courtyard in Runby Backe, Upplands-Vaesby.

expected to lessen housework.

Sweden has been progressive also in the commissioning of research to determine the effects of its housing endeavors. The current project is in that tradition. But addressing the issue of effects requires some understanding of the causes! In housing studies, causal sequences are by no means uniform. A crass social engineering perspective would make the housing structure (physical or organizational) the independent variable and the behavior subsequently observed dependent (with determinative causation). A less deterministic causal sequence involves self-selection, where people are conceptualized as desiring to carry out certain behavioral emphases in their home environments, selecting residences and areas in which physical or organizational features support these emphases, and then showing such behaviors on site subsequently (Bell, 1968). In a third perspective, people with common characteristics find themselves in the same residential settings. Observed behaviors in these settings reflect not contextual characteristics (which are spurious) but rather the residents' common social characteristics; this last perspective was used in several studies of behavior in post-war American suburbs (Whyte, 1956; Gans, 1967).

Students of the Swedish collective houses have noted that the collective

houses have attracted predominantly a middle-class intelligensia, seeking
social contact and collective activity at the same time that blue-collar workers increasingly pursue satisfaction of the suburban, single-family house
dream (Hjaerne, 1986; Woodward, 1987). Assuming that the behavioral
effects occur, are they a direct function of the residential context, of self-
selection to the particular context, or of the population characteristics?

These three alternatives can be diagrammed as follows:

A) deterministic view: housing $\longrightarrow$ outcomes
B) self-selection: pre-existing motivation $\longrightarrow$ housing $\longrightarrow$ outcomes
C) compositional: resident characteristics $\longrightarrow$ outcomes

Readers familiar with Claude Fischer's treatise on behavior at the urban scale (1976) will recognize this set of causal alternatives, with B) self-
selection equivalent as applied to housing to what Fischer calls the subcul-
tural theory. The self-selection perspective is also consistent with Stokols'
attempts within the field of psychology to create an appropriately interactive theoretical perspective for explanations of human behavior in the physical environment. Stokols points to theories which account for the mutual
effects of people's characteristics and the physical and social components
of environments (Stokols, 1986).

The Swedish experiments thus enable examination not only of the validity of the substantive hypotheses about housing and behavior but of the
dynamics by which this form of social engineering actually operates. This
paper will examine both as concerns the hypothesis of enhanced social contact. But before turning to that, a look at the design and methods used
might be helpful.

Research design and methods

Our research covers eight residential areas: four experimental and four
controls to specific experimental areas. The experimental areas include a
range of contemporary innovations, involving physical design innovations
and social organization, apart and in combination. All the areas had been
occupied approximately three to eight years by the time of the research in
the late winter and spring of 1988. The control areas, however, were more
conventional apartment blocks and did not include collective management.
Although it would be possible to compare data from all experimental to all
control areas in aggregate form, too much of the qualitative idiosyncrasies
of specific areas would be lost that way. Therefore, analysis will show four
sets of comparisons between experimental and control areas, as well as more

general intergroup comparisons.

Briefly, and in the order in which results are presented, the areas chosen can be described as follows: Praestgaardshagen is a small collective house in Stockholm with many activity rooms and collective spaces, a common kitchen and dining room with dinner made by resident teams every weeknight, and a daycare center on the premises. Its control for the purpose of this study is Runby Backe, a cooperative area in Upplands-Vaesby with a well-defined, grassy courtyard, and one or two meeting rooms, but whose projected ground-floor activity and meeting rooms had largely been converted to storage at early occupancy, making the buildings much more conventional.

Stolplyckan A, in Linkoeping, represents the conversion of half a many-building complex of point-tower buildings to a single collectively-run unit, connected on the ground level by heated, glassed-in corridors and with extensive lounge, meeting, hobby, and athletic facilities on the ground floor. About 10 per cent of residents receive special service support for handicaps of various kinds, and a hot lunch is made available in a dining room by the municipality to these persons, to the several school classes in the complex (along with daycare services), and to any other residents interested. A collective dinner is prepared by volunteers twice a week. Stolplyckan B is the adjacent area of buildings which have remained in their conventional design and rental conditions.

Gaardsaakra is a much-noted complex in Esloev of about three blocks of parallel, three-storey row houses with a glass roof over the centre "street" and huge amounts of growing plants all over. There are daycare and several schools inside the complex, and a store, but, apart from the mandatory sauna and laundry facilities, few commonly-available defined activity areas - just the expanses of walkways and plazas. Its control, Musikanten, is a cooperative area by the same corporation on an adjacent tract. But the housing units, while all low and multifamily, are scattered in small buildings around a large campus. There is a common clubhouse with laundry and sauna, but the greatest common space is on walkways, open green spaces, and play areas throughout the exposed campus.

Finally, Carlslund is a complex in Upplands-Vaesby. Its main feature is a tower building with extensive common facilities on the ground floor. These include a concierge desk, convenience store, library, cafe with television, laundromat, playroom, sauna, and party hall. Although rental in tenure, Carlslund represents a major investment in municipal personnel to operate the above features for resident use. Some surrounding buildings involve the rebuilding of courtyard homes to glass over the small-scale quadrangles. Bjoerkvalla, its control nearby, is a set of post-Modern high-rise cooperative buildings with a laundromat, sauna and a rooftop clubhouse, but little else in shared facilities. On the exterior is a roughly defined allotment garden and only the most rudimentary play facilities.

Both survey and observational materials were collected. The latter involved a coordinated attempt to observe the nature of and participants in social contact in common spaces at the same days and times in all the areas. The survey had two parts: A questionnaire for all adult residents addressed respondent characteristics, residential histories and rationales, expectations, behavioral characteristics and social contact being realized, and evaluations. A self-administered, pre-coded time-diary for each family member was for the assessment of what people do, where they do it (with codes reflecting the specific design aspects of the various projects), and with whom they do it.

The household data are based on 221 dwelling units, representing response rates in specific areas of from 93.5 to very low, depending on factors such as collective decision-making to fear of intruders. The size of areas dictated whether a random or 100 per cent sample was attempted. Between 20 and 41 households contributed survey responses within the areas. The conventional survey instrument was answered by 186 women and 151 men, from 99 one-adult and 122 two-adult households (in which 6 spouses declined to answer). Time-diaries were received from 144 men, 173 women, and 121 children.

Results

Previous analyses assessing the realization of greater social contact, based on the observational and time-diary data, support expectations that greater contact will be found in the experimental than in the control areas, with several caveats. First, the extent of social contact reflects design and organization independently, with areas combining innovations in both (i.e. the collective houses) showing the most. Second, the greatest differences between areas occur in cold weather, when protection against the elements means more. Third, innovations of a limited scope (e.g. appealing to only one segment of the population or focussed more narrowly on commerce) are likely to facilitate less widescale interaction. Finally, facilities designed to enhance contact appear to do so, particularly those like dining facilities built into the daily routine. (Michelson, 1989, 1990)

This chapter utilizes primarily the conventional survey data. These data will be assessed to further validate conclusions about the hypothesized differences in social contact. Then, the various dimensions of the alternative models explaining the dynamics of cause and effect will be examined and integrated.

Social contact as a dependent variable

The survey of adults in households contains several measures of self-perceived degree of social contact. Table 12.1 reports answers to a question (translated), "Compared with how you lived previously, do you meet people outside your own household more or less often (neighbors, relatives, employees, etc.)?" Residents of the experimental areas answer "more" to a much greater degree than those in the control areas, regardless of the specific characteristics of the experimental areas. Roughly two-thirds to three quarters report more contact in their current housing, while among the control areas, only 19-49 per cent do so.

The greatest increases are found in the collective houses. But there is another phenomenon found in one of them, Praestgaardshagen (the smaller collective), as well. Nearly a third of the respondents there note that while their contact with neighbors has increased in the collective, they have less contact with longer-term friends living elsewhere. They posit a trade-off between the cohesiveness of the collective and the time/freedom to connect with persons outside the residential environment to the same extent as before.

Subsequent parts of the above question shed light on increased social contact as an outcome of housing innovations and its relationship to the particular innovations. The great majority of those seen more often are in fact neighbors, though in some cases these include friends and relatives also. However, the causes of this increase vary according to the characteristics of the areas. Residents of Praestgaardshagen and Stolplyckan A, the two collective houses, with increased neighbor contact are most likely to attribute this to the organization of their areas (63% and 66%, respectively), though 50 per cent and 35 per cent of these respondents also mention physical design as a factor. In Gaardsaakra and Carlslund, with glass roofs and, in the latter, a conspicuous commitment of municipal services and facilities, design is cited by 61 per cent and 47 per cent, respectively, while organization is noted by only about 20 per cent. Thus, it appears that causes and effect are occurring much as expected in the experimental areas, and, moreover, this pattern does not change when controlled by gender.

Differences between the experimental and control areas appear as expected also in answers to questions about "how often you meet other persons from outside your household in [each of 17 specific]...locations." These locations include both those specially provided in the experimental areas and those typically available (often outside or as part of inside structure) in the absence of innovative design features. Respondents could rate their frequency of contact with other persons in the respective locations in one of the following categories: twice a day or more (weighted 6), about once a

Table 12.1: Social contact frequency in existing vs. previous housing

Housing Area:	No Change	More	More&Less	Less	N.A.	n=
Praestgaardshagen (E)	13.2%	50.0	31.6	5.3	0.0	38
Runby Backe (C)	45.5%	29.5	2.3	20.5	2.3	44
Stolplyckan A (E)	21.3%	70.2	2.1	6.4	0.0	47
Stolplyckan B (C)	66.7%	18.5	0.0	14.8	0.0	27
Gaardsaakra (E)	30.0%	62.5	5.0	2.5	0.0	40
Musikanten (C)	51.7%	46.6	0.0	1.7	0.0	58
Carlslund (E)	18.8%	65.6	0.0	15.6	0.0	32
Bjoerkvalla (C)	41.2%	35.3	2.0	19.6	2.0	51

Note:

- E = Experimental, C = Control.
- How adults resident in experimental and control housing areas compare the frequency they meet non-household members to frequency in previous housing (in per cent).

day (5), several times a week (4), about once a week (3), less than once a week (2), never or location not present (1).

Table 12.2 shows many different aspects of the various loci for contact. First, there are statistically significant differences in degree of contact in every location except the sauna/solarium, not generally a frequent source of contact. The variation in degree of contact between areas is significantly greater than the variation among individuals within areas. Although not specified in Table 12.2, variation by gender is very minor.

The means of contact for the housing areas taken over all the locations vary exactly as expected from the hypotheses and the previous findings with complementary methodologies. The experimental areas are always greater than their own controls, and all the experimental areas are higher than every control area. The two greatest levels of contact are from the two collective houses, followed by Gaardsaakra (the larger of the glassed-over areas) and then Carlslund (with commerce but no participatory organization).

Somewhat unexpectedly, these differences are so systematic that they hold for nearly all locations, regardless of content. Of 68 pair comparisons, the experimental area shows more contact in all but eight (underlined in table 12.2). In some cases, the exceptions are to be expected. For example, Stolplyckan B has only outside walkways, compared to internal equivalents

Table 12.2: Mean degree of social contact

Mean degree of social contact in specific locations by adults living in experimental and control housing areas (with significance of 1-way analysis of variance by area for each)

Location	P (38)	RB (44)	SA (47)	SB (27)	G (40)	M (58)	C (32)	B (51)
At home	4.16	3.07	4.09	2.85	4.18	3.34	3.41	3.27
Home of another	3.66	2.55	3.30	2.30	3.35	2.72	3.09	2.63
Hall; stairs	5.63	4.14	5.15	4.11	4.10	1.36	3.63	3.76
Entrance; lobby	5.00	3.84	3.98	3.96	4.40	2.67	3.59	3.26
Outside walkways	4.45	3.75	4.28	<u>4.78</u>	4.48	4.14	3.38	3.14
Glassed-over areas	1.87	<u>1.98</u>	2.85	1.62	**4.95**	1.16	**2.94**	1.31
Laundry room	3.16	1.86	2.55	1.78	2.23	1.38	1.56	<u>2.04</u>
Hobby room	**2.97**	1.20	**2.04**	1.04	1.28	1.16	1.00	<u>1.10</u>
Dining room/cafe	**4.76**	1.86	**3.23**	1.70	1.28	<u>1.41</u>	2.28	1.57
Sauna/solarium	1.63	1.36	1.40	1.15	1.40	1.32	1.47	1.43
Lounge	**3.53**	1.34	**1.94**	1.37	1.80	1.34	1.56	1.47
Private garden	2.26	1.55	1.79	1.26	**3.30**	<u>**3.45**</u>	2.09	1.71
Common space outside	3.32	2.66	3.55	1.96	2.88	1.86	2.66	2.08
Inside playroom	**2.89**	1.09	**2.60**	1.14	1.90	1.33	1.72	1.04
Outside playground	2.92	2.14	3.62	1.70	2.28	2.00	1.75	<u>1.76</u>
Daycare/eldercare	**2.68**	1.95	**3.66**	1.22	**1.90**	1.72	1.09	<u>1.23</u>
Local store	3.45	2.09	2.87	3.03	**4.43**	2.40	**3.31**	1.78
Mean Frequency	3.43	2.26	3.07	2.17	2.95	2.04	2.39	2.03

Note: Bold numbers = special area facilities; Underlined means = control areas greater than experimental; Significance is 0.000 for all locations except Sauna/solarium which is 0.260.

in Stolplyckan A. All Musikanten units studied have access to private gardens, compared to only a percentage of those in Gaardsaakra. Runby Backe features somewhat more glass than does Praestgaardshagen. Others of the exceptions are relatively trivial.

Finally, as indicated by figures in bold print in Table 12.2, it appears clear that many of the special features intended to foster social contact are indeed associated with evidence of success. For example, the hobby rooms, dining rooms, lounges, inside playrooms, and daycare facilities in the collective houses are all associated with relatively frequent social contact. The glassed-over street in Gaardsakra is one of the greater focal points, as are the private gardens (in warm weather) there and in Musikanten. The convenience store plays this part in Carlslund, as was documented by the observational data (Michelson, 1989).

Thus, evidence of the hypothesized effect is plentiful. The next question is whether this is a function of anything other than the environments created by the social engineers.

Resident desires and expectations

According to the earlier discussion on alternative causal dynamics, increased social contact would be caused deterministically if not part of a pre-existing agenda on the part of residents. If it were to be shown that residents moved to the various housing areas for matter-of-fact goals like obtaining more space, securing a desired location, or an absence of other alternatives but ended up with marked increases in social contact as a consequence of social engineering, then a good argument might be made for deterministic causation. But if, on the other hand, it could be shown that residents actively sought and expected the behaviors found in the respective areas, then the deterministic perspective could be rejected and the choice narrowed to either the self-selection or compositional model.

Basic elements of housing choice were addressed in both closed and open-ended format. In the former, respondents were presented with seven common, fundamental motives for choice of housing and asked to rate each in order of importance, including the option of zero for items of no importance at all. These scores were transformed to 8 for those ranked most important to 1 for not relevant.

Mean scores are reported in Table 12.3. In aggregate, dwelling size is given the most importance, followed by location, aesthetics, how the dwelling unit functions, and (not that surprising in view of Swedish housing allowance policy) costs. The two items potentially linked to behavioral outcomes, management organization and how the residential area functions were ranked last on this list.

Table 12.3: Mean ratings of common reasons for housing choice

Reasons	All	P	RB	SA	SB	G	M	C	B	Sig.
Costs	4.3	3.0	4.3	3.2	3.3	5.7	5.1	4.1	4.7	.000
Dwelling size	5.5	4.2	5.8	4.8	5.6	7.0	5.5	5.2	5.7	.000
Dw. funct.	4.9	5.3	5.6	3.9	5.7	5.2	4.6	5.0	4.4	.005
Area funct.	3.7	3.2	3.1	5.8	2.9	4.7	3.0	4.2	2.8	.000
Managem. org.	4.0	5.5	4.6	4.0	2.0	3.6	4.2	2.6	4.6	.000
Location	5.1	5.8	4.1	6.2	6.9	3.7	4.1	4.2	6.2	.000
Aesthetics	4.9	4.1	5.2	4.4	4.6	4.7	5.5	5.5	4.8	.049
n=	337	38	42	47	26	38	58	32	50	

Note:

- 1-way analysis of variance.
- 8 = highest; 1 = lowest.

Nonetheless, when the mean rankings are disaggregated by residential area, it becomes evident that the different reasons had varying relevance from area to area. Even the choice factors drawn on least in aggregate were highly pertinent to the choice of some areas. For example, how the housing area functions ranks only behind location in the very centrally-located Stolplyckan A collective house. The same is the case for management organization in the other collective house, Praestgaardshagen. This gives preliminary evidence that the hypothesized causes of increased social contact were relatively attractive to those in the collective houses, though not in exactly the same way. But the data also show that more traditional housing choice criteria also play a strong part in the choice of even collective houses.

In general, distinctive ranking patterns in the respective areas reflect their physical and organizational nature. This is supported by all the 1-way analysis of variance tests, which indicate significantly more variation in ranks between areas than among the residents within them (including inconsequential gender differences). My expectation was that the experimental areas would present evidence of a recognition of special features. As mentioned, this did come out in part regarding the collective houses; in addition, while area functioning is not a very high priority item in Gaardsaakra (where dwelling size and functioning, plus costs are ranked higher), this area is second highest in recognition of this choice factor, which probably reflects the glass-over street and institutional activity there. Rankings given to location reflect reasonably well the degree of access encountered by residents.

I expected also that more conventional housing choice factors like dwelling space and aesthetics would be cited by residents of the control areas, in the absence of special features. This last hypothesis was upheld in six of the eight comparisons. One exception is the extremely high rating given dwelling size in Gaardsaakra, an experimental area; but unusually spacious apartments there (often three storeys) give this an objective basis. The other exception is the high rating given aesthetics in Carlslund, in the absolute and also in comparison to Bjoerkvalla; although this is a subjective matter, there may be a basis in fact for these ratings, reflecting the aesthetics of the respective sites in particular.

More specific evidence of rationales for housing choice involving eventual increases in social contact come from answers to an open-ended question allowing up to five responses (listed in order of importance) to, "Why did you choose just that home you are living in now?" Table 12.4 shows that, in the aggregate, respondents cited a wide range of reasons for their choice. One of six had no choice in the matter; the home they got was the only one made available to them at their time of acute housing need, or they moved to be with another person, without reference to the nature of the housing. However, to counterbalance this evidence of nonselection, the factor of management organization was among the more frequently cited factors, both as the most important factor (column A) and over the maximum of five factors given (column B). Management organization is shown as high in salience by those choosing it, insofar as a relatively high percentage of those choosing it at all did so as the most important factor (column C). At a lower level of citation, but still chosen by a reasonable percentage of respondents, are potentially behavioral factors such as social interaction/characteristics of neighbors, suitability for children, and access to formal institutions. Once again, there are no appreciable differences according to gender.

As expected from the closed-ended question, mention of any particular choice factor varies greatly according to residential area. Exactly a half of Praestgaardshagen residents and nearly a third in Stolplyckan A cite management organization as the most important choice factor. But even with these fractions of their populations accounted for, they are highest in citation of the more specific interaction/neighbors factor by those remaining.

This breakdown is similarly rational in the other areas. Gaardsaakra residents stress their dwelling size most, followed by area design and access to formal institutions—all part of their special residential conditions. In neighboring Musikanten, with its campus arrangement, uniquely high citation is registered for access to the outside (from ground-level dwellings) and to green space. In Stolplyckan B, with the same location as "SA" but not its amenities and organization, it is location which attracted most res-

Table 12.4: Reasons for current residence selection

Reason	A. Most Important	B. Among 5	C. Salience (A/B)
No choice	16.6%	17.4%	.95
Location	16.6	37.1	.45
Management organization	13.9	24.0	.58
Dwelling size	13.1	21.1	.62
Aesthetics of dwelling	9.5	21.7	.44
Interaction/neighbors	4.5	10.2	.44
Area design	3.9	16.4	.24
Suitability for children	3.9	8.7	.45
Access to outside space	3.0	8.4	.36
Dwelling functioning	2.4	8.1	.30
Access formal institutions	2.4	6.6	.36
Access green space	2.1	13.4	.16
Other	6.9		
No answer	1.2	1.2	

Note: $n = 337$

idents. The three residential areas in Upplands-Vaesby, part of Metropolitan Stockholm's housing sphere, have lack of choice as their most frequent choice factor (from a quarter to nearly a third), followed by location for Carlslund and Bjoerkvalla and by dwelling aesthetics for Runby Backe.

What these data indicate is that while conventionally material factors in housing choice are part of decisions to live in all the residential areas, behavioral rationales are also given, and to a considerable extent for the choice of those areas with the most social engineering, the collective houses.

That behavioral effects are anticipated where "programmed" is indicated even more explicitly in Table 12.5. This table breaks down answers to the question, "When you chose this home, what expectations did you have then that the new home and environment would influence what you do on weekdays?" Expectations that their new housing would influence their everyday behavior were extremely high among those moving to the collective houses (92.1% in Praestgaardshagen and 70.2% in Stolplyckan A), but much less than half that in the other areas.

These data also shed light on the particular behavioral outcomes expected. Over 50 per cent of those in the collective houses who expected such influences, thought one form of outcome would be increased social contact. Virtually no respondents in the respective control areas thought the same, though 20 percent in Gaardsaakra did so. Thus, the greatest amounts

Table 12.5: Environmental influences in housing

Environmental influences on everyday behavior expected by adults in experimental and control housing areas.

Expected?	P	RB	SA	SB	G	M	C	B
	(% of those answering)							
yes	92.1	27.2	70.2	44.4	45.0	53.4	31.2	47.0
no	7.9	70.5	29.8	51.9	52.5	41.4	68.8	51.0
no ans.	0.0	2.3	0.0	3.7	2.5	5.2	0.0	2.0
n =	38	44	47	27	40	58	32	51
What Outcomes Expected (% of those answering yes):								
Soc. contact	52.6	2.3	55.4	11.1	20.0	6.9	9.4	13.8
Child care	15.8	6.8	25.5	0.0	7.5	5.1	9.4	0.0
Intgen. cont.	2.6	2.3	2.1	0.0	0.0	0.0	0.0	0.0
Housework	79.0	13.6	12.7	7.4	12.5	25.8	12.5	23.6
Defined act.	47.3	0.0	29.8	3.7	12.5	5.1	6.2	7.9
Ext. access	2.6	9.1	6.3	29.6	20.0	34.4	9.4	21.5

of increase in social contact found in the collective houses were largely anticipated, as were some of the respective amounts of increase in the other areas. The wording of and answers to this question and the rationales given for housing choice suggest that the characteristics of the residential areas were accorded some causal power by the respondents. More analysis of this question comes in the next section. In the meanwhile, it would appear that pure environmental determinism can be rejected, while self-selection and social composition should be examined further.

Meanwhile, Table 12.5 also sheds light on expectations concerning others of the design hypotheses. The collective houses are expected by some to facilitate child care, and their specialized facilities are expected to enable defined activities there; these may also facilitate social contact. Praestgaarden is unique in the percentage expecting reduced household work (probably reflecting daily availability of dinner, with commensurably less shopping, cooking, dishwashing, etc.), though some residents of Musikanten and Bjoerkvalla clearly expect that their modern apartments will ease household chores there, too. Little expectation appears in any area for increased intergenerational contact. Beyond specific design hypotheses, there is also evidence that residents of Gaardsaakra and Musikanten expect to utilize opportunities for activity on their outside garden areas, while those of Stolplyckan B and Bjoerkvalla expect to take advantage of the accessibility offered by their locations.

Social composition

Now that resident responses suggest that there were specific desires and expectations that preceded moves to many of the housing areas, we must examine whether these are accompanied by, or, more strongly, reflect differences in social composition in the various areas. As noted above, other observers in Sweden have noted the social class specificity of those moving to collective houses. Beyond that, stage in the life cycle is often related to housing choice.

Both compositional factors vary greatly by housing area. The two collective houses have the highest percentage of families with children; they are similarly greatest in the percentage of white collar workers. Thus, perceptions and behaviors recorded in these areas are likely to represent to a greater extent than in the other areas what middle-class families with children think and experience.

Nonetheless, for analytic purposes, it is critical to note that, despite such general tendencies, these are not the only residents of these collective houses. Between 20 and 34 per cent of residents of the collective houses do not have children at home, and a minority of blue collar workers is also found in each. Furthermore, not all the families with children studied live in the collective houses; indeed, the majority live elsewhere.

Moreover, there are notable differences between the two collective houses in composition, as well as between some of the other residential areas. The majority of households with children in Praestgaardshagen are single-parent households, while only a small percentage is found in Stolplyckan A. Stolplyckan B, Runby Backe, Carlslund, and Bjoerkvalla have no children in the majority of their dwelling units. In Musikanten and Carlslund, over 20 per cent of responses are from pensioners. Similarly, although the collective houses may be greatest in the percentage of white collar workers, these are the single greatest segment in every area but Musikanten, in which the split between white collar (32.8%), blue collar (38%), and those outside the labor market (29.3%) is relatively even.

Thus, while the housing areas reflect variations in social composition, the differences are not like day and night. No background characteristics are the unique preserve of any one area. Thus, it is possible to assess the extent that increased social contact is explained more fully by people's social characteristics or by the special features of their residential environments (or, indeed, by both in combination). If people with the same social characteristics act the same way regardless of where they live, then there is support for the compositional perspective. If features of the residential area are associated with certain outcome variables regardless of the characteristics of residents, then, given the degree of preceding desires and expectation, the self-selection perspective would appear more fruitful.

Before multivariate analyses are justified, though, it still has to be established whether compositional characteristics are related to increased social contact, the dependent variable. With family structure, the greatest increases in frequency people see persons outside their families are among the families with children (about 60%), followed by pensioners (just under 50%), and then by younger families without children (about 40%). While these differences are substantively understandable, the differences by category are not nearly as great as differences by housing area (cf. Table 12.1). Regarding how often people are encountered in the seventeen specific locations noted in Table 12.2, these vary significantly also by family structure in all but two (hobby room and sauna & solarium). There is not the same explanatory pattern shown, however, for the different locations. Those having to do with outside and inside common spaces, play facilities and institutions, other people's homes, and laundry facilities reflect families with children most fully. Some of the others, though, reflect considerably lower amounts of contact among pensioners living alone.

Thus, it is plausible to assess whether or not family structure directly affects the dependent variable of social contact, regardless of housing features. The plausibility of further assessment of the impact of social class is greatly reduced in view of few strong relationships with the dependent variables. While an increase in extrahousehold contact is somewhat greater among the white collar than among the blue collar workers (50.5% to 40.5%), this is a relatively small difference, compared to the other explanatory factors. Furthermore, social class is significantly related to frequency of contact in only 2 of the 17 locations [laundry facilities (white collar > blue collar) and outdoor gardens (blue collar > white collar)].

Therefore, multivariate analysis will focus on family structure and the housing areas vis à vis social contact.

For the question regarding greater, the same, or lesser contact in the current residential area, three-way contingency tables were computed with social contact as the dependent variable and family structure and residential area as independent variables, each of the latter serving as control in one of two sets of tables. When controlled according to residential area, the impact of family structure on social contact weakened considerably and showed inconsistency from area to area. In contrast, when controlled for family structure, the relationship between residential area and social contract remained relatively robust and consistent.

The data on the 17 loci of contact, having a more continuous dependent variable, lend themselves to more precise testing. Two-way analyses of variance were computed to assess the respective impact of residential area and family structure on social contact, controlling for the other and assessing the degree of statistical interaction between the two independent variables. Table 12.6 shows the significance levels for the F ratios of the competing variables and their interaction.

These statistics indicate that housing area explains variation in social contact with extremely great significance, even when the effects of family structure are considered. In contrast, when controlled for housing area, family structure explains social contact in far fewer locations, and in those cases where still significant, the levels of significance are often somewhat lower than those involving residential area. Substantively, family structure is shown to have a significant effect, independent of residential area, on frequency of social contact in the entrance/lobby, outside walkways, laundry room, dining area or cafe, inside playroom, outside playground, and local store—variously reflecting certain kinds of heightened contact among families with children and the reduced contact typical of single pensioners. In the cases of contact at home, in someone else's home, in lounges, private gardens, common outside space, and daycare/eldercare, residential area and family structure work interactively in explaining social contact (i.e. where the joint explanation explains more than the sum of the two influences taken independently).

So as to assure a complete view, similar two-way analyses of variance were computed for social contact as a potential function of residential area and social class, for the two loci for which social class significantly explained social contact (laundry areas and private gardens). In this context, residential area retained its extremely high level of significance, while social class lost nearly all of its explanatory power (sig.=.492 & .628, respectively).

Interpretation and conclusions

Thus, in our examination of the dynamics of social engineering, it is apparent that the physical and organizational features of the residential environment are indeed significant, not spurious, in their effects on social contact. But they facilitate what many people have decided they want to do, not determine behavior. These data complement previous findings suggesting that the residential environment provides opportunities for specific behaviors, which, if not unwanted, become the path of least resistance. Such "situated behaviors" are prevalent and positive to the extent that they are desired and expected (Michelson, 1977).

These data from specific Swedish residential contexts show that many people are aware of the potential behavioral implications of the home environments they choose. But the outcome of enhanced social contact is in part a function of a two-step process, self-selection of people to a context,

Table 12.6: Frequency of social contact in specific locations

Significance levels of 2-way analyses of variance, assessing frequency of social contact in specific locations as a function of residential area characteristics and/or family structure.

Locations:	Sig. of Res. Area	Sig. Fam. Structure	Sig. of Interaction
At home	.000	NS	.039
Home of another	.000	.021	.005
Hall; stairs	.000	NS	NS
Entrance; lobby	.000	.001	NS
Outside walkways	.000	.000	NS
Glassed-over areas	.000	NS	NS
Laundry room	.000	.000	NS
Hobby room	.000	NS	NS
Dining room/cafe	.000	.002	NS
Sauna/solarium	NS	NS	NS
Lounge	.000	NS	.037
Private garden	.000	NS	.044
Common space outside	.000	.003	.023
Inside playroom	.000	.000	NS
Outside playground	.000	.000	NS
Daycare/eldercare	.000	.000	.047
Local store	.000	.007	NS

Note: $n = 337$, NS = Not Significant

with a package of desires and expectations, and then exposure to the objective conditions distinguishing the setting. The settings serve to focus or diffuse preexisting intentions. Thus, while not deterministic, their effects are nonetheless real.

Certain backgrounds appear to predispose the choice of different residential environments. Collective houses, for example, appear to offer various kinds of extra support for child care, and they attract many families with children. But not all families with children want or need what collective houses offer, nor are all the residents exposed to the spatial and organizational opportunities of the collective houses nuclear families. So neither the environments nor the behaviors found there are synonymous with any single background. Their focus is intensified through the experiences of a wider population of residents. Thus, while some families with children and an orientation within parts of the middle class may be more predisposed to collective houses than are other segments of the population, their choice of this residential setting has more to do with how the context is expected to facilitate their life-style priorities than simply reflecting their social composition. And persons with other backgrounds, but the same priorities and subsequent exposure to the same residential context, come to act the same way.

But while the path from social composition to behavior appears clearly filtered by self-selection and explicit environmental opportunities, this does not mean that persons with a particular set of background characteristics are not predisposed to certain behaviors. Children want to play within the confines of local areas, and the desirability of child safety and the company of playmates commonly brings parents into contact. While some residential environments make it easier to satisfy these desires than others, and hence foster enhanced play and contact, parents of small children are more likely than others to have neighbor contact than other population segments. Similarly, the gerontological literature shows a gradual pattern of withdrawal by older persons.

Thus, it should not be surprising that the study data reported here show a less pervasive but nonetheless real set of relationships between social composition and frequency of social contact. In some cases, these are independent of housing characteristics, while in others, these work interactively with housing to further specify amount of social contact.

The over all implication for dynamics is that while housing is not determinative, its form and organization are extremely important. Experiments such as those represented in this study have considerable potential for social objectives in housing provided that they are consonant with the desires and expectations of sufficient numbers of individuals and families, who in fact have access to the appropriate residential settings. And while the behavioral components of social composition are not irrelevant, providing much potential for behavior, behavior itself is not carried out in a vacuum. The objective built environment, as designed and organized, plays a decisive role in the conversion of behavior from desired and expected to actual.

Therefore, both pure compositional and deterministic perspectives must be rejected in favor of one which includes self-selection and explicit consideration of the behavioral potential inherent in specific built environments, as well as the interaction between this and, as justified, compositional influences. Stokols' theoretical conception of people x (times) places is strongly supported by the current data.

For environmental planners, these results provide support in general for the benign potential of social engineering and in particular for the outcomes of several of the Swedish experiments, notably the collective houses but some other innovations as well. But these results make clear as well the value of attempting to optimize the selection of residents who both want and expect what specific residential settings have to offer. Lacking determinative power, but yet with a facilitative role to play, design professionals must understand the market for their products and how, through physical and social means, to provide conditions making possible the highest level of satisfaction of mutually-shared objectives.

References

Bechtel, Robert, Robert Marans, and William Michelson, Editors. *Methods in Environmental and Behavioral Research*. New York: Van Nostrand Reinhold, 1987.

Bell, Wendell. "The City, Suburb, and a Theory of Social Choice," in Scott Greer *et al.*, Editors, *The New Urbanization*. New York: St. Martin's, pp. 132-168, 1968.

Cooper, Clare, and Wendy Sarkissian. *Housing as if People Mattered*. Berkeley: University of California Press, 1986.

Fischer, Claude. *The Urban Experience*. New York: Harcourt Brace Jovanovich, Inc., 1976.

Franck, Karen, and Sherry Ahrentzen. *New Households, New Housing*. New York: Van Nostrand Reinhold, 1989.

Gans, Herbert J. *The Levittowners*. New York: Pantheon,1967.

Hjaerne, Lars. "Planning for Community in Swedish Housing," *Scandinavian Housing and Planning Research* Vol. 3, p.193-215, 1986.

Huttman, Elizabeth, and Willem van Vliet. *Handbook of Housing and the Built Environment in the United States*. Westport: Greenwood Press, 1988.

Michelson, William. *Man and his Urban Environment: A Sociological Approach*. Reading, Mass.: Addison-Wesley, 1976.

Michelson, William. *Environmental Choice, Human Behavior, and Residential Satisfaction*. New York: Oxford University Press, 1977.

Michelson, William. "Temporal and Seasonal Use of Indoor Common Spaces within Residential Complexes," paper presented to annual meeting of the American Sociological Association, 1989.

Michelson, William. "Time-Geography at the Micro Scale of Housing," paper presented to annual meeting of American Association of Geographers, 1990.

Stokols, Daniel. "Transformational Perspectives on Environment and Behavior," in William H. Ittelson, Masaaki Asai, and Mary Ker, Editors, *Cross-Cultural Research in Environ- ment and Behavior*. Tucson: University of Arizona, pp. 243-260, 1986.

Woodward, Alison. "Public Housing Communes: A Swedish Response to Postmaterial Demands," in Willem van Vliet *et al.*, Editors, *Housing and Neighborhoods: Theoretical and Empirical Contributions*. Westport: Greenwood, pp. 215-238, 1987.

Zeisel, John. *Inquiry by Design*. Monterey: Brooks/Cole, 1981.

Chapter 13

Housing Characteristics, Family Relations and Lifestyle: An Empirical Study of Estonian Families

TOOMAS NIIT
Institute of Philosophy, Sociology, and Law, Tallinn, Estonia.

The chapter, after a review of the housing situation in the Soviet Union, describes several approaches to family lifestyle used in psychological and sociological studies in Estonia. A framework for describing the functioning of a socio–physical system is presented. It proposes that we have to consider the system as a unity of place, activity and relations, for it cannot be understood without considering each relative to the others. Different levels of analysis are discussed and attempts to operationalise this framework in a study of families in new housing developments of Estonian cities are described. It discusses empirical facets of privacy preferences and possible approaches for analysing the activity structure of the family.

[0]A version of this paper was presented at the XII World Congress of Sociology, Madrid, July 9-13, 1990. The author is grateful to Prof. David Canter for the help in analyzing the privacy preference data and to Gun Frank and Swedish Building Research Institute for helping sponsor the Älvkarleby conference.

Introduction

Every year about 2 to 2.2 million apartments are built in the Soviet Union, with floor area more than 100 million square meters. At the present time, the average floor area per person is about 15.2 square meters, which is twice as much as the average thirty years ago. But still 15% of families in the cities and 2% in the country-side do not have separate apartments or houses. The task to give to each household a separate apartment is hoped to be solved by the year 2000, and the ideal as it is seen now, is to have about 28-30 square meters per person (Nikolayev & Feodorov 1989).

At the same time, the number of new flats built in a year per 1,000 inhabitants has decreased in the seventies, and probably in the eighties as well (e.g., 9.3 in 1970 and 7.5 in 1980) (Meerson & Tonsky 1983). 73.4% of the housing construction was funded by the state in 1976-80. In Estonia, about 70% of the houses built at the present time are large panel constructions. In many big cities this figure is higher than 75%. About 34% of houses built in 1980 in the Soviet Union were brick houses, and about 6% -wooden houses (Ibid.). The average size of the households in new apartments is about 3.15 persons and the average residential density ranges from 1.4 to 1.7 persons per room in different cities.

Most of the new houses are multi-storey buildings, the widest-spread being 9-storey units (40% of buildings built in 1980, and an increase to 45% was planned for 1985). Some 38% of houses built in 1980 were 5-storey units, 6% - 4-storey, and another 6%-one-or two-storey houses. The remainder were highrise blocks of 12 and more storeys (Meerson & Tonsky 1983). So, the number of floors is one of the few parameters by which the Soviet housing construction is on the first place in Europe.

To produce such amount of housing, about 650 construction industry plants have been established to produce amazingly uniform concrete panels either in Siberia, Central Asia or in Baltic states. For about 15 years the architects designing the panel houses at Central Research & Experimental Planning Institute of Dwellings in Moscow have been interested in studying lifestyle of families at the new housing developments they have designed. Most of this research has been coordinated by the Environmental Psychology Research Unit at Tallinn Pedagogic Institute. The aim of the architects has been to create regionally different norms for housing and neighborhood design and to find social and demographical bases for apartment layout typologies. The aim of psychologists and sociologists participating in this research has been to get some understanding about the general dimensions of urban lifestyle and transactions between people and the built environment.

Studies of lifestyle

Early approaches

Interest toward family lifestyles emerged in Estonia in the early seventies. The first empirical studies were carried out in the Laboratory of Sociology at Tartu State University under a grant from the All-Union Research Institute of Industrial Design (VNIITE) between 1970 and 1974. In connection with this project, a theoretical framework for characterizing lifestyle was elaborated (cf. Kruusvall, Niit & Heidmets 1984; Niit, Heidmets & Kruusvall 1987; Kruusvall 1988). Every activity is considered as a conventional "act of production" and the framework for analysing this activity consists of the subject of activity, the means of activity (object, instruments, activity space), the product of activity and the process (which characterizes the change of the components of the environment where activity takes place in time). The environment is characterized by parameters like the degree of organization, degree of multifunctionality, degree of ordinariness or originality, etc; the process was characterized, for example, by duration of activity, its frequency, attractiveness of activity, etc. (for details, cf. Kruusvall, Niit & Heidmets, 1984). A standardized interview consisting of about 1600 single items was developed and 2,000 families from the different types of settlements (from village to a big city) living in very different types of dwellings were interviewed in Estonia. As a result of computer classification, seven different types of domestic life were distinguished. Two types of parameters had greater power of differentiation: social distance of services (domestic, non-domestic, private, or public) from the consumer's home, and degree of mechanization of domestic activities. The first differentiated mainly among urban, the second among rural families (for details and the description of the types, cf. Kruusvall 1988).

"Family and Apartment" Project

Since 1974 the Environmental Psychology Research Unit has continued to study the domestic lifestyles with funding from the Central Research & Experimental Planning Institute of Dwellings. These studies have concentrated on families in public housing of new residential areas. As we said, different plants all over the Soviet Union produce almost identical apartments. Thus we can trace the influence of cultural differences in various regions of the country on behavior patterns at home and look for the effects of family size and family composition on the use of space and services. This project, called "Family and Apartment" has gone through three phases, and data have been gathered in more than 20 cities of different regions (including Moscow, Leningrad, Tallinn, Lvov, Tashkent, Tbilisi, Novosi birsk, Yakutsk, Norilsk, etc.). All in all, over 4,000 families were interviewed with comparable questionnaires. The selection of families in this project was directed. It was necessary to find a certain type of family (altogether 16 types were distinguished) and a certain type of apartment (from 1 to 4 rooms) and their main combinations. The central questions in this project were the use of space at home, the distance of services (actual and desirable) from home, frequency of domestic activities and frequency of using services, number of people engaged in joint activities at home, activities inside dwelling and in its vicinity, etc. (some results of this project are presented in Kruusvall 1988).

An alternative framework

Both of these large projects have devoted little attention to the psychological aspects of housing like family relations, attitudes toward other family members and toward neighbors, etc. Only one member of the family answered to the questions in these projects. To overcome the shortcomings of these studies we constructed a questionnaire where several aspects of family relations (family decisions, quarrels, attitudes toward each other), privacy preferences of family members, their satisfaction with various aspects of housing and life in general were included. The questionnaire contained several dimensions from Moos'(1974) Family Environment Scale (FES), a list of leisure activities, questions about TV-watching, Rotter's I-E Scale, etc. In each family, father, mother and a teenage child answered similar questionnaires. This makes it possible to compare the preferences and attitudes of different family members, and to construct indices of domestic behavior at the social unit level.

From this study a theoretical framework for describing the transactions between people and environments has gradually evolved. We have supposed that for analysing any sociophysical system (and a family in the dwelling certainly is such a system) on the level of social unit, we have to distinguish for analytical purposes at least three interrelated realities or categories place, activity, and relations (cf. Figure 13.1). This triad functions in the background of sociocultural norms which restrict the functioning of family or any other social unit. We must also remember, that such norms are generated during the functioning of a sociophysical system as well (but this will be a separate area of research, especially in cross-cultural studies). Such norms exist probably toward places (f.e., what a dwelling should look like), activities (f.e., what one can do in the living room or on the balcony), and relations (f.e., which family relations are considered "good ones"). In our analysis these norms are taken as something given in their general back-

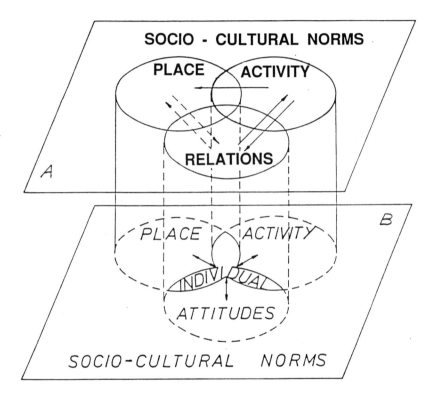

Figure 13.1: A framework for analysing people–environment transactions

Legend:

- Level A = the social unit; Level B = the individual.
- Arrows indicate the possible directions of influence.

grounds, although such norms are probably somewhat different for persons with different socioeconomic backgrounds.

The level of social unit

At the level of social unit we will be interested in the integral picture—the interrelationships between place, relations, and activities. In analysing the sociophysical system (or behavior setting in Roger Barker's terms (Barker, 1968)) we can distinguish the prevalent directions of influence (cf. arrows at level A in Figure 13.1), but we have to remember that the changes in one reality always lead to changes in the remaining ones (we have given examples of these influences in a recent paper, cf. Niit, 1988).

Place and relations are relatively stable, while activity is the dynamic component of a sociophysical system. We could declare that the activity is a reality where the restricting influences of place and relations become evident. As the studies in the tradition of ecological psychology (Barker 1968; Wicker 1979) demonstrate, a particular behavior setting is characterized by a relatively stable *pattern of activity*. On the level of a social unit we can speak of it as "behavioral lifestyle" (cf. Niit 1983), which could be characterized both quantitatively (the frequency of different activities, the variety of activity, etc.) and qualitatively (joint or separate activities, passive or active activities, etc.).

Relations in this scheme can be status or role relations, on the level of individual—or emotional or attitudinal relationships (relations toward each other, value orientations, etc.) as well. We could hypothesize that the more meaningful and essential relationships exist in a setting, the less successful will be the 'functional' architectural solution.

Places can be characterized in spatial, functional and other terms. Proceeding from the logic of a sociophysical approach, the participants of the situation as well as their sociodemographic characteristics (age, gender, etc.) should be included under the category of place.

We can hypothesize that the less transformable is the physical structure of the setting, while more probable is that changes will take place in the structure of relations or in behavioral lifestyle.

The level of individual. In some cases the analysis on the level of individual will be needed, to include her/his relations and attitudes emerging during the functioning of a social unit into the integral picture. If on the level of social unit the individual is a componental part of the sociophysical system, the analysis on the level of individual will be possible only when confronting her/him with the environment. At the same time, the individual unites in her/himself the characteristics of place (her/his physical body), relations and activities (cf. level B in Figure 13.1). At the level of individual we will not deal with relations between somebody, but with relations toward somebody or something—toward other people, their or one's own activities, or toward place. These attitudes may be favorable or negative, conflictual, dominant, etc. At this level the individual is restricted by parameters of place, the activities and relations (attitudes) of other people, and trying to balance these looks for a niche to "build her/himself into the environment", i.e. to find an equilibrium. The sociocultural norms as a general background influence her/his functioning as well. These may become components of her/his attitudes or (s)he may confront her/himself with these norms.

Different levels of analysis

Thus, the processes and phenomena we are studying on the different levels are partly overlapping and partly different, but by no means can we restrict ourselves in our studies with the level of the individual only. This excludes interpersonal relations which are an important facet of a sociophysical system. The more parametres or dimensions we can distinguish inside each of the three realities, the more adequate will be our picture or general understanding. It should be also evident that in different places (or situations) the same facets of relations or activities will not be equally relevant for the analysis. Therefore, in analysing various sociophysical systems we should try to distinguish preliminary the essential parameters of places, relations, and activities by a phenomenological or some other kind of approach.

We could suppose that for longer or shorter time periods such a system tries to maintain relative balance or quasi-equilibrium, i.e., tries to preserve the structure of relations, activity, and the place itself. This balance is disturbed by the activeness of participants (as well as their passivity, i.e. the lack of expected activity). The changes will occur in the most fragile facet of the system, and the system will stabilize for some period of time thereafter. It is very difficult to conclude which state would be optimal for the system, although comparing large number of similar systems or proceeding from the sociocultural norms we could distinguish the qualities of effectively functioning systems (e.g., "good family relations", "decent home", etc.).

The aim of this framework is to provide the researcher with a kind of "mental map" for dealing with various situations and places. It allows to organize the existing studies of people-environment transaction, but empirical research can proceed from it as well. The main area of application of such framework will be in studies concerned with various primary environments (homes, offices, etc.), where relationships between people are an important facet and moderator of human action in the man-made world.

Attempts of operationalizing

As the analysis of data from our research project is continuing, we will present here only some attempts to conceptualize the data and operationalize the proposed framework.

The structure of privacy preferences

As we said, the questionnaires contained similar scales and questions for three family members. The respondents were 200 families in new housing developments of Tallinn and Tartu (Estonia) who had at least one teenage child.

One of the instruments included in the questionnaire was a 45-item Privacy Preference Scale. It contained several items from the earlier privacy scales (Marshall 1974; Pedersen 1979) and several original statements (see Table 13.1). Privacy preferences are unique in the sense that they usually include both relationship, activity as well as place qualities. In our framework they are attitudes at the level of the individual. Using Smallest Space Analysis (SSA-2) we could distinguish six clear facets of privacy preferences (see Figure 13.2): solitude, openness, intimacy, reserve, avoidance of interaction, and anonymity (a factor–analytic interpretation of these data distinguished 8 much more ambiguous factors, cf. Niit & Lehtsaar 1984). These facets reflect the openness/closeness dialectics proposed by Altman (1975) and replicate several dimensions found by other authors (Marshall 1974; Pedersen 1979). What is important from our point of view is that we can construct six indices characterizing the privacy needs of each family member and correlate them with other parameters of the sociophysical system. Let us look, for example, at the averages of these indices for fathers, mothers and children (Table 13.2).

As it can be noticed, adolescents are more interested in solitude than their parents, but at the same time they are more open and less interested in avoiding interaction. They are also less interested in intimacy. The main reason for this is probably high residential density in the apartments studied. We have to deal with a complicated situation in most of our new housing estates. The adolescents want to direct their activities out of home, but they have actually very limited possibilities to do something in the neighborhood, as the architectural conception has not taken their needs and interests into account. This is even more complicated in the highly crowded homes. There is a high potential of conflict in the family and the adolescents' higher preference for solitude can only add to this conflict. At the same time the absence of semi-private areas in the neighborhood leaves few opportunities for adolescents to acquire privacy near their homes as

Table 13.1: Six facets of the privacy preference scale

SOLITUDE

(5)	I like to be at home alone
(25)	In my imagination I feel better than interacting with others
(26)	I like to walk alone
(28)	Sometimes I need to be alone and away from others, even from close friends
(30)	I am never happier than when alone
(32)	I like to be alone at home where it is peaceful and quiet
(34)	I would be happy living all alone in a cabin in the woods
(36)	It would be fun to be alone on a high mountain peak surveying the scene below
(37)	I like being in a room by myself

OPENNESS

(9)	I chat readily with strangers
(13)	I am interested in the personal problems of other people
(14)	I prefer to pay visits myself rather than receive guests
(20)	It is easier for me to talk about personal matters with a stranger rather than with close acquaintance
(22)	I like to talk much about myself, it makes me feel better
(29)	I like my friends to sympathize with me and cheer me up when I am depressed
(35)	I like other people to tell me what is happening in their lives
(44)	At workplace (at school) I live out my domestic worries
(45)	When returning from work (school), I like to meet acquaintances

INTIMACY

(1)	I like to walk in the woods in the company of an intimate friend
(12)	I interact readily only with limited number of people
(27)	I like to spend my vacation with my family
(31)	I do not like to be disturbed when I am home engaged in family activity

RESERVE

(3)	I do not like numerous gatherings
(10)	My home is my castle
(33)	I do not to sit next to strangers in a crowded bus
(41)	I would not mind living in a large city-at least everyone would not know everything about me

AVOIDANCE OF INTERACTION

(15)	Prolonged interaction with people becomes quickly boring for me
(18)	I am not longing to be in the company of friends
(24)	I do not like it when people talk much about themselves
(38)	Whenever possible, I avoid being in a crowd
(39)	Even if I chat sometimes with neighbors, I do not want to be bound with them too much
(42)	I do not like to talk about personal things with other people until I have known them a long time
(43)	At my workplace (at school) I like to work alone

ANONYMITY

(2)	I like to be unknown in the crowd
(6)	I like to help people, remaining myself unknown
(8)	Cars annoy me at the streets less than people, they do not stare at me
(11)	I like to observe people at the street, remaining unnoticed

Privacy Preference Indices

Table 13.2: Average values of privacy indices

	FATHER	MOTHER	CHILD
PRIVACY			
SOLITUDE	11.86	12.08	13.58
OPENNESS	10.32	11.00	12.35
INTIMACY	8.72	9.13	7.26
RESERVE	7.32	7.47	7.53
AVOIDANCE	13.41	13.49	11.36
ANONYMITY	6.08	6.45	5.99

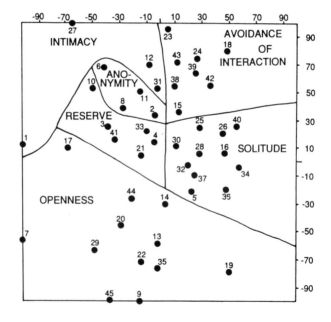

Figure 13.2: Smallest space analysis

Note: The smallest space analysis of privacy preference, scale items, and the privacy facets of public housing.

well.

It is possible to construct similar privacy indices for the whole family at the social unit level to analyse the mutual relationships between privacy profiles of the family and activity patterns at home.

Activity structure of the family

Our questionnaire contained a list of 35 leisure time activities (see Table 13.3) and the respondents had to rate on a 6-point scale the frequency they are engaged in these activities (from "almost every day," to "about once a year," or "not at all").

Using factor analysis, we could distinguish eleven dimensions in the activity structure to construct corresponding indices for each family member (the composition of these indices is presented in Table 13.3). These indices describe (1) orientation toward entertainment, (2) activeness directed out of home, (3) engagement in domestic activities, (4) active movement, (5) sociobality (6) orientation toward passive activities at home, (7) engagement in hobbies, (8) active information needs, (9) work oriented activities, (10) idling, and (11) engagement in culture-oriented activities. In addition, we have used the indices describing the number of activities the respondent is never engaged in, and the index of overall activeness based on the frequencies of all activities.

Such approach enables us to create activity profiles for different family members and for whole families (at the social unit level) and to relate them with different aspects of place and relations. We give only some examples here describing the relations between residential density (RD) and other parameters used in our study. RD is significantly related to the number of activities where it is never engaged in for "father", inversely related for "teenager", but not related for "mother." RD has also significant correlations with parents' passivity at home, supporting our general hypothesis that a passive pattern of behavior develops in the conditions of high RD (cf. Niit 1983). The indices of conflict between family members have also significant correlations with RD both for fathers and mothers. And finally, high RD has significant correlations with general satisfaction indices for the mother (-.41) and father (-.28), but not for the teenager.

Conclusion

The popularity of new housing developments in the Soviet Union is decreasing gradually. In 1978, 42.6% indicated the new developments as "a preferable place of residence," by 1985 this percent had decreased to 33.2

Table 13.3: Activity indices used in the study

	INDICES (See legend below)										
	1	2	3	4	5	6	7	8	9	10	11
GOING TO THE MOVIES	o	o								o	
GOING TO THE THEATER	o	o									o
GOING TO THE CONCERT	o	o									o
VISITING EXHIBITIONS	o	o									o
NIGHT AT THE RESTAURANT	o	o			o						
VISITING NEIGHBORS					o						
VISITING RELATIVES/FRIENDS	o	o			o						
RECEIVING GUESTS (W/FAMILY)	o		o		o						
RECEIVING GUESTS (ALONE)	o		o		c						
WATCHING TV						o		o	o		
LISTENING TO THE RADIO						o		o			
LISTENING TO RECORDER	o					o					
GOING TO TRIPS/EXCURSIONS	o	o									
TAKING BUSINESS TRIPS									F/M		
WANDERING IN SHOPS										o	
READING FICTION	o					o					o
READING LITERATURE							o	o			
READING NEWSPAPERS							o				
GOING FOR A WALK (ALONE)		o		o						o	
GOING FOR A WALK (FAMILY)	o		o	o	o						
GOING FISHING/HUNTING	o	o		o			F/M				
DOING MORNING EXCERSICES				o							
SPORTING/JOGGING		o		o							
WATCHING SPORTS	o	o					o				
PLAYING BOARDGAMES/CARDS	o				c	o					
PLAYING MUSICAL INSTRUMENT							o				
DOING PAPERWORK AT HOME									o		
CONSTRUCTION/HANDICRAFT			F/M				F/M				
NEETTING			M/C				M/C				
YARDWORK/GREENHOUSE			o	o							
GOING DANCING	o	o		c	o						
GOING TO HOBBY GROUPS		o					o		c		
GOING TO LECTURES/LIBRARIES		o						o	o		o
VOLUNTARY SOCIAL WORK		o						o			
RESTING AT HOME						o				o	

Legend:

- F = father; M = mother; C = child.
- 1 = orientation toward entertainment; 2 = activeness directed out of home; 3 = engagement in domestic activities; 4 = active movement; 5 = sociability; 6 = orientation toward passive activities at home; 7 = engagement in hobbies; 8 = active information needs; 9 = work–oriented activities; 10 = idling; 11 = engagement in culture–oriented activities.

(Heidmets 1987). This means that in the big cities only 1/3 of the residents of new housing developments live where they would like to live. The situation in Estonian cities is about the same.

In recent years "the social effectiveness of housing" has become a catch-phrase among architects and city planners. An attempt to conceptualize this effectiveness can be found in Kruusvall (1988). One of the main problems of our new housing developments is low social effectiveness of housing. The construction industry is producing houses but not neighborhoods, i.e., very little attention has been paid to the areas between houses and to services. The high-rise housing makes it almost impossible for the personalization of space around the houses, control over neighborhood, etc.

We hope that the proposed framework enables us to describe more thoroughly the effects of our new housing developments on family activity patterns, human relations, etc., and to show that what is cheap economically is rarely effective socially. We also think that this framework is a step towards the transactional approach recommended by Altman and Rogoff (1987).

References

Altman, I. (1975) *The Environment and Social Behavior.* Monterey, California: Brooks/Cole.

Altman, I. & Rogoff, B. (1987) "World views in psychology: Trait, interactional, organismic, and transactional perspectives." In D. Stokols & I. Altman (eds.), *Handbook of Environmental Psychology.* New York: Wiley, pp.7-40.

Barker, R.G. (1968) *Ecological Psychology.* Stanford, CA: Stanford University Press.

Heidmets, M. (1987) "Õhust ja maa pealt" (From air and from the ground). *Horisont,* No.1: 12-14.

Kruusvall, J., (1988) "Mass housing and psychological research in the Soviet Union." In D. Canter, M. Krampen & D. Stea (eds.) *Environmental Policy, Assessment and Communication.* Aldershot: Avebury, pp. 147-174.

Kruusvall, J., Niit, T. & Heidmets, M. (1984) "Mass housing and psychological research." In A. Lissner (ed.) *Perspectives on Environment and Action: Keynotes Given at IAPS 8.* Berlin: Hochschule der Kunste, pp.34-39.

Marshall, N.J. (1974) "Dimensions of privacy preferences". *Multivariate Behavioral Research,* 9: 255-272.

Meerson. V.G. & Tonsky, D.P. (1983) *Residential Construction in the USSR During the Eleventh Five-Year Period.* Moscow: Stroiizdat (in Russian).

Moos, R.H. (1974) *Family Environment Scale: Form R.* Palo Alto, CA: Consulting Psychologists Press.

Niit, T. (1983) "Activity patterns of the family and the experience of home." *Acta et Commentationes Universitatis Tartuensis*, 638: 79-85.

Niit. T., Heidmets. M. & Kruusvall, J. (1987) "Environmental psychology in the Soviet Union." In D. Stokols & I. Altman (eds.) *Handbook: of Environmental Psychology.* New York: Wiley, pp. 1311-1335.

Niit, T. & Lehtsaar. T. (1984) "Privacy preferences of family members." In H. Mikkin (ed.) *Problems in Practical Psychology.* Tallinn: Tallinn Pedagogic Institute, pp. 124-132.

Nikolayev, S.V. & Feodorov, Ye.P. (1989) "Main tasks and peculiarities in solving the housing problem", *Zhilishchnoye Stroitel'stvo*, No.2 (374):5-9 (in Russian).

Pedersen, D.M. (1979) "Dimensions of privacy". *Perceptual and Motor Skills*, 48: 1291-1297.

Wicker. A.W. (1979) *An Introduction to Ecological Psychology.* Monterey, CA: Brooks/Cole.

Chapter 14

Inheritability and Attachment: The Detached House in Japan

KUNIHIRO NARUMI
Osaka University

The desire of many Japanese families is to own a detached house. Given the fact that there is this strong desire to own a detached house, it is important to consider what should the future housing in Japan learn and adopt from the detached house. To this end, the chapter considers two points. First, it looks into the observation that even for a detached house, it is rare that a house is succeeded by a single "Ie" (a system of successive family genealogy), particularly in large cities; and therefore, it explores how privately owned detached houses are inherited as assets and how people think this inheritance should be. The second consideration analyzed is that a detached house can be easily improved by its physical reorganization through additions. Utilizing this analysis the chapter clarifies the role of the physical house in conveying culture from one generation to the next.

[0]I would like to express my appreciation and gratitude to the late Mr. Osamu Fujii and Ms. Eriko Oka respectively. The final two sections of this chapter are the results of cooperative studies with them.

Introduction

It is the desire of many Japanese to own a detached house. This is also the case in large cities, where a higher density land use is required. According to a recent survey conducted by the Japanese government, eight out of ten Japanese wish to own a detached house, while less than one expresses that mid- or high-rise housing will suffice. However, 55.7% of those who now live in rental housing can not expect to own a house due to the steep rise in land prices in metropolitan areas (*The Mainichi newspaper*, April 1, 1991). Judging from results of various surveys, it is considered that people wish to own a detached house for the following reasons: a) a desire to remain in close touch with the ground; b) to own a house as property; c) to provide for their old age; or d) as part of an ownership oriented trend.

It was after World War II when an enormous number of owner-occupied homes were built in Japanese large cities. During the period when large cities grew rapidly, a large number of people migrated from the country to large cities. At first, they lived in small rental apartments, but in due time wanted the detached house as a higher standard of living. This trend toward the possession of a detached house was based on personal desires, but it also depended greatly on the national housing policy that encouraged more home ownership.

Recently, social changes such as the "aging of society" and a "lower birth rate" are in progress. Although it is said that Japan, having been industrialized, has the same living standard as Europe and the U.S., many people do not expect social welfare services to guarantee their old age. Instead they expect their sons or daughters to do so. This characteristic of Japanese society helps bring together generations.

In Japanese traditional society, the concept of "*Ie*," (which literally means a house), played an important role in the family as a social unit. The "*Ie*," far from its literal connotation, means a system of successive family genealogy. This idea of placing an emphasis on "*Ie*" still remains strong in agricultural areas, where "*Ie*" should last forever with the farmland.

In the period of urban expansion, many of the young migrated from the countryside; mostly by themselves, formed nuclear families and are now faced with their advanced age. In doing so, they left the "*Ie*" which still remains strong in their home communities. However, many of these parents, now being faced with advanced age in large cities, wish to live together with a son or daughter's family, an arrangement which they themselves have not experienced. Additionally, they are going to leave a house behind which they did not inherit.

While many academic studies on housing carried out so far in Japan, they have focused principally on substandard houses and apartment houses.

Privately owned detached houses have been of comparatively high standard and their occupants have been regarded as "the blessed on housing." Therefore, these studies for the most part have not included privately owned detached houses since they are viewed as not been of major social concern. However, studies on the detached house have been carried out by the housing industry to guide the production of large amounts of prefabricated detached houses which have been supplied throughout Japan.

Owning a detached house is different from owning a car. A detached house not only has a higher value as an asset, but also reflects what its occupants think a family is. This may be in part the reason why a house is an object if inextinguishable concern and interest. Judging from the mentioned fact that there exists a strong desire to own a detached house, it is important to consider what should future housing learn and adopt from the detached house in Japan. To this end, the chapter considers the following points:

1) Even for a detached house, it is rare that a house is forever succeeded by a single "*Ie*", especially in large cities. First, the chapter clarifies the actual conditions on this matter, and then considers how privately-owned detached houses are inherited as assets and how people think this inheritance should be.

2) A detached house can be easily improved by its physical organization through remodeling or enlargement. The chapter analyzes what functions and forms are required according to the life stages of a family, what kind of space is valued, and how an image of a desirable house is realized. This observation clarifies the role of a house in conveying culture from one generation to the next.

Methods of the study

Methodologically, this chapter takes into account three general considerations in order to analyze the Japanese detached house. First it looks into the inheritability and attachment of unique spaces in the development of residential areas for detached houses. Second, it considers mobility and inheritability of detached houses. And third, it analyzes lives in detached houses and one's own unique space of attachment.

The first consideration is raised to introduce an outline of the historical development of Japanese detached houses. It is accomplished through an archival review of documents and official statistics kept for residential areas. To analyze this consideration, six residential sample areas for detached houses in Osaka and its suburbs were selected. For each sample

Table 14.1: Survey on mobility and inheritability of detached houses

Reference materials	district		no. of households
Housing Map *1	1. Kori		108
	2. Kusuno-sato		106
	3. Tezukayama	52	107
	Kita-batake	55	
Land Register *2	4. Tenno-cho		107
	5. Nansuien		103
	6. Sakurai		100

*1 "Detailed Housing Maps" published from 1960 to 1982 were used on each district.

*2 Land registers were used form 1958 to 1982.

*3 District numbers shown correspond to Figure 14.1

area, the changes in the owners of housing lots and those in the occupants were surveyed, using a land register and a housing map sold at book shops. The map identifies the changes of householders, and the land register shows transition of ownership of housing lots. Both have limitations. The map shows the changes of householders but does not clarify whether these changes were brought about by the transition of ownership; while the register does not clarify the ownership of buildings relative to whether the occupants changed or not when ownership remained the same, or whether the occupants changed or not when the land ownership changed. Regardless of these limitations, this survey gives a sufficient indication of mobility in privately-owned detached houses. The period of investigation, referential materials and the number of samples are shown in Table 14.1. The distribution of the investigated areas is shown in Figure 14.1. Furthermore, in order to investigate actual housing conditions and the intention for inheritance, two questionnaires were carried out. One in the above-mentioned six areas and another for residents in Osaka city.

Finally, to address the third consideration, seven detached houses were identified to examine which part of the house was valued more at the various life stages of a family. These houses are in the Senri New Town and its peripheral area. Senri is the first Japanese new town. It stretches over the areas 4 and 10 in figure 14.2. Its planned population was 150,000. The location of the houses, the time of construction, and the changes of family compositions are shown in Table 14.22. Prior to moving to their present

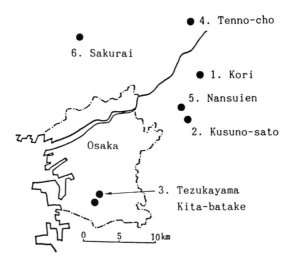

Figure 14.1: Location of surveyed areas

houses, five of the families surveyed had lived in rental apartment houses and two had lived in privately-owned detached houses.

A detailed survey was carried out by interviews. Although generalization from the survey results is difficult because the number of household samples is limited, the survey nevertheless provides clues about life of Japanese families in detached house and for those spaces valued by its residents.

Development of residential areas for detached houses

Before proceeding further with the chapter, the characteristics of the Japanese detached house need to be briefly introduced. This facilitates a better understanding of the various considerations and findings of the study.

1) Types of traditional residential areas

Morphologically, the Japanese traditional houses can be roughly divided into four types. The first prototype is the detached farmhouse. The second is the detached house with a walled-in garden for samurai, court nobles, and

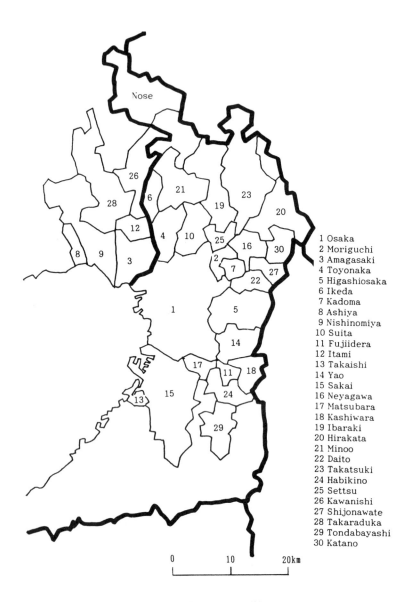

1 Osaka
2 Moriguchi
3 Amagasaki
4 Toyonaka
5 Higashiosaka
6 Ikeda
7 Kadoma
8 Ashiya
9 Nishinomiya
10 Suita
11 Fujiidera
12 Itami
13 Takaishi
14 Yao
15 Sakai
16 Neyagawa
17 Matsubara
18 Kashiwara
19 Ibaraki
20 Hirakata
21 Minoo
22 Daito
23 Takatsuki
24 Habikino
25 Settsu
26 Kawanishi
27 Shijonawate
28 Takaraduka
29 Tondabayashi
30 Katano

Figure 14.2: Osaka metropolitan area

Table 14.2: Outline of seven detached houses surveyed

	location	time of building	way of building	family composition at the time of moving in	family composition of today	frequency of enlargement/ remodeling	previous house
House A	Senri N.T.	1971	purchase of land made-to-order house	husband, wife, 1 child	husband, wife	2	rental apartment
B	Senri N.T.	1967	purchase of land made-to-order house	husband, wife, 3 children	husband, wife 2 children, 1 parent	1	own detached house
C	Senri N.T.	1972	purchase of land made-to-order house	husband, wife 2 children	husband, wife 1 child	0	rental apartment
D	Senri N.T.	1965	ready-built house	husband, wife 2 children 1 brother	husband, wife 1 child	1	company house
E	Senri N.T.	1963	ready-built house	husband, wife 1 child	husband, wife 2 children	1	rental apartment
F	Nose	1969	purchase of land made-to-order house	husband, wife 2 children	husband, wife	0	rental apartment
G	Senri N.T.	1968	ready-built house	husband, wife	wife	5	own detached house

*1 Survey interviews conducted in 1986.
*2 Nose location is shown in Figure 14.2.

priests. This type was called a mansion or manor house. The difference between the former and the latter is that generally the farmhouse does not have the clear demarcation of a privacy wall or a fence. The third proto-type is a house combined with a shop for townspeople who were engaged in commerce or industry. This type is located in lots which are narrow in width and long in depth, with little space between neighboring houses. This housing type for tradesmen is called "*Machiya.*" The fourth prototype is the row house for craftsmen and laborers. It is a single-story row house that shares a ridge and each housing unit is divided by a party-wall. Tra-ditionally, the row house provided the largest number of accommodations in towns.

In modern towns, these prototypes reinforce the clear division between districts. The mansions for samurai with thin walls clearly define the samu-rai district; temples, shrines, and priests' houses comprise another district; and tradesmen's houses and row houses are in the townspeople's district. In the townspeople's district, the tradesmen's houses stand facing the streets while the row houses are in back alleys. These two prototypes of houses are not located in separate districts of Japanese modern towns.

2) Development of the first suburban residential district

In the Meiji Era, when the Japanese Modern Period begins, the urban population rapidly expanded with industrial progress. In the case of Osaka City, the population was 280,000 in the first year of the Meiji Era (1868). It reached one million in 1904, two million in 1925, and in the next ten years, the population had reached three million by 1935. In the course of modernization, landowners and landlords ran the business of rental housing. Tradesmen and manufacturers who became rich, and the newly-appeared salaried men ran small rental housing as a business. These rental houses were generally row houses, which created the high-density urban areas. Some of these row houses were built with high quality standards, for the new high-salary earners to live.

As the population of Osaka City exceeded one million, the quality of the urban environment at the center deteriorated to extreme levels, and the suburb came to be recognized as the new residential area for families. In 1910, a private railway company in the Osaka metropolitan area issued a pamphlet under the title of "What kind of area should you choose? What kind of house should you live in?" On the pamphlet there were the following descriptions:

> "The beautiful city once well known for its canals has past-
> like a past dream, in the smokey town under a dark sky you

live, you miserable Osakaites? (omission) Those who are planning to leave the dusty Osaka and set up a residence in a suburb,
please look at the suburban residences built along the railway.
(omission) Those who are going to commute to the city to cud-
gel brains and ease tired bodies in their homes should wake up
in the morning by a rooster's cry in a backyard, enjoy in the
evening chirps of crickets in a garden, and taste home-made
fresh vegetables. ..."

Together with its opening, this railway company developed suburban
residential areas. It built 267 houses in Sakurai by 1911 (Figure 14.1),
and 200 houses in Ikeda-Muromachi the next year. This pamphlet was an
advertisement of these areas. The shape of the housing lots developed in
both areas was square; 28 meters in width and in depth (784 m^2) in Sakurai,
and 18 meters each (324 m^2) in *Muromachi* (Figure 14.3). The lot planning
in these new residential areas was similar to that in the lower-class samurai
district among the traditional residential districts of the city (Figure 14.4).

3) Influence of the Garden City

In Japan just in those days, there was an increasing interest in the Garden
City. In 1909, some voluntary members of the then Ministry of Interior
Affairs published the *Garden City*, which introduced and analyzed in detail
the construction work of the garden cities in Europe ("Garden City and
Japanese," Voluntary Members of the Ministry). In 1906, another railway
company in the metropolitan area, in order to promote the development of
residential areas along its line, issued the brochure entitled "Invitation to
a town life." This publication contained the chapter "Happiness of living
in a city and a garden suburb."

Based on these developments, it can be said that Howard's *Garden City*
did influence the suburban development in Osaka. Although Howard's was
a self-sufficient city, in Japan the idea resulted in the "bedroom town,"
similar to the "Garden Suburb" born in England around the same period
as the Garden City. The American and European suburban residential areas secured spaces worthy of the name "Garden City" or "Garden Suburb"
thanks to plans providing abundant green open spaces and gently-winding
roads. However, in the new Japanese suburban residential areas, the roads
are generally laid in grid pattern, similar to those of the *samurai district.*
A plan similar to that of European and American residential areas was
adopted in the Osaka metropolitan area, at the *Senriyama* residential district in 1922, in the *Ohmino* residential district in 1935; and in the Tokyo
metropolitan area at the *Denenchofu* residential district which was ready

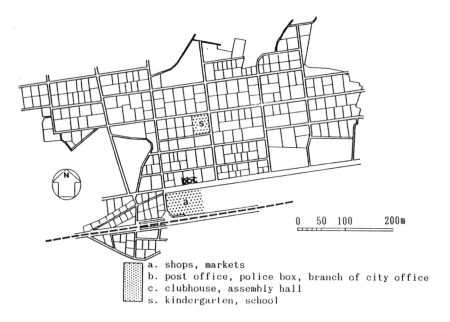

a. shops, markets
b. post office, police box, branch of city office
c. clubhouse, assembly hall
s. kindergarten, school

Figure 14.3: Town plan of *Sakurai* district

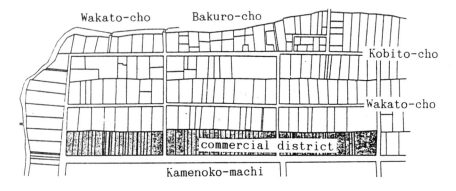

Figure 14.4: Town plan of lower-class *Samurai* district in *Hirosaki*

for house sales in 1923. It is said that *Denenchofu* was greatly influenced by the residential area called St. Francis Wood in San Francisco. All these suburban residential districts in Japan, developed during the first half of the 19th century, have now become high-standard residential areas.

4) Urbanization and development of residential districts in the postwar period

Osaka City was vastly destroyed in World War II. In order to secure rental houses in the war-damaged city, the Japanese Government in 1946 consecutively enacted the "Population Inflow Restriction Act," the "Open-Excessive-House Act," the "Temporary Management Act on Rental Lands and Houses in War-Damaged Cities," and revived the "Rent Control Act." Among them the Rent Control Act, while keeping rents for tenants from rising, decreased gains from rental housing. This lead to the selling of many of the rental houses to their tenants during the postwar. Therefore, while rental houses predominated in number after the war, privately-owned houses increased to account for a majority in the stock. In 1950, the housing loan corporation was established and further promoted the purchase of a house in Japan. As the postwar industry recovered, the population inflow to the metropolitan area began again. Against this policy and economic context, private developers actively started to build and sell houses. The houses in this period can be roughly divided into two types. One was ready-built houses in the outskirts of the existing cities where the access was comparatively high yet the land price would not rise rapidly. Most of these were small. The other type includes the high-quality standard houses built in suburbs along railway lines.

5) Statistics on privately-owned houses

The Osaka Metropolitan Area comprises Osaka City as its core and the surrounding cities (Figure 14.2). In these surrounding cities, the rate of commuting to Osaka City was over 30% by 1975 and the Densely Inhabited Districts (DID) spread almost throughout all the metropolitan area. At present, the total population of the area is approximately 9 million. Both figures 14.5 and 14.6 are related to the metropolitan districts map in figure 14.2. Together they clearly describe the spatial distribution of the residential growth in the Osaka Metropolitan Area. Figure 14.5 shows the housing stock classified by the time of construction in all the constituent cities in the metropolitan area, while Figure 14.6 shows the ratio of privately-owned houses and rental houses classified by type. In the earlier postwar period, privately-owned detached houses and more collective housing for rent were built, nearer to Osaka City (Figures 14.2, 14.5, and 14.6).

By 1985, the rate of house ownership was 50% in the whole Osaka Prefecture and 41% in Osaka City. The rate of owning houses is rather small in the central districts of metropolitan areas in Japan. Census figures show that, as of 1983, the proportion of detached houses was 38%, and that of non-wooden collective housing was 28%, of all the houses in the whole Osaka Prefecture. While detached houses in the study area increased by 90,000 units between 1978 and 1983, non-wooded collective housing increased by 180,000 units. This 2 to 1 increase rate in non-wooded collective housing remains the residential market conditions of the present, and most likely the future housing trends in Japan.

Mobility and inheritability of detached houses

1) Characteristic in transition of ownership: Mobility

Among the residential areas in the suburbs of Osaka, two districts were selected as samples for each of the three types of residential areas with detached houses. These three types are a "residential district developed in prewar days," a "residential district with comparatively large housing lots developed in the postwar period," and a "residential district with small housing lots developed also during the postwar period." The present situation on mobility of detached houses, i.e., the transition of ownership, was investigated in the sample areas selected. The average size of housing lots in the surveyed districts is rather large relative to those of detached houses and row houses located in Osaka Prefecture. Table 14.3 shows mobility of residence in privately-owned detached houses for each district. The mobility rates obtained from the housing map and from the land register are similar in the two districts for each type of residential development. There are two key characteristics of the detached house—transition of ownership and inheritability—both are central to the use and meaning of this housing type in Japan.

These three types of residential districts taken as samples were classified from the time of construction and the size of a house into "prewar high-standard residential district," "postwar high-standard residential district," and "postwar standard residential district." When analyzing them, three characteristics associated with the transition of ownership in each district are found. First, in the prewar high-standard residential district, both inheritance or transaction are frequent. The residential plots of land are fragmented by subdivision, and development of small-scale houses in-

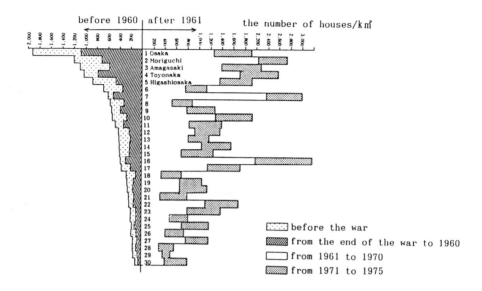

Figure 14.5: Housing stock by time of construction in *Osaka*

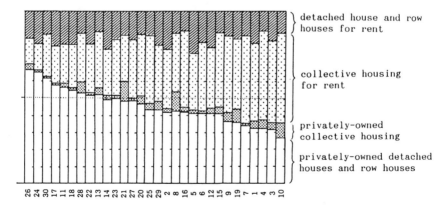

Figure 14.6: Privately–owned vs. rental houses by type

Source: Figures 14.5 and 14.6, Report on Housing Statistics, Osaka and Hyogo prefectural governments, 1978

Table 14.3: Patterns of ownership and occupancy in detached houses

	district	the period of observation	the rate of changes in ownership of housing/lots	the rate of changes per year	the average size of housing lots	the average of total floor areas
prewar high-standard residential district	6. Sakurai	25 years	68.0 %	2.72 %	390 m²	166 m²
	3. Tezukayama	21	34.5 *	1.64 *	346	171
	Kita-batake	22	55.8 *	2.54 *		
postwar standard residential district	5. Nansuien	18	46.6	2.59	127	89
	2. Kusunosato	18	44.3 *	2.46 *	164	93
postwar high-standard residential district	4. Tennocho	23	25.2	1.10	280	116
	1. Kori	17	22.2 *	1.31 *	327	126

1 * Observations from the housing map. "No marks" taken from the land register.
2   Size of housing lot and total floor area are averages compiled from the survey.

creases. Second, in the postwar high-standard residential district, transaction is minimal even though inheritance is frequent when compared to the mobility in postwar standard residential districts. The frequency of ownership transition is the lowest, making these the most stable residential areas. Third, in the postwar standard residential district, the opposite takes place. While there is frequent transaction, the inheritances are few.

The differences between these districts seem to be associated mainly with the time elapsed after development and the size of a house. In the case of the prewar high-standard residential district, more than 50 years have passed since the newest district was developed, yet the dwelling size is the largest among three types of districts. Both inheritance and transaction are frequent and the fragmentation of residential plots in these districts is in progress. Thess dynamics appear to depend on types of family needs. The housing lots were sold because it became difficult to maintain a large-scale house due to the inheritance tax at the time of inheritance from a generation to the next, or due to prevalence of the fixed property tax. Also, the necessity by families to sell or subdivide the housing lot and distribute the property at the time of inheritance explains fragmentation of housing property in these districts.

In the case of the postwar standard residential district, the transition of ownership by transaction was very frequent. Here the house, being of a small size, seems to serve as a house to live in for a certain period before the family moved to a larger house.

In the case of the postwar high-standard residential district, mobility is the lowest, making it the most stable. It is characterized by less than half of the mobility of the postwar standard residential district, yet developed at approximately the same period. This difference correlates with the dwelling size. In the postwar high-standard residential district, the dwelling size is rather large related to houses developed during the period and residents seem to have a strong consciousness of settlement. Actually, many of the first-generation residents are still living in these houses. However, in the future, when the original generation of residents will change to the next, there will be the possibility of mobility as it has been the case with the prewar high-standard residential district.

2) Characteristics of inheritance: Inheritability

Many people realize that it is quite difficult to acquire a house in large cities. In a discussion with students aimed at finding out how the recent young people think about the inheritance of a parents' house, the following opinions were often heard: "Enough houses will be available because of the low birth rate." "There are increasing such houses in a commuting distance that will be succeeded to the next generations, although the property value is not high." "It will be better to live in a local home town inheriting a parent's house, rather than to make a thrifty living in order to get a house in a big city." These students vaguely recognize the present-day difficulty to acquire a house in large cities. As they become more aware of such difficulty, their acceptance to live in a parent's house will increase.

While the above opinions composed a majority, there are some who strongly insist that: "Together with inheritance of a house, I will receive such matters as care of parents, finding a new job and conflict against memories in an old house;" or "If a man has a house to inherit, his actions will be restricted. It is a burden;" and that "A house functions unequally among brothers/sisters."

In the six districts sampled, a questionnaire was carried out to learn the inheritability of houses. The rate of inheriting the houses where they now live differs among the districts, but generally speaking, there is a tendency that the younger the occupants are, the lower is the rate of purchasing a house. In the age bracket from 30 to 50, the rate of inheritance from parents is as high as approximately 16%. Regarding the inheritability classified by the size of a housing lot, the tendency is that the larger the size of the house, the greater is the rate of inheritance. Meaning that in Japanese cities like Osaka, a house with a larger lot is not usually acquired by the resident's own resources. Figure 14.7 shows statistics of the ways of acquiring houses in the six districts. Only the houses whose times of inheritance/purchase was clear, were selected from the sample. In the prewar high-standard residential districts, acquisition by inheritance accounts for as high as 20%-30%.

In the same questionnaire, it was asked "whether your son/daughter will inherit your house and live there in the future." Less than half of the respondents answered "Yes, one of our children will live in," while only 7.5% answered "No, our children will not live in." The answer correlates with the number of children. The positive answer increased as respondents had more children. It became clear that they are not going to force their only son or daughter to inherit the house, but if they have many children, their expectations are for at least one of the children to inherit. More than 40% expressed uncertainty as to how inheritance traditions would be in the future. However, to the question, "which of your children will live in?", the answer of the "eldest son" predominated (77%). This proves that in Japan the idea that an heir to a family estate should be the eldest son remains strong.

Next, the question of "whether it will become necessary to sell your house at the time of distribution of property," the following results were found: 13.5% answered "Yes, I think so." This positive response was di-

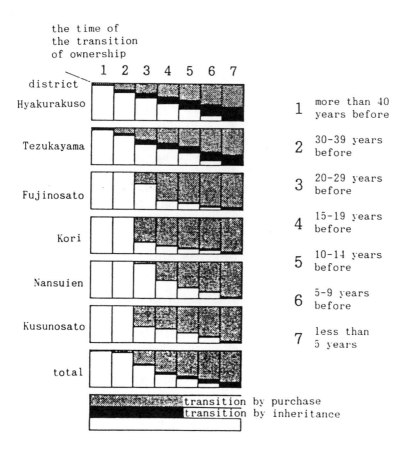

Figure 14.7: Purchase vs. inheritance acquisition by time

rectly related to the number of children in the family. On the other hand, nearly 40% answered "No, I don't think so." Judging from the results to the questions above, and taking the residents' intentions into consideration, it appears that about half of privately-owned detached houses will be passed on to a son or daughter.

Another interesting perspective to inheritability of housing in Japan results from the intentions of sons and daughters who are to receive the inheritance. Table 14.4 shows the results of our survey about the younger generation who lives in Osaka City and its peripheral areas. Those who expect to inherit a house account for about 30%. However, only about 20% of those who are inheriting expect to live in the house.

This lesser number of those who intend to live in the inherited dwelling is in part explained by the fact that all the houses are not necessarily in the Osaka region. These results begin to prove that the young recognize a house as a land asset rather that as a place to live. They also may reflect that the young do not want to live in an old house. In either group of "inheriting" or "inheriting to live," the younger respondents show the higher rate of inheritance expectation. This begins to reveal that in today's Japan, the younger generations have the stronger interest in their parents' housing assets, but not necessarily in their houses.

3) Living together: The parents and the family of a son or daughter

In what relation do parents and the family of a son or daughter dwell together? According to our survey, in the case of detached houses, over 30% live with the husband's parents, while only about 15% do so with the wife's parents. Another survey which includes a younger age group in detached houses, found that over 30% of this group lived with the husband's parents. This finding supports the results from our survey. In the case of rental houses, parents and a son or daughter have a different relationship. The rate of living within a walking distance to the husband's or wife's parents, is rather high in Japan. About 30–40% of the families seem to live with parents or live close to parents (Table 14.5).

Table 14.6 displays the rates from various countries of elderly (over 60) who live together with their children. This rate is remarkably high in Japan when compared to other industrialized countries. For example, the rate of households where the elderly live by themselves or the elderly couple lives alone, reaches approximately 80% in Europe and in the U.S.A., compared to about 30% in Japan. On the other hand, the rate of three-generation families reaches nearly 40% in Japan, but in Europe and the USA such

Table 14.4: Intentions of children toward inherited homes

classified by intention	the number of brothers						the order among brothers/sisters					average
							only son	only brothers		brothers/sisters		
	1	2	3	4	5	6		eldest son	second /later sòn	eldest son	second /later son	
I intend to inherit a parent's house	50.9	46.4	32.8	23.9	17.5	9.1	48.1	44.1	10.1	51.3	9.1	30.6
I intend t inherit a parent's house to live there	34.9	20.9	21.0	15.9	14.0	9.2	39.7	20.0	12.5	32.2	8.5	20.6

Rates (in %) from survey responses to "I intend to inherit" or "Probably I will inherit."

Table 14.5: Proximity between parents' and children's households

	Residents in detached houses		Those who reside or work in Osaka metropolitan area			
			Residents in detached houses		Residents in private rental houses	
	husband's parent(s)	wife's parent(s)	husband's parent(s)	wife's parent(s)	husband's parent(s)	wife's parent(s)
living together (in the same house)	30.6 %	12.3 %	34.0 %	7.3 %	10.6 %	3.6 %
living together (in separate houses in the same lot)	2.9	2.1				
living separately (in a walking distance)	7.6	10.3	5.5	9.4	22.7	27.3
living separately (in a non-walking distance)	58.9	75.3	60.5	83.3	66.7	69.1

Table 14.6: International rates of elderly living with children

	Japan	U.S.A.	England	France
single-person household	5.7%	41.3%	41.6%	30.0%
a couple only	25.1	40.0	46.1	46.3
a couple + unmarried children	15.2	8.3	5.0	9.5
three-generation family	36.9	1.6	0.7	3.5
others	17.0	8.8	6.6	10.6

Source: "Life and consciousness of the elderly," Subsidiary Chamber of the Prime Minister for providing for the elderly, Japan: 1982.

living arrangements are far less than 10%. If living with an unmarried son or daughter is added, the rate exceeds 50% in Japan.

Sociologists report that the rate of living together of the elderly parents with the family of a son/daughter is not less than 50%. However, this rate may be too high for large cities such as Osaka. In the survey, the carried out intention of living together accounts for less than 30% while that of living near-by exceeds 50%. Parents and the family of a son or daughter may be living together under unavoidable circumstances, when it may be desired by both parties to live apart.

Lives in detached houses and one's unique space of attachment

The two topics of concern, lives in detached houses and one's unique space of attachment in Japanese housing, are presented in terms of the pattern of enlargement and remodeling of a housing unit; valued, functional, and residential spaces in a house; one's own unique space of attachment in a house; and the attachementto family ties.

Pattern of enlargement and remodeling

The house is not only a container where a family lives but also a stage where the various generations of the family develop their daily lives. Especially in a detached house, the necessity becomes more visible as it is often characterized by ongoing enlargement or remodeling. In order to examine concretely the patterns of physical reorganization, we looked at a sample of seven detached houses. The frequency of enlargement or remodeling was "none" in 2 of the houses, "once" in 3 of them, "twice" in 1, and "five times" in another house.

The reasons for enlargement or remodeling are: a) to prepare for someone who lived together temporarily or for a long time; b) to improve daily use spaces such as kitchen, dining room, bathroom, and toilet; c) to provide for multiple dwelling in the future when parents or a son or daughter's family will live together; and d) to increase the ranking of a house by remodeling an entrance or a *Zashiki* room (Japanese-style reception room).

The enlargement or remodeling can be classified into five physical patterns. In the limited number of samples in the survey, there was a correspondence between the direction of enlargement or remodeling and its use, as follows:

	DIRECTION		USE
a)	horizontal addition...	addition of room(s) on the first floor	space for reception
b)	vertical addition...	addition of the second floor	children's room
c)	horizontal addition... upstairs	addition of room(s) on the existing second floor	main bedroom
d)	extension of a room...	making the existing room larger	kitchen dining room living room
e)	remodeling of the... interior	remodeling an interior, not changing a framework	Zashiki room

The ideas for an enlargement or remodeling were mainly conceived by housewives and their ideas were eventually coincidental in the sample houses in our survey. The enlargement or remodeling took place in the entrance, kitchen, dining room, living room, parlor, *Zashiki* room, bath room, and toilet on the first floor; and the children's room, main bedroom, and the second toilet on the second floor. Among the seven houses sampled, a house underwent enlargement and remodeling five times (Figure 14.8). This house

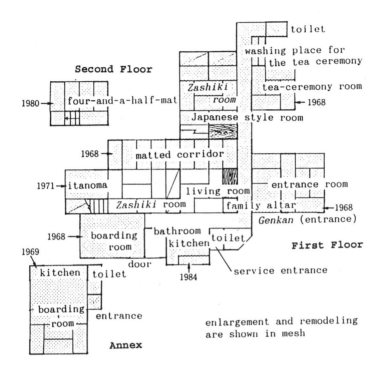

Figure 14.8: Expansion Case 1: A house of a tea ceremony master

was originally a wooden ready-built house with two rooms and a kitchen. The woman master of the house, taught the tea ceremony. Therefore she built over time a space suitable for a tea ceremony lesson. Now 70 years old, she lives alone and rents a room and an annex to boarders. From this sample we learn how the house has approached the resident's ideal function and image of a house through successive alterations.

Valued, functional, and residential spaces in a house

Genkan (entrance) *Zashiki* room (traditional spaces), Western-style parlor, residential rooms, corridor, and garden. *Genkan:* In the detached house, the *Genkan* represents the prestige of a house. It has been an important space for welcoming visitors. Originally, the Japanese house had a service entrance for ordinary use besides the front entrance. Among the houses surveyed, some have the service entrances, however it is the front entrance that now also serves ordinary use. Today there are few occasions when the entrance could be a stage for various functions. Close friends are immediately led into the house without stopping at the entrance. As for unexpected visitors, people talk over the entrance gate or through an interphone. This may be a reason why the approach from the gate to the entrance door is so elaborately designed in any house instead of the entrance space itself. While the formal importance of the entrance has decreased, the entrance gate and its vicinity are becoming more gorgeous. When a family member is sent home by car, for example, the only thing to be seen is the gate and gateposts. Families who have marriageable daughters or those who put emphasis on prestige pay special attention to the gate. The elderly want to have such an entrance as does not embarrass them in more public occasions such as a funeral.

Zashiki room: Among Japanese-style rooms, a room with *Tokonoma* (alcove for decoration) is called "*Zashiki*." This room is a multi-functional space but it was not being used for ordinary daily functions in any house surveyed. As the first three days of a new year are the most festive, this room is used for dining and playing. This room is also often used when people gather on special occasions. It is interesting that children stay in this room when they are sick. During engagements of daughters, a "shower of gifts" ceremony is held in the *Zashiki* room. This ceremony does not necessarily follow home traditions but is carried out strictly following various guide books or the advice of a betrothal gift shop. The gifts are decorated in the *Tokonoma*. In other words, the *Tokonoma* is provided for this purpose in a house where there are daughters. It is definitely the most decorative space in today's house. In those houses surveyed, this space was decorated with a hanging scroll on a wall and was not used for any other purpose.

The parlor is a western-style parlor. It is not used for daily activities even when a parlor is built in a house for more exclusive functions. The room is calm and quiet and japanese feel guilty even to sit there. Small children feel scared to enter the room. In the western-style parlor, a drawing room suite is placed. A piano is often found, since Japanese children, especially girls, often learn the piano and practice in this room. Sometimes the master of the house uses this room as a study room. Special ornaments of superior quality and family trophies are generally displayed in this room.

The dining room is more functional in the daily activies of the family. It is really a strange space. Even after the number of family members decreases, the number of chairs does not. The chairs for sons and daughters living away in a boarding house, or for a married daughter, remain there as if the children still live at home. When housewife's friends come, they are led to the dining room to enjoy a chat over tea and cakes. It can be said that the dining room is a kind of "gala" space to treat close friends.

The other functional area is the toilet. In any house, a toilet, washing area and bathroom are elaborately designed. At the time of building special attention is paid to make these areas spacious. The toilet particularly is "a place to be cleaned at first when visitors are expected." It is elaborately decorated.

Children's rooms, grandparents' rooms, and places for religion also have special placements, meanings and uses and are placed in a sunny side. Children's rooms are often on the second floor. Even after a son or a daughter moves away, their rooms are often kept. Although, sometimes a son's room is used as a cloakroom for his sister or mother. The daughter's room is equipped with a double bed and kept for the daughter and her husband for their two usual yearly visits. The grandparents' room is another residential space commonly found. There seems to exist a consciousness that a house which a son builds is also a house for his parents. A parent's room, even if it was not prepared at first, is generally provided later by adding a room for parents to come and live together. In any house at the time of construction, a place for religion is provided. A family altar is not installed. The altar is brought into the house when the grandparents move in. After the altar is brought in, the Bon Festival and other Buddhist services are carried out. Only in a single house from those surveyed a family shrine was enshrined.

The "Corridor" is another special space. "I don't like a house without a corridor" is a remark we often heard. When we think back to the house where we grew up, the scene of a long, winding corridor comes to mind. People say that a corridor is an ineffective space, but at the same time they enjoy the luxury of affording this "ineffective" passageway in detached houses. Finally, a garden is one of the important elements for which people desire a detached house. In Japan, in order to have a garden with a lawn, a housewife insisted on a detached house. For example, in the gardens surveyed, trees and flowers are transplanted every Sunday so that the view may change.

One's own unique space of attachment in a house

When people's expectations from and attachments to a house are examined it becomes clear that a resident's sense of value for a house changes according to life stages. There are own unique spaces of deep attachment which cannot be explained from functional viewpoints. Following, are some reasons why these spaces are regarded as "precious." First are attachments to a space which make a house deserving of its name. To use a concrete example, the house of one of the families surveyed has been selected and we will call it Mr. X's house (Figure 14.9). In this house, a living room

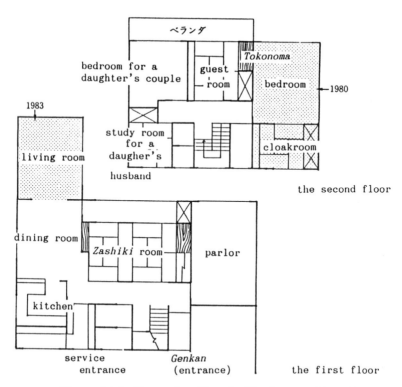

Figure 14.9: Expansion Case 2: The house of Mr. X

and a corridor where the master of the house relaxes are the "precious" spaces. As Mr. X grew up in a house with many corridors, much like a samurai house, he puts a high emotional value on the corridor. However, not only him, but also many Japanese say that without a corridor a house would not deserve its name. In terms of use, the corridor is often regarded simply as a space for passing through. However, in terms of meaning, it is also recognized as a space which makes a house deserving of its name.

Also, while a *Tokonoma* and a garden serve as spaces for decoration and relaxation, they are also regarded as spaces which make a house deserving of its name. As for the *Tokonoma*, many people insist that it should follow definite form conventions such as the *Nageshi*, a horizontal decorative timber at the upper frame of a *Tokonoma*. It is also thought that without a *Zashiki* room with a *Tokonoma*, a house would not be deserving of its name. A prototype of the "attachments" may be found in a house where the man grew up, or may be influenced by an impression of a house that he once happened to see. It may as well depend on the ideal image of a house that he has fostered as a status symbol.

Second is the "gala" space. It is also highly valued in the Japanese house. "Gala" means celebratory or formal. When children are small, such rituals as birthday and the Doll's Festival are enthusiastically celebrated and decorations for these ceremonies are set out in the house. For adults, the only celebration during the year is that of the New Year. Since the New Year's days are the most important days, special attention is paid to the decorations. In Mr. X's house, for example, many visitors may call for greetings during those days. Then, at the most inner part of the *Zashiki* room, Mr. X, as the master of the house sits, and dining settings for 24 guests are set in two adjacent rooms, after removing the dividing screen doors.

In a household with a daughter, when her marriage draws near, spaces for various ceremonies which accompany the marriage become important. The most important ceremony is that of betrothal gifts, and it is at this time that a *Zashiki* room with a *Tokonoma* performs its role. It may be a result of this role that some people regard the detached house with a *Zashiki* room as "a house appropriate for the marriage of a daughter." For a man like Mr. X who runs a company, the house has other functions to perform for his company. Therefore, Mrs. X adheres to her detached house; as a house appropriate for a company owner; as a desirable house which serves as a symbol for the employees to work for; and as a house appropriate to serve as a guest house for the company.

Attachment to family ties

When we call a house "*Ie* (house or home)," it means not only a place where a family lives but also it implies a place for the whole family to gather together after leaving home. In agricultural communities, an "*Ie*" has continuously existed as an imperishable and eternal concept. However, this is not the case in urban communities, where the possibility of greater family dispersion exists. Even though more in urban areas, people feel a strong attachment for family ties.

In order to see how it affects the structure of a house, let's take up the case of Mr. X's house. When he built his new house, his mother who lived on Shikoku island insisted, "If my son builds a house, I want my room there." So he added a "four-and-a-half-mat" Japanese style room for her. His mother stayed in this room only twice before she died. Assuming that their only daughter would get married and bring her husband home, a toilet was provided and services for an additional kitchen were prepared on the second floor so that the two-generation extend family could live together.

At the time of the first addition, rooms were constructed to have enough space if the daughter and her husband came to live with them, along with a guest room exclusively to accommodate visitors. However, soon after moving in to this house, Mr. X's business relocated to Tokyo. Since then, he stays in a hotel there, their daughter got married and lives in Tokyo.

Now, Mrs. X lives alone during the week. On Saturdays she cleans the house elaborately for Mr. X arrive. He returns late on Saturday evenings and usually goes out to play golf on Sundays. On the rare occasions he stays at home. Someone may come to meet with him, so, he dines together with them and stays overnight. On Mondays, he returns to his Tokyo apartment. The daughter who lives in Tokyo rarely comes home. On the Bon Festival and New Year days she and her husband do come back for a few days. Their contact is now maintained via the telephone. Hoping the day will come when her daughter's family will live with them, Mrs. X keeps on cleaning the house and sweeping the garden for her husband's once a week visits and those of her daughter's family twice a year.

Conclusion: A house to unite a family

Even in a detached house standing directly on its own land, occupants and owners are mobile and their children do not necessarily live there. Yet, under these conditions, the value of land as an asset still encourages home ownership. As a result, the house becomes more and more expensive, to the point of being almost impossible for the average worker to purchase a detached house in a metropolitan area of Japan.

Under these circumstances, people are currently attempting to adopt the idea of repaying a housing loan over two generations. Housing has become so expensive that we cannot acquire a reasonable one, unless the successive generations cooperatively invest in it. The trend towards permanent settlement in large cities due to the slowing population inmigration, low birth rates, and the longevity of the elderly, naturally encourages the idea of building a fine house cooperatively, and live there together from generation to generation. Just as once people did in the rural countryside. Thus, there is a possibility that a new type of "*Ie*" may emerge in large cities. The question is, how will it develop?

On the other hand, in large cities, resident populations of mid-or-high-rise collective housing, such as condominiums and apartment houses, are steadily increasing. However, many residents who own such condominiums do not consider them as their life-long house. In condominiums consisting of individually-owned units, maintenance and management can not be easily performed because of the difficulty in reaching consensus between all residents. Therefore, in the future, it may very well be that whole buildings will become substandard residential properties. Against such a possibility, residents who purchased these condominiums are not relieved from anxiety. While the maintenance and management system in collective housing has advanced, the processes of expansion and readaptation remain unclear since only a very few number of buildings have been reconstructed. Specially condominium buildings, consisting of individually-owned units, have many unresolved problems if they are to expand. Therefore, there exists a strong desire to own a house, even though the size of the Japanese household is steadily decreasing. The unmarried, married couples without children, and single-person households are steadily increasing. While this is a common trend in large cities of industrialized countries such as ours, I think that a new inter-generational family tie, appropriate to the forth coming urban age, will appear.

A house is not only a place to live in, but for many it is also a reservoir filled with "attachments and expectations" in life. Some may say that "a house with attachments" is only "a house of personal taste." However, taste is an important element in making our lives worth living. Among the "attachments and expectations," "family ties" are enormously important, especially for women in Japan. What form will housing take in Japanese culture in the future?

Professor Keiichi Sakuta mentions that there was a traditional consciousness in Japan that the "*Ie*" would continue. However, during the process in which the nucleus of a family changed from the parent-son (daughter) relationship to that of a husband-wife relationship, a family came to be divided by the marriage of each couple and the continuity of a family from generation to generation disappeared ("Sociology on Value," Keiichi Sakuta, Iwanami Publishing Inc., 1972). However, I think that intergenerational family ties will continue with every two or three generations as a unit. This hypothesis is supported by findings from a French-Japanese survey ("Parent-Child Relation in France and Japan," Toru Arichi, NHK publishing Inc., 1981). "A widower died and left a house for three children. While they are not rich, they are not in financial difficulty either. What would you think is best: a) to sell the house and to divide the money among the three children, or b) to keep the house as a place of mutual exchange among the children?" This question was asked to both parents and children participating in the survey. The results were that 56% of the parents and 50% of the children answered "to keep the house." Since France is regarded as a country of greater individualism than Japan, this result was an unexpected one, and it also raises the question regarding the role of the house in Japan as a place for the sharing of memories or family ties across a few generations, rather than the one of continuity as in the "*Ie*."

In metropolitan areas, when we consider the difficulty in purchasing a detached house sufficient for two generations to live in together, or rebuilding a condominium with individually-owned units, I think that there is a limitation in creating a new inter-generational family ties with a privately-owned house. However, even if each generation lives separately, the family tie does not fade away. Therefore, a new inter-generational family tie will be created in a network of houses rather than in a single house where multiple generations are forced to live together.

As mentioned, the number of children renting houses close to their parents, is high in Japan. If parents live in their own house, their children's families can live close to the parents by renting a house near their parents' and, when the parents become older and must be cared for, a son or daughter's family can move in to live with them. At that time, grandchildren may become independent. This is an idea to be considered not only in Japan. An owned house to be used as a base camp, and rented houses as the second and third camps. There will also be the opposite case of parents living in a rented house and a son or daughter's family living in their own house. Even if either family does not own a house, they can live in a similar arrangement. Thus, it may not be necessary to increase privately-owned houses any more.

An expression of inter-generational family ties is found in "enshrining ancestors." According to a survey, 87% of the elderly do not want to see an end to the enshrining of ancestors in Japan (Table 14.7). The ratio of maintaining a family altar is low in nuclear families and high in extended families. This proves that the altar is brought into a house with the grandparents. The high ratio of maintaining a family altar in commercial districts indicates that in such districts there are many families who have lived there for a long time, engaged in commerce (Table 14.7). There is no drastic decline over time as to changes of consciousness in ancestor worship.

Under the circumstances mentioned, it seems that the "space for enshrining ancestors" will continue to be valued in the future. It is said that in Western countries, furniture and tableware are taken as a symbol of continuous succession of a family or are given as a keepsake of parents, but such customs are not often found. I think this is because the family altar represents the continuity from generation to generation in Japan. "Attachments to and expectation" of a house affect its spatial structure in various ways. Comparatively, in a detached house the ' 'expectations" can be easily incorporated. This is one of the reasons why people prefer a detached house. However, we now have to consider how to embody these "expectations" in present and future collective housing.

There are a lot of points to be improved in the inner spaces of multi-family housing. It can be said that Japanese collective housing is too im-

Table 14.7: Family altars and ancestor worship

	1953	1973	1978
total	100 %	100 %	100 %
religious	77	67	72
normal	15	21	16
irreligious	5	10	10
others, including "I don't know"	3	2	2

	the rate of nuclear families	the rate of maintaining a family altar	the rate of maintaining a family altar in nuclear families	the rate of maintaining a family altar in extended families
commercial district	58 %	69 %	51 %	93 %
residential district	80	45	31	100

Top: The ratio of maintaining a family altar in *Tokyo.*
Bottom: Changes in a consciousness on ancestor worshipping.
Sources: "Japanese Religion," edited by Imon and Yoshida, 1970;
"Research on Japanese Nationality," Institute of Mathematical Statistics, 1980.

mature to be called a house. More elaborate considerations should be given to the *Genkan*, *Zashiki* room, *Tokonoma*, corridor, and garden mentioned above. A window is also an important element in a house, but in the existing multi-family housing, even the window is not appropriate for what is called a "house."

The poor quality of today's collective housing is surely the result of its small size. It also depends on their short history. Public housing, to be publicly accepted, is required to be rational and cannot afford to provide "one's own unique space." Condominiums are also built as rationally as possible under standardization in order to be selable. The only way to create "one's own unique space" in such collective housing is to remodel the interior of an apartment or to change furniture arrangements. In public housing, there are limitations to remodeling the interior, so the only method available is an alteration of the furniture. In the future, in both public and private collective housing, a method appropriate for remodeling the interior must be established in order to provide the fundamental "one's own unique spaces."

Gradually though, it appears that such collective housing units may adopt elaborate considerations as may be the case in cooperative housing and experimental company houses. The former are made-to-order condominiums, and the latter are apartment houses, which as company facilities are not a commodity for sale. From the experiences of these new housing types it is expected that a new style of collective housing will evolve in Japan.

This chapter concludes by introducing the following objectives as criteria which can lead to improvement of use and meaning in housing.

1) Life-style objectives for planning:

   a) eliminate unavoidable encounters and secure privacy in daily life;

   b) reduce pre-determined spaces and provide for their unrestricted, free use, in order to increase the value of multifamily dwellings;

   c) make a plan which provides opportunities for people to meet other residents of the areas as well as those of the company apartment; and

   d) make a plan which provides opportunities for people to meet other residents of the areas as well as those of the company apartment.

2) Spacial objectives for planning:

   a) provide windows where one may relax and enjoy reading;

Figure 14.10: Company houses of the DAIKIN Corporation, *Osaka*

- Top: Street view. Bottom: Small front garden.
- Architect Etsuo Tanda, conception by Narumi *et al.*

b) provide a deeper balcony;

c) provide a relaxing intermediate space between the outer street and the company flat; and

d) provide an attractive townscape and streetscape.

The meanings which these objectives implied were fully understood by an architect and realized in the DAIKIN Corporation company flats (Figure 14.10). The height of the building was restricted in order to maintain the spatial harmony with the surrounding area. Paths were created to provide as much as possible, an independent access to each apartment. A small garden was provided around each door, introducing the characteristics of the garden in traditional Japanese urban house. The construction work was rather difficult and its cost was high compared to simple-shaped collective housing. However this company project enjoys a high satisfaction by the company families living there. From attempts like this one, I do hope that new collective housing will involve a Japanese sense of value, utilizing the knowledge presented in this chapter.

References

The Mainichi Newspaper, April 1, 1991.

"Garden City and Japanese," voluntary members of the Ministry of Interior Affairs, Kodansha, 1980.

"Parent-Child Relation in France and Japan," Toru Arichi, NHK Publishing Inc., 1981.

"Sociology on Value," Keiichi Sakuta, Iwanami Publishing Inc., 1972.

Part VI
The Meaning and Use of Housing: Unconventional Arrangements

The Meaning and Use of Housing: Unconventional Arrangements

KATHRYN H. ANTHONY
University of Illinois at Urbana-Champaign

The international symposium on the meaning and use of home and neighborhood, held in Sweden in 1989, from which various contributions in this book are derived, was extremely stimulating. The cozy environment of the Alvkarleby conference center, complete with its small-scale, vernacular architecture, its striking natural setting, and its aromatic, tasty meals, along with the warm friendliness of our conference hosts, contributed to a wonderful albeit temporary sense of home for all participants. The symposium provided those of us fortunate enough to attend with the opportunity to hear the state of the art research on housing symbolism around the world. And it also offered us a unique opportunity, in a small-scale setting, to critically discuss and evaluate our own work and that of our colleagues. The unconventional format of the conference, where we each met with the same group of researchers for several successive sessions, rather than rotating around through various groups, allowed for an unusually in-depth set of discussions to occur.

Not only was the format of the conference unconventional, but so were many of the topics raised by the presenters. The following chapters in Part VI address three out-of-the-ordinary, non-conformist forms of housing: shared housing, the house trailer, and collective housing.

The methods used to study each of these non-traditional housing arrangements are worth noting. In her examination of shared housing, Depres uses a hybrid approach, a combination of both quantitative and qualitative data-gathering techniques, including face-to-face interviews as well as surveys. In his analysis of the house trailer, Wallis employs a longitudinal, historical perspective by examining the public record: court cases and legislation. And in his study of collective housing, Vestbro relies on surveys, individual and group interviews, spontaneous observations, participant-observation, and analyses of drawings and official documents. As in most research endeavors, no single technique is enough. Instead, a variety of complementary approaches has proven most fruitful. Both quantitative and qualitative methods, and the examination of archival data over a lengthy period of time have proven revealing ways of uncovering how people feel about their own homes and neighborhoods as well as those of others. In two of the three studies presented here, interviews with residents and open-ended survey questions proved to be unusually enlightening. The study of meaning is extremely rich, and the methodological approaches shown here reflect these complexities.

Throughout these three chapters, a number of issues and themes are raised. One issue is *non-conformity*. People who live in unconventional housing arrangements such as those described here have often become social curiosities. In societies where the house is one of the most powerful symbols of the self, an unusual dwelling arrangement can, at least in some people's eyes, connote an unusual type of occupant–that of a non-conformist. Unfortunately, people who live in mobile homes, houseboats, collective housing, and other unusual environments are often perceived as odd.

A second theme is *when "social deviance" in housing is tolerated*. While some housing arrangements are perfectly acceptable for certain stages in the life cycle, when people deviate from these stages they are often seen as transient. For instance, many Americans encourage their children to share dormitory rooms and off-campus apartments as college students. But once these adult children graduate from school, "settle down" with a job, a companion or spouse, and a family, they are expected to live on their own. Social and psychological currents of individualism and independence run very deep. At this more advanced stage in their life cycle, home-sharing is seen as only a temporary, transitional solution to the housing problem. Most adults share housing in times of economic or personal hardship, usually by force, but not by choice. People who choose to share housing often have to justify their choice to others.

A third issue is the *degree to which societies discriminate against occupants of non-traditional housing*. As Wallis points out, despite the fact that today's manufactured housing is dramatically improved both in appearance and in technology from the trailer homes of the past, many laws still reflect a strong negative class bias against them. The image of the house trailer has been confusing–it fails to fit into our existing schemas or categories of homes. Is it a house? It is a vehicle? Is it both of the above? Or is it neither? Society has been reluctant to accept wholeheartedly what it can not easily understand.

A fourth theme is *the role that nomenclature can play.* For instance, in an effort to make them more palatable to the mainstream elements of society, the term "park" has been used to describe the mobile home community. Since most such homes are no longer moveable, the term "manufactured housing" has replaced "mobile home". The current term "collective housing" is more neutral than is the 1960's expression "communal housing"— which, in some people's minds, conjures up images of hippies and flower children puffing pot and swimming in the nude. Terminology is important in helping to sway public opinion in favor of these innovative housing types. Reflecting upon all three contributions in Part VI, several questions come to mind: Why is the housing market, at least in the U.S., so conservative? Why haven't we seen more of the unusual housing prototypes presented here? Why have Sweden, Denmark, and the Netherlands taken the lead in housing innovation? Why do some people in so-called "civilized" parts of the world take pride in discriminating against those who live out of the mainstream? How can unconventional housing arrangements be made more socially acceptable? When many Americans, in the midst of a lengthy, painful recession, are also faced with exorbitant housing costs, what's wrong with sharing a home with a friend, living in manufactured housing, or thinking seriously about collective housing?

The American dream of a traditional, single-family, detached home, is one to which millions of Americans still aspire, but simply can not attain. Each of the three housing types presented in Part VI presents a viable, cheaper alternative to the status quo. But disseminating this type of information is essential. Perhaps we researchers need to take the lead in educating the public about the virtues of such housing options. Books like these can be used as a starting point from which to access trade publications of builders, developers, bankers, zoning officials, policy-makers, and others involved in the planning, design, and management of housing. Findings from contemporary housing research must also be brought to the attention of journalists whose articles in popular magazines and newspapers can help increase public awareness about a wider range of housing options. In an era where many individuals feel trapped out of the housing market and discouraged about their future, such options can offer them a few rays of hope.

Chapter 15

A Hybrid Strategy in a Study of Shared Housing

CAROLE DESPRÉS
Université Laval, Québec, Canada

This chapter discusses the advantages of combining qualitative and quantitative research methods in meaning of home research. The strength of hybrid methods is presented in the context of an empirical study on the meaning and experience of home for unrelated households in shared housing. The quantitative analysis indicates what categories of meaning homesharers valued most in relationship to first, their ideal home and second, their current shared home. It also indicates what dimensions of home are most critical in shared housing, that is, the ones that present the most discrepancies between homesharers' idea of what a home should be and their current experience of shared housing. The results of the qualitative analysis allowed to interpret "why" respondents' ratings of the statements for their ideal home and current shared home were so similar or dissimilar as well as to identify what human, societal, and morphological factors influenced most their answers.

[0] The results presented are part of a doctoral dissertation conducted at the department of Architecture at the University of Wisconsin-Milwaukee. This research was made possible through doctoral grants from the Canadian Council for Human Sciences and Université Laval, Québec.

Introduction

The last ten years have seen the publication of a fair amount of literature on meaning of home from both behavioral and human sciences. A number of books and collections of essays have highlighted some specific theoretical perspectives of home environments (for instance, Altman & Werner, 1985; Csikszentmihalyi & Rochberg-Halton, 1981; Lawrence, 1987; Low & Chambers, 1990) and the strengths and weaknesses of these mainstream behavioral/human approaches have been discussed (see Desprs, 1991; Dovey, 1988; Lawrence, 1989; Pred, 1983). It is however not the case of the methodologies used in conducting this type of research. In fact, researchers share very little on this issue. Space limitations in international conference proceedings and in professional journals rarely allow for more than a few paragraphs on methods. A direct consequence of this situation is the difficulty to appreciate the different research strategies put forward by researchers. The discussions of research methodologies brought out by this collection of essays constitute a major contribution to the field. An assessment of the state of the art in carrying out empirical studies on home environments is essential to the advancement of knowledge in this area of research. The respective strengths and limitations of quantitative and qualitative methodologies need to be exposed and innovative strategies diffused.

The methodology developed for the research presented in this chapter goes beyond the exclusive use of quantitative or qualitative data collection and analysis instruments. The general strategy was to put the two research traditions in a dialectical relationship so as to generate original sets of data. Exploring the meaning and experience of home for unrelated households in shared housing, the research design combined quantitative instruments from cognitive psychology and qualitative research procedures. These two types of research methods were not used separately or sequentially but rather put in an interdependent relationship. In other words, the final set of data would not have been possible without combining the instruments. The first part of this chapter discusses the conceptual issues and the methodological framework of this research, followed by the presentation of the study and its findings. The last section concludes on the limitations of the study and its implications for future research.

Conceptual issues and methodological framework

Two methodological trends seem to coexist in environmental meaning research. On the one hand, environmental psychology has favored quantitative data collection instruments and data analysis procedures. Cognitive approaches to meaning attempt to unfold the hidden structure of meaning in people's mind when talking about their home. It explores personal ways of making sense of the world and experiencing it, aiming at identifying the psychological categories and dimensions of the meaning of home. Data collection instruments such as the *semantic differential*, the *repertory grid*, and the *sorting task* were designed for this purpose.[1] The advantages of these methods are to provide first, means by which people's attention can be focused on very specific issues, and second, quantitative indicators of group trends. These latter, when considered alone, have limited power for the interpretation of environmental meaning. Even though cognitive approaches acknowledge that certain predispositions influence people's responses to the external world, it does not concern itself with identifying individual, societal or physical forces that gave birth to specific meanings.

On the other hand, many disciplines such as anthropology, human geography and phenomenological sociology generally favor qualitative research strategies that produce verbal data through unstructured interview techniques, participant observation, ethnographic methodology, etc. Even though it is now largely accepted that the study of environmental meaning calls for non-numerical data, qualitative methods are not without their limitations. If we take unstructured interviews, for instance, it is assumed that individuals are able to express their thoughts and feelings about their homes. And if we assume that they can to a certain extent (with the help of prompting), it is still very difficult to keep people's attention on questions being asked. Finally, researchers are often left with a quantity of verbal data to analyze that is difficult to manage. On a theoretical level, qualitative research have limited interpretative power. Because of their dependance on verbal material, qualitative research assumes a continuity between people's discourse and their experience. However, language is not transparent. Home cannot only be interpreted as a personal construct, it is also a social practice and a physical entity. Meanings expressed by respondents represent only a fragment of this reality. Their discourse is multi-vocal and researchers have to learn to read the hidden voices. In other words, people's personal discourses cannot be interpreted only in relationship to themselves but also in relationship to society (time, space, culture) of which they are part. Two levels of discourse can be uncovered when people talk about their home: (1) the immediate discourse, the one directly accessible through verbal data; and (2) the meta-discourse, the one that can only be uncovered through the identification of contradictions and preconceived notions in re-

---

[1] For more information, see: for the semantic differential, Osgood (1957); for the repertory grid, Kelley (1955); and for the sorting task, Garling (1976), Groat (1982) and Center, Brown & Groat (1985).

spondents' discourse about their home. The meaning of home can only be
constructed from people's immediate discourse and from the traces of the
meta-discourse found in the words that are expressed. Qualitative analysis
of verbal material about the home should then permit the identification of
these two levels of discourse (for a good discussion on this issue, see Gurney,
1990). We ought to find out not only *what* home means (categorization of
respondents' answers) but also *why* and *how*, that is, to identify the forces
that generated those meanings and the physical entities which carry them.
Data collection and analysis instruments that permit to do so should be
used in meaning of home studies. Structural data analysis techniques such
as multidimensional scaling (MDS) or structural text analysis allow to unfold levels of discourse that respondents are not always able to consciously
articulate. Structural built form analysis such as typomorphology as well as
analysis of ideological discourses are additional means by which the factors
that have shaped those meanings as well as their material representations
can be investigated.

The meaning of home study presented in the following section deals
with shared housing: a non-traditional type of housing practice. Shared
housing is defined as *the sharing of a one-kitchen dwelling unit by two or
more unrelated adults with or without children.* All household members
have their own private spaces and share some or all of the living areas
and sometimes a bathroom. Homesharers may cooperatively manage the
household or decide to have a different arrangement of responsibilities and
services (Franck, 1985; Horne & Baldwin, 1988). The general question
this research attempts to answer is *what is the meaning and experience of
home for singles and single-parents sharing a dwelling unit with unrelated
people?* The part of the study to be presented aimed at finding out (1) what
are homesharers' schemes for their ideal homes; (2) on what dimensions of
home is there more discrepancy between homesharers' schemes for their
ideal homes and their experience of shared housing, and (3) what sets of
factors can explain the gaps between homesharers' ideal homes and their
shared homes. Because very little empirical data is available on shared
housing, the research was designed to be "hypothesis-generating" rather
than "hypothesis-testing." It consisted of a cross-sectional survey of a non-
probability sample of 70 homesharers from the Chicago and Milwaukee
metropolitan areas.[2] Face-to-face interviews of about 1 1/2 hour took place

[2] Two thirds of respondents were women, one third, men. All were single (never
married, divorced/separated or widowed). Three quarters of respondents had no children
living with them at home, the others were single-parents. One third of respondents were
under 30 years old, another third were between 30 and 39 years old, while the last third
were over 40 years old. Nine out of ten had at least some college education or had
completed a degree in a technical school. Nearly two thirds had annual incomes of less

in respondents' homes.

Even though it was taken for granted that verbal data were essential to the study of environmental meaning, the strategy developed combined quantitative and qualitative instruments to take advantage of the strengths of both sets of methodologies. Three cognitive tasks—rating task, paired comparison task and sorting task—were used to provide quantitative indicators of sample trends but also as means to generate open-ended comments from homesharers on very focused issues. The rating task was designed to investigate the semantic dimensions of home most valued by homesharers; the pair comparison task, the spatial preferences of homesharers for different floor plans; and the sorting task, homesharers' visual preferences for different housing exteriors.

The three cognitive tasks proved to be efficient device for generating informal but very focused discussions on different aspects of shared housing. Because people were concentrated in proceeding with the tasks, they were less self-conscious about what they were saying. Moreover, since the focus of the interview was the tasks, homesharers were less apt to try to answer what they thought the interviewer wanted to hear. During long interviews (an average of 1 1/2 to 2 hours), cognitive tasks were also a way to keep homesharers' interest high by having them play a very active role by manipulating written and visual material. Because of space limitations, only the results of the rating task will be described in the following section.

Applications and findings

The general objective of the rating task was to evaluate the extent to which people living in shared housing agreed with statements about the home identified in behavioral/human studies of home environments. A most common way to measure people's agreement with different items is to use a rating scale. However, this technique does not necessarily provide comparable measures among respondents. An alternative to the rating scale technique is to have respondents freely express their thoughts on each of these statements using unstructured interview procedures. Although this type of interview is efficient in generating verbal data, respondents' answers may not be relevant to the original question, and the amount of verbal data

---

than $20,000. Over 80 percent were employed full-time, the rest worked part-time, were retired, or unemployed. Three quarters of the homesharers were renters, the others were homeowners. Three quarters lived in urban neighborhoods, the others in suburbs, small towns or villages. About a third of the dwellings were located in single-family detached houses; another third in two- or three- flat houses or small apartment buildings; and the last third in low-rise or small mixed commercial/residential multiplex buildings.

generated is often difficult to manage in the analytical phase. For these reasons, a hybrid strategy using both procedures was developed. Homesharers were read the 14 statements about the home written up from categories of meaning identified in behavioral/human literature on the meaning of home.[3] After each statement, they were asked to indicate on a seven-point scale their degree of agreement with the statement: first, in relationship with what they thought their *ideal home* should be; and second, in relationship to their current experience of *shared housing*. After completing the two ratings, homesharers were asked to explain why their answers were so similar or dissimilar. This procedure was efficient to generate focused open-ended comments without much prompting. Open-ended comments were recorded by the interviewer. Figure 15.1 illustrates this procedure for one of the 14 statements about the home.

In relationship with some conceptual issues discussed earlier, the analytical scheme for the quantitative and qualitative data collected during the rating task needed to identify: (1) preconceived notions or shared meanings about the home among the interviewed homesharers; (2) discrepancies between homesharers' expectations about what a home should be and their experience of shared housing; and (3) sets of factors that could account for the gap between homesharers' schemes for ideal homes and their current shared homes.

The ratings were first quantitatively analyzed. For each of the 14 statements, global rating scores were computed for ideal home and current home, along with median ratings and quartile deviations. From these quantitative measures, it was possible to determine first, which categories of meaning were most valued by homesharers in their ideal schemes; and second, which statements about the home were most experienced in shared housing. To determine which dimensions of home showed most discrepancy between what homesharers think a home should be and their experience of shared housing, the median difference between ideal home and current home ratings was computed for each statement along with the quartile deviation. Statements with higher median differences and variations represent the di-

---

[3] These statements were developed from the results of six important behavioral/human empirical studies that identified psychological/cognitive categories people use when talking about their home: Hayward (1977), Rakoff (1977); Csikszentmihalyi & Rochberg-Halton (1984); Sebba & Churchman (1986); Sixsmith (1986); Baker, Kramer & Gilbert (1989). Two statements which specifically related to shared housing were added to the list. These are: home as a place one feels comfortable bringing people in, and home as a place where one feels familiar with the spaces, the smells, the furniture and the objects. It was hypothesized that these statements about the home could be critical in shared housing. Two other statements which related to the financial aspects of housing were also added. These are : home as an investment from which one can expect to make money, and home as a protection for one's savings.

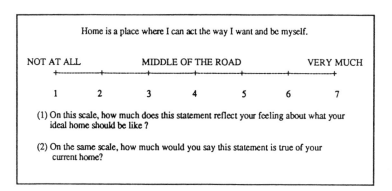

Figure 15.1: Example of rating task card for one of the 14 statements

mensions of home with the largest gap between the ideal and the shared home. Table 15.1 summarizes the results of the quantitative analysis.

The quantitative indicators, although describing general trends for the sample, do not provide any clues as to why homesharers rated in such ways for their ideal and shared homes. The results of the qualitative analysis of the comments recorded during the rating task are very insightful in this regard. For each of the fourteen statements read to respondents, the open-ended comments were transcribed on separate index cards.[4] The index cards were then sorted into piles by the investigator according to common themes or concerns. Overall, homesharers referred to eight important themes to account for the similarity or dissimilarity between their ratings for ideal homes and shared homes. Those can be grouped in three broad categories: personal factors, physical factors, and societal factors. Figure 15.2 illustrates these groupings.

These three series of factors—personal, societal and physical—were defined and discussed in the context of a critical review of mainstream behavioral/human empirical literature on home environments (Després, 1991). The author argues that these three series of factors must be pulled together to construct any interpretation of the meaning of home. *Personal*

---

[4]If a respondent had made more than one comment for a given statement, separate index cards were used to record each comment.

Table 15.1: Results for 14 statements on ideal vs. shared homes, and ideal vs. current home differences

MEANINGS OF HOME	IDEAL HOME SCORES			SHARED HOME SCORES			DIFFERENCES BETWEEN IDEAL AND SHARED HOME RATINGS	
	Rating Score	Median Rating	Quartile Deviatn	Rating Score	Median Rating	Quartile Deviatn	Median Differ.	Quartile Deviatn
Place where one feels physically safe;	471	7	0	403	6	1.0	1	1
Place where one can act the way s/he wants and be him/herself;	470	7	0	364	5	1.0	1	1
Place where one feels comfortable bringing people in;	457	7	0.5	357	6	1.5	1	1.5
Refuge, place where one can get away from outside pressures, find peace and quietness, and be alone when desired;	452	7	0	361	5.5	1.0	1	1
Enough space and rooms for one's daily needs;	446	7	0.5	345	5	1.0	1	1
Place one can modify and personalize;	445	7	0.5	332	5	1.5	1	1.5
Place of love and togetherness, place where one can strengthen the relationships with the people s/he cares for,	436	7	0.5	325	5	1.5	1	1.5
Storehouse for meaningful objects and material possessions;	422	7	0.5	353	5	1.5	0.5	1
Place in which one feels familiar with the spaces, the smells, the furniture, and the objects;	417	7	1.0	370	5.5	1.5	0	1
Place that gives one a sense of belonging somewhere, of having roots;	411	6	1.0	328	5	1.5	1	1
Place to own;	353	5.5	1.5	154	1	0	3	3
Protection for one's savings;	326	5	2.0	233	3	2.5	0.5	1.5
Investment from which one can expect to make money;	289	4	3.0	140	1	0	1	2
Place that tells people what status one has in society.	263	4	1.5	260	4	1.5	0	0.5

```
┌─────────────────────────────────────────────┐
│              SETS OF FACTORS                  │
├─────────────────────────────────────────────┤
│              PERSONAL FACTORS                 │
│   Homesharer's Personality, Lifestyle and Values │
│       Homesharer's Residential History        │
│         and Future Housing Aspirations        │
│    Presence of and Relationship to Housemate(s) │
│                                               │
│              PHYSICAL FACTORS                 │
│          Location and Neighborhood            │
│   Building & Dwelling Unit Formal Properties  │
│     Semi-fixed Features of Dwelling Unit:     │
│     (Safety Device, Upkeep and Maintenance,   │
│          and Personal Possessions)            │
│                                               │
│              SOCIETAL FACTORS                 │
│  Privileges, Cost and Meaning of Homeownership │
│    Privileges, Cost and Meaning of Tenancy    │
└─────────────────────────────────────────────┘
```

Figure 15.2: Thematic categories of comments made by homesharers during rating task

or micro-social factors have to do with the occupants of the home, their personal characteristics as well as their residential history and future housing aspirations. It also refers to their relationships to other household members, as well as friends, relatives, and neighbors. *Societal* or macro-social factors relate to variables that cannot be easily controled by residents but have different impacts on their experience of home. It includes legal and financial aspects of housing as well as ideological discourses about the home. *Physical* factors refers to the built environment itself. It includes the characteristics of the neighborhood in which a dwelling unit is located, the structural properties of the dwelling unit itself, as well as its semi-fixed features (furniture, upkeep and maintenance, etc.).

Table 15.2 lists the frequencies to which comments were associated with personal, societal or physical factors during the rating task. As the total frequencies indicate, some factors were more powerful than others to account for people's ratings depending of the statement about the home that was evaluated. For instance, statements about home as control and autonomy, as feeling rooted, and as the center of love and togetherness were almost exclusively related to personal factors. Statements about home of safety, as familiar environment and as status were equally related to personal and physical factors but not to societal ones. On the contrary, statements about home as ownership and as investment were mostly related to societal factors. As a general rule, comments expressed for most statements had to do with two sets of factors. Only home as personalization was significantly linked by respondents to the three sets of factors.

The results of the study are presented according to the three general questions of the research: first, homesharers' scheme for an ideal home; second, homesharers' experience of shared housing; and third, conflictual aspects between homesharers' ideal homes and shared housing. Quantitative indicators and qualitative material are both used in the discussion of the results.

What a home should be: Shared notions about the home

When referring to their *ideal home*, homesharers gave higher ratings to home as a safe environment, as control and autonomy, as a place to which bring friends and relatives, as a refuge, and as enough space for rooms for their daily needs. Statements with lower ratings had to do with home as a place to own, as a protection for one's savings, as financial investment and as social status. The first column of Table 15.1 lists the rating scores obtained for the 14 statements by decreasing order of importance. If we take a look at the median ratings (Table 15.1, column 2), the nine first statements listed obtained a "7"—the highest rating possible—with almost no variation among homesharers' answers.[5] This points out that even among non-traditional households living in non- conventional housing, these statements were considered as mandatory dimensions to feel-at-home.[6]

Home as a safe environment and as the locus of control and autonomy were the two statements about the home most highly rated by respondents. Homesharers were unanimous about the importance of these dimensions of home. The meaning of home as safety was related to issues of location and neighborhood. City, suburb or neighborhood crime rates, as well as the type of people living in a neighborhood were related to the feeling of safety in the home. Stable neighborhoods were perceived as safer, mixed-use neighborhoods as more dangerous. The proximity of public housing lowered people's perception of safety. Previous residential burglaries increas ed the importance of this statement in relationship to respondents' ideal home. Even though respondents were unanimous about the the importance of *control and autonomy* within the home, many homesharers who had lived by

---

[5] Quartile deviations of zero indicate statements on which there was almost no variation among respondents' ratings while a higher ones indicate more variation.

[6] We must however acknowledge that these 14 statements about the home were imposed on respondents and that this procedure did not allow respondents to identify other categories of meaning for the home that could have been more specific to homesharers.

Table 15.2: Personal, societal, and physical factors

MEANING OF HOME	SETS OF FACTORS			TOTAL
	PERSONAL	SOCIETAL	PHYSICAL	
Place where one feels physically safe;	55	0	51	106
Place in which one feels familiar with the spaces, the smells, the furniture, and the objects;	42	0	43	85
Place where one can act the way s/he wants;	80	0	11	91
Refuge, place where one can get away from outside pressures;	62	1	23	86
Place where one feels comfortable bringing people in;	56	2	25	83
Storehouse for meaningful objects and material possessions;	25	1	46	72
Enough space and rooms for one's daily needs;	17	0	95	112
Place one can modify and personalize;	53	18	23	94
Place that gives one a sense of belonging somewhere, of having roots;	72	6	12	90
Place of love and togetherness, place where one can strengthen the relationships with othersr;	72	0	1	73
Place that tells people what status one has in society;	31	4	35	70
Protection for one's savings;	50	26	2	78
Place to own;	31	56	0	87
Investment from which one can expect to make money.	13	19	7	39
TOTAL	649	144	374	1157

Note: Number of comments related to personal, societal, and physical factors for the 14 statements read to respondents about the home.

themselves prior to shared housing thought that total control and freedom of action could also limit one's experience of other dimensions of home such as center of relationship with others, center of activities, etc. . . Several respondents insisted that this feeling was not only possible or desirable within the home but also at work and among friends. A few homesharers said that because they were very flexible and adaptable people, they never felt limited in their control and autonomy.

There was a high level of consensus among respondents about home as place in which to bring people and friends and home as refuge. These two statements corresponds to the definition of privacy as the control over social interaction. Homesharers strongly felt that home was the locus *par excellence* for maintaining interpersonal relationship and answering people's desire for social intercourse. Home was also a place to get away from outside pressures. Many homesharers mentioned that home can be too much of a refuge when living alone. Walking in an anonymous crowd, driving a car, or walking in nature were other settings mentioned by respondents to fulfill this need.

In relationship to *home as enough space and rooms for one's daily needs*, people addressed to the spaciousness of the dwelling unit, to the number of separate living spaces, to the spatial organization of the floor plan, to the number and size of the bedrooms, as well as to the quantity of storage available. No mention was made of the housing type (detached houses, duplex, apartment building, etc.) in which they would like to live. Territories within the home were also related to this statement. Desirable additional rooms or spaces in ideal homes most commonly mentioned were den, workshop, office, and/or backyard.

Homesharers felt less strongly about home as as a place that gives one a sense of belonging somewhere, of having roots.[7] Instead, many felt attached to their region or their neighborhood but not to the specific dwelling unit in which they lived. Over one fifth of homesharers did not feel comfortable with being tied up to one specific home at this stage of their life. Rather, they valued mobility and changing environments. Many divorced people who had owned a home in the past did not want to feel a strong attachment to a home anymore. Single-parents gave more importance to this dimension of home because they had children and thought it was fundamental that they felt that way about their home. Generally speaking, older people were the most attached to their home. Memories and length of residency played important roles in people's evaluation of this statement.

---

[7]Many respondents saw two meanings of home in this statement. While most people related to home as sense of belonging somewhere, it was not so of home as rootedness. This might also explain why the statement did not get a higher rating (median rating=6, quartile deviation=1.0).

Homeownership was associated with financial security. The economic privileges of homeownership in the United States—its value as a good investment and the tax benefits attached to it—were referred to by respondents to account for their ratings. On the contrary, a good number of homesharers complained about the high cost and responsibilities of ownership. Additional people stated that homeowner taxes, insurance and maintenance costs were too high for them to think about purchasing a home.

Owning a home was thought to give a person complete freedom of action, as well as more credibility in society. It was said to be *what really makes a home feel like one's* by giving its owner a sense of accomplishment. The insecurity of tenancy in the U.S. was brought up: ownership prevents people from being evicted from their home and gives them more control over their destinies. Restrictions on lease regarding pets, decoration, and/or household composition, as well as management problems in rental apartment buildings were other reasons invoked for wanting to own a home. About one quarter of homesharers indicated that owning a home was not important at this point in their life, that ownership was not necessary to feel-at-home, or else that not owning a home was a pleasurable worry-free life style.

About a third of respondents related *home as a protection for one's savings* to tenure status. Overall, respondents thought that homeownership was among the best way to build equity in the United States. Renting was said to have no economic benefits. If most homesharers thought that owning a home was a protection for one's savings, many were very well aware that they could not afford it. Others doubted the fact that homeownership was such a great investment; the cost of purchasing a home, of maintaining it along with unstable markets and economy were thought to be factors challenging the rentability of owning a home.

The statements home as status symbol and home as financial investment were the two least valued meanings in homesharers' idea of what a home should be. More than a quarter of homesharers indicated that the dimension of home as symbol of social status was unimportant. These people defined their status by who they were—what they believed in and their intellectual backgrounds—rather than by the homes in which they lived. A quarter of homesharers did not make any comments about home as an economic investment; another quarter answered that they did not think of home that way, or that this aspect was unimportant to them. It seems that this statement, added for the purpose of this study, did not correspond to what homesharers thought of a home. Home was not seen as a financial return or an opportunity to make profit: "one can make money on a house, not on a home." Respondents were aware that homeownership was not the only form of investment but they still perceived it as the *best* one in North American society. Some homesharers felt frustrated because of the economic and legal privileges of homeowners compared to those of renters. Speculation was mentioned as one of the major reasons people are so tempted to buy.

The results discussed above indicate that the general categories of meaning for the home as described by the 14 statements were considered to be true in relationship to respondents' evaluation of what their ideal homes should be. No median ratings of less than "4" of a maximum possible of "7" were obtained for any of the statements. A relevant finding is the lower median rating given to *home as permanence and continuity*, which is directly related to the transitional character of homesharers' stage in life cycle. Also, *home as a symbol of social status* was the least important category of meaning for homesharers, even less so than *home as investment* and *home* as *protection for one's savings*. This, most likely, can be attributed to the high level of education of the respondents, along with the postmodern status of our society in which consumption is geared toward services (travels, health clubs, etc) rather than goods (house, furniture, etc.).[8] Finally, among the societal meanings of housing included in the statements, homeownership was rated the highest. People's comments on this statements were related to human/behavioral factors as well as to societal ones.

What home is: The experience of shared housing

The dimension most experienced in shared housing was *home as safe environment*. Comments made by homesharers to account for their ratings were equally related to personal and physical factors. A third of homesharers indicated that by living with adult homemates, they had increased their sense of safety since they would otherwise be living alone. Influential factors in people's perception of safety had to do with the larger scale environment (location, neighborhood) and with being surrounded by people one can trust or count on within and around the home. Good neighbors and homemates enhanced people's feeling of safety. "Feeling safe" was also a matter of personality and of past residential experiences. The floor location and the presence of safety features were perceived as efficient means for increasing security. By doubling up with others, homesharers could afford "safer" neighborhoods.

The second dimension of home most experienced in shared housing was *home as familiar environment*. This dimension of home was expected to get lower ratings because of the presence of homemates' personal belongings

---

[8] There are alternative hypotheses that this low rating is due to the instrument itself or to the purposive type of sample.

and furniture in the shared home. There was however some variation among respondents' ratings. A positive experience of this dimension of home was mostly related to the amount and use of personal possessions within the shared home. It seems that as long as homesharers had their personal belongings in the dwelling unit, this dimension of home could be experienced to a satisfactory degree. A relatively important group of homesharers that described themselves as very adaptable to change and with high tolerances for new environments. Some did not value familiarity as a quality for a home, at least at that point in their lives. The length of time people had lived in their shared homes was also found to be an important factor in accounting for people's ratings. Variations in ratings could be attributed to the status of the homesharer.[9] *Home providers* had their dwelling units furnished with their own furniture except for the room(s) they were renting out while, on the contrary, *home seekers* lived in homes where the only place they had personal belongings was their bedroom.

The third most highly rated statement was *home as a place where people can act the way they want and be themselves.* Respondents related the statement to issues of autonomy, control and privacy. Surprisingly, it came out as one of the most experienced dimensions of home in shared housing. In general, homesharers were respectful of their homemate(s)' need for privacy. Explicit or implicit behavioral rules helped this situation. People with similar personality, life style and values dealt better with this issue, so did homesharers who had known each other before moving into shared housing. Acoustical and visual privacy were found to be very much related to the formal properties of the dwelling unit. The number separate living spaces to entertain or find privacy, as well as their proximity to respondents' bedrooms were important variables on this issue.

The meaning of *home as refuge* was also expected to be less experienced in shared housing because of the presence of unrelated adults in the dwelling unit. A quarter of homesharers felt their shared homes were refuges while about a third said their experience was restricted because of the presence of their homemates, and/or because of the tightness of the dwelling unit or the lack of separate spaces. Interestingly, a good proportion of them indicated that they had chosen shared housing for companionship mentioning that home could be too much of a refuge when living alone. The bedroom came out as the locus of privacy in shared housing. People spent a lot of

---

[9] Three types of homesharer status existed in the sample: (1) home providers were homeowners renting out some extra rooms in their house, or else renters whose name was the only one written on the lease; (2) home seekers were people renting a room in an apartment or a house without having their names written on the lease; finally (3) equal partners were mostly people who shared a house or an apartment with equal legal rights, that is, all names were written on the lease.

time in their bedrooms reading, watching television, entertaining guests, etc...Bedrooms that allowed for unconventional placement of furniture as well as large bedroom with good lighting helped creating a private domain.

The high rating of *home as a place to which one feels comfortable bringing people* was unexpected since it was thought that by sharing their homes with non-family adults, homesharers would feel more restricted in bringing friends and relatives at home. There was however some variation in respondents' judgements. Homesharers who had most positive experiences were those who shared their home with friends or live in extended family type of households. Most respondents answered that it was a matter of deciding *when, how often* and *for how long* one would have guests over. A good proportion of homesharers entertained outside their homes; either they felt uncomfortable doing so at home or they preferred the social dimension of going out with friends. Some respondents felt it was really difficult to entertain friends in their shared homes without interfering with their homemate(s)' privacy. The lack of separate living spaces as well as the state of order of the dwelling unit were additional reasons mentioned for not entertaining at home.

Respondents related *home as a storehouse for meaningful possessions* to the amount of personal belongings they had with them. Most people indicated that they needed to see their things around to feel at-home. Once again, the bedroom came out as the locus of collection. A quarter of homesharers complained about the lack of storage for their own things inside the dwelling unit. Many had part of their belongings stored at either parents', relatives', or friends' homes. Most homesharers did not have difficulty with letting others using their personal belongings or with using those of others. In fact, many did not have much in terms of furniture and personal belongings. People under 30 were especially flexible on this issue. They rather related this meaning to their parents' homes, insisting that they did not own much at this stage of their life. Many single-parents indicated that they would live much lighter if it was not for their children. A category of people qualified themselves as non-materialistic, insisting that they were not collectors. They did not value the meaning of home as a familiar environment, enjoying more the excitement of discovering new environments.

Regarding the statement *home as enough space and rooms for one's daily needs*, about a third of homesharers thought they were living in comfortably sized home. Many mentioned that they had in fact more space than they needed. By splitting up the cost of housing with homemate(s), they were able to afford much larger homes. Others indicated that it was because they had extra space in their homes that they had decided to take in homemate(s).When people complained, it was mostly for the lack of separate living spaces, for the tightness of the bedrooms, or for the lack of storage. The desire for additional living spaces—formal dining room, den or study, etc.—and for additional storage and bathroom was mentioned. In relationship to home as locus of personalization, people's experience of this dimension of home in shared housing was related to the specificity of living with homemate(s). Differences or incompatibilities among homesharers' aesthetic sensibilities and tastes was found to be a most sensitive issue. Most of the time, one homemate was in charge of the decoration or consensus had to be reached among household members. Again, the locus per excellence for personalizing and decorating one's home was the bedroom. An important frustration on the issue of personalization was attributed to the legal restrictions imposed on decoration to tenant and condominium owners.

Comments used by respondents to account for their ratings of *home as providing a sense of belonging somewhere and having roots and home as center of love and togetherness* were the most significantly related to personal factors. Fourteen respondents did not see the nomadic character of shared housing as a problematic aspect of their experience of home since they did not want to feel rooted at this point in their life. Others did not feel that way because of the transitional character of their shared housing situation; t hey knew they would move out eventually. The length of residency of respondents in their shared homes was found to be related to feeling rooted. People who lives in shared households that resembled extended families felt a strong sense of belonging to their home.

The statement *home as a place of love and togetherness* was theoretically one of the most interesting dimensions of home to explore in the context of shared housing since it is often believed that by sharing their home with others, people recreate some kind of extended family. The results indicate that it is not not necessarily true. The type of relationship homesharers have with their homemate(s)—family-like, friendly, business-like—was found to be determinant in this respect. Only a third of homesharers described their shared households as extended families. Many were convinced that this meaning of home could only be experienced in households made up of couples and/or children. Young homesharers felt this meaning of home was true of their parents' home and single-parents that it was more important to their children than to them. Finally, many homesharers thought that home was not the only place where they could experience love and togetherness; travels and work could also enhance this feeling.

The group of statements least experienced by homesharers were *home as ownership, investment, savings and social status*. The limited extent to which these dimensions were experienced in these shared homes is in fact not surprising since three quarters of homesharers were renters. Two thirds of the comments made on *home as ownership* were related to societal factors, one third to personal ones. Homeowners, who knew about the real cost of homeownership, questioned the fact that it was such a great investment. These people were more critical of this meaning as a necessary condition for a home. It seems that once experienced, this legal and economic relationship to the home was perceived more pragmatically. Even though the experience of this dimension of home was low for a large proportion of homesharers, they did not feel the need for owning a home at this point in their life. For some, homeownership was perceived as restraining mobility by tying a person down to a geographical area. On the contrary, shared housing was seen as an option that permitted a more nomadic lifestyle and avoided the responsibilities of homeownership. Some respondents—mostly younger—saw shared housing as a transition toward the purchase of a home.

Regarding *home as a protection for one's savings*, it was the statement for which respondents' answers varied most. Some respondents thought that homeownership was the only way to protect one's savings while others indicated that shared housing allowed them to build up savings by cutting down on housing expenses. They saved money for various purposes—childcare, school tuition, travels, car payments, etc.—, or simply to make ends meet. On the issue of *home as social status*, many homesharers thought it had to do with the neighborhood and the maintenance of the building structure in which their homes were located. A prestigious location was said to give one a higher status while the proximity of public housing was perceived as lowering a neighborhood's reputation. Many people thought that by sharing housing expenses, they were able to afford better housing and neighborhoods and, as a consequence, had gained some status.

Ideal versus shared homes: measuring the gap between the dream and the reality

The next step, after describing homesharers' degree of agreement with the 14 statements in relationship to first, what they thought their ideal home should be and second, what their experiences of shared housing were, is to evaluate the gap between the dream and the reality. Dimensions of home highly valued but little experienced in shared housing could constitute lived contradictions for homesharers. The median differences between ideal home and current home ratings for each of the fourteen statements that are listed on Columns 7 and 8 of Table 15.1 were used as quantitative indicators of this discrepancy. The statement *home as a place to own* shows the highest median difference (3) between homesharers ideal and shared home ratings. Nine additional statements have median differences of 1, which seems to indicate a relatively small discrepancy between dream homes and experienced shared dwellings (although some statements show more variation among respondents' differences between their ideal home and shared home ratings). Finally, four statements have median differences of zero or 0.5 which indicate that these dimensions of home were experienced to an extent that somehow met homesharers' expectations for a home. These were: *home as familiar environment, home as storehouse for meaningful possessions, home as social status and home as protection for one's savings* (although the last dimension showed more variation among respondents' answers).

In general, shared housing fitted less men's aspirations for a home than it did for women. The median differences between their ideal and shared homes ratings being higher than those of women in 10 statements out of 14. They resented their incapacity to make an investment out of their monthly housing payment in shared housing. They were also more frustrated about not feeling comfortable to bring family and friends in their homes. Moreover, the transitional character of shared housing matched less their desire for home as providing a *sense of belonging somewhere, of having roots.*

For never married homesharers, it is as a *place of love and togetherness* and as *providing a sense of belonging and feeling rooted* that shared housing met least their expectations. The typical tenant status of homesharers did not match their desire for homeownership, as well as for home as a *protection for one's savings and an economic investment.* Divorced or separated people resented more the human and physical aspects of shared housing in relationship to their ideal of a home, especially in relationship to *home as place to which bring people and friends, refuge, enough space and rooms for one's daily needs,* and *personalization.* Shared housing matched better widows' ideals of what a home should be. Length of residency played a considerable role in this strong attachment to the home. The only small discrepancy was found for the statement *home as love and togetherness.* The death of a spouse and/or the departure of children making it harder to recreate this experience within the home.

Single-parents' ratings show larger median differences between ideal home and shared housing compared to singles. Important gaps between their expectations for a home and their shared dwellings were found on the issues of *home as control and freedom of action, refuge,* and place to personalize; although the largest gap concerned an economic aspect of housing— home as a financial investment. Singles felt more frustrated about *home as a place of love and togetherness.* The presence of children seemed to be sufficient to fulfill single-parents' expectations on this issue. Singles thought of shared housing as a friendly place but not as the center of intense emotional experience expected of family-living situations.

Conclusion

Quantitative indicators and qualitative data showed that shared housing can be a type of housing arrangements that without corresponding to the American Dream can fulfill people's need for a home at some stages of the life cycle. Because shared housing was perceived by homesharers as an intermediate phase toward the establishment or re-establishment of their home, it was not necessarily conflicting with their long-term housing aspirations but was rather perceived as a step toward reaching them. Homesharers generally agreed with meanings of home that had been identified in the context of more traditional households. Their dream homes were not that different from those of people living in more conventional housing arrangements. Young people expected to get marry, to have children, and/or to buy a house at some point in the future, single-parents wished to reconstitute a family, widowed women dreamed of a home that had disappeared at the death of their husband. The multiple frustrations of not-feeling-at-home in shared housing anticipated at the beginning of the study were not found to be experienced to significant levels. It is as if homesharers had different expectations for a home at that point of their lives. The transitional or temporary character of their shared housing arrangements allowed them to enlarge their vision of home. The comments made by homesharers to interpret the similarity or dissimilarity between ideal and shared homes' ratings of 14 meanings of home were not necessarily related to the specificity of shared housing, but also to respondents' personal characteristics and residential history, as well as to physical and societal factors.

The strengths of the methodological approach developed for this study are that: (1) it not only investigated the meaning of home for homesharers but compared it to their experiences of shared housing; (2) it identified commonly accepted meanings of home for a non-typical segment of the population; and (3), it explored how different meanings of home are associated by homesharers to human/behavioral, societal and physical factors. One of the weaknesses of the methodology is that, although the rating task was a very efficient device to elicit verbal data, the ratings obtained on the 14 statements for the two levels of questioning (ideal and current home) were quite similar. This instrument might not be strong enough as a quantitative indicator. A ranking or sorting task of the meanings commonly identified in literature on home environments might have been a more efficient technique. The investigation of the meaning of home through the analysis of respondents' spoken discourses is not sufficient. The structural properties of their dwellings as well as the use they make of them need to be considered. In fact, two additional cognitive tasks (not presented in the context of this chapter) using visual material were also part of the research instruments. Many respondents also had difficulties articulating their thoughts about societal factors even though the analysis of their open-ended comments indicated the need to measure their impact on the meaning of home. Regulations, ideological discourses having an influence on people's life in their home also need to be investigated objectively.

The results indicate that it is not so much the quantitative data from the rating task that provided the most useful information but rather the open-ended comments that were generated by respondents during the task. In other words, the combined use of quantitative and qualitative instruments produced a set of data that could not have been obtained by the exclusive use of one or the other. This type of combination of quantitative and qualitative methods should be further explored in meaning of home studies.

References

Altman, I., Werner, C. (eds) (1985) *Home Environments.* New York: Plenum.

Baker, M.W., Kramer, E., Gilbert, G. (1987) *The Pier Import 1 Study of the American Home.* Louis Harris and Associates, Research Report #871025.

Canter, D., Brown, J., Groat, L. (1985) A multiple sorting procedure for studying conceptual systems. In D. Canter (ed) *Facet theory: approaches to social research.* New York: Springger-Verlag.

Csikszentmihalyi, M., Rochberg–Halton, E. (1981) *The meaning of things: domestic symbols and the self.* New York: Cambridge University Press.

Despres, C. (1991a) The meaning of home: literature review and directions for future research and theory development. In R.J. Lawrence (ed) *The meaning and use of home and neighborhood.* Special issue of the *Journal of Architecture and Planning Research,* 8(2): 96- 115.

Despres, C. (1991b) *The form, meaning and experience of home in shared housing.* Doctoral Dissertation, University of Wisconsin-Milwaukee.

Dovey, K. (1988) Place, ideology and postmodernism. Proceedings of the Conference of the International Association for the Study of People and their Physical Surroundings (IAPS), (275-285). Delft, The Netherlands, 1988.

Franck, K.A. (1987) Shared Spaces, small spaces, and spaces that change: examples of housing innovation in the United States. In W. van Vliet, H. Choldin, W.Michelson & D. Popenoe (eds) *Housing and neighborhoods: theoretical and empirical contributions,* (157-172). New York : Greenwood Press.

Garling, T. (1976) The structural analysis of environmental perception and cognition: a multidimensional scaling approach. *Enviornment & Behavior*, 8(3): 385-415.

Gurney, C. (1990) *The meaning of home in the decade of owner occupation.* Working Paper. School for Advanced Urban Studies, University of Bristol, England.

Groat, L. (1982) Meaning in post-modern architecture: an examination using the multiple sorting task. *Journal of Environmental Psychology*, 2: 3-22.

Hayward, G. (1977) Psychological concept of home. *HUD Challenge*, February 1977.

Horne, J., Baldwin, L. (1988) *Homesharing and other life-style options.* Washington, D.C.: American Association of Retired Persons.

Kelley, G. (1955) *A theory of personality : the psychology of personal constructs.* New York: The Norton Library, 1963.

Lawrence, R.J. (1989) Structuralist theories in environment-behavior design research. In E. Zube & G.T. Moore (eds) *Advances in Environment, Behavior, and Design*, (37-70). Vol. 2. New York: Plenum.

Lawrence, R.J. (1987) *Housing, dwellings and homes.* New York: Wiley.

Low, S., Chambers, E. (1990) *Housing, culture, and design.* Philadelphia: University of Pennsylvania Press.

Moudon, A.V.–, Sprague, C. (1983) More than one: a second life for the single-family property. *Built Environment*, 8(1):54-59.

Osgood, C. et al (1957) *The measurement of meaning.* Urbana: University of Illinois Press.

Pred, A. (1983) Structuration and place : on the becoming of sense of place and structure of feeling. *Journal of the Theory of Social Behavior*, 13: 45-68.

Rakoff, R, M. (1977) The ideology in eveyday life: the meaning of the house, *Politics and Society*, 7(1): 85-104.

Sebra, R., Churchman, A. (1986) The uniqueness of the home. *Architecture and Behavior*, 3(1): 7-24.

Sixsmith, J. (1986) The meaning of home: an exploratory study of environmental experience. *Journal of Environmental Psychology*, 6: 281-298.

Chapter 16

The Study of Collective Housing: A Swedish Perspective

DICK URBAN VESTBRO
The Royal Institute of Technology, Stockholm

This chapter initially summarizes the goals for a variety of collective house forms developed in Sweden, as have been presented in research during the 80s. The possible biases and other theoretical problems in this type of research are then discussed. The main focus is on the application of an integrative methodology applied in one of the most comprehensive research projects. Nine different methods for the study of nine different aspects of collective housing are discussed. Among the nine methods are: analysis of municipal and other official documents; analysis of minutes, proposals and reports from residents' associations; key person interviewing; inquiries with structured questionnaires; group interviewing; observation; participant observation; and analysis of drawings.

The nine aspects of collective housing cover: the role of this housing type in the social policy of Sweden; how local governments and housing companies formulate their goals for housing experiments; the recruitment of suitable residents; how municipal services can be used as an instrument for social integration of the elderly and persons with disabilities; the problem of communal meals; tenant-management relations and resident participation in building administration; and the question of suitable spatial organization and other design considerations.

Introduction

Along with Denmark and Holland, Sweden has a leading position in the
development of collective housing with shared facilities such as dining hall,
club rooms, sauna and workshops. Apart from units for special categories
such as elderly and students, and communes living in large one-family apartments, the number of functioning Swedish collective housing units exceeds
50, comprising altogether 2,800 apartments. All except three of these units
were built in the 80s. The three are the surviving ones from Sweden's pioneering experiments with housing based on service through employed staff
in the period 1935-1970.

Compared to Denmark and Holland, where collective housing is even
more prevalent, collective housing in Sweden has been characterized by a
high degree of involvement by local governments and municipal housing
companies. This means on the one hand that collective housing is more
institutionalized than in other countries, and on the other, that it is accessible to ordinary tenants, and not only to an educated élite. Collective
housing units are mainly built for anonymous users, which in turn means
that housing companies to a large extent rely on documented experience
and research, rather than on direct contacts with the users, as in the case
of most Danish and Dutch projects.

Research on Swedish collective housing has probably been more extensive than in any other country. A few years back more than 20 Swedish
researchers were involved in studies related to communal living. Most of
these studies have been financed by the Swedish Council for Building Research. A review of this research has been made by Vestbro (1988), partially
summarized in English by Woodward (1988).

Goals of collective housing

What makes collective living so attractive for research is the fact that new
qualities in housing are addressed. Qualities usually referred to are those related to women's liberation, a better environment for children, good neighborly relations and meaningful leisure time activities. These qualities are
often advocated by groups which question traditional values related to family and housing.

In all Swedish collective housing units built before 1970 the dominant
goal was to reduce and simplify house work in order to enable for women
to join the labor market. The 18 units from that period were all based
on services through employed staff. Although the pioneers of collective
housing were members or sympathizers of the labor movement, the idea of

self help, as it existed in the impoverished workers' quarters, never reached the collective housing debate during this period. Instead collective housing was intended to be based on a division of labor as described by Caldenby & Walldén (1979) and by Vestbro (1982; summarized in English by Vestbro, 1989). Not until the Swedish housing crisis occurred in the middle of the 70s, were social goals such as elimination of alienation, promotion of neighborly cooperation and integration of the elderly and the handicapped were widely adopted, as reported by Sanne (1983) and Woodward *et al* (1989). Still these goals were more frequent in policy documents than in real housing projects.

In the '70s, feminist organizations started to object to the depreciation of women's work at home, as reflected in the earlier collective housing experiments. Instead feminists argued that house work was just as productive and valuable for society as work in the "productive sector". The negative thing about house work was that everyone has to do it alone in an isolated apartment. By carrying it out together with others, house work could be enjoyable, it was argued. The classical Swedish collective housing units were rejected as being too big (60-1250 apartments) and based on an unequal division of labor. A group of female architects, journalists and others developed an alternative model in a book by Berg *et al* (1982) which became a manifesto for a new type of collective housing based on a smaller unit (30-50 apartments) where residents could find a sense of community in carrying out house work together. The building programme presented in this report (widely publicized already since 1979) became the blueprint for about 35 collective housing units built in the 80s. Here this alternative is called the self-work model.

What opened the door to public support for collective housing was still another goal, however. In the 70s it was noticed by some observers that collective housing was an attractive solution for single parents, a rapidly growing type of household. While in conventional housing these parents and children were isolated in their private apartments, they could easily find friends and plenty of attractive indoor space in collective housing. Single parents could find babysitters for evenings allocated for tasks outside the home. As single mothers usually have had low incomes, their interest in collective housing contributed to the eradication of the idea that collective housing was a solution only for the privileged.

Equally important were ideas raised by local politicians and functionaries of social authorities to integrate the elderly and people with disabilities in collective housing. In Stockholm and some other Swedish cities social services such as restaurants, children's nurseries and care for the elderly were introduced as instruments for social integration in collective housing units. The social goals of integration were combined with economic goals such as efficiency in meal services and more intensive use of hobby rooms, sport facilities and workshops (Woodward *et al*, 1989). The most well known example of this type of integration was the Stolplyckan housing unit in Linköping, comprising 184 apartments, of which 35 were allocated for old and handicapped persons, as described by Krantz & Pedersen (1989).

All the new Swedish collective housing projects strove to promote a spirit of community. In the majority of cases this spirit was to be achieved not only through the sharing of certain spaces but also by sharing tasks such as cleaning and making food together. Yet another goal was to improve tenant-management relations and tenant involvement in building maintenance and management. Although public housing in Sweden has not been stigmatized as a solution for unprivileged groups, as in other countries, it has been evident that vandalism and lack of consideration for the environment have contributed to increases in maintenance costs. This has promoted a more positive attitude to collective housing by managements, which otherwise are sceptical to such alternatives.

Different types of collective housing

From the discussion above it is evident that there are various types of collective housing, and that the goals may vary widely. By describing the different house forms an operational definition of collective housing is obtained. In accordance with other scholars such as Woodward (1988) and Franck & Ahrentzen (1989), I use the word collective housing as equal to communal housing. The following types of collective housing can thus be distinguished:

1. *Housing communes*, housing where a group of persons, who are not relatives, live and eat together, usually in a one-family unit.

2. *Production communes*, units where a group of people, who are not relatives, work and live together.

3. *Collective housing for special categories* such as elderly people and students.

4. *Cohousing* (Danish: *bofællesskab*), where a group of people plan their houses collectively, often with other communal facilities than a central kitchen and not necessarily with indoor communications to common rooms.

5. *Service blocks* or *integrated service centres*, housing areas with collective services above the normal standard, spread out in the area.

6. *Collective housing units* (Swedish: *kollektivhus*), projects with a central kitchen, dining hall and other communal facilities connected by indoor communication to individual apartments.

7. The last type can be divided into three categories:

a. *The classical collective housing unit*, based on services through employed staff, including a restaurant.

b. Collective housing units combined with service housing for the elderly.

These two categories are sometimes referred to as *the service supported model*.

c. *The small collective housing unit* or *the self-work model*, based on the residents' own collective work.

While residents in housing communes form one household, residents in types 3 to 6 have their own apartments so that private life can be separated from communal activities. Production communes may consist of either one household or several private apartments. Collective housing for the elderly is usually called service housing in Sweden. For the 4th type, which is virtually non-existent in Sweden, there is no widely accepted term, except for the Danish *bofælleskab*. Two US housing experts have introduced the term cohousing for this alternative (McCamant & Durrett, 1989). This form of collective housing often consists of terraced or low-rise, high density housing around communal indoor and outdoor facilities. It is distinguished from the typical Swedish collective housing unit, where apartments in high or medium rise buildings are connected by indoor corridors and staircases to the communal rooms. Historically the Swedish collective housing unit has been defined by collective meal services, which does not always exist in the other types.

So called service blocks or integrated service centres—with facilities such as home service for the elderly, day care centres, meal catering, reception and maintenance services - were introduced in Sweden in the 1970s in order to raise the service standard without tying the services to certain buildings. This type is difficult to distinguish from conventional housing, but it is nevertheless logical to include it here, as it is based on collective services as in the classical collective housing unit. In fact, integrated service centres were introduced as an alternative to the collective housing unit by politicians who were opposed to what they considered to be lack of privacy in collective housing.

Våningsplan, 1:300

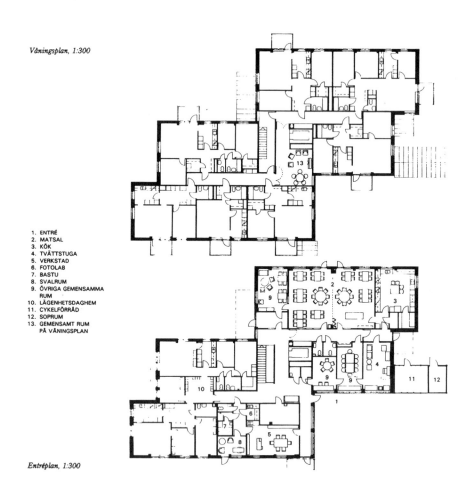

1. ENTRÉ
2. MATSAL
3. KÖK
4. TVÄTTSTUGA
5. VERKSTAD
6. FOTOLAB
7. BASTU
8. SVALRUM
9. ÖVRIGA GEMENSAMMA
   RUM
10. LÄGENHETSDAGHEM
11. CYKELFÖRRÅD
12. SOPRUM
13. GEMENSAMT RUM
    PÅ VÅNINGSPLAN

Entréplan, 1:300

Figure 16.1: Floor plan of the Prästgårdshagen collective housing unit

1. Ground floor of the Prästgårdshagen collective housing unit. 2. Dining hall, 3. Kitchen, 4. Laundry, 5. Ceramic workshop, 6. Photo lab, 7. Sauna, 8. Rest room, 9. Office/smoking room, 10. Children's nursery.

How to avoid bias

As collective housing constitutes a challenge to prevailing ideas and myths easily formed about implemented projects. Opponents are likely to look for failures, while the collectivists might have an interest in ignoring the negative aspects. Therefore research by independent persons, using reliable methods, is highly desirable. This does not mean that collectivists cannot make research about their own experiences. A good example of such a study is the report on the Hässelby family hotel, one of the surviving classical collective housing units. The study was carried out by five persons, four of whom lived in the Hässelby unit (Blomberg *et al*, 1986). The report does give a partial user view, for instance of conflicts with the housing company, but on the other hand the user view is very fruitful when coming to the description of the psychological dynamics of the collective.

Although some outside researchers have gone quite far in penetrating the personal motives for communal living in another Swedish unit, documented by Caldenby & Walldén (1984), the report on the Hässelby family hotel shows that personal involvement can be a rich source of knowledge. The vivid description of the frustrations involved when residents "get married" to the collective, does not seem to conceal the negative aspects since at the same time, the analysis is permeated by a basic sympathy for the idea of collective housing. Dedication could be a guarantee for objectivity in the sense that advocates of alternative house forms should be the first ones to bring out the negative aspects in order to trace its roots and possibly suggest measures to avoid them.

Most Swedish research on collective living has been carried out by persons who have been sympathetic to this idea, even if they have not practiced it themselves. This might have resulted in a tendency to be selective in favour of the positive aspects. On the other hand one may argue that, in a situation where the preconceived and hostile attitudes are dominating, it is the duty of the researcher to bring out the missing factors. I am confident that Swedish research into collective housing, and the debate accompanying it, has greatly contributed to counteract prejudicial ideas about collective living.

One of the preconceived ideas, which was frequently heard earlier, was the statement that the classical collective housing units were failures. It is true that some of them survived as collective experiments only a few years, and that others had their services "decollectivized" gradually. Does this mean that they actually were failures? Considering the over-optimistic goals of the early experiments, one may perhaps say that implementation was the failure, but if goals had been more humble, results might not have been so discouraging. Research by Vestbro (1982) shows that collective housing was not allowed conditions equal to other types of housing. Municipalities were, for instance, reluctant to offer attractive plots, and the housing authorities did not want to provide financial assistance at fair conditions. Therefore it can be debated whether the failure lay in the housing experiment itself or in the society.

Some of the classical Swedish collective housing units functioned well for a period of 30 years or more. Laundry and house cleaning services disappeared, but the meal service and a well established community spirit often remained. The latter factor was not among the goals from the beginning, but became the most important motive for collective housing later on. Thus failure can be noted in relation to certain goals, at the same time as success is documented in relation to other goals, added afterwards.

An interesting question is whether resistance from established society has contributed to success rather than to failure. Experiments carried out by dedicated people, welded together by a common vision, could have better chances to survive than those initiated from above. Perhaps the most interesting examples of such experiments are the communitarian socialists settlements of 19th century USA, discussed by Hayden in her book *Seven American Utopias* (1977).

Are conventional house forms successful? Although they dominate production, it is not difficult to find negative aspects. In the US context such factors have been elaborately analysed by Hayden (1981, 1984). Considering the fact that collective housing has constituted only a minute fraction of the housing stock, and that this type of housing has been the only serious alternative to conventional forms of housing, one may argue that research which presents the views of the pro-collectivists is much needed.

How to evaluate a building experiment?

When it comes to evaluation of single collective housing experiments, the discussion above has shown that such projects can be evaluated in many different ways. This is illustrated in figure 16.2.

Most studies of collective housing projects have described the selected experiment in comparison with conventional house forms (relation 2 in Figure 16.2). Often these comparisons have been based on assumed characteristics of conventional house forms, without regard for the large differences existing among these house forms. It has been apparent, for instance, that some of the conventional housing developments have shown a high degree of neighborly cooperation. This fact makes it difficult to draw conclusions about the influence of the house form upon cooperation between neighbors, as demonstrated by Bell & Westius (1972).

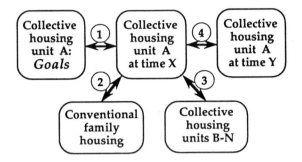

Figure 16.2: Alternate orientations of research project design

Possible alternative orientations of research projects designed to evaluate a single housing experiment

In journalistic descriptions of collective housing there has been a tendency to mix goals with reality. It could, for instance, be reported that residents spend three hours cooking once every second week, because this has been decided by the residents' association, whereas in practice some members keep avoiding their duties and others do more than their stipulated share. This tendency to confuse goals and reality may be explained by the fact that housing experiments have been considered interesting only when projects have just started, i.e. at a time when the participants themselves have been strongly influenced by goal discussions and when routine procedures have not yet been worked out. This journalistic bias has also been found in research reports, as there has been a tendency to initiate research projects when the issue is still "hot". In order to avoid such a bias, methods are needed which clarify the difference between goals and realized project (relation 1 in Figure 16.2).

It is well known that residents' behavior in any new housing area is characterized by a certain turbulence the first years after occupation. In Swedish rental housing there has been a high degree of mobility during the first years. Moreover, in collective housing there is a strong component of dynamism within the collective, which has often resulted in a continuously changing social situation. Surveys of attitudes and use of space therefore run the risk of being outdated already before the research report has been published. In order to counteract this, the same project could be studied with the same methods at different times (relation 4). Such studies may trace interesting changes in attitudes and functions, and reveal the degree of adaptability of the physical structure. In one of the Swedish research projects, presented by Krantz and Pedersen (1989), the study included interviewing before moving (documenting expectations), just after moving, and a couple of years after moving into the collective housing unit. Such an approach can be expected to provide the best possible basis for evaluation of a housing project. Unfortunately this research project has not yet resulted in a final report.

Another useful approach is to compare collective housing units with each other (relation 3 in Figure 16.2). This makes is easier to determine which features that are permanent and which are more temporary. McCamant & Durrett (1989: 36, 172f) have applied this approach fruitfully in their study of Danish cohousing. They could, for instance, draw some quite definite conclusions about common characteristics of the studied projects, and make useful remarks about design considerations. In my research I have used this approach in two different studies.

Methods of investigation

In a study made by Woodward, Grossman, and Vestbro four collective housing units of two different models, in two different towns (Stockholm and Uppsala) were compared. This study is documented in a Swedish report by Woodward *et al* (1989) and in two English essays by Woodward (1988, 1989). The major questions were: the extent to which the collective housing units lived up to their goals of social integration between residents, and of increasing tenant influence over housing management; the growth of a community spirit around aspects of everyday life, including meals and child care; and the importance of spatial organization and other design considerations. The units were studied from the planning stage onwards over a period of seven years, with the most intensive field work carried out between 1984 to 1986.

Considering the complexity of the problems, we decided to use a wide range of methods, most of which have been listed in Figure 16.3. Our study was the first one to make systematic comparisons between different collective housing units. Therefore we were obliged to have a representative sample of households. We decided to select all residents above the age of 12 in all four units (300 households) for an inquiry. This method, and group interviewing, both required the active participation of the residents.

Normally these methods are considered less useful because people are

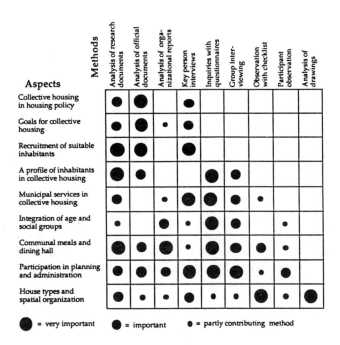

Figure 16.3: Investigation methods and their importance

Investigation methods and their importance for the study of selected aspects of four collective housing units in Stockholm and Uppsala. "Very important" implies either that the indicated method has been used substantially, or that this method was particularly fruitful for the specified aspect.

known to be reluctant to fill in inquiry forms, and because interviewing with a tape recorder in front of neighbors make respondents unwilling to participate. In case of residents of collective housing experiments, the situation could be expected to be different, however. The residents themselves were interested in the results of the study and could be expected not to hesitate to make their contribution. They even volunteered to distribute and collect the questionnaires. This resulted in an extremely high frequency of responses (78 per cent). Speculations have been made that scholars have given preference to this type of research just because they expect a high degree of cooperation by the residents, which is seldom the case in conventional housing studies (Lindberg, 1980).

As can be seen in Figure 16.3, *theoretical and empirical research docu-*

ments were used to analyse all selected aspects of collective living. Besides this, we found useful information in official documents of municipal and other authorities. Three of the four selected housing units were situated in Stockholm, where the collective housing initiative was taken by the city assembly. Also in cases when housing experiments are initiated by others, it has been standard practice in Sweden to refer proposals such as these to several local authorities, which are then requested to submit written statements before decisions are taken. In this case there turned out to be almost one hundred written documents produced by the city assembly, municipal authorities, housing companies, and other official organs. In order to get a full picture of the procedures behind the first collective housing units of the new type, a chronology of events was made, covering a period of more than 20 years.

The *analysis of the official documents* revealed that decision-makers' attitudes towards collective housing changed significantly at the end of the 70s, so that collective housing for the first time became part of the social housing policy of the city of Stockholm. Figure 16.3 shows that the official documents were the main sources of information for the analysis of collective housing as part of the official housing policy, and for the assessment of the goals of the selected housing projects. As we were aware that official documents such as these might conceal interesting conflicts, and perhaps other than official motives were behind the various decisions, we had to rely on other sources for the analysis of the two first aspects shown in Figure 16.3. A useful supplementary source of information was interviews with key persons. These helped us to interpret the written documents in a different way than we could otherwise have done.

A special source of information is constituted by the great number of *documents produced by the organization* of collectivists. In conventional rental housing there is no requirement that residents form an association, but in the new type of collective housing, it is stipulated that the contract holder belongs to a residents' association, which takes the responsibility to carry out certain tasks. The residents usually meet once a month and in most cases there are several working groups in charge of tasks such as purchase of food, activities for children, gardening, interior decoration, public relations, house rent negotiations, and revision of statutes. Most of these committees produce minutes, reports and written proposals, which are filed in archives available to the residents. In three of the four housing units studied the tenants had their own house journal.

All these documents were put at our disposal and we could use them for our chronology and for tracing interesting conflicts among the residents. They could also be used to illustrate certain problems in the words of the residents themselves, instead of our formulating the points in a less lively way. The organizational reports were especially useful when analysing the most controversial problems of the four units: the use of the dining hall and the organization of the common meals. The method was also used to trace problems related to the integration of various age groups and to the participation of residents in the administration of the building.

Interviews with key persons is a well known method, which does not require much commenting. Such interviews were started already in 1981 as part of another research project, which was later integrated into the main one. Key persons in this case consisted of politicians besides functionaries of housing companies, the town planning office, and of other local authorities. The method was used for all aspects except the analysis of the social composition of residents. We made it a principle that two of the three researchers should be present at each interview so that interpretation of replies could be more accurate. Besides tape recording the interview, we documented the interview situation by noting body language, what was said after the tape recorder was switched off, and other circumstances of interest. Key persons were frequently asked about their personal attitudes to collective housing, and we found that some of those in influential positions were quite hostile to the decision of the city assembly, thus contributing to the relative failure of one of the collective housing models used in Stockholm.

The most time-consuming method was the *inquiry* with all residents above the age of 12. We considered this method important for tracing the opinions of the passive residents. As complete anonymity was guaranteed, possible suppressed views could be revealed, as well as other types of odd information which would not be expressed publicly. The main reason for the inquiry to all households was, however, to get a proper base for statistical analysis. Sociologist Alison Woodward had the main responsibility for this part of the project.

A working group was formed in each housing unit to assist in distributing and collecting the questionnaires. These groups were also requested to propose questions of their own, and to participate in testing the preliminary version of the questionnaire. In this way new interesting questions were added, and unclear questions could be rephrased or taken away. Some of the questions were selected from studies of conventional rental housing, and of other collective housing units, in order to enable comparisons. As the four selected housing units were all different in some aspects, special questions had to be included for each unit, which meant that four different questionnaires had to be printed. Altogether 71 questions were included, many of which had subquestions. To write down so many answers is usually more than most respondents accept, but in this case the motivation was strong enough to result in a very high coverage.

Most of the questions had fixed alternative replies, but quite a few were open, allowing for the respondents' free articulation. In inquiries with questionnaires, open questions are usually avoided, because people tend to leave them out, and because the replies are difficult to classify for statistical analysis. In our case the replies to these questions turned out to be a gold mine of detailed and articulate information about aspects which we would otherwise have missed. The reason for this can probably be attributed to the fact that the residents were themselves unusually interested in their housing situation, and they had the capacity to express themselves in an articulate way. As could be expected, the inquiry could not very well cover the three background aspects or the question of spatial organization, but for all other aspects the inquiry method was very important.

Group interviewing was included in order to deepen the analysis on certain points and to provide supplementary information where the inquiry was insufficient. This method could also be used to trace problems in a formulative study. As the group interviews were carried out almost a year after the inquiry, this method was helpful in tracing changes in the social dynamic of the collective. We randomly selected ten persons in each building and prepared a checklist of aspects to be covered during the interview. Otherwise the intention was to let the respondents talk freely. Of course, there was a risk that respondents readjusted their replies in front of others, but we considered the group interviews to be quite useful for sorting out unclear points and for tracing contradictory attitudes to the functioning of the housing unit. From Figure 16.3 it can be seen that group interviewing covered exactly the same aspects as the inquiry. Group interviewing is, of course, cheaper than individual interviewing.

For the study of use of space *the observation method* is often applied. In this case we also wanted to use it for the study of social life in the dining hall, of integration of age groups, and of the various activities taking place in common spaces. For this purpose a special form was worked out. It turned out, however, to be very time-consuming and not as rewarding as expected. Therefore systematic observation was interrupted and replaced by more spontaneous observations. These were quite important for the analysis of spatial organization and other design aspects. The actual and possible use of space can be studied not only by observing people, but also by noting such things as furnishing, other types of equipment, sign boards, graffiti and other contributions made by the inhabitants, visual connections between spaces, how the light falls.

One of the researchers happened to get an apartment in one of the collective housing units selected for study. This created a problem in the sense that special loyalties could be expected to occur, at the same time as the method of *participant observation* could be used for more detailed information and for comparisons with other methods. We decided to proceed as planned, and to compensate for the possible bias by requesting the other two researchers to scrutinize the writings of the participant observer more carefully. The participant observer actually moved out of the house before the final manuscript was written.

In fact, all the three of us acted as participant observers in the sense that we invited ourselves many times for supper and to residents' meetings, at which occasions we took note of everything we could observe. In order not to affect the situation we decided from the beginning not to let ourselves become involved in conflicts or to express our opinions.

The method of participant observation has been applied to an even larger extent in other research projects, for instance by McCamant & Durrett in their study of Danish cohousing. Their conclusions seem to be coloured by their strong sympathy for the collectives where they lived, but they find no reason to make any reservations about possible biases.

A final method used was the *analysis of drawings*. This was applied to analyse the relationship between building type and the layout of the apartments. It was found that all four housing units deviated from established Swedish building practice, either by reducing the space of individual apartments, or by applying building types which have disadvantages in sun orientation or internal communication systems. Partly these deviations could be explained by the goal to obtain common space without raising the costs, i.e. by reducing private space accordingly. A supplementary explanation was, however, the fact that classical building types such as the "lamel block" and the "point block" (tower building) were gradually being abandoned in house production in general, as part of the rejection of functionalism, in favour of more complicated hybrids of classical multi-family building types. In the case of the Prästgårdshagen collective housing unit a point block solution and a unit based on internal corridor has been combined quite successfully.

For the analysis of the communication system in relation to the common rooms we took our inspiration from a study of transitional zones in collective housing units, made by Karin Palm Lindén of the Department of Building Function Analysis at the University of Lund. Palm Lindén in turn has applied a revised version of Bill Hillier's method for Space Syntax analysis. She has classified the Swedish collective housing units according to type of communication system and the location of common rooms into 20 different possible combinations (Palm Lindén, 1987; and in a forthcoming doctor's thesis).

One point of our study of the space system was to understand whether the various communal spaces are located at the right spot or not. Accessibility, integration and overview were the three key concepts in this analysis. Accessibility in this case was not only a question of proximity, but also de-

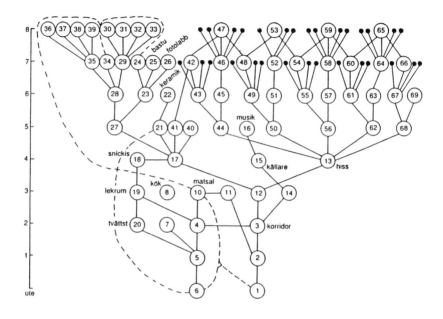

Figure 16.4: Room system in the Prästgårdshagen collective housing unit

Graphic illustration of the room system in the Prästgårdshagen collective housing unit.
Each ring with its number represents a common space (regardless of size). Filled black
dots represent private apartments and dotted lines represent outdoor connections (used
during the summer season).

pended on the likelihood that the residents would pass the common rooms
in such a way that they could easily drop in and leave casually. This spatial
quality was based on the assumption that community participation should
be fully voluntary and spontaneous. Thus common rooms should be located close to where everybody passed and have glass walls for maximum
overview.

How the room system is organized could also be expected to affect the
sense of security in the building. All four units had experienced burglaries
and minor cases of vandalism, which emphasizes the demand for overview.
This demand came into conflict with the demand for freedom of choice in
moving around in the building. Should it be possible to reach one's pri-

vate flat without being seen by other residents, or should the space system be organized in a way to force everybody to pass the communal rooms? None of the four selected buildings have solved this dilemma in a fully satisfactory manner, according to our judgement. The four units demonstrated interesting differences in space systems. The main conclusion is that the potential residents should be selected in such a good time that they have a chance to influence the design of the building. This was the case with the Prästgårdshagen unit, which greatly contributed to the relatively high level of satisfaction amongs the residents of this unit.

Conclusions about methods

The listing of research methods according to problem aspects as shown in Figure 16.3 provides a useful basis for an evaluation of methodologies in this type of housing research. Here only a few aspects will be discussed.

Figure 16.3 reveals an empty triangle in the top right corner. This is partly due to the fact that the residents had fairly little knowledge about the background to the respective housing project (the first three aspects). In Stockholm politicians and functionaries of municipal housing companies took the initiative in the three housing experiments selected for study, which means that the residents had very little to say about the planning process. In Uppsala the initiative was taken by a local association for collective housing, but most of the members of this association did not move into the new collective housing unit since they had to wait for the building to be ready. The few remaining initiators were interviewed as key persons, and not as ordinary residents, about background factors.

The empty triangle is also explained by the fact that almost all chosen methods turned out to be useful in one way or another for the five last aspects. This was not entirely planned from the beginning, but became a good source for cross-checking in the process of analysis. It turned out, for instance, that the tenants themselves discussed most of the selected research aspects during their meetings, documented in reports or house journals. We considered these sources valuable for articulating the views of the residents. Such documentation, of course, seldom exists among residents in conventional housing areas.

Most of the methods considered "important" or "partly contributing" have been included for supplementary information, and not necessarily for evaluating information acquired through another method. Key person interviews were, however, used for controlling information abstracted from written documents. Group interviewing had the same function in relation to the method inquiry with questionnaire. Thus key person interviews and group interviewing was used both for cross-checking replies and for interpreting information obtained through other methods. Yet it should be noted that there is still ample room for other interpretations than those made in our report (Woodward *et al*, 1989).

A pertinent question is whether some methods could have been avoided to save time and money. As mentioned above, systematic observation according to a check list was abandoned because it was considered to be too time-consuming in comparison to the expected results. The most time-consuming method was the inquiry. If this method had been excluded resources could have been saved only to the detriment of findings which could be generalized. Definite conclusions about differences between the four units could not have been made with any accuracy, and the opinions of the silent residents would not have appeared particularly well.

In other studies of collective housing quite a few interesting aspects are discussed, but they are often very weak indications of how typical the various observations are. Therefore it is well motivated to spend enough resources on methods designed to provide for generalizations and statistical processing for systematic comparisons between housing experiments.

References

Andersen, Hans Skifter: "Danish Low-rise Housing Co-operatives (bofællesskaber) as an Example of a Local Community Organization", *Scandinavian Housing and Planning Research*, Vol 2 No 2 (May 1985), p. 49-66.

Bell, Robert & Stefan Westius: *Några teorier om grannskap och grannrelationer* (Some theories about housing areas and neighboring), Stockholm: Byggforskningen R29:1972.

Berg, Elly *et al: Det lilla kollektivhuset. En modell för praktisk tillämpning* (The Small Collective Housing Unit. A Model for Practical Application), Byggforskningsrådet T14:1982.

Blomberg, Ingela *et al: Levande kollektivhus. Att leva, bo och arbeta i Hässelby familjehotell* (A Surviving Collective Housing Unit. Living and Working in the Hässelby Family Hotel), Stockholm: Byggforskningsrådet R19:1986.

Caldenby, Claes & Åsa Walldén: *Kollektivhus - Sovjet och Sverige omkring 1930* (Collective Housing Units in the Soviet Union and Sweden around 1930), Stockholm: Byggforskningsrådet T11:1979.

Caldenby, Claes & Åsa Walldén: *Kollektivhuset Stacken* (The Collective Housing Unit Stacken), Göteborg: Bokförlaget Korpen 1984.

Franck, Karen A. & Sherry Ahrentzen (eds): *New Households, New Housing*, New York: Van Nostrand Reinhold 1989.

Hayden, Dolores: *Seven American Utopias. The Architecture of Communitarian Socialism 1790-1975*, Cambridge, Mass.: The MIT Press 1977.

Hayden, Dolores: *The Grand Domestic Revolution: A History of Feminist Designs for American Homes, Neighborhoods, and Cities*, Cambridge, Mass.: MIT Press 1981.

Hayden, Dolores: *Redesigning the American Dream. The Future of Housing, Work, and Family Life*, New York & London: W W Norton & Co 1984.

Krantz, Birgit & Britt Pedersen: "The Stolplyckan Concept - a Meeting Place of Communal Living and Social Service", in Brech, Joachim (ed): *Neue Wohnformen in Europa. Berichte des 4. Internationalen Wohnbundkongresses*, Band I, Darmstadt: Verlag für Wissenschaftliche Publikationen 1989, p.332-340.

Lindberg, Göran: "Arguments for studying collective houses", paper for the International Sociological Association, Uppsala 1978. Printed in C. Ungerson & V. Karn (eds): *The Consumer's Experience of Housing*, Gover Publishing 1980.

McCamant, Kathryn & Charles Durrett: *Cohousing. A Contemporary Approach to Housing Ourselves*, Berkeley: Habitat Press/Ten Speed Press 1989.

Palm Lindén, Karin: *Mellanzonen i kollektivhuset. Metodbeskrivning och fallstudie* (The Transitional Zone in the Collective Housing Unit. Description of method and a Case Study), Byggnadsfunktionslära, Lunds universitet, R3:1987.

Palm Lindén, Karin: "The Physical Structure of the Swedish Collective House - Support or Limit in the Inhabitants' Everyday Life", in Brech, Joachim (ed): *Neue Wohnformen in Europa. Berichte des 4. Internationalen Wohnbundkongresses*, Band I, Darmstadt: Verlag für Wissenschaftliche Publikationen 1989, p.320-331.

Sanne, Christer: *Living People. Long-Term Pespectives for Human Settlements in the Nordic Countries*, Stockholm: Swedish Building Research Council D10:1983.

Vestbro, Dick Urban: *Kollektivhus från enkökshus till bogemenskap* (Collective Housing from One-Kitchen Houses to Communal Living), Stockholm: Byggforskningsrådet T28:1982.

Vestbro, Dick Urban: "Färdigforskat om kollektivt boende?" (Enough Research about Collective Housing?), *Tidskrift för Arkitekturforskning* (Swedish Journal of

Architectural Research) Vol 1 (1987), No 2 p. 33-52, published in 1988.

Vestbro, Dick Urban: "History of Collective Housing in Sweden", in Brech, Joachim (ed): *Neue Wohnformen in Europa. Berichte des 4. Internationalen Wohnbundkongresses*, Band II, Darmstadt: Verlag für Wissenschaftliche Publikationen 1989.

Woodward, Alison; Maj-Britt Grossman & Dick Urban Vestbro: *Den nya generationen kollektivhus. Experiment med social integration, förvaltning och rumsutformning* (The New Generation of Collective Housing Units. Experiments with Social Integration, Administration and Spatial Design), Stockholm: Byggforskningsrådet T16:1989.

Woodward, Alison: "Public Housing Communes: A Swedish Response to Postmaterial Demands", in van Vliet, Willem *et al* (eds): *Housing and Neighborhoods. Theoretical and Empirical Contributions*, Contributions in Sociology, No 66, New York etc: Greenwood Press 1988, p. 215-235.

Woodward, Alison: "Communal Housing in Sweden: A Remedy for the Stress of Everyday Life?", in Franck, Karen A. and Sherry Ahrentzen (eds): *New Households, New Housing*, New York: Van Nostrand Reinhold 1989.

Chapter 17

Assimilation and Accommodation of a Housing Innovation: A Case Study Approach of the House Trailer

ALLAN WALLIS
University of Colorado, Denver

The tension between the categorical system of regulations and innovations plays itself out in dual processes of assimilation and accommodation. This chapter provides a case study of assimilation and accommodation in the adoption of a housing innovation. The case For over sixty years mobile homes in various forms have served as both year-round and seasonal housing for a growing number of Americans. Today, almost 10% of the housing stock in the United States is composed of mobile homes. Despite their widespread utilization, mobile homes are still widely regarded as an undesirable form of housing which communities try to exclude through regulatory measures. This case traces mobile home development across four historical periods. Utilizing legal cases, evidence of physical design changes, it illustrates how the processes of assimilation and accommodation are evident in the adoption and diffusion of housing innovations.

Introduction

Twelve and a half million American households live in mobile homes. Over the passed two decades they have provided one fifth of all new single-family dwellings produced annually, and 90 percent of all homes purchased for under $50,000. Although mobile homes suffered from poor safety performance in earlier decades, for the last fifteen years their construction has been regulated by the federal government, and their soundness is now equivalent to site-built homes (Nutt-Powell, 1982).

Despite the contribution of mobile homes to American housing, and especially to the provision of affordable housing, mobile homes are often treated as a pariah. A majority of local governments utilize zoning and building codes to exclude mobile homes or confine them to rental parks. Even where they are allowed, minimum lot and unit size, along with appearance requirements, effectively reduce mobile home affordability, preventing many households from fully utilizing this innovative housing alternative (Wallis, 1991).

Explanations of mobile homes regulation

Why has mobile home use been so severely regulated? Is it because it is innovative, unproven, dangerous, ugly, or cheap? The legal foundation for regulating land use and building in general rests in the police power of the states, which allows them to protect the health, safety, and welfare of the public. While the regulation of mobile homes clearly falls under this power, the particular form its regulation has taken requires further explanation. The literature on government regulation in general, and mobile homes in particular, suggests three different explanations.

The first explanation suggests that restrictions placed on mobile home use were once amply justified by their poor record for safety combined with concerns about their suitability as environments for raising children. Although mobile home safety and liveability have improved dramatically over the last several decades, state and local regulations have failed to respond to its new condition. In effect, the regulatory system suffers from inertia, and lags behind the material realities of the object it is empowered to regulate (Ogburn, 1964). From this perspective, it follows that the regulatory system must be reformed in accord with material conditions.

An alternative explanation suggests that mobile home regulation is the result of vested interests who see their own concerns better served by preventing or restricting the use of new housing alternatives. These interests include property owners, real estate developers, and builders who see the widespread use of mobile homes as a threat to their property values and livelihood. From this perspective, regulations which restrict mobile homes don't suffer from inertia, rather, they are actively and intentionally set up to prevent certain perceived threats relating directly or indirectly to economic interests and class bias. It follows that when regulators argue that their restrictions are based on the fact that mobile homes have yet to prove their durability and safety that, in fact, their arguments are a subterfuge. Rather than protecting the health and safety of the community, regulators are serving special interests whose activities they are supposed to be regulating (Lowi, 1979).

A third explanation for regulatory restrictions against mobile homes is provided by structural-functional theory (Paiget, 1970). From this perspective housing is seen as embodying important social and cultural assumptions about family and community. These beliefs are often tacit but nevertheless deeply entrenched in building and land use regulations (Perin, 1977). This structure of beliefs provides a predictable environment in which to make individual and collective decisions and to coordinate action. When housing innovations like the mobile home are introduced they bump up against this underlying layer of beliefs and assumptions. Vested interests may be able to capitalize on these assumptions, but they do not create nor control them.

The approach taken to the analysis of mobile home regulation in the case study which follows utilizes a structural-functional approach. Before turning to the case a few concepts from the structural-function perspective are introduced, and the methodology for developing the case is described.

Elements of a structural-functional interpretation

From a psychological perspective, a basic function of environmental regulation and the regulation of housing is to limit the range of possible actions in a situation and hence increase the predictability of outcomes. In this capacity regulation serves to define the acceptable range of housing alternatives, which it arranges in a categorical system of preferred alternatives. The clearest expression of this categorical system in found in Euclidean zoning, where the single family detached house is given the greatest protection against nuisances.

Although regulation and the categorical system it constructs serve to provide a stable and predictable environment for housing related behavior, especially investment behavior, they can also have the effect of excluding

significant segments of society from the housing market because they lack
the means of securing a "proper" home. Changes in lifestyle, tastes, and
the availability of new technologies may also create pressure on gatekeeping
regulators, forcing them to open up the categories of housing and admit new
options.

If regulators fail to respond to these pressures they run the risk of undermining their authority. At the same time, if they do not monitor what is
allowed to enter the categorical system, they run the counter-risk of introducing other instabilities. The challenge facing regulators, then, is to adjust
their categorical system so as to maintain continuity with established types
of transactions while allowing for the introduction of options that better
satisfy current needs.

Regardless of their merits, innovative housing alternatives are rarely
accepted outright. From a structural-functional perspective their ultimate
adoption and diffusion involves dual processes of assimilation and accommodation (Marris, 1975). Assimilation consists of changes in the innovation
making it admissible to the categorical system. Conversely, accommodation consists of changes in the categorical system resulting from admission
of the innovation. The function of these dual processes is to maintain a
sense of continuity and hence predictability for the various parties engaged
in different aspects of housing.

Methodology

In attempting to understand how housing categories change to adjust to innovations it is essential to consider them in historical perspective. Looking
at a single period might suggest that only assimilation or accommodation
are at work, whereas a longitudinal perspective is more likely to reveal
the operation of both. Such a perspective may also serve to reveal significant shifts in categorization: changes in which a new and relatively stable
reinterpretation of the innovation has been established.

With respect to the system of housing categories, the basic data defining the system are public regulations, especially zoning and building codes.
However, only a small part of this material is typically implicated in responses to an innovation. Fortunately, the relevant portions are cited in
challenges to the use of the innovation. Court cases provide a useful and
accessible indication of where challenges are being mounted and over what
issues, thereby helping to identify points of strain in the categorical system.

Another area of conflict which helps to identify strain is the development
of state or federal legislation designed to reform local land use and building
regulation. These higher levels of government are traditionally reticent

about local land use and building issues. Consequently, their intervention usually indicates that a substantial abuse of power is occurring at the local level.

Both assimilation and accommodation have the effect of calling out features of the innovation which are points of tension in the effort to make it acceptable. The features that are called out are likely to be subject to modification. If modification does in fact follow, there is further confirmation that the features at issue were regarded as significant. The identification of such features also serves to indicate the nature of the underlying dynamic taking place as the innovation and the categorical system adjust to each other.

Beyond distinguishing significant from trivial changes, it is desirable to identify larger patterns of adjustment: i.e., points at which a new and relatively stable reinterpretation or categorization of the innovation has been achieved. These typically present themselves in terms of semantic changes, such as changes in the name of the object. Over a long period of time semantic changes may stabilize indicating a canonic interpretation of the object being categorized.

In summary, conflicts formalized as court cases and legislation provide basic data for studying the adjustment of the regulated system of housing categories in response to innovations. The significance of such data can be confirmed by evidence of changes in use, material, form, or location of the innovation. A longitudinal perspective is necessary to identify the full range of adjustments occurring in response to the innovation. Such a perspective may also serve to reveal the larger patterns of adjustments made both to the categorical system and to the innovation.

The case of the mobile home

Over the sixty year evolution of the mobile home four period of development are clearly distinguishable. The first period involves the use of trailers as autocamping accessories. The second commences with the Second World War, and is distinguished by the use of trailers as year-round temporary war worker housing. The third period is marked by the introduction of less transient, longer and wider models in the mid-1950s, used for year-round housing. The last period begins in 1980 when manufacturers successfully lobbied to have the mobile home officially renamed in federal legislation as "manufactured housing." By this time mobile homes had grown significantly larger, far more house-like in appearance, and virtually immobile.

The analysis which follows traces development of these homes-on-wheels through the four periods just described. In each period the tactics used to

Figure 17.1: The travel trailer era

The Travel Trailer is perceived as an automobile camping accessory—"The Machine Age" covered wagon, as illustrated by this 1940 Schult Trailer. Interiors have fold-up built-in furniture, borrowed from trains and yatchs designed to serve multiple purposes.

assimilate the innovation to the regulatory system of housing is considered, as well as evidence of how the categorical system accommodated their inclusion.

The travel trailer era

The mobile home first emerged in the mid-1920s as an automobile camping accessory. These "travel trailers" or "caravans" as they were then called, were primarily homemade affairs used for weekend and vacation camping trips (Figure 17.1). By the mid-1930s, there were approximately one million Americans camping in trailers, of which perhaps ten percent used their trailers as year-round housing. The latter consisted of itinerant workers who found a home on wheel suitable to their lifestyle.

At first, municipalities were anxious to attract trailer tourists, believing that they would bring business. But when trailerites began lingering on in towns, taking advantage of their services but failing to return their costs, fees were imposed and later ordinances passed restricting the period for which a trailer could remain (Belasco, 1984).

A particularly telling case from this period involved Hilred Gumsol and the Town of Orchard Lake, Michigan. In the summer of 1935, Gumsol set up his trailer on a rented lot. Rather than removing it at the end of the season, he placed it on blocks, added a porch, and left it for use the following summer. Suit was brought by nearby landowners concerned that if others followed Gumarsol's lead, Orchard Lake might soon be reduced to a trailer shanty town.

In his defense Gumarsol argued that his trailer was not a dwelling but an automobile accessory. Justice Green, however, ruled "that a house trailer of the type occupied by the defendant and having a great many appointments of a modern home would come under the scope of a human dwelling whether it stands upon blocks or the wheels attached thereto or whether it be coupled to or detached from an automobile" (Hodes & Roberson, 1974, 105).

While the Gumarsol ruling categorized the trailer as a dwelling, hence suitable for year-round use, the effect of that categorization is constructive exclusive: i.e., a trailer that could meet minimum dwelling space standards would be too large for legal towing on highways. Most courts were more direct in their categorization and exclusion. They fixed upon the fact that trailers had wheels, and held that a structure on wheels could not be regarded as a permanent dwelling. Indeed, this basis for classification remains to this day (Berry, 1985; Brown & Sellman, 1987).

By the late 1930s the passage of restrictive ordinances had become so widespread, they were perceived as a threat to the commercial trailer industry. Reasoning that if trailerites found it difficult to find camping sites, that trailer sales would decline, the industry organized itself to fight exclusionary ordinances. Their tactic was to argue that trailers were in fact designed to be vacation vehicles, and should therefore be confined to campgrounds where their stay could be limited. In effect the industry was saying it could live with these restrictions if trailers weren't banned altogether.

Manufacturers had another reason for wanting to promote the identity of trailers as automobile camping accessories, namely to distance themselves from the class of itinerant workers moving around the country in trailer housing. Commercial manufacturers perceived their market as coming from middle and upper-middle income professional households which employed trailers for vacationing. By contrast, they believed that year-round trailer dwellers were utilizing homemade rigs. The model ordinance could serve to preclude these people while helping the commercial trailer market.

In summary, during this period the trailer was treated as an invisible housing option. That is, the system of housing regulation ignored it, while vehicle regulators treated it as an automobile accessory. Categorization focused on the mobility of trailers, while simultaneously ignoring their use as year-round housing. Regulators found that they were allied with manufacturers in this approach.

The house trailer era

The position of manufacturers as well as the majority of trailer users changed radically with the out break of the Second World War. Suddenly there was tremendous need for temporary and preferably portable housing to serve war workers. For security reasons war production plants were being located in rural areas, and available housing in nearby towns was soon exhausted. Workers found trailers a preferable housing alternative. The obvious crisis created by war time conditions also served to loosen local regulations, permitting the use of trailer housing.

While the war created a new trailer market, specifically for trailers large enough to serve as year-round housing, construction utilized rationed materials. The manufacturers association, which only a year earlier had declared that trailers were too small to serve as year-round housing, found itself in 1940 lobbying in Washington for the use of trailers as war worker housing.

The Response of the War Production Board was to recognize trailers as "portable housing", a classification designating that they were to be removed at the end of the war. Under this categorization the government became the main purchaser of trailers, and over the course of the war it bought 35,000 trailers. By 1943, however, the government had changed its position, declaring that emergency conditions justifying the use of trailer housing were over, and that it would no longer utilize trailers for war workers. The effect on the industry was devastating. The number of trailer manufacturers dwindled, and those that remained dreamed of the end of war, expecting peace to bring a resurgence of the vacation trailer market.

In fact, when the war ended the major market for trailers was not for vacation use, but again as year-round housing. The post-war housing shortage had created a tremendous demand for housing (Figure 17.2). Moreover, the development of huge post-war federal construction projects (e.g., dams and atomic energy facilities) continued to fuel demand for portable housing. After the war, however, many municipalities returned to the practice of excluding trailer parks and trailers on individual sites. Consequently, parks were typically located outside of municipal boundaries. As these cities later expanded, they grandfathered the existing parks into their limits but continued to discourage new park development.

The majority of court opinions in this period upheld categorization of house trailers as vehicles, and consequently supported the idea that they be confined to parks where their duration of stay continued to be limited. These restrictions, however, did not affect the vast majority of buyers.

Figure 17.2: The house trailer era

House Trailer Era units have more house-like interiors supporting year-round housing. However, they are still vehicular on the exterior, with streamlined bodies designed for towing, as illustrated by this Spartan Manor 1947 model.

Military personnel in trailers generally lived in parks on bases, while construction workers lived at remote sites with no zoning.

An important aspect of the continued classification of trailers as vehicles is that they were exempt in most states from real estate taxes even when set up permanently. In 1954, twenty states taxed trailers as personal property, while most of the remainder imposed licensing fees. An exception to the general pattern was Florida, which based taxation on the manner of use. A trailer used for travel paid a license fees only; if used as a dwelling, but on a rental site, it was treated as personalty; but if it was permanently attached to a site then it was real estate (Meloan, 1954).

These types of classification appear to place trailer housing at a disadvantage, but in fact it enjoyed some distinct advantages as a result of its segregated status. This is evident in the experience of trailer manufacturers compared with industrialized home builders. During and after the war housing shortages created a demanded well suited for the development of an industrialized housing industry. But this industry never took off, in large part, because local building codes were used to excluded houses built in factories. Trailers, by contrast, were not regarded as housing, and therefore never provoked opposition from building and construction interests that effectively blocked the use of prefabricated homes (Drury, 1972).

The effect of regulation during this period was to move the trailer from the category of vehicle, where its dwelling functions were ignored, into the category of dwelling, but as a special type of dwelling that also functioned as a vehicle. Consequently, the use of trailer housing was bracketed by a great many restrictions. This is evident in the position that trailers are acceptable as dwellings on a year-round basis when restricted to parks which, in turn, are confined to commercial or industrial zones.

The mobile home era

The watershed event heralding transition from house trailers to mobile homes was introduction of ten-foot wide models beginning in 1954. The wider units were more spacious, but less mobile (Figure 17.3). They appealed to a new population of mobile home users. In the house trailer era the average trailer household was highly transient, but it enjoyed a higher level of income and education than the average American household. The reason for this was the concentration of trailer ownership among skilled itinerant construction workers and married military personnel. By the time the mobile home came into use, ownership demographics had changed and the average income level of users dropped below the national average. Class bias, which has always been an element in attempts to exclude this form of housing, now received new justification (Geisler & Mitsuda, 1987).

The new, more immobile, mobile home, required a different land use configuration. Rather than a campground it demanded a more residential setting. The term "park" became more common to describe mobile home communities, and the industry established a park design service to help promote new development standards. Problems remained in finding land on which parks were permitted.

The dominant regulatory practice of this period was to restrict mobile homes to parks on the grounds of sanitary requirements. Despite such restrictions, fully half of the sitings in this period are on single lots, the majority of which were owner occupied. Such lots were either in rural hinterlands or towns where there were no zoning ordinances. A study in the mid-1960s revealed that the most intense activity in park development was occurring at the outskirts of rapidly developing metropolitan areas (French and Hadden, 1965).

At this time there is evidence of refinement in the categorization of mobile home land uses, and indirectly—of mobile home households. One analyst suggested that parks could be distinguished as service-oriented or housing-oriented, with the former catering primarily to an older and more affluent household (Gillies, 1965). This distinction was already evident in the kind of zoning ordinances being constructed in sunbelt areas designed

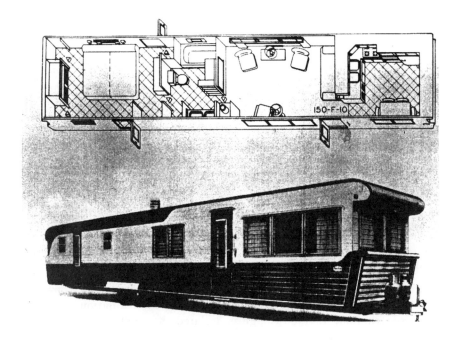

Figure 17.3: The mobile home era

Designs are boxier and less streamlined, with windows and doors providing a more house-like exterior as illustrated by this 1957 Peerless model. Likewise the interiors are more house-like with movable furniture, full-size kitchens and bathrooms.

to promote development of service-oriented parks. Park developers likewise promoted the distinction, finding that it helped win zoning approvals if they could demonstrate that their communities were likely to attract the "right kind of people."

The practice of restricting mobile homes to parks had an adverse if un-intended consequence for their tenants. Their rights to the full enjoyment of their homes was compromised by park owners' property rights. Park managers could impose rules or evict tenants in a manner that apartment tenants were protected against. Park managers defended their actions un-der the landlord's right to control property, while tenants sought protection under antitrust and consumer laws. By 1973, eight states had enacted mo-bile home tenant laws, in most cases as extensions of consumer protection laws.

In summary, the mobile home era is characterized by larger, less mobile units which were primarily used as year-round housing. Mobile homes were increasingly accepted as a housing type, but one to be segregated in parks. Minimum park standards were adopted in many localities to assure their suitability for year-round housing, but parks themselves continued to be relegated to non-residential zones.

Manufactured housing era

In 1974 Congress passed the Mobile Home Safety Standards and Construc-tion Act preempting all state and local codes in the regulation of mobile home construction. In 1980 Congress declared that mobile homes would, from that time forward, be referred to as "manufactured housing." The change in name was something that the industry itself had promoted in its efforts to reform public perceptions of its product (Bernhardt, 1980). By this time the term "mobile" had clearly become a misnomer in that only 10 percent of the units being produced were expected to be moved once they were established at a site (Figure 17.4). An important aspect of federal recognition of manufactured housing was improved federally guar-anteed mortgages for mobile home purchase. Today mortgage terms are comparable to site-built housing, whereas previously mobile homes were financed at higher automobile loan rates.

Despite this federal action, many localities have refused to reform re-strictive practices. A 1985 study found that at least 11 percent of com-munities surveyed still totally excluded mobile homes, and that at least 25 percent did not allow them in residential districts (Sanders, 1986). While lo-calities cannot alter provisions of the HUD code they continue to describe building standards in such a way as to exclude the placement of mobile homes. Through zoning practices they may attempt to exclude outright all

Figure 17.4: Manufacture housing era

The design of manufactured housing deemphasizes mobility and vehicle-like features. Manufactured housing is rarely moved once set-up on a site. This 1988 unit by Skyline Corporation is undistinguishable from site-built housing.

manufactured housing.

Several State Supreme Courts have ruled that it is constitutional to confine manufactured homes to parks. In 1984, for example, the Idaho Supreme Court upheld a local ordinance restricting mobile homes to parks and subdivisions on the basis that such restrictions preserved property values. A similar ruling was made by the Texas Supreme Court, but citing as its justification differences in construction leading to health and safety concerns.

Despite these court rulings, at least 14 states to date have enacted legislation prohibiting such discriminatory practices. In addition, several State Supreme Courts have ruled in mobile home discrimination cases deciding broadly to prohibit such practices. Michigan's Supreme Court was one of the first, in 1981, to recognize that manufactured housing was substantially different from mobile homes and trailers, and that its *per se* exclusion or confinement to parks was arbitrary. That court nevertheless preserved a community's right to control the appearance of manufactured housing sited in residential neighborhoods (Barewin, 1990).

State action, such as in Michigan, effectively requiring localities to provide for single siting, are often accompanied by appearance standards (Bair,

1981). In most cases these standards require the use of double-wide homes, with horizontal siding, shingled and pitched roofs, and other features that make units look like site-built homes. The appearance standard is telling in that it suggests that even when construction standards certify the safety of manufactured housing, that their integration with single family homes is to be based on conventional appearance. Unfortunately, meeting appearance standards usually results in a more costly house, undermining manufactured housing's principal advantage—affordability.

In summary, manufactured housing has enjoyed greater integration into the regulated housing system. Recognition has brought it more favorable loan rates and broader siting opportunities, but these have come at the expense of greater conventionality in design and higher costs.

Conclusions: strategies of assimilation and accommodation

The sixty year evolution of mobile home use in the United States reveals several basic strategies for the integration of innovations into the categorical structure of housing regulation. These strategies are directly related to the processes of assimilation and accommodation (Barnett, 1953). With respect to assimilation, the evolution of the mobile homes reveals two strategies. The first is syncretism in which the physical form of the mobile home remains a clear hybrid of vehicular and dwelling elements. Manufacturers along with regulators try to focus on particular features of the ensemble to justify categorization (Figures 17.5 and 17.6). In the travel trailer and house trailer eras they generally focused on vehicular aspects, whereas in the mobile home era they look more at dwelling features.

By the time of the manufactured housing era a different strategy is evident—conventionalization. The objective of this strategy is to make the innovation look as much as possible like an established option within the categorical system. Appearance standards suggests that if manufactured homes are to be placed in residential settings they will have to look like site-built housing.

With respect to accommodation, two strategies are also evident. In the early eras of mobile home development, the basis mode of accommodation is independence: i.e., setting the housing type off in a category of its own. Its use is highly restricted, but it is nevertheless recognized as housing. Again, by the time of the manufactured housing era there is clearly a shift in strategies, in this case to structuralization. Structuralization involves a fuller integration of the housing option into the categorical system. It is

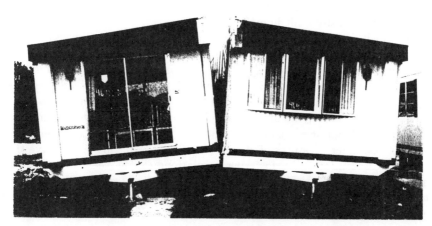

Figure 17.5: Challenges to regulatory categorization

The fundamental challenge to regulatory categorization posed by the mobile home is that it is both a vehicle and a house. Local building and zoning regulations in the U.S.A. treat houses as objects built on-site, not as packages delivered to it.

Figure 17.6: Site additions to mobile homes

Site additions to mobile homes compound the categorization problem. Once permanently attached to a site with built additions does the mobile home become real estate or is it still personal property? Should the factory-built and site-built sections be subject to the same building code?

evident in the ability of manufactured home buyers to more freely locate their housing and to enjoy the benefits of mortgage programs similar to those offered on site-built homes.

In conclusion, the structural-functional approach to the analysis of housing regulation and innovation focuses on the importance of maintaining continuity between established ways of knowing and acting. Continuity is maintained through dual processes of assimilation and accommodation. As distinction from an interpretation of regulation as inert and lagging behind technological change, the structural-functional approach views regulation as part of a dynamic system which operates to maintain its structure and boundaries under pressures of change. Similarly, from this perspective the role of vested interests in fostering regulations can be seen as an aspect of the processes of assimilation and accommodation. Lessons derived from the case of the mobile home undoubtedly apply to housing innovations in general, especially in modern societies.

References

Frederick Bair; *Regulating Mobile Homes*; Chicago; American Planning Association, Planning Advisory Service publication 360; April 1981.

Howard Barewin; "Rescuing Manufactured Housing From the Perils of Municipal Zoning Law"; Washington University Journal of Urban and Contemporary Law, 37 (1990).

Homer Barnett; *Innovation as the Basis of Cultural Change*; New York; McGraw Hill; 1953.

Warren Belasco; *Americans on the Road*; Cambridge, MA; MIT Press, 1984.

Arthur Bernhardt; *Building Tomorrow: The Mobile/Manufactured Housing Industry*; Cambridge, MA; MIT Press, 1980.

Rita L. Berry; "Restrictive Zoning of Mobile Homes"; Idaho Law Review, 21 (1985).

James Brown and Molly Sellman; "The Invalidity of the Mobility Standard"; The Urban Lawyer; 19, 2 (Spring 1987).

Margret Drury; *Mobile Homes: The Unrecognized Revolution in Housing*; New York; Praeger, 1972.

Robert French and Jeffery Hadden; "An Analysis of Distribution Characteristics of Mobile Homes in America"; *Land Economics*; May 1965.

Charles Geisler and Hisayoshi Mitsuda; "Mobile Home Growth Regulation and Discrimination in Upstate New York;" *Rural Sociology*; 52:4 (1987).

James Gillies; *Factors Influencing Social Patterns in Mobile Home Parks*; Los Angeles; Trailer Coach Manufacturers Association; 1965.

Barnet Hodes and Gale Robertson; *The Law of Mobile Homes*; Washington, D.C.; Bureau of National Affairs; 1974.

Theodore Lowi; *The End of Liberalism*; New York; W. W. Norton; 1979.

Peter Marris; *Loss and Change*; Garden City, NY; Doubleday; 1975.

Taylor Meloan; *Mobile Homes*; Homewood, IL; Richard D. Irwin; 1954.

Constance Perin; *Everything in Its Place*; Princeton, NJ; Princeton University Press; 1977.

Jean Piaget; *Structuralism*, trans. Maschler; New York; Basic Books; 1970.

Thomas Nutt-Powell; *Manufactured Housing: Making Sense of a Housing Opportunity*; Boston; Auburn House; 1982.

William Ogburn; *On Culture and Social Change*; Chicago; University of Chicago Press; 1964.

Welford Sanders, *Regulating Manufactured Housing*; Washington, D.C.; American Planning Association, Planning Advisory Service Report Number 398; December 1986.

Allan Wallis, *Wheel Estate: The Rise and Decline of Mobile Homes*; New York; Oxford University Press; 1991.

Part VII
The Meaning and Use of Housing:
Overlooked Populations

The Meaning and Use of Housing: Overlooked Populations

KAREN A. FRANCK
New Jersey Institute of Technology

Introduction

This book demonstrates the attention researchers are starting to give to the variety of households and housing, meanings and uses of housing that exist. As we continue to study this variety, we need to be thorough and inclusive in our conceptualizations and investigations, paying attention to the social construction and hence the social and political aspects of each of these four components. This requires that we draw upon a variety of research methods and sources of information.

Much of what we study and learn in any field depends upon the categories we use: what they include and exclude, what they combine and separate, and what values they represent . The problem is not that we use categories; we must use them. The problem is that we are often unaware of how they structure and dictate the content of research, policy, and design. As categories in all these domains become more numerous with finer distinctions, we need to become more keenly aware of what the implicit and

[0] This essay does not review the existing literature in any thorough or systematic way. For that, please refer to other chapters in this volume as well as to Despres (1991) and other articles in the special issue of Journal of Architecture and Planning Research on meanings of home (Volume 8, Numbers 1 and 2, 1991). I appreciate comments from Nora Rubenstein and Joan Sprague on an earlier version of this introduction.

explicit distinctions are, what values they hold, and what consequences they have.

This introduction reviews the kinds of households, housing, uses and meanings of housing that we do, or need to, consider in housing research. It suggests the rich complexity of issues and relationships that merit our attention.

Household characteristics

The prototypical household of husband, wife and young children, which still serves so centrally in the U.S. as a norm of what a "family" should be, is statistically in decline. In the U.S. the proportion of all households meeting this definition has decreased from 40 percent in 1970 to 26 percent in 1990. While the percentage of married couples without children has remained fairly constant (about 30 percent in both 1970 and 1990), the proportions of all other kinds of households have increased: notably people living alone (from 17 to 25 percent of all households) and single parent families headed by women (from 5 to 7 percent). In 1970 12 percent of families with children under 18 were headed by single women; in 1990 it was 24 percent. The U.S. is not alone in experiencing these changes: world wide the number of households headed by women and the number of people living alone have increased.

Another world-wide phenomenon is the increase in households with no permanent residence. In Western industrialized countries, the increasing number of people living in shelters or public places has become a serious and highly visible problem. In the U.S. a high many of these people are single women with children while in England they are often single young people. While many of homeless persons only lack funds to afford housing, others suffer from additional problems including drug or alcohol abuse or mental illness. After even a short period of homelessness, these or other debilitating conditions can quickly develop.

To address these conditions, social service providers and non-profit housing organizations are developing programs and housing to serve particular kinds of homeless individuals and families including single mothers with children, single mothers or individuals with substance abuse problems and the mentally ill. Similarly, more and more distinctions are being made between elderly persons of different ages and health status. This has led to new kinds of programs and housing accommodations including home care services, respite care for family care givers, retirement communities, life care communities, and housing for people with alzheimers.

Feminist researchers have pointed out that within the prototypical household of mother, father and children, all household members do not have the same needs. Viewing the two-parent family as a homogeneous unit and assuming that all benefits (and difficulties) accrue to each member equally privileges the traditional patriarchal role of the male head and extends advantages to the male head of household while undermining the experiences and rights of women (Olkin, 1989). It is becoming conceptually more difficult to make this assumption as women are participating in the work force in greater numbers, as women take on responsibility for caring for aging parents, and as more and more women take on sole responsibility for raising children (Skolnick, 1991). Yet, despite these changes, the planning and designing of housing and neighborhoods are still based on the prototypical ideal.

There is no doubt that as a society we are recognizing a much greater diversity of needs regarding housing and services. Some of these needs always existed but were not acknowledged; others are newly emerging. A great many of them have implications for the uses, meanings, and design of housing, even though these implications are not as widely recognized as is the diversity. Understanding what the differences between different kinds of households may be, and what implications they have for policy and design requires careful conceptualization and empirical research.

Housing as accommodations

Just as the prototypical household in the U.S. has been the two parent family with children, so the prototypical dwelling, which still serves both as dream and standard, has been the single-family detached house in a residential neighborhood. Some variation is recognized but this consists largely of variations upon the standard. Two family houses, row houses, or apartment buildings all possess some of the essential features of the single family house. They are as socially and spatially independent of other units as possible and each is intended to house only people who are related to each other by blood or marriage (Franck, 1987). Other kinds of arrangements that support a greater degree of sharing between households are almost exclusively intended for special populations — college students, the elderly, or the homeless.

One response to homelessness has been the increasing development of specialized housing: single room occupancy hotels and private or shared apartments, often with special programs and services. Some projects are completely residential in character. Others possess some, or even many, attributes of institutions in terms of rules, maximum length of stay, and management responsibilities. All of these types respond to, and thereby help to construct, what is seen as the "problem" that the putative residents have. All of the residents who move in then have that problem. Depending upon the intentions, scale, and quality of management of the program, this can be a very beneficial approach, particularly when the programs and services are aimed at, and achieve, the empowerment of residents. However, since these types are just now being developed, we still need concepts and empirical research to understand the similarities and differences between them and to evaluate them. Such work requires that we broaden our definitions of housing and its meanings and uses.

Housing is also a social ordering device (Perin, 1977). The emergence of more and more types for special populations suggests a finer and finer grain of ordering, and segregation. The development of alternative housing for special populations does not change mainstream housing design and policy. It leaves the social and spatial self sufficiency of the single-family home or apartment untouched. Indeed, that may be one of its purposes as a social ordering device. Recently, the development of cohousing in the U.S. has provided one alternative to that model of complete separation and self-sufficiency (McCamant and Durrett, 1988; Fromm 1991). Other models of sharing either within or between individual dwelling units have been proposed and a few have been built (Franck and Ahrentzen, 1989) but much more exploration of alternatives for non-marginalized households is needed. Alternatives can and must be developed that meet the needs of both mainstream and special populations that encourage a greater degree of integration of kinds of households and kinds of uses than is now allowed in conventional housing and neighborhoods.

As all kinds of alternatives must be developed. It makes sense to take a more inclusive and a more detailed view of what "housing" is and to consider both permanent and temporary accommodations, those that are service enriched and those that are not, those that are close to the conventional forms of housing and those that possess some attributes of institutions. At the same time, we must seriously question the increasing classification of populations and accommodations when it generates a higher degree of permanent social and spatial segregation. In housing research, we need to develop a conceptual framework that fully embraces complex variations in types that will enable us to study existing and potential diversity of kinds of households and kinds of housing. Crucial to that framework is a more systematic way of looking at the activities and meanings that are supported by different kinds of accommodations.

Accommodations and activities

"Use of housing" can be viewed as the activities that occupants pursue in and near their accommodations. Daily, mundane activities help produce and reinforce the meanings of environments. But discussing meanings without attention to the practical daily life activities that we commonly pursue in the home generates a level of abstraction that misses some of the most fundamental purposes of housing.

Safe and sanitary accommodations of some type allow occupants to get adequate sleep, to be protected from the elements, serious diseases, and assault by others, and to wash and care for themselves and their clothing. These are the most basic ways we reproduce our selves each day of our lives – not just our self – identities but our embodied selves. This process of maintaining our bodies and our appearance is fundamental to the functioning and the identity of any human being (Giddens, 1991). It may be the most important activity that safe and secure accommodations support and the one most taken for granted and, hence, overlooked in housing research. For some long-term homeless men the first change after moving to a well-maintained single room occupancy hotel is that they begin to wash and shave on a regular basis. This is the beginning of renewed dignity and self-esteem. The biggest difference between living in a domicile of any kind and living on the street or in emergency shelters may be the ability to maintain the bodily self with ease. In considering the many meanings and uses of housing this fundamental ability must not be overlooked.

Safe and secure accommodations also allow occupants to develop a spatial, temporal, and social order to daily life (Dovey, 1986) and to take the routines of daily life for granted (Rivlin, 1986). This gives people the time, the energy and the daily predictability to pursue other activities, such as jobs, and to develop and maintain relationships with others. At a similarly basic level, having a fixed residential location-represented by an address and a phone number — allows one to receive mail and to be visited or called by others.

The inability to maintain proper health and appearance, to assume any order or predictability in daily life or even to be located in the world contributes to making the homeless "non-people" in our society. People living on the street, in cars, or in a shelter, not only do not have "homes" with the myriad meanings that carries, they do not have residences in the most practical and basic sense. Without a residence, one is a nonperson. The most fundamental purpose of housing is to enable one to be a person, both in the sense of maintaining one's embodied self and being acknowledged by others.

While all accommodations, beyond emergency shelters, allow people to maintain their embodied selves and to develop daily life routines, they differ significantly in the manner in which they support personal identities and relationships. The physical design, social, and management characteristics of a given type of housing or a given project may encourage particular kinds of activities, relationships and self identities and discourage others. However, the characteristics of a type do not fully determine or fully restrict activities or relationships. Single room occupancy (SRO) housing presents a good lesson on this point. For many years, researchers and policy makers assumed that, simply by virtue of the type of housing they occupied, residents of single room occupancy hotels were socially isolated. Recent research by Hoch and Slayton (1989) shows that is far from true. Similarly, researchers and laypeople alike may assume that the single family house is the most ideal residential setting where safety, privacy, and autonomy are at their zenith. However, this is not true for all occupants nor for all activities. It is not true for women or children who are abused nor is it true when zoning restricts the use of the home for wage work, or for group worship, or for occupancy by more than a given number of unrelated people. Some of the autonomy, privacy and security so strongly associated with the single family house may indeed be more ideological than accurate. The connections between type of household, type of housing, and activities and experiences of residents are rich and complex. All of these connections deserve theoretical and empirical investigation with attention to the detailed nature of each component.

One component that needs such attention is the sharing of facilities by unrelated households and the rationale for such sharing. Some of the transitional housing for mothers and children referred to by Huttman in this section and studied by Rivlin (1986), requires households to share kitchens and baths and to follow various rules concerning curfews and visiting hours. These are the attributes most criticized by residents and most clearly limit the kinds of activities and relationships residents can pursue by restricting their autonomy and control of space. Residents report feeling that they are being treated like children. This may be quite true but researchers also need to consider the *purpose of sharing* and the *purpose of the rules* in transitional housing to understand more fully its nature and how it differs from other kinds of accommodation, particularly conventional houses or apartments. It is misleading to evaluate one kind of accommodation, such as transitional housing or SRO housing, exclusively according to the characteristics of another kind of accommodation.

In other cases, using a kitchen with other households may not feel constraining to residents, particularly when residents have chosen that kind of housing and when they manage the housing themselves (Research by Michelson and Vestro in this volume addresses the sharing of facilities).

The characteristics of the households and the housing and the reasons for sharing are all significantly different from those of transitional housing. Certainly, the sharing of meals and other activities is a prime reason people choose to develop cohousing but the shared spaces supplement complete, private dwellings and the residents not only manage but typically have also designed and developed the communities themselves. The presence and kind of activity spaces that are shared by different households, the rationale for the sharing, and the degree of choice and self management by residents all constitute important differences between different types of accommodations and different cases of the same type.

Even in accommodations with shared facilities, the privacy and autonomy afforded individuals may differ. There may be shared bathrooms, but how many people can use the space at one time? Can the shower or commode be locked? These physical design details can ensure greater, or lesser, degrees of privacy and autonomy. Equally important, the philosophy and attitude of management and the underlying goals of the housing significantly affect residents' perceptions of the reasonableness and desirability of sharing. Understanding the consequences of all these characteristics for personal relationships and self identity should help housing providers self-consciously adopt the spaces, design, and, rules appropriate for the philosophy and population they serve. It will also increase our understanding of the full range of housing accommodations that is emerging.

Meanings and ideology

Just as we need to broaden the range of populations and accommodations we study, we need to broaden the range of meanings of housing that we consider, both at the individual and the societal level. As Despres (1991) has pointed out, most of the research on the meanings of home has been conducted among couples and conventional nuclear families in middle class apartments and houses. This has generated findings that may be limited to those particular circumstances or to the idealized household and house that those circumstances represent in the U.S. One may well ask how much this research reveals about the meanings of home among individuals and how much it reveals about the North American ideology of home. The more troublesome meanings, such as the home as a consumer product, a means of investment, a heavy financial burden to its occupants, a place of violence for abused women and children, a place of unpaid work, or one means of preserving the segregation of gender roles and economic groups also need to be explored. It will be difficult to conduct this research if we continue to view the uses and meanings of housing primarily in benign and idealized

terms. Our idealization of housing as home, and often as a particular type
of home, makes it difficult to examine what else is going on.

To uncover overlooked meanings and uses at the individual level, we can
expand the kinds of households and accommodations we study and the research methods we employ in research. Chawla, in her chapter, does this by
exploring poets' memories of their childhood homes; ElRafey and Sutton
through interview-observations look into daily life activities of Egyptian
women; while Despres is studying the meanings of home for people who
share houses and apartments. Less conventional research methods may
also give us insight into the less obvious meanings of home. Cooper Marcus
(1986) has drawn upon Gestalt therapy to develop role playing techniques
were participants play the role of themselves, talking to their homes, and
then of their homes talking back. She finds that the home can be both
"haven" and "trap." Rubinstein (1992) asks her students to write environmental autobiographies where they describe places they "love that love
them back." She has found revelations of abuse and memories of the home
as a place of trauma. Harvey (1992) is adapting a body work approach that
involves deep breathing, voice work, and movement in front of projected
photographic images of homes one has occupied. The purpose is to uncover
memories and desires through one's response to these images and thereby
to discover hidden aspects of identity that have implications for the design
of housing and community. All of these methods encourage individuals to
focus in depth on particular places they have lived and their experiences
of those places. Previously hidden or unacknowledged meanings and uses
of home emerge from these approaches. They are not elicited or framed by
fixed choice questions, ratings or sorting techniques.

It is not just the meanings of home described by individuals that need
to be explored further; it is also the meanings of home that society creates
and perpetuates. Researchers need to take an inclusive social, political
and economic view of housing and to recognize that not all the uses and
meanings of home are benign, either on the individual or societal level. Uses
and meanings, and housing itself, do not develop in a social or political
vacuum. In large part they are socially produced and reproduced for the
benefit of special interest groups whose interests, and influence, are often
obscured or ignored. As King has stated so succinctly "... buildings are also
social and political resources. They are a contested terrain. They are never
neutral but become platforms for promoting particular interests" (1992, p.
132). Who are the various parties involved in the production, regulation,
and management of housing? What are they trying to achieve with respect
to particular types of accommodations and particular types of meanings
and uses that they promote? How do they benefit from the achievement
of those goals? The recent emergence of new types of accommodations as

well as the dramatic development of single-family detached houses after World War II deserve this kind of analysis. The social production, if not the manufacture and manipulation, of the meanings and uses of housing by parties who have vested interests in those meanings and uses is also an essential topic to pursue (see Dovey, forthcoming). Once we begin to fully acknowledge the close connections that exist between housing and social order, between housing and special interests, and between housing, meaning, and ideology we can begin to develop a more complete picture of all of its meanings and uses.

We can also begin to develop a richer and more complete picture of what housing can be. Until very recently, the power of the single-family detached house as dream, symbol and standard has impoverished the range of housing provided or envisioned. Its idealization helped create homelessness by making the earlier residences of many low income single people — the SROs — substandard and socially unacceptable (Franck 1989, Groth, 1989). And it is the influence of this idealized image that makes it so difficult to see other kinds of accommodation, like SROs, as "housing" at all or to explore what could be their true benefits under particular conditions. The dream of the single family house impoverishes our vision of what housing is and what it could be — of the yet unrealized meanings and uses it could have. We need to conduct research that does justice to the variety of housing, households, meanings and uses that presently exist and that could be developed.

Conclusion

I have suggested in this introduction that research on housing should embrace a wide range of kinds of accommodations, kinds of households, and kinds of uses and meanings and that it should pay careful attention to the detailed nature of these four components and their interconnections at the individual as well as at the social and political levels. I have further suggested that we look more carefully at the ways that housing, households, meanings and uses are socially constructed and socially perpetuated, serving the interests of particular parties and restricting the interests of others. To be both more inclusive and more cognizant of complexity, at least conceptually if not empirically, is an ambitious goal but much of the research presented in this book suggests that we are already moving in that direction.

454   *K. Franck*

References

Cooper-Marcus, Clare. "Home-As-Haven, Home-As-Trap," in Quinn, Patrick and Robert Benson (eds.) *The Spirit of Home*. Washington, D.C.: Association of Collegiate Schools of Architecture, 1986.

Despres, Carol. "The Meaning of Home." *The Journal of Architecture and Planning Research*, 1991, 8(2), 96-115.

Dovey, Kim. "Home and Homelessness," in Altman, I. and C. M. Werner (eds) *Home Environments*. New York: Plenum, 1986: 33-64.

Dovey, Kim. "Dwelling, Archetype, and Ideology." Center. Austin, Texas: University of Texas, forthcoming.

Franck, Karen. "Shared Spaces, Small Spaces and Spaces that Change," in Van Vliet, W. et al. (eds), *Housing and Neighborhoods*. Westport, CT: Greenwood Press: 1987, 157-172.

Franck, Karen and Sherry Ahrentzen. *New Households, New Housing*. New York: Van Nostrand Reinhold, 1989.

Franck, Karen. "Overview of Single Room Occupancy Housing," in Franck, K. and S. Ahrentzen (eds) *New Households, New Housing*. New York: Van Nostrand Reinhold, 1989, 245-262.

Fromm, Dorit. *Collaborative Communities*. New York: Van Nostrand Reinhold, 1991.

Giddens, Anthony. *Modernity and Self Identity*. Stanford, California: Stanford University Press, 1991.

Groth, Paul. "Non-people: A Case Study of Public Architects and Impaired Social Vision," in Ellis, R. and D. Cuff, *Architects' People*. New York: Oxford University Press, 1989: 213-238.

Hoch, Charles and Robert A. Slayton. *New Homeless and Old: Community and the Skid Row*. Philadelphia: Temple University Press, 1989.

King, Anthony. "Building Institutionally Significant Histories," in Schneekloth, Lynda et al. (eds), *Changing Places*. Fredonia, N.Y.: White Pine Press, 1992, 124-136.

McCamant, Kathryn M. and Charles R. Durrett. *Cohousing*. Berkeley: Habitat Press, 1988.

Olkin, Susan. *Justice, Gender and the Family.* New York: Basic, 1989.

Perin, Constance. *Everything in Its Place.* Princeton, N.J.: Princeton University Press, 1977.

Rivlin, Leanne. "A New Look at the Homeless. *Social Policy,* 1986 Spring: 3-10.

Rubenstein, Nora. Personal Communication, July 1992.

Sherman, Harvey. Personal communication, April 1992.

Skolnick, Arlene. *Embattled Paradise: The American Family in an Age of Uncertainty.* New York: Basic, 1991.

Sprague, Joan. *More Than Housing: Lifeboats for Women and Children.* Boston: Butterworth Architecture, 1991.

Chapter 18

The Homeless and "Doubled-Up" Households

ELIZABETH HUTTMAN
California State University

The chapter discusses how a growing number of persons, both singles and families, lack a permanent abode of their own in the U.S.A. The National Coalition for the Homeless has estimated the number as high as two million. This chapter, utilizing a narrative approach, demonstrates how for all homeless, the main hope is to have one's own unit, that is, a permanent home, however substandard. In addition, the chapter analyzes why the "meaning of home" can also be defined in terms of having privacy and safety—for singles, one's own room where you can lock the door and keep your possessions, and or families, an apartment rather than a communal accommodation, even if one has a separate room.

Introduction

In the U.S. homelessness and "doubling-up" and use of other temporary shelter arrangements is a common condition for an increasing number of poor households. Some are on the street, some in massive city shelters, some families in single rooms in transient "welfare" hotels, some in motel rooms, and some in makeshift church facilities, some in specialized small shelters such as those for battered women and families in general, some in cars, RVs or even tents. For these people "the meaning of home" concerns, above all, some of the very basic elements of shelter. To them, much more than the households with a regular abode, having a home is an essential ingredient that will give their life structure and meaning, and stop their feeling of being like unneeded garbage pushed about and discarded (Rosenthal, 1989). To them "home"—a permanent accommodation–will provide the setting in which to start their life over, to get things right, to provide a place to allow a regular routine or pattern of living to go on. It will end the "nothingness"— the horror of no place to be, no home to go back to. For many, it will give them private space, rescue them from the continual stress of living in public space and from the incongruence between need and present living arrangements.

Populations without permanent accommodations

In the U.S. the potential for homelessness is great; unconventional households without sufficient income represent a noticeable proportion of the inner city households. For example, female headed households have greatly increased, now making up about half of all black households, most living in inner city areas. Some are recent divorcees but many are long-time solo households; a number are unwed young mothers and their children. Others are battered women who have left violent households. The singles men population has also grown. Many are unemployed, with a sizeable number of minorities living in inner city ghettos. A number are disabled and/or alcoholics, mentally ill, and possibly drug users (Wright, 1987a). For these and others, a level of living below the poverty line exists; benefits, if any, do not any where near cover housing costs (Wright, 1987b). Even if cheap housing existed, many of the above are ill-equipped to locate and keep it.

External factors

A number of economic factors, especially, decreased availability of older cheap housing units, less need for unskilled workers, and a noticeable drop in income versus rents, have made homelessness or doubling up more likely for these population groups, female-headed households, single young males, many who are minority members, and those with such problems as alcoholism, mental health, and drug addiction. The income gap between those on AFDC, General Assistance or other benefits, and the stable working class is increasing as benefits fail to rise with cost of living (Rossi, 1989). Income of single males in unskilled work, including service sector jobs, are also falling behind normal budgetary needs, with the minimum wage far below medium wages.

As far as housing, there has been a very significant decrease in the traditional transient hotels in inner cities that these populations, especially single men and mentally disabled persons, used (Huttman, 1990). Many of these hotels have been torn down or converted to condominiums or tourist hotels. The board and care homes the mentally ill have traditionally been placed in, after mental hospitals were closed, have also closed in large numbers. And subsidized housing, whether public housing or nonprofit units, are not being built, and, in fact, a substantial number of the present stock of subsidized units, nonprofit and public, built under 20 year contracts with private investors, are moving out of the low rent category as investors, after this time period comes to an end, put them back on the private market at higher rents. Section 8 housing allowance type assistance also becomes less available as fewer private rentals can be found at HUD's (U.S. Housing and Urban Development's) allowable rent, that is their fair market rents. In fact, in general in many U.S. cities affordable rental units for low income are no longer available; most low income must pay 40-60 percent or even 70 percent of their low income for rent, and usually these households get a bare substandard unit in an undesirable city area for that amount. And not all find that because with a scarcity of cheap rent units, landlords can take their pick, screening out unconventional households, whether women with children and no husband, those who are alcoholics or obvious drug addicts or noticeably mentally ill, or simply unemployed and/or on welfare checks.

It is not surprising then that those without permanent shelter, either homeless, doubling up, sleeping in cars or RVs, or even tents, has continually increased in the last five years. When no units can be located with rents below $250 as in Boston or even $350-400 in San Francisco, one can expect people out on the streets. Many sources (Conference of Mayors, 1989; National Coalition of the Homeless) number this population at 2 million or more. It no longer is just made up of the transient bum, the alcoholic, or even the mentally ill. It now includes many families, many of them female headed, but also a number of two parent families where the male head has fallen on bad times or the family recently moved to a new area.

In some areas half or more of the homeless are families, equalling over three-fourth of a million persons, according to Bassuk (1988) and the National Coalition for the Homeless estimates (1989). In the City of Oakland over two-thirds of those in shelters are families and the U.S. Conference of Mayors 1988 survey, in different cities, found that a third or more of the homeless were families.

Types of temporary housing

Before discussing meaning of home for these groups in temporary accommodations, it is useful to provide a description of the types of housing they live in now. For some, the temporary shelter is an accommodation with relatives or friends, a short term "doubling-up." These "guests" often try to be on their best behavior, while occupying the living room sofa or basement room or storage bedroom. Rosenthal (1980) points out how "doubling-up" is common for divorced women; he describes how these divorced women try to keep up appearances so their unorthodox temporary housing state is not known to relevant others.

If these persons are moving in with family they may be able to integrate back into the household. However, because of children the returning divorced or unwed daughter may not fit in, causing instead disharmony in the home. If the single relative, the family may after a short stay react negatively to his circumstances, such as unemployment, alcoholism, mental or physical illness, or possible drug use (Wright, 1987a). The welcome starts to wear thin and finally the situation becomes intolerable for the household.

The car or RV are other likely temporary quarters for the family or single. Families of even five persons have been found living in a car in a park or on a back street, without toilet or washing facilities. Meals are from a fast food facility or a soup kitchen, and the washup may be at a gas station. Often such living is interspersed with shelter stays, as McChesney (1987a) found in Los Angeles. A motel unit may represent another type of temporary accommodation, one either acquired by the household itself or one provided through the city's housing voucher assistance. Not only is the one room too small for the family, but the motel setting is not conducive to family life, due to use by such undesirables as prostitutes. And, as a SUNY study showed, the motel usually lacks play space and a school stop nearby (Brandwein, 1987). Another similar type of accommodation is the transient "welfare" hotel, where families share occupancy with singles, often alcoholics or drug users. These rundown units often only have toilets at the end of the hall and completely lack play space. Yet many homeless families are relegated to them by welfare departments in big cities, such as San Francisco and New York. These authorities heavily subsidize these welfare hotels, often at a rate of $3000 a month per room (Kozol, 1988). In fact the irony in this situation is that single men whose life style was somewhat congruent with living in these transient hotels have been pushed out so that owners could rent, at a higher price, the rooms to families housed by cities (Hoch and Slayton, 1989). Of course, there is even a shortage of these transient hotels with many recently demolished or converted to higher economic uses, such as offices, apartments or tourist hotels.

For many homeless, use of city or nonprofit agency shelters is the alternative to the street. These shelters vary in type. There are the massive city shelters, including the winter armory type, where there are rows of cots and large dining areas & mass communal use of wash facilities (Hope and Young, 1986). Such allow little privacy, even for the family; teenage boys may be separated from their mothers (Redmond and Huttman, 1991). Regulations are strict, with volunteers often setting and enforcing rules, including for the children; child rearing is no longer a private matter for the mother. For example, reporting on a public shelter, Boxill and Beatty (1987) point out shelter mothers are externally controlled with: "someone other than mother deciding when and where the family should rest, bath or secure housing and health care. Others determine when her family eats, evaluates her abilities as a parent, judges her need for supportive services, parent training for fitness to retain custody of her children."

For the homeless using massive city shelters, they may have uncertainty each day as to whether they will have an accommodation there that night. They at the most will be allowed a short stay and must then move on to other accommodations or another shelter. Each day they will be forced to leave the shelter from early morning to evening and are unlikely to get the same bed each night. This type of accommodation is indeed the most temporary of accommodations and the most public living, unlikely to provide any feeling of having a home.

Some small non-profit—often church—shelters try to do better, giving a specific sense of place to the user for the short period of time that he/she or the household is allowed to stay, although still subjecting them to daily eviction during daylight hours, sometimes only mornings, and to numerous regulations and communal living. Some are temporary shelter in a church working with other churches to supply, on a rotating basis, overnight accommodation.

Other non-profit shelters are improvements on these; they usually are ones serving a specialized family population. It may be battered women, or women being rehabilitated from drug use, or simply all families. This family shelter may be a sub-part of a larger shelter. The family shelter usually has more privacy, with a private room for the families, although in some cases two families share a room. The dining in some cases is less communal, with each family cooking separately. One main feature is a longer allowable stay period, after an initial trial period; this is often as long as 60 to 70 days (Redmond and Huttman, 1991). However, regulations are still strict and this may cause impairment of family functioning, including child rearing. And day time eviction is mandatory though often of shorter length, and not required of women with babies (Redmond and Huttman, 1991).

None of these temporary shelter arrangements equals a home. There is complete incongruence between the household's needs and the situation these types of shelters provide. The idea of the home meeting needs cannot even be approached in these unconventional shelter arrangements, where the shelter or hotel room sink must be used to wash babies or clean food, or where, in the welfare hotel or motel, a hot plate is used to cook the children's food. Ideas on space use of the home cannot be explored when the living arrangement is such an inadequate one (Altman and Werner, 1985; Korosec, 1985).

In this paper the homeless are shown to be lacking, even at the minimal level, the basic elements of a satisfactory home environment. For these users of temporary accommodation wishes for improvements are of a very simplistic survival level, for example the wish for a private room or for one's own cooking facility, rather than the more luxurious demands for interior living space that the average American family has, such as a recreation/family or television room. In comparison, for example, one homeless family of mother and son was overjoyed at obtaining a small room, with bunk beds, from a family shelter, after having been in a very basic church shelter of one large room full of sleeping bags (San Francisco KRON TV, 1990). A homeless man on the street was glad to find an SRO hotel room, with its basic but private room (Hoch and Slayton, 1989). This illustrates our point that for groups lacking a permanent home, demands/wishes are for striped-down elementary accommodation attributes that meet the most primitive meaning of home. Yet, obviously the intensity of these desires for these minimal basic needs is the main focus of this person's life. What the average citizen takes for granted, is the intense desire or dream of the homeless. The search for any shelter of the most basic type occupies much of the day of the homeless, and the lack of such is their main sorrow in life. For mothers with children it becomes an even more dominant matter, not only because of worry over care of the children, but in addition a very real fear that if they find no housing the welfare department may take the children away and put them in foster care, especially if these children are teenage boys that often are not welcomed in shelters.

The next major part of this chapter details the meaning of home for different types of homeless. This includes an evaluation of what attributes of a normal home homeless most find missing in their present situation, both from our study of opinions of staff in 25 shelters, and from other studies of such staff and of homeless users themselves.

The former home of the homeless

Before proceeding to this section, we want to remind the reader that what the shelter or hotel/motel user actually desires in his/her home environment may be far from what the household had in its prehomelessness state; in some cases some desirable features may have been met but others not found in the former home. For example, for many battered women in shelters, they and their children had previously lived in a violent environment of physical and emotional abuse before coming to the shelter (in our survey of shelter staff half felt over 75 per cent of the shelter children they knew had witnessed violence in the home); yet these women often lived in the pre-shelter period in a comfortable attractive home of standard quality which afforded considerable privacy, such as a single family owner-occupied home. Others did live in slum area apartments, especially if minority battered women.

For single men, their former unit was often a substandard transient hotel room, with bath down the hall and poor lighting. Yet, as Hoch and Slayton say, it at least gave them privacy.

Another type of housing not considered desirable by the average citizen, public housing, may also be considered desirable by the homeless. As one homeless mother of two children exclaimed to the author, she was finally going to get a unit in San Francisco public housing; her joy was that she would be able to stop rotating between welfare hotels the social service agency put her in. She would have a bedroom and kitchen. Yet, to the author this particular public housing project seemed very undesirable because of the dominance of drug gangs with their shootings.

The basic nature of meaning of home

Before discussing different types of wishes for the home environment in detail, let us present an overview. While many desires may be mentioned, there is both an obvious hierarchy of wishes for the home, from a basic one of a roof over one's head, to a separate bedroom for each child, and in addition there is the fantasy of the "dream home" seen on television. For example in our staff survey giving data on shelter mothers and children, there was evidence of their desire, or "dream" of a perfect home, with the many meanings involved, and at the other extreme, there were very

simple wishes of what a home should include. In Hughes' (1986) study
of battered women's shelters she found the children had fantasies of better
living... "fantasies about a different home life." While children in Redmond
and Brachman's research on shelters for women found the children dreamed
of a better home, their main wish, in some cases, was simply "that we can be
safe and happy" and for others, it was even more basic, that "we have some
place to stay." Children suffered emotionally from the continual uncertainty
as to whether they had to move from the shelter and find another place to
sleep that night. Their fear was very realistic, for in big city shelters, the
stay was often uncertain from day to day.

The dream for single men was also of a basic nature, as shown in the
Gibson's community study where their wish was as basic as just wanting
provision of showers and toilets, and for any type of roof over their head,
even a leaky dumpy house boat.

Basic desires for a home and direction of government policy

Even these basic meanings of home are ignored by American policy makers
who have directed their main funding for the homeless toward provision
of shelters where any basic attributes of home are lacking. Most of the
$2 billion of the federal McKinney Act money has gone toward shelters
and services related to shelter use; in addition a large hunk of state and
city monies has gone toward providing temporary shelters (Huttman, 1991;
Hoch and Slayton, 1989). The latter researchers point out that "emergency
and transit shelters have been created as a response to compassionate ap-
peals but officials and the public are slow to take up the cause of affordable
housing for the poor." They add: "although most large shelters are unpopular with the homeless and their advocates, they remain the primary
source of housing for the homeless in big cities because of their low operation cost." Because of federal cutbacks of housing subsidies, there has been
little ability to move homeless into a regular apartment.

Yet many researchers stress the urgent need for a higher level of shelter, considering the temporary solutions very harmful to the users (Hoch
and Slayton, 1989; Rosenthal, 1989; Stoner, 1987; 1989). Levenson and
Rivlin (1990) argue for the need for a higher level of shelter that better
provides "a haven, a home, as a place of personal meaning, safety, comfort
and nurtuance." They state that: "a review of the growing literature on
contemporary homelessness, especially the situation in the U.S., finds little
attention to the concept of housing as home, as something more than shelter. This is a dangerous situation because it creates the impression that
minimal settings for poor people and homeless people may be sufficient.

It raises serious questions when evaluating facilities for homeless persons," Hoch and Slayton add, that the success of shelters mean even liberals take this as the solution, while in reality shelters are dismal and demoralizing and help make people feel dependent.

Even in the half way solution, transitional housing with its private and larger family unit, Levenson and Rivlin argue we should not have it a place that increases the stress of the homeless, but that it is one where meaning of home is considered, even though it can never be a real home.

Maybe the below description of attributes of a home will help move policy makers toward provision of permanent units for the homeless rather than policy makers' present orientation of accepting the shelter with all its deficiencies as the solution, as Hoch and Slayton (1989) complain.

Desired attributes of a home and lack of such in temporary units

With this above overall introduction to the topic, let us now list specific attributes homeless, including those in motels and welfare hotels, and those "doubling-up", want in their home.

Diverse population

Before doing this one should remind the reader that the homeless population is a diverse population ranging from singles that are unemployed and may also be alcoholic or have a physical disability or mental problem, to a variety of types of female households, and even elderly. The meaning of home and its desired attributes are common to all. Since our own research and that of a number of researchers we quote is on mothers and children in temporary quarters, some of the desired attributes of home apply especially to them. Even among this group one must be reminded that some are battered women, who as McChesney (1987a) points out, had, in their pre-shelter period, an employed husband and often a comfortable home; some recent divorcees also had such before the separation. Other women are poverty cases of long standing, on AFDC for months or years, no longer able to pay the rent due to its increase but lack of noticeable increase in AFDC benefits; others are women waiting for AFDC.

Added to these household types are couples with children who have recently moved to the area and who have an unemployed household head; others have lost shelter due to demolition of the building. Singles also fall into a number of categories as mentioned above.

Physical shelter as a desired attribute of home

To all, a basic meaning of home is a physical shelter, a place to shield one from the rain, snow, or sun, and to provide a location for sleeping and eating in comfort.

One of Feltey's (1990) respondents said "home ... it is a place to stay ... some place to put my head and put my stuff." Even this most basic of wishes, to have a roof over one's head, as vocalized by the homeless in Feltey's study of women shelter users, and Gibson's (1990) of street-walking singles, mostly male, is not met for many homeless, except in very temporary ways.

Shelters, transient welfare hotels, motels, and certainly the street, do not offer the normal physical comforts. Some shelters are cold; many are communal with cots in a large room; some are make-shift bedding in a church or such used for other purposes in the day. The physical amenities are certainly at a minimum; showers and baths are shared and can only be used at prescribed hours.

Physical conditions of welfare hotels are little better; landlords often do not keep up maintenance and do repairs such as to toilets, nor supply sufficient heat. Many have problems of leaking roof, roaches and mice (Kozol, 1988). The bathroom may be down the hall, a hall used as a locale for drug addicts and winos, a hall that is the only play space available for the homeless family housed there. Doubling-up arrangements are often as bad, with use of the living room couch after the family goes to bed, and sharing their bath facilities. And car living offers little more than a roof, crammed car seat sleeping, and minimal storage facilities and of course no bath or cooking facilities. Most temporary arrangements lack a place to cook one's own food; in small shelters sharing of cooking equipment and food storage space often causes havoc, with distrust over whether someone has borrowed your food. In many shelters they forbid storage and preparation of food in one's room, if one has such; the shelter has its own cook and does not allow individual cooking, as true in many of our studied shelters. This bothers mothers who consider cooking for the children part of their job; the kitchen formerly may have been the center of their home life, a setting for functioning, and a place to nurture their family and carry on social interaction.

The noise and strangeness of the shelter and the crowded conditions also make it a poor physical setup. Noises may cause sleeplessness and nightmares by children, as staff in our study reported.

A place to keep belongings

A "normal" home is also thought of as a place to keep one's belongings, to store away one's momento of the past, one's extension of self. These temporary accommodations usually do not allow a place for such; for those experiencing the day-to-day use of massive shelters, they must usually carry their belongings out with them each day, for the period the shelter is closed, or in some shelters, use a minimal storage facility provided to them. Often the person or family must move from shelter to shelter, exhausting the allowable days of use of one shelter; with such a situation, one must keep cutting down on belongings. In family shelters and other specialized shelters the family again is limited in number of items; such a situation is even truer for those doubling-up with one's family or friends. Sometimes the car becomes the place of storage. One of Feltey's (1990) respondents shows how precarious the doubling up is and how belongings must be limited. Her respondent says: "you wear out your friends, you know, you sleep on their couches, and probably eat a couple of meals at their house and they start looking at you kind of funny." Imbimbo (1990) found for a welfare hotel population, it was the children that most missed their belongings. She says: "they're angry, all their beliefs are gone. They've lost everything, their toys, everything."

A place for healthy living

The meaning of home includes a clean sanitary place free of health hazards; it also means a place to recover from injuries or illnesses. The homeless suffer from very unsanitary conditions both in shelters where one shares communal baths and toilets, often not kept clean; sleeps in cold barrack like rooms next to many ill people, or welfare hotels/motels with their unclean conditions, or in cars without provision for sanitation or toilet facilities. Those living on the street suffer from cold, unclean conditions, and lack of facilities. Wright (1987a), an authority on health conditions of the homeless, reports; "the homeless, of course, are prey to all the ills to which the flesh and spirit are heir, but the incidence, prevalence, and severity of these ills are magnified by disordered and frequently dangerous living arrangements, exposure to the physical environment, inadequate provision for daily hygiene, poor nutrition, overcrowded and unsanitary shelters (when shelter is even available) and various sociopathic behavior patterns." Wright (1987a) adds: "Life in unsheltered circumstances is extremely corrosive of physical well-being. Minor health problems that most people would solve with a palliative from their home medicine cabinet become much more serious for people with no access to a medicine cabinet. Ailments that are routinely cured with a day or two at home in bed can become major health problems if one has neither a home nor bed." (Even those using a shelter, lack such during the day, and are on the street). For children, shelter living causes serious health problems (Bassuk, 1984). In the St. Louis Homeless Children's Project clinical medical observations found "homeless children malnourished, with significant untreated medical problems, developmental delays in such basic areas as cognitive development, language and motor functioning" (Whitman, Stretch and Accardo (1987).

A place that is safe and secure is a desire both homeless adults and children have

The city massive shelters are so unsafe many homeless do not want to use them. People are robbed and even beaten, with drug addicts and mentally ill the most offensive to others. In welfare hotels drug users again make the locale unsafe. And of course day-time living on the street is hardly safe with mugging and robbery likely, or unpleasant assaults by locals. Car living suffers some of these same problems, especially robbery. Children must be continually warned of the dangers.

Home as a haven and source of emotional satisfaction

As compared to the street and shelter, "home is a haven, a psychological protection from an unfamiliar and sometimes threatening world, as a place with familiar people who can help you", as Levenson and Rivlin (1990) state.

In description of meaning of home by a group of professionals, a major attribute of home was "an oasis and retreat," "warm," "a haven", as Levenson and Rivlin (1990) report. In our survey of shelters staff said mothers missed this. Home is a place where stresses of the outside world can be forgotten, where peace exists from neighborhood intrusions, including gangs on the street, or from unpleasant encounters with authority figures. Home is a place where the effects of poverty, such as not possessing certain material goods others in the community have, can be forgotten; or anger over one's poverty versus others' affluence be ignored; where dreams can exist, or television or VCR films or alcohol or drug use can alleviate the sorrow over one's own life situation.

For a child, home is a haven against a strange outside world; it is a place where warmth and bonding to the mother can take place; it is a place where peer group pressures of school and societal demands can be forgotten. Where the stigma of being poor can be ignored. If one lacks a home all these pressures of every day life are continually with you; escape from this is difficult.

Home is a place of belonging

As one shelter user said: "home is a place to come back to." To lack such, another said means "you don't have your own place to return to ... you are left out... you are just not in this world." As Rosenthal (1989) says, to be without a home is to be cut off from the world.

Home gives us an identity. As Proshanaky et al (1983) say "this is where I belong ... it is a place from which the world can be viewed," "this is my roots."

Even in the poor slums this feeling can exist as Fried (1963) showed in "grieving for a lost home," in this case a slum area of Boston occupied by Italian immigrants. While quality of housing improved for many leaving this slum area designated for urban renewal, they grieved for their former home for as long as two years. Home is a place of personal meaning, as many of the studies of the elderly show (Huttman, 1985) and Levenson and Rivlin point out (1990).

For children loss of their past home is very hard; staff in our study reported children crying and angry over the loss, and often puzzled as to why it had occurred, asking "when, mommy, will we move back to our own home" or "when will we have a real home?" In several studies, shelter users wanted to move to apartments, seeing that as a "permanent residence" (Levenson and Rivlin; Redmond and Huttman, 1991). In the Boxill and Beaty (1987) study of public shelters, one respondent said: "You are in a situation where you have a place to stay today but everyone knows there is a due date; you don't have a permanent place."

Freedom of action and control over environment

Home is a place you can do what you wish when you wish. It is somewhere you don't need to answer to anyone else. You, in a real home, don't have to go along with a program, just because you are staying there, or go to sleep when everyone else does. You have freedom from this in your own home (Fealtey, 1990). The shelter is unlike this; shelter life is a regulated routinized atmosphere as our study showed. As Hoch and Slayton say it is a very institutionalized atmosphere of many rules and regulations. In our surveyed family shelters, a number had regular getting-up hours, times to leave and enter the shelter, and often curfews, such as 8:30 p.m. in one. Often no visitors were allowed for the family. Regarding discipline for the children, physical punishment was not allowed. Many of these rules are necessary at the meagerly staffed shelters with their dense population of troubled people. Yet the rules emphasize this is not a home. For shelters with religious orientations rules may include attending service; for social service orientated shelters, they often include mandatory counseling attendance (Marin, 1986). As Rosenthal (1989) says for Santa Barbara: "Those seeking a meal or night's shelter at Santa Barbara's Rescue Mission, for instance, must attend a mandatory religious service. Even those seeking entrance to Transition House, the least religiously orientated of the local shelters, must stand in line for a long period to be admitted, fill out an application sheet, provide proof of looking for work, and follow rules which determine the time you must enter the shelter for the night, when you eat and go to sleep, how much noise you can make, what substances you may not imbibe, and so forth." (p.8)

The Philadelphia Committee for the Homeless, made up of homeless, in proposing to run a shelter with FEMA (Federal Emergency Management Agency) money, said: "We wanted a shelter of our own... We wanted to be different from the other shelters. At almost all those places, they tell you what to do and when. You've already lost control over your own life, living on the streets. In shelters you lose whatever control and dignity you have left." (Hope and Young, 1986, p.244).

In Feltey's study (1990) users also considered this a major complaint of shelter life; 28 percent of family users expressed frustration with this fact of shelter life, as one woman said: "I feel like I am a little girl at home. You have to be in at eight o'clock. I have a curfew at 30 years old. I feel like I am back under my mother's wing."

Another user added: "They say we are not allowed to have food in our rooms. We are not allowed to have candy in our rooms."

In the Levenson and Rivlin transitional housing study (1990) they say "rules set in place by each facility, which did differ somewhat across settings, were the single most criticized elements." The curfew requirement, the restrictions on visitors (most places did not permit outside visitors of any kind in the residents' room or apartments), the prohibitions against sitting or standing outside the buildings were other reminders that their lives were managed by an authority other than themselves... When asked about what they would like to change in the place, the rules were most frequently cited. Rules decreased independence and as Hoch and Slayton (1990) strongly feel, make people dependent.

Rules mean loss of control. For mothers, this could include control over their children. As our surveyed shelter staff said, discipline by mothers of children was prescribed by staff. And it goes farther than that. As Hope and Young (1986) state: "The parents lose their dignity, partly because staff take over and run the lives of the family, tell them when to get up, when to go to bed, where they can play, where they can't. Parents lose the respect of the child, who sees they don't have control of their lives."

To Boxill and Beaty (1987) "it is a peculiar context for living—for mother/child relations." They again point out agency personnel and volunteers control eating, sleeping and recreational hours. They feel it hurts the mother's functioning and bonding with her child.

It certainly means this shelter is not a home, not a place of freedom of action.

Another rule that makes a shelter not a home is the one concerning length of stay. For city massive shelters it may be only a few days while with family and other specialized shelters it may be 45 to 60 days, as we found for our surveyed shelters (Redmond and Huttman, 1991). Stay is often related to the mother's looking for work and for housing; if the staff deems the effort inadequate they may not let the person stay.

Privacy in the home

The meaning of home is not only that it is a haven where you can shut yourself off from the world and have a private life of your own; it is a hiding place (Levenson and Rivlin, 1990) away from public view. It allows individuality and independence. In our survey many staff commented that families lacked this in shelters. Levenson and Rivlin's transitional housing respondents considered these apartments an improvement over shelter living because the apartments allowed privacy and individuality; it was the feature the users liked best. And Hoch and Slayton (1989) see single men better off in traditional SRO transient hotels than their present likely accommodation, city shelters, because the former have private rooms, even though crude, while in city shelters there are only large rooms with rows of cots. In our family shelters, even though families have their own room, they must share this little space with all family members; second, they must use communal dining and bath facilities. Those doubling-up with relatives or friends lack privacy, and families living in a car have no privacy from other members. For our surveyed shelters families faced many communal aspects of living, from dining to bath facilities.

Privacy was a major wish of shelter women in Feltey's (1990) study, with a fourth of the sample naming it. Some said they wanted:

"just some place where you can just go and have your thoughts to yourself and be yourself."

This sharing facilities, instead of having a place of your own, no matter how small or dinghy, is a degree of intimacy not natural to most persons, and certainly not their idea of a home. As Levenson and Rivlin state: "it could be said that sharing intimate and personal tasks with strangers (in transitional housing) is something that does not occur in most households ... it echoes the message that this form of living is a shelter more than a home."

Children cry out against this situation. Surveyed staff in our study said children suffer from the problem of being surrounded by strangers. The communal life interfered with their sleep and normal bonding relations with mother. The continual contact with strangers means they pick up bad habits, and bad language, as shelter mothers in Imbimbo's (1990) study report.

A place to develop and grow

For children, another aspect of home environment is its provision of a setting for developing and shaping of personality (Horwitz and Tognoli, 1982). Neither a temporary shelter or a welfare hotel in most cases provide such a supporting setting. Our staff reported withdrawal a common trait of children; for some, instead it was aggressive behavior. Bassuk's early Harvard research, using psychological screening instruments, found developmental delays and learning difficulties to an alarming degree (Bassuk, Rubin and Lauriat, 1986). And from the St. Louis hospital project, Whitman et al (1987) reported that of 107 homeless children they tested on cognitive scales, 45 percent were in the slow learner group or mildly retarded (11 percent). On the Peabody Picture Vocabulary Test, using percentile ratings, 80 percent of these children fell at the 50 percentile level or lower.

In a study of homeless families McChesney (1987a) found children experienced developmental delays—they didn't walk, talk or sit up on time. And some children exhibited developmental regression, such as one child moving from potty training back to diapers. As a shelter director said: "the long term effects of homelessness are much more severe on children. How can they develop a healthy self-image? Parents who must devote all their energy to the fight for survival often ignore the educational and emotional needs of their children, according to those who have worked with homeless families. The children live without privacy or the opportunity to develop normally" (Mark Story, quoted in Gorden, 1987).

Our interviewed shelter staff pointed out that children had no place to study in a shelter, and second, the homeless experience was so devastating they were too emotionally upset to study. Many did not go to school.

As Imbimbo (1990) said from her shelter study: "homelessness disrupts every aspect of a child's growth and development. Insufficient sleep, poor nutrition, unsanitary living conditions, and the absence of medical care contribute to the development of illness and disease." These factors certainly harm chances of normal development and growth for the child.

A home provides a place to lower emotions and tensions– a shelter increases them

Home is a place of quiet and tranquility in many cases, helping keep emotions from the world stresses in check. (Hayward, 1975). The actual shelter situation causes non-normal emotional reactions. Staff in our surveyed shelters felt many children were depressed; half felt the most noticeable characteristic or behavior of homeless children related to depression and being withdrawn, confused or insecure. Nearly one third of these staff respondents saw anger from children over their present situation, and aggression, a noticeable characteristic resulting from such. Hughes (1986), in her study of battered women in shelters, also found aggressive behavior and nervousness among children. In several studies it was found children fought often (Redmond and Brachman, 1990; Phillips et al, 1988). Of course, some of the children's emotional behavior started in the pre-shelter period (many have suffered child abuse), but the shelter situation exacerbated it (Redmond and Huttman, 1989).

Shelter life also effected mothers' emotions. In our shelter survey, nearly forty percent of the staff responses, when asked about this, were that mothers felt fear, guilt and anger.

The home as a place providing self-esteem, status and dignity

Meaning of home is thought to include a setting for providing status and positive identity. Many writers on social class have mentioned home as a source of status. While many of the homeless did not inhabit a very enviable type of housing before they were homeless, just having their own apartment or house gave them a positive identity and self-esteem.

Obviously living in a shelter, in a welfare hotel or motel, or a relative's house, or worse, a car, or being on the street hardly gives one self-esteem or a positive identity. Rosenthal (1989) speaks of how homeless are given labels of being "transient", of being unstable—not having a fixed address labels them to an employer or benefit source. He also states:

"Precisely because they share so many values with housed people, homeless people are acutely aware of how straight society perceives their state and how this perception extends to a degrading of their personal worth. Every day is a lesson in their non-status. Housed people avert their eyes or look through them when they pass on the street. Police and merchants treat them as potential problems..." (p.14). Even agency contact often have negative images of them (DeGarmo et al, 1990). Marin (1986) relates what this stripping of social identity can mean "They (homeless) reduce their world to a small area, and thereby protect themselves from a world that might otherwise be too much to bear... Pavlov, the Russian psychologist, once theorized that the two most fundamental reflexes in all animals, including humans, are those involving freedom and orientation. Grab any animal, he said, and it will immediately struggle to accomplish two things: to break free and orient itself. And this is what one sees in many of the homeless. Having been stripped of all other forms of connection, and of most kinds of social identity, they are left only with this: the raw stuff or nature, something encodes in the cells—the desire to be free, the need for familiar space. Perhaps this is why so many of them struggle so vehemently against us when we offer them aid. They are clinging to their freedom and their space, and they do not believe that this is what we, with our programs and our shelters, mean to allow them." This is certainly a statement saying a shelter is not a "home".

For children, the shelter or welfare hotel again does not give status or self-esteem. In our shelter study some staff said children were so ashamed of having the shelter as their address that in school they made every effort to hide the fact. Kozol (1968) writing of New York welfare hotel, and also Kosof (1988) reported that homeless children are teased as "homeless kids" and how they have the school bus drop them off blocks from their accommodation. One reason homeless children do not go to school is this shame.

For children in a battered women's shelter, Hughes (1986) found they had below average self-esteem scores as pre-schoolers. And Imbimbo (1990), studying shelter children in New York, says: "the development of identity and self esteem is impeded in an environment where a child lacks control, privacy, stability and security."

Conclusion

The purpose of this chapter is to show how the homeless lack the normal "meaning of home" that authors in Altman and Werner (1985) discuss. Certainly the lack of status and self-esteem from the home environment, just described above, is one. In this chapter, it also has been pointed out that the attributes of the home, such as a place to belong, a place for privacy, a place that is comfortable physical shelter with adequate space (Horwitz and Tognoli, 1982; Korosec-Serfaty, 1985), and many others are lacking for the homeless. For example, the rules and regulations of the shelter mean freedom of action is limited for these people, just as true in a "doubling-up" situation. And a shelter or welfare hotel or motel is not a place free from health hazards, but one inducing health problems; nor is it free from crime. Nor is the shelter a place to store one's belongings and mementos; there is no or very little space provided.

While most homes have the meaning of a "haven" and place of emotional satisfaction this situation if not true for the homeless, with the shelter or streets hardly providing such. Nor is it a place for growth and development for children; in fact, as studies show, the shelter or welfare hotel/motel inhibit growth.

In the end, to the homeless the meaning of home is very basic desires, such as a decent roof over one's head, a bedroom for the children, and private bath and toilet. In today's America, there exists a group so far from mainstream housing conditions that their wishes as almost those of 1700 tenement dwellers, although the latter might have been better situated than our homeless today with their temporary non-private abode.

References

Altman, Irving, and Carol Werner (eds.) *Home environments.* New York: Plenum Press, 1985.

Bassuk, Ellen. "The homeless problem." *Scientific American.* 251. 1984. 40-85.

Bassuk, Ellen, and Margaret Daly. "America's homeless families." *Better Homes and Gardens.* December 1988. 27-28.

Bassuk, Ellen, L. Rubin and L. Luriat. "Characteristics of sheltered homeless families," *American Journal of Public Health*, 76 (9), 1986. 1097-1101.

Boxhill, Nancy, and Anita Beaty. Prepared statement. Hearings. "The Crisis in homelessness: Effects on children and families." Washington: U.S. House of Representatives. Select Committee on Children, Youth, and Families. 100th Congress. 1st Sess. 1987. 117-123.

Brandwein, Ruth. Prepared statement. Hearings. "The Crisis in homelessness: Effects on children and families." Washington: U.S. House of Representatives. Select Committee on Children, Youth, and Families. 100th Congress. 1st Sess. 1987. 117-123.

DeGarmo, David, Kathryn Feltey and Brian Pendleton. "Perception and attitudes of service provided to homeless women." Paper presented at the Society for Study of Social Problems meeting, Washington, August 1990.

Feltey, Kathryn. "The social construction of home by homeless women: Symbolic versus lived reality." Paper presented at the Society for Study of Social Problems meeting, Washington, August, 1990.

Fried, Marc. "Grieving for a lost home," In L.J. Duhl (ed.) *The urban condition.* New York: Free Press, 1963. 151-171.

Gibson, Dorothy. "A study of the apparent homeless in Sausalito." Report prepared for the Sausalito, California City Council. 1990.

Hayward, D.G. "Home as an environmental and psychological concept," *Landscape,* 20 (1), 1975. 2-5.

Hoch, Charles, and Robert Slayton. "The limits of shelterization," In Charles Hoch and Robert Slayton. *New homeless and old: Community and the skid row hotel.* Philadelphia: Temple University Press, 1989.

Hope, Marjorie, and James Young. "Work with the homeless: Emerging trends," In Marjorie Hope and James Young (eds.) *Faces of homelessness.* Lexington, MA: D.C. Heath, 1986.

Horwitz, J. and J. Tognoli. "The role of home in adult development," *Family Relations,* 31. 1982. 335-341.

Hughes, H. "Research with children in shelters: Implications for clinical services," *Children Today* March/April 1986. 21-25.

Huttman, Elizabeth. *Social services for the elderly.* New York: Free Press-MacMillan, 1985.

Huttman, Elizabeth. "Homelessness as a long-term housing problem in America." In Jamshid Momeni (ed.) *Homelessness in the United States: Data and issues.* Westport, CT: Greenwood Press, 1990.

Huttman, Elizabeth. "Short-time Horizons: U.S. policy for the homeless." Paper presented at the International Housing Research Conference, Oslo. June 1990.

Imbimbo, Josephine. "The educational experience of children living in temporary housing." Paper presented at the International Housing Policy conference, Paris. June 1990.

Korosec-Serfaty, P. "Experience and use of the dwelling." In Irving Altman and Carol Werner (eds.) *Home environments.* New York: Plenum Press, 1985. 65-86.

Kosof, Anna. *Homelessness in America.* New York: Franklin Watts, 1988.

Kozol, Jonathan. *Rachel and Her Children.* New York: Crown, 1988. Levenson,

Conrad, and Leanne Rivlin. "Transition Housing: Evaluating A New Conception of Housing." Paper presented at International Housing Policy conference, Paris. June 1990.

Marin, Peter. "Helping and Hating the Homeless." *Harper's Magazine.* January 1986. 40-49.

McChesney, Kay. Statement. Hearings. "Crisis in homelessness: Effects on children and families." Washington: U.S. House of Representatives. Select Committee on Children, Youth and Families. 100th Congress. 1st Sess. 1987a. 62-68.

McChesney, Kay. "Paths to family homelessness." In M.J. Robertson and M. Greenblatt. *Homelessness: The national perspective.* New York: Plenum, 1987b.

National Coalition for the Homeless. "New HUD report: Dramatic increase in homeless families, low shelter occupancy." *Safety Network*, 8 (4), 1989. 1-4.

Phillips, M., N. DeChillo, D. Kronenfeld, and V. Middleton-Jeer. "Homeless families: Services make a difference." *Social Casework*, 69, 1988. 48-53.

Proshansky, H.M., A.K. Fabian, and R. Kaminoff. "Place-identity: Physical world socialization of self." *Journal of Environmental Psychology*, 3. 1983. 57-83.

Redmond, Sonjia, and Joan Brachman. "Homeless children and their caretakers." In Jamshid Momeni (ed.) *Homelessness in the United States: Data and issues.* Westport, CT: Greenwork Press, 1990.

Redmond, Sonjia, and Elizabeth Huttman. "Battered women and homelessness: Evidence of need to look beyond to long-term social services assistance and permanent housing." Paper presented at National Council of Family Relations. New Orleans, November 1989.

Redmond, Sonjia, and Elizabeth Huttman. "Women and homelessness: Evidence of need to look beyond shelters." *Journal of Sociology and Social Welfare*, forthcoming.

Rosenthal, Robert. "Worlds within worlds: The lives of homeless people in context." Paper presented at the American Sociological Association meetings. San Francisco. August 1989.

Rossi, Peter. *Without shelter: Homelessness in the 1980s.* New
San Francisco KRON. "Homeless families." Television film. 1990.

Stoner, Madeline. "A non-homeless world: Ending America's shelter system." Paper presented at Society for Study of Social Problems. Session on Homeless.

Atlanta. August 1987.

Stoner, Madeline. "Beyond shelter: Policy directions for prevention of homelessness." *Social Work Research and Abstracts.* 25 (4), 1989. 7.

Story, Mark. Quoted in Gorden, R. "Homeless families suffering." *San Francisco Chronicle.* September 29, 1987. 9.

U.S. Conference of Mayors. "A status report on hunger and homelessness in American cities, 1988: A 27 city survey." Washington: U.S. Conference of Mayors, 1988.

Whiteman, Barbara, Jack Stretch, and Pasquale Accardo. Statement. Hearings. "The crisis in homelessness: Effects on children and families." Washington: U.S. House of Representatives. Select Committee on Children, Youth, and Families. 100th Congress. 1st Sess. 1987. 125-136.

Wright, James. "The national health care for the homeless program." In Richard Bingham, Roy Green and Sammis White (eds.) *The homeless in contemporary society.* Newbury Park, CA: Sage, 1987a. 150-169.

Wright, James. Statement. Hearings. "The crisis in homelessness: Effects on children and families." Washington: U.S. House of Representatives. Select Committee on Children, Youth and Families. 100th Congress. 1st Sess. 1987b. 73-124.

Chapter 19

Home is Where You Start From: Childhood Memory in Adult Interpretations of Home

LOUISE CHAWLA
Kentucky State University

Both housing researchers and the people whom they study necessarily adopt cultural frameworks of interpretation in defining the meaning of home. This chapter examines some major cultural interpretations of the significance of remembered childhood homes through the medium of four men and women who are articulate and self-conscious about the traditions that they draw upon. Through these case studies, it looks at how childhood memories persist in adult constructions of the meaning of home. In each case, choices of meaning are adaptive rather than passive: subjects select and shape cultural possibilities in keeping with parental relations and social and political status. Their resulting concept of home synthesizes adult conclusions with childhood origins. The results indicate that to understand childhood sources of the meaning of home, it is necessary to integrate remembered physical qualities of the home and neighborhood, family relations, sociopolitical status, and adult world view.

Introduction

This chapter is about how childhood homes and neighborhoods get turned into something less and something more through the alchemy of memory. It is something less because the hard or soft immediacy of reality is reduced to a vestige of itself, an insubstantial idea. It is something more because this idea takes fragments of memory and a vague general sense of how it was and embellishes a durable scheme of the meaning of home.

This chapter reviews this process in the life spans of four diverse men and women, with a focus upon the connections to childhood memory that they have established at the approach of old age. Its method is phenomenological, as it seeks to attend to their descriptions of the quality of memory as openly as possible. It is also hermeneutic, because rather than stressing shared qualities of human experience (Husserl, 1970), it explores how self-understanding is an interpretive act in which memories acquire meaning and value within an individual's particular time and place in history. In the terms of Gadamer (1975), whether we seek to understand ourselves or to understand others in the course of research, we proceed through a "conversation" with tradition in which we assimilate and adapt our culture's customs of language, thought and action to the conditions of our experience. As this exchange proceeds, words and images fill with meaning from the particulars of our lives, and our choice of available terms tells us where we are. The purpose of this chapter is to observe how culture and experience interact during the life process of giving meaning to remembered childhood homes.

This research is based upon interviews and close readings of poetry, essays, and autobiographical pieces by four men and women who are distinctive in that they are successful contemporary American poets: Audre Lorde, one of the most anthologized and reprinted African-American women poets; Marie Ponsot, who was hailed by Lawrence Ferlinghetti as "one of the most important young Catholic poets of the post-World War II period" when she began publishing in the 1950s, who interrupted her career to raise seven children and resumed it with two well-received collections in the last decade; David Ignatow, who as a young man won the attention and encouragement of William Carlos Williams and who has continued Williams' tradition of uncompromising urban poetry in more than a dozen books; and William Bronk, who won the National Book Award in 1982 for poems that now span more than forty years. Theirs is a distinctiveness that involves representativeness. By holding readers' attention, they have shown that they speak not only for themselves but for many, and that they do so with admired articulateness. In the words of Lorde (1989, p. 37), the poet's task is to "help give name to the nameless so it can be thought." In this respect, poetry is itself a phenomenology as the poet seeks to illuminate what he or she observes to be general human truths.

These four people have contributed to this chapter's hermeneutic as well as phenomenological purposes because they are highly literate and well informed about different cultural traditions regarding the significance of memory and the meaning of home, and therefore they have been able to identify the cultural heritages that they draw upon with unusual self-awareness. These heritages, however, are not theirs alone. They influence many—even environmental researchers; and so their work may help define some of the cultural assumptions embedded in research approaches as well as subjects' responses.

Another great value of the poets' careers is that their poetry, essays, and autobiographical writing constitute a trail of evidence of different orientations to memory at different periods of their lives. It is, in effect, a longitudinal record. Finally, these four people express diverse but certainly not unique conditions: two are men, two, women; two were born into settled upper-middle class homes and two to struggling immigrant families; one is an African-American who has reclaimed African philosophy for herself, one is Catholic, one Jewish, one Protestant; three have raised children of their own and one has not. Through the variety of their lives, they express a variety of beginnings and conclusions.

A recent review of literature on the meaning of home by Despres (1991) notes an interpretive bias that has favored behavioral and psychological dimensions to the neglect of societal and material contributions. This chapter will observe how some material features—notably the childhood dwelling's size, space for privacy, and surroundings—have remained important in memory. Perhaps more important, however, have been the quality of the home's internal family relations and external social, political, and economic conditions. They have made it either easy or difficult to accept childhood origins; and as these people have moved through new conditions in adulthood, their relations to their beginnings have changed. In research by Tognoli and Horwitz (1982) and Cooper Marcus (1992), childhood memories have proved an important part of adult relations to home. This chapter will explore how this childhood legacy can be sustaining or ambivalent.

Cultural constructions of the meaning of home

In the concept of home, body and soul meet. The word implies a physical frame in which we satisfy physical needs, as well as intangibles: love, security, ease, privacy. Therefore, the two great competing paradigms of modern thought are engaged by this word: that the world is a material mechanism, or that it is an ensouled organism in which a whole that is greater that the sum of its parts is intuited through a sense of goodness, beauty, harmony. For more than three hundred years, the first paradigm has dominated the scientific world view—which some would now call scientistic as it has been challenged by twentieth century physics but remains entrenched in popular thought (Griffin, 1988). According to Descartes' (1982/1637) original formulation of this position, the soul or mind is separate from the body, and body and world are machine-like; but paradoxically, the end of science is to make the world serve this soulless body. In practice, the concept of the soul became irrelevant and the mind became a by-product of the body's functions. The second, organic paradigm is Platonic, but it was reformulated by the Romantics in opposition to the rising power of science. Rather than a mechanistic world and mind, it identifies correspondences and creative exchanges in which the imagination has the power to apprehend truth (Abrams, 1971).

According to the first paradigm, a home is reduced to a house; and in keeping with this paradigm's dominance, most housing research since the beginning of the century has focused upon physical variables like hygiene, crowding, building height, and behavioral adjustments to the size and layout of rooms, or upon analyses of policies for the basic provision of housing. The Romantic focus upon qualities of consciousness and interdependence of world and mind has been inherited by hermeneutic and phenomenological methods. In recognition of the importance of both the physical and qualitative dimensions of home, the present book has collected chapters from both approaches.

These two paradigms have influenced more than research methods. They also influence people's use of memory. Like the word "home" itself, poets in particular stand in the middle of these two traditions. As twentieth century men and women, they are confronted by the materialist paradigm, at the same time as they are literary heirs to the Romantic tradition. As the poets that this chapter studies have picked their way between these competing claims, their choices have determined the significance of their childhood places; and their examples may give insight into how memory operates in other lives.

In the middle of his life, in the 1960s, Ignatow evaluated his experiences by the mechanical principles that he had assimilated.

> There is no intimation of divinity in even the most exalted
> and mystical moments. There are merely physical reactions to
> certain states of mind while the mind is a function of the body
> so that what happens to the mind or body is an interaction. I

am fighting for the scientific view of man. (1973, p. 248)

Measured by these principles, his memories of his childhood world appeared either foolish or wise. Most of his memories date from when he was nine, when his father opened a bookbinding shop and bought a house in a new Brooklyn development where the son was free to play games under sheltering trees, ride bikes, explore convivial streets, and read at leisure at home. During this time, his world usually appeared a positive presence.

> These were among my first thoughts on earth: I had been placed here as some kind of reward, given the gift of being what I was, and I loved by bike, praising it for moving at the command of my pedaling and steering in the right direction at my touch... The wind upon my face was like the hand of approval. (1981, p. 16)

Judged by his scientific view, these memories of a responsive, benign world appeared delusions fit only for mockery. Before this time, however, there was a darker family period when his father ran an unsuccessful butcher shop, when the son had the after-school chore of making deliveries and taking orders for the next day. His route took him past a cemetery on dark winter nights, where he felt afraid of "the mysterious, the something that was always behind me and yet threatened me" (1980, p. 269). In retrospect, this intuitive dread of death appeared accurate.

For Bronk too, a dread of nature as an overpowering immensity that engulfs human concerns began in childhood, although he could not articulate it until early manhood. In one of his rare poems about childhood, "Home Address" he associates a feeling like that of Ignatow beside the cemetery with his family's sprawling unmanageable Victorian house. When he or his sisters returned home, "In the winter, coming alone from school, / we waited outside till there was at least a light / and someone else inside" (1982, p. 16). In his seventies now, he lives alone in the same house, and the sense of a brooding power remains. "Something nourishes, / as a plant might, in the dirt of the floor, grows / in the light from the window or in the dark at night./ Horror is what it is called" (1982 p. 222). Bronk has personally internalized science's description of the world as an almost infinite field of recombining atoms within unimaginable magnitudes of time; and against this backdrop, attempts to construct a stable identity, including indulgence in memory, appear ludicrous. Within this context, his childhood house serves as a metaphor for general human efforts to create artifacts and mental constructs as shelters against this vastness—ultimately in vain.

Both Ignatow and Bronk express what they understand to be "the scientific view of man." It makes childhood memory, at best, a usable metaphor and, at worst, a laughable fiction. Their examples show that an atomistic, materialistic paradigm can only accommodate a limited range of memories, as a remembered sense of a cooperating, responsive world contradicts its basic assumptions.

There is a scientific explanation of both buoyant and brooding childhood memories within this paradigm that both Bronk and Ignatow have alluded to: Freudian theory. For Freud (1960/1905) too, the essential tragedy of human existence is that we are one with nature, so that no matter how heroically we try to bend it to our desires by extracting wealth and raising shelters and defenses against it, we return to it in death. The closest parallel to this utter subjection is an infant's helpless dependence on its mother, so that memories of the mother—or images of other women that substitute for her—often personify our dread of dissolution into Mother Nature at death.

The mother represents the positive pleasures of nature as well, because our infant bliss in being fondled and fed is our introduction to nature's sensual allures. According to Freud (1961/1927), it is the origin of the "oceanic feeling" of at-oneness with the universe which sometimes resurfaces in later life—as in mystics' ecstasies that they mistake for revelation. Oceanic feeling is the Freudian explanation for Ignatow's exultant memories.

In Freud's analysis, the house is a common symbol for women's sexual attractions. Freud (1935) believed that houses regularly represent the human body, and often woman's body, because they contain what he called "the essential thing in woman," that she encloses space. Because the childhood home is directly associated with the mother, it can be expected to signify her.

Although Bronk would consider Freudian theory one more clever attempt to give order to a world that is ultimately incommunicable and blind to our systems, he has played with its application. It explains his sense of a brooding menace in his childhood house as a justified fear of nature's power, combined with anxieties about sexual competition with his father for the love of his mother. Bronk recalls that his relations with his mother were close. In a recent poem about his life, he writes of "my not being able ever to set up house / somewhere with youthful mother for fear / young father will one day want to take me / to all the places he always goes himself" (Bronk, 1985, p. 9).

Also in keeping with Freudian theory, Ignatow connects his positive childhood moods and sense of home to his mother's nurturance. During a period of intense pressure and anguish in mid-life, he wrote in his notebook:

> I am trying to find out what memories, what experience in
> the past hold me to life. Not too much hardship. A memory of
> ease in my childhood. Going to the library, being able to sit at

a window and read, being free to leave and enter the house at will. What made me believe life was worth living? My mother's largeness. She wore a corset that reached from her breasts to her thighs. My mother's largeness felt protection for me against harm. I never saw it in violent motion and I imagined all was well (1973, p. 238).

Ignatow's entry illustrates the process of "life review" predicted by Freud's student, Erikson (1963), and empirically described by Butler (1963), which observes that people reminisce and reevaluate their past in times of trauma and at the approach of old age. Erikson suggested that the quality of care we receive in childhood—which usually means a mother's care—determines our world's general emotional tone, whether it be in the house or in nature at large. He also suggested that this initial world feeling provides a foundation for the assessment of life's integrity in old age according to cultural beliefs about the relations between nature and society.

Long before Erikson—and probably familiar to him through poetry, novels, and autobiography—the Romantics made a similar connection between childhood memory and mature integrity which may be described as a "life return." More than a simple review, it recommended a return to childhood spontaneity and unity with the world to the extent that the changes of adulthood allow.

Abrams (1971) has traced the Romantic model of development in the literature of nineteenth and twentieth century England, France, Germany, and the United States. In order to maintain a spiritual vision of the world in the face of mechanistic science, it transferred the idea of paradise—a place of union with God or the Good where the world's divine order is perceived—home in the ultimate sense—from Platonic preexistence or the Christian afterlife to the present universe, and it elaborated a faith in the agency of the imagination to perceive the world's goodness and amplify it through human creativity. The Romantics added that children enjoy a spontaneous attunement with the world which becomes a redemptive memory in maturity. They described a process of alienation from the world in mid-life as people are divided by adult worries and ambitions, followed—if one is fortunate—by renewed harmony in old age. In this search for peace and receptive vision, childhood memories provide a guide. Many Romantic authors sought this return in memory through a physical return to their childhood home.

Freudian analysis, life review, and the Romantic return present three versions of the significance of childhood memory. For Freud, the blissful source, the "nostalgia for paradise," is union with the mother in infancy; but we must relinquish this temptation of the childhood home in order to erect houses and other shelters of civilization as protections against piti-less Mother Nature. The recovery of childhood memory is redemptive—as the Romantics suggested—but only so that we can recognize its irrational, sexual nature and free ourselves from its compulsions. In a life review, the significance of childhood memory is that it provides a foundation for succeeding or failing to fulfill our culture's basic virtues. For the Roman-tics, childhood memories offer true insights into a world that we need to make home; and although adult suffering and labor may forever distance us from our first unthinking union with the world, we need to integrate these insights into the wisdom of maturity and the creations of art.

A critical issue in the above versions of memory is the interpretation of the imagination. When the imagination is a fictive defense against a real self-obliterating unity with nature—as it has been for Bronk and for Ignatow during his young adulthood and mid-life–then any faith in a co-operative universe—as in Ignatow's memories of sidewalk play—appears imaginative in the most pejorative sense of delusion. In Romantic phi-losophy, in which the imagination can intuit truths and contribute to the world's creative processes, childhood can be a time of insights and memory a way of preserving these sustaining perceptions. The importance of these conceptions is illustrated by Ignatow's eventual reevaluations of his mem-ory. In his sixties, he softened his scientific view, concluding that reality and the imagination are not separate, but that they are united by a common principle of metamorphosis, of "change, renewal, reassertion, reaffirmation of itself in constantly emerging new forms" (Ignatow, 1983, p. 98). His conclusion was prompted by his reading popular presentations of quantum physics which replace the old world of mechanistic relations with a new world of reorganizations in which human vision–for Ignatow as a poet, the imagination—has a shaping role. Within this new climate of beliefs, he has been able to accept the playful character of his childhood memories of well-being. As the Romantic model predicts, Ignatow has moved through unity with his world, to alienation, to reintegration (although never as far as renewed belief in an ensouled world). A later section of this chapter will examine how this development has been related to social and economic transitions in his life.

Ponsot's and Lorde's interpretations

Neither Ponsot nor Lorde have appeared yet in this discussion of the mean-ing of childhood homes and surroundings in memory because, as women, the preceding theories and models have left them out. The Romantics paid women the tribute that they retain their childlike unity with nature throughout life, making the care of children in the home their ideal role (Massey, 1985). Therefore women never have to pass through men's stages of alienation and recovery—or their stages of progression. As the Romantics wrote, middle and upper-class women were being physically enclosed in the "separate sphere" of the home, away from the ugly, dangerous, industrializing public realm (Lasch, 1979). Freud deepened this identification by determining that the house commonly symbolizes woman in the psyche.

In empirical confirmation of these differences, when Peskin and Livson (1981) analyzed longitudinal interviews that traced men and women from their teens through their fifties, they found that men tended to distance themselves from childhood memories while they were busy making their way in a "man's world," only entertaining them after they had achieved security in their forties, but women did not go through this distancing. The researchers attributed this difference to women's socialization into child care. In a study of residential histories, Horwitz and Tognoli (1982) also found that women maintained continuity with their past more easily than men, experiencing less disruption in moving out of their parental home to establish dwellings of their own. They attributed the difference to women's socialization into home-making.

For Lorde and Ponsot, as aspiring women born in the first third of the twentieth century, this cultural identification with the home, children, and childhood has presented both a problem and an opportunity. It has been assigned to them, not made by them, as part of social restrictions. Therefore they have had to redefine these connections on their own terms. In this process they have used memories of their childhood home flexibly, creating new variations of existing perspectives. To understand these meanings, and to better understand Bronk's stasis and Ignatow's transitions, it is necessary to reconsider the meaning of home within its social contexts.

Social contexts of the meaning of home

The preceding sections have presented different cultural explanations of the meaning of childhood homes as options that people select; but the social, political, and economic contexts of this choice are not chosen. In the light of personal circumstances, certain versions of home fit and others appear dissonant. This section will examine how these four poets have adapted existing definitions of home to the given realities of their experience.

There are three levels on which cultural ideals of home correspond or clash with personal experience: physical, familial, and sociopolitical. Home at its best is a place that meets physical needs and desires, where one enjoys emotional security within the family, which is nested in turn within general economic and political security within society at large (Chawla, 1985). For all four people, one or more levels of this ideal have clashed with their childhood or adult realities.

Both Bronk and Ponsot were born to upper-middle class parents with good addresses in graceful surroundings; and in their work they assume they belong where they were born and that it belongs to them emotionally, whatever their emotions may be: a sense of "insideness" (Relph, 1976) that corresponds to their parents' actual deeds of ownership and secure place within society. Their comfortable acceptance of their origins is shown by the fact that he still lives in the same house where he grew up, she in the same neighborhood. In Bronk's case, the big Victorian house that he moved into at the age of two was a sign of his father's success as an entrepreneur in housing construction, lumber, heating fuels, and real estate; and its Hudson Falls location rooted him within the river valley settled by his seventeenth century Dutch ancestors. Ponsot's father sold fine wines and liquors to a New York clientele. The family lived in a genteel neighborhood of Queens, New York where there were still undeveloped corners where her mother taught her bird-watching and the identification of wild flowers.

A primary theme of Bronk's poetry, however, is that attachments to homes and places are a cage as well as a comfort. As a child, he felt this ambivalence in the terms that the house was too big, drafty, and dark, eluding the family's control and vaguely threatening. In adulthood, its function as both refuge and trap intensified. He came of age with a young man's common ambitions: to find lasting love and success and to establish a home of his own. When he was still in his twenties, however, his father died; so that he moved back home with his mother to oversee the family business until a manager could be found. This "temporary" move proved permanent. He never married or moved away again, but watched his mother decline into old age and death within an aging house, and exchanged his youthful ambition to make a name for himself in the New York literary world for the responsibility of the family business until his retirement.

Bronk has concluded that his frustration of desires is not just his but universal. Similarly, the Freudian theory that he has played with identifies universal conflicts between ideal social roles and realities in a world in which the ultimate fulfillment is death. In the context of this scientific world view, Bronk's childhood intuition that home is a futile defense against overpowering forces is a metaphorical truth.

For Ponsot, raised in a cohesive Catholic family, life began and remained something different. The center of her childhood is embodied in her religion's image of the holy: mother and child. In a sonnet series in memory of her mother, "Late," she identifies her mother's legacy of love and trust with images of herself and her mother reading in the family garden.

Reading, sunned, outside,
I see your lit hand on the page, spirea
Shaking light on us; from your ring I see slide
A sun, showering its planets across skies
Of words making, as you read or I or we,
A cosmos, ours. (1981, p. 73)

It is not coincidence that she chooses natural images from the garden, because her mother connected her to the natural world by teaching her habits of attention and reverence, naming what they discovered, watching quietly, and reciting Wordsworth from memory.

When Ponsot grew up, this domestic model of generativity and intimacy became an obstacle as well as opportunity for fulfillment. By the time her first book of poetry was published when she was in her thirties, she had had five children, and two more followed. As she became absorbed by child care, her husband grew distant, eventually leaving her to support the children financially as well as imaginatively by doing translations of children's books at home. Heroically, she continued to write poetry, but not to publish, cut off as she was from public readings and contacts by her enclosure in the home, and feeling that her intimate maternal subjects were inappropriate for the public roles that male poets modeled.

"I say I wanted what I found at your side," Ponsot (1981, p. 73) has written in the poem "Late," affirming the connections to nature and generativity that her mother taught her and that she has reproduced. As with Bronk, however, her life has not matched her expectations. Her identification with home and children excluded her from the world of her husband, an artist, and artistic opportunities for herself. In a poem written after her mother's death and the sale of her childhood house, she welcomes the objects that she has inherited. "My mother instructed me in your behalf. / I have made room for you," she writes (1981, p. 65). Then the poem concludes, "And you, old hopes of the house of my mother, / Farewell."

For Ponsot, the way out of this exclusion was a divorce. By seeking it, she broke her society's and church's definition of her role and initiated her independent redefinition of her past. Whereas Ignatow has become more tolerant of his childhood memories as he has aged, she has become more critical. In an interview, she observed that all public roles—whether they be good daughter or wife or the poet as a dramatic oracular figure—are stereotypes that distort memory, which is never simple, and with it liberty to think and act. Like the Romantics, she believes in an ensouled world in which the imagination is the faculty that perceives truth; but in her case, it does so by detecting glosses and half-truths in stereotypical memory and working to recreate experience accurately. For her, contrary to Bronk, memory can be either a self-comforting fiction or a revelation of a real world of moral significance. She has published two post-divorce volumes of poetry in which many pieces incisively reconstruct her childhood home and family and the domestic circle that she recreated for her own children.

Both Bronk and Ponsot have embodied conflicts between their youthful hopes and reality in their experience of home. They have taken for granted, nevertheless, that their dwelling is home, whatever its limitations. For Ignatow and Lorde, born as outsiders within their society, defining what home is has been a struggle in itself, in which their childhood experience has been pivotal.

Ignatow's parents were Jewish immigrants who fled poverty and persecution in Eastern Europe. During his childhood in the 1920s, they moved residence a few times within Brooklyn as his father tried several jobs unsuccessfully, until he opened his own bookbinding business. Most of Ignatow's childhood memories date back to this final settled period when his father made marginal but adequate profits: memories of ease at home and on the streets and of his mother's presence. In school, he was taught that he lived in "the home of the free"; and in the seventh grade, he discovered Walt Whitman, whose celebrations of America expressed his own hopefulness, and who became a model for the type of poet that he wanted to become. Given his social background, however, writing became agonizing. He has named a recent collection in which he admits childhood memories *Leaving the Door Open*, because by early manhood he had begun to shut his door tensely against the noise in his parents' small house in order to write; and he continued to shut it against his wife and only son in cramped apartments of his own as he tried to continue writing after exhausting days in his father's sweatshop or a series of equally menial, consuming jobs. In the beginning, he still believed in "Whitman's America" and the goad to his despair was his inability to become a part of it. As years went by, he noticed that he was not alone in his predicament, and his poetry turned into an analysis of the duplicity of the American dream.

Paradoxically, Ignatow's success in finding a style and subject matter in keeping with American realities brought him acclaim, university positions, economic security, and time to write. Because his identity as a person and poet was closely tied to New York, he took a permanent position at York College in Queens and rented an apartment nearby; but after he was mugged in his apartment lobby, he became a Long Island commuter. He suddenly found himself at ease again among quiet tree-shaded streets like those of his Brooklyn childhood, where his memories began to return. His hard-won security restored continuity with his past.

I enjoy this world in its squirrels and cats and birds, its

silence after dark, its darkness outside my window and the peace
with which it is happening. In other words, that part of my life
which I remember from childhood that I love has been returned
to me and through my efforts at getting it back (1973, p. 332).

Added to his contentment, he and his wife had a daughter in this peaceful
period of life. With this achievement of a comfortable home of his own, he
has been able to "open the door" to memories of his childhood.

Lorde, like Ignatow, was the child of immigrants—with a crucial difference. For his parents, there was never any possibility of returning to the
poverty and persecutions they had left behind; whereas her parents were
black West Indians who came to New York before the Depression in order to work and save enough money to return to establish a good life for
themselves on their native island. The Depression defeated their plans; but
Lorde and her older sisters grew up with the expectation that they might be
told any day to pack their bags to go "home" to the island of Carriacou in
the Grenadas. Her mother never referred to the United States as more than
"this place." To prepare her daughters for its rigors, she demanded strict
obedience and kept her strong-willed youngest under constant supervision
in their small apartment. On the other hand, she nourished her children
on stories of the island's people, songs, waters, healing plants, flowers, and
fruits; and her youngest daughter would lie in bed at night in their Harlem
tenement piecing together the details of this magical place called "home."
Adding material to her imagination, at the age of four she began to read her
way through the children's room of the Harlem Public Library, where she
learned about other tropical countries of sun-browned people. The United
States, in contrast, was a land of foreigners, where white classmates called
her names and excluded her from their activities. As she put it later in a
poem, "This is a country where other people live" (1982, p. 55).

By the time Lorde was an adolescent, her parents had abandoned hope
of going "home," and she had gained freedom to explore New York's attractions in the company of a schoolgirl friend. On holidays and weekends,
they took possession of Manhattan's downtown streets and parks. The city
began to compete for the claim of "home"; but she was not able to reconcile
herself to it until she made some unexpected connections. After she had
established herself as a poet and college teacher, she was able to travel to
Benin in West Africa, which she believed to be her ancestors' source, judging from her facial features. Here she was startled to discover that many
of her family's behaviors were recognizably African—relations among family members, her father's role, the treatment she received as the youngest
daughter. After Africa, she visited Carriacou for the first time, to find it
remarkably African also. "This place," the Harlem of her childhood, she

realized, was one of the reaches of the African diaspora, as her ancestors moved from Africa to the West Indies to the United States. Therefore it was an extension of the range of home.

Another reason to learn to be at home in "this place" was the birth of a son and a daughter. When her own patience with the city's violence wore thin, she saw her children move into its streets as she had done in adolescence; and she decided that the city's contrasts between harshness and opportunity were their best preparation for the realities of their native land. Therefore she bought a home on Staten Island where she could have trees and a garden and overlook water, like the Carriacou of her mother's stories, linked by bridges to the city of her birth, Manhattan, which she now recognizes to be another island home.

Both Lorde and Ponsot, as women, have described generative links to their childhood home in a world that is essentially spiritual. Ponsot remembers that her mother created a magic circle in which she gave her daughter what she has described as a life-sustaining elixir to pass on (Ponsot, 1981, pp. 109-113). Lorde, growing up in a ghetto tenement without privacy or beauty, credits her mother with two great lessons. One was survival under any odds; but softening this harsh lesson were her descriptions of Carriacou that gave her daughter a lasting sense that "this is not all," that there were other possibilities beyond the limits of Harlem. This connection to Carriacou, which Lorde eventually carried back to Africa and then to the United States, was a racial connection through generations. In the African philosophy that she has made her own, the earth is animated by the guardian spirits of ancestors. "I get this sense more and more and more the older I get," she has said in an interview, "that I am part of a chain, I am part of a continuum. It did not start with me and it will not end with me, but that my piece is vital." Both women's interpretation of home as a place for bearing and caring for life is part of their mother's broader legacy of a sense of nature that primarily sustains rather that destroys.

Discussion

In the preceding four interpretations of home, childhood memories have expressed the internal family relations that the house as a building contained and the external social context within which it was contained. The house has not, however, been entirely dematerialized. In these four cases, remembered physical provisions of ease and beauty persist: the window where Ignatow read; the tree-lined streets where he played; the garden where light, leaves, and flowers amplified Ponsot's pleasure with her mother. Where memories are mixed with dread or anger, the physical environment collaborated here too. Lorde's mother's strict supervision of her daughter was successful within the confines of a tenement apartment; and Bronk's sense of an uncontrollable, time-assailed world was embodied within his family's over-large house. In these cases, the physical qualities of childhood places have colored memories' mood and meaning.

Despite the importance of this material foundation, these four cases show the potency of social relations in memory as well. In each case, family relations pervade vivid images of the childhood house. Where parents have suffered from political upheavals and economic or racial vulnerability, the children have inherited their struggle to secure a sense of home.

This midway position of the house itself between the internal drama of the child's place within the family and the family's external place within society requires a limited conception of design's contribution to the making of a sense of home. Important as design features may be to lasting images of comfort and pleasure, beyond the walls of the house the absence or presence of general social conditions of political opportunity and tolerance shape the experience of home. These four cases suggest that attempts to understand how a house becomes a home must take social conditions of equity and opportunity into account.

In addition to family content and social context, the meaning of childhood homes in memory reflects adult beliefs regarding the universe of nature, society, and the self. "If the meaning of home as identity is both collective and personal," Dovey (1985, pp. 40-41) has observed, "it is also in a sense universal." He has noted connections between representations of home, self-identity, and world view in indigenous cultures, and argued that Cartesian dualism and rationalism erode these connections through contemporary design, planning, and management processes. According to the four lives reviewed here, home, self-identity, and world view are related in modern as well as indigenous cultures, and the scientific world view derived from Descartes erodes a comfortable sense of home within the psyche regardless of the environment's plan or management. This chapter suggests that a comfortable continuity between an adult and childhood sense of home depends upon a general sense of "at-homeness" in the universe. As the examples of Bronk and Ignatow show, the universe can appear alien and threatening to a child as well as an adult; and according to the scientific world view that Ignatow in mid-life and Bronk throughout his life endorsed, these fears embody existential truths. In order to accept imaginative childhood bonds with the physical world, it is necessary to hold a world view that legitimizes them.

Mechanistic and behaviorist research assumes this scientific world view that makes memory and identity futile in a world that is not a comfortable human home. An interactive metaphysics in which natural processes and the human imagination continually reorganize into new forms, such as Ignatow came to adopt, or a metaphysics in which bonds of care and renewal join human and natural worlds, as in Ponsot's and Lorde's adaptations of Catholic and African spirituality, require other forms of knowing (Griffin, 1988). Methods chosen to explore childhood memory or a sense of home are therefore not neutral. The philosophical premises of both research and personal memory, this chapter suggests, shape conclusions. An exciting feature of the subject of home is that it requires that research attend to the simultaneous effect of physical experience, social conditions, and interpretive world views.

References

Abrams, M. H. (1971). *Natural supernaturalism.* New York: Norton

Bronk, W. (1985). *Careless love and its apostrophes.* New York: Red Ozier Press.

Bronk, W. (1982). *Life supports.* San Francisco: North Point Press.

Butler, R. N. (1963). "The life review." *Psychiatry,* 26, 65-76.

Chawla, L. (1985). "Knowing your place." In S. Klein, R. Wener, and S. Lehman (Eds.), *Environmental change/social change.* Washington, DC: Environmental Design Research Association, 155-161.

Cooper Marcus, C. (1992). "Environmental memories." In I. Altman & S. Low (Eds.), *Place attachment.* New York: Plenum Press, 87-112.

Descartes, R. (1982). *Discourse on method, and meditations.* Trans. L. J. Lafleur. Indianapolis: Bobbs-Merrill. Original editions 1637 and 1641.

Despres, C. (1991). "The meaning of home." *The Journal of Architectural and Planning Research,* 8(2), 96-115.

Dovey, K. (1985). "Home and homelessness." In I. Altman & C. M. Werner (Eds.), *Home environments.* New York: Plenum, pp. 33-64.

Erikson, E. (1963). *Childhood and society.* New York: Norton.

Freud, S. (1961). *The future of an illusion.* Trans. J. Strachey. New York: Norton. German edition 1927.

Freud, S. (1960). "The theme of the three caskets." In J. Strachey (Ed.), *The standard edition of the complete works of Sigmund Freud,* Vol. 4. London: Hogarth Press, pp. 244-256. German edition 1913.

Freud, S. (1935). "Symbolism in dreams." In *A general introduction to psychoanalysis*. Trans. J. Riviere. New York: Liveright Publishing, pp. 133-150.

Gadamer, H. G. (1975). *Truth and method*. New York: Seabury Press.

Griffin, D. R. (Ed.) (1988). *The reenchantment of science*. Albany: State University of New York Press.

Horwitz, J., & Tognoli, J. (1982). "Women and men living alone describe their residential histories." *Family Relations*, 31, 335-341.

Husserl, E. (1970). *The crisis of European sciences and transcendental phenomenology*. Trans. D. Carr. Evanston, IL: Northwestern University Press.

Ignatow, D. (1983). "From the notebooks (1972-1974)." *Ironwood*, 21, 98-105.

Ignatow, D. (1981). *Whisper to the earth*. Boston: Little Brown.

Ignatow, D. (1980). *Open between us*. Ann Arbor: Michigan University Press.

Ignatow, D. (1973). *The notebooks of David Ignatow*. Chicago: Swallow Press.

Lasch, C. (1979). *Haven in a heartless world*. New York: Basic Books.

Lorde, A. (1984). "Poetry is not a luxury." *Sister outsider*. Trumansburg, NY: Crossing Press.

Lorde, A. (1982). *Chosen poems old and new*. New York: Norton.

Massey, M. (1985). *Feminine soul*. Boston: Beacon.

Peskin, H., & Livson, H. (1981). "Uses of the past in adult psychological health." In D. H. Eichorn (Ed.), *Present and past in middle life*. New York: Academic Press, pp. 152-181.

Relph, E. (1976). *Place and placelessness*. London: Pion.

Tognoli, J., and Horwitz, J. (1982). "From childhood home to adult home." In P. Bart, A. Chen, & G. Francescato (Eds.), *Knowledge and design*. Washington, DC: Environmental Design Research Association, pp. 321-328.

Chapter 20

The Elderly and Housing Relocation in Sweden: A Comparative Methodology

BERTH DANERMARK
University of Örebro

MATS EKSTRÖM
University of Örebro

This chapter stresses the importance of acquiring greater knowledge as to what methodological considerations should be taken into account when looking at the elderly's housing situation. To this aim, it focuses on prescriptive methodological approaches to the study of the meaning and use of elderly housing. It introduces an intensive process-oriented design, focusing on the development of events in case studies of individuals. The purpose is to clarify concrete mechanisms, connections and relations between various circumstances, events, acts, meanings and states. Instead of seeking statistically significant correlations, causal relations are clarified through "contra-factual reasoning" and through "intra" and "inter-individual" comparisons.

[0] Funded by the Delegation for Social Research, Ministry of Social Affairs, and the Swedish Council for Building Research.

Introduction

From the political, planning and research point of view there is a real need
to gather information from and about the elderly and their environment.
During the forthcoming decades the number of elderly people will increase
substantially, by about 50% in Europe and a little over 100% in North
America (Myers, 1985). This development applies particularly to the very
old, i.e. people over 84 years of age. Another important change in this
context is that the standard of health among the elderly is steadily improving, as can be seen, for example, from the constant increase in the
average life-expectancy in developed countries. One consequence of these
two trends will be an increase in the number of elderly people living in their
own homes.

A major part of the research considering elderly people and their environment has focused on the problem of relocation in old age (Lawton,1985;
Pastalan, 1983; Schooler, 1976). Besides descriptions of relocation patterns
and willingness to move, a considerable body of research has been directed
partly towards the reasons and motives which are determining factors for
whether elderly people move or not, and partly towards the consequences
of relocation in terms of mortality and morbidity. The latter problems are
basically of causal nature.

The frequency of moving among elderly people is said to be relatively
low, (O'Bryant and Murray, 1986; Lawton, 1985; Newman, Zais and Struyk,
1984; Serow, 1987). However, relocation at the same time can be regarded
almost as a natural part of the aging process. Relocation can be seen as
a preparation for, a way to cope with, the changes which occur in old
age, e.g. reduced functioning, retirement and widowhood (Crivier, 1980;
Litwak and Longino, 1987; Speare and Meyer, 1988; Serow, 1987). The
home often has a special meaning for elderly people by providing control,
continuity, competence, security, identity, feelings of belonging to a social
and physical environment. (O'Bryant and Murray, 1986; Danermark and
Ekström, 1990). The attachment to home is an important reason why many
of the elderly want to stay put. An extensive research also indicates that,
for certain groups under certain circumstances, relocation causes negative
consequences with regard to social situation, psychological well being and
health (Borup et al, 1979; Bourestom, 1984; Lawton, 1977; Pastalan, 1983;
Schooler, 1976).

A prominent feature of the research on the elderly and relocation is the
dominance of purely empirical and quantitative variable-oriented studies.
These studies have been focusing on, for example, the relative significance
of different reasons for relocation, the correlation between willingness to
move and background variables, and the correlation between relocation,

background variables and morbidity. Intensive process oriented studies are rare (Rowles, 1983) and there are only a few contributions to the development of theories, both regarding the process preceding a move (Bowles, 1980; Wiseman, 1980) and the consequences of relocation (Danermark and Ekström, 1990; Schulz and Brenner, 1977).

Our position is that different types of correlation analyses, based on statistical techniques, have decidedly limited usefulness with regard to the clarification of the relatively complex patterns of causal interaction which form the process of relocation. Instead of routinely applying multivariate statistical techniques for most kinds of enquiry and reformulating the questions of causal mechanism as questions of statistical correlation, we argue in favor of a methodological approach which seeks to integrate extensive and intensive designs.

Before we present the characteristics of the intensive and extensive designs, the relationship between them, and our application, we will consider two basically different accounts of causality. A strong connection exists between different views of causality and methodological approaches.

The rise in the proportion of elderly people in the population in many countries and the increase in gerontological research, have not led to a corresponding evaluation and development of different methods. The ability of the elderly to take part in empirical studies has been questioned and the very old have often been excluded from investigations. In the last part we will deal with two problems concerning quality in the study of the elderly.

Complex causality and the combination of an extensive and an intensive methodology

Our judgments regarding research questions, and our methods of collecting and analysing data, are based on methodological assumptions about how to define and how to approach the phenomena which are of concern. The position advanced here involves a realist generative perspective, treating relocation as a process of complex causal interactions. This perspective emphasises that reality must be viewed as a complex whole, consisting of a continuously ongoing interaction between interrelated and mutually modifying phenomena and processes (Bhaskar, 1978a, 1978b, 1989).

Causality is, from the realist point of view, a question of internal powers and properties within objects, rather than a question of constant correlations between objects. Causal powers function in many cases as intervening mechanisms between internally related phenomena. These mechanisms are looked upon as tendencies. They reinforce or neutralise each other, which means that causal relations in their pure forms are not necessarily manifested empirically. From this perspective, causal statements express abstractions and not empirical generalizations. Observed regularities are not a necessary criterion of causality (Bhaskar, 1978a, 1978b, 1989; Harré and Madden, 1975; Keat and Urry, 1975; Sayer, 1984).

This perspective differs from the empiricist succession view of causality as a question of empirical regularities. The observation of constant correlations—of how one event is repeatedly followed by another—is seen to be a necessary condition for causal conclusions. The relationship between cause and effect is regarded as an external relationship. Behind this concept lies a picture of reality which consists of discrete, clearly distinct and independent objects and events. Reality is regarded as a closed system. The empiricist perspective finds expression in the extensive methodology which is characterised by the attempt to study, in a large population, with the help of standardised and structured data-collection methods, common properties and general statistical correlations between a limited number of previously defined variables.

However, the traditional extensive design provides no opportunity to study relocation as a process of complex causal interactions. From the generative and process-oriented point of view, the extensive design is useful in giving descriptive information about general patterns, but we are doubtful about the possibility of translating these correlations into causal relations. In order to clarify the active causal mechanisms behind the general pattern, it is necessary to use an intensive case-oriented design (Sayer, 1984; Qualitative Gerontology, 1988; Ragin, 1987). The following are central characteristics of the intensive case-oriented design (see Sayer, 1984; Ragin, 1987; Glaser and Strauss, 1967).

Intensive process-orientation: In this design, focus is on how different processes work, on how different phenomena and circumstances are produced and how they are constantly changing in a dynamic and reciprocal process. This can only be carried out if the researcher intensively and exhaustively follows a limited number of cases over a period of time and in context. In contrast to the variable-oriented design, this design uses non-standardised and non-structured methods, for example depth-interviews and participant observation. The design can be either prospective or retrospective. The latter is common within gerontological research in the form of life-course studies.

Interpretation and sensitivity: Interpretation of the implications is given a prominent role through the entire research process and is not limited—as it is in extensive designs—to questions of how certain previously collected empirical data should be interpreted in the light of a theory or a model. Methods used are sensitive to the different meanings people give their environment, their social situation and their actions.

Contextualisation: This design sets in focus the interrelation and transaction between various phenomena and the context. Phenomena are not regarded as discrete entities, separate from one another and from a larger context. Causal mechanisms are not additive but transactive.

Abstraction and the construction of concepts and theories: Contextualisation combines with abstraction to show causal relations in their pure form. Aspects of objects and relations are isolated from their complex chronological, socio-cultural and spatial contexts.

Comparison: The construction of relevant groups for comparison is a crucial part of the research process. Two basically different but complementary forms of comparison are: on the one hand, comparisons of the same individual or group over a period of time, in the context of different events and situations (interindividual comparisons), and on the other hand, comparisons between different individuals/groups in similar circumstances (intraindividual comparisons). The comparisons form a continuously ongoing process in that new objects of comparison can always be set against a background of previously acquired experience.

Many gerontologists today seem, in the main, to support the generative and process-oriented perspective illustrated above. However, causal explanatory research on, for example, aging and relocation is dominated by extensive designs, which in practice imply that parts of reality can, in a meaningful way, be regarded as isolated and as consisting of clearly distinct and independent objects and events.

Application

A study of old people living in a middle-size Swedish town who have moved during 1989 and 1990 has been carried out. The aim has been to investigate the social and health consequences of relocation among elderly people. In the study we combine an extensive design with an intensive one. The position advanced here is that the extensive and intensive designs are complementary, i.e., they give answers to different questions, and are not viewed as sequential, for instance as an explorative and hypotheses-testing phases in a research process.

The Register study

The register study is a quantitative investigation of all elderly people who have moved during 1989 and 1990 (about 2,800 individuals). The informa-

Table 20.1: Examples of indicators included in the register study

Background Variables	State of Health	Housing	Other
Age	No. of days of illness	Type of property owner	Distance of move
Sex	No. of occasions	Type of tenure	Home help
Civil status	medical treatment	Type of building	
Income	was required	Year of construction	
	Diagnoses	Length of residence	
	Cause of death		

tion comes from different authorities' registers, which means that sampling problems, which are otherwise common in studies of this kind, do not arise. Background variables information about state of health and housing have been collected. Examples of different indicators which are registered are shown in Table 20.1.

Control groups are made up and in the statistical analysis we seek to answer questions about which patterns can be illustrated, e.g. we look for correlations between relocation and a change in state of health and mortality. We also seek to define the study population in terms of categories, so that possible changes can be related to background variables and home circumstances. The quantity of material allows for sophisticated analysis, but what we do not discover through this kind of analysis is the causal mechanisms. Which are the actual linking processes and how do these processes work? The quantitative section of the study is decidedly limited with regard to explanatory power on these aspects.

The telephone interviews

The purpose of this investigation is to complement the register study with data about people's reasons for moving, how the decision was made and how people felt about the move. It was a total investigation inasmuch as all those households which had moved during a specific period of time were included in the study. The interviews were short and included only a few areas of inquiry, e.g. experience of the move, reasons for the move.

The home interviews

The next stage of the study was a small-scale survey consisting of home interviews. In contrast to the telephone interviews, these are, by their nature, more intensive. They aim to grasp the process of relocation, the reasons, consequences, and how the elderly coped with it. One hundred elderly people were included in an initial sample, and fifty of them participated. (The problem of non-response will be dealt with below).

The investigation was largely standardised, but at the same time the interviews were interactive and provided a lot of additional information. Two interviews with the same respondent, the first just before and the second just after the move, were conducted. The study included questions about e.g. civil status, family situation, previous occupation, current residence, attachment to the home and neighbourhood, the meaning of home, coping, control, reasons for moving, experience of moving, state of health and ADL and social relations. The analysis is based on intra- and inter-individual comparison.

The depth interviews and participant observation

The aim of this part of our approach is to identify different meanings of relocation, how the relationship between people and their environment is changing over time, and to explain the consequences of relocation, this in the context of the elderly's social position, living environment, life experiences, or patterns of action.

The study is conducted as a prospective longitudinal study. It is necessary to follow the people involved fairly closely over a period of time. The prospective design also counteracts the risk of retrospective bias, which is important because people tend to interpret previous experiences in the light of their current situation. Ten elderly people were visited three to five times in their homes. The first interview took place a few months before and the last a few months after the relocation. In order to follow the people involved closely, we also kept in contact with them by telephone in between the interviews. The open-ended interviews revolved around themes such as residence, biography, the relocation in terms of appraisal and action patterns, social network and social support, daily activities, mental well-being and health. The informants represent a diversity in social backgrounds, age (65-90), social relations, and health. Knowledge about the context such as housing condition, relationships with authorities in terms of power and dependence has also been gathered by participant observation.

The conversations were in most cases recorded on audio tape and were analysed qualitatively. The analysis is characterised by a constant interplay between contextualisation and abstraction in terms of concept formation. Two such central concepts which identify central causal mechanisms are control/power and the meaning of home.

Quality problems in the study of the elderly— evaluation and discussion

The quality of the information is determined by a number of factors. In an extensive design these are, for example, sampling and representativeness, operationalization and the validity and reliability of the measuring instruments, the possibility of isolating parts of reality from the influence of non-included variables, and also the characteristics of statistical analysis. In an intensive design, the quality is determined by the degree to which the sample includes people with different characteristics and under different circumstances (the sample is strategic, not random), the extent to which the interaction between the interviewer and the interviewee facilitates the clarification of the meaning people place on various events, situations and processes, the interviewee's willingness to talk openly and in depth about his/her situation, the researcher's sensitivity and ability of interpretation.

Research on methodological problems which are specific to gerontology has focused mainly on several aspects of quality which are central to the extensive design, sampling problems (Cartwright and Smith, 1987; Gentry and Shulman, 1985; Hoinville, 1983; Kalton and Andersson, 1989; Lee and Finney, 1987; *New Methods For Old-Age Research*, 1986), the development of measuring instruments for research on the elderly and on aging, upon the validity and reliability of these instruments (George and Bearon, 1980; Helmes, Csapo and Short, 1987; Lawton, 1975), and age-related problems with regard to standardised and structured interview and questionnaire studies (Andrews and Herzog, 1986; Gibson and Aitkenhead, 1983; Herzog, Rogers and Kulka, 1983; Herzog and Dielman, 1985; Herzog and Kulka, 1989; Rogers and Herzog, 1987).

We have chosen to deal with two largely age-related methodological problems which we see as central indicators of quality in both extensive and intensive research studies, even though the problems have different implications, depending upon which strategy is applied: the problem of selective bias and the problem of the reliability of information from elderly people.

Selective bias and quality in gerontological research

The risk of selective bias is a basic problem in research on the elderly. Experience shows that those who are particularly frail and vulnerable to changes in housing and the environment (the very old, the ill, those who are alone, those with a low income) are often under-represented and sometimes completely excluded from investigations. This is serious because the picture

Table 20.2: Participation according to age (%)

	Age			
	65-74	75-84	85+	Total
Participating	76	62	50	69
Non-participating	24	38	50	31
Total	100	100	100	100

given by the investigation can be far too positive and contribute to the reproduction/persistence of inequality and other disparities. In extensive research strategies this limits the possibility of reaching general conclusions. In intensive research (which does not aim at empirical generalization) the important breadth and variety of the cases studied and the ambition to include different aspects of a given phenomenon is impeded by selective bias.

There is some evidence that there is a decline in response rates with increasing age when using the most common (and cheapest) survey methods like mail and telephone surveys (Herzog and Rogers, 1988; Herzog and Kulka, 1989). The results from a Swedish large-scale survey of people's standard of living, carried out as standardised home-interviews, indicate the presence of a threshold at around 85 years of age, above which there is an increasing problem of non-respondence (SCB, 1988).

Relatively poor health among non-respondents in comparison with respondents seems to be a fairly general pattern in gerontological research, which has been observed in a number of studies (Atchley, 1969; Milne, Maule and Williamson, 1971; Norris, 1985; Rockwood *et al*, 1989), even though there are a few studies which do not corroborate it (e.g., Akhtar, 1972). This selective bias becomes particularly noticeable among the very old. Other characteristics that have been observed among non-respondents or drop-outs in panel studies are relatively low income (see, for instance, Atchley, 1969; Norris, 1985) and weak social networks (Atchley, 1969).

In our telephone interview survey which included 184 respondents, there was a decrease in the level of response as age increased (Table 20.2).

If we pick out a particularly vulnerable group, consisting of those who were 75 years of age or older with low income/pension (below SEK 50,000 in taxable income) and had spent 10 or more days in hospital during the preceding year, we find that the number of responses is lower than in the rest of the group, 2% compared with 6%. It is extremely important to

Table 20.3: Stated reasons for non-participation

Reason	No	%
Unavailable	16	27
Prevented from taking part	20	34
Refused to take part	21	36
Death	1	2
	58	100

develop knowledge about elderly people in order to adjust methods so as to reduce selective non-response. Reasons stated for non-response in our telephone survey are shown in Table 20.3.

The largest category, 'prevented from taking part', includes for the most part people with temporary or long-term physiological or psychological illnesses/disabilities or those temporarily in hospital or other health-care institution. This indicates that the number of health-related reasons is greater than the number which can be described as outright refusals (see also Herzog and Rodgers,1988).

In the small-scale longitudinal survey we found four types of non-participants to be particularly common: (1) those who just refused without giving any particular reason, (2) a relatively large group who gave health-reasons, (3) a large group who referred to problems and difficulties connected with the relocation, and (4) a number who for various reasons couldn't manage to, or didn't want to, receive visitors. If we add together the last three categories, we get a group, making up 58% of the non-respondents, which can be assumed to be in general particulary vulnerable to the changes which relocation involves.

There are, in principle, two strategies in order to deal with the problem of selective bias. The first is to complement information collected through interview and questionnaire studies with existing data and statistics or by interviews with relatives or other closely related persons. The second is to develop research strategies which suit the very old, the sick, in order to make it possible to a greater extent, for these people to take part in the studies.

People's motives for refusing to be interviewed are always related to notions about what participation may involve, about who the researcher could be, or what the interview situation might demand. Many elderly people may be uncertain as to whether they have anything scientifically interesting to tell or are even afraid of the interview and interviewer (Schmidt, 1975; Qualitative Gerontology, 1988). This uncertainty and unwillingness cannot be reduced by traditional, formal means of contact (i.e. by letter or telephone) which the researcher normally uses before an interview. We have tried a different, less formal procedure. After sending the elderly people an informal, hand-written letter, we paid them a visit. Such a visit gives one a chance to explain at leisure what the interview involves. It gives people a chance to see what kind of person the interviewer is and also to take an active part in deciding what form the interview should take. This means that the standardised interview is replaced by an interview suited to the capacities of the old old. As a result even very vulnerable elderly people participated. Our hypothesis is that a more informal, personal approach, and a non-standardised interview, is a feasible way of reducing the risk of selective bias (Qualitative Gerontology, 1988).

Reliability and the quality of information in gerontological research

Certain researchers have maintained that reliability is a particularly serious problem in the study of the elderly due to lack of concentration and comprehension, distress and the fact that elderly people need more attention and explanation (Hoinville, 1983; Colsher and Wallace, 1989). However, there are studies indicating that older respondents are as accurate as respondents of younger ages (Herzog and Dielman, 1985).

In this context it is not possible to talk about 'the elderly' as a homogeneous group (Schmidt, 1975). Underlying the kind of picture which Hoinville (1983) so clearly and explicitly draws, are assumptions about physiological limitations such as hearing defects and senile dementia, the latter being assumed to impair the memory and cause difficulties in understanding and expressing oneself. However, the discussion of methodological problems is not related to knowledge about how common various reductions in mental and physical capacity are in different age-groups. For example, Johansson and Zarit (forthcoming) show that the occurrence of dementia only becomes common in the 80-85 and above age-group. Amongst people in the age-group 64-80 it is relatively uncommon. A Swedish longitudinal study shows that the occurrence of severe dementia increases from 1.8% at about 70 years of age to 7.4% when the population has reached 79 years (Berg, Nilsson and Svanborg, 1988; Nilsson and Persson, 1984). The study also shows that very few of the people of about 70 years of age have hearing or sight defects which could limit their ability to take part in a questionnaire or interview study (DSF, 1980). Both the problem of non-respondence and the problem of reliability due to specifically age-related problems occur first and foremost around the age of 85 and above.

However, it is important not to limit the discussion of reliability to a question of the physical and mental state or other personal characteristics of elderly people. The interview must be seen as a social interaction and a communicative event (Briggs, 1986; Jones, 1985). The reliability of the information is related to at least five aspects of this interaction: (1) how co-operative the respondent is and how well he/she can identify with the aim of the interview and the interviewer's questions; (2) the relationship between the interviewer and the respondent (whether or not it is trusting, filled with anxiety); (3) the degree to which it is controlled and structured by the interviewer (how far the respondent is allowed to answer independently and spontaneously); (4) the respondent's ability to give a picture of his/her situation, views and feelings; and (5) the interviewer's ability to interpret the information (Gordon, 1970).

The experiences from our study indicate that elderly people often have plenty of time, are co-operative, and are interested in talking to other people about life experiences, which is a basic criterion for quality particularly when it comes to depth interviews (Qualitative Gerontology, 1988). Only in a very few cases have questions about health, loneliness, etc., been felt to touch upon a sensitive issue or to be threatening (see also Gibson and Aitkenhead, 1983).

An adequate interview requires knowledge and understanding concerning communicative norms and the social situation, attitudes, and capacity of the respondents. The quality of the interview can be limited by a lack of common experience and understanding. More qualitative research strategies have the advantage here. The less structured depth interview, especially when the informants are visited more than one time, gives the researcher a chance to understand and to take into consideration the old people and his/her context and it is possible to develop a trustful relation. This is of special importance when it comes to interviewing the very old.

Conclusion

Relocation is a process formed by a complex transaction between elderly people and their environment. This process involves various motives, decisions, patterns of action and consequences. A research review indicates that there is a lack of studies employing a design adapted to this process–oriented perspective. The dominating methodological approaches are of an extensive character, showing statistical correlations between a limited number of key variables.

With the starting point in a generative view of causality we present an approach which can integrate an extensive longitudinal and an intensive research design. The former gives descriptive knowledge about general patterns of correlations, and the latter informs us about the complex causal mechanisms behind observed phenomena. The position advanced here is that the extensive and intensive designs are complementary, i.e. they give answers to different questions, and are not viewed as sequential, for instance as explorative and hypothesis–testing phases in a research process. This approach is illustrated in a study of the relocation of elderly people and their social and health consequences.

Old-age research brings several specific methodological problems to the foreground. Two such central issues discussed here are that of selective bias and of reliability in information from elderly people. The study presented above, and experiences from earlier research, question the view of the elderly as being unable to participate in different types of studies, due to visual and hearing defects, confusion, senility, difficulty in remembering and fear of being interviewed.

However, the elderly cannot be treated as a homogeneous group in this respect. Problems with low response rates and deficient reliability appear in a significant way when the respondents are very old, i. e. about 80-85 years and above. The most vulnerable people, people with low income, poor health, or few social contacts, are often extremely over-represented among the non-respondents. At the same time, the very old are the most rapidly growing group in many countries, yet the knowledge about them is very limited. It is necessary to develop and test methods designed with regard to the characteristics of this population group. Here, the traditional, standardised survey methods are too limited. One way to cope with these problems is to use the non-standardised, depth interviews of informal character. Another way is to include data from existing registers and documents. A combination of these two methods fits into the integrated extensive and intensive approach advocated by this chapter.

References

Akhtar, A.J. "Refusal to Participate in a Survey of the Elderly," *Gerontology Clin.*, Vol. 14, 1972, p. 205-211.

Altman, I., M.P. Lawton, and J.F. Wohlwill, Editors. *Elderly People and the Environment.* New York: Plenum Press, 1984.

Andrews, F.M. and A.R. Herzog. "The Quality of Survey Data as Related to Age of Respondent," *Journal of the American Statistical Association*, Vol. 394, 1986, p. 403-410.

Atchley, R.C. "Respondents vs. Refusers in an Interview Study of Retired Women: An analysis of Selected Charateristics," *Journal of Gerontology*, Vol. 24, 1969, p. 42-47.

Berg, S., L. Nilsson and A. Svanborg. "Behavioural and Clinical Aspects of Longitudinal Studies," in J.P. Wattis and I. Hindman, Editors, *Psychological Assessment of the Elderly*. London: Churchill Livingstone, 1988.

Bhaskar, R. *A Realist Theory of Science*. Sussex: The Harvester Press, 1978a.

—— "On the Possibility of Social Scientific Knowledge and the Limits of Naturalism," *Journal of Theory of Soc. Behavior*, Vol. 8, 1978b, p. 1-28.

—— *Reclaiming Reality: A Critical Introduction to Contemporary Philosophy*. London: Verso, 1989.

Borup J.H., D.T. Gallego and P.G. Heffernan. "Relocation and its Effect on Mortality," *The Gerontologist*, Vol. 19, 1979, p. 135-140.

Bourestom N. "Psychological and Physiological Manifestation of Relocation," *Psychiatric Medicine*, Vol. 2, 1984, p. 57-90.

Bowles, G.K. "Age migration in the United States," *Research on Aging*, Vol. 2, 1980, p. 137-140.

Briggs, C.L. *Learning How To Ask: A Sociolinguistic Appraisal of the Role of the Interview in Social Research*. Cambridge: Cambridge University Press, 1980.

Cartwright, A. and C. Smith. "Identifying a Sample of Elderly People by a Postal Screen," *Age and Aging*, Vol. 16, 1987, p. 119-122.

Colsher, P.L. and R.B. Wallace. "Data Quality and Age: Health and Psychobehavioral Correlates of Item Nonresponse and Inconsistent Responses," *Journal of Gerontology*, Vol.2,1989, p. 45-52.

Crivier, F. "A European Assessment of Aged Migration," *Research on Aging*, Vol. 2, 1980, p. 255-270.

Danermark, B. and M. Ekström. "Relocation and Health Effects on the Elderly: A Commented Research Review," *Journal of Sociology and Social Welfare*, Vol. 17, 1990, p. 25-49.

DSF (Delegationen för social forskning). *Frisk eller sjuk pääldre dar* (Healthy or unhealthy in old age). Report No.1980:4. Stockholm, 1980.

Fry, C.L. and J. Keith, Editors. *New Methods For Old Age Research.* Massachusetts: Bergin and Garvey Publishers, 1986.

Gentry, M. and A.D. Shulman. "Survey of Sampling Techniques in Widowhood Research, 1973-1983," *Journal of Gerontology*, Vol. 5, 1985, p. 641-643.

George, L.K. and L.B. Bearon. *Quality of Life in Older Persons: Meaning and Measurement.* New York: Human Sciences Press, 1980.

Gibson, D.M. and W. Aitkenhead. "The Elderly Respondents," *Research on Aging*, Vol. 2, 1983, p. 283-296.

Glaser, B. and A. Strauss. *The Discovery of Grounded Theory.* New York: Aldine Publishing Company, 1967.

Gordon, H. *Intervjumetodik* (Interview methods). Stockholm: Almqvist and Wiksell, 1970.

Harré, R. and E.H. Madden. *Causal Powers—A Theory of Natural Necessity.* Oxford: Basil Blackwell, 1975.

Helmes, E., K.G. Csapo and J-A. Short. "Standardization and Validation of the Multidimensional Observation Scale for Elderly Subjects (MOSES)," *Journal of Gerontology*, Vol. 4, 1975, p. 395-405.

Herzog, A.R., W.L. Rodgers and R.A. Kulka. "Interviewing Older Adults: A comparison of Telephone and Face-to-face Modalities," *Public Opinion Quarterly*, Vol. 47, 1983, p. 405-418.

Herzog, A.R. and L. Dielman. "Age Differences in Response Accuracy for Factual Survey Questions," *Journal of Gerontology*, Vol 3, 1985, p. 350-357.

Herzog, A.R. and W.L. Rodgers. "Age and Response Rates to Interview Sample Surveys," *Journal of Gerontology*, Vol. 6, 1988, p. S200-205.

Herzog, A.R. and R.A. Kulka. "Telephone and Mail Surveys with Older Populations: A Methodological Overview," in M.P. Lawton and A.R. Herzog, Editors, *Special Research Methods of Gerontology.* New York: Baywood Publishing Company, Inc, 1989.

Hoinville, G. "Carrying Out Surveys Among the Elderly. Some Problems of Sampling and Interviewing," *Journal of the Market Research Society*, Vol. 3, 1983, p. 223-237.

Johansson, B. and S.H. Zarit. "Dementia and Cognitive Impairment in the Oldest-old: A Comparision of Two Rating Methods," *International Psychogeriatrics*, (in press).

Jones, S. "The Analysis of Depth Interviews," in R. Walker, Editor, *Applied Qualitative Research*. Brookfield: Gower Publishing Company Ltd., 1985.

Kalton, G. and D.W. Anderson. "Sampling Rare Populations," in M.P. Lawton and A.R. Herzog, Editors, *Special Research Methods for Gerontology*. New York: Baywood Publishing Company, Inc.,1989.

Keat, R. and J. Urry. *Social Theory as Science*. London: Routledge and Kegan Paul, 1975.

Lawton, M.P. "The Philiadelphia Geriatric Center Moral Scale: A Revision," *Journal of Gerontology*, Vol. 1, 1975, p. 85-89.

Lawton, M. P. "The Impact of the Environment on Aging and Behavior," in J. E. Birren and K. W. Schaie, Editors, *Handbook of the Psychology of Aging*. New York: Van Nostrand Reinhold Company, 1977.

Lawton, M. P. "Housing and Living Environments of Older People," in R. H. Binstock and E. Shanas, Editors, *Handbook of Aging and the Social Sciences*. New York: Van Nostrand Reinhold Company, 1985.

Lee. G.R. and J.M. Finney. "Sampling in Social Gerontology: A method of Locating Specialized Populations," *Journal of Gerontology*, Vol. 6, 1977, p. 689-693.

Litwak, E. and Longino, C.F. "Migration Patterns Among the Elderly: a Developmental Perspective," *The Gerontologist*, Vol. 27, 1987, p. 266–272.

Milne, J.S., M.M. Maule and J. Williamson. "Method of Sampling in a Study of Older People with a Comparision of Respondents and Non-respondents," *British Journal of Preventive Social Medicine*, Vol. 25, 1971, p. 37-41.

Myers, G.C. "Aging and Worldwide Population Change," in R. H. Binstock and E. Shanas, Editors, *Handbook of Aging and the Social Sciences*. New York: Van Nostrand Reinhold Company, 1985.

Newman, S.J., J. Zais and R.J. Struyk. "Housing Older America," in I. Altman and J. F. Wohlwill, Editors, *Human Behavior and Environment*, Vol. 1. New York: Plenum, 1984.

Nilsson, L.V. and G. Persson. "Prevalence of Mental Disorders in an Urban Sample Examined at 70, 75 and 79 Years of Age," *Acta Psychiatrica Scandinavia*,

Vol. 69, 1984, p. 519-527.

Norris, F.H. "Characteristics of Older Nonrespondents Over Five Waves of a Panel Study," *Journal of Gerontology*, Vol. 5, 1985, p. 627-636.

O'Bryant, S.L. and C.I. Murray. "'Attachment to Home' and Other Factors Related to Widow's Relocation Decisions," *Journal of Housing for the Elderly*, Vol. 1, 1986, p. 53-72.

Pastalan L. "Environmental Displacement: A Literature Reflecting Old-person-environment Transaction," in G.D. Rowles and R.J. Ohta, Editors, *Aging and Milieu*. New York: Academic Press, 1983.

Qualitative Gerontology, S. Reinharz and G.D. Rowles, Editors, New York: Springer Publishing Company, 1988.

Ragin, G. *The Comparative Method: Moving Beyond Qualitative and Quantitative Strategies*. Berkeley: University of California Press, 1987.

Rockwood, K., P. Stolee, D. Robertson and E.R. Shillington. "Response Bias in a Health Status Survey of Elderly People," *Age and Aging*, Vol. 8, 1989, p. 177-182.

Rodgers, W.L. and A.R. Herzog. "Interviewing Older Adults: The Accuracy of Factual Information," *Journal of Gerontology*, Vol. 4, 1987, 387-394.

Rowles, G.D. "Between Worlds: A Relocation Dilemma for the Appalachian Elderly," *International Journal of Aging and Human Development*, Vol. 17, 1983, p. 301-314.

Sayer, A. *Methods in Social Science*. London: Hutchinson and Co. Publishers Ltd., 1984.

SCB (Statistics Sweden). Unpublished Documents, 1988.

Schooler K. K. "Environmental Change and the Elderly," in I. Altman and J. F. Wohlwill, Editors, *Human Behavior and Environment*, Volume 1. New York: Plenum, 1976.

Schulz, R. and G. Brenner. "Relocation of the Aged: A Review and Theoretical Analysis," *Journal of Gerontology*, Vol. 32, 1977, p. 323-333.

Serow, W.J. "Why the Elderly Move," *Research on Aging*, Vol. 4, 1987, p. 582-597.

Schmidt, M.G. "Interviewing the 'Old Old'," *The Gerontologist*, Vol. 6, 1975, p.

544-547.

Speare, A. and J.W. Meyer. "Types of Elderly Residential Mobility and their Determinants," *Journal of Gerontology*, Vol. 3, 1988, p. S74-81.

Wiseman, R.F. "Why Older People Move. Theoretical Issues," *Research on Aging*, Vol. 2, 1980, p. 141-154.

Chapter 21

Egyptian Norms, Women's Lives: A New Form and Content for Housing

MOSHIRA EL-RAFEY
University of Michigan

SHARON E. SUTTON
University of Michigan

This chapter presents an ethnographic study that provides insight into how Egyptian women's cultural reality affects daily routines and compromises their capacity to achieve a sense of "at homeness" in contemporary housing. The study included middle-income women with differing degrees of adherence to traditional values who lived in two complexes located in desolate desert areas near Cairo. Composite portraits are presented which illustrate typical afternoons in the lives of four women, drawn to illustrate the spatial problems that women encounter depending on their cultural and religious values. The study is narrated against the history of Islamic domestic architecture which offers a road map of Egyptian culture. To address women's inequality, embodied in their inadequate housing design, the chapter concludes with a model for elaborating physical and social change.

Introduction

Female silence is incontestable in Egyptian housing design, where cultural norms block women's participation to create residential environments, whether as designers or users. In both roles, their voices are hidden behind the male figure. Yet as we will show, many women in this Islamic country continue to be secluded in their homes. Those who venture into the public arena to pursue careers may do so with great reluctance while they, and even the most liberated, continue to place great value on homemaking.

In addition to being a silent voice in crafting housing schemes,[1] Egyptian women bear an added burden of living during a transitional period when the centuries-old cultural traditions that clearly specified their behavior have been diffused by the influx of Western values. Egyptian feminist writer, Amina Al-Sa'id (1977, pp. 380-381) assesses Arab women's situation in this way:

> One of the most important challenges facing the Arab woman is that of trying to equate her inner self, her thoughts, attitudes, and feelings, with the contemporary social reality about her. It is not easy to resolve the contradictions, both personal and societal, which are bound to occur between the old inherited traditions and the new currents of thought. Society may move at an astonishing speed, but the mind is not able to keep up with the pace, and this applies especially to matters related to women... We have yet to achieve a balance between the development of the form of our new societies and the development of the content of those societies.

In short, Egyptian women face a double-edged problem of being excluded from advancing new housing forms while having lost the inherited personal and societal content that gives meaning to space. Modern residences simply mimic Western housing without considered attention to the climatic or sociocultural context, a situation that is especially difficult for women whose lives are centered in domesticity. As Saegert and Winkel (1980, p. 58) suggest: "The home for women is the place where they spend most of their time and on which they focus most of their activities.... Clearly the home environment represents both a set of significant satisfactions and a set of responsibilities that must be traded off with the pursuit of goals outside the home." The tradeoffs are even more

---

[1] The invisibility of women in housing design is not peculiar to Egypt. Cooper and Sarkissan, among others, lament women's underrepresentation in the design professions in the United States despite the fact that they are the primary users of the home (See Cooper and Sarkissan, 1986, p. vii).

exaggerated in an Islamic country where the cultural acceptance of men's superiority gives them unabridged control over women's private lives.

Background to the ethnographic study

Overview of a three-stage research process

The ethnographic study allows women to voice their silenced housing needs while providing a closeup understanding of how culture affects day-to-day routines, and therefore, the capacity to achieve a sense of "at homeness." It consisted of a nine-month, three-stage study. The first stage included four to six hours of open-ended interviewing with each of five women living in family housing at the University of Michigan in Ann Arbor. Two were American, three were Middle-Eastern, all were married with children. Different from the Americans, the Middle-Eastern women disclosed sizable concerns about their need for privacy (especially in the kitchen), and spoke of their husbands' control over shared spaces in the house. In addition, these exploratory interviews suggested that any investigation of Middle-Eastern women's housing needs would have to be read against an assessment of their personal and societal values.

Because the design of the entry[2] seemed critical to Middle-Eastern women's satisfaction with their apartments, two multi-family housing projects with different entry designs were selected for the second and third phases of the research which were conducted in Cairo. One complex, Madinet-Nasr, was designed with the front door leading directly to the living room while the other, New Maadi, had an entrance foyer that permitted the living room to be closed off. Both projects were built in the 1970's to house middle-income families.[3] They were located on the outskirts of this center of Islamic culture in an expansion into the desert. Both contained apartments of comparable size, and were constructed of similar materials on super blocks with three to four medium-rise buildings per block. In addition to questions regarding satisfaction with the disposition of specific spaces, a series of questions were asked to determine a respondent's degree of adherence to traditional values.[4] While there was no clearcut correlation

---

[2] In one instance, curtains were used to divide a tiny entrance hall in two so that one space led to the living room (used by men) while the other led to a nicely decorated basement (used by women).

[3] Middle-income Egyptians are primarily professionals who work for the government earning considerably less than laborers. Few are home owners.

[4] To assess whether a woman tended to be more modern or traditional in her values, thirty-five questions were developed centering around five themes—privacy, religion, family relationships, food habits, and sex roles—taken from the exploratory interviews and from classical Islamic texts (See El-Rafey, M. "Chapter Three," 1992).

between values and satisfaction, a survey questionnaire administered to 120 married women in both projects revealed that almost seventy-five percent of the respondents who valued privacy also preferred the apartment with an entrance foyer. Furthermore, religious beliefs emerged as a crucial factor, accounting for more than one-third of the variations in satisfaction with various aspects of the apartment design (El-Rafey, 1992, chap. 4).

However, what remained unanswered which subsequently was addressed in the ethnographic study was the immediate spatial experience of women as they organized their domestic routines according to cultural and religious beliefs. Additionally, it would be the first opportunity to speak directly with Egyptian women without the male presence that overshadowed the survey.[5] Conducted in the homes of eight women, about three hours were spent on each of four days with every informant while preparation for the biggest meal (lunch) was in progress, but before the husband arrived home. Major activities were recorded as to duration and place, and conversations were both open-ended and directed.[6] Here we present composite portraits which illustrate a typical afternoon in four Egyptian women's lives in order to clarify the range of environmental problems that are emerging as women accept or resist new social realities. Through their voices and actions, varied spatial constraints are unveiled as each person attempts to reinvent her domestic environment to reflect a perceived position in the broader society as well as a degree of personal commitment to inherited cultural and religious values.

The first subject, Amal, whose placement on the values scale confirms her strong adherence to traditional values, lives in Madinet-Nasr, as does Amira, whose placement is modern. The two New Maadi informants are Mouna, a traditional woman, and Madiha who is modern. However, before permitting these women to share their stories, we set the stage with a brief history of Islamic domestic architecture which discloses critical themes that are later recanted by the informants. We also describe the neighborhood environments of the two projects, their relationship with the city of Cairo and other support services which, as it will be seen, are other limiting features in the women's spatial landscape.

After visiting the four apartments, we summarize the major themes that have emerged, then translate them into a conceptual model which consid-

---

[5] Since the government agency overseeing field research felt it would be unsafe for female researchers to go door-to-door by themselves, male researchers were used who generally interviewed the women respondents in the presence of their husbands.

[6] The eight women who participated in the ethnographic study were between the ages of 32 and 41 because survey data suggested that older respondents in both housing projects were significantly less satisfied with apartment size, room size, and number of rooms. The group contained an equal number of traditional and modern informants living in each project, with and without careers (See El-Rafey, M. "Chapter Five," ibid.).

ers physical space as well as a dialogic process for addressing the social inequities embodied in Egypt's contemporary housing. While this chapter is specifically about the spatial needs of Egyptian women, it is also a blueprint for understanding how all disempowered persons are compromised by limitations in the physical environment and by cultural conditions that maintain the status quo. Through the conceptual model, we hope to illuminate a process for enabling any disempowered voice to invent new forms for culturally-sensitive environments.

A social history of domestic architecture

The daily experiences of our four informants must be narrated against the history and evolution of domestic architecture which is itself a road map of the progress of Egyptian culture. Prior to 1881, when British occupation began, the design of homes reflected the sex segregation that is required by Islamic religious rules, distinguishing between private and public through space-planning and interior decoration. The typical Islamic house, of which there are still many examples in Cairo,[7] was two to five stories high, depending on whether it was a private or multifamily residence. Windows on the ground floor were small, rectangular, and heavily latticed while those on the upper floor were configured to allow light and ventilation while assuring privacy for female members of the household, their placement high enough to prevent a passenger on camelback from seeing inside.

Rooms with openings covered by mushrabeya, or perforated wooden screens, faced inward to a private hosh, or interior courtyard, that brought people in touch with the sky, and thus with God. A male visitor entered through a curved passageway, curved to prevent any direct view of the hosh from the front door. The female members of an extended family were confined to the hareem, or women's quarters, where they socialized together, playing the piano, dancing, knitting, preparing young girls for marriage. The hareem was usually situated on an upper floor, separated from the hosh by a stairway and many closed doors. The semi-private mandara, or guest room for male visitors, was most often located on the ground floor while the qa'ah and maq-ad were respectively interior and exterior spaces located above (Encyclopedia of Islam, 1971, p. 209). Thus the Islamic house contained private areas for females where family activities occurred, and semi-private areas for males and their guests.

Well-to-do women had servants inside the home to assist with child care,

---

[7] For an overview of existing Islamic housing in the old city of Cairo, including private houses, palaces, low-income housing and mixed-use residences (See El-Rafey, M. "Chapter Two," ibid.).

but husbands supervised shopping outside the home. Women only went out
to visit the mosque, physician, or other women's homes, maintaining their
privacy by wearing the hegab, a long dress with long sleeves and scarf, and
the yeshmak or veil covering the mouth and nose. While privacy in Western
cultures is generally equated with power, in traditional Egyptian society it
was not a reflection of women's power, but of men's authority to entrap
them into isolation. Unquestionably, the traditional Islamic house form
was in every detail a footprint of female subservience, carefully configured
to hide women from non-family members in restricted areas of the home
where they performed domestic activities. Despite spatial limitations, it is
notable that high-density, low-income housing in which as many as 4,000
people lived and worked achieved these privacy requirements through the
discreet disposition of doors, corridors, and window treatments.

At the neighborhood scale, space was equally hierarchical with housing
being organized into distinct clusters each containing a shared semi-public
space centering around a mosque with carefully controlled access to a public
marketplace. The width of the streets with their tightly-hugging, impen-
etrable walls communicated which areas were semi-public, i.e., where only
local residents were permitted, and which areas were public. By clustering houses into discreet districts, familiarity among a group of families was
increased, thus confirming through the physical environment the Islamic
requirement to assume responsibility for your neighbors up to the seventh
house.

However, as early as 1805, Egyptians began to change their lifestyles
as secular education was offered to males and later to females. Numerous young Egyptian men began attending European universities, and a
steady stream of Western technical experts came to Egypt, thus diffus-
ing cultural traditions (Shaarawi, 1986). From 1863 to 1879, King Ismail
specifically encouraged Western development, constructing the Suez Canal
and a European-style opera house. The ambitious Suez Canal project put
the country in debt and resulted in a seventy-one year occupation by the
British. According to sociologist Saad-Eddin Ibrahim, "between Ismail's
demise and the liberal age (1881-1952) when Egypt was under complete
British occupation, development did not cease, but it was a development
mostly initiated by an alien power, designed to serve its interests and carried out mostly by foreigners" (Ibrahim, 1984, p. 25).

Westerners brought new standards for housing and neighborhood design which Egyptian architects and planners applied despite centuries of
traditions regarding rigorous social segregation that was expressed through
clear progressions of space from private to public. The hareem vanished as
did the hosh and narrow, walled streets; the kitchen was placed near an
entrance that opened unceremoniously to the living area; bedrooms were

sometimes given balconies facing the street or other dwelling units; windows had unobstructed views of wide thoroughfares laid out on a gridiron that no longer expressed a specific clustering of families. Built to accommodate the rapid migration from rural areas, the less ornate, distinctive enclosures of mass housing were also less responsive to the hot, arid environment.

Paralleling these changes in domestic architecture, Quasim Amin, an advocate for women's education, also called for freedom from wearing the yeshmak and being secluded at home. As modern trends began to clash with traditional norms, many women began to distinguish between those norms resulting from Islamic religious laws and those regulating the status of women that arose from male domination. However, although 150,000 women earned university degrees between 1928 and the early 1980s, thereby accessing professions that were once exclusively male (Sullivan, 1986, p. 35), the acceptance of men's superiority has remained. In addition, there is a duality in the expectations of their private and public life as described by Naila Minai (1981, p. 29):

> School opened women's eyes to wider horizons and prepared them to take active roles in their society, while home restricted their freedom in order to guard their reputation and marriage-ability. The best career in the world was tangential to the sacred feminine roles of wife and mother.

According to Ibrahim and Hopkins (1977), the contemporary Arab family is not as traditional as it used to be, but it is not totally modern either. The changing structure, functions, and values create tensions for women who have lost the clarity of their inviolable position in the home. Although there has been a relaxation of the norms of women's segregation, their spatial needs appear to be more or less under constraints inherited from the hareem.[8] As for the women interviewed, both Mouna and Amal, the two more traditional women, attempt to maintain their seclusion through the use of curtains, screens, and additional doors. Even the liberated Madiha has a recall of the ancient mandara for guests, enclosing a balcony to create a private family area, and, to a certain degree, all acknowledge, and Amal wholeheartedly embraces male superiority if only in religious and financial affairs. However, most poignant is Mouna, who simultaneously dwells in

---

[8] Survey data showed that eighty-one percent of all respondents, modern and traditional, thought the kitchen should have a door while seventy-six percent believed in male superiority, sixty-eight percent felt the wife should always obey her husband in economic matters, while sixty-five percent concurred that a woman's place is in the home and that the entry hall should not permit the view of strangers (See El-Rafey, M. "Chapter Three", ibid.).

the past and present, being a subservient Muslim wife at home while reluctantly assuming a career outside the home, the duality of her life amplified by the harshness of her physical environment.

Journey to Madinet-Nasr

Surrounded by dessert and mountains that magnify its pollution, the city of Cairo is packed with international-style office buildings and hotels that primarily are American owned. The Nile River acts like New York's Fifth Avenue. Its central, prestigious location generates the highest rents. Since all governmental, commercial, and educational facilities are concentrated in Cairo, this city of almost ten million attracts another two million commuters. Its metropolitan area has one of the world's highest densities with 82,900 inhabitants per square mile (Ibrahim, 1984, p. 31) as compared to 66,800 on the island of Manhattan. However, high rents and lack of opportunities and services in these new developments, thwarts attempts to disperse the population to satellite cities.

The journey to Madinet-Nasr from downtown Cairo takes at least thirty-five minutes by car and more than an hour by public transportation. Along the way, there are abundant opportunities for delays as you traverse the old city on a double-deck road, built to alleviate congestion, to Salah-Salem (Cairo's longest road which leads to the airport), past a dense middle-income district to the edge of Madinet-Nasr where a 100,000-seat stadium and the Central Agency for Statistics are located. With construction beginning about thirty years ago, the development has almost thirty successive neighborhoods of varying income levels which are strung out along Salah-Salem. The proximate ones are more affluent, their concrete buildings softened by landscaping, the presence of human activity, and a number of neighborhood services. However, as the road penetrates the desert, landscaping, human life, and services disappear making the boxy concrete structures appear even more brutal against the hot sun.

Afternoons spent with four Egyptian women

Dwelling in the past and present

In Amal's and Amira's neighborhood, undifferentiated buildings faced one another in a staggered design. Many of the terraces off bedrooms were enclosed, including Amal's which was used as an additional bedroom so that the one provided could function as a family area (Figure 21.1). Windows were covered over with heavy curtains or awnings to block the sun and the view. The building corridor was clean, its white walls lit by small plastic light fixtures, its stillness filling the concrete of a single, seven-story, open stairwell.

Amal's attempts to maintain seclusion through curtains, screens, and doors.

Both the physical appearance of the forty-year-old Amal and her apartment authenticated her traditional values. Opening the door with a wet hand, she disclosed that lunch preparations had begun. From a couch in the living room, only her head could be seen over the top of a white, louvered, swinging door, a door she added to separate the guest area from the family's private space as a remedy for her foyerless apartment.

> Privacy gives time to relax and a feeling of comfort from the outside world pressure. I like my private living room where we can be together as family without being seen from the outside, and I hate the kitchen window because it is overlooked by the neighbors.

Maintaining eye contact over the swinging door, she explained that her daily schedule starts at five A.M. and continues nonstop till nine P.M. Returning from her job as an assistant professor around two in the afternoon

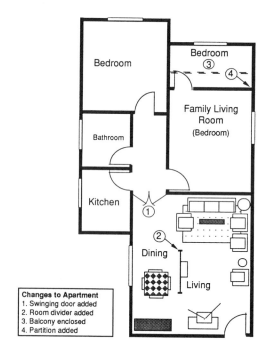

Figure 21.1: Amal's apartment

Floor plan and exterior adaptations of her apartment in Madinet–Nasr. Exterior view
of her balcony enclosed with dark glazing.

to prepare lunch, Amal's decision to work came out of economic need, not choice.

> No matter what position a woman reaches in her career, she must remember that her major role in life is her family's well-being because God created her to perform these responsibilities. God mentioned in the Holy Book that men are superior to women because they can perform religious requirements better than us, not because we are less, but because our natural creation requires for us to carry the children and to care for them.

The apartment was clean, but not very well-organized on that particular day. Amal apologized for her children's mess, saying that there had not been time to clean up. A double layer of curtains covered the window and a decorative wooden partition carved out a dining area from the living room.

> We eat our everyday meals here in front of the TV. It is close to the kitchen, but still it is not very convenient to my needs to save time and energy. Besides, I don't feel comfortable eating in front of the door because every time the doorbell rings, I have to cover my hair and the food.

Going out of her way to squeeze this appointment into the day's overloaded schedule, Amal appeared nervous, especially when talking about women's unequal rights.

> We have inherited from Islam some rules that have been misinterpreted by men to entrap women and we are still inhabiting these norms. These male-oriented, exaggerated rules add to the complexity of our lives as Islamic women.

The double burden of meeting career and family responsibilities was visible on Amal's strained face as she made tea. Rushed to finish the meal before her children and husband were scheduled to arrive, she graciously accepted assistance. With robot-like movements, Amal quickly snatched at a row of ingredients, working up a such sweat in the hot apartment that she apologetically removed her hegab. The value system of Egyptian society is unfair, she explained, because women carry the load inside and outside the home, but no one pays attention to their needs. Lacking housekeeping assistance, daycare facilities, and viable transportation, women's liberation has led to an even more enslaved life.

> Travel-to-work is a problem that I have to face every day. It is time-consuming because public buses do not come on a regular basis, and I truly find all these problems very exhausting. In order for a woman to combine career and family, she must be made out of iron, like a machine.

After about an hour of frenzied activity, two of Amal's three children returned from school going directly to their rooms to wash up and pray. Lunch was ready, and the visit ended.

Leisurely days socializing with neighbors

Amira was very excited about this visit and the chance to tell the story of her furniture. Encircled by Italian wallpapers, doors, curtains, chandeliers, carpets, and even a nonfunctional glazed-stone fireplace, Amira looked for affirmation of her design ability.

> I like my house; every piece in this apartment expresses my taste. I made it all after we returned back from our honeymoon. We had the traditional furniture that all Egyptian girls must have when they get married, like their grandmothers. I have changed it all. I could not stand it any more.

It was eleven o'clock in the morning and Amira's husband was out of the country on a business trip. Sounds of children at play could be heard coming from the bedroom.

> I think that if these apartments were given to us without any inside partitions except for the bathroom, it would have given us more freedom to adapt them according to our needs without any more expense than what we have now.

As she served coffee and homemade cookies in the living room, everything about Amira, her mannerisms, dress, apartment design, lack of concern for privacy, appeared modern. Yet when she began to talk about men and women's roles, a traditional perspective emerged.

> I believe that men are created stronger to do the hard work for us and provide our needs. Therefore, we're expected to provide them with a comfortable environment where they can relax to continue their hard jobs. I also believe that women's work outside their houses must be for economic needs only.

One child appeared in the doorway, curious to know what was going on, but he obediently responded to Amira's disapproving look by returning to his room. It seemed that her children were used to playing together inside.

> My children are not allowed to go outside by themselves.
> They play every Friday in the club, but not outside since we
> have had many security problems.

An interior designer by avocation, Amira continued the discussion at a leisurely pace, opening the doors of built-in cabinets in the bathroom and foyer to show-off neat stacks of stored goods.

Amira's Italian decor apartment

> An ideal house for me is a house where everyone can attain
> a feeling of well-being. In this apartment, it is the place where
> my husband has his space near the fireplace to drink coffee and
> read the newspaper quietly; and where I have space to relax
> after finishing my domestic work; where I have space for my
> hobbies (I am using the dining table for that purpose); and my

kids have a place to play safely; and where they have a nice
bedroom to decorate according to their taste.

The door bell rang and a male servant, hired to run errands and clean
house, appeared with groceries. While Amira was talking to him, the
youngest child began crying because the eldest took his toy. She chastised
all three children, making it clear that she did not want any more inter-
ruptions. Nor did any occur during the next hour-and-a-half while Amira
sketched relaxed days spent with neighbors, painting, knitting, sharing family problems, recipes, and ideas on child-rearing and apartment refurbish-
ing.

A life devoted to family and tradition

Mouna and Madiha lived in New Maadi which was similar to Madinet-Nasr
except that it had more landscaping and facilities and the buildings were
smaller in scale with four apartments per floor instead of eight. However,
the surrounding area had the same deserted quality as Madinet-Nasr, and
many of the terraces had also been enclosed, including those of both informants (Figure 21.2). For household items, they had the choice of commuting to Cairo to shop or of purchasing goods in the adjoining and expensive
Maadi neighborhood where the American community was located.

The visit to Mouna's began around 11:30 A.M. She was anticipating it,
her apartment clean and well-organized, her time more flexible since she
was not employed. Since Mouna's children were at school, it was quiet—a
quiet that was magnified by her calmness and the smile that brightened her
face whenever she referred to God.

> The Koran states that *"Men are the managers of the affairs
> of women for that God hath preferred in bounty one of them over
> the other."* Based on God's say, I believe in men's superiority.
> If this were not true, why do you think that God has mentioned
> it?

Surrounded by framed passages from the Koran hanging on all four
walls of the living room, and facing a french door that was painted with a
religious scene to block the view of the bedrooms, Mouna explained that
she takes care of daily family needs while her husband provides all financial
resources.

> My happiness and satisfaction comes from sharing my every-
> day life with my family. What counts for me is how to create
> an agreeable atmosphere that can make my family happy.

Figure 21.2: Mouna's apartment

Floor plan adaptations of her apartment. Like Madinet-Nasr, the area around New Maadi is unsafe, desserted, and not suitable for childrens play.

Mouna served tea and homemade cookies, then seemed a little embarrassed to say that she needed to start preparing lunch. Her kitchen was clean, lovingly decorated with white and red wooden cabinets that were installed floor-to-ceiling. Mouna cooked raw vegetables first, then spaghetti, and finally meat.

> The kitchen is my private space where I can retreat alone
> and enjoy cooking and organizing my utensils. It is where I
> spend my time and I don't like to share it with anybody.

After lunch was almost ready, Mouna began setting a formal dining table which was at the far end of the living room in a space created by enclosing the terrace. When asked whether eating in the kitchen might not be more convenient, she responded that she would not be happy to change their customs because the dining room was a big part of their daily life. She finds happiness when she sees her family dining around the table, enjoying the meal that she prepared. As she decorated the table with a lace table cloth and put out plates and silverware, Mouna turned her attention to the neighborhood.

> One of the things that I can't adjust is the outside of this
> building. We are far from everything, but I don't feel that it is
> safe for me to walk alone, even in the middle of the day.

Visual markers should be installed, she thought, to indicate where guests are permitted and where families can be private—as prescribed by Islamic law—and apartments ought to be arranged so that neighbors can not see into other apartments.

> There will be no present to our society without the foundation of our past. I believe that it is the only way for our generation to develop our identity. We must preserve our Islamic traditions in our daily life activities.

After finishing up her chores, Mouna changed her clothing to pray and get ready for her family's return home. It was almost 2:30 P.M., and the visit ended.

Professionalism nets a practical approach to homemaking

The visit with Madiha was different from the others because it was after lunch when the pressures of being a professional woman and a Muslim wife were perhaps most profound. Madiha's schedule as a chemist was intense — so intense that this meeting could only be arranged during a break one evening when her husband happened to be working late and her two small children were being cared for by her mother. Office files covered the dining table, and a male servant was cleaning. Madiha sighed, then began to relax.

> Sometimes I feel that I can't any more bear these maternal instincts that push me to cook, clean, and take care of my children, and my ambition to earn a successful career. However, I would never leave my children to be raised by a baby-sitter. It is a problem for me but I want both.

Reflecting on the resistance to change in Egyptian society, she said:

> Our mothers were like that and our daughters will also be like that. Despite the fact that women are professional and are holding career responsibilities, they are also required to hold household domestic chores. It is rare that any of our husbands will have modernized ideas and believe in the importance of sharing the chores.

Madiha had purchased a cake on the way home which she served with tea. She came across as a practical woman who minimized her domestic chores by hiring a cook once a week, and by shopping for large quantities of food which was stored on the shelving that she had installed in the kitchen. Convinced that women's advancement would only occur if women bore fewer children, became self-supporting, and learned how to stand up to men by questioning the norms that they had contrived.

> These traditional norms are men's creation to subordinate their wives in order to have freedom outside their houses. They imprisoned women under the flag of Islam which is a wrong interpretation because the Islamic religion gives women full rights.

Despite her modern outlook, Madiha had converted the balcony into a second living room, equipping it with a bookcase, lamp, and comfortable chair. Of the necessity for creating a private zone, she said:

> I feel that an ideal house will have two different spaces, one a private area, and one a public area that can be shared with guests. The outside public area has to be relatively large to accommodate all our activities and it can also be open to the kitchen area.

The servant announced that he was ready to leave. Madiha paid his salary and continued the conversation till six P.M. when it was time to chauffeur her children home.

Summary of women's cultural and spatial constraints

Continuity and change in the sociospatial environment

These four case studies and the research leading up to them suggests that Egyptian women are caught in a double-bind between the forces of continuity and the forces of change which affect every aspect of their personal existence and their position in society. While a spectrum of values coexist from modern to traditional, Madiha shows how a modern woman may still treasure nurturance, thus increasing her daily responsibilities. Amal is forced into the workplace by the rising cost of living but leaves the seclusion of her home with painful reluctance. Societal changes have increased educational opportunities for Amira, but the intimacy and emotional security provided by large, extended families with servants has also disappeared; rendering Amira's relaxed existence rare. More typical is the lone Amal who performs "like a machine" to shoulder the responsibilities of homemaking while succeeding in a competitive workplace. Yet despite their own stellar performance, each one of the women accepts men's superiority in some way, thus rendering their own voices silent in decision-making whether at the personal or societal level.

These contradicting forces are magnified by their poorly designed physical environments which require an additional investment of time and money without yielding a better quality of life. Both housing projects are located in remote areas that are destitute of services and public transportation which adds travel time (getting to work, shopping, chauffeuring children to school) as well as a cash investment (paying servants to shop, buying goods at more expensive stores, wear and tear on cars). These increased costs primarily are borne by our informants who are obliged to spend more time on domestic chores, get around without the family car, take an unwanted job to balance the household budget, or recreate an apartment that violates cultural norms.

The visual quality and spatial configuration of both neighborhoods with their vast, undefined areas and paucity of landscaping, pedestrian walkways, play spaces, or opportunities for visual surveillance, discourages their use for prosocial activities while encouraging criminal behavior.[9] The lack of security in the neighborhood environment also disadvantages our informants, restricting their mobility, increasing their stress, and eliminating the possibility for their children to play in the natural environment.

A framework for environmental change

Since physical space is a reflection of the cultural values which shape it, simply redesigning the residential environment will do little to improve the lives of our informants unless some consideration also is given to changing the structural inequities that allow such housing projects as these to be built. An environmental psychologist Maxine Wolfe (1985, p. 4) points out,

> ...In order to understand the role of the physical environment in affecting people's lives and to act on this understanding in ways that would actually improve people's lives, we have to have a framework for understanding the physical environment in relation to the political, economic, and social environments of which it is a part.

Wolfe, among others, calls attention to the resistance to changing this broader framework which requires dominant groups to give up a social order that benefits their superior position, a resistance that is complex in a developing country where multiple layers of domination exist. One layer is due to foreign and royal interests which conspired to intensify urbanization, increase land values, and make Egypt part of the world's capitalistic system (Ibrahim, 1984, pp. 26-30). Another is caused by the blurred line between religious law and male power which, as our informants conveyed, has created a male-oriented society that is sanctioned by the flag of Islam. "Cairo's overcrowding, deteriorating physical infrastructure and public services are made worse for the majority of its population by glaring inequities of power and wealth" writes Ibrahim (1984, pp. 33), and for women these injustices are exaggerated by the cultural norms relating to gender that silence their individual and collective voices.

In our view, women's inequality—and the inadequacies in housing design that embody it—can only be reversed by enabling them to develop a collective voice that has the power to transform the physical environment as well as women's position in society. We subscribe to the approach taken

---

[9] Merry (and Newman) argues that prosocial spaces are created by the way buildings are designed and grouped to provide for visual surveillance and physical demarcation of space. (See Merry, 1987, p.40)

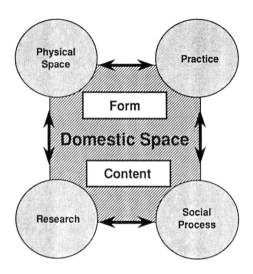

Figure 21.3: Model for elaborating new forms and content for housing

by Saegert and Leavitt who characterize a model for improving inner-city communities in the United States in this way: "The goal of the community-household model is not simply to transform housing and neighborhoods, not even whole cities; it is to facilitate the transformation that individuals, households, and communities seek for themselves."

Although what follows is tentative, we conclude by outlining an interdependent approach to the physical and social transformation of domestic space in Egypt.

A model for reinventing the physical and social environment

In this last section, we sketch out a conceptual model for elaborating a new form and content for the residential environment which considers the configuration of physical space as well as a dialogic social process for addressing the personal and societal values that give meaning to space. We propose that both components - physical space and social process - be elaborated through research and practice (Figure 21.3).

The parameters for physical change include a reconsideration of the activities that occur among specific groups of people in different types of space - all focused on increasing a sense of at-homeness among middle-

Table 21.1: Parameters for physical change

Type of Space	Users	Activities	Major Considerations
Private 2/3 of interior space	Family members	Socializing Dining Watching TV, etc. Sleeping Hygiene	No view from outside No view from semi-private Storage Flexibility
Semi-Private 1/3 of interior space	Family members Guests	Socializing Dining, etc. Cooking Entry	Kitchen with swinging door Also connects to private Foyer with door Storage Flexibility
Semi-Public	Building residents	Socializing Siting Meeting Gardening, etc. Homemaking Washing clothes Washing cars, etc. Playing	Security Control of access Lighting Visual surveillance Landscaping and screening
Public	Neighborhood residents	Going to school Shopping Walking Going to mosque	Police presence Public transportation Pedestrial amenities

income Egyptian women. Since the study reveals a strong cultural preference for distinct spatial hierarchies, the parameters of physical space are organized accordingly, looking at the users and activities occurring in four types of areas from private to public. We define private interior space as that place in the apartment which is reserved for shared and private family activities, including dining and watching television. Semi-private interior space comprises the entry, kitchen, and an area for socializing with guests. Two-thirds of the apartment is devoted to private space while one-third is semi-private space. Semi-public exterior space is that area which is restricted to building residents and contains the intimate recreational and service spaces that adults and children need on a frequent basis. Public exterior space is the area that is close enough to one's home to be considered "my neighborhood" where the facilities required by homemaking and childcare are located (Table 21.1).

Additionally, we propose several formal and informal arenas in which women (and supporters of women's equality) can break their silence and find a voice for exploring the parameters of social change, especially as it pertains to the environment. Because no one person can bring about significant change except in relation to a broad-based "we," a strategy is needed to place the individual accommodations that women are making in their homes into a collective medium. Social theorist Amitai Etzioni (1968, pp. 2-3) explains the mechanism for change in this fashion:

> While individual action is possible, it cannot be understood except against the background of the social action of which it is a part, on which it builds, or against which it reacts...Social change is chiefly propelled by social selves, by acting collectivities. Individuals participate, some even lead others, but the vehicle of change is a social grouping.

He proposes a model of an "active society" in which the generation of knowledge, shared values, and goals enables a group of people to develop a collective purpose and bring about social progress. We have adapted this idea and propose that parameters for social change be explored through a formulation of shared values, means, and ends.

To enable the creation of social selves, "safe places" are needed in which women can unpeel the layers of social inequity that are reflected in the physical world—places where they "not only can gain a shared understanding of the social, economic, and political sources of oppression in their lives, but where they can act independently of this oppression" (Feldman & Stall, 1992)—where they can invent a personal and societal content for domestic living that moderates tradition with the need for change. We imagine these safe places occurring in various arenas, informal as well as institutional, involving professionals as well as citizens, youth as well as adults (Table 21.2). As Feldman and Stall (1992) point out, the appropriation of a safe place is in itself a source of the resistance to subordination.

One arena of discourse is in the Ministry of Housing where formal or informal networks might form to advocate for changes in housing policy and design. Another is in the university where applied and theoretical approaches to addressing women's housing needs might be developed. A third is in primary and secondary schools where curricular and extracurricular activities might be designed to stimulate an awareness of the effect of the environment on the quality of life. A fourth arena is in the community where women can begin to define for themselves their sociospatial needs.[10] Each of these arenas can serve to forge the shared values, strategies, and outcomes that are needed to fundamentally change the way domestic space in Egypt is designed and used.

---

[10] Like Madinet-Nasr and New Maadi, most newly built middle-income housing projects seem to be without any communal facilities where meetings could occur. Therefore, this place is necessarily in someone's home.

Table 21.2: Parameters for social change

Safe Place	Values	Means	Ends
	Religious Cultural Social justice	Envisioning Taking action Reflecting Evaluating	Participatory process Physical design Research Practice
In the Ministry of Housing			
In the University	Cells developed through dialogue		
In the Schools			
In the Community			

While the task is enormous, Egyptian woman—and all women of color bring a wealth of skills to the situation. Women of color who are relegated to the margins of society have learned to live in multiple realities, to accommodate their behavior to externally-imposed rules, to shoulder the burden of providing life support for their families often in situations of economic hardship. If the skills that Egyptian middle-income women have developed to manage their private lives can be extended into their communal lives, we can imagine a situation in which they are able to transform their residential environment and, in so doing, to transform themselves and their race.

References

Al-Sa'id, A. "The Arab Woman and the Challenge of Society," in *Middle Eastern Women Speak*. Texas: The University of Texas Press, 1977, pp. 380-381.

Cooper, C.M. and Sarkissan, W. *Housing as if People Mattered: Site Design Guidelines for Medium Density Family Housing*. California: University of California Press-Berkeley, 1986, p. vii.

El-Rafey, M. *Housing in Egypt: Reconstruction of a Women's Point of View*, Unpublished doctor of architecture dissertation at the University of Michigan, 1992.

Encyclopedia of Islam, 1971:209, (Reference forthcoming).

Etzioni, A. *The Active Society: A Theory of Societal and Political Processes.* New York: The Free Press, 1968, pp. 2-3.

Feldman, R.M. and Stall, S. "The Politics of Space Appropriation: A Case Study of Women's Struggles for Homeplace in Chicago Public Housing" in *Women and the Environment*, Altman and Churchman (eds). New York: Plenum Press, 1992, in press.

Ibrahim, S-E. Cairo: "A Sociological Profile" in *The Expanding Metropolis: Coping with the Urban Growth of Cairo.* Malaysia: Eurasia Press, 1984. p. 25.

Ibrahim, S-E. and Hopkins, N. *Arab Society in Transition: A Reader.* Cairo, Egypt: The American University in Cairo Press, 1977.

Merry, S.E. "Crowding, Conflict, and Neighborhood Regulation" in *Neighborhood and Community Environments*, Altman and Wandersman (eds.) New York: Plenum, 1987, p. 40.

Minai N. *Women in Islam: Tradition and Transition in the Middle East.* New York, New York: Seaview Books, 1981, p. 129.

Saegert, S. and Winkel, G. "The Home: A Critical Problem for Changing Sex Roles" in *New Space for Women*, Wekerle, Petersen, and Morley (eds.). Colorado: Westview Press, 1980, p. 58.

Shaarawi, H. *Harem Years: The Memories of an Egyptian Feminist (1879-1924)*, translated by Margot Badran. London: Virago Press ltd., 1986.

Sullivan, E. *Women in Egyptian Public Life.* New York: Syracuse University Press, 1986, p. 35.

Wolfe, M. "Environmental Change, Social Change, and Environmental Design Research." Paper published by the Environmental Psychology Program at the City University of New York Graduate School, 1985, p. 4.

Part VIII
Conclusion:
Directions and
Implications
for Future Developments

Chapter 22

Getting From What Is to What Should Be: Procedural Issues

RAYMOND G. STUDER
University of Colorado

Procedural issues in housing research and housing praxis are differentiated, with a primarily focus on procedural issues in praxis. The procedural research agenda of housing praxis is characterized as including the application of general knowledge, the generation of instrumental knowledge, and the processes and methods of housing design and decision-making which link social and behavioral ends to built environmental means. Given that one of the major challenges in praxis involves linkages between sociophysical knowledge and sociophysical problems, the kinds of questions encountered in housing decision processes are critically reviewed in order to illuminate contemporary procedural issues. Four metastrategies are presented for generating knowledge required in housing praxis, concluding that all of these should be considered as components of a general program to address the multifaceted substantive and procedural issues involved.

Introduction: Housing research and housing praxis

Are inadequate responses to society's housing problems due to our lack of knowledge, or to our inability to use the knowledge we have? In other words, is the underlying problem one of substance or procedure? While most would argue as this volume does, that it is both, the purpose of this chapter is to reflect on certain procedural issues embodied in housing as praxis. In the succeding chapter, which focuses on substantive issues, van Vliet– illuminates the various disciplinary perspectives on the central theme of this volume, concluding that "the important differences in meaning and use of housing express themselves in the daily experiences of individuals." Organizing these experiences through organization of the built environment is the purpose of sociophysical planning, design and management, the processes which underlie praxis.

Some of the difficulties we face in addressing procedural issues in housing grow out of the scientification movement which impacted various fields of praxis during the sixties and seventies. Significantly influenced by this movement were such fields as policy analysis, planning, design and management. A by-product of scientification efforts was *instrumental rationalism*, a form of reasoning which focuses on the identification, assessment and selection of the most effective means, the value of which are taken for granted (Leiss, 1975; Dunn, 1982). This development, together with the so called rationality debate which it stimulated, was discussed in the introduction to Part I. What we now understand is that while they clearly overlap, procedural issues in housing research differ significantly from those in housing as a field of praxis. Housing as an area of research is driven by an interest in documenting what is (and possibly what will be). Investigations are generally undertaken with a view toward " testability, generalizability, and replicability of findings and theories" (Altman and Rogoff, 1987). That is, the focus of housing research is on factual claims, and the generation of knowledge of housing products and processes, generalizable to wider populations and contexts.

Housing as a field of praxis is, by contrast, concerned not only with what is, but also with what *should* be in a particular problem context. Procedural issues in housing praxis are thus integrally linked to intervention, decision making, and the generation of instrumental, i.e., situation specific, knowledge directly relevant to the selection of ends and means for a particular system or setting. Intervention and decision making thus involves an amalgamation of both factual and valuative claims. While housing researchers can select and bound problems according to their interests, practitioners must take problems as they come. That is, housing researchers seek general knowledge, while housing practitioners must solve situation-specific sociophysical problems. Although praxis incorporates both factual and valuative claims, decision making per se is intrinsically normative. For example, in documenting the conditions of a problematic setting, the needs and propensities of users should be empirically assessed. However, the decision to accommodate these through intervention in the built environment, constitutes a normative act.

Both general and instrumental knowledge is required to support decision processes in praxis, and like those of research, the execution of these processes is conditioned by the axiology, including the methodological commitments of the actors involved.[1] As is the case in other areas of praxis, that of housing struggles with a number of contemporary issues, including conflicting axiological platforms, quantitative versus qualitative methods, and positivist versus post-positivist perspectives. Indeed, even fundamental positivist assumptions regarding objectivity and rationality have come under critical scrutiny (Bernstein 1983, Alexander 1984, McCarthy 1978). Such issues, as noted above, grow out of challenges to the pervasive scientification of praxis. While the agendas of housing research and housing praxis are intrinsically different, they are, in certain respects, highly overlapping. Current procedural issues in housing research was the central focus of Chapter 2 by Jon Lang. The primary focus of what follows is on procedural issues of praxis.

The conceptual and procedural research agenda of housing praxis would seem to include three interrelated areas: 1) identifying and applying relevant general knowledge to specific housing contexts, 2) generating instrumental knowledge required for intervention in specific contexts, and 3) development of more effective decision-making processes and methods.

Procedural issues in housing praxis

As is amply documented in this volume, the research agenda of praxis includes the search for linkages between the social and behavioral sciences and the practical problems of planning, designing, and managing housing environments for human use. To refine this linkage requires a firm understanding of how questions and issues emerge in decision processes involved in realizing housing systems and settings. Setting aside differences among particular of design and decision making process models, let us briefly, but

---

[1] Axiology refers to the world view—the ontological, epistemological, paradigmatic, and theoretical platform—upon which investigations of phenomena are predicated (e.g., Sutherland 1979).

critically, review the major questions and issues that must be addressed in accommodating the housing needs of a population. The intent of the following is not to address specific intervention methodologies, but rather to examine certain issues that inform the invention or selection of appropriate methods for this purpose. The major questions which must be addressed in decision making include the following: what is?, what should be?, what could be?, what would happen if?, and what happens when?

What is?

The act of intervening in the built environment is predicated on the presumption or perception of a population of stakeholders that something is amiss (or will be if existing trends continue).[2] Since the enterprise is directed toward changing the state of human social and behavioral affairs (via intervention in the built environment) from an existing to a more desirable state, the process logically begins with an assessment of the existing conditions.

Assessment of the existing state of sociophysical affairs translates to "what are the facts?" The response is clearly linked to the axiological posture of one who would observe, describe and model the situation. The objective of such an analysis is intendedly empirical; however, to the extent that any observation is biased by the axiological predicates underlying such observations (Dunn, 1982), the data that emerge can be challenged. The model of man embraced by the analyst will determine the units of analysis, that is, the elements and structure of the analytical framework or model that guides observation of the system or setting. Beyond these analytical (ontological, epistemological, theoretical) biases, whose ideological and practical interests are involved and implicated in the outcomes of such an ostensibly factual analysis?

While assessment of what is may be "intendedly factual," there are any number of realities depending on the axiological assumptions underlying them. In short, facts and values are not so simply disentangled. Moreover, while documentation of the existing sociophysical state of affairs informs decisions regarding future states, it cannot produce such decisions. That is, "facts as such have no meaning; they can gain it only through our decisions" (Popper, 1962). This reality brings into question certain procedures conventionally employed, and suggests a reexamination of the related procedural research agenda.

---

[2] Stakeholders are "all parties who will be affected by or effect an important decision" (Mitroff, Emshoff and Kilman, 1979); stakeholders in housing decision processes include users and various affected non-users.

What should be?

It is the disparity between what is and what should or ought to be that defines a built environmental problem, confirms that one actually exists, and clarifies its nature. Externalizing, assessing, and documenting the preference orderings of participating stakeholders, that is, establishing the goals of a population or setting, is of a fundamentally different order than assessing the existing state of affairs. Whatever the nature of the fact-value dichotomy (ontologically), the establishment of goals is a *normative* function. Although the proposition would seem plan enough, its implementation in practice has, in one way or another, led to some of the excesses of instrumental rationalism. The procedural difficulties of defining goals as a precondition for defining the problem or requisite state of sociobehavioral affairs are essentially 1) conceptual (what is a goal?), and 2) methodological (how are a population's sociobehavioral goals to be externalized, assessed, and consensually weighted and ordered?).

Human problems ultimately come down to disparities between existing and requisite states. The purpose of intervening in a population-s housing environment is to facilitate the realization of goal-related outcomes—to move the system or setting from where it is, to where it should be. This is the problem to be addressed in the selection or invention of built environmental means.

Assessment of the disparities between existing and requisite states is ostensibly an empirical issue. But conflicts in the axiological posture, the underlying assumptions guiding such an analysis, impact this function precisely as they do assessing the existing system in the first place. Moreover, classifying a disparity as sufficiently critical to indicate intervention is yet another kind of decision issue. Which is to say that the decision to classify a situation as a problem is itself a normative one. Moreover, the manner of defining a problem establishes the universe of discourse within which both factual and valuative issues will be addressed. The unresolved procedural issues in goal setting and problem definition in the context of the fact-value dichotomy require attention.

What could be?

If the existing housing environment is ill-related to the stakeholder's goals, aspects thereof need reorganization. The task is to describe characteristics of an environment required to facilitate the requisite state of sociobehavioral affairs Required is the development of a *program* describing the quantitative, qualitative, and relational requirements of a new sociophysical ensemble. Implicit in this program is a prediction, i.e., "If a particular (built environmental) configuration is implemented, the requisite conditions will emerge."

The properties of this sociophysical program are obviously predicated on the axiological posture, including the model of man invoked. Specification of a requisite environment, in essence, involves a prediction regarding the performance of a sociophysical system yet to be realized. A handy resource to support this task would be nomological knowledge of human sociophysical processes. As things stand, not only is there a great deal of axiological conflict among relevant experts, but there are limits to the predictive capabilities of any known system of sociobehavioral science. Whatever the difficulties of assessing the "facts" regarding an existing state of affairs, these are compounded when we attempt to render reliable predictions regarding new states. Given the lack of universal agreement on how to go about consummating this task, the issue is: What are the assumptions underlying a set of requisite environmental specifications and their predicted human impacts?

What would happen if?

Having specified the general characteristics of the requisite system, the task is to transform these specifications into a real functioning system. The issue here is that while the basic characteristics of the requisite system have been described, many solutions or possible configurations could be proposed. There are no algorithms for solving this class of problems, and direct implementation of untested sociophysical interventions may carry considerable social, economic, political, and even physiological risk. We are thus committed to a process of heuristic search–a process of generating and evaluating proposed concrete solutions. At this point the technical demands of real-world constraints (economic, physical, social, and political) impinging on the proposed solution come into play. The conclusion of this search-assessment process is the selection of the built environmental means to achieve the ends,i.e., the goals, of the population under analysis. The development and assessment of various alternative environmental arrangements, and the selection of that configuration deemed most effective in realizing the goals established for the setting identifies a task for which certain known procedures may be relevant. However, this is also an area of needed methodological innovation.

Appropriate built environments, including those of housing, are thus organized via heuristic search processes, aspects of which are not well understood beyond recognition that these involve invention and comparative assessment of alternative configurations (see Simon, 1957, 1973; Rittel and Weber, 1973). In any event, the characteristics of the means selected to facilitate requisite stakeholder goals and objectives are again predicated on the axiological postures of those generating and evaluating various alternatives. Within any population of stakeholders these are generally conflicting both technically and practically.

What happens when?

Assuming that both the stakeholder's goals and the built environmental means have been consensually formulated, implementing the selected system in the larger environment presents only technical and logistical problems. That is, appropriate technical procedures are employed to bring the selected built environment into reality and then to evaluate its performance.

If there is consensus among stakeholders regarding both the ends (goals) and the means (built environment) implemented, the process of evaluating the new sociophysical system is straight forward and involves no procedural issues beyond those encountered in assessing the existing system initially. Required here is assessment of emergent sociobehavioral states and comparison of these with the stakeholder's goals–a confirmation of the effectiveness of the implemented built environment. If there is a disparity between requisite and resultant states, or if and when stakeholder goals or external conditions change, this would (theoretically) call for reiteration through the entire decision making process until requisite and resultant states reach consonance. Extant physical technologies of course make this kind of dynamic responsiveness problematic (Studer 1970, 1987). The execution of this function embodies precisely the same issues, that is, axiological conflicts among relevant actors, as those encountered in assessing a sociophysical system prior to intervention.

Under the influences of scientification, an impressive array of methodological resources has been, and continues to be developed to deal precisely with the procedural issues depicted in the above. However, the way we view the methodological problem has been changing in recent years. The purpose of this brief review of decision-making issues has been to emphasize that: 1) the procedures for realizing housing environments involve an amalgamation of two distinct ontological classes, (probabilistic) facts and values (Michalos, 1980; Studer, 1982), 2) our knowledge of both sociophysical problem and solution spaces is highly limited; and 3) the manner of effecting the procedures involved is predicated on the axiological postures of those involved in the enterprise.

Metastrategies for research in housing praxis

Proposed elsewhere (Studer 1988) is a four part typology which builds on a proposal by the late Horst Rittel. To improve housing praxis in the future we could consider four investigatory metastrategies: research *on* decision processes, research *for* decision processes, research *in* decision processes, and generative decision processes.

Research on decision processes

Research *on* decision processes is predicated on the assumption that sociophysical intervention embodies a set of unique procedural and substantive issues that define a discrete field of fundamental inquiry. Modeled after fields of basic (deductive) science, the objective is the realization of a body of nomological knowledge, a science of sociophysical design and decision making, that "trickles down" to areas of application. This level of inquiry is highly theoretical and deals with "essences" arrived at through reductive processes characteristic of other fields of basic research.

Basic inquiry in the procedural realm draws from such areas as mathematical decision theory, artificial intelligence, and topology in the development of formal decision-making models applicable to all sociophysical interventions. Formal logics, as well as mathematical and computer modeling, figure heavily in this level of procedural inquiry.

Basic substantive inquiry can be seen to include two foci: 1) general theories of physical system organization and 2) general theories of sociophysical phenomena. At more advanced levels of development decision processes would be driven by formal sociophysical models (structures and processes). Investigations at this level would generally take the form of theoretical, transdisciplinary modeling, and the resultant product might be seen as a system of functional, rather than discursive, models of sociophysical phenomena. At this level of inquiry substantive and procedural phenomena tend to merge. The resultant models would not only depict dynamic sociophysical systems, but the processes (functional relationships between independent and dependent variables) of their organization and evolution.

Characterized in this manner, research *on* design sounds more like science fiction than contemporary social science. While elements of such a program are ongoing, its realization in terms of providing usable knowledge within any reasonable time frame is highly problematic. A commitment to this level of basic inquiry, unencumbered by real-world complexities, is predicated on the hope that a theoretical breakthrough might occur and "trickle down" to practice.

Research for decision processes

Research *for* decision processes is essentially what we are involved in at the present. It is an arrangement in which a wide variety of research programs generate knowledge deemed relevant to housing design and decision making. The assumption is that although executed in the context of a variety of interests, foci, and axiological platforms, the building up of a massive knowledge base will, in time, surely lead to more effective, congruent housing environments.

Procedural research is this category generally involves appropriation of decision models from the so-called systems sciences in an attempt to rationalize conventional design and decision making processes. Design and decision making models are of two general classes, i.e., empirical (how decisions are actually made), and normative (how decisions ought to be made). Normative decision models are more or less formal arguments for the most effective procedures for linking ends to means. We have a plethora of these models competing for recognition and adoption. Since normative models cannot be verified empirically, their merits must be argued in terms of their utility vis-a-vis rival variants.

Substantive research for design consists of a collection of primarily descriptive investigations, usually unconnected directly to design and decision making processes. Attempts to catalog and organize the findings of these investigations into a general framework (Moore, Tuttle, and Howell, 1985) may help to illuminate their potential relevance, but no amount of cataloging and classifying will overcome the problems of utilizing the findings of these various studies in situation-specific problem settings. The underlying issue is, of course, generalization. We have a large collection of descriptive studies focusing on place, people, and sociobehavioral variables (Moore, Tuttle and Howell, 1985), the findings of which, while relevant, are generalizable only within the limits of the studies. The prospects that any one or a combination of these investigations will match a particular problem setting (for example, population, place type, sociobehavioral variables) is quite remote. Moreover, it is simply not feasible to develop a comprehensive catalog of investigations from which could be selected one (or even a combination of them) that precisely matches a particular problem context. In short, notwithstanding the value of enhancing our scientific understanding of sociophysical phenomena, the direct application of this knowledge in the planning and design of housing environments in the near future appears highly limited.

Research in decision processes

Research *in* decision processes characterizes an arrangement wherein sociophysical knowledge is produced *within*, and in response to, a situation-specific design and decision-making context. This direct, situation-specific knowledge-generating process, of course, produces highly usable knowledge; but its generalizability across a wide range of problem settings is unlikely. What is generally appropriated for research *in* decision processes are the *methods*, rather than the substance of sociophysical inquiry. Such an arrangement suggests close collaboration and mutual learning opportunities for both practitioners and researchers, and no doubt produces more congruent housing environments. Over time a cumulative instrumental knowledge base applicable to a range of interventions could be realized.

Notwithstanding the positive impacts of this metastrategy, there is the inevitable trade-off with respect to participating social scientists. Few situation-specific design and decision making contexts lend themselves to research within the norms of social science. The controls required to assure validity (Campbell and Stanley, 1963) are not readily implementable (for example, sample selection or numbers of subjects). In short, research *in* design must generally be seen as applied social science. This is no problem for housing practitioners or users, but it may be for potential social science collaborators.

Generative decision processes

Generative decision processes, a variant of research in design, constitutes a fourth metastrategy, one based on a post positivist axiological platform (Dunn 1982; Mason and Mitroff 1981). In this arrangement stakeholders are directly involved in decision making processes, and it essentially bypasses major aspects of the knowledge generation-utilization problem. In generative (collective, participatory) processes stakeholders' values, needs, preferences and goals are played out directly as a function of reaching collective decisions. Generative processes require a supporting instrumentality that guides and manages decision processes, analyzes stakeholder responses to various decision making issues, and illuminates consequences of alternative environmental configurations.

While this arrangement does not overcome all of the problems associated with incomplete sociophysical knowledge, it does have the advantage that built environmental ends and means are identified, analyzed, and selected via direct responses of stakeholders engaged in structured dialectical discourse. Over time, these kinds of decision making contexts are likely to produce sociophysical knowledge unattainable through other means. In any event, the challenge here is in the development of a generative methodology (Mason and Mitroff 1981; Dunn 1982; Studer 1982, 1987) and the instrumental support necessary to effect inter subjective decision processes.

The above characterizations of alternative metastrategies are offered to illuminate the range of possible approaches to generating usable procedural and substantive knowledge in housing praxis. The plurality of interests and goals among housing researchers and practitioners is quite apparent. All of the above metastratagies—variants or combinations thereof—should perhaps be embraced if we are to address more comprehensively the procedural issues in housing.

Conclusion

In this chapter reflecting on procedural issues, the missions of housing research and housing praxis were differentiated. The focus has been primarily on the latter, and the procedural research agenda of housing praxis was characterized as including: the application of general knowledge, the generation of instrumental knowledge, and the processes and methods of housing design and decision-making. The kinds of questions encountered in housing decision processes were reviewed in order to illuminate the procedural issues in praxis. Four metastrategies were presented for generating knowledge required in housing praxis, concluding that all of these should be considered as components of a general program to address the multifaceted issues involved. Implicitly suggested is development of some sort of technology (analogous to established physical technologies) linking basic and applied sociophysical knowledge to situation-specific housing problems The procedural issues discussed herein are no doubt quite familiar to housing policy analysts, planners, designers and managers. What has complicated the procedural agenda in housing praxis, however, is recognition of the problems associated with scientification, instrumental rationalism, and the related challenge of the post-positivist rationality debate.

References

Altman,I. and B. Rogoff (1987). "World Views in Psychology: Trait, Interactional Organismic and Transactional Perspectives," in D. Stokols and I. Altman (eds.) *Handbook of Environmental Psychology and the Built Environment.* New York : John Wiley, 7-40.

Alexander, E.R. (1984). " After rationality What? A Review of Responses to Paradigm Breakdown." *Journal of the American Planning Association*, 50, No.

1: 62-69.

Bernstein, R.J. (1983). *Beyond Objectivism and Relativism*. Philadelphia: University of Pennsylvania Press.

Campbell, D.T. and J.C. Stanley (1963). *Experimental and Quasi-Experimental Designs for Research*. Chicago: Rand McNally.

Dunn, W.N. (1982). "Reforms as Arguments," in E.R. House et al (eds.), *Evaluation Studies Review Annual*, Vol. 7. Beverly Hills, CA: Sage: 117-128.

Leiss, W. (1975) "The Problem of Man and Nature in the Work of Frankfurt School". *Philosophy of Social Science*, 5: 163-172.

Mason, Richard O., and Ian I. Mitroff (1981). *Challenging Strategic Planning Assumptions: Theory, Cases, and Techniques*. New York: John Wiley.

McCarthy, T. (1978). *The Critical Theory of Jürgen Habermas*. Cambridge: MIT Press.

Michalos, Alex C. (1980). "Facts, Values and Rational Decision-Making." *Policy Studies*, 9: 544-551.

Mitroff, I. and J. Emshoff (1979). "On Strategic Assumption Making: A Dialectical Approach to Policy and Planning." *Academy of Management Review*, 4, no. 1: 1-12.

Mitroff, I., J. Emshoff, and R. Kilmann (1979). "Assumptional Analysis: A Methodology for Strategic Planning." *Management Science*, 25, no. 6: 1-12.

Moore, G.T., D.P. Tuttle, and S.C. Howell (1985). *Environmental Design Research Directions*. New York: Praeger.

Popper K. (1962). *The Open Society and Its Enemies*. Volume 2. New York: Harper and Roe.

Rittel, H.W.J., and M.M. Weber (1973). "Dilemmas in a General Theory of Planning." *Policy Sciences.*, 4: 155-169.

Simon, H.A. (1973). "The Structure of Ill-Structured Problems." *Artificial Intelligence* 4: 181-210.

Studer, R.G. (1970). "The Dynamics of Behavior-Contingent Physical Systems," in H.M. Proshansky, W.H. Ittelson, and L.G. Rivlin (eds.), *Environmental Psychology: Man and His Physical Setting*. New York: Holt, Reinhart and Winston,

56-76.

Studer, R.G. (1982). "Normative Guidance for the Planning, Design and Management of Environment-Behavior Systems." Ph.D. dissertation, University of Pittsburgh.

Studer, R.G. (1987). "The Prospects for Realizing Congruence in Housing Environments," in W. van Vliet–, H. Cholding, W. Michelson, and D. Popenoe (eds.), *Housing and Neighborhoods: Theoretical and Empirical Contributions.* Wesport, CT : Greenwood Press, 29-41.

Studer, R.G. (1988). "Design of the Built Environment: The Search for Useable Knowledge," in E. Huttman and W. van Vliet– (eds.) *Handbook of Housing and the Built Environment." Wesport, CT : Greenwood Press: 73-96.*

Sutherland, J. (1974). "Axiological Predicates of Scientific Research." General Systems, *19: 3-13.*

Chapter 23

A House is not an Elephant: Centering the Marginal

WILLEM van VLIET–
University of Colorado

Differences in the meaning and use of housing are usually not random, but, instead, follow systematic patterns. This concluding chapter focuses attention on differences arising out of inequities that are created and reinforced by systems of housing provision. These differences are largest in nations where housing is foremost treated as a commodity, to be produced and traded for profit. In these countries, households that are too poor to translate their housing needs into an effective market demand become residualized. Such marginality characterizes the daily life of a majority of the population of the less industrialized world. Relationships of economic dependency on the industrialized world set an important constraining context for ameliorative policies. The argument here proposes that the processes that marginalize poor households ought to be a central concern of designers and planners.

Bases of perspectival divergence

There is a story about six blind men called upon to describe an elephant. The first man bumps against one of the elephant's legs. Feeling its shape and size, he proclaims that the elephant is like a tree. The second one approaches from the front. Getting a hold of its trunk, he likens the elephant to a big snake. The third, coming from the rear, grabs the tail and compares the elephant to a rope. Each of the remaining blind men touches a different part of the elephant and consequently reports a different simile.

Like the elephant, housing, too, can be many different things. This point is amply illustrated by the chapters in this volume. Individually, each emphasizes a particular aspect of housing. Together, they bring out a wider span of relevant considerations. Indeed, the very multiplicity of meanings and uses of housing can itself be seen as a defining characteristic of the field.

However, in the field of housing, unlike in the story of the elephant, different observers do not just stumble by happenstance upon divergent perspectives. The different meanings and uses of housing are not coincidental or random. The differences derive from the different positions that different observers occupy. These positions are anchored in more or less orderly patterns. These patterns, in turn, are structured along different dimensions—professional, cultural, political, economic, et cetera.

Within the context of this book, an obvious pattern is that created by disciplinary precepts. Economics have dominated the meaning and use of housing. Typically, housing investments constitute between 2 and 8 percent of GNP, between 10 and 30 percent of gross capital formation, between 20 and 50 percent of accumulated wealth, and between 10 and 40 percent of total household expenditures. Housing loans account for between 10 and 40 percent of all loans in banking systems. Housing occupies about 50 percent of urban land. In addition, housing construction has numerous forward and backward linkages, so that investments in it have significant multiplier effects. Hence, housing has been a common policy tool for affecting levels of employment and inflation. Not surprisingly, economic approaches have informed much of the research on housing.

This book fulfills an important function by representing a substantial amount of housing research undertaken from other disciplinary perspectives. These perspectives bring into focus different aspects of housing. For example, architects will likely stress issues of physical design, whereas anthropologists will tend to be more oriented to aspects of culture as they relate to housing and the framework of sociologists frequently guides them to a concern with social behavior. The preceding chapters reflect these various professional paradigms and illustrate the broad multidisciplinary nature of the field of housing. Ultimately, the important differences in meaning and use of housing express themselves in the daily experiences of individuals. These experiences are significantly shaped by their linkage to the surrounding context. Political and economic structure are cardinal ingredients of context, and aspects of inequity are of paramount importance in this connection. Unlike the blind men in the story, not everyone in the field of housing shares the same handicap, creating vastly different housing experiences.

The view developed here is purposely selective in order to emphasize an aspect of housing that I deem to be important: inequity. However, this view is not intended to be reductionist or exclusive of other considerations. It remains cognizant of other parameters, such as culture, that help structure differences in housing experience as well.[1] Also, at another level, different perspectives on housing may stem from different positions across the life span. For example, children's use of the housing environment is closely related to their developmental stage (e.g., Hart 1979; Pollowy 1977).[2] Likewise, the diminishing mobility that often accompanies advancing age has clear implications for the elderly's experience of their housing environment (e.g., Wachs 1979; Regnier and Pynoos 1987).

In cases such as these, the differential meanings and uses of housing can be traced to (a variety of) prior factors—disciplinary paradigm, cultural value system, stage in the life cycle, and so forth. There are, of course, other ways of differentiating meanings and uses. For example, in Chapter One, Francescato points to aspects of scale. However, in this last case, and others like it, the differentiating variable is itself an element of the environment. Although it can *describe* different experiences of housing, it cannot *explain* the mechanisms underlying the differences.

The concern of this concluding chapter is with differences in housing experiences that are systemic, that is, differences whose etiology is endemic to the existing systems of housing provision. Relevant questions in this connection ipso facto relate not as much to the different meanings and uses of housing as to their antecedents.

An important development in this regard is the growing reliance on pri-

[1] In a recent interdisciplinary cross-cultural study of domestic architecture and the use of space, culture is seen to include technology, symbolism, economics, social structure, and political organization (Kent 1990). Used this way, culture becomes a conceptual passe-partout that is of limited use in developing the analytical distinctions necessary to gauge the independent and interactive effects of a complex of interrelated factors. For excellent coverage of culture and built environment, see Altman and Werner (1980).

[2] A case in point are the age-related evaluations of residential suburbs as reported by Gans (1967). He found that teenagers, with few things to do within their home range, spoke much less positively about life in Levittown, NJ, than did their parents who had selected this environment as the family's place to live.

vate sector mechanisms for housing provision in countries worldwide. This trend means, among other things, that ability-to-pay is becoming more important. Suppliers will respond to those who can translate their needs into a market demand that provides a profitable return for private investors. However, this same trend makes life increasingly difficult for those peripheral to the economic and political processes of society. These households are too poor to articulate an effective market demand. Increasingly, their needs go unmet. Witness the growing number of homeless.

The resulting polarization has been well documented. This polarization does not occur in a vacuum. Whether intended or not, it is the outcome of current policy orientations that further reinforce existing inequities between, for example, renters and owners and between the industrialized and the industrializing world.[3] As we examine the different meanings and uses of housing, these inequities are all too rarely addressed. However, without a doubt, they are extremely salient. The argument here is that the experiences of those at the margin and, more importantly, the processes that marginalize them should be made central to the discussion of meaning and use of housing.

Housing as symbol

About 20 years ago, Clare Cooper (1972) presented a view of housing as a symbol of self-identity. Among the examples she cited was a study by Werthman (1968). He found that homeowners with occupations in the helping professions, whose goals revolve around personal satisfaction rather than financial success, tended to opt for quiet, inward-looking house designs. Extroverted, self-made businessmen chose somewhat ostentatious, mock-Colonial "display" homes. Subsequently, there has been further research along similar lines. For example, Rybczynski (1986) has provided an historical account of how the design of houses and their interiors can be seen as the physical articulation of evolving notions of family, privacy, intimacy, and comfort. Other work has been more narrowly focused and has examined, for example the correspondence between inferences by observers of dwelling interiors regarding personality characteristics of the occupants and the image intendedly projected by the occupants through their selection

---

[3] In general, statements like this demand corroborating evidence and responsible source documentation. In this case, none is presented. The tale spun here is important and bears repeating. However, it is not new. It weaves together strands from earlier work that contains abundant references to substantiating materials. Rather than unduly larding the present discussion with same, skeptics are referred to van Vliet– (1990a, 1990b and, in particular, 1991) for information supportive of the points made here.

and arrangement of furniture and the like. Without question, symbolic aspects of housing are a relevant domain of inquiry. It is important, however, to see these aspects in their proper context.

For about 20 years, the feminist Gloria Steinem lived in a two-room brownstone apartment that meant to her little more than a "pitstop" and "crashpad". A few years ago, having received a $700,000 advance for her first book, she bought two adjoining rooms and had a connecting spiral staircase installed. After chartering also the services of an interior decorator, "these days she is able to recognize her apartment as 'a symbol of the self"' (Bennett 1992, p. 91), stating "I don't know why it took me so long to realize you need to have a home" (ibid.).

It is perhaps interesting to note the meaning of home for an outspoken critic of women's domesticity like Ms. Steinem. However, it is more important to note that her ability for self-expression is not universal. The situation of Rachel and others down-and-out like her, so vividly described by Kozol (1988), form a stark contrast. Living under absolutely squalid conditions in so called welfare hotels, most of these destitute women do not even have enough food. For them, having a house that symbolizes their self-identity is pie in the sky. And so it is for innumerable households at the economic and political fringes of society. Of course, there are many examples of how also the poor seek to personalize their domestic environment. However, their opportunities for doing so are greatly restricted and the primary needs that dominate their concern with housing relate to shelter, access, and security of tenure.

Housing as a symbol revisited

In San Francisco, a well intentioned architect has designed 4 x 8 foot plywood dog houses at $500 a piece to house the local homeless (People 1987). In Atlanta, activists have constructed similar 6 x 8 foot boxes for those without a home with the tacit blessing of the mayor (Stein 1988). In the United States, it is also possible to find a $15,000 miniature Victorian mansion for a Doberman pincher, designed with a redwood cathedral ceiling, Italian porcelain tile flooring, solid brass fixtures, cedar-shake roof, double-pane windows, pool and rock garden (Andrews 1990).

Housing can also be seen as a symbol in these contrasting situations in the wealthiest country of the world. However, in these instances it symbolizes foremost the prevailing national commitment to a view of housing as a commodity. This view not only condones, but helps produce a system of housing provision that is propelled by the profit-seeking motive, a system whose requirement is a return on private investment and that is supported by public policies that benefit most those who need it least, aimed at providing investment incentives for the rich, first, and housing opportunities for the poor, last. The small proportion of public housing in market systems, and its designation as a place of last resort, symbolize the same ethos.[4]

Although other systems of housing provision are scarcely free of problems either, it is market systems that are most likely to sustain uneven outcomes.[5] The disparities between the haves and the have-nots are greatest in market systems. However, we need to look beyond the internal workings of national systems. As we examine housing on a global scale, the most grievous problems are suffered by the peoples of the less industrialized countries.

The context of housing at the margin

Notwithstanding important differences among them, almost all of the less industrialized countries continue to experience very high urban growth rates. Between 1950 and 1990, the urban population of the industrialized world increased by 80 percent; during the same period, the urban population in the industrializing world increased by more than 400%. The pace and scale of urbanization exacerbate all sorts of problems, including housing. Supply produced by the formal sector has fallen far short of demand. As a result, large numbers of people live in shelter fabricated through informal processes of housing provision. Although precise counts are difficult to obtain, the United Nations Centre for Human Settlements (1987, p. 77) has come up with estimates for 1980 that have been widely accepted (for example, Lima: 33%; Karachi: 37%; Mexico City: 40%; Manila: 40%; Ankara: 51%; Bogota: 59%; Dar es Salaam: 60%; Addis Abbeba: 85%). It is generally agreed that these figures have increased since that time. In many cities, squatters and slum dwellers now make up 50 to 75% of the population. Not only do most of the less industrialized nations face formidable quantitative housing deficits, they also suffer serious problems of housing quality, deficient physical infrastructure and inadequate services. What is the context for solutions to these problems?

A few statistics are informative. Forty percent of all children under five in the less industrialized nations are malnourished; 40,000 children in this

---

[4] In contrast, in welfare states and in centrally planned systems, most of which are now in transition, public housing generally is much more common and without intense negative connotations, representing national commitment to housing as an entitlement.

[5] The underlying ideology was succinctly captured by David Stockman, former president Reagan's first budget director and a major protagonist of "free" markets. Opposing entitlement to any kind of service he stated: "I don't accept that equality is a moral principle" (Kozol 1988, p. 163).

age group die every day from malnutrition and infectious diseases, most of which are easily and inexpensively preventable (UNICEF/UNEP 1990, p. 22, p. 48).[6] In 1987, in the countries with very high child mortality rates, only 34 percent of the population had access to safe water and just 41 percent had access to health services; in 1985, the literacy rates for men and women were 43 and 22 percent, respectively; in 1988, one-half of all boys and one-third of all girls were enrolled in primary school; only 40 percent completed primary school; average life expectancy was 48 years (UNICEF 1990).

Many more statistics could be added, but the point is clear: housing is not the only problem. Nor is it the problem given the highest priority. In national development, goals of health, education, economy and, with few exceptions, military capability, are seen to be more important.

However, the context of housing needs in the less industrialized nations is not formed by competing claims alone. All of these problems are framed by the relations between the industrialized and the less industrialized world. A significant aspect of these relationships is the transfer of funds from the latter to the former. Annual debt and interest payments are now more than triple the aid received. At present, Latin America's debts are four times as large as its total annual exports. Each percentage point increase in interest rates requires a 4 percent increase in exports merely to keep up the tempo of payments. The debt burden of Africa, in relation to its export earnings and ability to pay, is twice that of Latin America (UNICEF 1990). Trade barriers further put the less industrialized countries at a disadvantage.

Under these circumstances, the resources allocated to housing are obviously very limited. Public housing projects have commonly benefitted government employees and other privileged groups. Site-and-services schemes have generally been unable to reach the poorest 30% of the population. Slum upgrading has not been able to reach the most impoverished segment of the population either. The emerging orientation to "enabling strategies" is certain not to change this situation. The position of the poor is more difficult yet in the ways and to the extent that domestic exclusionary processes tend to residualize them further (Durand-Lasserve 1986).

Conclusion

When studying the meaning and use of housing, researchers have at their disposal a rich arsenal of methods. The development of the field during

---

[6]For example, it is estimated that 2.5. million deaths attributed to diarrhoeal diseases in 1988 could have been prevented by the use of oral rehydration salts available in sachets costing just 7 U.S. cents each.

the last two decades has been greatly aided by continuing methodological advances. The chapters in this book contain many fine examples of this progress in quantitative as well as qualitative approaches to housing research. However, as we strive to perfect these tools we must not forget about the contexts within which they become useful. Just as we must be committed to rigor in the application of scientific methods to the collection and analysis of data, so also must we be committed to rigor in the selection of the ends to which they are applied. We must ensure that our application of methods is impartial to these ends. We must also ensure that our selection of these ends is partial to the values that we seek to uphold. In this regard it is as important to avoid the pretense of neutrality as the folly of dogma. While acknowledging other worthy domains for research on the meaning and use of housing, this brief concluding chapter purposely focuses attention on distributional questions, issues related to poverty in the face of affluence.

Clearly, the housing experience of any given individual is significantly shaped by his or her niche in a broader system. Systems that generate inequities effectively disenfranchise persons at the economical and political margins. In the Global Strategy for Shelter, adopted by the U.N. General Assembly in 1988, housing for low-income groups is an explicit and central component (United Nations Centre for Human Settlements 1990). By the very nature of their professional canons, architects and planners are concerned with intervention. They should target their interventions to help redress the most acute and iniquitous situations. They should place the plight of the marginal on center stage.

References

Altman, Irwin and Martin M. Chemers. 1980. *Culture and Environment.* Monterey, CA: Brooks/Cole Publishing Company.

Bennett, Leslie. 1992. "Deconstructing Gloria." Vanity Fair, January, pp. 88-91, 137-141.

Cooper, Clare. 1972. "The House as Symbol." *Design & Environment from Design & Environment,* Vol. 3, No. 3 (Fall).

Durand-Lasserve, Alain. 1986. *L'Exclusion Des Pauvres Dans Les Villes Du Tiers-Monde.* Paris: L'Harmattan.

Gans, Herbert J. 1967. *The Levittowners: Ways of Life and Politics in a New Suburban Community.* New York: Random House.

Hart, Roger. 1979. *Children's Experience of Place*. New York: Irvington.

Kent, Susan. 1990. *Domestic Architecture and the Use of Space*. Cambridge University Press.

Kozol, Jonathan. 1988. *Rachel and Her Children*. New York: Random House.

Pollowy, Anne-Marie. 1977. *The Urban Nest*. Stroudsburg, PA: Dowden, Hutchinson & Ross, Inc.

Regnier, Victor and Jon Pynoos. 1987. *Housing the Aged: Design Directives and Policy Considerations*. New York: Elsevier Science Publishing Co.

Rybczynski, Witold. 1986. *Home: A Short History of An Idea*. Penguin books.

Stein, Karen D. 1988. "Guerilla welfare." *Architectural Record*, November.

United Nations Centre for Human Settlements (Habitat). 1987. *Global Report on Human Settlements 1986*. Oxford University Press.

United Nations Centre for Human Settlements (Habitat). Nairobi, 1990. *The Global Strategy for Shelter to the Year 2000*. As adopted by the General Assembly of the United Nations at its forty-third Session in Resolution 43/181 on 20 December 1988.

United Nations Children's Fund (UNICEF). 1990. *The State of the World's Children 1990*. Oxford University Press.

United Nations Environment Programme/United Nations Children's Fund. 1990. *Children and the Environment*.

Van Vliet–, Willem. 1991. Human Settlements in the U.S.: Sustaining Uneven Development, Research paper 183, Centre for Urban and Community Studies, University of Toronto (a shorter version is included in *Sustainable Cities: Urbanization and the Environment in International Perspective*. Edited by Richard Stren, Rodney White and Joseph Whitney. Westview Press. 1992).

Van Vliet–, Willem. 1990a. The Privatization and Decentralization of Housing, Ch. 1 in *Government and Housing*. Edited by W. van Vliet– and J. van Weesep. Sage Publications.

Van Vliet–, Willem. 1990b. Cross-national Housing Research: Analytical and Substantive Issues. Ch. 1 in *The International Handbook of Housing Policies and Practices*. Greenwood/Praeger.

Wachs, Martin. 1979. *Transportation for the Elderly: Changing Lifestyle, Changing Needs*. Berkeley: University of California Press.

Werthman, Carl. 1968. "The Social Meaning of the Physical Environment" Ph.D. dissertation, University of California, Berkeley.

Contributors

IRWIN ALTMAN is Distinguished Professor of Psychology at the University of Utah. There, he has been the past Chair of the Department of Psychology, Dean of the College of Behavioral Science, and Vice-President for Research. He is a leading figure in social and environmental psychology which he has advanced through numerous seminal books and articles. Presently, he edits the prestigious series *Human Behavior and Environment: Advances in Theory and Research*, published by Plenum Press.

KATHRYN H. ANTHONY is an Associate Professor in the School of Architecture and in the Housing Research and Development Program, as well as an associated faculty with the Department of Landscape Architecture at the University of Illinois at Urbana–Champaign. She has authored numerous publications on social and phychological issues in design, applied environment–behavior research, and design education. Her research on housing has focused especially on the needs of single–parent families, the elderly, and those with physical disabilities. Ms. Anthony is the author of *Design Juries on Trial: The Renaissance of the Design Studio* (New York: Van Nostrand Reinhold, 1991). Her research has been funded by the Graham Foundation as well as the National Endowment for the Arts. Ms. Anthony currently serves on the Editorial Board of the *Journal of Architectural Education*, and recently served on the Board of Directors of the Environmental Design Research Association. She holds a Ph.D. in architecture from the University of California at Berkeley. She has lectured extensively in the United States and abroad.

ERNESTO G. ARIAS is the chair of the Planning Option at the College of Environmental Design at the University of Colorado, Boulder, Colorado, where he founded and directs the Urban Simulations and Information Systems Laboratory, a research and teaching resource focusing on the relationships between theory and practice in the study of socio-physical systems and the investigation of new methods to include user participation and simulation approaches in planning, design and management. He is the recipient of two Fulbright Scholar Fellowships for teaching and research growth management and housing concerns in the Third World, and is a Fellow at the Center of International Research and Education Projects of the University of Colorado-Boulder. His housing research has been presented at national and international meetings of learned societies and published in various publications.

GILLES BARBEY teaches at the School of Architecture at Lausanne, and serves as a permanent consultant in the Preservation of the Built Heritage in Switzerland. He is the co-founder of the Institute of Research on the Built Environment, at the Polytechnical School, Lausanne (IREC), and has been the Chairman of the International Association for the Study of People and Their Physical Surroundings (IAPS) since 1984. He is currently a senior research officer at the Institute of Architectural History and Theory at the Federal Institute of Technology, Lausanne (ITHA), and acts as an architectural historian in his association with the Inventories of Swiss Architecture (INSA).

YVONNE BERNARD is a professor of psychology at the Universite Rene Descartes, Paris. The high quality of her research work has lead to her appointment as the Director of the Centre National de la Recherche Scientifique of France. Dr. Bernard's research focusing on residential environments is carried out within the "Laboratoire de Psychologie de L'Environnement." She is the author of numerous articles and books in psychology and is widely read in France and throughout Europe.

P. WIM BLAUW is associate professor of sociology at Erasmus University Rotterdam, and was at the Rotterdam School of Architecture. He is teaching courses on urban sociology and the sociology of housing. He did research into the spatial context of housing of several social categories, like immigrants and suburbanites. Dr. Wim Blauw has published, in addition to his numerous articles in scientific journals on housing, books on segregation in Dutch (*Soort Bij Soort*, 1978) and english (co-edited, *Urban Housing Segregation in the U.S. and Western Europe*, to be published by Duke University Press), a book on suburbanization (*Suburbanisatie on Sociale Contacten*, 1986), as well as his recently edited book on public spaces—*Ruimte Voor Openbaarheid*, 1989.

LUCIA MARIA M. BOGUS received her Ph.D. in Urban and Regional Planning from the Universidade de Sao Paulo, Faculdade de Arquitetura e Urbanismo, in Brazil. She has been researching and lecturing on the subject since 1978. Presently she is teaching Post-Graduate courses in Urban Sociology at Pontificia Universidade Catolica de Sao Paulo, She holds bachelor's and master's degrees in Architecture from Laval and is a doctoral candidate in the Department of Architecture of the University of Wisconsin-Milwaukee. In addition to her studio teaching, she gives a lecture class on sociology and housing. Her research interests include the meaning and symbolism of the built environment, women's studies, and housing as it relates to issues of meaning and use, planning and design, alternative life-styles and innovative housing forms. Her most recent writings include: "Beyond theoretical purism: the search for an integrated paradigm" in *Environmental Meaning Research, The Meaning of Home*, "Literature review and directions for future research and theoretical development," *From bourgeois to modern home*, and "Domesticity, aesthetics and feminine sensibility" (In French).

GIUSEPPE BOVE got his doctorate in Methodological Statistics at the University of Rome. He is presently researcher at the Statistics Department of the University of Rome "La Sapienza". His research intersts concern Multivariate Analysis and Multidimensional Scaling and their application in the psychological field. He has published articles concerning the improvement of Correspondence Analysis and Principal Component Analysis and some new methods to deal with asymmetric proximity matrices.

THEREZA C. CARVALHO is a Brazilian architect and urban designer, and foreign correspondent of Projeto, a major Brazilian architectural journal in Sao Paulo. A lecturer in the Housing Diploma Course in the School of Planning at Oxford Polytechnic where she has recently completed her doctoral work on specialized housing studies. She has been elected Councillor of the Brazilian Institute of Architects, a designer at Ateller Integrado de Arquitetura and research jobs for the National Housing Bank, a coordinator of the National Programme of Municipal Housing Staff Development, and a consultant of the National School of Housing and Loans for Self-Help Housing Policies in Brazil. This record is the basis of the "British Council Technical Cooperation Grant" bestowed by the government and National Housing Bank of Brazil to pursue her doctoral work in Britain. Already her work has been selected for presentation in two major international housing conferences.

LOUISE CHAWLA is an associate professor at an interdisciplinary honors college within Kentucky State University, teaching courses that integrate social science, philosophy, and literature. Her research interests have been housing and community resources for children, the significance of early environmental experience in memory, the origins of environmental concern and protection, and developmental theory that accommodates diverse forms of environmental experience. She has published book chapters and articles on these subjects and given numerous conference presentations.

BOYOWA ANTHONY CHOKOR is a Senior Lecturer in the Department of Geography and Regional Planning, University of Benin, Nigeria, where he teaches Environmental Cognition, Urban Geography and Planning at both undergraduate and postgraduate M.Sc. and Ph.D. levels. He received his Ph.D. from the University of London (University College). He has published widely in professional academic interdisciplinary and geographical journals in the area of man-environment-behaviour relationships, environmental/housing quality, landscape assessment and values. He has also been at the forefront in advocating a more critical humanistic geographical studies for the Third World. His current research aims to clarify the cultural, social meanings and symbolic quality of houses and neighbourhoods in the African urban context for planning and redevelopment purposes. He is currently compiling a book titled: Environmental Evaluation and Planning in the Third World, to be published by Avebury, England, U.K.

BERTH DANERMARK, received his Ph.D. in Sociology from the University of Uppsala. The title of his doctoral thesis from 1983 is "Class, Income and Housing. About segregation in some cities." He is a researcher at the Centre for Housing and Urban Research at the University of Orebro. At present he is conducting a study on the health consequences of the relocation of the elderly. He is the pro-Vice-Chancellor of the University.

CAROLE DESPRÉS is Associate Professor at the School of Architecture at Laval University in Québec, Canada. She received her bachelor's and master's degrees in Architecture from Laval, and her doctoral degree in Architecture from the University of Wisconsin–Milwaukee. In addition to her studio teaching, she gives a lecture clas on housing. Her research interests include the meaning and symbolism of the built environment, women's studies, and housing as it related to issues of meaning and use, planning and design, alternative life styles and innovative housing forms. Her most recent writings include: *Beyond theoretical purism: the search for an integrated paradigm in environmental meaning research*; *The meaning of home: literature review and directions for future research and theoretical developments*; *From bourgeois to modern home. Domesticity, aesthetics and feminine sensibility* (In French).

MATS EKSTRÖM, studied Sociology, Political Science and Economy at the University of Orebro, where he graduated 1986. He is currently a postgraduate student at the University of Uppsala. Since 1987 he has been a research assistant at the Centre for Housing and Urban Research at the University of Orebro. At present he is conducting a study on the health consequences of the relocation of the elderly (together with Danermark).

MOSHIRA EL-RAFEY holds a doctoral degree in architecture from the University of Michigan where she examined the relationship between societal values and the design of housing in Egypt. Her goal was to cultivate greater awareness among design professionals for meeting womens' needs and to augment the body of research in behavior, perception, and housing design. Her dissertation data also yileded several peer-reviewed papers. El-Rafey has been an assistant lecturer at Helwan University, Egypt, since 1979. She encourages students to understand the clients' sociobehavioral background—especially when working with minority clients. In 1983, she was awarded a Peace Fellowship to pursue master's degree in architecture at the University of Michigan, and in 1987 received a scholarship from the Egyptian Ministry of Higher Education to obtain her doctorate in architecture. She was awarded the prestigious American Association of University Women (AAUW) International Fellowship in 1991.

GUIDO FRANCESCATO is a professor of Architecture and an affiliate professor of Urban Studies and Planning at the University of Maryland, College Park. He has conducted national studies of housing satisfaction, design aspects and management factors for the Ford Foundation and the U.S. Department of Housing and Urban Development, and has acted as a consultant on environmental design issues in public schools and office buildings. His most recent publications include chapters on an attitudinal model of residential satisfaction in W.F.E Preiser (ed.) Building Evaluation, with S. Weidemann and J.R. Anderson, and on the concept of type in architectural knowledge in K. Franck and L. Shneekloth (eds.) Building Type and the Ordering of Space. He currently chairs the International Housing Research Network of the Environmental Design Research Association (EDRA).

KAREN A. FRANCK is Associate Professor of Architecture at the New Jersey Institute of Technology in Newark. With Sherry Ahrentzen, she edited *New Households, New Housing* (Van Nostrand Reinhold, 1989) to which she contributed chapters on shared housing and single room occupancy housing. Over the years she has written about women and environments, feminism and architecture, and physical determinism. She continues her research on alternative housing with the intention of writing her own book on this topic. She is presently editing a book on the idea of type in architecture and research with Lynda Schneekloth, to be published by Van Nostrand Reinhold

M. VITTORIA GIULIANI is senior researcher at the Istituto di Psicologia of the Consiglio Nazionale delle Ricerche (C.N.R.) in Rome. Her research on residential settings has been widely presented at international scientific conferences and published in several articles. She is presently member of the board of I.A.P.S.

ELIZABETH HUTTMAN is Professor of Sociology at California State University, Hayward. She has written Housing and Social Services for thees, and authored "Transnational Housing Policy" in *Home Environments* (edited by Irving Altman and Carol Werner). She is co-organizer of the International Committee of Housing and the Built Environment.

JON T. LANG is Professor of Architecture at the University of South Wales, Australia. Dr. Lang is the past chair of the Urban Design Program at the Graduate School of Fine Arts and the director of the Environmental Research Group at the University of Pennsylvania. He has held various visiting teaching positions and fellowships in universities around the world. He is the recipient of an Indo-American Fellowship to study culture and housing in India, and a Ford Foundation Fellowship to teach in India. Additionally, he has been a UNESCO consultant to T urkey. Dr. Lang has written extensively on design methodology, behavioral factors in design, and design and planning education. He co-edited the pioneering book *Designing for Human Behavior: Architecture and the Behavioral Sciences*, and is the author of the recent book *Creating Architectural Theory: The Role of the Behavioral Sciences in Environmental Design* (Van Nostrand Reinhold Co., 1987).

RODERICK J. LAWRENCE is currently appointed to the Centre for Human Ecology and Environmental Sciences at the University of Geneva. He has been a Consultant to the Committee for Housing, Building and Planning of the Economic Commission for Europe, a faculty at the Ecole Polytechnique rale de Lausanne, Switzerland, and a Visiting Research Fellow at the School of Social Sciences at the Flinders University of South Australia. He has published numerous articles and chapters of monographs in both English and French concerning the reciprocal relations between architectural and behavioural parameters in house planning from cross-cultural, societal and psychological perspectives that address historical processes. He is also the author of two books: *Le Seuil franchi: logement populaire* *et vie quotidienne en Suisse romande, 1860-1960* (Georg Editeur, Geneva, 1986) and *Housing, Dwellings and Homes: Design Theory, Research and Practice* (John Wiley, Chichester, 1987).

DONNA LUCKEY is an Associate Professor in the School of Architecture and Urban Design at the University of Kansas, Lawrence, Kansas. She holds a Ph.D. in Architecture from the University of California, Berkeley where she focused on Design Methods. Her research includes the areas of land *aménagement* and environmental planning, based on work at the California Coastal Conservancy. She has recently returned from Sabbatical on a Fulbright Research Grant to Costa Rica where she has been studying housing forms and issues.

WILLIAM MICHELSON is Professor of Sociology at the University of Toronto, where he is also associated with the Centre for Urban and Community Studies. His research interests concern how people's contexts bear on their lives; this has led to work on such topics as housing, urban children, and maternal employment. Author of widely used books such as *Man and His Urban Environment: A Sociological Approach*, or more recently—*From Sun to Sun: Daily Obligations and Community Structure in the Lives of Employed Women and Their Families*, and *Methods for Environmental and Behavioral Research* (coedited with Robert Bechtel and Robert Marans).

KUNIHIRO NARUMI is an associate professor in the College of Engineering at Osaka University in Japan, where he is the Chair of the Department of Environmental Engineering. Dr. Narumi is a highly respected Japanese urbanist planner/engineer who has published widely in the areas of use and meaning of Japanese urban environments. He received the prestigious Suntroy Arts and Sciences Award in 1988 for his research on Urban Climax—Life-spatiology as Phenomenology, Chikuma-shobou Co., in Japanese (1987), and the OKUI Award by the Society of Urban Studies of Japan for his editorship on Urban Arrangement from Town-scape Design, Gakugeishuppansha Co., in Japanese (1988).

JACK L. NASAR is an Associate Professor of City and Regional Planning at the Ohio State University, Associate Editor of the em Journal of Planning Literature, and the Architectural Critic for the *Columbia Dispatch*. His research deals with human aspects of urban form. He edited the book *Environmental Aesthetics: Theory, Research and Application* (Cambridge University Press, 1988).

TOOMAS NIIT is a faculty member of the Department of Sociology at the Institute of Philosophy, Sociology & Justice, Estonia, USSR. Dr. Niit's methodological approaches to study families in dwelling environments in Russia have been presented in a variety of scientific conferences and journals in his country and internationally such as his seminal chapter in H. van Hoogdalem *et al.* (eds.), "Looking Back to the Future," Vol.2 (IAPS 10 Proceedings). Delft: Delft University Press, 1988, pp. 382-391.

GIUSEPPINA RULLO graduated in Psychology at the University of Rome, Italy, and got her Master of Science in Environmental Psychology at the University of Surrey, U.K. Since 1984 she has done studies on the interaction between people and their residential environments at the Istituto di Psicologia of the Consiglio Nazionale delle Ricerche (CNR) in Rome. Her publications focus on meaning and use of home interiors as well as on users' representations of urban places.

RAYMOND G. STUDER is Dean of the College of Environmental Design, University of Colorado, at Boulder. He formerly headed the program in Man-Environment Relations and the program in Community Systems Planning and Development at The Pennsylvania State University. His interests include theoretical and methodological issues in planning, programming, design and management of sociophysical systems and settings; application of behavioral technology and behavioral ecology in sociophysical intervention; and other areas of sociophysical research, including those relevant to the fields of architecture, urban planning and public policy. His current focus is upon generative decision processes and methods to support planning, design and management.

SHARON E. SUTTON is associate professor of architecture at the University of Michigan and coordinator of the Urban Network, an award-winning program in urban design for youth. She uses a background in music, art, architecture, and psychology to search for humane relationships between space and the quality of life for specific groups of people. A frequent speaker at colleges, universities, and conferences, Dr. Sutton is the author of numerous articles and commentaries on the aspirations of disadvantaged groups as they relate to the physical environment. Her book, *Learning through the Built Environment,* was published in 1985; and another, *Weaving a Tapestry of Success,* is in progress. Dr. Sutton was in private practice in New York City for eight years and has taught at Pratt Institute, Columbia University, and the University of Cincinnati.

DICK URBAN VESTBRO is an architect and Assistant Professor of Building Function Analysis, School of Architecture, The Royal Institute of

The Meaning and Use of Housing

Technology in Stockholm. Dr. Vestbro has been carried out research on collective housing over a period of more than 25 years. The two main reports from this research are "Kollektivhus från enkökshus till bogemenskap" (Collective Housing from One- Kitchen Units to Communal Living), 1982 and "Den nya generatione kollektivhus" (The New Generation of Collective Housing Units), 1989 (together with Alison Woodward and Maj-Britt Grossman), both published by the Swedish Council for Building Research. He has also presented his research at conferences in Zürich, Hamburg, Tokyo and Canada. Besides collective housing, Dr. Vestbro's research also covers the problem of shanty towns and housing in third world countries.

WILLEM VAN VLIET— is an urban and environmental sociologist at University of Colorado, Boulder. His research interests concern cross-national analysis, urban and community planning, and housing. His published work includes contributions to anthologies and journals in the field and a number of edited books, including most recently *Housing Markets and Policies under Fiscal Austerity* (1987), *Women, Housing, and Community* (1989) and the *International Handbook of Housing Policies and Practices* (1990).

ALLAN WALLIS is director of research for the National Civic League and assistant professor of public policy at the Graduate School of Public Affairs, University of Colorado, Denver. He holds a Bachelors of Architecture from Cooper Union, a Masters in Public Administration from Harvard University, and a Ph.D. in Environmental Psychology from the Graduate School of the City University of New York. Professor Wallis is author of *Wheel Estate: The Rise and Decline of Mobile Homes*, published by Oxford University Press.

MARIA M. YEN is a doctoral student in City and Regional Planning at the University of California, Berkeley. She holds a bachelor's degree in Chinese and Political Science and a Master's degree in Urban Planning from the University of Michigan, Ann Arbor. Her research and practice interests involve cross-cultural comparison of community planning in Asia and North America. Maria spent a year in Visakhapatnam, Andhra Pradesh, India, researching migration from villages to urban squatter settlements.

Index